# Some Like It Wilder

# SCREEN CLASSICS

Screen Classics is a series of critical biographies, film histories, and analytical studies focusing on neglected filmmakers and important screen artists and subjects, from the era of silent cinema to the golden age of Hollywood to the international generation of today. Books in the Screen Classics series are intended for scholars and general readers alike. The contributing authors are established figures in their respective fields. This series also serves the purpose of advancing scholarship on film personalities and themes with ties to Kentucky.

Series Editor
Patrick McGilligan

# SOME LIKE IT
# WILDER

## The Life
### and
## Controversial Films
### of
## Billy Wilder

**GENE D. PHILLIPS**

THE UNIVERSITY PRESS OF KENTUCKY

Scholarly publisher for the Commonwealth,
serving Bellarmine University, Berea College, Centre College of Kentucky,
Eastern Kentucky University, The Filson Historical Society, Georgetown
College, Kentucky Historical Society, Kentucky State University, Morehead
State University, Murray State University, Northern Kentucky University,
Transylvania University, University of Kentucky, University of Louisville,
and Western Kentucky University.
All rights reserved.

*Editorial and Sales Offices:* The University Press of Kentucky
663 South Limestone Street, Lexington, Kentucky 40508-4008
www.kentuckypress.com

14 13 12 11 10   5 4 3 2 1

Library of Congress Cataloging-in-Publication Data

Phillips, Gene D.
  Some like it Wilder : the life and controversial films of Billy Wilder /
Gene D. Phillips.
    p. cm. — (Screen classics)
  Includes bibliographical references and index.
  ISBN 978-0-8131-2570-1 (hardcover : alk. paper)
  1. Wilder, Billy, 1906-2002.  2. Motion picture producers and directors—
United States—Biography.  I. Title.
  PN1998.3.W56P45 2010
  791.4302'33092—dc22
  [B]                                                2009045857

This book is printed on acid-free recycled paper meeting
the requirements of the American National Standard
for Permanence in Paper for Printed Library Materials.

Manufactured in the United States of America.

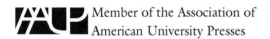 Member of the Association of
American University Presses

For Fred Zinnemann
Another exile in Hollywood

When you think about the breadth and scope of what
Billy Wilder has written, produced, and directed, and then
take into consideration that English is not even his first
language, then you see that his entire output is staggering.
—Stanley Donen, film director

# Contents

*Illustrations follow page 162*

# Foreword

## Fred Zinnemann Speaking

After I finished film school, I got work as a cameraman in Berlin. I was fortunate to be the assistant to Eugene Schüfftan, one of the best German cameramen during the golden age of German cinema in the 1920s. One of the films that Schüfftan photographed was *Menschen am Sonntag* (*People on Sunday*), a semidocumentary made in 1929 about four young people spending a weekend in the country. The film was written by Billy Wilder and directed by Robert Siodmak.

I only carried the camera around and measured the focus, but I was pleased to be working with talented people like Billy Wilder and Robert Siodmak. The picture was made on a shoestring, and we had to stop every two or three days to raise more money. It was a smash hit, and Billy, Robert, and I all eventually migrated to Hollywood and became directors there.

My career in Hollywood in some ways ran parallel to Billy's. For example, each of us made a picture in the ruins of Berlin after World War II, in 1948. I directed *The Search,* about displaced European children, and Billy directed *A Foreign Affair,* about the Allied occupation of Berlin. Both pictures were successful at the box office.

The cold war years, a period of uncertainty in the aftermath of World War II, spawned Senator Joseph McCarthy's witch hunt for Communists, and the House Un-American Activities Committee hearings. In 1950 Cecil B. De Mille, who was very right wing, persuaded the board of the Screen Directors Guild (SDG) to require a loyalty oath of the membership. Joseph Mankiewicz, the president of the SDG, opposed De Mille's resolution. Billy Wilder and I, among others, signed a petition supporting Mankiewicz.

The De Mille faction sent out messengers on motorcycles late at night with a letter to each of us who supported Mankiewicz's stand. There weren't any direct threats in the letter, but there were heavy hints that our careers were on the line if we didn't endorse De Mille's resolution.

At the general meeting of the SDG membership, the crunch came when

De Mille read our petition to reject his demand for a loyalty oath. De Mille said it was signed by "Mr. Vilder and Mr. Zinnemannnnn," indicating that we were foreigners and that our petition was un-American. With that, the membership booed De Mille. John Ford got up and said, "Cecil, you're a good picture maker, but I don't like what you stand for." Then Ford moved that De Mille's motion for a compulsory loyalty oath be rejected, and it was.

Billy and I seemed to have kept pace with each other throughout our careers. We both won Academy Awards for directing features—two apiece. Billy won for *The Lost Weekend* and for *The Apartment;* I won for *From Here to Eternity* and *A Man for All Seasons.*

Although Billy and I began our careers in Germany, we have always thought of ourselves as Hollywood directors—not just because we worked in the American film industry for so many years but because we both believed in making films that would entertain a mass audience. Neither of us wanted to make pictures that were aimed at an elite—intellectual or otherwise. We always believed that motion pictures were a popular art, meant to entertain the public at large. And that is the kind of movie that we made.

# Acknowledgments

To begin with, I am most grateful to Billy Wilder for granting me an extended interview in his Hollywood office, which was the starting point of this book. In addition, I wish to single out the following among those who have given me their assistance in the course of the long period in which I was engaged in remote preparation for this study. I conducted interviews with filmmaker Fred Zinnemann about how he and Wilder started their careers together in Berlin; with Otto Preminger about acting in Wilder's *Stalag 17;* with Howard Hawks, for whom Wilder cowrote *Ball of Fire;* and with Wilder's friends and fellow directors William Wyler, George Cukor, John Huston, and Garson Kanin.

I met with actors Olivia de Havilland (*Hold Back the Dawn*), Fred MacMurray (*Double Indemnity* and *The Apartment*), Pat O'Brien (*Some Like It Hot*), and Christopher Lee (*The Private Life of Sherlock Holmes*) about working with Wilder; with playwright-screenwriter Samuel Taylor in New York about collaborating with Wilder on *Sabrina;* with screenwriter Ernest Lehman at the Cannes Film Festival about working with Wilder on *Sabrina;* with film executive Edward Small in Hollywood about executive producing *Witness for the Prosecution;* and with Ted Schmidt about serving as an assistant editor on *Some Like It Hot.*

Many institutions and individuals provided me with research materials. I would like to single out the following: the staff of the Celeste Bartos International Film Study Center of the Museum of Modern Art in New York; the staff of the Motion Picture, Broadcasting, and Recorded Sound Division of the Library of Congress in Washington; the staff of the National Archives and Records Administration in College Park, Maryland; the staff of the National Film Archive of the Library of the British Film Institute in London; and the staff of the Department of Special Collections of the Newberry Research Library in Chicago.

Research materials were also provided by the Paramount Collection of the Margaret Herrick Library of the Academy of Motion Picture Arts and Sciences in Beverly Hills, California; the Department of Special Collections of the Charles E. Young Research Library of the University of California at Los Angeles; the Billy Rose Collection of the Theater and Film Collection of the New York Public Library at Lincoln Center; the Film Archive of the George Eastman House in Rochester, New York; the script repositories of Paramount, United Artists, Twentieth Century–Fox, and Universal Studios; film historian and documentary filmmaker Kevin Brownlow; movie critic and film historian Andrew Sarris; Wilder scholar Bernard Dick of Fairleigh Dickinson University; Lester Keyser, professor emeritus of the City College of New York, who tracked down hard to find research materials on Wilder's films; film historian Charles Higham; and the staff of the Rush Medical Center in Chicago, who advised me about Wilder's films *The Lost Weekend* and *Buddy Buddy.*

Fred Zinnemann's recollections of Billy Wilder, which appear as the foreword of this book, were adapted from my interview of Zinnemann. Some materials in this book appeared in completely different forms in the following publications: *The Movie Makers: Artists in an Industry* (Chicago: Nelson-Hall, 1973), copyright by Gene D. Phillips; "Billy Wilder: An Interview," *Literature/Film Quarterly* 4, no. 1 (1976): 2–12, copyright by Salisbury University; *Exiles in Hollywood: Major European Film Directors in America* (Cranbury, NJ: Associated University Presses, 1998), copyright by Associated University Presses; and *Creatures of Darkness: Raymond Chandler, Detective Fiction, and Film Noir* (Lexington: University Press of Kentucky, 2000), copyright by the University Press of Kentucky. These materials are used with permission.

# 1

# From Berlin to Hollywood

## The Early Screenplays

I was a very small fish in the German celluloid pond. I had worked at the Ufa studios in Berlin, but I had only been a tiny wheel in that big machine.

—*Billy Wilder*

"Are we rolling?—as we say on the set?" Veteran film director Billy Wilder eyes the tape recorder before him on his desk and the interviewer across from him. It is hard to believe that this energetic, articulate man began his career in films many years ago in Berlin by writing film scripts, most notably for a semidocumentary called *People on Sunday* (1929). After he migrated to Hollywood in the 1930s in the wake of the rise of Hitler, Wilder continued his career as a scriptwriter for such major directors as Ernst Lubitsch. When he graduated to film direction with *The Major and the Minor* (1942), he continued to collaborate on the scripts for his films, and he finally took over the task of producing the films he directed to ensure his artistic independence. He was, therefore, able to create motion pictures that bore the unmistakable stamp of his own artistic vision.

Although Wilder made comedies as well as dramas, his satirical purpose was the same in film after film: to expose the foibles and flaws of human nature to the public eye to stimulate audiences to serious reflections about the human condition. It has been said that if a satirist like Jonathan Swift had lived in the twentieth century, he would have written screenplays for Billy Wilder.

Wilder's office was richly endowed with memorabilia associated with the greats of Hollywood history with whom he had worked in his long career. There was, for example, a photo of Marlene Dietrich, whom he first knew in Berlin in the early 1920s. Some of the awards he had received over the years were inconspicuously stashed on bookshelves (he won no fewer than six Oscars); they easily went unnoticed by visitors. A veteran like Wilder had no need for self-advertisement.

# Early Years

Billy Wilder was born on June 22, 1906, in Sucha, a town in the Austrian province of Galicia, about one hundred miles east of Vienna, in what was then the Austro-Hungarian Empire but is now part of Poland. He was christened Samuel, but his mother Eugenia, who had lived in New York City for a time in her youth, nicknamed him Billy. She had seen Buffalo Bill's Wild West Show in Madison Square Garden and was fascinated by stories about Billy the Kid.[1] Billy had a brother, Wilhelm, one year older than Billy, whom his mother nicknamed Willie. Maximilian Wilder, their father, ran a chain of railway restaurants at the depots where the trains on the Vienna line stopped. In due course Max moved on to owning a hotel for transients in Krakow called (in English) Hotel City. "My father was a failed entrepreneur; none of his business enterprises ever succeeded," Wilder said.[2]

Billy Wilder was born during the reign of Emperor Franz Josef, who would figure in Wilder's film *The Emperor Waltz* (1948). "Billy Wilder was part of the crowd that watched Emperor Franz Josef's funeral procession in 1916," writes Geoffrey Macnab. "He marveled at the scale of the pageant and the sight of the tiny Crown Prince Otto amid the black clad mourners."[3]

The Wilders moved to Vienna at the outbreak of World War I and remained there after the war. The gymnasium Wilder attended in Vienna was for recalcitrant students. He had earned a reputation early on as a problem student because he sometimes rebelled against the "iron discipline" of the Vienna schools, and he often played hooky. He preferred to skip school and go to the movies. American films were widely available, and his favorite silent film star was Charlie Chaplin.

A crucial incident of Wilder's youth occurred when he noticed a postcard addressed to his father in the afternoon mail. It was an invitation to attend the graduation of his son Hubert from boarding school. The lad in question was Max Wilder's illegitimate son, about whom his immediate family knew nothing. Later Billy silently handed the card to his father, who made no comment about it. "My father and I had an unspoken agreement about the matter," Wilder explained. Hubert was their secret, and that created something of a bond between father and son.[4] In light of this episode, young Billy began to sense at this early age that deception was the normal climate of life—an attitude that would later surface in his films.

Wilder graduated from high school in 1924 at age eighteen with barely passing grades. Soon after, he had another traumatic experience. Having become a rabid fan of American jazz, he frequented a record shop in downtown Vienna, where he bought imported jazz recordings. One of the clerks was an attractive girl named Ilse, and Wilder began dating her—until two of his friends told him that they had noticed Ilse leaning against a lamppost in the red-light district of Vienna, soliciting customers. Wilder went to see for himself. He confronted Ilse, slapped her across the face, and angrily broke off their relationship.

According to biographer Maurice Zolotow, this bitter experience destroyed Wilder's faith in women, and it explains the hard-bitten, cynical females who turn up in his movies, from femmes fatales like Phyllis Dietrichson in *Double Indemnity* to the seductive spy named Ilse in *The Private Life of Sherlock Holmes*. Wilder even employed a similar episode in *Sherlock Holmes*, wherein Holmes recalls, in a flashback, discovering that his girl was a harlot (a scene deleted from the release prints of the film). But Wilder maintained that Zolotow's remarks amounted to a kind of "primer level" Freudian analysis. "He tried to explain why I hate women," Wilder fumed. "Well, I don't hate women"; so, he said, there was nothing to be explained. He added that Ilse made no lasting impression on him whatever.[5]

Wilder was eager to contradict Zolotow on a related point. Zolotow hazarded that Wilder fell into such a deep depression after his breakup with Ilse that he dropped out of law school after only one semester.[6] It is true that Billy's parents had hoped that he would become a lawyer and urged him to enroll in the University of Vienna after high school. But Wilder insisted, "I never attended the university at all, I would have been bored stiff studying law; and I told my parents so."[7]

In any case, after he quarreled with his parents about his future, they finally relented and inquired what career he had in mind. Wilder stubbornly replied that he had set his sights on becoming a newspaper reporter. He had liked writing for his high school newspaper and thought that the life of a journalist would be more interesting and eventful than a job in an office.

In 1924 Wilder moved out of his parents' home and got himself a tawdry flat of his own. He started his writing career by becoming a reporter for *Die Stunde* (The hour), a Viennese tabloid. The paper wanted to feature celebrity interviews for its special Christmas issue in 1925, so Wilder, a cub reporter full of bravado and ambition, sought out renowned Viennese figures for interviews. He succeeded in snaring composer Richard Strauss and playwright Arthur Schnitzler, but he got his comeuppance from Sigmund Freud. Wilder showed Freud his press card, and Freud promptly showed Wilder the door. The controversial founder of psychoanalysis was understandably wary of journalists, but Wilder was proud to have met Freud at all and took this rejection with equanimity.

Because he was an aficionado of jazz, Wilder was particularly interested in interviewing American bandleader Paul Whiteman, the King of Jazz, in the summer of 1926, when he came to Vienna for a concert. Whiteman's lead vocalist was Bing Crosby, who would star in Wilder's musical *The Emperor Waltz* two decades later. Whiteman was pleased with Wilder's write-up of his Vienna concert, so he asked him to come to Berlin and cover his concert there. Wilder cagily notified his parents that he was going to stay in Berlin for a few days after the concert, when he had actually decided to stay there for good.

When Wilder arrived in Berlin at age twenty-one, it was a heady center of the arts that drew ambitious young people from all over Europe. He soon earned a reputation as a freelance crime reporter for Berlin tabloids like *Tempo*. Wilder was already cynical by nature; hence the exposés of greed, lust, and political corruption that he reported for the scandal sheets in Vienna and Berlin served to deepen his cynical attitude toward human nature—an attitude that was later to surface in his films.

Wilder's earnings as a freelance journalist were meager, since he got paid only for the pieces that were accepted. Indeed, he was sometimes reduced to sleeping in the waiting room of a railway station. To make a fast buck in the autumn of 1926, he conceived the idea of writing a series of articles on gigolos, so he posed as a dancing partner for elderly ladies at the Hotel Eden. It was the hotel's custom to hold a thé dansant every afternoon, when young men steered lonely matrons around the dance floor. According to protocol, a lady would ask the waiter for an *Eintanzer* (dancer): "Waiter, I'd like to order one extra-dry dancing partner." The dancer then went through the ritual of asking her to dance with him. "One had to say enchanting things while dancing divinely with those dreadful creatures," Wilder commented. His outré series of articles, "Waiter, Bring Me a Dancer: The Life of a Gigolo," was published in January 1927 in four installments. The series caused quite a furor. Wilder coyly implied that some of the boys provided services for the ladies beyond ballroom dancing, but he always contended that he was not one of them. "I was a newspaper man, gathering evidence for a story"; he maintained that he was not inclined to bed down with any of these "corpulent old ladies," even for a considerable hunk of cash.[8]

Wilder liked to hang out at the Romanisches Café, a Bohemian tavern frequented by people in the film industry as well as newspapermen. He began moving around the edges of the German film industry by making contacts at the café. It was there that he encountered Joe Pasternak and Paul Kohner, managers of the Berlin office of Universal Pictures in Hollywood. He also met a rising young actress named Marlene Dietrich, who would star in two of his films years later.

## The Film Apprentice in Berlin

Berlin in the 1920s was the film capital of Europe; indeed, this period became known as the golden age of German cinema, when directors like Ernst Lubitsch (*Madame Du Barry*), F. W. Murnau (*Nosferatu*), and Fritz Lang (*Metropolis*) produced major silent films in Germany that were seen around the world. So Wilder, while still working as a newspaperman, began writing film scenarios on the side, with a view to pursuing a career in the movies. He could not sell any script under his own name, since he had no standing in the film industry. So he became a ghostwriter: he would collaborate on a script with an established screenwriter but would not receive an official screen credit for his efforts as coauthor of the script.

In all, Wilder worked on close to fifty scripts for silent pictures from 1927 to 1929, receiving twenty-five to fifty dollars per script. The number of screenplays is somewhat misleading, since scripts for silent movies were usually about thirty pages long—there was no dialogue, only action.

In 1928 Max Wilder came to Berlin to visit his son, only to be stricken with severe stomach pains while there. Max expired of an abdominal rupture on November 10, 1928. Wilder buried his father at the Jewish cemetery on Schönhauser Allee in Berlin, since he could not afford to ship the corpse back to Vienna. He was eking out an existence in Berlin. Sometimes he was compelled to borrow money from a man named Nietz, leaving his typewriter as collateral. Wilder would use this incident in *The Lost Weekend* (1945), when a failed writer decides to hock his typewriter.

Wilder was making enough money from ghostwriting to rent a modest accommodation in a slightly disreputable rooming house. It was there that he sold his first solo script. "I was living in a rooming house where there was also living Lulu, the daughter of the housekeeper. Lulu was engaged, but she was also playing around a little on the side. One night, when she was at it again," Heinz, her muscle-bound fiancé, "stormed up the stairs and pounded on the door." Suddenly Wilder saw a frightened man on the ledge outside his window, carrying his clothes in a bundle under his arm. He hauled the man into his room. Wilder recognized him as Herr Galitzenstein, the president of Maxim Films. Wilder seized a script that had been turned down all over town and informed the producer that the price of his hiding out in Wilder's room was that he purchase the screenplay. "Send it along to my office," the producer said. Wilder replied, "Tomorrow you'll forget you ever met me," and demanded payment on the spot. Galitzenstein gave Wilder five hundred marks and beat a hasty retreat down the back stairs.[9]

## *Der Teufelsreporter* (1929)

Carl Laemmle, studio chief at Universal Pictures in Hollywood, sent word to Pasternak and Kohner that he wanted them to produce a low-budget silent picture starring Eddie Polo, a has-been Hollywood Western hero who was trying to revive his sagging career in Germany. Pasternak and Kohner immediately commissioned Wilder to concoct a script for Polo.

Writing the script, Wilder was able to draw on his own experiences as a journalist. Polo had been an action star at Universal in his heyday, so Wilder had him playing an intrepid reporter who captures a mob of kidnappers singlehandedly. Wilder endeavored to enliven the proceedings with a climactic car chase in which Polo gallantly pursues the kidnappers. He even has Polo gamely holding the gang at gunpoint while phoning in his story to his editor—before calling the police! Alas, it was too late to salvage Polo's stalled career, given his advanced age; he was no longer credible as an action hero. *Der Teufelsreporter* (The daredevil reporter) opened on June 19, 1929, in Hamburg and was quickly forgotten. Wilder nursed a grudge against Polo, who had seduced Wilder's current girlfriend, so he wanted to forget Polo and the picture—except for the fact that the film represented his first official screen credit as a scriptwriter, and a solo credit at that.

Wilder developed the habit of writing on the title page of each script "Cum Deo," Latin for "With God." He did so because he was convinced that whatever talent he possessed came from above. He picked up the practice, he said, from another writer whom he worked with in Germany. Then, perhaps a little embarrassed by expressing some religious sentiment, he added, "It can't hurt; it's the cheapest way I know of to bribe that being up there in the clouds."

Wilder's contacts at the Romanisches Café were beginning to pay off, not only in terms of his relationship with Pasternak and Kohner but also in the case of Robert Siodmak, an aspiring filmmaker. Robert's brother Curt suggested that Robert assemble an independent film unit to make a low-budget semidocumentary, shot entirely on location in and around Berlin.

The story was about a group of young Berliners sharing a Sunday afternoon outing on their day off at Lake Wannsee on the outskirts of Berlin. Wilder's scenario was based on Curt's concept. *Menschen am Sonntag* (*People on Sunday*) was the projected title.

## Menschen am Sonntag (1929)

The picture was to be shot on a shoestring; Siodmak drew up a budget of five thousand marks (roughly five hundred American dollars at the time). He then set about cobbling together the financing. He borrowed a goodly sum from a relative. In addition, Edgar Ulmer, a friend of Siodmak's and the assistant director on the film, cofinanced the picture with money that he had earned as a production assistant on Lang's *Metropolis* and other movies.

The balance of the crew included cinematographer Eugene Schüfftan and assistant cinematographer Fred Zinnemann. Schüfftan, who had served as one of the cinematographers on *Metropolis*, was the only pro in the film unit. "Four nonprofessionals were selected to play themselves," remembered Zinnemann, "because we couldn't afford professional actors." They could shoot only on Sundays because all of the actors had regular jobs during the week.[10] The cast included Edwin Splettstösser, a taxi driver; Wolfgang von Walterschausen, a wine salesman; Christl Ehlers, a movie extra; and Brigette Borchert, a salesgirl in a record shop. Each weekend Wilder would meet with Siodmak and Ulmer at the Romanisches Café to flesh out the scenes in Wilder's scenario to be shot that Sunday. Wilder would scribble the additional material "on pieces of scratch paper," the backs of envelopes, and even the café menus.[11]

No one on the team owned a car, so they had to travel by bus to the location sites. During the week, Wilder and Siodmak would take the footage shot on the previous Sunday to the laboratory to be developed. One day they got into a heated argument about a brainstorm that Siodmak had, which departed significantly from the script. To Wilder, the script was always "scripture." They both stormed angrily off the bus, "leaving the film negative behind them—a whole day's work, which was never seen again and had to be reshot."[12]

During production Wilder wrote an article for *Tempo* in which he explained that the film aimed to render a portrait of daily life in Berlin, focusing on a cross-section of typical Berliners. He and his fellow filmmakers wanted to bypass the conventional methods of traditional German cinema. So the movie avoided the "clearly contrived situations" characteristic of the schmaltzy pictures being turned out by the big studios.[13] Since the actors could shoot only one day a week, the filmmakers worked at a fevered tempo each Sunday, to get as much accomplished as possible before having to shut down until the next weekend. When filming finally wrapped, the four principals in the cast retired permanently from the screen. But work on the film continued.

Siodmak and Schüfftan edited the footage into a one-hour film and finished postproduction on December 11, 1929. Wilder and his partners beat the bushes for a distributor, until finally Hanns Brodnitz, who was in charge of distribution at Ufa, the enormous studio at Babelsberg outside Berlin, bought the exhibition rights. (Ufa was the acronym for Universum Film-Aktiengesellschaft, the Universal Film-Production Company). *Menschen am Sonntag* was given a limited release on the art house circuit in Germany in December 1929. It opened in Berlin on February 4, 1930.

Critics noted enthusiastically that the ordinariness of the characters was captured with unvarnished realism. Edwin and Christl loll languidly about on the beach together, while Wolf and Brigette go off into the woods, where he seduces her. The camera coyly pans up to the treetops and descends to the lovers. Brigette then removes a pinecone from under her back; it has been poking her and making her uncomfortable all the time that Wolf was on top of her. She feared that if she mentioned it during their lovemaking, it would ruin the moment. Both Brigette and Wolf laugh nervously as they stare at the cone. At the film's end the four individuals go their separate ways, realizing that they never got to know each other at all. They part nonchalantly, with no plans to see one another on the following Sunday. A printed epilogue declares, "The actors went back into the nameless crowd from which they came."

*Menschen am Sonntag* is a movie of honesty and simplicity. Wilder's script brings "zest, humor, and enthusiasm to what could have been dull material," noted *Sight and Sound* when the film was released on DVD.[14] "The film did make quite a splash at the time it was released," Wilder remembered. "People talked about it. It was a semidocumentary type film, which was very novel for its time. We had a fresh approach to our material because we made the film on our own, and we were therefore not caught up in the quagmire of banality of some of the big studio films. We were chiefly concerned with learning our craft and trying from the beginning of our careers to avoid the clichés of the average commercial pictures."

Wilder and his colleagues were fortunate that their picture was a big success, despite that it was released when silent movies were going out of favor. "*Klangfilm,* that is, sound movies, were introduced in America with

Alan Crosland's *The Jazz Singer*, starring Al Jolson," on October 6, 1927, Zinnemann said. The film had a musical score and four musical numbers, but only one dialogue sequence. "It was followed in July 1928 by Brian Foy's *The Lights of New York*, a gangster movie that was the first all-talking picture," he continued. "The coming of the sound era took Berlin by storm," and there was a frantic rush to convert studios to sound in Berlin.[15] Movies have not shut up since. *Melody of the Heart*, a musical released in Germany in late 1929, formally inaugurated the era of talking pictures in Germany. Wilder welcomed the advent of sound because it allowed for spoken dialogue and thus for more character development. Individual characters could now reveal themselves more effectively through the nuances of speech.

Wilder, Zinnemann, Siodmak, and Ulmer would all become Hollywood directors, but at the time he scripted *Menschen am Sonntag*, Wilder pointed out, he was still making the rounds of the studios. He remembered sounding off at the Romanisches Café about how the studios should be more willing to hire young talent. Robert Liebmann, head of the story department at Ufa, went over to Wilder's table and announced, "If you are as talented at screenwriting as you are at shooting your mouth off, I might give you some work." With that, Wilder began to obtain writing assignments, mostly at Ufa, which was presided over by Erich Pommer, a canny impresario who had helped to make it the top German film corporation.

Between 1930 and 1933, the year that Wilder left Germany, he received official screen credits on at least a dozen films. He said he also made uncredited contributions to some other screenplays, for example, *Ein Burschenlied aus Heidelberg* (The student song from Heidelberg, 1930). One of the most noteworthy films for which Wilder was granted a screen credit was *Emil und die Detektive* (*Emil and the Detectives*, 1931), a fresh, vigorous movie about a lad who secures the help of a gang of street urchins to help him catch a thief. The film was derived from the 1928 novel of the same title by Erich Kästner, which had become an instant children's classic.

Film historian Kevin Brownlow thinks very highly of *Emil und die Detektive*. It "is brilliantly written and directed; it keeps up a tremendous pace. . . . Gerhardt Lamprecht, the director, has a marvelous light touch; the children are appealing and very well directed." The documentary-style use of locations, Brownlow continues, makes the film of special interest. "The freshness and vitality of the street scenes must have been astonishing to audiences accustomed to all of the studio-bound talkies." He concludes, "This is one of my top favorite German films."[16] The movie was a big hit in Germany when it premiered on December 2, 1931, and it went on to be booked on the art house circuit in the United States.

The last German movie Wilder collaborated on was *Was Frauen träu-men* (*What Women Dream,* 1933), which stars Peter Lorre, one of Wilder's pals from the Romanisches Café, as a police detective on the trail of a female jewel thief.

When Hitler officially became chancellor in January 1933, Wilder real-ized his days in Berlin were numbered. The Nazis were tightening their grip on every aspect of German society, including the film industry. Wilder was very much aware that, as a Jew, he had no future in Germany.

# Exile in Paris

Wilder opted to emigrate to France, since he was fairly fluent in French, which he had studied at school. Twenty-four hours after the Reichstag fire, Wilder took the midnight train to Paris. All the money he could scrape together was hidden in his hatband. He was wise to leave Germany when he did; a few days after his departure, the front office at Ufa carried out an offi-cial "purge" of the Jewish employees at the studio.

The twenty-six-year-old Wilder arrived in Paris on the morning of March 1, 1933. He holed up at the Ansonia, a shabby boardinghouse near the Arc de Triomphe, where several Jewish expatriates whom he had known at Ufa had taken lodgings: Lorre; composers Frederick Hollander and Franz Waxman; and screenwriters Max Kolpe, Hans Lustig, Walter Reisch, and Robert Liebmann. Wilder would work again with Hollander, Reisch, and Waxman in Hollywood. Right now he got together with Kolpe and Lustig and hashed out a screenplay for a low-budget caper film about a gang of delinquents who specialize in stealing cars. Waxman committed himself to scoring the picture once they got the project off and running. The screen-play was titled *Mauvaise graine* (*Bad Seed*), using a term for a youngster who is incorrigible and usually becomes a delinquent—thus the auto thieves in the script.

## *Mauvaise graine* (1933)

Wilder and his team had difficulty obtaining financial backing for the movie, since none had established themselves in the French film industry. One pro-ducer offered to fund the picture, provided that his girlfriend could play the female lead. Wilder sarcastically noted that the young lady could not act her way out of one of her cashmere sweaters and turned her down, thereby alienating the producer.

To save money, Wilder's partners persuaded him to direct the movie.

He in turn recruited a Hungarian immigrant, filmmaker Alexander Esway, to codirect the picture with him. Wilder had no experience in directing, but Esway had already codirected two French movies, including *Le jugement de minuit* (The judgment of the moment, 1932). It was Esway who in turn secured producer Edouard Corniglion-Molinier to finance the picture for one hundred thousand American dollars—a small budget by today's standards, but a king's ransom for an independent film in 1933.

Danielle Darrieux, who played Jeanette, remembered that the cast considered Wilder the principal director of the picture. He coached the actors during rehearsals, while Esway kibitzed from the sidelines. Wilder added, "Most of the interiors were shot in a converted garage, even the living room scenes."[17]

Wilder shrewdly incorporated into the film several sequences that were shot silent, with only the addition of background music and sound effects. Waxman's lively jazz score was filled with fox-trot tunes.

Wilder came up with some inventive directorial touches for his first effort as a filmmaker. Jeanette first appears holding up her compact mirror while checking her makeup. Then she lowers the mirror to reveal her lovely face. Jeanette, it develops, is the only female member of the mob of youthful auto thieves to which her brother Jean (Raymond Galle) also belongs. After Henri (Pierre Mingand) joins the gang, he soon falls for the beguiling Jeanette, and their relationship blossoms into love. Wilder slyly introduced a veiled homosexual subplot into the film. Baby-faced Jean has a crush on Henri, whom he invites to share his flat and sleep on his couch. Jean proudly proclaims more than once that Henri is his best friend, trots around after him like an adoring puppy, and is on hand when Henri undresses for bed. Yet none of the other characters seem to notice, perhaps because Henri is seriously preoccupied with Jeanette.

When Henri and Jeanette are spotted by the police riding in a stolen vehicle, the cops give chase. The speeding car careens off the road and crashes into a ditch. Henri and Jeanette manage to survive the accident and elude the police, but the harrowing experience motivates them to go straight. The film concludes with the young lovers' embarking on a steamship bound for America and a new life.

Like Wilder's earlier German film, the present French picture was shot documentary style in the streets and alleyways of the city and on country lanes. "We didn't use a single studio soundstage. We shot mostly outdoors on real locations," Wilder explained, just as François Truffaut and his comrades would later advocate.

Long unavailable for viewing, *Mauvaise graine* was released on DVD in the United States in a spiffed-up digital package in 2002. Wilder's directorial debut cleverly weaves bouncy comedy with high-octane thrills. This movie is significant because it fills in a gap in Wilder's filmography; it is a potboiler that mixes comedy with crime melodrama, as Wilder would later do again in *Some Like It Hot* (1959).

*Mauvaise graine* went into general release in France in the summer of 1934, greeted by mostly positive reviews. "I cannot say that it made me very happy" to have directed a feature film, Wilder said, since the pressure of directing his first film on the double and on the cheap made the production experience a real ordeal. "But now I knew I could do it."[18] He still preferred writing to directing, and by the time *Mauvaise graine* was in the cinemas, he was already in Hollywood pursuing his career as a film writer.

After finishing *Mauvaise graine,* Wilder sent an original script, "Pam-Pam," to Joe May, a German who had known him at Ufa and was now a producer at Columbia Pictures in Hollywood. On the strength of Wilder's screenplay, May arranged to bring him over to Hollywood at the studio's expense for a brief writing stint at Columbia. Several of Wilder's fellow refugees, including Lorre and Reisch, also decamped for Hollywood around this time.

Wilder left Europe for New York on the *Aquitania* on January 22, 1934. His brother Willie, who had preceded him to the United States by some years, met him at the dock. Willie had developed a successful line of women's handbags in New York. Billy stayed a few days with Willie and his family in their home on Long Island, where he got his first impression of America. When he got up one snowy morning, he noticed a big, black Cadillac stopping in front of the house. A boy with a stack of newspapers got out and tossed one on the porch. The weather was bad, so the news-boy's family, it seems, was driving him on his paper route. "What kind of a country is this?" Wilder exclaimed. "Newspapers delivered by Cadillac!"[19] A few days later, Wilder arrived by train in Los Angeles.

A decade later, Willie followed Billy to Hollywood, where he produced and directed a variety of cheapies under the name of W. Lee Wilder to avoid being confused with his brother Billy. Willie's only film of note was *The Great Flamarion* (1945), a low-budget film noir starring Erich von Stroheim, whose career was in decline, and directed by Anthony Mann, whose career was on the rise.

Soon after Billy's arrival in Hollywood, he set to work at Columbia expanding his scenario for "Pam-Pam" into a full-length screenplay. Looking back, he said,

> Basically you would have to divide the influx of German picture makers into the United States into two categories. First there were

the ones that were hired by the American studios because they were outstanding geniuses like Murnau and Lubitsch, to mention just the very prominent ones. These were the people who came over in the '20s who were sought after by studio executives because they had made enormously successful films in Europe. That was the first group.

Then in the middle '30s came an avalanche of refugees who were looking for jobs on the basis of their experience in German pictures such as Zinnemann and myself. We didn't come because we were invited like the first group; we came to save our lives, and from the first we desperately tried to learn English so that we could get work in Hollywood. So you see in my case I was a job seeker, not an accomplished motion picture maker. Moreover, Austria, my country, no longer existed for me. I really had to make good here. It wasn't a question of my saying to myself, "Well, if things don't work out here I can go back to Austria or to Germany." For me it was a question of fighting it out here and surviving, or going back and winding up like most of my family in the ovens of Auschwitz.

Since my profession at the time was writing, it was especially important for me to learn English, and here I was knowing only German and French. It was a very tough period for me. I had sold an original story to Columbia while I was still in Paris and I made $150 a week for a short time because of that when I first arrived in Hollywood.

Though Wilder spoke no more than a smattering of rudimentary English, he admitted to knowing about a dozen words that the industry censor would not tolerate. He taught himself the language by regularly listening to baseball games on the radio and by going to American movies.

# Hollywood Immigrant

The studio boss of Columbia was Harry Cohn, an obstreperous, volatile, vulgar-tongued Hollywood mogul; he was once called a thug in a front-office suit. Sam Briskin, Cohn's chief assistant, was an equally gruff, outspoken type.

During his first meeting with Wilder, Briskin was chagrined to observe Wilder's poor command of English. When Briskin inquired about Wilder's nationality, Wilder froze; his English temporarily deserted him and he muttered, "I . . . been . . . Austrian." Briskin dispatched Wilder to the writers' compound, where he was assigned to a six-by-eight cubicle. Wilder was severely handicapped by his elementary English. "I kept writing in German, and some of my pals who were a little ahead of me would translate my stuff into English." Years later, he examined the translation of one of his scripts and suffered "a mild coronary" when he discovered that his translators were not always accurate in rendering his work into English.[20]

Wilder's six-month contract with Columbia expired; so did the visitor's permit with which he had entered America. He had to go to Mexico to obtain an immigration visa because the U.S. quota for immigrants from Europe had been filled. Wilder crossed the border into Mexico and rented a squalid hotel room in Mexicali, where he presented his case to the official at the U.S. Consulate. "I knew I needed a bunch of documents to present to the consul," he said later, "but all I had was my birth certificate and my passport." Wilder explained to the consul that he had left Berlin on very short notice; if he went back to Germany to obtain additional credentials, "they would ship me to Dachau on the next train." Finally the consul asked him how he hoped to support himself in the United States. "I write screenplays," Wilder answered. The consul paced up and down his narrow, dilapidated office, then returned to his desk and said, "Write some good ones!" With that, the consul, a movie buff, stamped Wilder's passport, allowing him to stay permanently in the United States. Wilder concluded, "I have tried ever since not to disappoint that dear man in Mexicali." For the record, Wilder became an American citizen in 1939, a date he remembered as one of the shining days of his life.

When he returned to Los Angeles from Mexicali, however, life was still bleak; he went hungry for weeks on end while he continued to study English. He endeavored to find employment as a scriptwriter on the basis of his previous work in Germany. "I had collaborated on German films that most people in Hollywood had never heard of. . . . I had to entice an agent to handle me because my list of credits from Germany was not impressive. There was no *Nosferatu* behind me as there was behind Murnau. I had none of the accomplishments of an Ernst Lubitsch."

For a time Wilder got a cramped room at the tacky Château Marmont, an actors' hotel on the Sunset Strip. During the Christmas season, however, the hotel was fully booked, and Wilder was reduced to living in the lounge adjoining the women's restroom, since that was all he could afford. The ladies eyed him suspiciously as they passed through his "quarters" en route to the lavatory. Later on he bunked with Peter Lorre in a fleabag hotel for ten dollars a week. They survived "in dignified starvation" on one can of Campbell's soup a day, warmed on a hot plate. "I had leather patches on the elbows of my jacket," Wilder recalled, "not because it was fashionable, but because there were holes in them."

Wilder's poverty did not last, but he always retained his German accent. "You could lose your accent if you came over from Europe as a youngster," he explained; "if you went to school here. But I was nearly twenty-eight when I arrived. It was too late for me to lose my foreign accent."[21] Elsewhere, he remarked, "If you think *I* have an accent, you should have heard Ernst Lubitsch," for whom Wilder would work as a screenwriter. Wilder continued, "But he had a wonderful ear for the American idiom and slang; you either have an ear or you don't, as Van Gogh said. I suppose I have it; many foreigners do."[22]

Wilder also never lost his outsider's view of American life. "We who had our roots in the European past, I think, brought with us a fresh attitude towards America, a new eye with which to examine this country on film, as opposed to the eye of native-born moviemakers who were accustomed to everything around them. Hence there was some novelty about our approach to the films that we made here from the start."

As Wilder's English improved, so did his fortunes. Joe May was offered a chance to direct films at Fox Studios, and he managed to wangle a short-term contract for Wilder there. Wilder collaborated on the script for May's *Music in the Air* (1934), which was based on a dated operetta by Jerome Kern and Oscar Hammerstein II. The movie was produced by Erich Pommer, another immigrant for whom Wilder had worked at Ufa. Wilder received his first official screen credit on an American film, but the hummable Kern-Hammerstein score could not redeem the flimsy plot, and *Music in the Air* failed at the box office.

When Fox merged with Twentieth Century in 1935, Wilder was out of a job. He continued to live a hand-to-mouth existence in the film colony, not having much luck as a screenwriter. He collaborated on scripts for a string of forgettable pictures, sometimes uncredited; these included love stories, crime melodramas, and musicals.

Finally, in 1936, Wilder was placed under contract to Paramount by Manny Wolf, head of the story department. Wolf, a short, nattily dressed chap with Coke-bottle glasses, was a shrewd judge of talent. He saw that Wilder was a promising writer and hired him at a salary of $250 a week. The writers' building on the Paramount lot, which housed 104 screenwriters, had been christened the Tower of Babel because it housed so many writers who were exiles, like Wilder himself.

One of the writers whom Paramount employed around this time was American novelist F. Scott Fitzgerald. Wilder was unimpressed by Fitzgerald's screenwriting abilities: "It seemed to me as though he could never get beyond page 3 of a script. He made me think of a great sculptor who is hired to do a plumbing job. He did not know how to connect the fucking pipes, so the water would flow." Fitzgerald was a great novelist, Wilder concluded, but he did not know how to construct a scene in a screenplay.[23]

During his first couple of years in Hollywood, Wilder shied away from dating women in the German refugee colony who, like himself, were employed in the film industry. Instead, he acquired American girlfriends who could help him master English. As a freelance screenwriter, he played the field and did not think seriously about marriage. Once he had a steady job on salary, however, he decided that he was in a position to marry.

Wilder had been introduced by another screenwriter to Judith Iribe, a sophisticated lady from a prominent California family. They had been dating for more than a year when he finally popped the question; they eloped to Yuma, Arizona, on December 22, 1936. The newlyweds moved into an apartment on South Camden Drive in Beverly Hills and eventually into a house on North Beverly Drive. Their daughter Victoria was born on December 21, 1939, one day before their third wedding anniversary.

Judith was courtly and reserved; Billy was brash and indelicate. Not surprisingly, they gradually grew apart, and Billy sought companionship elsewhere. Judith and Billy became increasingly estranged as the years went by and eventually divorced.

Wilder formed an important professional relationship in 1936, the year of his first marriage, that proved to be far more viable than his personal relationship with his wife. Wolf decided to team Wilder with another contract screenwriter, Charles Brackett. Fourteen years Wilder's senior, Brackett was a graduate of Harvard University. He had become the first drama critic for the *New Yorker* while publishing short stories in slick magazines with big circulations like the *Saturday Evening Post*. He had been associated with a number of minor movies like *The Last Outpost* (1935), a flaccid Cary Grant starrer about British troops in the desert, codirected by Louis Gasnier and Charles Barton. Brackett was an accomplished wordsmith. So it was that, on the morning of July 17, 1936, Wolf called Wilder into his office and said, "Meet Charles Brackett; from now on you're a team." Brackett declared solemnly that a team was made up of those "whom God had joined together."[24]

Once Brackett and Wilder joined forces, their screenwriting careers flourished. The two partners could not have been more dissimilar. Wilder was a feisty middle European Jew; Brackett was an East Coast patrician. "Brackett and I had nothing in common but writing," said Wilder. It was precisely because he and Brackett were so different that their collaboration worked. "If two people think alike, it's like two men pulling at one end of a rope," Wilder commented. He was a firm believer that the best scripts emerged from the friction between the writers who collaborated on them. "If you are going to collaborate, you need an opponent to bounce things off of."[25] Moreover, Wilder welcomed a writing partner who could polish his uncertain English. He wrote, "I was lucky enough to be teamed with Charles Brackett," an experienced writer for whom he already had great respect.[26]

The creative association of Wilder and Brackett was to last for more than a decade. They functioned perfectly as a writing team: Brackett, who had an impeccable command of English, fine-tuned the dialogue, while Wilder concentrated on plot construction, at which he had become proficient in his Berlin days.

The first film that Brackett and Wilder coscripted was a comedy titled *Bluebeard's Eighth Wife* (1938), derived from a French farce that had been filmed in 1923 with Gloria Swanson. The remake would be directed by none other than Ernst Lubitsch, Wilder's idol.

# 2

# Champagne and Tears
## *Ninotchka, Midnight,* and *Ball of Fire*

> In a film, marriage is a beautiful mistake that two people make together.
>
> —*Ernst Lubitsch*

When he was preparing *Bluebeard's Eighth Wife* for filming, Ernst Lubitsch wanted Charles Brackett to write the screenplay. He did not ask the studio for Billy Wilder as well because he did not want to give the impression that he was a German-born director who favored hiring members of the German immigrant colony in Hollywood. But Manny Wolf told Lubitsch that Brackett and Wilder were a team, so Wilder was part of the deal.

Lubitsch, a stout, cigar-chomping little man with a thick German accent, had a genius for making Hollywood pictures, like *Trouble in Paradise* (1932), marked by sophisticated Continental humor. In his first meeting with Brackett and Wilder, he posed a thought-provoking question. In romantic comedies, he explained, the hero and the heroine should not meet in an ordinary way. They should "meet-cute," as the saying goes; that is, they should meet in an unexpected manner that will get the audience interested in them. Lubitsch accordingly asked his writers, "How do the boy and girl get together?"

Wilder, who kept a notebook of clever ideas for use in screenplays, volunteered this proposal: Wealthy Michael Brandon (the character eventually played by Gary Cooper) is trying to buy pajamas in a men's store on the French Riviera where he is vacationing, but he sleeps only in the pants. He is thrifty, as millionaires go, so he insists on purchasing only the pants. The clerk says he must buy the tops as well. Nicole de Loiselle (who would be played by Claudette Colbert) comes into the store and asks to buy the tops only, because she sleeps only in the tops. So Michael and Nicole divide a pair of pajamas. Lubitsch was enthusiastic about Wilder's suggestion, which was the ultimate meet-cute scene.

Wilder continued the habit of scribbling ideas into a pocket notebook throughout his career. "I have always been an inveterate note-taker, because you never know when the muse will touch your brow." These bright ideas, he concluded, could come in handy on the days "when the muse goes out to have her hair done."

## Collaborating with Ernst Lubitsch: *Bluebeard's Eighth Wife* (1938) and *Ninotchka* (1939)

Lubitsch was just finishing another picture. So he told his writing team to go ahead and work out the narrative structure of the entire scenario, and he would have story conferences with them from time to time. The French farce by Alfred Savoir that they were adapting provided the skeleton of the scenario, including certain tentpole scenes that they had to work into the script for *Bluebeard's Eighth Wife*.

Lubitsch was a perfectionist who insisted on polishing a screenplay until it was as good as possible. "Preparation is everything," he wrote; it was vital that every scene in the script "be detailed down to the last raising of an eyelid."[1] He never allowed actors to improvise on the set—an attitude that Wilder picked up from his mentor when he became a director. Wilder clearly found in Lubitsch a kindred spirit.

During script sessions, Lubitsch would act out each role as he tested the writers' dialogue. He would periodically prod Brackett and Wilder with queries like "Is this the best we can do?" Wilder declared, "If the truth be known, Lubitsch was the best writer who ever lived." Most of the "bright ideas" came from him. In the script, when the American Michael is looking for a clothing store in France, he notices a sign in a store window: "English is spoken here." Lubitsch penciled into the screenplay at this point the following addition to the sign: "American understood."[2]

Michael is a millionaire who has married and divorced seven women; he paid each of them a generous settlement when he got bored with her. After marrying him, Nicole learns that she is the eighth Mrs. Brandon and nicknames him "Bluebeard." She decides to divorce him for a huge amount of alimony. But after many twists and turns, Nicole realizes that she really loves Michael, and she decides to remain Bluebeard's eighth—and final—wife.

*Bluebeard's Eighth Wife* began principal photography on October 11, 1937. Lubitsch allowed Wilder to observe him at work on the set whenever he got the chance. "His technique was totally subordinated to storytelling,"

Wilder recalled. "His theory—and mine—is that, if the viewer notices direction, you have failed." Whenever the camerawork calls attention to itself, it is mere showmanship. For example, a living room should not be filmed with a camera inside the fireplace, shooting out at the room through the flames, "unless it is from the point of view of Santa Claus coming down the chimney."[3]

Shooting wrapped in January 1938, and postproduction was completed in time for a New York premiere on March 23. Some reviewers scored the picture as a near miss, complaining that Cooper never seemed at home in the role of a much-married millionaire. Moreover, the film seemed to gradually lose its sparkle after the buoyant opening scenes, when marital discord sets in. Other critics thought the picture a winner, noting that the Brackett-Wilder script provided some fine comic moments and that Lubitsch knew how to make the most of them. Despite these mixed reviews, the picture turned a profit, and Lubitsch was more than willing to collaborate with Brackett and Wilder again.

Only a few days before the opening of *Bluebeard's Eighth Wife,* Hitler annexed Austria to the Nazi empire, and Austrian Jews were summarily deprived of their civil rights. The Nazis had been actively promoting a so-called *Anschluss* (union) between Austria and Germany since 1935. Wilder had visited his mother in Vienna in 1935 and entreated her to come to America with him. But at the time she was convinced that Germany would not take over Austria in the foreseeable future. Besides, his widowed mother intended to marry again; she was engaged to a businessman named Siedliska, whom Wilder never met. "She was set in her ways," Wilder said, and she decided to stay in Vienna with her new husband.

Wilder never saw his mother again. In the wake of the *Anschluss,* he lost contact with her. After the war, he was informed by Auschwitz survivors he had met when visiting Vienna in the summer of 1945 that his mother had been taken to the death camp in a cattle car. He finally learned through the Red Cross that his mother, his grandmother, and his stepfather were all gassed at Auschwitz in 1941. "The Nazis just threw my family away," he said.

No doubt Wilder's own view of human nature was indelibly shaped by his experience of the twentieth century's violent events. "I learned many things about human nature," he said of those days, "none of them favorable." To the end of his life, he felt "fury, tears, and reproaches" over the loss of his family to the Holocaust. He believed that he should have insisted that they come with him to America in 1935, and not left them behind in Vienna. But, he concluded stoically, paraphrasing Shakespeare, "What is done is done, and cannot be undone."[4]

After the theatrical release of *Bluebeard's Eighth Wife,* Lubitsch's tenure at Paramount was at an end. He moved over to Metro-Goldwyn-Mayer to shoot a vehicle for Greta Garbo, at her request. Lubitsch accordingly arranged for Paramount to loan Brackett and Wilder to MGM to write the screenplay. He also hired Walter Reisch, a screenwriter with whom Wilder had worked at Ufa. The picture was to be titled *Ninotchka.*

Wilder welcomed the opportunity to observe the director applying his celebrated "Lubitsch touch" to another film. Because the term was coined by a publicist, no one, least of all Lubitsch, ever elaborated on it. Wilder finally described it as "a gracefully sophisticated, mischievous way of getting a provocative point across to the audience by innuendo." Thus in Lubitsch's films there are women of easy virtue, but no sluts; masked balls, but no orgies. "Lubitsch could do more with a closed door than most directors can do with an open fly," Wilder explained. Beyond the closed door, the filmgoer imagined, the naughty lovers "were accomplishing outrageous things." In sum, the Lubitsch touch was a cosmopolitan yet outré kind of humor, "an incomparable ability to present delightfully barbed and suggestive dialogue in such a way that it never seemed vulgar, but charming and discreet."[5]

The screenplay for *Ninotchka* evolved from a brief story synopsis scribbled in a notebook by writer Melchior Lengyel. He in due course submitted it to MGM, suggesting that it would make a vehicle for Garbo: "Russian girl saturated with Bolshevist ideals goes to imperialistic Paris. She meets romance and has an uproarious good time. Capitalism not so bad after all." MGM liked the concept enough to pay Lengyel fifteen thousand dollars for the three-sentence scenario.[6]

Lubitsch closeted himself with his troika of writers, and together they hammered out a detailed screenplay. Commissar Ninotchka Yakushova (the Greta Garbo character) is sent from Moscow to Paris to check up on three inept envoys from the Kremlin who have been assigned to sell jewels confiscated by the Communist regime from a czarist aristocrat. The diamonds once belonged to the exiled Grand Duchess Swana (Ina Claire). But the three Russian stooges, Iranoff (Sig Ruman), Buljanoff (Felix Bressart), and Kopalski (Alexander Granach), have been seduced by the decadent pleasures of Paris and have all but disregarded their mission. Lubitsch's Paris is a place of infinite elegance, wit, and sexual tolerance; it represents a flight from everyday reality. Ninotchka intends to retrieve the jewels and get on with selling them to a Paris jeweler herself, to raise money for the state. But Swana coaxes her urbane lover, Leon d'Algout (Melvyn Douglas), to deflect Ninotchka from her set purpose by romancing her.

The razor-sharp dialogue in the streamlined screenplay by Wilder and his cohorts provides Garbo with some pungent lines. Asked by her three bungling comrades how things are in Moscow, Ninotchka, with her unbecoming granite face, replies in a tombstone voice. Speaking of Stalin's purges, she intones, "The last mass trials were a great success. There are going to be fewer but better Russians."

Leon takes Ninotchka under his wing, and they go to a bistro for lunch. In an effort to melt her ice-cold exterior, he tells her some stale jokes. Ninotchka steadfastly declines to laugh at any of them. Leon is nonetheless carried away by his own comic routine and falls off his chair; at the sight of his pratfall, Ninotchka bursts into gales of laughter. When Garbo let loose with uproarious laughter during rehearsals for this scene, Lubitsch said, "From that moment on, I knew I had a picture."[7] Ninotchka develops a crush on Leon, and the feeling is mutual.

Principal photography commenced on May 31, 1939, and lasted fifty-eight days. Garbo had no problems with the double entendres in the script. For example, on a date with Ninotchka, Leon observes, as the clock strikes twelve, "It is midnight; one-half of Paris is making love to the other half." Continuing his amorous badinage, he says, "Look at the clock: one hand has met the other hand, and they kiss." Then Leon bestows a kiss on Ninotchka.

Garbo insisted that anyone who was not absolutely necessary to the shooting of a scene was not to be on the set. This prohibition included the screenwriters. But Wilder contrived to sneak onto the soundstage occasionally to watch Lubitsch direct a scene with a skeleton crew. One day Wilder was hiding behind a piece of scenery, watching the filming, when two production assistants put a screen in front of him. "Nobody said for me to leave," he remembered; "they just put it there. But I knew that Garbo had felt my presence. She had eyes in the back of her head."

Wilder explained that the film was a "serious satire," with references to the repressive Bolshevik regime endured by the Russian people. Back in Moscow after her sojourn in Paris, Ninotchka is reunited with Buljanoff, Iranoff, and Kopalski at a party in the cold-water flat she shares with her roommate Anna in a dreary tenement. One of the other tenants walks by while Anna is chatting with Ninotchka, and Anna suddenly lapses into stony silence. "I never know whether he is going to the washroom or to the secret police," Anna explains.

Lubitsch invited his screenwriters to a sneak preview of the picture in Long Beach. Afterward he read through the stack of preview cards turned in by the audience; suddenly he roared with laughter at one card. "I was wondering what the hell was so funny," said Wilder. Finally Lubitsch handed him the card, which read, "Funniest film I ever saw; I laughed so hard that I peed in my girlfriend's hand."[8] Wilder howled too. "Garbo laughs!" was the slogan of the movie's publicity campaign, a reference to the many humorless roles she had played in the past.

Wilder's high regard for Lubitsch never diminished. "Many of us have tried so hard to imitate the Lubitsch Touch," Wilder said. "Oh, we may get lucky: a few feet of cunning film once in a while, . . . that is *like* Lubitsch—but *not* Lubitsch."[9] He added later, "I have sometimes been called the heir of Lubitsch. My God, if I could write and direct like Lubitsch, I would be a very happy man. . . . No one but Lubitsch could make a Lubitsch picture."

## Collaborating with Mitchell Leisen: *Midnight* (1939) and *Hold Back the Dawn* (1941)

Brackett and Wilder coauthored the screenplay for another comedy in 1939, *Midnight,* which they wrote just before *Ninotchka*. It was directed by Mitchell Leisen, for whom the pair would also write *Hold Back the Dawn* (1941). Whereas Wilder developed quite a rapport with Lubitsch, he never got along with Leisen. In fact, he dismissed Leisen as Paramount's second-string Lubitsch.

Leisen had graduated to directing after serving as Cecil B. De Mille's set designer on films like *The King of Kings* (1927). He became a prominent director of screwball comedies, a brand of farce that flourished during the Depression era, when audiences hungered for escapist entertainment. This style of comedy combines sophisticated repartee with slapstick; it depends on fast, witty dialogue and usually focuses on the battle of the sexes. The main characters often represent different classes of society. Leisen's *Easy Living* (1937), for example, deals with a rich playboy (Ray Milland) falling for a typist (Jean Arthur). It was written by Preston Sturges, who helped to make it a frenetic farce that was one of Leisen's best screwball comedies.

*Midnight* was intended as a vehicle for Claudette Colbert, Paramount's biggest box office draw; hence producer Arthur Hornblow Jr. judged it important enough for him to splurge on a topflight cast and crew. In addition to Colbert, the cast list boasted Don Ameche (*In Old Chicago*), John Barrymore (*Grand Hotel*), and Mary Astor (*Dodsworth*). Cinematographer Charles Lang and editor Doane Harrison would later work on Wilder's own films. So would composer Frederick Hollander, who had written the music for one of Wilder's earlier German films.

The scenario of *Midnight* centers on Eve Peabody (Claudette Colbert), an out-of-work showgirl stranded in Paris, who catches the eye of taxi driver Tibor Czerny (Don Ameche). But Eve is a gold digger who is looking for bigger game than a cabbie. As in *Bluebeard's Eighth Wife*, Brackett and Wilder came up with a pip of an opening scene. Eve arrives one evening in a Paris depot, sitting on a wooden bench in a third-class coach with no luggage. An ex-chorine down on her luck, she is wearing the only finery she has left, a gold lamé evening gown. Tibor is much taken by her and offers her a free ride in his cab. She asks him to drive her around town while she looks for work. Asked what kind of work she wants, she replies, "Well, at this time of night and in these clothes, I'm not looking for needlework." Eve implies, with an innuendo reminiscent of Lubitsch, that she is a mercenary young woman who is not above latching on to a wealthy beau now and then. At the moment, however, she is hoping to find a singing job. Tibor drives her around to several nightclubs, but her auditions come to nothing. Eve shrugs that she is prepared to sleep in the waiting room of the train station (evoking Wilder's early days in Berlin). But she soon crashes a society party by proffering a pawn ticket as an invitation. There she encounters millionaire Georges Flamarion (John Barrymore), and the screenplay shifts into high gear.

Georges is willing to pay Eve handsomely to pose as a baroness to lure Jacques Picot, a dapper gigolo, away from his straying wife Helene (Mary Astor). Impishly appropriating Tibor's surname, Eve calls herself Baroness Czerny, a Hungarian aristocrat. The deal includes Georges inviting Eve to a lavish party at his swank country estate. He tells her in the course of the soiree that she is the belle of the ball. She replies, "Every Cinderella has her midnight." Tibor traces Eve to Georges's villa, where he quickly sizes up the situation and introduces himself as Eve's husband, Baron Czerny. Eve endeavors to keep Tibor from exposing her as an impostor by maintaining that her hapless husband is incurably insane. Eventually Eve tires of the masquerade and declares her love for Tibor, while Georges and Helene are reunited.

Leisen jealously guarded his prerogatives as a director, revising and deleting lines without consulting Brackett and Wilder—unlike Lubitsch, who always compared notes with his writers. Wilder was fit to be tied when he learned what Leisen was up to; he took to sneaking onto the set to ascertain whether Leisen was shooting a scene as written. When Leisen caught him hiding behind a flat on the soundstage one day, he had Wilder barred from the set, claiming that Wilder was spying on him. Wilder was outraged when he was escorted from the set by a security officer, but Brackett, who was always a calming influence on him, got him to cool off.

Wilder was acerbic in describing Leisen. If Leisen put down Wilder for being a "foreigner," Wilder poked fun at Leisen, who was bisexual, for flamboyantly flaunting his homosexual proclivities. It was an open secret in the movie colony that Leisen "turned his home into a homosexual rendezvous," according to Zolotow. With that in mind, Wilder fumed, "Leisen was too goddamned fey. I don't knock fairies; but Leisen . . . was stupid." Leisen, the former set designer, spent more time arranging the silverware and dishes on the table of a dining room set "than he did discussing scenes with the writers." Wilder smirked that Leisen was still a set designer, not a director; he was a "window dresser." What's more, Leisen "didn't know crap about narrative construction; and he didn't care."[10] Wilder, who would eventually gain a reputation as a master of the well-made screenplay, maintained that each detail should have a precise, interlocking function in the script. "In a good script, *everything* is necessary or it ain't good," he contended. "And if you take out one piece, you better replace it with a different piece or you got trouble."[11]

By the time he appeared in *Midnight*, Barrymore was a drunken relic of the dashing matinee idol he had been in silent pictures like *Don Juan* (1926), when he was dubbed the Great Profile. One night during the shooting period, Barrymore went on a binge; he was so fuddled with drink that he went into the ladies' room of a Hollywood nightclub by mistake. A woman came in while he was relieving himself and exclaimed in outrage, "Sir, this is for women!" Undismayed, Barrymore turned around and declared, "So is this."[12] Little wonder that Barrymore's addled mind could not retain his lines. *Midnight* represented the culmination of his long career, which ended with Barrymore's death from cirrhosis of the liver on May 29, 1942.

When the film opened on March 24, 1939, the notices not only praised the picture for being an outstanding screwball comedy but also singled out the superior screenplay; indeed, one reviewer, according to Tom Wood, called it "a script of diamond brilliance."[13] When the film was released on DVD in 2007, the *New York Times* termed it "a diverting comedy" with Colbert and Ameche "running amok."[14] When, in 2006, film scholar David Kipen picked the top five Hollywood screenplays of all time, among them was *Midnight*, a "magnificent, overlooked screwball comedy."[15]

Brackett and Wilder reentered the lists with Leisen when they were assigned to write the screenplay for *Hold Back the Dawn*. Wilder's interactions with Leisen were once more marred by several testy exchanges. In the years ahead, Wilder would consistently refer to Leisen as "that fag who ruined my scripts."[16]

By this juncture, Brackett and Wilder had developed a standard method of composing screenplays. Wilder paced back and forth in the office, chain-smoking and swinging a walking stick or riding crop, sometimes whacking a piece of furniture to drive home a point to his partner. "I needed something to keep my hands busy," Wilder explained, "and a pencil wasn't long enough." It was Brackett who wielded the pencil. Brackett curled up on the sofa with his shoes off, making notes with a legal pad and pencil. Their script conferences inevitably degenerated into shouting matches. "We fought a lot," Wilder remembered. "Brackett and I were like a box of matches. We kept striking till it lit up. He would sometimes throw a telephone book or a lampshade at me."[17]

Still, Wilder valued Brackett's presence. "It's such an exhausting thing, facing that empty page in the morning," he explained. "One of the best things about a collaborator is that he stops you from committing suicide. You have to have specific talent to be a collaborator. It's like a marriage."[18] Wilder acknowledged that Brackett "didn't think like I did at all, didn't even approve of me. But, by God! When we started mapping out dialogue, there were sparks!"[19]

A Brackett-Wilder screenplay was not committed to paper until every line of dialogue had been discussed thoroughly. To offset the possibility of their finished screenplay being passed on to another writer to fiddle around with, as happened with *Midnight,* they adopted the practice of doling out their scripts a few scenes at a time, just before each one was to be shot. Producers accepted their tight security over their scripts because Brackett and Wilder were by now the most renowned writing team in town. Nevertheless, when Leisen was shooting a scene, he was still prone to modifying the screenplay. That was precisely what happened on *Hold Back the Dawn,* their last screenplay for him.

The film is principally set in a small town on the Mexican border, where Georges Iscovescu (Charles Boyer), a European refugee, desperately waits to obtain an American visa. Wilder drew on his own experience in obtaining an immigration visa to enter the United States in 1934.

The movie has a clever narrative frame: Georges sneaks onto the Paramount lot, where he encounters Mr. Saxon, a film director played by Leisen, who is shooting *I Wanted Wings* (1941), the war picture that Leisen was actually shooting at the time. Georges proceeds to tell his story to Saxon with the hope that the director will want to film it. His story plays out in an extended flashback.

Georges is a down-at-the-heels roué from Romania. He admits to having been a "dancer for hire" and a "ladies' escort" back in Romania—precisely what Wilder had been in Berlin in 1926. Georges romances a visiting tourist, an American schoolteacher named Emmy Brown, as his one-way ticket to the United States. Georges and the innocent, gullible Emmy become engaged. He plans to obtain a quick divorce once he has his American visa and is settled in the United States, but he gradually realizes that he really loves Emmy. In an unexpected crisis of conscience, Georges offers to let her off the hook, but Emmy forgives him his deception and still agrees to marry him.

Shooting commenced on February 18, 1941. For one scene Brackett and Wilder devised a monologue for Georges to deliver to a cockroach crawling up the wall of his room in the wretched Hotel Esperanza, a hostel that does not promise the hope of its Spanish name. In this scene an unshaven Georges dramatizes his plight as if he were a border official delaying the cockroach's passage across the wall. On March 15, the day that the scene was to be filmed, Boyer complained to Leisen that it was idiotic for him to address an insect that could not respond to him. Leisen deemed the lines superfluous and canceled the monologue without notifying Brackett and Wilder.

Wilder was having lunch at Lucy's, a bistro near Paramount, when he came across Boyer, who made the mistake of casually informing him that he had gotten Leisen to cut the cockroach speech. When Wilder objected, Boyer added defensively that the scene was running too long. Wilder told Brackett after lunch that Leisen apparently did not appreciate how the cockroach monologue encapsulated the wretched Georges' own situation. Georges, the lonesome alien, is so desperate for communication that he converses with this bug.

The irony and dark humor in the speech could have permeated the rest of the movie. "It is not necessary for a director to know how to write," said Wilder sarcastically; "it helps, however, if he knows how to read." Wilder pounded his fist on the desk and threatened to beat Boyer's brains out. But then he reflected that actors did not have any brains and abandoned the notion. Later in the day, Brackett entered their office suite and found Wilder "wildly scratching out lines in the script." When Brackett inquired what his partner was doing, Wilder answered with maniacal glee, "Cutting Boyer's lines; if the son-of-a-bitch won't talk to a cockroach, then he's not going to talk to anybody!"[20] Brackett and Wilder were still revising the last third of the screenplay, so they proceeded to favor Olivia de Havilland by giving her the best lines of dialogue. Boyer's part dwindled appreciably in the last segment of the movie, and de Havilland ended up with an Oscar nomination for her performance. Brackett and Wilder were also nominated for best screenplay.

But Wilder was not yet finished getting even with Boyer. A year later, while directing his first Hollywood feature, *The Major and the Minor,* he included a bit in which a little girl asks her mother to buy her a movie magazine at a newsstand in a train station. The lurid cover story is titled "Why I Hate Women," by Charles Boyer. Even years later, the *Hold Back the Dawn* episode still rankled. When Wilder filmed *The Spirit of St. Louis* (1957), he had James Stewart as Charles Lindbergh address a fly buzzing around the cockpit of his plane. Wilder defied anyone to suggest that he cut the fly monologue.

The shooting of *Hold Back the Dawn* was finished on May 5, 1941; Doane Harrison completed the edit in time for release in September. Like *Midnight,* it collected a sheaf of favorable notices. It was described as a first-rate soap opera that would please "the washboard weepers," yet the movie never becomes maudlin. It was also called a touching romantic melodrama with mass appeal.[21]

Wilder had become increasingly disgruntled about Leisen's meddling with the screenplays he and Brackett had written for him. He began to consider more seriously than ever the possibility of directing his own screenplays, to keep directors like Leisen from interfering with the scripts he wrote. But before he could pursue this ambition, he had to fulfill one more commitment. Independent producer Samuel Goldwyn had asked Brackett and Wilder to script a film for a major Hollywood director, Howard Hawks (*His Girl Friday*). The resulting film would be *Ball of Fire,* a daffy screwball romp along the lines of *Midnight.*

## Collaborating with Howard Hawks: *Ball of Fire* (1941)

Goldwyn was renowned for assembling top-notch collaborators to work on his productions. In addition to Hawks, *Ball of Fire* boasted the services of the distinguished cinematographer Gregg Toland (*Citizen Kane*) and the ace editor Daniel Mandell (*Wuthering Heights*). Mandell would subsequently edit no fewer than six of Wilder's own films. The stars of *Ball of Fire,* Gary Cooper and Barbara Stanwyck, would likewise both appear in Wilder movies. There was no doubt that Brackett and Wilder were in good company on this picture.

Wilder dug out of his trunk an unused fourteen-page scenario titled "From A to Z," which he had composed in his threadbare days in Berlin. He handed it to Thomas Monroe, a junior writer at Paramount, for a quick polish. In a story conference with Goldwyn and Hawks, he summarized the plot for them: Bertram Potts, a professor of linguistics, is coauthoring an encyclopedia with seven other scholars. He recruits sassy nightclub singer Sugarpuss O'Shea to aid him in writing the entry on slang after hearing her warble "Drum Boogie" at the club. The song is filled with picturesque slang phrases like "The hepcat's a killer diller." Wilder, we recall, was a jazz enthusiast from his youth in Vienna. Hence he loved having Sugarpuss O'Shea belt out the jazzy "Drum Boogie" as the lead singer for Gene Krupa and his band, who would appear in the picture. Sugarpuss invades the fuddy-duddy professors' mausoleum for a few days to help Bertram with his research on slang. Hawks liked the scenario very much. He commented at the story conference, "It's just *Snow White and the Seven Dwarfs*": the brassy showgirl is Snow White, and the eccentric professors are the seven dwarfs. Hawks concluded that Wilder brightened and said, "We'll have it for you in a few weeks."[22]

Production began on August 6, 1941, with a forty-eight-day shooting schedule. Wilder obtained permission to be on the set during filming to observe the top director at work. Hawks did not mind Wilder's presence on the set "as a fly on the wall."[23] When Wilder had observed Lubitsch at work, he had not been thinking of moving up to directing. Now he spent more time on the soundstage. "I wanted to see a picture from beginning to end, before I started directing myself," he said. One of the things that Wilder admired in Hawks, according to Andrew Sarris, was that he "never betrayed the script for the sake of a personal flourish of visual virtuosity."[24] Wilder noted that, like Lubitsch, Hawks avoided a display of fancy visual style for its own sake; his objective was to tell the story as efficiently as possible.

Hawks had developed the custom of changing any dialogue in the screenplay that no longer fit the flow of the shooting as it had been progressing. "I was not really improvising," he emphasized; "I was simply modifying the dialogue to better fit the action of the scene." Since Wilder was usually on the set during shooting, Hawks would sometimes have a give-and-take session with him on the soundstage, along with the actors, just before the cameras rolled, to revise passages of dialogue.[25]

The picture was released on December 2, 1941, just days before the outbreak of World War II, and it was a huge success. The critics lauded the hilariously mismatched couple—the bashful academic and the snazzy nightclub siren—who provided the makings of a madcap screwball comedy. Hawks biographer Todd McCarthy writes that *Ball of Fire* remains utterly charming for the brash cleverness of the dialogue, the heartwarming geniality of the professors, and the expert comic playing of Cooper and Stanwyck.[26]

But Wilder was still smarting from his unpleasant experiences with Mitchell Leisen, particularly on *Hold Back the Dawn*. When Wilder decided to establish himself as a writer-director, he implicitly asserted that a filmmaker should be in control of his projects from the script stage onward. "I got very incensed with directors, good directors, but people who did not have the proper respect for the script. I was just very incensed," Wilder remembered. "You know, once you finished the script, they grab it and rewrite it. If they're behind schedule, they tear out eight pages, and they're on schedule again. It made me so furious, I decided to go on and become a director."[27]

Wilder always considered himself a writer first and foremost, even after he started directing. There were two screenwriters who had made the transition to directing shortly before Wilder made his bid in 1941 to do the same: Preston Sturges and John Huston. Sturges (*The Miracle of Morgan Creek*), a contemporary of Wilder's at Paramount, recalled that it was not uncommon for a platoon of screenwriters to work on the same script. "Writers worked in teams, like piano movers," he recalled.[28]

Wilder persuaded the studio to give him a shot at directing. According to Wilder, Paramount figured he would do something artsy-smartsy: "What? Crazy Wilder? We're going to give him one picture; he's going to fall on his face. Then he's going to come back and be a writer again," having gotten it out of his system.[29] The front office was expecting him to reach back to his Berlin days and do a warmed-over version of a film he had written then, such as *Menschen am Sonntag*. He had other plans. "I set out to make a commercial picture I wouldn't be ashamed of, so my first picture as a director would not be my last."[30]

One thing that was in the budding director's favor was his versatility. His Hollywood scripts had ranged from musicals like *Music in the Air* to comedies like *Ninotchka* and melodramas like *Hold Back the Dawn*. "I can't understand how anybody can always work in the same genre," Wilder said. "I get bored and jump around to make different types of films." In fact, writes John Russell Taylor, Wilder "stands as one of the most famous and successful of a whole group of émigrés who from the start could and did turn their hands to almost anything" with equal success.[31] The first picture Wilder was slated to direct was *The Major and the Minor*. If the people in the front office thought he would fall on his face, they were in for a surprise.

# 3

# New Directions

## The Major and the Minor and Five Graves to Cairo

The American moviegoing public has the mind of a twelve-year-old. They must have life as it isn't.

—*Ernst Lubitsch*

A director must be a policeman, a midwife, a psychoanalyst, and a bastard.

—*Billy Wilder*

In the fall of 1941, Joseph Sistrom, a junior executive at Paramount, volunteered to search through the stockpile of unproduced scenarios in the story department's files to find a property that Wilder could dust off and spruce up for filming. He unearthed a reader's report on a Broadway play, *Connie Goes Home* by Edward Childs Carpenter, adapted from a *Saturday Evening Post* short story by Fannie Kilbourne, published in 1921 and titled "Sunny Goes Home." The reader's memo was unfavorable, pointing out that the action of the stage play goes steadily downhill and that the play closed after a mere twenty performances. The reader accordingly recommended that Paramount not acquire the play for filming.

Still, Sistrom thought the scenario was promising, and Wilder agreed that the plot had comic possibilities that had not been exploited in the original short story or the stage play. The tale concerns a young woman who fails to establish a career in New York and decides to return to her home in Iowa. Short of funds, she has to disguise herself as a child to buy a half-fare ticket. A man her own age becomes interested in her during the train trip, but he, of course, fears that he will be robbing the cradle if he gets involved with her.

In December 1941, Paramount purchased the screen rights to both the short story and the stage play. In the years ahead, Wilder would become known for his ability to revamp old narrative formulas for the screen. The two sources of *The Major and the Minor* are but the first of many forgotten stories that Wilder revitalized for film.

# *The Major and the Minor* (1942)

Arthur Hornblow Jr., who had produced two popular films from Brackett-Wilder screenplays, *Midnight* and *Hold Back the Dawn,* agreed to act as producer on Wilder's maiden voyage as a director. By mid-January 1942, Brackett and Wilder had nearly completed the first draft of the screenplay, now titled *The Major and the Minor.* But the plot, which had seemed innocuous enough in outline, now made some of the Paramount executives doubt its acceptability to the industry censor, Joseph Ignatius Breen.

The heroine is called Susan Applegate in the screenplay; in the course of her train journey back to Iowa, she masquerades as twelve-year-old "Sue-Sue." She is befriended en route by Major Philip Kirby. When he becomes subconsciously attracted to Sue-Sue, the script seems to be dallying with pedophilia. The studio was aware that, only a few years earlier, film critic–novelist Graham Greene had suggested that John Ford's *Wee Willie Winkie* (1937), which featured child star Shirley Temple, flirted with pedophilia. Though Twentieth Century–Fox had won its libel suit against Greene, Paramount wanted to avoid a similar scandal erupting over *The Major and the Minor.*

The "safety curtain" that the story and dialogue of *The Major and the Minor* provided was that the audience is aware that Susan Applegate is a grown woman pretending to be a child. This takes the edge off the shocking implications that the film might otherwise have. Wilder defended the script of *The Major and the Minor* to Breen, explaining that Philip takes a fatherly stance toward Sue-Sue and is not conscious that he may be physically attracted to her. Consequently, Wilder contended, Philip is convinced that he merely finds Sue-Sue a charming little girl, as when he jokingly observes, "It's not often that a boy my age gets a smile from someone whizzing by in a kiddy car." When she finally reveals herself to him as a grown woman at film's end, Philip is so delighted that he fails to realize that his affection for Sue-Sue may not have been as paternal as he assumed. "The major is sexually aroused by her; he couldn't help himself," Wilder explained. "We had here the first American movie about pedophilia," featuring a pre-*Lolita* pseudo-nymphet. "I worried that the audience would be shocked by the story, but it seems that they were not."[1] It may have been clear to the cognoscenti who were on the right wavelength that Philip was attracted to a supposedly underage girl, but most moviegoers apparently did not pick up on the fact that this picture was about "a man who gets a hard-on every time he looks at this woman he *thinks* is a twelve-year-old."[2]

Wilder retained in his Hollywood screenplays the wry, brittle humor he had perfected as a scriptwriter in Berlin. Indeed, it was the Wilder wit that prompted Leslie Halliwell to deem him "Hollywood's most mischievous immigrant." Another film historian, who found Wilder's sardonic humor less to his taste, described his wit as "curdled Lubitsch."[3]

A salient example of Wilder's mordant humor occurs early in the screenplay of *The Major and the Minor,* which contains a smattering of piquant sexual references. Albert Osborne, a lecherous middle-aged businessman, attempts to seduce Susan Applegate, who has come to his apartment to give him a scalp massage. Osborne leers at Susan, who has just come in out of the rain, and says suggestively, "Why don't you slip out of that wet coat and into a dry martini?" This line of dialogue is usually attributed to humorist Robert Benchley, who played Osborne. But Benchley did not ad-lib the line; Charles Brackett overheard comedian Charlie Butterworth make this sally of wit at a Manhattan cocktail party.[4]

When it came to casting, Wilder hoped to get thirty-one-year-old Ginger Rogers to play Susan. Rogers had won an Academy Award for *Kitty Foyle* (1940), in which she played a working girl whose infant dies, and the actress was a big box office draw at the time. It so happened that Wilder and Rogers shared an agent, Leland Hayward. Of course, Hayward cottoned to the notion of two of his clients working together, and he encouraged Rogers to take the part of Susan in *The Major and the Minor.* Wilder, who never missed a chance to spice up an anecdote, commented that Rogers agreed to do the film "in the middle of a screw" since Rogers and Hayward were lovers.[5]

When Rogers was asked why she was willing to play a woman who pretends to be a child, she replied that she had played a youngster in pigtails in a flashback of *Kitty Foyle* that portrays the heroine's early life. Furthermore, Brackett and Wilder had written "one hell of a part" for her.[6] Rogers, in the course of the film, played not only twelve-year-old Sue-Sue but also Susan Applegate as a mature woman, as well as Susan's mother, Mrs. Applegate, whom Susan impersonates late in the movie. (Mrs. Applegate also appears in the film, played by Lela Rogers, Ginger's own mother.)

Wilder secured Ray Milland to play Major Philip Kirby by a rather unorthodox means: He followed Milland's car out of the Paramount parking lot one afternoon. He caught up with Milland at a stoplight and yelled at him, asking if he would like to be in his picture. Milland remembers smiling and responding, "Sure!"[7] It did not matter to him, Milland explained, that it was the first picture Wilder was directing in Hollywood, since Milland had acted in *Arise, My Love* (1940), a very good film about the Spanish civil war that Brackett and Wilder had written. Benchley, a celebrated humorist and sometimes movie actor (*Foreign Correspondent*), was content to play the lascivious Albert Osborne because he and Brackett had both been on the staff of the *New Yorker* in the 1920s.

Wilder endeavored to round up the best crew he could muster at Paramount for his first venture as a Hollywood filmmaker. "I needed all the help I could get," he said. Cinematographer Leo Tover, film editor Doane Harrison, and camera operator Ernest Laszlo had all done good work on *Hold Back the Dawn*. (Laszlo would later serve as director of photography on Wilder's *Stalag 17*.)

In February 1942, the studio drew up a budget of $928,000, a rather standard budget for an A picture. Brackett, who had seniority over Wilder at Paramount, was to receive $27,000 for coauthoring the screenplay, while Wilder was allocated $17,200 as coauthor of the script. Wilder's services as director merited a measly $9,800. Hence his combined salary for cowriting and directing the film came to the same amount Brackett would receive for cowriting the screenplay. As Wilder noted sardonically, that meant that he virtually directed the picture for free.

Wilder confided to Lubitsch that he was terrified at the thought of directing his first Hollywood film. Lubitsch invited several immigrant directors to come to the set on March 12, 1942, the first day of shooting, to give Wilder moral support. Among them was William Wyler (*Wuthering Heights*). Preston Sturges, a native-born American, showed up on his own because he wanted to encourage Wilder, only the second screenwriter to become a writer-director at Paramount. As it happened, Sturges's *The Lady Eve* was the leading moneymaker for Paramount at the time. Wilder cleared the set of well-wishers by 10:00 A.M., and at 10:25 he called Ginger Rogers to the soundstage for the first shot.

The first thing Wilder learned about directing was that there could be only one boss on the soundstage. He knew he would be lost if he allowed the actors to push him around. "Making a movie is like flying a plane," he explained. "Once you get off the ground you must be in full control of the flight if you are to avoid a crash."[8] Even though *The Major and the Minor* was Wilder's first Hollywood film, said Rogers, "from day one I saw that Billy knew what to do." He was very self-confident but would listen to the actors' suggestions.[9] He began each rehearsal by having the actors read the scene together; then he had them walk through it on the set; finally he would figure out where to put the camera and where the camera moves would be. At that point he would do the first take.

Charles Coleman Jr. was appointed Wilder's assistant director, a post the dependable individual would hold for fifteen years, through *The Spirit of St. Louis* (1957). Coleman was also second unit director on *The Major and the Minor;* he was sent to Delafield, Wisconsin, to shoot background exteriors at St. John's Military Academy, which stands in for Wallace Military Academy in the movie.

It was during the making of *The Major and the Minor* that film editor Doane Harrison became an important member of Wilder's production team. Harrison, a lanky, laconic individual, had begun as an editor of Mack Sennett comedy shorts in the 1920s; he spent most of his career at Paramount. Wilder asked Harrison to be by his side while he was shooting and frequently conferred with him about composing the shots and selecting the camera angles. He planned each scene with Harrison's advice because he wanted to make the film on the set and not allow the editor to remake it in the editing room—under the watchful eye of the producer. Wilder, from the outset of his career as a director, learned from Harrison to shoot just enough footage to enable the editor to put together a given scene one way—his way. For example, if Wilder decided that he did not want a close-up in a particular scene, he simply did not film one. In his opinion, a close-up was a special thing that should be used sparingly, like a trump in bridge. Wilder did not give the producer extra footage "to monkey around with" in the cutting room: "When I finish a film there is nothing on the cutting room floor but cigarette butts, chewing gum wrappers and tears."[10]

Beginning with *Sunset Boulevard* (1950), Harrison would be designated as supervising editor; he would continue to advise Wilder as associate producer from *The Seven Year Itch* (1955) through *The Fortune Cookie* (1966). Wilder's creative association with Harrison was one of the most enduring professional relationships of his career. "I went to Doane Harrison College," said Wilder in tribute.[11] In all, Harrison collaborated with Wilder on twenty-three pictures over three decades.

Principal photography was finished on *The Major and the Minor* on May 9, 1942. Perhaps because the war does not figure in the plot in any significant way, Richard Armstrong incorrectly states that Wilder "completed shooting a month before the Japanese attack on Pearl Harbor" on December 7, 1941.[12] Rather, it is because the film's literary sources date from the 1920s that it more or less ignores the impending war.

For the record, Wilder brought in his first Hollywood movie within striking distance of the budget and only six days behind schedule. Perhaps his experience a decade earlier of making *Mauvaise graine,* a low-budget independent picture in Paris, had taught Wilder how to cut corners during filming. He fell behind schedule, he pointed out, only while filming the scenes set in the military academy, such as the school dance, which involved two hundred teenagers as extras.

After principal photography wrapped, Wilder plunged into postproduction. Since he and Harrison had planned the total editing scheme during shooting, Harrison cut the film at a brisk pace, conferring with Wilder along the way. Robert Emmett Dolan wrote the background music for the picture after consulting with Wilder. Dolan was a young composer fresh from providing the incidental music for the Bing Crosby–Fred Astaire vehicle *Holiday Inn* (1942). Dolan employed Victor Shertzinger's waltz "Dream Lover" as one of the numbers played at the cadets' school dance. Then he did variations on it throughout the rest of the background score. Dolan borrowed the melodious waltz from Ernst Lubitsch's 1929 musical *The Love Parade.* Perhaps Wilder suggested it to Dolan as an homage to his mentor.

Wilder's first Hollywood picture opens with a printed prologue, a practice he would follow intermittently throughout his film career. This prologue states, "The Dutch bought New York from the Indians in 1626, and by May 1941, there wasn't an Indian left who regretted it." The first shot of the movie focuses on a street sign that reads "Park Avenue." It is night, and the camera pans down to Susan Applegate on her way to Albert Osborne's apartment to give him a scalp treatment.

Osborne attempts to ply Susan with liquor and clumsily tries to coax her into doing a rumba with him ("We could make beautiful music together"). But Susan resists Osborne's blandishments and reads the riot act to him in a speech that provides a nifty example of Brackett and Wilder's crisp, clever dialogue. Susan declares that she has had quite enough of wicked New York City: "From the bargain basement to the Ritz Tower, I got myself stared at, glanced over, cuddled up against." She is fed up. "This is Susan Applegate signing off!" But the libidinous Osborne is not to be deterred, so she baptizes him with a generous dollop of egg shampoo. She escapes his clutches by hightailing it to the nearest elevator, while Osborne literally has egg on his face. By now Susan is determined to escape the bevy of male admirers who constantly plague her.

Susan soon boards the train for Stevenson, Iowa, disguised as a preteen named Sue-Sue, and encounters Major Philip Kirby on board. Wilder said that, when he first saw Ginger Rogers with her bosoms taped down, wearing pigtails and bobby socks, carrying a balloon and sucking on a lollypop, "I knew I had a picture"—a favorite phrase of Lubitsch's.

Donning a disguise is a recurring element in Wilder's movies. As we have seen, in *Midnight,* Claudette Colbert masquerades as a Hungarian baroness. In addition, Wilder's very next film, *Five Graves to Cairo,* features a British officer who impersonates a deceased espionage agent.

The plot of *The Major and the Minor* goes into overdrive when Susan accepts Philip's invitation to spend the weekend visiting the exclusive Wallace Military Academy for Boys in High Creek, Indiana, where he is on the faculty. Susan must maintain her charade while at the institute. Philip's vision is impaired in one eye, which suggests that he is not perceptive in sizing up others; he fails to "see through" Susan's disguise. He calls himself Sue-Sue's "Uncle Philip."

Philip takes Sue-Sue to stay with the family of his huffy fiancée Pamela Hill (Rita Johnson). Philip belongs to the local elite social set, as does Pamela. She and her precocious kid sister Lucy (Diana Lynn) are alone in suspecting that Sue-Sue is a phony. Pamela says pointedly to Philip at one point, "When you felt the urge to become an uncle, you should have found a less inflammatory niece." Lucy confronts Susan directly. When Sue-Sue gazes into Lucy's fishbowl and says the goldfish "wants his din-din," Lucy snaps, "Stop that baby talk, will you? You're not twelve just because you're acting like six. Maybe you can fool the grown-ups, but you can't fool me!" Yet Lucy does not give Susan away. As a matter of fact, Lucy does not approve of the way that her older sister bosses Philip around and in no time at all decides that Philip would be better off with Susan. "You're much more my sister than Pamela," she tells Susan later.

Susan must fend off the hot-blooded cadets who begin making advances on her as Sue-Sue. One of the cadets, Clifford Osborne, turns out to be the son of Albert Osborne. Clifford even uses one of his father's lines on Sue-Sue: "We could make beautiful music together"—like father, like son! Another cadet, a randy young man named Anthony Wigton (Raymond Roe), maneuvers Sue-Sue into a clinch and a kiss on their first encounter. The second time around, she distracts him by coaxing him to tap-dance with her.

Dismayed by the manner in which the cadets are pursuing Sue-Sue, Philip summons her to his office for a helping of paternal advice. In the course of his mini-lecture on the facts of life, he confesses, "When I look at you with my bum eye, you look almost grown-up; Sue-Sue, you're a knock-out!" William K. Everson observes, "The sexual implications . . . of the major's growing fondness for a girl he believes to be only twelve [are] surprisingly risqué for a film of 1942."[13]

Sue-Sue is invited to the cadets' school dance, where Albert Osborne, who has come to the institute to visit his son, shows up. He inevitably recognizes Susan in the guise of Sue-Sue and informs Pamela who Sue-Sue really is. Pamela accordingly issues an ultimatum to Susan: she must depart immediately, or Pamela will reveal her true identity to Philip. Susan hotfoots it out of town, without bidding goodbye to Philip, and presses on for her home in Stevenson. When Susan's mother asks her what happened to her on the trip from New York City, Susan replies cryptically, "I went to a masquerade."

Philip decides to stop over in Stevenson on his way to the West Coast to see Sue-Sue. Susan dispatches her mother to the attic so that she can impersonate her mother with Philip, since she does not want her mother to meet him. Susan dons her mother's apron and spectacles and waits for Philip on the front porch. Philip informs her that Pamela broke their engagement to marry Anthony Wigton's wealthy father. He proceeds to the depot. While standing on the platform, awaiting his train, Philip notices an attractive woman dressed in a tailored suit and picture hat who bears a strong resemblance to Sue-Sue. She tells him she is off to marry a major. Philip instantly recognizes her and cries, "Sue-Sue!" With that, they board the train together. A cloud of steam billows up from the train engine and blots the couple from view; they vanish, as if by magic.

The critics found *The Major and the Minor* a fresh, funny comedy, as did the mass audience.[14] Rogers gave a refreshingly flavored and rounded performance as the preadolescent Sue-Sue, as the mature Susan Applegate, and as Susan's mother. Her one regret was that she never had the opportunity to work with Wilder again. She remarked on TV talk shows that, as a star at the time, she helped his career along while he was making his first Hollywood film, but Wilder did not seem to appreciate the favor she did him. Asked about this, he answered, "I showed my appreciation—she got top billing."

*The Major and the Minor* is a startlingly assured film, with none of the cheap tricks or showiness of a tyro director desperate for a studio calling card. "Everyone expected me to make something 'fancy-schmancy,'" said Wilder. "Yet I made something commercial; I brought back the most saleable hunk of celluloid I could."[15] Wilder always stubbornly maintained that his films did not qualify him to be named the heir of Ernst Lubitsch, but with *The Major and the Minor,* Wilder proved what he inherited from Lubitsch: Wilder brought to his first Hollywood picture a sophistication and wit that were totally lacking in the film's literary sources. For his film, "Wilder wrote dialogue that ran the gamut from wisecracks to double entendre," Bernard Dick writes. It was the sort of dry wit and banter that would come to define the Wilder touch in his subsequent films. For example, when Philip asks Sue-Sue how she feels, she responds, "Sue-Sue is so-so." Moreover, the scene between Susan and Albert Osborne is peppered with Osborne's saucy bons mots. In the present film, Wilder's wit is not heavy-handed, says Dick; "Wilder winks rather than leers."[16] *The Major and the Minor* is a crazy screwball comedy in the best tradition.

The front office was more than satisfied with Wilder's handling of *The Major and the Minor,* which he brought in nearly on schedule and only slightly over budget. "They were obviously not going to send me back to my typewriter, but allow me to continue directing," he said, since the picture was a commercial success. After directing this film, he convinced the studio to allow Brackett to act as the producer of the subsequent films they coscripted, to make doubly certain that their screenplays would be committed to celluloid without interference from the front office.

Wilder wanted a change of pace for his next film. He did not want to be typed as a director of romantic comedies, so he was looking for a solid melodrama. The literary source for his next film was an obscure play by the Hungarian playwright Lajos Biró, *Hotel Imperial,* a World War I espionage drama. It had never been produced on Broadway. Biró had written the play after the First World War and brought it with him when he immigrated to Hollywood in 1924 to become a screenwriter.

Paramount had made a silent film of *Hotel Imperial* in 1926 starring Pola Negri, which was directed by Mauritz Stiller and produced by Erich Pommer. This was one of the two American films that Pommer, for whom Wilder worked at Ufa in Berlin, produced in his brief sojourn in Hollywood in the 1920s.[17] Ernst Lubitsch planned to remake the picture at Paramount in 1936 as *I Loved a Soldier,* with Marlene Dietrich in the lead. But Lubitsch abandoned the production when Dietrich bowed out of the project. Journeyman director Robert Florey eventually filmed it in 1939 with Isa Miranda replacing Dietrich, and it flopped.

Both the 1926 and the 1939 versions of *Hotel Imperial* follow the original play pretty carefully. The play is set in a Balkan border town; by sheer coincidence, the town is Sucha, Wilder's birthplace. "Sucha is a small Galician town" that, in the play, the Russians capture from the Austrians.[18] The town's shabby hotel serves as the Russian army's headquarters. An Austrian officer stays on at the hotel in the guise of a waiter to spy on the enemy. When the officer kills a Russian soldier who has uncovered his identity, he escapes to the Austrian lines. A Polish chambermaid is accused of the murder by the Russian general; she is about to be shot when the Austrian officer returns with a squad of soldiers and rescues her.

## *Five Graves to Cairo* (1943)

Biró himself brought the play to Wilder's attention in 1942. He suggested that Wilder update the story to World War II and build it around Field Marshal Erwin Rommel and his Afrika Korps, who were then fighting the British in the desert. The play appealed to Wilder because it involved a character perpetrating a deception by assuming a disguise—already a favorite theme of his. Still, to transplant the story from World War I to World War II would require considerable overhauling. Brackett and Wilder changed the title to *Five Graves to Cairo* to dissociate their project from the 1939 fiasco.

Paramount officially assigned Brackett and Wilder to the film on August 10, 1942. The studio allocated a budget of $825,000 for the production. The budget for *The Major and the Minor* had been somewhat larger, mostly because Rogers commanded a star's salary; there were no expensive stars in *Five Graves to Cairo*. For example, Erich von Stroheim, who would play Rommel and be featured prominently in the publicity layouts for the film, would receive a mere $30,000 for his efforts. Wilder was to receive a bigger piece of the pie than he had on the previous film. He would pocket $31,500 for coauthoring the screenplay and $21,000 for directing the picture, for a total almost twice the amount he had been paid for cowriting and directing *The Major and the Minor*. Clearly, Wilder's status was improving at Paramount.

Brackett and Wilder changed the setting from a Balkan village to a town on the Libyan border in North Africa. The Austrian officer in the play became a British officer, John Bramble; the Polish chambermaid was now a French servant girl named Mouche; and the Russian general was transformed into Rommel, the Desert Fox.

By and large, Wilder and Brackett's negotiations with the studio brass over production plans went fairly smoothly. They agreed to shoot the location scenes in the desert near the Camp Young army base, eighteen miles outside Yuma, Arizona, and at Salton Sea, near Indio, California, at the southern end of the Mojave Desert. The studio did, however, object repeatedly to the title, *Five Graves to Cairo*, and made several alternate suggestions, such as "Rommel's Last Stand." One executive disliked the word *graves* in the title, since it had morose connotations. Why not simply call the movie "Five to Cairo"? Brackett and Wilder passed over this suggestion in silence. One member of their production unit at the time said that there was no use in disputing with Brackett and Wilder once they made up their minds about an issue: "They were like solid iron and quicksilver."[19]

42

Brackett and Wilder set the film in 1942, right after Rommel, a born tank commander, has driven the British from Tobruk on June 21. As the story develops, Rommel uses the faded Empress of Britain Hotel in the village of Sidi Halfaya as his temporary headquarters. This is where most of the action takes place. Brackett and Wilder completed the first draft of the screenplay in October 1942, but they kept revising it, in keeping with the press reports of the African campaign. Wilder liked to boast that the screenplay was torn from the headlines. The screenplay was so up-to-the-minute that the final shooting script, dated December 17, 1942, contained a reference near the end to the decisive defeat of Rommel's Afrika Korps by British general Bernard Montgomery's Eighth Army at El Alamein in November 1942, when Rommel's men and machines were worn out. That spelled the beginning of the end of the German resistance in North Africa.[20]

Wilder noted that the finished screenplay ran a mere 120 pages, which would make a film of less than one hundred minutes. Screenplays had to be economical, he explained, in order not to bore the audience with scenes that go on too long.

Wilder had learned early in the game that one way of placing his personal stamp on the films he directed was to assemble a production crew that went from picture to picture with him. His team of regulars by this time included screenwriter-producer Charles Brackett, editor Doane Harrison, and assistant director Charles Coleman, all of whom he had worked with before. On *Five Graves to Cairo,* he added, among others, cinematographer John Seitz, whom he would call on often throughout the next decade. Seitz was an experienced director of photography whose career dated back to the silent days, when he photographed Rex Ingram's *Four Horsemen of the Apocalypse* (1921), Rudolph Valentino's career-making movie. These creative collaborators could almost intuit what Wilder wanted from each of them as the shooting period progressed.

In casting *Five Graves to Cairo,* Wilder chose Franchot Tone (*Three Comrades*), a competent actor but a star of the second magnitude. For the role of Mouche, the French maid, Wilder picked twenty-year-old Anne Baxter, who had made a name for herself the previous year in Orson Welles's *Magnificent Ambersons.* Akim Tamiroff (*The Great McGinty*), a reliable character actor, was tagged for Farid, the oily Egyptian proprietor of the Empress of Britain Hotel; he specialized in playing unsavory foreigners with heavy accents.

For the movie's drawing card, Wilder was banking on Erich von Stroheim in the role of Rommel. After Stroheim's career as a director foundered with the coming of sound, he had devoted himself to character parts, usually villains. He was familiar to audiences. Wilder had admired Stroheim as both an actor and a director from his youth. When Wilder was still a struggling young writer in Berlin, in April 1929, he contributed a profile of Stroheim to the journal *Der Querschnitt* (The cross section). Wilder extolled Stroheim for writing, directing, and starring in Hollywood films like *The Wedding March* (1926), in which he frankly portrayed the debauchery of the decadent Austrian aristocracy prior to World War I; the picture was thought shocking at the time. Referring to Stroheim's reputation for playing nasty villains, Wilder titled the *Der Querschnitt* article "Stroheim, der Mann den man gern hasst" (Stroheim, the man you love to hate). Stroheim earned that epithet in *The Heart of Humanity* (1919), when he played a German officer who has invaded an enemy village; the brute picks up a wailing infant and throws it out the window. The moniker had subsequently been used in ad campaigns for films in which he appeared.[21] He continued to play stiff-necked, inflexible Prussian types in both American and European films, including, most famously, the monocled commandant of a German prisoner-of-war camp in Jean Renoir's *La grande illusion* (1937).

When Wilder returned to his office at the studio one afternoon early in production, he was informed that Stroheim, who was working in Hollywood during the war, had arrived and was over at the Western Costume Company on Vermont Avenue, trying on uniforms. Arthur Lennig, author of the definitive biography of Stroheim, recounts that Wilder rushed over to the store and found Stroheim. "I clicked my heels, introduced myself, and said, 'This is a very big moment in my life: that little Wilder . . . should now be directing the great Stroheim.'" Stroheim did not answer, so Wilder added, "to make him feel good," a reference to the classic films Stroheim had directed. "Your problem, I guess, was that you were ten years ahead of your time." Stroheim stared at Wilder with a vulpine look and barked, "Twenty, Mr. Wilder; twenty!" Wilder concluded, "He possessed grandeur. Even his mistakes were grandiose; and when he succeeded he had real class."[22]

Characteristically, Stroheim made sure that his contract with Paramount for *Five Graves to Cairo* stipulated that he could personally supervise his costumes. He was a firm believer in utilizing "costume and decor to define the personality within."[23] Stroheim had carefully examined newspaper photos of Rommel, and he told Wilder during their meeting at Western Costume that he must have genuine German field glasses and an authentic German-made Leica camera slung around his neck. The camera, he emphasized, must be loaded with unexposed film. Wilder tactfully inquired who would know whether the camera had film in it. Stroheim replied that an audience would sense that the camera had no film inside it and that it was merely a prop. Besides, he added, "*I* will know!"[24]

Although principal photography would not go into full swing until January 1943, Wilder aimed to get some of the desert exteriors in the can ahead of time. In the film's opening scene, John Bramble (Franchot Tone), a survivor of the fall of Tobruk, climbs out of a British tank that is rumbling across the desert sands. He crawls toward the oasis hotel in the nearby village of Sidi Halfaya. Wilder was acutely aware that the first scene in a picture was crucial. Some people might walk out on a picture in the first few minutes, he explained. "You have to have something arresting, telling them what they're going to see."[25]

On Tuesday, November 3, 1942, Wilder boarded the Sunset Limited for the train trip from Los Angeles to Yuma, Arizona, the town closest to the desert location. He was accompanied by Seitz, Harrison, and Coleman. Tone was scheduled to arrive on Thursday, November 5. Wilder and Brackett, who had studied news photos of the Libyan desert in planning the film, thought the Arizona sand dunes an ideal approximation of the Sahara desert.

Wilder spent two days with his skeleton crew lining up shots for the opening scene. He rose at four o'clock on Thursday morning and proceeded to the desert location for a last-minute check. He was chagrined to discover tire tracks all over the sand dunes where he planned to shoot the opening scene. Some GI from Camp Young had taken a joyride in his jeep all over the area the afternoon before. The script, of course, called for a clean, untrammeled expanse of desert sand. Wilder was determined to surmount this unforeseen obstacle. When the film unit arrived, he immediately ordered the production assistants to make a foray into Yuma and obtain every broom they could buy when the stores opened. When they returned, Wilder pressed the whole unit into service, industriously sweeping away the tire tracks. Wilder himself, Tone, the camera crew, and some volunteer citizens from Yuma all joined in. "We cleaned up every goddamned tire track," he said; "I shot the scene, and it was perfect."[26]

Principal photography got under way in earnest in early January 1943. Interiors were filmed on the soundstages at Paramount, with exteriors filmed at Salton Sea. It was there that the replica of the oasis hotel, the Empress of Britain, was erected; it was situated in the village of Sidi Halfaya, whose main street had also been built. British Major David Lloyd, a veteran of the tank warfare in the Libyan desert, was on hand as a technical adviser.

"By the time of shooting we generally had a pretty good idea of the mood we wanted," John Seitz remembered. "There was a lot of night work" on *Five Graves,* "and we just kept that style throughout."[27] Seitz became renowned for his use of low-key lighting on Wilder's films. In the present film, he helped to establish the menacing atmosphere of the Empress of Britain Hotel, which is occupied by the Germans, by throwing a dim, low-key light on the set. He thereby summoned up night-shrouded rooms and ominous corridors. For example, in the scene in which Bramble encounters a Nazi officer in a shadowy room and kills him, the only visible light source is Bramble's flashlight. Seitz had to make the illumination in the dark room seem to be coming solely from the flashlight, and he created a dark, sinister atmosphere for the murder in the bargain.

Stroheim was a short man, but Wilder made him an imposing figure from the first moment his image flashes on the screen. We first see Rommel from the back and from above, as he strides back and forth in the hotel lobby, dictating a message to the führer. He first dictates the memo in German, then repeats it in English, he explains, "to save the British the trouble of translation when they intercept it." Fresh from his victory at Tobruk, Rommel declares, "Nothing can save the British Eighth Army from a colossal catastrophe. They say the Red Sea once opened by special arrangement with Moses. A similar mishap will not occur this time."

At this point Wilder's camera moves in for a close-up of "the back of Stroheim's neck, damp with sweat," Lennig writes. "Only at the end of the speech does he turn, so we can see his face. What a striking and dramatic introduction" for the Desert Fox. When one of the other actors asked Stroheim why he delivered this speech rather slowly and deliberately, he answered, "To be on-screen a little longer." Wilder later commented, "Standing with his stiff, fat neck in the foreground, he could express with his face more than almost any other actor."[28]

It was common in American films at the time to have foreigners speak English with a foreign accent, even when they were addressing each other, instead of speaking their own language. In the course of this picture, however, Wilder has Stroheim as Rommel bark orders at his subordinates in German lines that are not subtitled. That makes Rommel seem all the more threatening to Bramble and Mouche, since they are ignorant of his plans.

Wilder portrayed the Nazis in the film as civilized individuals who have gone terribly astray, not as uncivilized brutes. By the same token, Stroheim and Wilder agreed that he should not play Rommel as the sort of vicious Hun that had been Stroheim's stock-in-trade in other films over the years. Two decades later, I asked Kurt Richter, a veteran of the Afrika Korps, what he thought of Stroheim's portrayal of Rommel. He responded, "Stroheim rightly gave Field Marshal Rommel a dignified, even gentlemanly demeanor.

After all, Rommel was a quintessential professional soldier, respected even by his enemies."[29]

Doane Harrison did the first edit at a good clip, since he and Wilder had, as usual, mapped out the editing plan during filming. Wilder hoped to get composer Franz Waxman, but Waxman had a contract with Warner Bros. and could not moonlight at Paramount. Hence Wilder chose Miklos Rozsa (*The Thief of Bagdad*), who, like Lajos Biró, was a native of Hungary. Rozsa composed a score filled with driving rhythms, jolting chords, and some discordant passages. Wilder was pleased with what he heard, but Louis Lipstone, the head of the music department at Paramount, was not. Lipstone called Wilder and Rozsa to his office and asked Rozsa to make the music more pleasant by eliminating the dissonant passages. Wilder bristled; he told Lipstone that he was a second-rate musician who had begun his musical career sawing on a fiddle in a cheap bistro. He therefore advised Lipstone "to leave the composing to the real composer."[30] Wilder saved Rozsa's score, but his overbearing manner made some enemies in the front office. At any rate, the postproduction was finished, and the film was shipped to the New York office of Paramount in April. The movie was released in May.

The opening credits of *Five Graves to Cairo* are impressive. They appear on the screen in typescript, as if the story that is about to unfold has been taken from the official files of the War Department. In the sequence that follows, a phantom tank lumbers across the sand dunes of the Sahara desert. Inside, the corpses of the crew are slumped over, except for one soldier who is still alive. Half-conscious, he climbs out of the tank's open hatch and is pitched onto the ground as the tank lurches forward. Wilder's camera tracks in on the soldier as he lies prostrate on the scalding sand; the camera pauses in close-up on the dog tags on the soldier's chest: "J. J. Bramble." He is the solitary survivor of a British tank crew that has been cut off from the rest of the army during the retreat from Tobruk. The delirious Corporal John Bramble, suffering from sunstroke, drags himself across the blazing desert toward the outpost of Sidi Halfaya. He staggers into the ramshackle Empress of Britain Hotel and collapses in the lobby. Wilder demonstrates his penchant for visual storytelling in this virtually wordless opening sequence.

Bramble is revived by Farid, the hostelry's Egyptian proprietor, and Mouche, the French chambermaid. He learns that the British regiment detachment that had been billeted in the hotel has departed and that Rommel, along with his staff, will arrive soon and take over the hotel as his temporary headquarters. The obsequious Farid hastily hauls down the Union Jack and hoists the Nazi flag with its swastika in its place. He later places a veil over the portrait of Queen Victoria, in whose honor the hotel is named.

When Rommel and his entourage arrive, Mouche applies lipstick and primps before a mirror to make herself look attractive to the German officers. She hopes to employ her feminine wiles to coax Rommel or one of his aides to arrange for the release of her wounded brother from a Nazi prisoner-of-war camp.

Bramble finds out that Paul Davos, an Alsatian hotel waiter, has been killed in an air raid and lies buried beneath the rubble of a bomb explosion in the cellar. Bramble assumes Davos's identity to spy on the Nazis and promptly commandeers Davos's uniform. Since Davos had a club foot, Bramble must from now on hobble about as if he were lame. Thus in Wilder's second film, as in his first, a character assumes a disguise to deceive others.

Bramble finds out from Lieutenant Schwegler (Peter van Eyck), Rommel's adjutant, that Davos was an espionage agent spying on the British for Rommel. Hence Bramble finds himself in the unenviable position of a double agent; he must manufacture information about the British battle plans that will sound plausible to Rommel while attempting to get Rommel to divulge military secrets that he can relay to the British general headquarters in Cairo.

Mouche takes Rommel's breakfast tray to him the next morning so she can broach the question of her brother's plight to him. Expecting a male servant, Rommel, who has his breakfast in bed, says it is inappropriate for a female to approach him at this hour in his bedroom. As Mouche leans forward to hand him his tray, he snaps, "Two steps back." When she presents her petition about her brother to him, he launches into a sardonic speech that Stroheim delivers masterfully. "You are suggesting some kind of bargain," he begins, implying that she plans to repay him for her brother's release with sexual favors. "This is a familiar scene, reminiscent of *bad* melodrama. Although usually it is not the brother for whose life the heroine comes to plead; it is the lover. The time is midnight; the place, the tent of the conquering general. Blushingly the lady makes her proposal and gallantly the general grants her wish. Later the lady very stupidly takes poison." He concludes by informing her that such requests must be made through the Red Cross or the Quakers—in triplicate. Then he dismisses her.

In a later sequence, captured British officers are brought to the desert inn to have lunch with Rommel. He gloats over his victories while giving them a lecture on military strategy as he maneuvers saltcellars and pepper shakers around on the tablecloth. Bramble, in his role as a waiter, places a whiskey decanter in front of Colonel Fitzhume (Miles Mander). Wilder's camera moves in for a close-up of the bottle to show the viewer that Bramble has draped his dog tags around the bottle. In this manner Bramble adroitly reveals to Fitzhume that he is a British soldier. Wilder even mines some humor from this interchange. When another officer notices the dog tags on the bottle, he assumes that *Bramble* is the brand name of a whiskey he has not heard of. Unruffled, Bramble replies that it is a choice brand that Rommel saves for special occasions.

During his lecture to the British officers, Rommel refers to the mysterious five graves to Cairo. He firmly refuses to give away the answer to the riddle but adds, "After I've taken Cairo, I will send a postcard to number 10 Downing Street with the correct solution." At the end of the luncheon, Fitzhume surreptitiously tells Bramble to uncover the secret surrounding the five graves, which Rommel says is the key to his success in the desert campaign.

In the course of ransacking the hotel for some clue to the puzzle, Bramble discovers a telltale newspaper clipping in a desk drawer. Dated February 17, 1937, it concerns a German archaeologist named Cromstaetter who led an expedition to Egypt before the war to explore ancient tombs. The photo accompanying the article reveals that the so-called archaeologist is really Rommel. He was scouting strategic sites for supply depots in the desert—in anticipation of the African campaign. Bramble ultimately figures out that the five graves are actually five plots of ground between Tobruk and Cairo in which ammunition and other supplies are buried. The exact locations can be identified on Rommel's map of Egypt, since each of the five letters on the map that spell out *Egypt* marks the site of a supply dump.

One criticism of the picture, which originated with the French film historian Georges Sadoul, centers on the character of Mouche. After she fails to make a bargain with Rommel for her brother's freedom, she offers herself to Lieutenant Schwegler, who deludes her by making empty promises to save her brother just to manipulate her into a sexual liaison. Sadoul was outraged that Mouche personified France "as a softhearted whore at the beck and call of Nazi supermen" like Schwegler. Sarris comments that Sadoul's criticism is symptomatic of the way that Wilder "has been penalized for being more honest and more open about the realities of human sexuality than most of his Hollywood colleagues."[31]

It is Lieutenant Schwegler who discovers Davos's body among the debris in the hostelry's basement; he rightly guesses that Bramble is masquerading as the deceased Davos. So Bramble is forced to liquidate him. Bramble is convinced that it is his duty to relay the strategic information about Rommel's supply depots to the high command at the British headquarters in Cairo. Mouche enables Bramble to make good his getaway and carry out his mission by taking the blame for Schwegler's murder. Rommel suspects that Mouche killed Schwegler to punish him for duping her into a sexual relationship. He tells her, "To prove to you that we are not the Huns you think we are, you will be tried according to your own French law—the Napoleonic Code." Rommel presides over a court of inquiry, which finds her guilty, and she is summarily executed by a firing squad. Pace Sadoul, Mouche is one of Wilder's most admirable heroines, since she valiantly sacrifices her life for the war effort.

Montgomery's rout of Rommel is presented in a montage. It consists mainly of Harrison's skillful manipulation of stock newsreel footage, but it is nonetheless quite effective. (Incidentally, Mander looked all the more impressive in the part of Colonel Fitzhume because of his coincidental resemblance to General Montgomery, who appears in the footage of the battle sequence.) And so on November 12, 1942, the British army comes back to Sidi Halfaya. Bramble returns to the little desert inn as a newly made officer in Montgomery's Eighth Army. The gutless Farid has restored the portrait of Queen Victoria to its former place of prominence in the hotel lobby. Farid tells Bramble of Mouche's execution.

In the film's source play, *Hotel Imperial*, the hero arrives in time to save the heroine from being executed by the enemy general. But Wilder rejected a contrived, last-minute rescue for Mouche. He consigned her to a tragic death, which occasions Bramble's stirring eulogy. Bramble places on her grave the pearl-handled parasol she had always wanted, which he had intended to give to her personally as a present. He addresses her spirit, concluding, "Don't worry, Mouche, we're after them now. We're going to blast the blazes out of them."

In directing *Five Graves*, Wilder made a film for the eye as well as for the ear, as exemplified by the movie's visual metaphors. In several scenes Wilder had Stroheim carry a fly swatter, which takes on symbolic implications in various situations. Several reviewers called it a riding crop, but the script identifies it as a "fly swisher." It resembles a whisk broom with a foot-long handle, "which Rommel flicks repeatedly to shoo away flies." Rommel at times wields the fly swatter as if it were a royal scepter, implying to all and sundry that he is a person of power and authority. At one point he employs the fly swatter as a whip, to strike Mouche across the face while he is interrogating her about Schwegler's death. It thus serves as a warning that Rommel is quite capable of harsh measures whenever he feels that they are necessary. Moreover, Lennig reminds us, "it prevents Rommel from appearing too likeable, a necessity for wartime propaganda."[32] Stroheim dominates the screen with his imposing presence in every sequence in which he appears. "*Five Graves to Cairo* is notable for its unsensationalized, nonstereotypical view of Rommel," writes Kevin Lally; "the film treats him with deference, respecting him as a brilliant tactician and mighty opponent."[33]

*Five Graves to Cairo* was hailed as an ingeniously plotted melodrama with uniformly fine performances, a beautiful, dark gem among World War II films. The lion's share of the praise, of course, went to Stroheim's peerless portrayal of Rommel. In fact, the movie rejuvenated Stroheim's acting career; he would repay Wilder by giving one of his last and best performances in *Sunset Boulevard* seven years later. *Five Graves to Cairo* still holds up as a top-notch espionage thriller with nary a sag. In Wilder's estimate, it is one of the best pictures he directed.

For his next film, Wilder chose to do a thriller, an adaptation of James M. Cain's *Double Indemnity*. Cinematographer John Seitz, film editor Doane Harrison, and composer Miklos Rozsa were committed to move on from *Five Graves* to *Double Indemnity*. Much to Wilder's surprise, after collaborating with him on the screen treatment, Charles Brackett begged off, saying that a grim and gory crime novella like *Double Indemnity* was simply not his cup of tea. Since Wilder's partnership with Brackett had often been described in the press as a marriage, Wilder accused Brackett of infidelity and went looking for another screenwriter to replace him on this project.

4

# The Rise of Film Noir

## Double Indemnity

> During the war a new mood of cynicism, pessimism, and darkness
> had crept into the American cinema. *Double Indemnity* was the best
> written, the most characteristically film noir of the period. *Double
> Indemnity* was the first film which played film noir for what it
> essentially was: small-time, unredeemed, unheroic.
> —*Paul Schrader, film historian*

In his book on film noir, William Hare repeats the story that one day Billy
Wilder could not find his secretary. He was told by one of the women in the
office that she was holed up in the ladies' room, reading a novella titled
*Double Indemnity*. After she emerged with the novelette "pressed against
her bosom," Wilder decided to read it himself.[1] A nice anecdote, but
apocryphal.

Wilder maintained that Joseph Sistrom, the enterprising young executive who had suggested that Wilder turn the play *Connie Goes Home* into
*The Major and the Minor*, "had read the [Cain] story and brought it to my
attention."[2] Sistrom was a devotee of popular fiction and was familiar with
the pulp fiction turned out by Cain and others. He had read *Double
Indemnity* as it was serialized in *Liberty* magazine, in back issues from
February 15 through April 4, 1936, which he had found in the story department's archives. When *Double Indemnity* was published in book form in
1943, he suggested the property to Wilder.

The story, a turgid tale of greed, lust, and betrayal, was right up
Wilder's street. After all, "the Berlin of the 1920s had taught Wilder to
recognize decadence when he saw it," as Richard Schickel writes in his
monograph on this film.[3] *Double Indemnity* portrayed a decadent, depraved
world of violence and duplicity. Wilder would give us a foreigner's vision
of the underside of American life, as represented by the back streets of Los

Angeles where the film is set. It is a drab world, devoid of beauty and decency.

Wilder was aware from the get-go that Cain's story would present him with censorship problems. The novella had already been considered and rejected by the major studios in 1935, shortly before it was serialized in *Liberty* magazine. This lurid tale describes how a villainess named Phyllis lures Walter, an insurance salesman, into a conspiracy to murder her husband for his insurance money—a conspiracy that becomes a recipe for their destruction. Metro-Goldwyn-Mayer had inquired of Joseph Breen whether Cain's novelette was suitable for filming. Breen shot back a letter to MGM executive Louis B. Mayer, dated October 10, 1935, in which he asserted, "The story deals improperly with an illicit and adulterous sex relationship. The general low tone and sordid flavor of this story make it . . . thoroughly unacceptable for screen production," according to the censorship code implemented by the industry in 1934.[4] Moreover, Breen noted, the novella portrayed the actual planning and carrying out of a murder plot in minute detail, and "filmmakers were forbidden to depict details of a crime that might permit its imitation in real life." Indeed, Breen considered the novella to be a "blueprint for murder," which could show potential criminals how to kill for profit.[5] Breen's letter scared off not only MGM but also every other studio in town from considering *Double Indemnity* as a viable film project.

Cain remembered his agent's showing him a copy of Breen's report: "It started off, 'UNDER NO CIRCUMSTANCES,' and ended up, 'NO WAY, SHAPE, OR FORM.' My agent asked me if I wanted to hear what was in between, and I told him I could guess." Eight years later, when *Double Indemnity* was published in book form, "my new agent, H. N. Swanson, sent it again to eight studios," Cain recalled. Sistrom passed it on to Wilder, who snapped it up and immediately "took it home and read it." Wilder arranged to buy the screen rights for a mere fifteen thousand dollars—there were no other bids.[6]

On September 21, 1943, Paramount sent Breen a screen treatment of *Double Indemnity,* a detailed synopsis that Wilder had prepared in conjunction with Charles Brackett. The censor felt that the revised story line, which they had composed according to his specifications, had overcome in large measure his original concerns. Breen added that, after all, "adultery is no longer quite as objectionable" as it once was in motion pictures.[7]

Sistrom agreed to produce *Double Indemnity* in Brackett's stead, although the self-effacing young exec declined to accept a screen credit for doing so. He was listed officially as associate producer. But Wilder still needed someone to replace Brackett as his cowriter on the screenplay. Wilder had hoped to engage Cain himself to help him adapt his novella for film, but Cain was then under contract to Twentieth Century–Fox and could not accept a writing assignment at another studio. Sistrom suggested another eminent crime novelist, Raymond Chandler, to collaborate with Wilder on the screenplay. Wilder had read Chandler's 1939 novel *The Big Sleep* and knew of his regular contributions to pulp fiction magazines like *Black Mask*, which specialized in crime stories. He was impressed with Chandler's lively narrative style and pungent dialogue. Although Chandler had no previous experience in screenwriting, Wilder accepted Sistrom's suggestion to engage Chandler, especially because Chandler "could put a nasty spin on dialogue."[8]

Chandler was interested in working with a writer-director who had already made an important wartime thriller, *Five Graves to Cairo*. His one hesitation was that he personally did not much care for Cain's crime novels. In a letter to Blanche Knopf, the wife of his publisher, Alfred Knopf, on October 22, 1942, Chandler said of Cain, "Everything he touches smells like a billygoat. He is a *faux naif*, a Proust in overalls, a dirty little boy with a piece of chalk," scrawling obscenities on a board fence when no one is looking. In short, Chandler disapproved of novelists like Cain "not because they write about dirty things, but because they do it in a dirty way."[9] Withal, Chandler welcomed the opportunity to increase his income, since the sales of his short stories to pulp magazines proved woefully insufficient to pay his living expenses.

*Double Indemnity* deals with the great American pastime of cheating an insurance company, and it does so with deadly seriousness. According to Wilder, Cain based his novella on the notorious Snyder-Gray case, which fascinated Wilder as well. John McCarty agrees that Cain's novelette offers striking parallels to "the real-life murder case of Ruth Snyder and Judd Gray, who conspired to kill Snyder's husband for $100,000 in insurance money" in Queens Village, New York, in 1927. "Unlike Cain's fictional couple, however, Snyder and Gray were caught and sent to the electric chair."[10] Snyder achieved tabloid immortality when she became the first woman in New York to be executed. Moreover, a photojournalist smuggled a camera into the execution chamber at Sing Sing on January 12, 1928, and snapped a picture of Snyder just as the juice was turned on. The next day, the photograph appeared on the front page of the *New York Daily News*. Certainly the photo would have drawn Cain's attention to the trial, if he had not been following it already.

When Wilder scheduled a preliminary meeting with Chandler in his office on the fourth floor of the writers' building at Paramount on May 12, 1943, he expected the author of hard-boiled detective fiction to be a burly, tough-looking type. Instead, Wilder recalled, he beheld a fifty-five-year-old gentleman wearing a frayed tweed jacket that made him look like a somewhat eccentric British schoolteacher. Chandler also had a sickly complexion, which to Wilder betokened that Chandler was "a man who has drowned himself in drink."[11]

It is true that Chandler had officially sworn off liquor by the time he went to work at Paramount, Al Clark comments, but the writer was a closet alcoholic who kept a pint bottle of bourbon stashed in his briefcase. Wilder was sure that Chandler would take a nip from the bottle whenever Wilder went to the restroom while they were working together. "Chandler responded all too easily to the climate of genial dipsomania" that prevailed among many of the writers, and he regularly drank with them at the end of the day at Lucy's, a bistro frequented by Paramount employees.[12] Wilder put up with Chandler's drinking habits, he said later, because "he was one of the greatest creative minds I have ever worked with, though more trouble than any other writer I've ever worked with."[13]

At all events, during their first story conference, Chandler informed Wilder, "This is already Tuesday; I cannot promise you the script until next Monday." Chandler was obviously laboring under the misconception that he was expected to write the screenplay on his own and in record time. Wilder responded that the studio was prepared to offer Chandler $750 a week for writing the script in collaboration with Wilder himself. To the mystery writer, accustomed to paltry payments from pulp publishers, this seemed a handsome sum. Still, Wilder warned Chandler, "You don't know how scripts are written."[14] Wilder gave Chandler a copy of Cain's novella, plus a copy of his own script for *Hold Back the Dawn* as a model screenplay, and told him to get to work.

Not heeding Wilder's warning, the neophyte screenwriter showed up at his next meeting with the director toting sixty-five pages of script, whereas Wilder had turned out three pages of the opening scene. For the most part, Schickel records, "Chandler had typed up Cain's dialogue in the best imitation he could manage of screenplay form." Wilder, with typical Wilder exaggeration, claimed Chandler had added camera directions like "the camera slips in through the keyhole and sniffs her undies."[15] Wilder took one look at Chandler's batch of script pages, tossed them back at him, and barked, "This is crap, Mr. Chandler." "You don't know a damn thing about writing for the screen," Wilder reiterated. "But I'll teach you."[16]

Wilder went on to explain that Cain had written the novella in a hurried, slapdash fashion because he needed money, as Cain was the first to admit.[17] As a result, the story's narrative structure and character development needed shoring up. Wilder concluded by advising Chandler to forget about inserting camera directions into the script, since that was the director's business. "Just let's write characters and situations."[18] A morose, touchy man, Chandler preferred to work alone, so he resented the script conferences Wilder imposed on him, terming them "godawful jabber sessions." Specifically, Chandler resented having to collaborate with this brash, opinionated filmmaker on a daily basis. He grew testier and more disagreeable as time went on.[19]

Admittedly, Wilder was an excitable man who had his share of eccentricities, and they bothered Chandler. After all, Chandler had never before been forced to write in the same room with another person. Wilder paced back and forth while they discussed the screenplay, often brandishing a malacca cane, which he sometimes rudely waved in Chandler's face as he emphasized a point. Chandler saw this as the height of incivility.

Wilder had some grievances of his own. Chandler smoked a pipe from which emanated clouds of noxious smoke but insisted that the office windows remain tightly shut because he was convinced that the Los Angeles smog was hazardous to his health. One day, in exasperation, Wilder snapped, "Ray, would you raise the window just this once, for Chrissakes?"[20]

Finally, one morning four weeks into coauthoring the script, Chandler, who was an inveterate collector of injustices, real or imagined, declined to report for work. Instead, he issued a written ultimatum to Wilder. It was a letter of complaint, the director recalled, in which Chandler maintained that he was fed up with Wilder's rudeness. The letter insisted that Wilder "is at no time to swish under Mr. Chandler's nose or to point in his direction the thin, leather-handled Malacca cane which Mr. Wilder is in the habit of waving around while they work. Mr. Wilder is not to give Mr. Chandler orders of an arbitrary nature, such as 'Ray, will you open that window?'"[21]

Sistrom acted as mediator; he contacted Chandler, who told him succinctly, "I don't want to work with that son-of-a-bitch any more."[22] Nevertheless, Sistrom coaxed him into reporting for work the following morning. Wilder and Chandler made a truce, although Wilder reminded him, "For God's sake, Ray, we don't have court manners around here." But he apologized just the same, simply because he still admired Chandler's writing ability and very much wanted him to continue collaborating on the script. For a tyro screenwriter to exact an apology from an influential film director was deemed something of an achievement at the writers' table in the Paramount commissary. The rancor that characterized Wilder and Chandler's relationship, however, did not interfere with their collaboration on the script.

The completed script is dated September 25, 1943; filming began the following week. Chandler was kept on salary throughout the shooting period to help Wilder revise any scene that needed work. In all, Chandler was on salary for six months, from May through November 1943, netting him eighteen thousand dollars—more money than he had made in a long time.

During the shooting period, Chandler agreed to do a silent cameo for the film. Sixteen minutes into the film, Walter Neff leaves the office of Barton Keyes and passes a lone figure sitting in the corridor, reading a magazine and facing the camera. Neff does not notice him, but he notices Neff: Raymond Chandler looks up from his magazine and gazes at Neff for a moment, and then returns to his reading.

Chandler and Wilder had initially planned to borrow as much of Cain's tough, spare dialogue from the novelette as possible. As time went on, however, Chandler realized that the novella's dialogue needed reworking for the screen. Wilder disagreed, Cain remembered, "and he was annoyed that Chandler wasn't putting more of it in the script." To settle the matter, Wilder enlisted a couple of contract players to read passages of Cain's original dialogue from the book. "To Wilder's astonishment, he found out it *wouldn't* play," said Cain. After the actors read a scene straight from the book, Chandler pointed out to Wilder that the dialogue sounded like "a bad high school play. The dialogue oversaid everything and, when spoken, sounded quite colorless and tame."[23]

As Chandler later told Cain in a consultation, "Jim, that dialogue of yours is for the *eye*," not for the ear. "I tried to explain it to Billy." Chandler continued, telling Cain that his clipped dialogue had no sting and even sounded flat when it was spoken aloud. Chandler added that the book's dialogue, particularly the exchanges between Phyllis and Walter, had to be "sharpened and pointed" for the screen. Cain graciously replied that he fully understood why Chandler and Wilder had not used more of his "deathless dialogue" in the picture.[24] The upshot is that the film's taut, cynical dialogue owes more to Chandler and Wilder than it does to Cain. "We improved it quite a bit," Wilder said later. He was impressed with the way Chandler could "get the flavor of California" into his flip and mordant writing, in both his scripts and his novels.[25] Chandler, after all, was a native of Chicago who had been educated in England.

The title of the film refers to the double insurance benefit paid out in the event of accidental death. Phyllis Dietrichson seduces Walter Neff, an insurance agent, into helping her murder her husband and making it look like an accident so they can cash in his insurance policy. Phyllis is confident that Walter can aid her in defrauding the insurance company, since he is employed by the firm that has insured her husband.

Walter's willingness to buy into Phyllis's sordid moneymaking scheme brings clearly to prominence a theme that often surfaces in Wilder's films. As Wilder himself formulated that theme, "People will do anything for money, except some people, who will do *almost* anything for money." This is Wilder's satirical comment on the erosion of values in our modern acquisitive society. Without a doubt, Walter is just as willing as Phyllis to do anything for money, not excluding homicide. In fact their love story is fundamentally grounded in their mutual desire to collect the death money.

Although Chandler and Wilder had to revise Cain's dialogue, at times they were able to employ a passage from the novella just as Cain wrote it. For example, in the book Walter admits that he had considered bilking the insurance company that employed him long before he met Phyllis; Chandler and Wilder reproduced this passage virtually intact in the film. Walter begins by explaining how he has become an expert in heading off policyholders who try to defraud the company. He continues, "You're like the guy behind the roulette wheel, watching the customers to make sure they don't crook the house. And then one night you get to thinking how you could crook the house yourself and do it smart, because you've got the wheel right smack under your hands. You know every notch in it by heart. And you figure all you need is a plant out front, a shill to put down the bet. Suddenly the doorbell rings, and the whole set-up is right there in the room with you."[26]

Andrew Sarris complained that Wilder offered no satisfactory explanation for Neff's transformation into a killer: "I have never been able to perceive the motivational moment in which Walter Neff, the breezy insurance salesman and devil-may-care womanizer, is transformed into a purposeful murderer."[27] John Gregory Dunne responded, "The answer has always seemed obvious to me: Phyllis Dietrichson gave Walter Neff an erection, and from that moment on Neff's underdeveloped common sense took up residence in his scrotum."[28] In sum, Alan Woolfolk says, "The manipulative Phyllis Dietrichson provides the opportunity and perhaps some additional incentive, to which Walter is entirely susceptible."[29]

The dark, brooding atmosphere of the film, coupled with the equally somber vision of life reflected in this tale of obsession and murder, marks *Double Indemnity* as belonging to that class of American melodramas that French film critics christened around that time *film noir* (dark film). This trend in American cinema was just surfacing when Wilder made *Double Indemnity* during World War II. The pessimistic view of life exhibited in such movies was an outgrowth of the disillusionment that would continue into the cold war. Others see film noir as a specific style of filmmaking that can be applied to various genres. To be precise, a noir film can be identified by its grim, sinister tone and its bleak, cynical thematic vision. Film noir depicts a stark night world peopled by characters who are trapped in a decadent, crime-ridden society.[30]

Foster Hirsch opines that "the best *noir* directors were German or Austrian expatriates who shared a world view that was shaped by their bitter personal experiences of . . . escaping from a nation that had lost its mind." Thus some of Wilder's films, like *Double Indemnity*, can be deemed examples of film noir. "The group of expatriate directors who were to become the masters of the *noir* style," Hirsch continues, brought to their American films a predilection for "stories about man's uncertain fate, and about psychological obsession and derangement."[31] *Double Indemnity* is very much in keeping with the conventions of film noir, with its spare, unvarnished realism, typified by the stark, newsreel-like quality of the cinematography, especially in the scenes that occur in sleazy places at night.

Ed Muller noted that "*Double Indemnity* was a trend-setting film, which helped to establish film noir."[32] That *Double Indemnity* was in the vanguard of film noir movies is evident from a seminal essay on film noir by French film critic Nino Frank, published in the August 28, 1946, issue of *L'écran française* (The French screen). In it Frank terms *Double Indemnity* an example of "a new type of crime film" coming out of Hollywood, which he designates as film noir. Frank thus coined the term and was the first critic to use it in print. He also singled out John Huston's *Maltese Falcon* (1941), with Humphrey Bogart as a hard-boiled private eye, as significant in the development of film noir.[33]

Both *The Maltese Falcon* and *Double Indemnity* feature a crafty, malevolent femme fatale, who uses men and then discards them. Brigid O'Shaughnessy in *The Maltese Falcon* and Phyllis Dietrichson in *Double Indemnity* are both prototypical femmes fatales; each is a heartless, double-dealing female. The femme fatale would become "one of the mainstays of classic noir," writes Jason Holt—"fatal not only to the sap who falls for her, but also to herself."[34] That, in a nutshell, describes Phyllis Dietrichson.

Nevertheless, Wilder said, "Although *Double Indemnity* has quite a reputation today as an example of film noir, I was not aware of being part of a trend at the time." Indeed, Wilder never thought of any of his movies as belonging to the category of film noir when he made them. "I didn't set out to make a particular style of film," he declared. "You're trying to make as good and as entertaining a picture as you possibly can. If you have any kind of style, the discerning ones will detect it."[35]

Y. Frank Freeman, vice president of Paramount, shared Charles Brackett's opinion that *Double Indemnity* was a sordid movie. Freeman, who came to Paramount with experience in the soft drink industry, belonged to the religious Right. He hated the idea of Paramount's making the film, but he was outvoted by other executives, including the head of production, B. G. "Buddy" De Sylva. Wilder disliked Freeman, and he was not alone. Indeed, the standing joke around the lot about the high-handed, narrow-minded mogul was for someone to ask, "Why Frank Freeman?"[36]

At any rate, Freeman did not encourage any of his top actors to appear in *Double Indemnity.* So Wilder had trouble casting the leads—except for the role of the insurance claims investigator, Barton Keyes. Edward G. Robinson accepted the part because "at my age it was time to begin thinking of character roles, to slide into middle age. . . . I was never the handsome leading man; I could proceed with my career growing older in roles that would grow older, too."[37]

Wilder told me that every leading man in town turned down the role of the randy, womanizing murderer Walter Neff. "I confess that I even sank so low as to offer the role to George Raft," the second-string star of mediocre melodramas like *Background to Danger* (1943). "And that's pretty low!" Raft had an assistant read the screenplay for him, Wilder continued, "because he couldn't read." When Raft advised Wilder that he would take the part only on the condition that Neff turn out to be an FBI agent and arrest Phyllis at the end of the picture, Wilder replied that that was out of the question. "So George Raft turned down the role; and that's when we knew we had a good picture."[38] (Raft was not noted to be a shrewd judge of roles; he also passed up the lead in *The Maltese Falcon.*)

Wilder finally turned to Fred MacMurray, who hesitated to accept the part because he normally played "happy-go-lucky good guys" in light comedies. "You're making the mistake of your life!" he exclaimed to Wilder. Playing a serious role required acting, he explained, "And I can't do it."[39] Wilder responded that he was confident that MacMurray could play Neff and that he could guide him through the part. MacMurray had one other reservation about taking the part: he feared that Wilder's wish to cast him against type as a cad and a scoundrel would ruin his screen image.[40] But Wilder wanted MacMurray to play Walter precisely because Walter's charming manner and affable grin belie the lust and larceny inside him, and MacMurray's surface charm would make his performance all the more chilling as a result.

Similarly, Barbara Stanwyck hesitated to accept the role of Phyllis Dietrichson, a woman so thoroughly malicious and unscrupulous. Stanwyck had been paired with MacMurray in the 1940 romantic comedy *Remember the Night,* which was written by Preston Sturges and directed by Mitchell Leisen, and she likewise wanted to maintain a positive image with her fans. But Stanwyck too relented because she trusted Wilder: "I knew him a little from *Ball of Fire,*" she explained. "You couldn't help but notice how he cared about his script."[41]

Stanwyck's portrayal of Phyllis won her a place in film history as a legendary femme fatale. Wilder gave Stanwyck a tacky blonde wig because he wanted it to project "the phoniness of the girl—bad taste, phony wig," with cheap perfume to match.[42] Wilder said that, after he made *Double Indemnity,* "MGM made another James M. Cain novel into a picture, *The Postman Always Rings Twice* [1946], with Lana Turner as the wife of the proprietor of a hot dog stand. She was made up to look glamorous instead of slightly tarnished the way we made up Barbara Stanwyck for *Double Indemnity,* and I think *Postman* was less authentic as a result."

The studio allocated a budget for *Double Indemnity* of $980,000, which Wilder adhered closely to. The budget allowed him a salary of $44,000 for the four months he spent writing the screenplay with Chandler and $26,000 for the two months he spent directing it. But his total take was still less than the $100,000 apiece that MacMurray, Stanwyck, and Robinson were paid for starring in the picture.

Principal photography began on September 27, 1943. Wilder wanted to present an uncompromising picture of a corrupt, essentially lawless urban environment by shooting on location in the crooked streets and back alleys of Los Angeles. Schickel remarks, "Wilder's judicious use of locations around Los Angeles is noteworthy; it is enough to take the film out of the studio context. Los Angeles was a city which was somewhat amoral; Wilder noticed that when he first came to town."[43] In the film, the gray atmosphere reflects the bleak lives of the characters, who live in run-down neighborhoods that have seen better days. Walter occupies a chintzy bachelor flat, and Phyllis lives with a husband who is nearly twice her age in a crumbling stucco bungalow. (The house used for exteriors is located at 6301 Quebec Street in the Hollywood Hills.) Wilder said, "I strove for a strong sense of realism in the settings in order to match the kind of story we were telling. I wanted to get away from what we described in those days as the white satin decor associated with MGM's chief set designer, Cedric Gibbons [*Ninotchka*]."

Hans Dreier, head of Paramount's art department, had, like Wilder, started his career at Ufa in Berlin in the 1920s. He assigned Hal Pereira as production designer on *Double Indemnity.* Wilder instructed Pereira to design the interiors of the Dietrichson house to appear drab. Thanks to

Pereira's astutely placed venetian blinds, the faces of Walter and Phyllis, when they converse in the house, are at times barred with shadows that imply imprisonment of body or soul. Once the set was ready for shooting, Wilder said, "I would go around and overturn a few ashtrays in order to give the house in which Phyllis lived an appropriately grubby look, because Phyllis is a poor housekeeper—an index of her indifference to her husband." Wilder got on well with Pereira, and they would work together again. Dreier, who supervised Pereira's work, was likewise pleased with the results. Wilder continued, "I also worked with the cameraman, John Seitz, to put dust in the air, to give the house a sort of musty look. We blew aluminum particles into the air, and when they floated down into a shaft of sunlight, they looked just like dust." (Real dust is invisible to the camera's eye.) "It was just right for that creepy house in the Valley," Wilder concluded. "I like that kind of realism."

Principal photography wrapped on November 24, 1943, just short of two months. When it came to postproduction, Miklos Rozsa contributed a portentous, dissonant score that establishes from the start an overall sense of dread and foreboding. It was not typical of the usual melodic Hollywood score, and Wilder soon discovered that Louis Lipstone disliked its discordant, morose themes even more than he had disapproved of Rozsa's similar background music for *Five Graves to Cairo*. When Lipstone informed Wilder of his negative judgment of the *Double Indemnity* score, Wilder stared him down and barked, "You may be surprised to hear that I *love* it. Okay?"[44] So Wilder overruled Lipstone again, and he was ultimately vindicated. Rozsa's brooding score for *Double Indemnity* influenced the background music for subsequent noir films "like no other soundtrack of the 1940s," writes Robert Horton. "The opening credits alone—a doom-laden thump of a funeral march," all pounding chords and throbbing drum beats—"establishes the noir vibe with brazen audacity."[45]

The opening credits of the film show the silhouette of a man hobbling toward the camera on crutches; his shadow grows larger until it fills the screen. This menacing image prefigures Walter's temporary impersonation of Phyllis's crippled husband after Walter murders him.

The film proper opens with a stunning sequence: A speeding car careens down a dark street late at night; a stoplight in the foreground of the shot changes from go to stop, but the auto runs the light. "This is, of course, a visual symbol for everything we are about to learn about the car's occupant, Walter Neff," says Schickel. Walter will "run all the stoplights in his relationship with Phyllis Dietrichson."[46]

Nursing a gunshot wound in his shoulder, Walter lurches into the building that houses the offices of the Pacific All-Risk Insurance Company, where he is employed. He settles down at his desk, inserts a cylinder into the Dictaphone, and begins a memo to Barton Keyes, chief claims investigator for the insurance company. The memo takes the form of a confession, which Walter narrates, in voice-over on the sound track, while the story of his deadly alliance with Phyllis is portrayed in flashback. Wilder said that the secret of doing a voice-over in a movie was to "be careful not to describe what the audience already sees. Add to what they are seeing."[47] He followed this rule in the script for *Double Indemnity;* Walter's caustic voice narration provides a running commentary on the events the viewers see unfolding on the screen.

Since Walter is dictating an office memorandum, he supplies some vital statistics, starting with the date, July 16, 1938. Dating Neff's memo, explains Peter Evans, "represents a common way at the time of avoiding reference to the war."[48] Walter identifies himself as "Walter Neff, insurance agent, thirty-five years old, unmarried." He glances down at the bullet wound in his shoulder and adds, "No visible scars, until a little while ago, that is." Then, with a line lifted from a later scene in the book, Walter observes stoically that he killed Dietrichson: "I killed him for money and a woman. I didn't get the money and I didn't get the woman."[49] Remarks such as this lend the film a fatalistic atmosphere, for the viewer knows that Walter is doomed from the start.

With that, Walter begins to tell his tale. Wilder reminds the viewer that Walter is relating his own story by periodically returning to him sitting before the Dictaphone; each time Wilder does so, the bloodstain on Walter's suit coat is larger. As Walter starts to narrate his story, he begins with lines once more taken directly from the novella. He says, "It all began last May. I remembered this policy renewal on Los Feliz Boulevard, so I drove over there," to the home of the Dietrichsons.[50]

When Walter sees Phyllis for the first time, she is standing on the staircase landing, looking down at him. She is draped in the white bath towel she has donned for sunbathing. Phyllis's apparel suggests purity in color only, for, as the story unfolds, she will display her true colors. As she descends the stairs, Walter notices her gold ankle bracelet, which is shown in close-up. Evans writes, "The anklet dangles invitingly in front of him as she crosses her legs in the living room." It is "an anklet which Walter relishes all the more for cutting into her flesh," as Walter admits in his voice-over.[51] Walter's obsession with the anklet implies that it is for him a sexual fetish by which he is chained to Phyllis.

Walter also notices the scent of Phyllis's cheap perfume, which reminds him of the honeysuckle he smelled on the way to the Dietrichson house. He comments, in voice-over on the sound track, "It was a hot afternoon, and I can still remember the smell of honeysuckle all along the street. How could I have known that murder can sometimes smell like honeysuckle?" The cloying aroma that pervades the area is an emblem of "the rotten, sickly-sweet corruption" of Phyllis Dietrichson's domain.[52]

Chandler and Wilder concocted some salty, innuendo-strewn interchanges for Walter and Phyllis not found in Cain's novelette. A striking example occurs during their first encounter. Walter gets fresh with Phyllis after eyeing her provocatively draped towel: "I'm an insurance agent, and I can see you are not fully covered." Phyllis responds in a playful, coy fashion that demonstrates that she is Walter's match when it comes to naughty innuendo: "There's a speed limit in this state, Mr. Neff." Walter replies, "Suppose you get down off your motorcycle and give me a ticket." "Suppose I let you off with a warning this time," Phyllis answers with a smirk.

As Walter prepares to leave, he inquires suggestively whether Phyllis will be home when he returns to see her husband. "I wonder what you mean," Phyllis says. Walter retorts, "I wonder if you wonder." As a matter of fact, when Walter returns, Phyllis is home, but she has made sure that her husband is not. Phyllis then broaches to Walter the possibility of his drawing up a double indemnity accident policy for her husband. In due course, this leads to their planning Dietrichson's death for the insurance money.

Walter's better judgment tells him not to get involved with a femme fatale like Phyllis, writes Frank Krutnik, and Walter's "voice-over commentary provides a suggestively phallic metaphor for the danger and excitement" of the enterprise.[53] "I knew I had hold of a red-hot poker," Walter muses, "and the time to drop it was before it burned my hand off." Walter ignores his misgivings, however, and goes along with Phyllis's plot. In short, although Walter is capable of recognizing evil when he sees it, he still succumbs to it.

A central metaphor in the Chandler-Wilder script is that of a trolley car one must ride to the end of the line.[54] When Walter agrees to help Phyllis liquidate her husband, he says that their plan "has got to be perfect, straight down the line." Walter immediately comments in a voice-over, "The machinery had started to move, and nothing could stop it." As Walter prepares to kill Dietrichson later that same night, he reflects on the sound track that fate "had thrown the switch. The gears had meshed." The trolley "had started to move, and nothing could stop it."

After the murder, Keyes parallels Walter's "straight down the line" perception. Keyes suspects Phyllis of engineering her husband's death with the help of an unknown accomplice. "They've committed a murder," he says, "and that's not like taking a trolley ride together, where each one can get off at a different stop. They've got to ride all the way to the end of the line. And it's a one-way trip, and the last stop is the cemetery."

The scene in which Walter murders Phyllis's husband provides a dramatic high point in Walter's narrative. Dietrichson is determined to take a train trip, despite the fact that he has a broken leg and must walk with crutches. As Phyllis drives him to the train station, Walter crouches unseen in the backseat of the car. When Walter suddenly pounces on Dietrichson and chokes him to death, the camera moves in on a close-up of Phyllis, who stares unflinchingly at the road ahead. Wilder allowed the audience to imagine the murder while it takes place off camera, "because what the audience does not see can sometimes be more frightening than what they do see."

Because Dietrichson is slain when he has a broken leg, Walter must board the train on crutches when impersonating him, recalling the image of the dark figure on crutches in the opening credits. Walter must make it appear that the crippled man was killed as the result of an accidental fall from the train. He accordingly rides the train for a few miles and then jumps off, crutches and all, at the prearranged spot, where Phyllis is waiting for him with her husband's corpse still in the car. Walter dumps the body, along with the crutches, on the railroad track.

The low-key lighting that John Seitz employed in *Five Graves to Cairo* creates an even darker, more sinister atmosphere in *Double Indemnity*. In the scene in which the lovers implement their plan to murder Dietrichson, they are enveloped in almost total darkness. The lighting emphasizes how the guilty lovers are trying to hide their evil deed under a cloak of darkness. In retrospect, it is evident that in this film Seitz set the standard for the shadowy, somber lighting for the noir films to come.

It certainly looks as if Walter and Phyllis's plan has worked and fate is on their side. But Keyes proves to be an obstacle to the success of their plot. Walter and Phyllis fear that he may eventually finger Walter as Phyllis's partner in crime if he happens to see them together.

In one scene Phyllis is about to knock on the door of Walter's apartment when she hears Walter talking with Keyes inside. As the door opens and Keyes comes out, Phyllis quickly hides behind the half-open door. Fred MacMurray told me that Wilder "tampered with realism" in that scene by having the door open outward into the hall, so that Phyllis can conveniently disappear behind it as Keyes leaves—despite the fact that doors normally open inward.[55] Be that as it may, the scene provides another suspenseful highlight in the film, as Cain himself noted: "I wish I had thought of something like that."[56]

Later on, Walter's relationship with Phyllis unravels when he discovers that she has been using him to help her obtain the payoff from the insurance company. She actually plans to double-cross Walter by taking the money and running off—not with him but with still another, younger man. Walter forces a showdown with Phyllis in her stifling, shuttered living room. "Tangerine" is being crooned somewhere in the night, "probably from a neighboring radio" (as the script has it), and the romantic ballad wafts into Phyllis's living room.[57] The love song is an ironic comment on the romantic illusions Walter nurtured about the faithless Phyllis.

Walter tells Phyllis about Keyes's theory that two people who commit murder are trapped on a trolley car and their only way out is death. He then informs Phyllis that he is not going to ride the streetcar to the end of the line; rather, he plans to get off the trolley "right at this corner." With that, the pair shoot it out. Phyllis grievously wounds Walter and is about to fire again when she experiences a split second of remorse. She admits that she is "rotten to the heart." Then she looks into his eyes and begs Walter to embrace her. She hesitates to fire the second shot, which will finish him off, and instead professes her need for him. As Bernard Dick describes Phyllis, "We see what Neff sees—a face that, for an instant, loses its rodent-like sharpness and becomes almost human. But it is only for an instant."[58] Walter, convinced of her deep duplicity, has trusted her for the last time. "I'm sorry, Baby; I'm not buying," he mutters. "Goodbye, Baby." Walter embraces her; then he fires two shots and kills her on the spot. Thus Walter's final embrace of Phyllis ends when he ejaculates bullets into her; it is the logical consummation of their sordid liaison. Walter, though gravely wounded, still has enough life in him to make it to his office and record his confession for Keyes.

After viewing *Double Indemnity,* Cain remarked that it was "the only picture I ever saw made from my books that had things in it I wished I had thought of; Wilder's ending was much better than my ending."[59] It is easy to agree with Cain on that point. The novelette ends with Walter and Phyllis fleeing to Mexico onboard a steamer. But they have reason to believe that they have been recognized aboard ship, and so Phyllis, who has by now sunk completely into madness, convinces Walter to join her in a suicide pact by jumping overboard. Phyllis, a grotesque figure dressed in a blood-red shroud, with her face painted a deathly white, materializes like a ghostly apparition in Walter's cabin to summon him to his doom. They both are prepared to die. The mass audience, Dick quite rightly judges, "would not understand anything quite so operatic."[60]

Keyes, in describing his job as a claims investigator for Walter earlier in the movie, defines his role as "a doctor, a bloodhound, a cop, a judge, a jury, and a father-confessor, all in one." Certainly Keyes is Walter's father-confessor, since it is to Keyes that Walter confesses his crimes on the Dictaphone. In fact, the father-son relationship between Walter and Keyes is evident throughout the film. "The real love story is not between Neff and Phyllis, but between Neff and Keyes," Jeffrey Meyers declares. "Neff's criminal betrayal of his friend and mentor gives the tawdry story a new dimension."[61] Cain noted that "there's a hint" of the filial relationship of Walter to Keyes in the book, "but it was extended in the movie."[62] As Schickel puts it, "Keyes's part was expanded in the film to flesh out his relationship with Neff, which almost doesn't exist in the book."[63]

In the film, as Walter finishes dictating his memo to Keyes, he looks up and sees Keyes, who has been summoned by the night porter; he has been standing in the doorway, unobserved, for some time. Walter tells Keyes that he could not identify Dietrichson's murderer "because the guy you were looking for was too close. He was right across the desk from you." Keyes replies, "Closer than that, Walter." Neff responds wryly, "I love you too." Despite his offhand, almost mocking tone of voice, the remark reflects the deep affection and respect he nurtures for Keyes.

Walter's strength is ebbing away, but he still manages to put a cigarette in his mouth, and Keyes lights it for him. In doing so, Keyes performs for Walter the ritual gesture of friendship that Walter has often performed for him. Throughout the film Walter lights Keyes's cigar for him as an implicit gesture of filial feeling for his father figure. Now Keyes, with a veiled display of affection, returns the favor, as they await the police.

Some critics have inferred a hint of homosexuality in the relationship of Walter and Keyes. Parker Tyler goes so far as to say that Keyes is "secretly hot" for Neff, as evidenced by the scene described above. But such a reading of a Wilder movie misconstrues the value the director placed on male companionship in a number of his films.

*Double Indemnity* was originally intended to conclude with Walter's execution. Wilder even filmed him dying in the gas chamber at San Quentin. The scene took five days to shoot and, according to Lally, cost a whopping $150,000. Actually, the itemized budget for the picture included only $4,700 for the set.[64] Perhaps Wilder had the Snyder-Gray execution in mind when he developed the execution scene with Chandler. He shot the scene with minute precision: there were the pellets of poison dropping and the fumes they caused; in addition, "I had the priest from San Quentin, and I had the warden and the doctor."[65]

The execution scene was shot before the scene portraying the last meeting between Walter and Keyes was filmed. Once that final, intimate exchange between Walter and Keyes was in the can, Wilder began to wonder if the execution scene was not superfluous. Without the execution scene to follow it, the viewer easily infers that Walter will soon die of his fatal wound. Moreover, after Wilder viewed the completed execution sequence, almost eighteen minutes of footage, he felt uneasy about it. He found it unduly gruesome and too harsh for the mass audience to digest, so he decided to end the film with Walter lying grievously wounded in the company of his fatherly friend. Thus, when Walter begs Keyes to give him time to make it across the border to Mexico, Keyes replies, "You'll never make the elevator." Walter staggers toward the exit, only to collapse helplessly in the doorway, where he lies at death's door. One assumes he will die in Keyes's arms, perhaps even before the police arrive.

The final version of the screenplay omits not only the execution scene but also a line of dialogue spoken by Walter to Keyes just after Walter says, "I love you too"—which is the last line in the final script and in the film as released. At this point in the original draft, Walter makes a final request of Keyes: "At the end of the trolley line, just as I get off, you be there to say goodbye, will you, Keyes?"[66] This line was meant to serve as a transition to the execution scene, for, as James Naremore remarks, the initial version of the script "went on to show Keyes at the penitentiary, honoring his friend's wishes."[67] Walter's reference to the trolley car hearkens back to Keyes's earlier observation that Phyllis and her partner in crime were trapped on a trolley car that would carry them to their doom. With or without the execution scene, Keyes's ominous prediction comes true.

William Hare assumes that the ending of the released version of the film constitutes "new material" that Wilder and Chandler devised as a substitute for the execution sequence.[68] A comparison of the original version of the screenplay (dated September 25, 1943) with the final version (dated November 27, 1943) shows his assumption to be false, however. The final script is shorter than the original simply because it omits the death chamber sequence and ends the film with the final encounter of Walter and Keyes in the insurance office.[69] In any case, the gas chamber sequence seems to be a postscript to the story. The ending of the movie as it stands is much more powerful and moving, and could not be bettered. Wilder excised the execution scene while working on the final edit of the film with Doane Harrison.

Wilder remembered that, after a sneak preview of the picture in a theater in Westwood in July 1944, Cain waited for him in the lobby and told him that he much admired the film. His story, he told Wilder, "has been put on the screen exactly as I wrote it, only more so."[70]

Critics hailed the movie as a thriller deftly served up by master chefs, with a superior script and inspired direction. The movie grossed more than $2.5 million on its initial release and garnered Oscar nominations for best picture, director, screenplay, cinematography (John Seitz), musical score (Miklos Rozsa), and actress (Barbara Stanwyck). Leo McCarey's *Going My Way*, a sentimental Paramount picture with Bing Crosby as a priest, also received multiple nominations. The studio campaigned mostly for McCarey's heartwarming picture, reasoning that it had a better chance of snagging Oscars than Wilder's nasty movie. Wilder felt betrayed by his own studio and was miffed when his picture won no Academy Awards at the ceremony on March 15, 1945. When McCarey was on his way up to the podium to accept the best director award for *Going My Way*, Wilder recalled, he stuck his foot out and deliberately tripped McCarey. Wilder chortled, "Mr. McCarey stumbled perceptibly."

When a reporter asked him after the ceremony for his reaction to the losses, Wilder snapped, "What the hell does the Academy Award mean, for God's sake? After all, Luise Rainer won it two times—*Luise Rainer!*"[71] (Rainer had won a best actress award for *The Great Ziegfeld* [1936] and another for *The Good Earth* [1937], but within three years her career had inexplicably evaporated, and by 1945 she was all but forgotten.) Nonetheless, even with no Oscar for his direction of *Double Indemnity*, Wilder was widely considered Paramount's resident genius, since Preston Sturges, the only other writer-director on the lot, had severed his connection with the studio in December 1943.

In recent years commentators on *Double Indemnity* have steadily come to recognize it as quintessential film noir. "*Double Indemnity* was a milestone in opening new avenues for the frank portrayal of sexuality and criminality on the screen," writes Gaylyn Studlar. "Wilder confirmed that Hollywood filmmakers could take a sophisticated, artistically complex approach to crime, even while operating under the moral restrictions" of the industry's censorship code.[72]

Even though, Wilder said, Charles Brackett "thought I cheated on him with Raymond Chandler," they were reconciled: "Charles and I got together again for *The Lost Weekend*," a psychological study of an alcoholic.[73] In addition to collaborating with Wilder on the screenplay, Brackett again acted as producer, and Wilder continued to direct. The word around the film colony was that the dynamic duo was back in action.

# 5

# Through a Glass Darkly

## The Lost Weekend and Die Todesmühlen

I have supp'd full with horrors.

—*William Shakespeare, Macbeth*

Billy Wilder was on his way by train to New York for a holiday in the spring of 1944. He picked up a copy of Charles Jackson's novel *The Lost Weekend* at a kiosk during the stopover at Union Station in Chicago. Wilder sat up all night reading it. By the time he reached Pennsylvania Station in New York City the following morning, Wilder had finished the book. He was convinced that it would make an engrossing movie.

Wilder phoned Paramount executive Buddy De Sylva from the station and requested that the studio purchase the screen rights to the book. De Sylva informed him that Y. Frank Freeman was out of town but said that he would buy the novel for Wilder on his own authority. So De Sylva plunked down fifty thousand dollars for *The Lost Weekend*.[1] De Sylva had started in show business as a lyricist for major songwriters like Jerome Kern, with whom he had composed "Look for the Silver Lining." He graduated to producing pictures and became Paramount's head of production in 1939. He supported Wilder in the making of *Double Indemnity*, which turned out well, and he was more than willing to sponsor another Wilder project. Wilder then sold Brackett on the book; both were eager to collaborate again.[2]

When Freeman learned what De Sylva had done in his absence, he was outraged. As a Bible Belt Baptist, he did not approve of Paramount's making what he considered a sordid movie about a disreputable souse. Wilder did not relish having to face Freeman, who had likewise strongly disapproved of *Double Indemnity*. Freeman called an executive meeting to rake Wilder over the coals.[3] Wilder presented an inspired talk at the meeting, in which he emphasized that the movie would not be a dreary message picture about temperance. "If you want to send a message," he commented, "go to Western Union." He said that the script would focus on the romance between the main character and his loyal girlfriend. He devised on the spot a classic "meet-cute" to rival the one he had pitched to Ernst Lubitsch for the script of *Bluebeard's Eighth Wife*. In the present instance the hero and heroine would meet over the mix-up of their coats in the cloakroom of the Metropolitan Opera House. But Freeman remained intransigent; he stated emphatically that *The Lost Weekend* would be made "over my dead body." Wilder muttered under his breath that that could be arranged.[4]

There is a saying in Hollywood that a director is only as good as his last picture. Although *Double Indemnity* would not be released until the fall, the buzz about the picture in the film colony was enthusiastic, a point in Wilder's favor. Furthermore, De Sylva was in Wilder's corner. Consequently, the board of executives at the meeting finally green-lighted the project. Their decision was ratified by Barney Balaban, president of Paramount, whose office was at the studio's headquarters in New York City. Balaban, who had run a lucrative chain of theaters in the greater Chicago area before taking over at Paramount, was a canny judge of potential film projects.

## *The Lost Weekend* (1945)

After the conference, Wilder commented to a journalist that *The Lost Weekend* was not going to be the ordinary Hollywood fare. "Hollywood is in a rut," he said. Speaking of the run-of-the-mill movies the studios churned out, he noted that Hollywood was a slave to formula. "They don't make pictures, they remake them." *The Lost Weekend,* he continued, would be the first mainstream film to take alcoholism seriously.[5]

Prior to this movie, drinking was primarily employed on the screen as comic relief. "In those days an alcoholic was something you roared with laughter about," Wilder explained.[6] The drunkard would be a comedian like W. C. Fields, who would get plastered in a bar, then bump into the furniture and put on his hat backward as he left. But Don Birnam, the writer in *The Lost Weekend* whose addiction to liquor leads him into the wretched world of the alcoholic, is not a comic drunk, Wilder said: He does not stagger; he is a dignified man. In fact, there is nothing at all funny about Don Birnam.

Asked if he modeled Don in the screenplay for *The Lost Weekend* on Raymond Chandler, the alcoholic writer he collaborated with on *Double Indemnity,* Wilder replied, "Not consciously; I may have had him in mind subconsciously. But many screenwriters back then were heavy drinkers." As a matter of fact, Wilder said that he had another American writer with a serious drinking problem in mind when he wrote the script: F. Scott Fitzgerald.

For Brackett, *The Lost Weekend* had some painful parallels in his own family. His wife Elizabeth had suffered from alcohol dependency for more than a decade and had not profited from hospitalization. In addition, one of Brackett's daughters, Alexandra, was a heavy drinker; she would eventually be killed by falling down a flight of stairs while in an alcoholic stupor.[7] In the script of *The Lost Weekend*, Don tumbles down a staircase, but his fall is not fatal.

When Charles Jackson published the novel in 1944, he was often asked, "How much of Don Birnam is you?" Jackson would reluctantly concede that there was some resonance of his own drinking problem in the book. By the time the novel was reprinted in 1963, however, Jackson was prepared to admit that it was decidedly autobiographical. In point of fact, only a couple of "minor incidents were pure invention."[8] For example, Jackson did not pawn his girlfriend's expensive coat.

Literary critic Philip Wylie has termed the novel "the most compelling gift to the literature of addiction since De Quincey," referring to Thomas De Quincey's *Confessions of an English Opium Eater* (1822). Some commentators on Jackson's book have described it as more of a case history than a novel. On the contrary, Don's addiction is dramatized with the novelist's skill, rather than merely analyzed as a clinical study. Said Brackett, the novel has "more of a sense of horror than any horror story I ever read."[9]

Wilder researched the subject of alcoholism before beginning to fashion the screenplay. He not only consulted with Jackson but visited Alcoholics Anonymous, where he talked with alcoholics and physicians. "When I researched it," said Wilder, "I realized that the novel was no exaggeration, but an accurate picture of an alcoholic."[10] Wilder and Brackett proceeded to turn out a screenplay that was an unflinching portrayal of dipsomania. For good measure they engaged Dr. George Thompson, an expert in alcoholic studies, as a medical adviser on the script.

The writing team decided to stick primarily to depicting Don's wild weekend, keeping flashbacks to Don's past life to a minimum (there are only two flashbacks in the film). Some of the deletions Wilder and Brackett made in the novel's plot were at the behest of Joseph Breen. For example, Jackson's intimations that Don drinks to excess because he cannot acknowledge his repressed homosexuality could not be brought up in the movie. The industry's censorship code decreed that explicit references to "sex perversion" were prohibited. Consequently, "any filmic adaptation of plays or novels that had homosexual content . . . had to be revised to eliminate the offending subject matter."[11] In the book Don is nagged by memories of his "passionate hero-worship of an upperclassman during the very first month at college, a worship that led, like a fatal infatuation, to scandal and public disgrace."[12] Don was expelled from his fraternity for writing a love letter to the student he idolized. But this episode is not mentioned in the screenplay. "Look," said Wilder, "I think I had enough problems already, making an alcoholic a sympathetic character," which was hardly standard movie fare at the time. "If, on top of that, he also was a homosexual . . ."[13] Therefore, in the script, Don Birnam, a once promising novelist, turns to drink to assuage the frustration and depression he experiences as a result of his failure to produce a salable piece of fiction.

Actually, Breen was less concerned about the portrayal of Don than he was about the depiction of Gloria, a woman who hangs around the bar that Don frequents. "The characterization of Gloria as a prostitute is definitely unacceptable," Breen pronounced; he suggested that Wilder make her a "hostess" at the bar.[14] Wilder was sure that, although Gloria seeks to ingratiate herself with Don and other male customers, nowhere in the script was she designated as a whore. He therefore judiciously ignored Breen's complaint about Gloria, and Breen let the matter drop.

*The Lost Weekend* was to some degree influenced by the years that Wilder spent in Berlin during the heyday of the expressionist movement, which made a significant impact on German cinema. The bizarre dream sequence that Wilder wrote into his script for the 1931 German film *Emil und die Detektive* smacked of expressionism. In *The Lost Weekend,* when Don's liquor supply runs out, he spies the shadow of a whiskey bottle, which he has earlier stashed in the chandelier, and the magnified shadow of the bottle falls across his face, signaling how alcohol has cast a shadow across his whole life.

*The Lost Weekend* is another superlative example of film noir. Wilder, in consultation with cinematographer John Seitz, planned to employ expressionistic lighting, which readily lends itself to the ambience of film noir. "The nighttime hours predominate in film noir," Foster Hirsch explains, as we have seen in another noir classic, *Double Indemnity.* So in the present film Wilder conjures up, with the help of Seitz's low-key lighting, the grim, isolated atmosphere in which the alcoholic exists: dimly lit, claustrophobic sets with elongated shadows looming on the walls and archways. As Joan Didion notes, the Wilder world "is one seen at dawn through a hangover, a world . . . of stale smoke, and drinks in which the ice has melted; a true country of despair."[15] In sum, "the character's breakdown is presented in a vivid noir style," typified by Seitz's expressionistic lighting.[16]

Because Jackson's novel was so tightly constructed, Wilder and Brackett found that adapting it for film was relatively simple. In fact, Brackett stated, "*The Lost Weekend* was the easiest script we wrote, thanks to the superb novel."[17] They finished the rough draft in July 1944, having spent only two months, rather than the usual four months, on the preliminary draft. They had plenty of time to rework the script, since shooting was scheduled to commence in late September.

While revising the screenplay, Wilder got involved with casting. He wanted José Ferrer for the male lead—a curious choice. Admittedly, Ferrer had made his mark in *Othello* as Iago on Broadway in 1942, opposite Paul Robeson as Othello. But Ferrer had not yet appeared in a film, so he was an unknown quantity to the mass audience. Hence De Sylva nixed Wilder's choice of Ferrer. "Take a leading man," De Sylva advised Wilder, "because then the audience will feel with him, even when he slides into degradation. They will wish that he would reform."[18] So Wilder selected Ray Milland, a Paramount contract player who specialized in light comedies like *The Major and the Minor*. Still, Milland had earned his spurs as a serious actor by playing a former mental patient in Fritz Lang's *The Ministry of Fear*, which he had made earlier that year.

De Sylva gave Milland a copy of the novel with a note attached: "Read it. Study it. You're going to play it." Before he finished the book, Milland had misgivings about playing an alcoholic on a bender. He was put off by the "depressing story," he writes in his autobiography. More important, he saw that "the part was going to call for some pretty serious acting," and he was not sure that he was equipped to do it. Furthermore, Frank Freeman assured Milland that playing a disheveled drunkard on a spree would be career suicide. But Milland's wife, Mal, convinced him to give it a try.[19] Andrew Sarris points out that both *Double Indemnity* and *The Lost Weekend* involved "a casting coup," in which Fred MacMurray and Ray Milland were persuaded by Wilder "to switch type from glossy leading man to gritty semi-villain."[20]

Wilder also opted to give Jane Wyman a chance with a meaty dramatic role, that of Helen St. James, Don Birnam's long-suffering girlfriend. Wyman usually played secondary roles in comedies like *Brother Rat* (1939) at Warner Bros., so she too would be cast against type. Jack Warner was pleased to loan Wyman to Paramount for "that drunk film," since she was not in demand at her home studio.[21] *The Lost Weekend* proved to be a turning point in Wyman's career, for it established her as a serious actress. For the part of Helen's mother, Wilder selected Lillian Fontaine, the mother of Joan Fontaine, who would also be in his next movie, *The Emperor Waltz*.

Wilder targeted Howard Da Silva for the role of Nat, the understanding barkeep, in *The Lost Weekend*. Da Silva was a character actor with a long list of credits, including *Sergeant York* (1941). Wilder's choice for the role of Gloria, the bar girl at Nat's tavern, raised some eyebrows in Hollywood. He chose his mistress, Doris Dowling, a twenty-three-year-old starlet who had been marking time at Paramount. As Dowling tells it, one day when she and Wilder were lunching with Charles Jackson at Lucy's, Jackson hazarded that "it was too bad that I wasn't a more common type, so I could play Gloria." Wilder never looked up from his plate; he just replied, "She is."[22]

By September Wilder had assembled both his cast and crew. In addition to John Seitz, film editor Doane Harrison and composer Miklos Rozsa were back on board. Wilder insisted to the studio that he would have to do some location work in New York to give the picture documentary-like realism. Production designer Earl Hedrick, a newcomer to Wilder's production team, scouted locations around New York that would be suitable for the picture. Shortly before filming began, Milland went on a crash diet of toast and boiled eggs to assume the look of a haggard alcoholic who habitually forgets to eat.

Wilder and Brackett arrived in New York on September 24, 1944, with a film unit of twenty cast and crew members. Principal photography started on October 1. Wilder shot about a third of the film on location in New York, just as he had filmed *Double Indemnity* in part around Los Angeles, to get away from the studio back lot. In *The Lost Weekend*, "we used P. J. Clarke's bar at the corner of Third Avenue and Fifty-fifth Street," Wilder said, "because that is where Charles Jackson did his drinking; and that is where his friendly bartender, called Nat in the movie, worked."

Wilder got some exterior shots of the apartment house between Second and Third avenues on East Fifty-fifth Street where Charles Jackson lived during his drinking days. Axel Madsen writes that this motion picture's "vision of New York remains among the most unsparing ever recorded on film. Here is a nightmare of litter-strewn streets, a cluttered apartment looking onto a desolate cityscape, the elevated train clanging up Third Avenue in the dirty light of a summer morning."[23]

Pauline Kael notes that some scenes in the movie are indicative of the "distinctive cruel edge" that was the Wilder-Brackett writing team's specialty. In this regard she points to Don's "long, plodding walk along Third Avenue in an attempt to hawk his typewriter, when the pawnshops are closed on Yom Kippur."[24] Wilder explained that he shot this scene in New York "because there was simply no other way to reproduce Don's thirty-block trek up Third Avenue." The sequence was shot in a single day, on a Sunday, when all the pawnshops would be closed. Milland trudged up Third Avenue from Fifty-fifth Street to 110th Street, lugging a typewriter. John Seitz recalled that he captured this particular scene as unobtrusively as possible, by means of a hidden camera, "so that people on the street would not know we were there. All these pedestrians walking leisurely by" added to the documentary feel.[25] The camera was hidden along the route in the backs of delivery trucks, behind huge packing crates on the sidewalk, and in the windows of empty stores.

Wilder enhanced the film's realistic atmosphere by photographing a sequence in Bellevue Hospital in which Don is forced to spend the night in the hospital's alcoholic ward. To prepare for this scene, Milland had Wilder arrange with the hospital authorities for him to check himself into the alcoholic ward a few days before. "I was given hospital pajamas and a threadbare terrycloth robe, and assigned to a narrow iron bed," writes Milland. "The place was a multitude of smells, but the dominant one was that of a cesspool. And there were the sounds of moaning; two of the inmates had to be restrained, strapped to their beds." During the night Milland was awakened by a new arrival, a hysterical man whom the guards were attempting to subdue. "Suddenly the room was bedlam," Milland remembers; "I knew I was looking into the deepest pit."[26]

Milland bolted from the ward when no one was looking and attempted to hail a cab on Thirty-fourth Street. But a policeman, who recognized the Bellevue bathrobe Milland was wearing, grabbed him and hustled him back inside. He was able to convince the attendant on night duty to allow him to notify Wilder of his predicament. Wilder soon showed up, brandishing documentation that proved that Milland was no derelict but a movie star making a film. Milland was duly released, and Wilder utilized the very same ward to shoot the Bellevue scenes a few days later.

The officials at Bellevue subsequently regretted allowing Wilder to film on the premises, claiming that he had made Bellevue look more like a jail than a hospital. Director George Seaton said that, when he later asked Bellevue's managing director for permission to shoot some scenes there for *The Miracle on 34th Street* (1947), "the hospital manager practically threw me out. He was still mad at himself for having given Wilder permission to shoot at the hospital."[27] Ed Sikov writes that the hospital manager complained that Wilder had given him a bogus copy of the script: "He showed me one script, which I approved, but then he filmed a different script!"[28]

Wilder finished filming on New York locations by October 19, 1944, and filming resumed at the studio in Hollywood on October 23. Production designer Earl Hedrick built an exact replica of P. J. Clarke's bar on a soundstage at Paramount to serve as Nat's bar in the film.

Wilder sometimes described the shooting period as a battle, which made some journalists wonder how agreeable he was when working with actors. He would reply that he always tried to be flexible and listen patiently to actors' suggestions—except when they wanted him to alter lines in the script. Wilder explained that the dialogue that the director takes out to satisfy an actor may be "very important," while what he substitutes on the spur of the moment may be "plain stupid."[29]

Principal photography wrapped on December 30, 1944. By April 1945, Harrison had finished his preliminary edit of the film with Wilder's collaboration. The studio arranged a test screening at a Santa Barbara theater. Wilder stood in the back of the house before the screening began; when the house lights dimmed, a hush of expectation fell over the audience.

The picture plunges into the world of the alcoholic with the very first shot. The camera pans across the New York skyline and pauses outside the window of Don's East Side apartment, where a liquor bottle dangles from a rope attached to the windowsill. The camera then glides through the window and focuses on Don as he moves about his bedroom. Don casts a furtive glance in the direction of the bottle from time to time, hoping that it will not be noticed by his fiancée, Helen, when she visits his apartment shortly. Don plans to spend the evening having a drink or two but not drinking to excess. This is surely not a realistic expectation. As his long-suffering brother, Wick (Phillip Terry), tells him later in the film, for an alcoholic like Don to assume that he can drink moderately is the same as believing that "he can step off a roof and expect to fall only one floor."

Later on in the evening, Don stops in at Nat's bar for a few drinks. Gloria makes a pass at Don, whom she fancies. "You do like me a little, don't you, honey?" she is fond of saying to him. She has genuine feelings for him, but he usually ignores her to chat with Nat. He explains to Nat that, when he is sober, he is troubled by the nagging fear that he will never succeed as a writer, and drinking makes him feel supremely self-confident. In due course Don relates to Nat how he met Helen, his faithful fiancée. With that, Wilder launches into a flashback, showing Don at a performance of Verdi's *La traviata* at the Metropolitan Opera House.

The chorus raise their glasses for a toast and burst into a drinking song, "Libiamo, ne' lieti calici" (Let's drink from the joyful glasses). The shot of the chorus dissolves to a shot of a row of coats on a rack in the cloakroom. Then the camera focuses on Don's trench coat; by means of a double exposure, Don's coat becomes transparent, making the whiskey bottle in one of the pockets visible. Don craves a swig of whiskey, so he walks out on the opera to retrieve the bottle from his coat. Wilder's portrayal of Don's fantasy demonstrates the influence of German expressionism on the director. In fact, this scene, with its emphasis on visual imagery, could have been transplanted complete from the German silent cinema.

Don arrives at the cloakroom, only to discover that he has been given the wrong coat check, and he must wait until the opera is over to set things right. When Helen appears in the lobby, she and Don exchange coat checks, so that he gets his trench coat and she gets her leopard-skin coat. With that, the flashback ends. "The Wilderian 'meet-cute' packs a pungent punch," writes Richard Armstrong, and it is, of course, a bit of an homage to Lubitsch.[30]

In the course of Don's chat with Nat, the bartender pointedly suggests that Don consider drying out. Nat's philosophy is that, for an alcoholic, "One drink is too many and a hundred are not enough." But Don disregards Nat's advice. "I'm on a merry-go-round," Don answers, "and I have to ride it all the way." Don goes back to his apartment, where he finishes off a bottle of liquor he has concealed in the chandelier. The next day he endeavors to begin his confessional novel, *The Bottle*, but he cannot get past page 1. Don despairs of ever rekindling his writing career, and he decides to drown his sorrow in booze. He aims to pawn his typewriter for money to buy some more liquor. He is, in essence, willing to sacrifice his career to his addiction. But Don's painful trek up Third Avenue carrying his typewriter is all in vain, because the pawnshops are closed in observance of Yom Kippur. Later on, however, Don succeeds in snatching a bottle of booze, gets smashed all over again, and falls down a flight of stairs. He comes to later in the city alcoholic ward at Bellevue.

"Bim" Nolan (Frank Faylen), the nurse who attends Don, is a gay man who gives homosexuality a bad name. He is a leering, malevolent individual who enjoys taunting his charges about the horrors of delirium tremens (d.t.'s).[31] "This is Hangover Plaza," he tells Don. "Your blood is straight applejack—96 proof. There will be a floor show, when the guys . . . start seeing little animals. That stuff about pink elephants is the bunk; it's *little* animals, like beetles, that they see." Bim reminds Don that "delirium is a disease of the night" just before he switches off the lights and leaves Don to suffer the tortures of the damned with the other inmates of the ward. "I did manage to portray the orderly at Bellevue's alcoholic ward as a homosexual, even though homosexuality was a taboo subject in American films in those days," Wilder commented. "I directed the actor how to play his role as a homosexual. The film industry's censor couldn't nail me on it, however, because I had been subtle about it, and he couldn't pin anything down to which he could object. The cognoscenti, those who looked and listened, got the implications of the scene." Wilder laconically commented, "Those were different days." Indeed they were; by 1970, he was able to make homosexuality an issue in *The Private Life of Sherlock Holmes*. But in 1945, Judy Cornes reminds us, "audiences were not prepared for any references to homosexuality in mainstream Hollywood films."[32]

Don manages to escape from Bellevue the following morning. He makes it back to his apartment, where he suffers hallucinations of "little animals" resulting from d.t.'s, just as Bim said. In this harrowing scene, Don fantasizes that a mouse is sticking its head out of a hole in the plaster on his apartment wall. Suddenly a bat swoops down and pounces on the helpless rodent, and blood oozes down the wall. In the grim world of the alcoholic portrayed in the film, there is no place for pretty pink elephants.

Gordon Jennings, head of the special effects department at Paramount, was responsible for creating Don's hallucination. In fact, he was given a special Academy Award at the Oscar ceremony in 1944 for his technical achievements. Jennings sometimes borrowed gimmicks that were used to produce visual tricks in stage plays. He created Don's delirious fantasy of the ravenous bat attacking a hapless mouse by an old-fashioned method: he employed a mechanical bat attached to thin wires, which are invisible on the screen, zeroing in on a real mouse. Seen today, the sequence is as frightening as it ever was.

Wilder had initially planned to include other surreal images in Don's hallucination. But Brackett worried that he was going overboard with German expressionism in the sequence. Wilder said that Brackett warned him that, if he made Don's vision any more grotesque than it already was, the sequence "would be conspicuous and out of style for this picture; and worse, people might laugh. So I settled for the bat and the mouse."[33]

As the apparition fades, Don is cowering in a chair, screaming at the predatory bat, when Helen bursts into his apartment. He pulls himself together, and before Helen realizes what he is up to, he seizes her leopard-skin coat and disappears out the door. Don is convinced that he is at the end of his rope and proceeds to pawn Helen's coat to obtain a gun with which to commit suicide. Ironically, this is the same coat that brought them together.

By the time Don returns to the apartment, Helen has figured out that he has swapped her missing coat for a gun, and she beseeches him not to end his life. At this point Nat, the bartender, shows up at Don's door. He has come by to return the battered typewriter Don carelessly left behind in the bar after he failed to hock it. Nat assures Don that "it still writes pretty good," even though it has been kicked around. He implies that the same can be said of Don himself: Don too can still write, despite what he has been through.

After Nat leaves, Helen coaxes Don to write a novel about his lost weekend, in hopes that putting some words down on paper may keep him off the bottle. She finally convinces him that he has a powerful personal experience to write about; Don promises her that he is "going to put this whole weekend down, minute by minute." As an emblem of his resolve to stay on the wagon, he douses a cigarette in a glass of whiskey. From now on Don intends to be running on empty. With that, Don begins to punch the keys of his portable.

The opening shot is reversed at the end of the film so that the camera pans away from Don's apartment and back to the New York skyline. Don says, in voice-over on the sound track, "Out there is that great big concrete jungle. I wonder how many others there are like me, poor bedeviled guys . . ."

Cornes comments, "The movie ends . . . with an upbeat note, far different from Charles Jackson's original, grittier, more realistic ending."[34] Unlike the movie's Don Birnam, the novel's Don Birnam implies that his self-destructive pattern of behavior will probably continue. He even minimizes the agony that he endured during his recent binge. "This one was over and nothing had happened at all. Why did they make such a fuss?"[35] Cornes is not the only critic who finds the film's more conventional ending unsatisfying. Stephen Farber maintains that Don's new lease on life is not consistent with the rest of the movie. "Wilder's eleventh hour conversions are troublesome," writes Farber. "Certainly such conversions are possible. But Wilder is rarely successful at dramatizing them. His commitment seems to be to the cynical attitude expressed through the first three-fourths of these films; the morally uplifting conclusions are played almost invariably without conviction."[36] Sarris makes Farber's point more bluntly: "Billy Wilder is too cynical to believe even his own cynicism."[37]

"The so-called happy ending of *Lost Weekend* was not something imposed on me by the studio or by the censors or anyone else," Wilder said. He himself sees the ending of the film as ambiguous: "When Don promises his girl that he is going to stop drinking, this is not a pat happy ending at all. He says he will *try* not to drink anymore. The film does not imply that he will never drink again, because, for all we know, he may have gotten drunk again the next day. We end on a note of promise, that he is going to make one more attempt to reform, but that is as far as the picture goes." Wilder concluded, "Don sees the bottle as his worst enemy, but Don Birnam is his own worst enemy." One can say safely that the ending of any Wilder picture is just as uncompromising as the story requires, and *The Lost Weekend* follows this rule.

Wilder created a fine piece of cinema with this film. *The Lost Weekend* is an intense and intricate story of spiritual meltdown, told with invisible dexterity and emotional acuity. But that is not how the first preview audience judged the picture. The Santa Barbara preview in early April 1945 was an unmitigated catastrophe. The audience did not know about the novel, which had just been published and had not yet become a best-seller. Consequently, Wilder said, "they did not know the movie was going to be a serious picture about drinking"; they were not prepared for the drama that unspooled. They giggled uproariously, as if it were a comedy about a slaphappy drunk, à la W. C. Fields. When they discovered that the picture was not about a comic souse, they started walking out in droves. "Three hundred people turned into fifty," Wilder recalled forlornly. The preview cards uniformly denounced the picture as dull and disgusting.[38] Frank Freeman, Wilder's nemesis, used the Santa Barbara movie preview as a stick to beat Wilder with. Having vehemently but unsuccessfully opposed making the picture, Freeman was now against releasing it. He pointed out that *The Lost Weekend* had cost $1.3 million to make; for the studio to spend another $2 million on prints and advertising would be throwing good money after bad. Freeman threatened to shelve the picture indefinitely.

Wilder was not licked yet; he was already planning some damage control. For one thing, the print of *The Lost Weekend* screened in Santa Barbara had a temporary music track, since Rozsa had not yet finished his score. The temporary score comprised prerecorded music and at some points had a "jazzy, Gershwinesque" flavor, according to Rozsa, which was "disastrously inappropriate."[39] He told Wilder that he wanted to do a full symphonic score, which was what was indicated for a picture about a self-destructive alcoholic. Wilder told him to go ahead. To supply the haunting background music the movie required, Rozsa made extended use of the theremin, an electronic musical instrument that produces a high-pitched, quavering sound that perfectly augments the weird atmosphere of the picture. Rozsa had skillfully utilized the theremin for the first time in his score for Hitchcock's *Spellbound* (1945), and it likewise proved a highlight of his music for *The Lost Weekend*. For example, the bizarre quivering of the theremin helped to transform Don's delirium tremens scene into something really bloodcurdling. Rozsa's score "demonstrated that film music could be serious and contemporary, while still remaining within the symphonic tradition."[40]

In addition to conferring with Rozsa about the background music for *The Lost Weekend*, Wilder tinkered with the movie's final cut with Harrison. Wilder on principle had always abhorred sentimentality in a movie, but Harrison reminded him that a scene could have sentiment without descending to sentimentality. A case in point was the final scene of *The Lost Weekend*, when Helen attempts to dissuade Don from suicide. Harrison felt that, if Wyman delivered the speech with more emotion, the entire scene would be more arresting, especially when Helen says, "I'd rather have you drunk than dead!" Harrison commented on the scene to Wilder, "You didn't break my heart; go back and do it again." Wilder trusted Harrison's intuition and complied. Members of the cast and crew reconvened on April 10, 1945, to reshoot the final scene, and the production wrapped for good on April 11. Both Wilder and Harrison thought the revised scene represented a marked improvement in the final cut of the movie.[41]

After *The Lost Weekend* was in the can, Wilder accepted the invitation of the Office of War Information (OWI) in May 1945 to join the armed forces temporarily as a liaison between the American army of occupation and the people of Germany. He knew that Paramount's decision about the fate of *The Lost Weekend* would not be forthcoming, so he might as well make himself useful to the U.S. Army. During the summer of 1945, Wilder collaborated on an anti-Nazi documentary before returning to Hollywood in mid-September.

While he was away, the liquor industry joined in lobbying against *The Lost Weekend*. Stanley Barr, head of public relations for Allied Liquor Industries, issued an open letter to Paramount, warning that the "professional prohibitionists" would use the movie as a weapon in their campaign to reinstate Prohibition.[42] The powerful liquor lobbyists were not above double-dealing behind the scenes to get the picture buried. Mafioso Frank Costello was authorized by the liquor interests to make a clandestine offer to the studio brass of $5 million to buy the original negative of the film and all existing prints, in order to burn them. Since Freeman had already considered writing the picture off as a loss, Costello's offer was tempting. But Balaban was not inclined to accept a bribe from the mob to destroy the picture. Balaban, never one to mince words when discussing business, overruled Freeman by declaring flatly, "Once we make a picture, we don't just flush it down the toilet."[43]

Accordingly, on August 9, 1945, Paramount held a private screening of *The Lost Weekend* for members of the industry. The final cut shown included not only Wilder's refurbished final scene but also Rozsa's stunning score. The picture was received enthusiastically. In addition, the advance reviews in the trade papers were very favorable; they applauded the honesty with which the movie had been made, pointing out that *The Lost Weekend* "hasn't any laughs; or games." It "required courage for Paramount to violate cardinal box-office principles about what makes a hit to film it."[44]

When Wilder returned to the studio, he was greeted with the news that Paramount had officially decided to release the picture. It opened to rave reviews on November 16, 1945, almost a full year after principal photography was completed. James Agee, who was himself known in critical circles to be an avid drinking man, ended his positive notice with a little joke on himself. Referring to Barr's open letter, Agee delivered this punch line: "I understand that the liquor interesh are rather worried about thish film. Thash tough."[45]

In the light of the movie's success, the liquor lobbyists opted to abide by the old adage, "If you can't beat them, join them." The House of Seagram issued a press release declaring, "Paramount has succeeded in burning into the hearts and minds of all who see this vivid screen story our own long-held and oft-published belief that *some men should not drink!*"[46]

For his part, Charles Jackson endorsed the movie in an interview in terms that echoed James M. Cain's comments about Wilder's *Double Indemnity:* Wilder "thought of things I wish I had thought of first."[47] There is, for example, the sardonic Wilder wit, which of course is not in the novel, as when Don "reassures" a clerk in a liquor store that he is buying alcohol to fill his cigarette lighter.

The movie's somber subject matter did not dissuade the mass audience from making the film a box office favorite. *The Lost Weekend* brought in $4.3 million in domestic rentals. One of the reasons that the movie was a commercial success across the country was that the reputation of the novel had caught up with it. The book had become a best-seller, with the help of its being a selection of the Book-of-the-Month Club. By the time the picture was released, audiences knew they should expect a serious picture about a dipsomaniac and not a farcical film about a slaphappy drunkard.

Sarris summarizes the virtues of the movie by saying that its punishing portrait of an alcoholic is still shocking today. "It has stood the test of time as an expressionistic forties film noir, principally for such factors as the theremin of Miklos Rozsa's score and the hallucinatory images of a swooping bat and a bleeding mouse."[48]

At age thirty-eight, Billy Wilder was ushered into the class of top directors by *The Lost Weekend*. As Wilder himself put it, "It was after this picture that people started noticing me."[49] Indeed they did. *The Lost Weekend* went on to become the most honored film of the year. It won the Grand Prize at the first postwar Cannes Film Festival. In addition, Academy Awards were conferred on the film for best actor, Milland; best screenplay, Brackett and Wilder; best director, Wilder; and best picture of the year, which went to Brackett as the film's producer. Cinematographer Seitz and editor Harrison were also nominated.

When the Academy Awards ceremony took place at Grauman's Chinese Theatre, William Wyler, Billy Wilder's fellow immigrant, presented the best director award to him. Wilder noted afterward that Leo McCarey was nominated as best director for yet another picture with Bing Crosby as a priest, *The Bells of St. Mary's*. He said jokingly that he was afraid that McCarey might trip him as he marched up the aisle to accept the award, just as he had tripped McCarey the year before. Speaking seriously, Wilder said that he had a hunch that the academy named him best director for *The Lost Weekend* because they passed over him in 1944 for *Double Indemnity*. "So in 1945 they made up for it. It is very gratifying to win, because it is a validation of the work."[50]

After Milland had accepted his award, Bob Hope, the master of ceremonies, gingerly observed, "I'm surprised they just handed it to him. I thought they'd hide it in the chandelier!"[51] Wilder was not surprised that Milland won. As he said years later, "I knew the guy who played the drunk would get the Academy Award." He added, "Mr. Ray Milland was surely not an Academy Award–worthy actor. He's dead now, so I can say it." Wilder explained, "If you are a cripple, if you stammer, if you are an alcoholic, people think that is great acting. An actor could not win an Oscar playing Cary Grant parts," he concluded. "There is nothing astonishing there, coming in and saying, 'Tennis, anyone?'"[52]

Perhaps Wilder's fondest memory of the 1946 award ceremony was that on the following morning, as he drove onto the Paramount lot, he noticed that from every window of the writers' building was hanging a whiskey bottle suspended on a cord.

## *Die Todesmühlen* (1945)

In the late spring of 1945, Wilder had joined the film unit of the Psychological Warfare Division (PsyWar) of the U.S. Army with the rank of colonel. He flew to Europe on May 9 in a seaplane and arrived in due course at PsyWar's headquarters in Bad Homburg, north of Frankfurt. He had a conference with two Russian officers who were assigned to help rejuvenate the German film industry. When they discovered that Colonel Wilder was an American movie director, one of them beamed and exclaimed, "*Mrs. Miniver!*" This 1942 film, a stiff-upper-lip movie about the British war effort on the home front, had been in fact directed by William Wyler, but Billy Wilder accepted the Russian colonel's praise.[53]

One of Wilder's chores was to collaborate on a documentary about the concentration camps, to be titled *Die Todesmühlen* (*Death Mills*). The filmed record of the Nazi atrocities, a frank account of man's inhumanity to man, was to be shown in German cinemas. Wilder viewed the raw footage of the extermination camps filmed by official army photographers who had accompanied the liberating armies. He found the shots of the gas ovens, mass graves, and skeletal survivors shattering.

By the time Wilder joined the project in August 1945, Hanus Borger, a U.S. colonel in PsyWar and a documentary filmmaker, had produced a compilation of the footage. His rough cut of *Die Todesmühlen,* which ran eighty-six minutes, had been shipped to the PsyWar branch in London. Ivor Montagu, a British documentary filmmaker who was supervising *Die Todes-mühlen,* judged Borger's preliminary edit to be much too long. Borger's version of the film was accordingly shipped back to Bad Homburg, where Wilder condensed and polished it for a documentary short running half an hour.[54]

Wilder left Germany with the outline of a film he hoped to make about the American occupation of Berlin firmly in mind. The movie would focus on a GI's romance with a German woman. "As for the GI," Wilder wrote in a farewell memo to the OWI, "I shall not make him a flag-waving hero," but something of a cynic.[55] The picture, when it was finally made in 1948, would be called *A Foreign Affair.*

On the credit side of the ledger, as we know, Wilder returned home to find that he had a successful film on his hands, *The Lost Weekend.* On the debit side of the ledger, however, Judith Wilder, his estranged wife, sued him for divorce two weeks after he returned. This came as a surprise to no one, least of all Billy Wilder. Wilder's marriage had for all practical purposes ended by the time he finished shooting *The Lost Weekend.* It was an open secret that his mistress was Doris Dowling, whom he had cast in the movie. What's more, he had started dating Audrey Young, a bit player who played a hat-check girl in the film. Young was not much of an actress; she was better known as a singer with Tommy Dorsey's band. Thus Wilder, while cheating on his wife with Dowling, was also "cheating on his mistress by pursuing Audrey Young." That spelled the end of Wilder's stormy relationship with Dowling. Young "got her man, but her part wound up on the cutting room floor," David Freeman observes.[56]

Judith Wilder officially filed for divorce on October 2, 1945; the divorce decree was finally granted on March 6, 1947. In the meantime, Judith and Victoria, their only child, took up permanent residence in the San Francisco Bay area. Wilder always blamed himself for the breakup of his first marriage. "I thought I was in love with Judith," he reflected, "but I didn't know what love was."[57]

When Wilder started dating Young, he discovered that she lived in an unfashionable district of Los Angeles. "I would worship the ground you walk on," he quipped, "if you lived in a better neighborhood."[58] Audrey learned from the outset of their relationship to roll with the punch lines of Wilder's jokes.

Billy Wilder and Audrey Young were married on June 30, 1949. Audrey recalled that Billy was self-conscious about getting married a second time and wanted to keep the occasion as simple and unostentatious as possible. They drove to Linden, Nevada, and were married by a justice of the peace. They tied the knot, she remembered, "for $2.00 in three minutes." He bought her a wedding ring for $17.95, which Audrey has worn ever since.[59] Billy's marriage to Audrey lasted till the end of his days. On their first wedding anniversary, Audrey greeted her husband at breakfast by reminding him of the date. Without looking up from his copy of the *Hollywood Reporter,* he exclaimed, "Please, not while I'm eating!"[60] When asked whether she felt that her husband placed his movie career ahead of his marriage, Audrey answered, "You're always going to come second."[61]

Wilder wanted his film about an American GI in occupied Berlin to be his next project for Paramount. But he realized that it was too soon after the war to attempt extensive location shooting in the streets of Berlin. Berliners were understandably resentful of the American occupation forces. They would not welcome a Hollywood film crew taking over whole blocks of downtown for shooting. So he postponed *A Foreign Affair.* When Hollywood gossip columnist Louella Parsons asked him in February 1946 what his next film would be, he responded that he was going to make a musical called *The Emperor Waltz.* "Instead of the bat and the mouse in *The Lost Weekend,*" he added, "we're having Bing Crosby and Joan Fontaine."[62]

# 6

# Wunderbar

## The Emperor Waltz and A Foreign Affair

I never knew the old Vienna with its Strauss music, glamour, and easy charm. I really got to know it in the classic period of the black market after the war. Vienna didn't look any worse than Berlin—bombed out.

—*Graham Greene*

When Wilder returned to Hollywood from Europe in the fall of 1945, he turned his back on war-ravaged Vienna. Instead he decided to make a lush musical about pre–World War I Vienna, after the manner of the Waltz King, Johann Strauss ("The Blue Danube"), and Franz Lehar. Wilder remembered the Viennese operettas of Strauss and Lehar from his youth in Vienna. Furthermore, Wilder had collaborated with Lehar himself on a musical film in Berlin back in 1932, *Es war einmal ein Walzer* (*Once There Was a Waltz*). One of Strauss's finest waltzes, "The Emperor Waltz," would provide the title of Wilder's present film and be featured in the movie's score.

Wilder was, of course, bracketed with Brackett, his writing partner, in the film colony, and not always to his advantage. Brackett, it was whispered in industry circles, "exercised a restraining, civilizing influence on the cynical, callous, morbid tendencies of Billy Wilder."[1] Yet *The Emperor Waltz* was to be a fluffy Viennese musical confection, a project that obviously appealed much more to the Austrian Wilder than to the New England Brackett. "I don't suppose I ever understood it very well," said Brackett.[2]

Wilder returned to Paramount in mid-September 1945. "After cutting . . . a thirty-minute documentary about the concentration camps," he explained, he wanted to get those images out of his mind. During a conference with the studio brass one afternoon, an executive noted that the studio did not have a suitable vehicle for Bing Crosby. Wilder picked up on the idea. Speaking on Brackett's behalf, as well as for himself—as he always did at these meetings—Wilder ventured, "Why don't we just do a musical?"[3]

## *The Emperor Waltz* (1948)

At the time, making a picture with Crosby seemed like a good bet. Crosby had won an Academy Award for playing a priest in *Going My Way,* and his other recent pictures had been hits. In addition, Wilder had personally liked Crosby as a top vocalist ever since he had met him in Vienna in 1926, when Crosby was touring with Paul Whiteman's band. Crosby was to play an American by the name of Virgil Smith, peddling phonographs in Austria.

Joan Fontaine excelled in playing refined heroines. She had won plaudits for playing the title role in *Jane Eyre* (1944) opposite Orson Welles. She was to take the part of Countess Johanna Augusta in Wilder's film. Richard Haydn, who specialized in playing elderly types twice his age, such as Professor Oddly in *Ball of Fire,* was called on to take over the part of the aging Emperor Franz Josef after Wilder decided that Oscar Karlweis, who had originally been cast, was not right for the part.

The story that Wilder devised with Brackett was set at the beginning of the twentieth century in Vienna, when Wilder was himself a child; he clearly looked back on his boyhood and homeland with affection. The plot was derived from an actual incident: a Danish inventor had demonstrated a primitive talking machine to Emperor Franz Josef, who rejected it out of hand as a newfangled innovation.[4] In the film, Virgil Smith endeavors to get the emperor to endorse his gramophone to spark European sales of his product. While visiting the imperial palace, Virgil's fox terrier, Buttons, takes a fancy to the persnickety poodle of Countess Johanna Augusta, and Virgil, in turn, becomes enamored of Johanna.

Wilder had been frustrated when he collaborated on movie musicals in his Berlin days, such as the one he worked on with Franz Lehar, because the musical numbers were merely appendages to the plot. He wanted each song in *The Emperor Waltz* to be an extension, not an interruption, of the plot. For example, the song "Friendly Mountains" in *The Emperor Waltz* expresses how dazzled Virgil is when he visits the Tyrolean Alps, where he has a rendezvous with Johanna. Wilder envisioned *The Emperor Waltz* as an homage to Ernst Lubitsch, who had directed some delightful musical films, like his version of Lehar's *Merry Widow* (1934).

When Wilder and Brackett finished the first draft of the screenplay in late May 1946, they submitted it to the industry censor. After the troubles they had encountered with Joseph Breen over *Double Indemnity* and *The*

*Lost Weekend,* they thought their featherweight musical would pass muster with ease. Not a bit of it. Breen's report to Wilder stated flatly that the censorship code would not tolerate the "offensive sex-suggestions inherent in a parallel between the mating of two dogs and the love affair of their respective owners." Wilder and Brackett accordingly met with Breen and his chief assistant, Geoffrey Shurlock; the authors agreed to excise explicit references to canine mating habits. They also were willing to delete the phrase *son of a bitch* in reference to a male character. Wilder said he was tempted to playfully ask Breen whether he could substitute the circumlocution "If you had a mother, she would bark." But he let that remark pass. Finally, the screenwriters agreed to delete references to the dogs' "wetting," because of the "vulgar connotations."[5]

Once the screenplay was approved by Breen, Wilder and Brackett circulated a memo around the studio addressed "to all concerned with the production." They began by declaring that *The Emperor Waltz* "is a comedy with a smattering of songs. Just because it plays in Vienna in 1906, don't let's have everyone talk like Herman Bing," a German-born character actor with a thick German accent who had appeared in *Bluebeard's Eighth Wife.*[6] The only character in the film who speaks with a pronounced German accent is Dr. Zwieback, the court veterinarian, played by Sig Ruman (*Ninotchka*). Dr. Zwieback employs Freudian psychology in diagnosing the illness of Johanna's ailing poodle Scheherazade. "Was your home life always congenial?" the doctor inquires of the whimpering poodle. Apparently Wilder never forgave Sigmund Freud for tossing him out the front door when Wilder sought to interview him for a Vienna daily.

Wilder and Brackett's office memo about *The Emperor Waltz* continued, "And just because it's in Technicolor, don't let's have the Emperor wear canary-yellow jaegers and a purple jock strap." As a matter of fact, *The Emperor Waltz* was Wilder's first film in color. Paramount utilized color sparingly in the 1940s, usually limiting it to lavish musicals and costume pictures—both of which criteria *The Emperor Waltz* met. Wilder admitted to being prejudiced against color movies. "Everything looked like it was in an ice cream parlor," he observed; "a little raspberry, a little lemon. I was against color."[7] Despite his misgivings about Technicolor movies, Wilder went ahead. He picked George Barnes as his director of photography on *The Emperor Waltz.* Barnes had skillfully photographed Leisen's *Frenchman's Creek* (1944), a swashbuckler with Joan Fontaine, in Technicolor. In fact, Barnes was renowned for his color palette. He supplied rich colors for the opulent ballroom sequence and subtler, softer hues for the love scenes.

The front office allotted $2,879,000 for the budget of *The Emperor*

*Waltz*—more than twice the budget allotted to *The Lost Weekend*. The huge budget allowed Wilder to shoot the Alpine scenes on location in the Canadian Rockies, rather than on the studio back lot. Wilder and Doane Harrison departed from Los Angeles for Jasper National Park in Alberta, in western Canada, on May 19, 1946, to scout locations. The full unit of three hundred cast and crew followed over the next two weeks. Principal photography was set to begin on June 1, and the location shooting would continue throughout June.

The breathtaking Canadian Rockies were not quite grand enough for the director. "Not that we disagreed with nature," he said, "but Technicolor is sometimes a little harder to please." Once he had committed himself to filming in color, Wilder became very conscious of the movie's color scheme. He imported four thousand daisies from California, but Technicolor bleached them out. "White photographs too glaringly," he explained. So he had all the daisies painted with a cobalt blue tinge. Furthermore, the park's pine forest did not have enough pine trees to suit Wilder. So Paramount paid to transport several dozen pine trees from California and had them planted exactly where Wilder wanted them. The total cost of Wilder's improvements of mother nature: $120,000.[8]

Word reached Hollywood about Wilder's wholesale remodeling of the landscape. Screenwriter Herman Mankiewicz commented wryly, "It only goes to show you what God could do, if he had the money."[9] Nevertheless, in fairness to Wilder, all the money spent was displayed on the screen. Barnes's color photography in the Alpine sequences was rapturous, making splendid use of the Canadian wilds.

There was a good deal of late-night carousing on location. Wilder posted an edict declaring, "We are here as representatives of a great American industry and a great country; and we are judged by our actions. Everyone will behave as if you were at home." Wilder let it be known that any member of the company caught drinking or making love with one of the natives would be fired forthwith. Some members of the unit denounced Wilder as a "goddam hypocrite," since on his previous picture he had romanced both actress Doris Dowling and bit player Audrey Young. But their grumbling never reached Wilder.[10] In any case, location shooting wrapped on June 30, and the production team was back in Hollywood in July, shooting the interiors at Paramount.

Given Crosby's screen image as Mr. Nice Guy, it is astounding to find that he was not popular with cast or crew during shooting. He comes across on film as affable and warm, but off camera he was aloof and cold to the unit—even to the director. Crosby snidely told Fontaine at one point that "he had some trouble understanding Wilder's funny accent." Fontaine said that Crosby, as one of the studio's biggest box office draws, thought of himself as the emperor of Paramount. "Crosby had the power over Billy Wilder," she said.[11]

With the studio's endorsement, Crosby even brought in his own writer, Barney Dean, to revise his dialogue. Dean had been fiddling with Crosby's lines in the pictures he made since the 1930s. Fontaine remembers Crosby showing up on the set one morning and cavalierly handing Wilder some new lines, saying, "This is what we're going to do." Said Fontaine, "It must have been very demeaning for Billy."[12] Dean's emendations to the dialogue of *The Emperor Waltz* are not very impressive. For example, he has Virgil seek to ingratiate himself with Johanna by calling her "Honey Countess," a cloying phrase that must have made Wilder wince. Wilder commented that "Crosby was a big star; . . . he operated for himself, not for the group or the film."[13]

Filming ended on September 20, 1946, twenty-eight days over schedule. The final cost of the production was $4,070,248. Wilder, whose pictures had usually come in on budget, had some explaining to do to the front office. For a start, he pointed out, there was the unpredictable Canadian weather; heavy rains had complicated location shooting and delayed filming on several days. Wilder explained that he could not begin shooting a scene in sunshine on one day and then continue filming the scene the following day in a cloudburst.[14] There were other variables, Wilder continued. When Karlweis had proved unsatisfactory in the role of the emperor, all of the emperor's scenes that had already been shot had to be redone with his replacement, Haydn. Wilder was hoping that the picture would come together in the editing room as he worked with Harrison on the rough cut during postproduction.

To score the picture, Wilder chose Victor Young, who had been scoring Paramount films for over a decade and was De Mille's favorite composer. Of course, Young took no part in putting together the sheaf of songs that Crosby warbled in the movie; he rather composed the incidental music for the rest of the picture. Young did a masterful job of meshing his own original melodies with excerpts from the Strauss waltzes used in the picture.

The opening credits are presented on a background of yellow brocade, as the sound track evokes old Vienna with the title waltz. There follows the kind of printed prologue that Wilder had gotten into the habit of using: "On a December night some forty years ago, His Majesty, Franz Josef, the First Emperor of Austria, . . . King of Galicia, and so forth, was giving a little clambake at his palace in Vienna." Trust Wilder to slip in a mention of the Austrian province where he was born.

In the opening shot, Virgil Smith climbs up the terrace to the balcony of the imperial palace, smashes a window, and goes inside. He stands above the elegant ballroom, looking at the waltzing couples below, while still wearing his earmuffs. Virgil is looking down on the Austrian nobility, both literally and figuratively, as a class of people he no longer views as being above him. This implies that "Wilder's sympathies are not with the Viennese royalty, but with the American salesman."[15]

Then Virgil spies the radiant Countess Johanna Augusta waltzing in the elegant ballroom, and he impertinently cuts in on her partner to dance with her. The snobbish Princess Bitotska (Lucile Watson), an elderly gossip, recounts to her companion Isabella the events that have led up to Virgil's brazenly gate-crashing the gala. Like *Double Indemnity*, this film is mostly narrated in flashback.

"This vulgar and obnoxious American is a traveling salesman from New Jersey," Princess Bitotska begins. She describes Virgil as having only average looks, "with ears like a bat." (It is surprising that Crosby let that line pass, since he did have protruding ears.) As the flashback begins, Virgil shows up at the imperial palace, wearing his straw hat tilted jauntily, accompanied by his fox terrier, Buttons. He hopes to coax Emperor Franz Josef into endorsing a new contraption called a phonograph, thereby increasing sales throughout the empire. The emperor is unimpressed by Virgil's sales pitch, however. Virgil even uses his terrier to simulate the famed RCA Victor trademark: he positions Buttons in front of the gramophone and has him peer into the horn on top of the machine, just like the dog on RCA's emblem. But it is no go.

Virgil meets Countess Johanna at the palace; she gives him the brush-off, just as the emperor did. By contrast, her French poodle, Scheherazade, takes a fancy to Virgil's mongrel Buttons. In the end, the palace guard gives Virgil, who is only a common drummer, and his pooch the heave-ho.

Johanna is officially informed that "his Majesty's dog is asking for the paw of Scheherazade." She hopes that her pedigreed poodle will mate with the emperor's black poodle, Louis. But Scheherazade suffers a nervous breakdown, and Johanna takes her to be examined by the royal veterinarian, Dr. Zwieback. After hearing about the high-bred poodle's regard for Virgil's low-bred terrier, Zwieback decides that Scheherazade is pining for Buttons. He states that the two dogs must be allowed to become friends. Virgil and Johanna likewise strike up a relationship; Virgil melts her icy coolness gradually, and their friendship ripens into love. Princess Bitotska smirks in her narration that Johanna is going to the dogs.

But the emperor tells Virgil regretfully that he cannot give his consent to the union of Johanna and Virgil. He explains that Johanna would never survive as a housewife married to a commoner in Newark, New Jersey. The extended flashback ends, and we are back at the gala. Virgil soon learns that Scheherazade is about to give birth. He rushes to the imperial stables, where he discovers that Scheherazade has brought forth three white puppies. That signals that Buttons, not Louis, sired the pups. Virgil snatches up the basket of puppies and takes them to the ballroom. He presents them to Franz Josef, who dotes on the cute, scrappy pups and decides to keep them as his own.

Virgil bluntly tells Franz Josef that, if Buttons and Scheherazade can overcome class barriers, he and Johanna can transcend the conventions of her tradition-oriented homeland and wed. The emperor gives their marriage his blessing and makes this telling remark to Virgil: "You Americans are simple; you are stronger than us. Ultimately the world will be yours." The cocky Virgil responds, without batting an eyelash, "You bet it will!"

Meanwhile, since the subject of marriage has been raised, the aging Princess Bitotska turns to the impoverished aristocrat who wants to marry her for her money and inquires cynically, "How does the richest woman in Austria look to you?" The gold digger replies obsequiously, "Ravishing!" She has bought herself a younger man with whom she can have one last fling. So much for the decadent Austrian aristocracy. The orchestra strikes up "The Emperor Waltz," and Virgil invites Johanna to waltz with him as he sings the lyrics for Strauss's waltz written especially for the movie.

When Wilder and Brackett looked at the rough cut, both were rather disappointed. "I can't imagine what went wrong," Brackett said afterward; "we *did* have Bing Crosby. The final result was quite dull."[16] Wilder said, "I can't get it into my head that people break into song" in an operetta, "but they do." He concluded, "I was handicapped; I was not up to making a musical."[17]

Because Wilder had intended *The Emperor Waltz* to be an homage to Lubitsch, he had a private screening of the rough cut for Lubitsch and his wife. Some time back Lubitsch had told Wilder that one day he hoped to make a movie about a squabbling couple who are reduced to utilizing their dog as a go-between. As *The Emperor Waltz* began unreeling, Lubitsch saw how the two dogs brought their owners together, and he said to his wife in a stage whisper, "The son-of-a-bitch has taken my story!"[18] Otto Preminger, who was part of the German film colony in Hollywood, thought that Lubitsch overreacted by accusing Wilder of plagiarism. "Lubitsch had been demoralized by a severe heart attack," said Preminger, "and continually worried about his heart condition." So he really was not himself. "At another time he would not have made such a fuss."[19]

Withal, Wilder remained friends with his mentor until Lubitsch's untimely death at fifty-five, on Sunday, November 30, 1947. Lubitsch was in the middle of filming an operetta with Betty Grable, *That Lady in Ermine* (1948). (Preminger finished the picture.) Lubitsch had spent the afternoon with a call girl, suffered a postcoital heart attack, and died before a doctor could reach him. He was buried at Forest Lawn Memorial Park on December 5, 1947, with Billy Wilder acting as a pallbearer and Charles Brackett delivering the eulogy. Lubitsch's death was a blow to Wilder. William Wyler said that, when he and Wilder left Forest Lawn after the funeral, Wilder said to him, "No more Ernst Lubitsch." Wyler responded, "Worse than that: no more Lubitsch pictures."[20]

When Wilder screened the final cut of *The Emperor Waltz* for the Paramount executives in the fall of 1946, they judged the lavish production "only moderately and spasmodically amusing."[21] They thought it would be a hard sell for the publicity department and decided to postpone its release until the marketers could come up with a suitable ad campaign. Frank Freeman employed the same logic to delay the release of *The Emperor Waltz* that he had used to shelve *The Lost Weekend* for months. *The Emperor Waltz,* he reminded the other executives, had cost more than $4 million to make, so why spend an additional $2 million on prints and advertising for a movie the studio did not have much faith in?

The delay in releasing the picture stretched to nearly two years. Once again Barney Balaban finally insisted, as he had about *The Lost Weekend,* that Paramount did not make pictures just to have them languish in the studio vault. The studio finally got around to arranging for the movie's world premiere at the Paramount Hollywood Theatre on May 26, 1948, about a month before the general release. Fearing critical brickbats for the picture, Wilder did not attend the premiere but took off for a European vacation instead.

When the movie opened across the country in July, it received mixed reviews, but none were hostile. Some reviewers felt that the movie was an entertaining piece of strudel whose witty dialogue and tuneful score compensated for its hokey plot. One critic found the movie mildly diverting but hazarded that "*The Emperor Waltz* was entrusted to Wilder because of his birth certificate, rather than his sensibility."[22] James Agee's notice straddled the fence, with both positive and negative observations: "At its best this semi-musical is amusing and well-shaped, because Charles Brackett and Billy Wilder have learned a fair amount from the comedies of Ernst Lubitsch." Agee could not resist ending with a sly vulgarity: "At its worst, it yaps and embraces every unguarded leg in sight."[23] Other reviews were decidedly positive. The Hollywood trade papers observed that "Bing was never better than in *The Emperor Waltz* and not as good since *Going My Way*," and "Charles Brackett and Billy Wilder get better with every picture."[24]

Indeed, *The Emperor Waltz* has some virtues that are frequently overlooked. One cannot deny that the film entrances the eye. The visual richness of the movie is reflected in the way Wilder skillfully shot the rugged, beautiful Canadian landscapes that stood in for the Tyrolean Alps, with roseate dawns and dusks. His shooting style is fluid and imaginative throughout. He shot individual sequences, like the ballroom scenes, with great flair.

*The Emperor Waltz* is frequently referred to as a financial failure, but it was not. It attracted a fairly large audience and turned a modest profit. After all, Crosby's loyal fans, who bought his recordings by the millions, could be counted on to see a Crosby picture.

Although Wilder always maintained that the less said about the movie, the better, he made a veiled reference to it in *Stalag 17* a few years later. In a sly dig, Wilder has Sefton, an American soldier in a Nazi prisoner-of-war camp, don an Alpine hat similar to the one worn by Crosby in *The Emperor Waltz* and quip, "I'd look pretty stupid in this, yodeling my way across the Alps."

What is fascinating about the movie today, says Cameron Crowe, is how un-Wilder it is—all waltzing couples, sumptuous ballrooms, and glittering candelabra. "For that reason it stands alone and apart from his other work," and it is frequently ignored by commentators on his films.[25]

Wilder began preparing a movie that would "cure the whipped-cream hangover of *The Emperor Waltz*."[26] He decided to make the movie about postwar Berlin that he had envisioned while working in the U.S. Army's Psychological Warfare Division in Germany. Wilder wrote about the bombed-out cities he visited during his tour of duty, "The destruction is unbelievable; . . . the people are still living in this rubble, in the cellars, in ruins with just two walls standing."[27] Wilder later filmed exteriors for the film, *A Foreign Affair* (1948), on location in Berlin. It was the first film Wilder had been associated with that was shot in Berlin since *Menschen am Sonntag*.

In his last memo to the OWI before leaving Germany, Wilder outlined the feature film he planned to make back in Hollywood. "I have spent two weeks in Berlin," he wrote. "I found the town mad, depraved, starving—fascinating as background for a movie. My notebooks are filled with hot research stuff. . . . I have lived with some GIs and put down their lingo."[28] Wilder was confident that he had more than enough material to serve as the basis of a screenplay.

Even though Wilder had made a misstep with *The Emperor Waltz*, he was still the Paramount director par excellence. He had outlasted Preston Sturges, whose career had declined, and he had outlived Ernst Lubitsch.

# *A Foreign Affair* (1948)

While Wilder was mulling over some preliminary ideas for the screenplay, Brackett ran across the sketch for a proposed film titled "Love in the Air" in the stockpile of the studio's unproduced scripts; it was credited to David Shaw. It told the story of an officer in the U.S. Air Force who accompanies a congresswoman on a tour of American army installations in postwar Europe. He falls in love with her en route and proposes to her on the return flight to Washington. Shaw's seventy-two-page screen treatment begins with this preamble: "The Second World War was not only witness to the most enormous movement of material goods in the history of the world; it also saw the greatest mass movement of lust in recorded time."[29] Since Shaw's synopsis was the property of Paramount's story department, Wilder and Brackett were free to incorporate elements from it into the script of *A Foreign Affair*. But Wilder added a romance between an American officer and a German siren to pep up the story line.

Wilder and Brackett finished a forty-three-page treatment of the movie by May 31, 1947. Paramount assigned Richard Breen (no relation to Joseph Breen), a junior writer in the story department, to assist them in composing a full screenplay. The front office was uncomfortable with the movie's working title, *A Foreign Affair*, since it suggested hanky-panky between American soldiers in Berlin and German women. They proposed a substitute title, "Operation Candybar"; this was a reference to the manner in which GIs ingratiated themselves with fräuleins by offering them American chocolate bars and other hard-to-get items. Wilder and Brackett scoffed at the proposed title, just as they had earlier refused to consider "Rommel's Last Stand" as a title for *Five Graves to Cairo*.

As Wilder and Brackett worked on the screenplay, Brackett became extremely uneasy about the film's problematic portrayal of American GIs in Berlin. He and Wilder had several serious disagreements while they were constructing the screenplay for this movie. One of the first sequences that Brackett took exception to begins with U.S. Army captain John Pringle, a wheeler-dealer and a cad, trading a dozen candy bars for nylon stockings at the black market near the Brandenburg Gate. Then he jumps into his jeep and drives through the rubble-strewn streets to the digs of his German mistress, Erika von Schluetow, who lives in a bombed-out apartment building. Along the way he whistles "Isn't It Romantic?" which, given the movie's grim backdrop, lends an ironic twist to the scene. As Pringle enters Erika's ramshackle flat, she is standing at the bathroom mirror, wearing a bathrobe, and rinsing her mouth with mouthwash. She turns to Pringle and playfully squirts him full in the face with mouthwash. Pringle responds by wiping his face in her hair; then he hands her the nylons.

Brackett protested that it was revolting to show "a woman spitting lovingly in a man's face." He fumed, "Hell, it offends me beyond words, Billy."[30] Wilder responded, "Charlie, that's just how a broad is, if she really likes the guy. We show how close they are—physically." Brackett replied, "You're sick, Billy! Sick!" as he hurled the Los Angeles telephone book at Wilder's head, just missing his target.[31] But the scene stayed in the script. Like Erich von Stroheim, Wilder was ahead of his time when it came to portraying sexual relationships on the screen frankly.

Wilder was becoming fed up with Brackett's squeamish attitude toward the material he wanted to film. When he recalled their frequent, vociferous quarrels over their previous screenplays in the course of their increasingly stormy professional relationship, he began to consider breaking off their creative association for good.

But their feuding was never reflected in their screenplays. The crackling dialogue they wrote for *A Foreign Affair* is pure backroom Wilder and Brackett. For example, Colonel Rufus J. Plummer, who is in charge of the twelve thousand American troops in Berlin, comments at one point about the GIs' getting involved in the seamier side of Berlin by openly dealing with the venal, tawdry black market: "This isn't a Boy Scout camp. Some of the boys do go overboard once in a while. But you can't pin sergeant's stripes on an archangel."

Wilder and Brackett completed the bulk of the screenplay at the beginning of August 1947, but they continued revising it off and on until the end of November, right before shooting started. All the time he was writing the script, Wilder had Marlene Dietrich in mind for the role of Erika, the sultry chanteuse at the Club Lorelei and the mistress of Captain Pringle. "I had known Marlene from Germany before I came to this country, when I was a newspaperman in Berlin," Wilder said, "and we were very friendly."[32] When Wilder offered her the part of Erika, however, Dietrich declined. Erika hobnobbed with Nazis, and Dietrich was afraid that her longtime anti-Nazi stance would be tarnished by playing the role. Wilder ran the screen test by June Havoc (*Gentleman's Agreement*) for Dietrich. He cleverly persuaded her that no American actress could play Erika convincingly. Dietrich concurred and accepted the role. She writes in her autobiography that she learned that "you can't refuse Billy Wilder." Moreover, she had a high regard and trust for him as an artist. In addition, quite frankly, she needed the money.[33]

Dietrich's daughter, Maria Riva, writes in her biography of her mother that Dietrich's credentials as an anti-Nazi were confirmed when the U.S. government selected her to receive the Medal of Freedom—the highest honor the nation could bestow on a civilian—for her bravery in entertaining the troops at the front throughout World War II. As Wilder put it, "She was at the front more than Eisenhower." Dietrich, the first woman to be so honored, proudly accepted the award in November 1947, shortly before filming started at Paramount on *A Foreign Affair.*[34]

Dietrich was not pleased with her costars, John Lund, who was to play Pringle, and Jean Arthur, who was to play Phoebe Frost, the straitlaced congresswoman investigating the morale and the morals of the American army of occupation. Dietrich referred to Lund as a "petrified piece of wood" and dismissed Arthur as that "funny little woman with that terrible American twang."[35] Dietrich's assessments of Lund and Arthur were hardly fair. Lund was not a matinee idol by any means, but he had given a creditable performance in his first picture, Leisen's *To Each His Own* (1946), opposite Olivia de Havilland. And Arthur's midwestern accent was just right for her to play a congresswoman from Iowa. She had been in films since 1923 and was always appealing as the girl next door. She had excelled in screwball comedies in the 1930s and more recently had appeared in George Stevens's *The More the Merrier* (1943). She would receive top billing in *A Foreign Affair.*

Furthermore, Arthur was being paid more than Dietrich. Arthur's salary was $175,000; Dietrich's was $110,000. Wilder's take-home pay now exceeded that of his stars; he was allotted $116,000 for directing the picture and $89,000 for coauthoring the screenplay. Brackett's paycheck for producing the picture and coauthoring the script was $135,000 total.

Wilder chose Marlene Dietrich to play the key role of Erika von Schluetow, "the Berlin bombshell," because her appearance in the film "helped to give the movie a more authentic atmosphere. There was a natural similarity between Lola, the café singer that she portrayed in von Sternberg's *The Blue Angel* [*Der blaue Engel,* 1930], and the Berlin nightclub singer she played in my film." Dietrich's songs in *A Foreign Affair* were composed by Frederick Hollander, the German composer who had written the songs for *The Blue Angel.* "That made the connection between Dietrich's two roles even closer," Wilder added.

Most critics of *A Foreign Affair* assume that Wilder commissioned Hollander to write the songs expressly for this movie. Actually, Hollander composed them for the Tingeltangel Club, his failed attempt to establish a bistro in Hollywood "recreating a disenchanted Berlin cabaret." When the club closed, Wilder arranged to have Paramount purchase the screen rights to the songs for Dietrich to warble as the torch singer of the decadent Lorelei

Club in *A Foreign Affair.* The songs are sardonic and mockingly sentimental; Dietrich, said Wilder, "sold a song very well."[36] The three cabaret songs Hollander composed evoke the disenchanted mood of a devastated, defeated people. In one of the musical numbers, "Black Market," the lyrics describe how "salami and soap . . . are traded for black lingerie." In another, "Illusions," Erika sings of her "broken-down ideals" and her illusions, which are "slightly used, secondhand, and for sale." One journalist noted that, given the collaboration of Wilder, Dietrich, and Hollander, the picture has such an authentic atmosphere of Berlin that one expects to see the logo of Ufa, not Paramount, on the movie. Wilder replied that it was really Dietrich who brought the authentic atmosphere of Berlin to the movie: "Marlene is Berlin incarnate!"[37]

Wilder secured Charles Lang as his director of photography. Lang, who had photographed *Midnight*, which Wilder cowrote for Leisen, was, along with John Seitz, one of the best cinematographers for black-and-white movies in Hollywood. Lang gave *A Foreign Affair* a documentary-like quality with his spare cinematography. He adroitly captured the jagged edges of the Berlin cityscape. "The cinematography of *A Foreign Affair* by Charles Lang is a masterplay of shadow and light among the grey ruins," writes Robert Dassanowsky-Harris.[38] This was the first of four Wilder films that Lang photographed, culminating in *Some Like It Hot* in 1959.

The opening credits state that "a large part of this film was photographed in Berlin," but that is not precisely true. Wilder and his camera crew did spend three weeks in Berlin, photographing actual locations, but most of the film was shot at Paramount Studios in Hollywood. German film historian Oliver Kuch, the principal expert on this film, writes that "Wilder's familiarity with Berlin shines through the picture, as bombed-out images of the city come together with studio sequences so seamlessly that the entire movie looks as if it had been shot on location."[39] The skillful meshing of the location footage with the studio material is, of course, the handiwork of Wilder's longtime editor Doane Harrison.

Location filming lasted from August 17 through September 6, 1947, prior to the start of principal photography in Hollywood. Erich Pommer, who was studio chief at Ufa when Wilder was a tyro screenwriter there, had joined the exodus to Hollywood before the war. Pommer returned to Germany in 1946 and was now head of the film unit of PsyWar, with which Wilder had been associated immediately after the war in 1945. Pommer was charged with revitalizing the German film industry. He helped facilitate Wilder's obtaining official permission from the U.S. army of occupation to film in Berlin. Wilder filmed the movie's opening shots of Berlin from a plane. "It was absolute ashes, Berlin; rubble," he recalled.[40] Wilder's cameras captured the black market at the Brandenburg Gate and the GIs flirting with the fräuleins near the rutted Tiergarten (zoo). As Wilder had feared, some Berliners objected to an American film crew invading downtown Berlin and disrupting traffic. But, Steven Bach writes, "Wilder cut them down to size in his acidic, Austrian-spiced German."[41]

While Wilder was shooting in the ruins of Berlin, he wanted to "reconnect with the Berlin" he had once known. He remembered filming *Menschen am Sonntag* there in 1929, when Berlin was, he said, "the most beautiful and the fastest city on earth."[42] After Wilder returned home, he collaborated with Harrison in editing the location footage together, with a view to integrating it into the studio material.

The only time Wilder expressed his deep-seated hatred of the Nazis while making this picture came in the editing room. After running the aerial shots of the widespread devastation in Berlin, an assistant editor noted how the Allied bombings had destroyed the city. Wilder jumped up and shouted that the Allies were not responsible for the destruction of Berlin; ultimately the Nazis were. "To hell with those bastards!" he exclaimed. "They burned most of my family in their damned ovens! I hope they burn in hell!"[43] After that outburst, Wilder never mentioned the fate of his family again during the making of this picture.

Wilder and Brackett had finished the revised version of the script after taking into consideration the industry censor's objections to the screenplay. Joseph Breen reminded Wilder that the U.S. Army and the members of Congress were not to be ridiculed. He pointed to the Production Code: "The just rights, history, and feelings of any nation are entitled to consideration and respectful treatment."[44] Breen accordingly required that certain offensive lines of dialogue be eliminated from the script, such as the description of Congress as "a bunch of boobs that flunked out of law school." The writing team complied. Breen also complained about "the over-emphasis on illicit sex that seems to run through most of the picture."[45] Wilder and Brackett removed a few blatantly offensive lines of dialogue. But these were merely token gestures to make Breen favorably disposed to approving their screenplay, which he finally did.

Principal photography began at Paramount on December 1, 1947. Dietrich had to shoot a simulated newsreel that showed Erika socializing with the Nazi high command at the opera. Dietrich glared at Wilder while filming this scene and said, "Only you, Billy, could make me play a part like this." He replied, "Relax! It's only a movie."[46]

Wilder invited Dietrich, his Berlin buddy of old, to move into his house for the duration of the shoot. During her stay, Dietrich regaled Wilder, at his prompting, with stories about her multiple love affairs with directors like Sternberg and costars like Gary Cooper. She acknowledged that she had had liaisons with members of both sexes, which was an open secret in film circles.[47]

Jean Arthur saw Wilder's inviting Dietrich to be his houseguest during filming as an example of his favoritism toward Dietrich, a complaint that she would register often during the shoot. She was jealous of the bond between Dietrich and Wilder, and it unnerved her when the two joked in German on the set. Moreover, Dietrich would invite Wilder to lunch in her dressing room, where she would cook German dishes for him, while Arthur retreated to her dressing room in tears. Arthur was an insecure and skittish actress, although it never showed in her performances on the screen. "During the making of *A Foreign Affair* her nervousness . . . and natural timidity made her finicky and difficult about how well she was being filmed, which caused Marlene to detest her," writes Ean Wood.[48] Arthur resented Dietrich's line of dialogue, which she thought Dietrich delivered with too much relish, in which Erika describes the prim, plain-looking Phoebe (Arthur) as having a face "like a well-scrubbed kitchen floor." Arthur had convinced herself that Wilder would allow Dietrich to upstage her in every scene they played together and that ultimately Dietrich's performance would eclipse her own.

Wilder was aware that Dietrich was somewhat narcissistic and possessed a frank fascination with her own glamour and beauty. Sternberg, Dietrich's mentor, had taught her to check the lighting of a scene before the cameras turned. "This spotlight," she would say to the camera crew, "is not in the right place" to illuminate her face properly. "Could you put it over there?" When the crew ignored her orders, she would say to Wilder, "Billy, tell the lighting crew they should change the lights." Wilder would respond that the lighting of a scene was up to the director of photography; "leave me out of it."[49] He exclaimed, "What a picture; one dame who's afraid to look in a mirror, and one who can't stop!"

Wilder admired Arthur as an actress, but he grew impatient with her paranoia. Things came to a head in the middle of shooting. One night Wilder's doorbell rang after midnight; there was Arthur in a frenzy, with her eyes bulging. Her husband, producer Frank Ross, was standing behind her on the porch for moral support. "What is it, Jean?" Wilder asked. She answered, "What did you do with my close-up? The one where I look so beautiful!" Wilder asked her what she meant. "You burned it," she replied; "Marlene told you to burn that close-up; she does not want me to look good." Wilder responded, "This is madness; that I should destroy something." The next morning he took Arthur to the editing suite and had Harrison show her her close-up, still intact. "This is typical," he commented wryly. A movie set "is a little insane asylum," and the actors "are all inmates."[50]

Over the years, various commentators on *A Foreign Affair* have taken Wilder to task for the way he handled Jean Arthur in this movie. Richard Corliss, in his book *Talking Pictures,* asserts that Arthur looks far from her best in this film. Wilder photographed her, he continued, "with all of the gentleness of a mug shot."[51] The most outspoken of Wilder's detractors on this subject is Andrew Sarris. In his 1968 book *The American Cinema,* Sarris denounces Wilder for his thoughtlessly "brutalizing a charming actress like Jean Arthur in *A Foreign Affair*."[52] Yet in his 1977 essay "Billy Wilder, Closet Romanticist," Sarris reassesses his harsh judgment: "Am I blaming Wilder too much and the devastating Dietrich too little for what happened to Miss Arthur in *A Foreign Affair*? After all, Hitchcock once told me that Jane Wyman burst into tears when she saw how she looked next to Dietrich in *Stage Fright* [1950]; and yet I never condemned Hitch for his cruelty."[53]

Perhaps the most salient defense of Wilder in this regard comes from Dassanowsky-Harris, who emphasizes that Arthur's Phoebe Frost is the dowdy, stridently prudish congresswoman only for the first half of the picture. When she gradually becomes enamored with Captain John Pringle in the second half of the movie, "Arthur's shy, lovely beauty eventually surfaces in her portrayal; she becomes relaxed and even girlish."[54]

Moreover, Arthur herself ultimately changed her tune about Wilder's treatment of her on this picture. Some forty years later, in 1989, Arthur phoned Wilder to say that she had finally seen *A Foreign Affair* on TV. Karasek writes that she declared, "It was a wonderful film, and even the close-ups were wonderful!" Arthur asked Wilder to forgive her for her behavior while making the picture. Wilder gallantly answered that there was nothing to forgive.[55]

The shooting of *A Foreign Affair* wrapped on February 12, 1948. Harrison had a rough cut ready in two weeks. Hollander, who wrote Dietrich's songs, also supplied the background music for the film; he wove throughout his score the themes of the three cabaret songs that Dietrich sang.

The film opens impressively with the aerial shots of the bombed-out city of Berlin. The devastation reflects the desolate lives of the German civilians, who inhabit a world of disillusionment and cynicism. The plane flying overhead is carrying some members of Congress, including the prim, puritanical Phoebe Frost. She and her colleagues are members of a fact-finding committee charged with investigating the "moral malaria" that seems to be infecting the soldiers attached to the American occupation forces in Berlin. She is determined to "fumigate Berlin with all the insecticides at our disposal."

Congresswoman Frost is shocked to discover that the American troops are openly trading with civilians on the black market and "fraternizing" with the fräuleins. She is further upset to learn that Erika von Schluetow, the former mistress of a high-ranking Nazi, Hans Birgel, is singing at the Lorelei, an off-limits café frequented by American GIs. To make matters worse, Erika is now rumored to be the mistress of an American officer. Phoebe enlists the help of Captain John Pringle in her effort to smoke out Erika's American lover. Little does she know that the officer she is trying to identify is Captain Pringle himself.

Erika explains away her opportunism by observing sardonically, "A woman picks out whatever is in fashion, and changes it with the seasons, like wearing a spring hat after winter." Wilder does not appoint the audience Erika's hanging judge, however. "Erika is the film's most problematic character," writes Dassanowsky-Harris, because she has learned to cultivate "the survival spirit." She is a worldly-wise and war-weary individual who knows how to survive by making the best of a bad situation.[56]

To distract Phoebe from her official mission, randy John Pringle woos her. He accompanies her to the army intelligence file room, where she plans to investigate Erika's records. John makes advances toward her, and she resists his blandishments by opening one file drawer after another between them. But John closes every drawer that she opens; he finally traps her in a corner between two drawers and kisses her. "You are out of order!" Phoebe blurts out. "Objection overruled," replies John.

Phoebe becomes romantically inclined toward John, but she vows to sever their relationship when she finally discovers that he is Erika's lover. John seeks to mollify Phoebe by telling her that he pursues his affair with Erika only to smoke out Birgel, who is still at large. Erika is indeed being used by the American military police as bait for the trap to snare her jealous, most-wanted Nazi lover. He eventually takes the bait and shows up at the Lorelei in disguise, looking for Erika. But the military police are lying in wait for him, and he is killed in an exchange of gunfire. Erika is slated for a labor camp because she is tainted by her Nazi affiliations. Unrepentant to the last, she gives a seductive wink to the two young MPs assigned to escort her to prison. She hikes up her skirt to her knees and asks coyly, "Is it still raining? If there are any puddles, you'll carry me, won't you, boys?"

Hence the filmgoer infers that the incorrigible Erika will most likely slip away from the two bedazzled soldiers and never see the inside of the prison camp. Farber is probably right when he writes, "Wilder cannot quite abandon such a bewitching character to her fate without a hint of possible reprieve."[57] Perhaps only a Hollywood filmmaker who grew up in Europe amid the privations of World War I and experienced the decadence of Berlin between the wars could have presented Erika as a somewhat sympathetic character to the viewer. As John Russell Taylor puts it, Wilder "had become an American filmmaker, though with continental trimmings."[58]

As for the frigid Phoebe Frost, once Erika is out of the picture, she thaws out and warms up to Pringle once again. "Wilder's choice of ending has Capt. Pringle selecting Phoebe over Erika," writes Malene Sheppard Skaerved, "but would any man really have chosen Arthur over Dietrich?"[59] Actually, Pringle does not have a choice between the two women: Erika is gone for good at the film's end, whatever may become of her, and Phoebe alone is left to him.

With *A Foreign Affair*, Wilder was denounced on the floor of the U.S. Senate for making a movie in which "our occupation forces appear undisciplined and ill-behaved."[60] Certain members of the Department of Defense also criticized the film, specifically because some of the American GIs were depicted as taking advantage of the citizenry of Berlin whenever they got the chance.

Stuart Schulberg, who was involved with the Motion Picture Export Association of America, determined whether or not American films could be exhibited in Germany. He banned *A Foreign Affair* from being released in Germany. "Our initial disappointment with the picture later escalated to outrage and disgust," he subsequently wrote in an essay defending his decision. "We could not excuse a director who played the ruins for laughs and cast Military Government officers as comics." He condemned the picture as "crude and superficial. . . . Berlin's trials and tribulations are not the stuff of cheap comedy."[61] (Oliver Kuch notes that *A Foreign Affair* "was first shown in West Germany as a successful television special in 1977, and only hit the German big screen in 1991," when it was a smash hit.)[62]

Wilder's response to the film's detractors at the time of its release was to point out that he put into the movie what he had himself observed during his German tour of duty in the summer of 1945. He was not criticizing the American occupation forces alone, he continued; "every occupying, victorious army . . . plunders, steals. That is a rule that goes way back to the Persians."[63]

At all events, *A Foreign Affair* had its American premiere at the Paramount Theatre in New York on July 1, 1948, a scant two months after the long-delayed premiere of *The Emperor Waltz*. The picture collected a sheaf of mostly favorable reviews. Critics pointed out that, even in a landscape of ruins, "Billy Wilder sets off a firework display of witty dialogue." Still Wilder's masterly control of the plot ensures that "this movie is anything but a formless string of gags" or a mere sideshow. Nevertheless, some reviewers expressed reservations about the movie, saying that it was too soon after the war to joke about a tragedy of this magnitude.[64]

Because of the hostile reaction to the movie in official circles, Paramount is said to have discreetly withdrawn *A Foreign Affair* from distribution. Actually, the studio delayed doing so until the movie had fulfilled most of its dates across the country. So Paramount's action seems a token gesture, since the film certainly was exhibited long enough to make money.[65]

The movie ultimately weathered the storm that had brewed in Washington at its original release. What is more, it has come to be regarded as a sophisticated dark comedy, distinguished by Wilder's astringent, cynical wit. Wilder himself said, "*A Foreign Affair* I regard as one of my better pictures." Set in the still-smoky ruins of postwar Berlin, the picture leaves a bitter aftertaste of defeated hopes and soiled illusions. A warts-and-all account of U.S. military corruption in Berlin after World War II, the movie riffs on themes of deception and moral relativism. Yet the caustic bite of the dialogue does not keep the film from being entertaining. It is a warmly acted, briskly paced movie. Jean Arthur came in for her share of critical praise for her performance; with her apple-pie features and no-nonsense air, she is well cast as Phoebe. The movie was a personal triumph for Marlene Dietrich. As Erika, Dietrich sports a succession of attractive costumes, which the camera caresses. She exudes a wry, world-weary dignity.

Charles Brackett maintained that he endured working on *A Foreign Affair*, although he disapproved of its satire on the U.S. military officialdom in Berlin, because Wilder promised that their next film would be more to his liking. It would be about a silent film star who attempts a comeback twenty years later. This was a concept that Brackett had suggested to Wilder more than once. The picture would be a comedy with perhaps some dark undertones, but a comedy nonetheless, thought Brackett. He was anxious to give it a whirl.

# 7

# Dark Windows

## Sunset Boulevard

You don't know what it means to stand in front of a camera again.
This picture will put me right back where I was.
—*Bette Davis as Margaret Elliot in the film* The Star

"I was working with Mr. Brackett, and he had the idea of doing a picture with a Hollywood background," Wilder recalled. "Once we got hold of the character of the silent picture star, whose career is finished with the advent of the talkies, . . . we started rolling."[1] It was the comeback story, he concluded, that appealed to them, so they tackled it.

Wilder had a staunch belief in having a resourceful cowriter on every picture. During the story conferences, he said, "there is no muse coming through the window and kissing our brows. We just sit together and discuss, . . . and we fight it out." Then too the collaborator comes in handy "when you're arguing with the front office," he added. "You need somebody there, preferably with a machine gun on his shoulder."[2] The aim of the writers was to make the screenplay as airtight as possible, to forestall having to improvise dialogue on the set. "Sometimes, if a scene does not work during shooting," Wilder explained, "we withdraw into a corner and rewrite it . . . during lunchtime." But, he emphasized, this was quite different from shooting off the cuff. They would not just "sit down and slap it together. No, never."[3]

Wilder and Brackett press-ganged D. M. Marshman Jr. into joining their team, since they had much admired his insightful movie reviews for *Life* magazine. The trio began work on the scenario on August 9, 1948. "We closed the doors and asked ourselves, 'What kind of story shall we do?'" Brackett remembered. It was Marshman who suggested "a relationship between a silent-day queen and a young man. She is living in the past, refusing to believe her days as a star are gone, and is sealed up in one of those rundown, immense mansions on Sunset Boulevard, amid a clutter of mementoes," like a gondola-shaped bed.[4] "We saw the young man as a screenwriter," Brackett continued. "He's a nice guy, maybe from the Middle West, a man who can't make the grade in Hollywood." They did not see the older woman as a horror; "she was someone who had been given the brush by thirty million fans."[5] This last sentence would find its way into the screenplay almost verbatim.

Then the writing team got stuck; they were unable to figure out what would happen next. Wilder, from the beginning of his screenwriting career in Hollywood, had kept a notebook in which he scribbled clever ideas for use in screenplays. When he consulted his notebook, he found this fragment: "Silent picture star commits murder. When they arrest her, she sees the newsreel cameras and thinks she is back in the movies."[6] Wilder remarked to his partners, "Suppose the old dame shoots the boy."[7] That suggestion put them back on track.

They decided to call the aging movie queen Norma Desmond. Her first name was a reference to Mabel Normand, the silent film comedienne. Her surname referred to William Desmond Taylor, a director of silent films who was murdered on the night of February 2, 1922. Taylor had had love affairs with several actresses, among them Normand, who was implicated in Taylor's unsolved murder. The scandal ended her career.[8] So Norma Desmond's name was tinged with tragedy.

Joe Gillis, the aspiring screenwriter who gets involved with Norma, resembled Wilder himself at the beginning of his career in Hollywood, when he was a struggling scriptwriter. Concerning his affinities with Joe, Wilder explained, "Any writer draws on things he has seen and lived through. . . . I submitted God knows how many scripts and synopses and was turned down," just like Joe Gillis.[9] Wilder opted to have the male lead narrate *Sunset Boulevard*, as he had done with *Double Indemnity*. In the present instance, Joe Gillis would narrate the film from beyond the grave, making *Sunset Boulevard* one of the rare Hollywood films narrated by a dead person. "I have always been a great man for narration," said Wilder, "and not because it is a lazy man's crutch." Narration allows for economical storytelling because "it saves you a lot of exposition," he continued. "You can say in two lines something that would take twenty minutes to dramatize, to show, and to photograph."[10]

On December 21, 1948, Wilder and Brackett submitted to the studio a sixty-one-page preliminary draft of the screenplay. They attached a cautionary note: "Due to the peculiar nature of the project, we ask all our co-workers to regard it as top secret." To disguise the true nature of the film's plot, Wilder and Brackett employed the spurious working title "A Can of Beans."[11] They feared that, if word got out that they were planning a movie about Hollywood, members of the film colony would assume that it was to be a *film à clef*—that is, a sardonic tale presenting unflattering portraits of individuals whom Wilder and Brackett had known and worked with.

Paramount tendered a vote of confidence to Wilder and Brackett by green-lighting the project on the basis of their preliminary draft. On March 21, 1949, they turned in a script of 126 pages, the standard length for a feature picture. Wilder, Brackett, and Marshman continued revising the script throughout production. Sometimes they found it difficult to stay one jump ahead of the shooting schedule. Consequently, they would dole out pages of the screenplay to the cast and crew for a scene only a day or two before it was to be shot. The revisions were mostly the work of Brackett and Wilder, with occasional assists from Marshman, according to Wilder.

Wilder sent the screenplay to Joseph Breen on April 11, 1949, a mere week before production was scheduled to start. Wilder indicated that the script at that point did not contain the final sequence. "We're still working on it," Wilder explained. "We haven't quite decided how the picture ends."[12] Wilder had some trepidation about Breen's evaluation. After all, as James Agee notes, "A sexual affair between a rich woman of fifty and a kept man half her age is not exactly a usual version of boy meets girl."[13]

Wilder did not receive a detailed response from Breen until May 24, 1949. Breen replied that, because the script lacked the last sequence, he could not render a final verdict on the acceptability of the entire story. He did complain, however, about the sexual relationship of Joe Gillis and Norma Desmond: "There is no indication of a voice for morality, by which the sex affair would be condemned, nor do there appear to be compensating moral values for the sin."[14]

George Cukor, Wilder's friend and colleague, explained, "According to the provisions of the code at that time, the main character could not have an extramarital affair without suffering some kind of dreadful punishment, like breaking a leg or falling down a well." Consequently, Cukor concluded, Breen warned Wilder in his letter about *Sunset Boulevard* that, in the ending that Wilder contrived for the film, some clear-cut punishment must be meted out to Norma as the main character for her moral transgression.[15] Even though the film's ending was not finalized, Wilder and Brackett were planning a tragic conclusion for the picture, one that should satisfy Breen.

As the characters took shape in the screenplay, Wilder and Brackett naturally began to discuss who should be cast in the picture. Wilder wanted an old-time star to play Norma Desmond. "God forgive me, I wanted Mae

West," Wilder confessed.[16] When Wilder interviewed her, it was apparent that West, who was nearing sixty, thought that she was as sexy as she had ever been. She was insulted when Wilder asked her to play a has-been, even though she had not made a picture since 1943—*The Heat's On,* a tasteless musical that had flopped. West would not consider playing an older woman who is eventually dumped by her younger lover. On the contrary, West assured Wilder, she would have seen to it that Joe was too exhausted from their sexual bouts in her boudoir to get out of bed![17]

Next on the list as a candidate to play Norma was Mary Pickford, known as America's Sweetheart in her heyday in silent pictures. Pickford demanded, for openers, that the part of Norma Desmond be built up; it must be abundantly clear that Pickford was the star of the picture. Scott Eyman notes, "Wilder could foresee that Pickford, who was now a movie executive, desired more control over the picture than he was prepared to grant her."[18]

Finally, Wilder sounded out Cukor, who had been directing pictures for nearly two decades. Cukor suggested Gloria Swanson, who had been one of the brightest stars of the silent period. Indeed, at the height of her career, Cukor pointed out, "She was carried in a sedan chair from her dressing room to the set."[19] But her career had faltered after the coming of sound. By the time Wilder cowrote *Music in the Air,* a stale musical, for her in 1934, her Hollywood career was for all practical purposes defunct. Wilder remembered, when he was considering her for *Sunset Boulevard,* that Swanson was thought to be "sort of an old bag from silent picture times."[20] She was only fifty-two.

Cukor assured Wilder that Swanson could play a movie goddess hoping for a comeback convincingly, since at that point she was a Hollywood has-been.[21] But Swanson had not withdrawn into seclusion. By the time Wilder wanted her for his movie, she had moved to New York and become the host of a local TV talk show. Brackett, in his function as producer, officially phoned Swanson in New York and told her that Billy Wilder was much interested in her playing the lead in his next film. When he added that the studio wanted her to do a screen test, Swanson was indignant. "I made two dozen pictures for Paramount," she replied; they might well serve as her "screen test." After all, her successful silent pictures had helped to build Paramount. "Without me, there would be no Paramount Pictures," she told him—a line Norma Desmond would repeat in the film. She concluded acrimoniously, "You want a screen test . . . to see if I am still alive?"[22] Brackett tactfully responded that she should think of the test as a mere formality. Swanson accepted Brackett's invitation to come out to Hollywood and discuss the project.

Another actor on Wilder's wish list for *Sunset Boulevard* was Erich von Stroheim. After the war Stroheim had moved back to France, where he continued to be considered one of the all-time great directors, a titan of the silent era. Wilder contacted Stroheim at his home outside Paris and told him he wanted him to play Max von Mayerling in *Sunset Boulevard*. Like Stroheim, Max had been a director of silent films; in fact, Max directed Norma Desmond in a silent picture, just as Stroheim directed Gloria Swanson in one. But, like Stroheim's, Max's directorial career did not survive the coming of sound. Max has wound up as Norma's dignified butler and last admirer.

At first, Stroheim wanted no part of the role. Max von Mayerling was no Field Marshal Rommel but a Hollywood has-been, a character similar enough to Stroheim himself to be disturbing. Stroheim reflected ruefully that, if he took the part, he would be returning to Hollywood to appear in a movie that was exploiting his own downfall as a film director. Moreover, he was offended by the mention of his return to Hollywood in the gossip column of "that old bitch" Louella Parsons, who said that he was a relic of Hollywood's past.[23]

What's more, Stroheim learned, Cecil B. De Mille was very likely going to do a cameo in the picture, playing himself. The idea of appearing in a movie with De Mille was galling to Stroheim. As Arthur Lennig, author of the definitive biography of Stroheim, writes, "Here was De Mille, a lesser talent, still making films, still a success, still a foremost director; and here was Stroheim playing a butler." Withal, Stroheim accepted the role because, as usual, he was short on funds, since he always lived beyond his means. But ever after, Stroheim referred to the role of Max von Mayerling as "that goddamned butler."[24] John Seitz, the director of photography on the film, attested to the fact that Stroheim thought the role of Max demeaning to him. "He would walk around the set muttering, 'Why are they doing this to me?'"[25]

Montgomery Clift was set to play Joe Gillis, Norma's young lover. Clift's first movie was Fred Zinnemann's *The Search* (1948), in which he played an American GI in war-ravaged Berlin. Wilder learned that Zinnemann had nothing but praise for Clift and engaged him. But two weeks before Wilder began shooting *Sunset Boulevard*, Clift's agent phoned him to say that Clift had bailed out. Clift's alleged motive was that he did not believe that he could be convincing making love to a woman twice his age. "Bullshit!" Wilder hollered at the agent. If he were a serious actor, he could be convincing "making love to ANY woman!!"[26]

Brackett knew the facts behind Clift's reneging on his commitment to play Joe Gillis, and he set Wilder straight. Clift had been carrying on an affair with Libby Holman, a faded star of the New York stage in the Roaring Twenties, since 1942. Brackett, who had known Holman since his days at the *New Yorker* in the 1920s, was aware that she was fifteen years older than Clift. In 1932 Holman had been accused of shooting her wealthy young husband Zachary Reynolds, although his death was eventually declared a suicide. Holman, who was by now a hopeless alcoholic, had convinced herself that the plot of *Sunset Boulevard,* which Clift had relayed to her, was a thinly disguised version of her relationship with Reynolds. She threatened to kill herself if Clift made *Sunset Boulevard.* So Wilder gave up on Clift.[27]

Wilder combed the list of Paramount contract players and settled on William Holden, who had given a solid performance as a prizefighter in *Golden Boy* (1939) but since then had been more or less wasted as a second lead in some frivolous comedies. Holden was afraid he simply was not talented enough to play a serious role like Joe Gillis. But Wilder brushed aside his misgivings: "That's easy. You know Bill Holden? Then you know Joe Gillis." Wilder was aware that Holden's career had begun to slide. Furthermore, he was becoming a problem drinker and was getting a little frayed around the edges.[28] Holden himself had agreed that the story of Joe Gillis was his story. Joe is supported by an aging actress, he pointed out, and he had himself once been "a whore" like Joe. "When I was a young actor starting out in Hollywood, I used to service actresses who were older than me," he confessed.[29]

Holden desperately wanted to give his career a boost, and Wilder convinced him that this was the part that would do it for him. Holden finally agreed to play Joe a scant three days before shooting began.[30] As things turned out, Holden was better in the part than Clift would have been. Holden retained a vestige of the features of the all-American boy that he had been when he made *Golden Boy.* So in *Sunset Boulevard* he was the all-American boy being corrupted—a subtle dimension to the part that Clift could not have matched.

If Cukor had to encourage Swanson to play Norma, Swanson, in turn, had to coax Cecil B. De Mille to take a cameo role in the film. Swanson had heard by the grapevine that De Mille had agreed to do a scene but was having difficulty learning his lines, "and he was very nervous about appearing in front of the camera." Swanson accordingly sent him a telegram, declaring, "Mr. De Mille, if you're just yourself, you'll be wonderful."[31] Swanson signed the telegram "Young Fellow," which was De Mille's pet name for her. Swanson had become a major star in the films she had made for De Mille between 1919 and 1921, including *The Affairs of Anatol* (1921), a saucy comedy about the battle of the sexes, in which she costarred with Wallace Reid. The nickname was a reference to the spirit and energy she brought to the parts she played. When he saw how Swanson had signed the telegram, "he lit up."[32] De Mille would call Norma "young fellow" in the film.

De Mille drove a hard bargain with Wilder for appearing in *Sunset Boulevard*. He got ten thousand dollars for one day's work, a sequence in which Norma visits De Mille on the set of *Samson and Delilah*. Then Wilder asked him to come back and do one more close-up. "It was shot outside the soundstage, where he says goodbye to Norma. He came back"—and he got the studio to buy him a new limousine as compensation for the extra work.[33] "We used his sets when Norma visits him," which were still standing, Wilder remembered.[34]

In the screenplay Wilder and Brackett mention that Norma has Max screen "one of Norma's old silent pictures" for Joe.[35] Wilder wanted to use a clip from one of Swanson's silents in this scene but was at a loss as to which of her pictures to choose. Stroheim suggested that Wilder take an excerpt from his *Queen Kelly*, an unfinished silent movie from 1928. Wilder told me, "It was an interesting tie-in, that the clip of Gloria Swanson as a younger film star was actually from the one picture in which she was directed by Stroheim, who was playing Norma's former director in *Sunset Boulevard*. This added a more genuine flavor to the film." *Queen Kelly* was produced by Gloria Swanson and financed by Joseph Kennedy (father of John F. Kennedy), a Boston financier who was also Swanson's lover. Swanson played Patricia Kelly, a young girl whose affair with a handsome prince ends abruptly when he is forced to marry the neurotic queen who rules the land. "Stroheim was painstaking and slow during filming because of his relentless perfectionism," Swanson said. They had numerous clashes on the set. After one shouting match with Stroheim, who simply would not be hurried, she stalked off the set. She phoned Kennedy and stated flatly, "Our director is a madman!" Kennedy soon called Stroheim. He said that it was time to shut down the picture because it was clear that talking pictures were here to stay; there was little hope of releasing a silent film successfully.[36] In *Sunset Boulevard*, it is while looking at a close-up of herself in this silent film that Norma utters the celebrated remark, "No dialogue—we didn't need dialogue. We had *faces* then."

Swanson, as producer of the picture, gave Wilder permission to use an excerpt from *Queen Kelly* in *Sunset Boulevard*. "Of course I didn't mind," she writes in her autobiography. She and Stroheim "had long since reconciled our differences over *Queen Kelly*."[37] When I asked Wilder why he substituted his own intertitle for the one in the scene he was using from *Queen*

*Kelly,* he replied, "I couldn't use the intertitle from *Queen Kelly* because *Queen Kelly* was a movie starring Gloria Swanson, while the clip being projected in *Sunset Boulevard* was supposedly from a film starring Norma Desmond."

While location scouting around Hollywood, Wilder found the house that would serve as Norma Desmond's mansion at 3810 Wilshire Boulevard, although the address is given as 10086 Sunset Boulevard in the film. The real house "was owned by billionaire John Paul Getty," Seitz remembered. Paramount rented it for the duration of the shoot.[38] Getty had given the house to his ex-wife as part of their divorce settlement, but she did not reside there. The baroque edifice was built in 1924 to resemble a French-Italian Renaissance castle. The swimming pool was added to the grounds for the film, and the former Mrs. Getty kept it as partial payment for the use of the house when shooting was completed.

Joe characterizes Norma's "mausoleum" in his voice-over narration of the film as "the kind of place that crazy movie people built in the crazy '20s." Wilder had Joe describe the old mansion this way: "A neglected house gets an unhappy look—this one had it in spades. It was like that old woman in *Great Expectations,* that Miss Havisham, with her rotting wedding dress and her torn veil, taking it out on the world because she had been given the go-by."

Hans Dreier, head of Paramount's art department, took a special interest in the set designs for *Sunset Boulevard,* as he had for *Double Indemnity.* Dreier appointed John Meehan production designer on *Sunset Boulevard,* but he supervised Meehan's work very closely. The Getty house was used for exteriors; interiors were filmed on sets built in the studio. Tom Wood, unit publicist on the film, describes in his book on Wilder the elaborate sets Meehan designed in consultation with Dreier for Norma's florid palazzo. There were "stained glass windows in the front hall, palm trees . . . in the conservatory," heavy velvet drapes, and a pipe organ in the living room. The gondola-shaped bed in Norma's boudoir once belonged to Gaby de Lys, the legendary exotic dancer.[39] To top it off, Wilder borrowed from Swanson a gallery of vintage photographs of herself to serve as pictures of Norma; they transform Norma's living room into "a museum."[40]

Beginning on March 26, 1949, prior to the start of principal photography, Wilder commandeered the camera crew to shoot various locations around Hollywood and Beverly Hills. His purpose was to establish the authentic atmosphere of the film colony for the movie. He photographed the Alto Nido Apartments at 1851 North Ivar Avenue, near Hollywood and Vine, where Joe Gillis lives in a seedy bachelor flat. (The apartment building is still there.) The set that Meehan designed for the interior of Joe's digs was created in the studio. Wilder also took some exterior shots of Schwab's Drug Store on Sunset Boulevard, which was a hangout for young hopefuls—both writers and actors. Joe and his friends congregate at Schwab's.

Principal photography commenced officially on April 18, 1949. During shooting, writes Swanson, "Erich von Stroheim kept suggesting things and asking if scenes might be reshot—very much in his grand old manner of perfectionism, regardless of schedule or cost."[41] Still, Wilder found some of Stroheim's suggestions helpful. Wilder told me, "It was he who suggested that Norma be receiving fan letters that are ultimately disclosed as having been written by Max. Stroheim had a fine celluloid mind; he knew what worked." As Stroheim told Wilder, Max writes the letters "because Max still loves her and pities her." Wilder commented, "Erich had another idea, to dramatize that Max was still crazy about Norma." Stroheim wanted Max to "be shown washing some of her undies, and caressing them lasciviously." This was precisely the kind of sexual fetish that Stroheim had gotten away with in his silent films like *Foolish Wives,* in the days before the censorship code. Wilder convinced Stroheim that such a titillating scene would get them arrested.

Stroheim had one difficulty in playing Max that Wilder had not anticipated. Swanson writes, "Erich as Max, Norma's butler and chauffeur, drives her and Joe to Paramount in her old Isotta-Fraschini, with its leopard upholstery. Erich didn't know how to drive."[42] So the camera stayed close to him as he faked turning the steering wheel, while the ancient auto was towed by ropes attached to a truck. And yet Stroheim still managed to crash into the Paramount gate on Marathon Street!

There was a technically difficult shot in the opening scene in which Joe's corpse, floating facedown on the surface of the swimming pool, is viewed from below. Wilder instructed Seitz and Meehan, "The shot I want is from a fish's viewpoint." Meehan placed a six-by-eight-foot mirror at the bottom of the pool. Seitz then positioned his camera on the edge of the pool, pointed it down at the mirror, and filmed Holden's body as it was reflected in the mirror. This proved to be a simple way of getting the shot, Meehan explained, without "the use of expensive underwater camera equipment."[43]

When Norma and Joe tango together on New Year's Eve on the tile floor of the deserted ballroom of her once-elegant mansion, Norma observes, "Valentino said there's nothing like tile for a tango." Swanson had actually tangoed with Rudolph Valentino in the one picture they made together, Sam Wood's *Beyond the Rocks* (1922). Seitz had shot *The Four Horsemen of the*

*Apocalypse* in 1921, in which Valentino danced a terrific tango with Alice Terry. Seitz utilized the same technique to photograph the tango in both films. He had the camera mounted on a platform on wheels. "Men behind the camera moved the camera platform" so that Seitz could photograph Swanson and Holden "making a complete 360-degree turn around the room."[44]

When Joe later that night threatens to leave Norma, she attempts suicide by slashing her wrists. For the subsequent scene, in which Norma lies on her bed with her wrists bandaged, Seitz asked Wilder what kind of camera setup he wanted. Wilder replied impishly, "Johnny, it's the usual slashed wrist shot."[45]

Swanson writes that no picture "challenged or engrossed" her more than *Sunset Boulevard*. For example, Wilder asked her to do an imitation of Charlie Chaplin, whom Swanson had known since 1915, when both were starting out in silent pictures. She had done a Chaplin imitation in Alan Dwan's *Manhandled* in 1924. Rehearsing a party scene with Dwan, Swanson snatched a derby from a crew member and clapped it on her head. "Then I grabbed a cane from somebody and started wobbling around in an impersonation of Chaplin."[46] She virtually repeated in *Sunset Boulevard* the Chaplin routine she had done in *Manhandled*. This time Swanson borrowed Wilder's malacca cane for her imitation.

Principal photography wrapped on June 18, 1949. The final scene to be shot was also the final scene in the picture; it took two days to shoot. It was Norma's mad scene, when she descends the grand staircase of her mansion in a trance, fantasizing that she is at last making her comeback film. Her eyes are glazed as she walks toward the camera lens, and the shot gradually goes out of focus and fades to black. "I hated to have the picture end," Swanson writes. "When Mr. Wilder called 'Print it!' I burst into tears," while the cast and crew burst into applause.[47]

Although the filming itself went smoothly, Wilder had some bitter quarrels with Brackett during postproduction. Brackett had originally perceived the film's premise as that of a silent screen star's attempt at a comeback, which would fundamentally be a comedy with some serious undertones. As the production progressed, Brackett became increasingly uneasy about the grotesque touches Wilder was adding to the mix. As producer of the picture, Brackett had a right to complain, but Wilder did not often heed his objections. One bone of contention was a montage of Norma preparing for her return to the screen by subjecting herself "to a merciless series of facial treatments, in order to have her image as the ageless star."[48] An army of beauticians employ massages, sweat boxes, mudpacks, and rubber masks, "as Norma tries to recapture the face of her celluloid image."[49]

When Brackett viewed the rushes of this footage with Wilder and William Schorr, Wilder's production assistant, he was apoplectic. He reminded Wilder that the script merely called for "a short montage of various beauty treatments applied to Norma."[50] Brackett insisted that Wilder had turned the montage into something grotesque and vulgar, and he demanded that Wilder excise the montage from the film. Wilder responded that he wanted to portray the torment an older actress would endure to make a comeback. Wilder and Brackett finally exchanged blows, and Schorr had to intervene to stop the fistfight. Schorr was then asked to resolve the conflict. *Sunset Boulevard* was the first film he had worked on at Paramount, and Wilder was his immediate boss. Not surprisingly, he sided with Wilder. Brackett stormed out of the screening room, shouting obscenities at both men. It was at this time that Wilder confided to Schorr that very likely "this was the last film he would ever make with Charles Brackett."[51]

Doane Harrison became supervising editor of Wilder's movies starting with *Sunset Boulevard*. Arthur Schmidt was assigned to edit the film, in collaboration with Harrison. Usually Harrison was on deck to consult with Wilder about cutting the film. He brought a combination of intuition and experience to his discussions with Wilder. "It's likely that Harrison's eye . . . did much to ensure that no scene goes on too long and that no scene is truncated," writes Sam Staggs. "Harrison's contribution to *Sunset Boulevard* surely helped to make the picture a seamless, balanced, measured work of art."[52]

During his career Harrison was nominated for three Academy Awards, for *Five Graves to Cairo, The Lost Weekend,* and *Sunset Boulevard.* Inexplicably, he never won. For the record, John Seitz was nominated for the same three pictures, plus *Double Indemnity,* and the inscrutable members of the academy never voted him a single Oscar either.

Composer Franz Waxman, who scored *Sunset Boulevard,* was, like Wilder, an émigré from Berlin who came to Hollywood during the Nazi period. By the time he composed the background music for *Sunset Boulevard,* he had written scores for some outstanding Hollywood films, including Hitchcock's *Rebecca* (1940). He began working on his music for *Sunset Boulevard* immediately after principal photography was completed in June 1949; he labored all summer and finished in August. "The main theme is one of a tango character," Waxman explained; "it stems from a scene in which Gloria Swanson makes reference to the early days of Hollywood and dancing the tango with Rudolph Valentino. This is the atmosphere in which she still lives in 1950. The tango theme recurs throughout the film, changing keys and instrumentation as called for, right up to the film's climactic scene, when Norma has gone completely mad." At this time the tango theme is repeated "in twisted and tortured harmonies"; it has become "as disjointed as her mind is at this moment."[53] John Caps, who named Waxman's score for *Sunset Boulevard* among the best ever composed for a film, states, "The dark, pulsing introductory passages place the audience in the sonic world" of a thriller—all tense strings and strident brass. "Waxman spins his material into an essay on dead dreams and self-delusion." By the end, Waxman himself added, the main theme "has become a powerful tango into madness," to accompany Norma's ghastly descent of the staircase.[54]

Since Norma is playing Salome as she sweeps down the stairs, Wilder employed Richard Strauss's "Dance of the Seven Veils" from his opera *Salome* during rehearsals. Wilder said, "Then we got better than Strauss: Waxman!"[55] Waxman wrote his own *Salome* music for the last scene, which he titled "The Comeback" in his score. Wilder commented, "Waxman and Rozsa, two Europeans, provided my best scores. They knew my work intuitively."[56]

The original draft of the screenplay, dated December 21, 1948, begins with a prologue that was to appear after the opening credits but did not make it into the finished film. This sequence, which takes place in the Los Angeles County Morgue, was written by Wilder alone, since Brackett would have nothing to do with it. As he had done with Norma's beauty treatment montage, Brackett pronounced the prologue disgusting and morbid. The camera pans from the pavement to the rear of a black hearse; painted on the back of the hearse is the word *Coroner.* The vehicle pulls up to the receiving entrance of the Los Angeles County Morgue, a low, narrow building. Two attendants wheel the corpse on a cot from the hearse into a large, window-less room. Along the walls are twenty sheet-covered corpses lying on metal slabs in two orderly rows. One of the morgue attendants removes the shoes and socks of the latest arrival. A tag is attached to the left big toe that reads, "Joe Gillis, homicide, 5/19/49." After the attendants leave, Joe sits up on his slab and begins to recount to the other cadavers how he came to be there.

In January 1950, Wilder had a sneak preview of the picture at the Coronet Theatre in Evanston, Illinois, just north of Chicago, near Northwestern University. Wilder chose a town far from Hollywood because he did not want a lot of Hollywood insiders at the preview of this picture about the industry. "At the moment they tied the name tag to Holden's big toe," Wilder recalled, "the people roared with laughter." When some of the audience began to walk out, Wilder followed; he sat disconsolately in the lobby, on the steps leading downstairs to the restrooms. As a well-dressed woman passed him on the stairs, he inquired how she liked the picture. She barked, "Have you ever seen such a pile of crap in your life?" Wilder replied, "Never!"[57]

Seeking to do some damage control, Wilder figured that, just as in the case of the sneak preview of *The Lost Weekend,* the audience did not know whether the movie they were going to see was a comedy or a drama. They did not know what mood to be in for *Sunset Boulevard,* and they found the morgue scene ludicrous. Wilder decided to lop off the prologue.

Many film historians assume that Wilder devised a whole new opening sequence, on which he expended additional time and money filming. But that is not the case. John Seitz testified that the footage of Joe's corpse floating in Norma's pool while the police try to fish him out had already been shot for use toward the end of the film. "We already had both"—the morgue sequence and the scene at the pool.[58] Wilder himself stated, "No new footage was shot." He simply added a voice-over narration by Joe, telling posthumously of the events leading up to his demise.[59]

Paramount hosted a full-dress preview screening at the studio in April 1950, to which three hundred members of the Hollywood industry were invited. Wilder was concerned about how the film community would accept the picture. He reassured himself that the new opening sequence was going to get the movie off to a good start. At the first strains of Waxman's score, with its strident brass and surging strings, the picture got rolling.

After the opening credits, in which the film's title is seen stenciled in wedge-shaped letters on a curb, the police are shown swarming around a swimming pool. The pool is on the grounds of an immense baroque estate on Sunset Boulevard; it is just after dawn. A corpse is floating facedown in the pool. The dead man is Joe Gillis, who begins to tell the filmgoer his story in voice-over on the sound track. Joe narrates the film "from beyond the grave," writes Avrom Fleishman, "from the detached perspective of the dead."[60]

As Joe's story unfolds in flashback, we see him as a debt-ridden, failed screenwriter. One day Joe's car has a blowout on Sunset Boulevard, and he turns into the curving private driveway of a garish, shuttered villa that belongs to Norma Desmond, a faded star of the silent screen. When Norma learns that Joe is a screenwriter, she promptly engages him to revise her elephantine screenplay for *Salome,* a biblical epic in which she desperately hopes to make her comeback. The film scenario that she sketches for Joe is clearly derived from Oscar Wilde's play *Salome* (1894), "the version that invented the Dance of the Seven Veils."[61] Joe is to be her amanuensis or, more precisely, her "ghostwriter"—laboring over a script for Norma, who is but a ghost of her former self. "Poor devil," Joe muses, "still waving to a parade that has passed her by."

Norma plays bridge once a week with some old friends whom Joe wryly christens "the Waxworks, dim figures from the silent days." Wilder strove to give the film documentary-like realism by having three stars of silent pictures join Norma's bridge game: H. B. Warner, Anna Q. Nilsson, and Buster Keaton. Warner had played Christ in De Mille's 1927 biblical spectacle *The King of Kings;* Nilsson was imported to Hollywood from Sweden in 1911—a dozen years before Garbo—to appear in silent pictures like Raoul Walsh's *Regeneration* (1915); and Keaton was the silent clown who made the comic masterpiece *The General* (1927). "The cameo appearances of these silent film stars added a more genuine flavor to the film," as an evocation of the old Hollywood, Wilder said. Swanson writes that "Keaton muttered in his unmatchable deadpan, 'Waxworks is right,'" as the four assembled for the scene, "and we all howled with laughter. . . . Keaton looked ravaged, as indeed he had been, by alcohol."[62]

The bridge game was filmed on May 3, 1949. The actors all performed like professionals, requiring only two or three takes for each shot. By 5:15 Wilder had finished shooting the bridge game. The reunion of the four stars of silent movies for a single day, Keaton observed, was "like old home week."[63]

Cecil B. De Mille also enjoyed playing himself in *Sunset Boulevard.* Wilder said, "He was very disciplined and gave a subtler performance, I thought, than any actor ever gave in a film that he directed." In the sequence in which Norma visits De Mille while he is shooting *Samson and Delilah,* De Mille puts her in the director's chair so she can watch a rehearsal. "While she is sitting there," David Freeman observes, "a boom microphone passes behind her, disturbing her hat and casting a shadow over her face. . . . Norma scowls at the microphone, the very thing that ended her era."[64] Norma mentions to De Mille that the studio has been calling her urgently, but it is not, as she thinks, about making her *Salome* movie; it is merely to arrange to borrow her venerable Isotta-Fraschini for a Crosby picture. Jeffrey Meyers notes that "De Mille manages to suppress this fact, to forestall her humiliation."[65]

On New Year's Eve, Joe has a quarrel with Norma, who is drunk; he walks out on her. But Max soon phones him to inform him that Norma has attempted suicide. Joe returns to the house and finds Norma lying in bed, and they are reconciled. "At the stroke of midnight, as the strains of 'Auld Lang Syne' waft into the room, she reaches up and pulls him toward her with nails that look like talons," comments Morris Dickstein.[66]

The film's title refers to the passing of the old Hollywood: It recalls the tragic lives of has-been film stars like Norma Desmond, whose careers in silent pictures were eclipsed by the advent of sound. The sun set on their careers when they failed to make the transition to sound films. The decaying swimming pool on Norma's estate, in which John Gilbert swam ten thousand midnights ago, is a relic of the grandeur of Norma's long-lost heyday as a superstar in Hollywood. It is cracked and empty at the film's start, but after Joe enters her life, Norma restores the pool and fills it. "Still, I didn't conceive the pool so much as a metaphor for Norma's personal decay, but as an authentic depiction of the way a woman like Norma, living in the past, would allow her property to slide into ruin," Wilder explained. "Even today there are old Hollywood estates with empty swimming pools, with rats running around in them, and cracked tennis courts with sagging nets. That is part of our community; people are up, and then they are down. I also used the neglected pool for a dramatic purpose, because later when Joe enters Norma's life, it would be natural that she would have the pool cleaned and filled as an indication of her renewed interest in life."

Norma's romance with Joe is doomed to be short-lived, however; as time goes on, Joe finds it intolerable to be supported by a wealthy, aging woman. He realizes that he is an opportunist who has sold himself to the highest bidder. He thus reflects Wilder's favorite theme: Joe can no longer bring himself to do *anything* for money. Joe strikes up a relationship with Betty Schaefer (Nancy Olson), another aspiring screenwriter. She calls one sequence in "Dark Windows," a scenario of Joe's, "moving and true." She is confident that it could be made into a screenplay about "teachers and their threadbare lives." Joe catches her enthusiasm, and he works on it surreptitiously with her several nights a week. But Norma inevitably discovers that Joe is seeing Betty and becomes insanely jealous.

One fateful night, Joe finally summons the courage to tell Norma that he is terminating their sordid liaison once and for all. "Norma, you're a woman of fifty," Joe tells her. "There is nothing tragic about being fifty, unless you try to be twenty-five!" When she threatens to kill herself if he leaves, he replies, "You'd be killing yourself to an empty house. The audience left twenty years ago." Norma, who has been emotionally disturbed for some time, finally crosses the brink into insanity. As Joe leaves her spectral mansion and walks across the patio, the deranged woman empties a revolver into his retreating figure; he pitches forward into the swimming pool. She shoots Joe dead, comments Steffen Haubner, "to prevent him from abandoning her, as everyone else did long ago."[67] As Joe is fished out of the floodlit pool by the police, he comments laconically on the sound track to the filmgoer, "Well, this is where you came in."

Shortly afterward, a crew of newsreel cameramen enter the mansion to photograph the fallen star as she is taken away by the police. But Norma mistakes the newsreel cameramen for the camera crew on a movie set and accordingly believes that she is at long last making her comeback film. Max, who has supported her fantasies about a new career all along, makes believe, for her sake, that he is Cecil B. De Mille directing her in *Salome*. A look of anguish crosses Max's face when he directs the cameras toward Norma as she sweeps down the grand staircase of her exotic mansion for her final close-up. "So they were turning after all, those cameras," Joe says over the sound track. "Life, which can be strangely merciful, had taken pity on Norma Desmond. The dream she had clung to so desperately had finally enfolded her." The stunning finale of *Sunset Boulevard* makes for one of the greatest moments in all cinema.

American films at the time tended to have more positive endings than this film does, because the studios feared that the public would reject downbeat endings. "*Sunset Boulevard* did not have a happy ending," said Wilder, "because it was inevitable that Norma would go mad. No other ending would have worked for the film, and the studio at no point questioned this."

Most of the audience at Paramount's advance screening of *Sunset Boulevard* for the Hollywood community on that April night in 1950 stood up and cheered at the film's conclusion. Gloria Swanson writes, "Barbara Stanwyck fell on her knees and kissed the hem of my skirt." Swanson looked around for Mary Pickford, but an old-time producer told her, "She can't show herself, Gloria. She's overcome; we all are."[68] Not Mae Murray, another diva of the silent screen, whom Stroheim had directed in *The Merry Widow* (1925). She thought the movie was overdone; "None of us floozies was *that* nuts!" she exclaimed.[69]

Louis B. Mayer, the pompous chief executive of MGM, threw a tantrum in the lobby. "We should horsewhip this Wilder; . . . he should be sent back to Germany," Mayer ranted.[70] Then, spying Wilder, he shook his pudgy fist at him, denouncing him as a disgrace to the industry. "You have dirtied the nest. You should be kicked out of this country, tarred and feathered, you goddamned foreigner son-of-a-bitch." In the heat of the moment, Mayer apparently lost sight of the fact that he too was an immigrant, having been born in Minsk, Russia. Tom Wood, the film's publicist, diplomatically reported afterward that Wilder merely stuck his tongue out at Mayer. But, by Wilder's own testimony, he responded to Mayer in kind. "Yes, I directed this picture," Wilder said. "Mr. Mayer, why don't you go fuck yourself!" When a friend later told him that his offensive remark might have cost him some Oscar votes, Wilder replied, "You are so right. Remind me to cut out my tongue in the morning."[71]

Wilder insisted that *Sunset Boulevard* "was not anti-Hollywood," as Mayer contended. Joe Gillis was a hack and Betty Schaefer tried "to put Joe back on the right track," Wilder explained. "I don't say anything derogatory about pictures" in this film.[72] One might even say that *Sunset Boulevard* proves that Hollywood was fundamentally all right, if it could turn out a picture like *Sunset Boulevard,* so unlike the bland, well-scrubbed "heartwarmers" being churned out by Mayer at MGM in those days.

Very few critics panned *Sunset Boulevard* when it premiered at Radio City Music Hall on August 10, 1950. Admittedly, one reviewer dismissed it as "a pretentious slice of Roquefort," but he was the exception that proved the rule.[73] James Agee, who was committed to writing capsule film reviews for the *Nation,* contributed a five-page essay on the picture to the November 1950 issue of *Sight and Sound.* "It is one of those rare movies," he rhapsodized, "that can be talked about, almost shot for shot and line for line, for hours on end. . . . I am willing to bet that it will be looked at and respected long after most of the movies too easily called great have been forgotten."[74] (For example, Compton Bennett's *King Solomon's Mines,* thought to be a major epic in 1950 and nominated, along with *Sunset Boulevard,* for best picture, is no longer remembered.)

*Sunset Boulevard* is blessed with a superb screenplay and inspired direction, topped off by Gloria Swanson's superlative performance as Norma and Erich von Stroheim's indelible portrayal of Max. Moreover, the movie is sterling for Wilder's consummate craftsmanship in producing well-defined, plausible characters. Swanson, as the obsolete screen star, has the threat of madness throughout—the cockeyed glint in her eyes implies the unruly and unmanageable passions that lie beneath her surface glamour. This keeps us watching as she leads us down the treacherous path to tragedy.

When the Academy Awards rolled around, *Sunset Boulevard* nabbed eleven nominations, including best picture; Holden and Swanson for best actor and best actress; Stroheim for best supporting actor; Wilder for best director; Wilder, Brackett, and Marshman for best original screenplay; Waxman for best score; and Meehan and Dreier for best production design. On Oscar night, March 29, 1951, the only winners for *Sunset Boulevard* were Wilder, Brackett, and Marshman for best original screenplay; Waxman for best score; and Meehan and Dreier for best production design.

At the Oscar party that Paramount held at the Mocambo nightclub after the ceremony, Wilder commiserated with Holden: "It was a miscarriage of justice, Bill."[75] Since Paramount had come away from the Academy

Awards almost empty handed, Wilder endeavored to cheer up the gathering at the Mocambo with his sardonic humor. He told the journalists present that Barbara Stanwyck had just related to him an anecdote about an aging actress like Norma Desmond whose toy boy was spending her money extravagantly. According to Wilder, Stanwyck had inquired of the dowager, "Tell me, darling, is the screwing you're getting worth the screwing you're getting?"[76]

Stroheim did not make the trip from Paris for the Oscar ceremonies; he was offended that he had been nominated for best supporting actor instead of best actor. So he had an additional reason to hate the role of the subservient butler to the end of his days.

Over the years, *Sunset Boulevard* has continued to be singled out as a masterpiece. When the American Film Institute (AFI) honored the best one hundred films made during the first century of American cinema with a special on CBS-TV on July 3, 2003, *Sunset Boulevard* was near the top of the list. The release of the picture on DVD in 2008 was the occasion for renewed acclaim. The transfer to DVD is a triumph of digital technology—it is amazingly sharp, clear, and free of perceptible blemishes, and it boasts detailed commentaries.

Wilder never forgot the very moment he decided to call it quits with Brackett once and for all. One day he was having a discussion with Brackett while they were sitting in Wilder's car, parked in the studio lot. "He kind of flew off the handle," said Wilder. The discussion turned into a violent quarrel, and they both got out of the car angry, "and that is how it ended."[77] The next morning Wilder said to Brackett with studied casualness, "You know, Charlie, after this, I don't think we should work together any more. I think it is better for both of us if we just split up."[78]

Nearly twenty years later, one rainy Sunday afternoon at Brackett's Bel Air home, when he was dying from a stroke, Brackett talked with Garson Kanin about his breakup with Wilder. "I never knew what happened, never understood it," Brackett lamented. "We were doing so well; I always thought we brought out the best in each other. . . . It was shattering; it was such an unexpected blow that I thought I'd never recover from it. And, in fact, I don't think I ever have." Brackett concluded, "We had our disagreements, of course; but they were always professional, never personal."[79]

The point that Brackett had lost sight of was that their disagreements never ended. They had been quarreling incessantly, amid flying telephone books and ashtrays, for years. "It's like with married people," Wilder explained candidly; they have to argue in such a way that they don't destroy anything basic about the relationship. "You have to be able to come back for more. Like lovers, it's better not to go to sleep angry."[80] The collaboration of Wilder and Brackett had often been described as a marriage, but by now it was a bad marriage, according to Wilder. "We had been squabbling about every little thing."[81] Moreover, Wilder had broached to Brackett the subject of *Ace in the Hole,* a dark satire about yellow journalism, and Brackett wanted no part of what he termed a lurid scenario. And so the professional marriage of Wilder and Brackett finally ended in divorce, after twelve years and thirteen pictures.

After their separation, Wilder stayed at Paramount, but Brackett moved to Twentieth Century–Fox, where he continued cowriting and producing movies. In 1953 Brackett produced and coauthored the script for *Titanic* for director Jean Negulesco (remade by James Cameron in 1997). Brackett, *Ninotchka* cowriter Walter Reisch, and *A Foreign Affair* cowriter Richard Breen won an Academy Award for their screenplay for *Titanic.*

Wilder would stay at Paramount for another three pictures before moving on to other studios. After he broke off with Brackett, he took over from his former partner the responsibility of producing the films he directed, to safeguard his artistic autonomy. From now on, as cowriter, director, and producer of his films, Wilder would bear the brunt of whatever praise or blame accrued to his films.

8

# Barbed Wire Satire

## Ace in the Hole and Stalag 17

> Billy Wilder is a tall, loose-jointed man with a brain full of razor blades.
>
> —*William Holden*

Writing in the mid-1950s, film critic Manny Farber praised certain Hollywood directors like Billy Wilder who would "tunnel" beneath the surfaces of the stories they were filming and seek to illuminate, in a shrewd and unsentimental fashion, deeper truths, usually about the unglamorous side of the human condition. These directors did not get bogged down in "significant" dialogue but told their stories in a straightforward fashion that nonetheless implied subtle themes beneath the surfaces of their basically plot-oriented scripts.[1] Tunneling underneath the plot to reach a deeper meaning is a particularly apt metaphor for *Ace in the Hole*, which deals with a mine cave-in.

## Ace in the Hole (1951)

*Ace in the Hole* takes place in a rural town on the edge of a wasteland. Nevertheless, as Foster Hirsch shrewdly stresses, "Chuck Tatum merely transports a city mentality to an out-of-the-way setting." Tatum, a former metropolitan newspaper man reduced to working for a rural rag, is "a city reporter type at heart with all the animal cunning of characters who inhabit the city jungle."[2] Tatum callously exploits the plight of Leo Minosa, who is trapped underground in a crumbling mine shaft, to advance his career. Tatum was to some extent based on Wilder, who worked for a scandal sheet in Berlin in the 1920s. "I was doing the dirty work of crime reporting," he said. "Some of this I remembered for *Ace in the Hole*."[3] Wilder recalled taking the streetcar in Berlin to interview the parents of a murder victim and then taking another trolley to interview the parents of the murderer. He confessed that he made up the answers to the questions about how the murderer's parents felt about their son, because he could not bring himself to ask.

When Wilder delivered the finished print of *Sunset Boulevard* in early February 1950, severing his professional connection with Brackett for good, he began casting about for a replacement writer. He continued to feel that he had an erratic command of English. Besides, "after Brackett and I split up, I found it too lonely to write by myself." He added, "I sure miss him."[4]

Wilder's new writing partner was Walter Newman, a twenty-three-year-old radio writer. Wilder had heard one of Newman's plays on his car radio and contacted him about collaborating on a screenplay. It was Newman who suggested to Wilder the concept of *Ace in the Hole*. After they had kicked around several possible ideas for a movie, Newman suggested the story of Floyd Collins, a cave explorer who had been the victim of a Kentucky mine cave-in twenty-five years earlier, as a good premise for a script. Wilder liked the idea of an updated version of the Collins tragedy and commissioned Newman to lay out a preliminary screen treatment of the plotline, under his supervision.

Wilder turned over Newman's scenario to the story department in March 1950 with the tentative title "The Human Interest Story." About that time, Wilder invited Lesser Samuels, a former newspaperman and a contract writer at Paramount, to join the team. The front office gave the project the green light after considering Newman's treatment. The production was budgeted at $1.8 million; Wilder's combined salary as cowriter, producer, and director was $250,000.

Newman's scenario clearly followed the Floyd Collins story. On January 30, 1925, Collins was trapped by a landslide in a sandstone cavern near Mammoth Cave in central Kentucky. Robert Murray and Roger Brucker write in their book *Trapped! The Story of Floyd Collins* that William Miller, an enterprising reporter from the *Louisville Courier-Journal*, crawled into the cave "on his hands and knees" and was able to get close enough to Collins for a brief interview. Collins's plight soon made national headlines. Throngs of sensation-hungry tourists from near and far descended on the cave site. "It was like a county fair," Murray and Bruckner observe; "con artists abounded." The crowds behaved as if they were at "a carnival midway. . . . In the process the majority forgot about the imprisoned man underground."[5] Miller continued to cover the rescue operation until Collins's death finally ended his ordeal. He had been trapped in the mine for eighteen days. In May 1926, Miller won a Pulitzer Prize for his reportage.

Wilder, Newman, and Samuels toiled on the first draft of the script throughout the spring of 1950. Studio insiders were anxious to see whether Wilder could succeed without his former writing partner. In some quarters Wilder was considered a heartless cynic whose excessive contempt for humanity had been controlled and toned down by his wise partner. Without Brackett's steadying hand, they were certain, Wilder would fall on his face. But Wilder did not play it safe on his first film without Brackett as his chief collaborator. After all, he had chosen for his next film a story with an unsympathetic lead character: a cocksure newspaper man who exemplifies the American mania for making a quick buck, even at the expense of someone else's personal tragedy. Furthermore, Wilder was starting from scratch on an original screenplay, instead of buying the rights to a successful play or novel. "Usually the studio prefers to bank on a sure-fire property," he explained. Wilder was aware of the gossip in the commissary about his next film. He always viewed making a movie as climbing up to the peak of Mount Everest. The studio wags "can't wait for me to slip into a crevasse," he mused ruefully.[6]

The first draft of the screenplay, dated May 31, 1950, has a handwritten note stapled to the first page: "Do not give out under any circumstances to anyone!" Wilder was worried that news of this scenario, which was designed to skewer the newspaper business, would find its way into the local gossip columns, precipitating an uproar in the press. The draft begins in the Albuquerque train depot, where Jacob Boot, a newspaper editor, watches a pine box being loaded into the baggage car of a train. "Good-bye, Mr. Boot," says Chuck Tatum in voice-over; "when you write the obit, lay it on the line. All you've got on me! What I wanted, and what I did to get it. Remember the very first day I hit this God-forsaken town of yours?"[7] It is Tatum in the box; Wilder was repeating the concept of having a talking corpse narrate the film, as Joe Gillis had narrated *Sunset Boulevard*.

In the final shooting script, however, Wilder scrapped the original opening in the train station for one in which Tatum arrives in Albuquerque in a coupe with New York license plates. His convertible breaks down because of burned-out bearings and is laid up for repairs in a local garage. Tatum, who is down on his luck, takes the occasion to inquire about a job on the *Albuquerque Sun-Bulletin*. He makes his pitch to Jacob Boot, managing editor of the *Sun-Bulletin*, but Boot is not particularly impressed. Tatum, it develops, has been kicked off some top eastern dailies for dishonesty and drinking on the job. When Boot inquires whether Tatum drinks a lot, Tatum replies with a typical Wilder witticism: "Not a lot, just frequently."

Boot prominently displays his paper's motto, "Tell the truth," in an embroidered sampler hanging above his desk, "as a sign of his and the newspaper's guiding ethic."[8] Tatum, whose ethical standards are "flexible," to say the least, sees that Boot will need a lot of persuasion to hire him. So he launches into a high-pressure spiel: "Apparently you haven't seen my byline; that's because you don't get the Eastern papers out here. Mr. Boot, I'm a $250 a week newspaperman. I can be had for $50. I can handle big news and little news. And if there's no news, I'll go out and bite a dog, to create some. . . . Make that $45."[9] Boot is overwhelmed by the sheer force of Tatum's braggadocio and hires him for a salary of $60 a week.

"Tatum's a hungry guy who bites off more than he can swallow," Wilder explained with gusto. "What we have is an indictment of a reporter like Tatum who has recently been writing for cheesy tabloids." Tatum has no scruples about sensationalizing a news event to sell more papers, Wilder continued. "On the other side, we have a publisher, an old-time newspaperman, Jacob Boot, who makes some telling points about honor in his profession." Boot is the only individual in the film who stands for journalistic integrity.[10]

On July 6, 1950, just four days before the beginning of principal photography, the shooting script was finished. Wilder sent a copy to Joseph Breen, who responded that the script was lacking "a proper voice for morality" at the end.[11] He was especially concerned about the portrayal of the local sheriff as corrupt. As Richard Armstrong notes, Sheriff Gus Kretzer has "all the scruples of the rattlesnake he carries around with him" in a cardboard box.[12] Tatum knows how useful to the sheriff "the prolonged publicity of an extended rescue operation would be in the sheriff's forthcoming election campaign."[13] He arranges to prolong the rescue operation by convincing Sheriff Kretzer to employ outmoded methods in digging Leo out. This will give Tatum more time to dramatize the rescue and the sheriff's part in it. Breen was relatively easy on the script of Wilder's nihilistic movie because Tatum ultimately pays for his transgressions with his life. But Breen and his advisers believed that "Sheriff Kretzer breezes out of the story a little too easily, considering the malice of his misdeeds throughout the story." The censor expected Wilder to provide some additional dialogue, "which will make it clear that Kretzer will be answerable for his evil in the near future."[14] Wilder made a concession to Breen by having Boot declare that he plans to write an exposé about the sheriff, which will ruin Kretzer's chances at reelection. Breen accepted this change.

Wilder signed Kirk Douglas for the pivotal role of Chuck Tatum. Douglas had played the career-making part of the unscrupulous boxer in

Mark Robson's *Champion* (1949); consequently he seemed right to enact the role of the selfish, scheming, cocky Chuck Tatum in *Ace in the Hole*. But Douglas had some misgivings about the character. When he approached the part, he wrote Wilder a letter, stating, "Look, Billy, I think I'm being a little too tough. . . . For God's sake, Billy, please understand that I am not being one of those typical actors who is trying to write a screenplay."[15] Douglas thought the character was too unlikable and would forfeit audience sympathy. Wilder conceded that he had not made Tatum sympathetic but noted that he was an interesting, even riveting character. "He didn't see it my way," Douglas concluded, "so I did the best I could."[16] Douglas recalled that Wilder sent him "to work at the *Herald Examiner* as a rookie reporter for a week before shooting began." He learned the ropes of the newspaper business during that week.[17]

The only substantial woman's role in the picture was Lorraine Minosa, Leo's slatternly wife, who has become increasingly bored with working in Leo's souvenir shop. The part went to Jan Sterling, who had recently played a jailbird in John Cromwell's *Caged* (1950). Sterling accepted the role of Lorraine because "it was the first really good part I'd had."[18] Richard Benedict, who usually played heavies in films like Maxwell Shane's *City across the River* (1949), was called on to play Leo, one of the few sympathetic roles in his résumé.

Wilder stuck to his usual team behind the camera. Supervising editor Doane Harrison was with him as always, as were editor Arthur Schmidt, who was the cutter on *Sunset Boulevard*, and director of photography Charles Lang, who shot *A Foreign Affair*. Hal Pereira, who was production designer on *Double Indemnity*, was now head of Paramount's art department, replacing Hans Dreier. At Wilder's behest, Pereira appointed Earl Hedrick, who had designed the sets for *The Lost Weekend*, as production designer on *Ace in the Hole*. Pereira, of course, monitored Hedrick's work, as Dreier had monitored his.

Principal photography began on July 10, 1950, with location work on the streets of Albuquerque around the offices of the *Sun-Bulletin*. The following day, the film unit moved to a barren stretch of land outside Gallup, New Mexico. It was there that Hedrick and his production team had set up Leo Minosa's souvenir shop, known as the local trading post. The exterior of the cave in which Leo is trapped was not far away (the cave interior was built on a soundstage at Paramount). There was plenty of room in the arid landscape outside Gallup to accommodate the crowds of extras, recruited from the nearby towns, who were playing the curious tourists attracted by the mine catastrophe.

"I looked up the Floyd Collins story," said Wilder. "There was a circus up there. There were hustlers trying to make a fast buck; they were selling hot dogs. . . . They composed a song." So in Wilder's film, throngs of morbid gawkers flock by the hundreds to the isolated outpost that is the site of Leo Minosa's ordeal. The protracted rescue operation thus evolves into a carnival. The fairground that Hedrick designed encompassed concession stands, a Ferris wheel, a press tent, and a parking lot. It was one of the largest outdoor sets ever constructed for a movie: twelve hundred feet wide and sixteen hundred feet long.[19]

As for the lugubrious "anthem" composed for the event, Wilder took the liberty of having a song played while the rescue mission is in progress. The actual song inspired by Floyd Collins's tragedy, "The Death of Floyd Collins," was recorded by country singer Vernon Dalhart in 1925 and sold 3 million copies.[20] For the song in the movie, "We're Coming, Leo," Wilder called on the songwriting team of Jay Livingston and Ray Evans, who had done a cameo in *Sunset Boulevard,* playing their hit song "Buttons and Bows" in a party scene. Wilder commissioned them to write "the worst song you can, with bad rhymes and everything else bad."[21] They obligingly came up with a promotional jingle designed to lure the sensation seekers to the site of the mine cave-in:

We're coming, Leo, so don't despair.
While you are cave a-hopin'
We will finally make an openin'.

The climax of the location shooting came on July 25. It was a helicopter shot of the media circus surrounding the cave; seven hundred extras participated, mostly local citizens. The location footage that Wilder accomplished in conjunction with Charles Lang is vivid and authentic. Wilder declared that paying close attention to milieu was the only way he could approach his characters, so that their situations came to life on the screen. Commenting on Lang's cinematography, Wilder said that too many cinematographers—unlike Lang—"are working for the goddamned Academy Award," and hence want to use a lot of elaborate shots. Wilder emphasized that he did not admire "fancy camerawork, with the camera hanging off the chandelier. That's to astonish the middle-class critics."[22] Both Wilder and Lang wanted *Ace in the Hole* to have the unvarnished look of straight reportage. Their work on this film has what Manny Farber terms "a chilling documentary exactness."[23] Wilder wrapped up the location shooting on August 2, 1951, and the film unit decamped for the soundstages of Paramount in Hollywood.

Filming ended on September 11; it had lasted a total of forty-five days—fifteen days shorter than the shooting schedule of *Sunset Boulevard*.

The composer available to score the picture was the Academy Award–winner Hugo Friedhofer (*The Best Years of Our Lives*). "It is not important for the audience to be aware of the technique by which music affects them; but affect them it must," he once said. "The listeners should be aware subliminally how the score winds through the movie . . . and integrates the film experience."[24] Initially Wilder wanted Friedhofer to compose a more melodic score than the dissonant one Friedhofer wrote for him. Wilder "was upset that I hadn't written a schmaltzy score," Friedhofer remembered, perhaps because Wilder wanted the score to offset the harshness of the story line. "It's a good score; but there isn't a note of melody in it," Wilder complained. Friedhofer answered, "Billy, you've had the courage to put on the screen a bunch of really reprehensible people. Did you want me to soften them?"[25]

The most reprehensible character in *Ace in the Hole*, of course, is Chuck Tatum, who cajoles Jacob Boot into giving him a job as a reporter after he has flunked out as a journalist on some New York dailies. Tatum chafes at being exiled to a burg like Albuquerque. In fact, he looks on his job on the *Albuquerque Sun-Bulletin* as a stopover in this "sun-baked Siberia" on his way back to the big time.

One of the routine assignments that Boot gives Tatum is to cover a rattlesnake hunt in the wilderness on the outskirts of town. Stopping for gas en route, Tatum pulls into Leo Minosa's trading post, which is near an ancient Indian cave dwelling. Tatum learns that Leo, who entered the abandoned cave in search of ancient artifacts and relics to sell in his souvenir shop, is now trapped in a mudslide. Tatum immediately recognizes that the disaster has the makings of an exclusive news story for him to write—with a byline. Leo Minosa is Tatum's "ace in the hole." Indeed, Tatum's scoop will result in headlines all over the country and will get him back in "the big leagues." (Because Wilder learned English by listening to baseball games on the radio, his film scripts abound in baseball metaphors.)

Tatum enters the cavern and digs his way to the place where Leo is up to his waist in sand and shale. He assures Leo that help is on the way. The two-faced Tatum then convinces Sheriff Kretzer not to have the rescue party shore up the crumbling wall of the tunnel with timber, in order to extricate Leo from the mine shaft in a matter of hours. Instead, he persuades the sheriff to instruct the engineers to drill through solid rock from the top of the cave, a lengthy process that could endanger Leo's life. This will give Tatum several days in which to build his big news story to produce maximum publicity. The sheriff agrees in return for having a sign posted at the cave entrance reading, "Reelect Sheriff Kretzer." Tatum loses no time in phoning in the lurid story of the mine catastrophe to Boot: "Unless war is declared tonight, here is your front-page feature!" Afterward he says to himself, "Now that they've pitched me a big one, I'm gonna smack it right out of the ball park!"

That same day, Leo's jaded wife, Lorraine, who has been looking for a chance to get free of her dead-end marriage, decides to desert her trapped husband. Lorraine finds life dull, living in a wasteland on the edge of town and clerking in Leo's trading post. "We sell a case of soda pop a week," she whines to Tatum, "and once in a while a Navajo rug." Tatum intercepts her just as she is preparing to fly the coop, and he begs her to stay. He needs her to help him give his news dispatches some human interest. "Your husband is stuck under a mountain; you're worried sick," Tatum explains. "That's the way the story goes." Lorraine insists that she is leaving anyway. "You'll just have to rewrite me," she says with a shrug. Finally Tatum, shrewdly appealing to her greed, persuades her that the souvenir shop will become a gold mine once the press and the carnival promoters lure crowds to the cavern where Leo is entombed. Lorraine catches on quickly; soon she is charging admission to the cave site and hawking souvenirs at Leo's trading post. At one point Wilder shows Lorraine in close-up biting into an apple, implying that she recalls Eve in the Old Testament. Lorraine, a temptress in this decadent Eden, coaxes Tatum into committing adultery with her.

Swarms of sensation mongers begin to converge on the fairground surrounding the cave, arriving aboard a train, "the Leo Minosa Special." They are greeted by a band blaring out "We're Coming, Leo," the theme song of this media circus. A traveling carnival has set up shop near the cave. An announcer, speaking over a public address system, welcomes the crowds to "this community of tents and trailers"; a billboard assures the customers that "proceeds go to the Leo Minosa Rescue Fund." Wilder's satire is unrelenting.

Meanwhile, Tatum's relationship with Lorraine has become strained. He says to her testily, "It's Sunday. Aren't you going to church?" She replies, "I don't go to church; kneeling bags my nylons." Wilder credited this gem of a line to his wife, Audrey—"How would I know a thing like that?" But Tatum is not to be deterred by Lorraine's indifference. He insists that she attend the rosary service at the local Mexican church so he can get photographs of her for his press coverage as the "grief-stricken wife," praying for her husband's safety.[26] (Tatum obviously chooses to overlook that Lorraine has made several passes at him.)

Becoming more impatient with Lorraine, Tatum snaps, "Wipe that smile off your face." After all, she is playing the role of the anxious wife. "Make me!" she replies, defiantly. Tatum responds by slapping her across the face. Lorraine finally agrees to go to the Catholic service, but she adds, "Don't ever slap me again, Mister." Then she smiles. She says she is relenting only because Tatum wrote a flattering piece about Leo's "loyal wife" in the afternoon edition of the *Sun-Bulletin*. "Tomorrow this will be yesterday's paper," he retorts, "and they'll wrap fish in it."

When Tatum pays another visit to Leo in the cavern, Leo expresses his growing anxiety that he cannot survive much longer. He asks Tatum to deliver to Lorraine a fur stole that he bought for her as an anniversary present, since he probably will not live to see their anniversary. Tatum is all too aware that Lorraine is not the devoted wife that Leo thinks she is, but he keeps that to himself. Instead he simply promises to do what Leo asks. But Leo's wife takes one look at the mangy fur piece, which is all that Leo could afford, and sneers, "He must have skinned a couple of hungry rats." Then she drops it on the floor with disdain. Tatum is appalled by the floozy's cold indifference to her hapless husband. In a fit of rage, Tatum snatches up the stole, wraps it around her neck, and begins to choke her with it. Lorraine is nearly asphyxiated; in self-defense she turns on Tatum, grabs a pair of scissors, and plunges them into his stomach. When Wilder called, "Cut!" Douglas noticed that Sterling's face was blue and she was gasping for breath. He exclaimed, "Good God, Jan! If I was squeezing you too hard, why didn't you tell me?" She answered weakly, "I couldn't, because you were choking me!"[27]

Tatum receives word that Leo is dying of pneumonia. Tatum is painfully aware that he has placed Leo's life in jeopardy unnecessarily, just to get his scoop. He recalls that, during his last visit with Leo in the mine shaft, Leo requested that he bring a Catholic priest to administer the last rites. The guilt-ridden Tatum does so. As Leo recites the act of contrition, Wilder cuts to a close-up of the anguished, remorseful Tatum, who is the real sinner present. Leo, the poor chump, lies dying, still convinced that Tatum is his best friend. He will die without knowing about Tatum's treachery. Compelling scenes like this one prevent the film from becoming a tasteless sideshow.

Inevitably, Leo expires in the dank pit with Tatum standing by. Tatum, who is gradually losing blood from his stab wound, goes outside the cave, grabs a microphone, and announces to the crowd that Leo Minosa is dead. "Now go home, all of you; the circus is over." The carnival tent collapses and the gaping sightseers evaporate. Lorraine hits the road with her suitcase;

she is last seen in extreme long shot, hitching a ride on the highway, aimlessly headed for nowhere in particular.

Meanwhile Tatum, filled with self-loathing, attempts to file his final dispatch, in which he confesses the part he played in Leo's demise. But none of the wire services are interested; not even the *Sun-Bulletin* will print his confession. "He realizes, of course, that a dead man is no longer a news item," comments Bernard Dick, and Leo Minosa is dead.[28] Now that his grand deception has turned sour, Tatum realizes that he will never be able to tell the world of his gigantic hoax. The only one around to hear Tatum's confession is Herbie Cook (Robert Arthur), a cub reporter who once looked up to Tatum as a role model. But now even Herbie is thoroughly disillusioned with Tatum.

Tatum lurches into the office of the *Sun-Bulletin;* he is leaking blood from his fatal wound, as Walter Neff does at the end of *Double Indemnity.* In a variation of the spiel he delivered to Boot at the beginning of the film, Tatum proclaims, "Mr. Boot, I'm a thousand-dollar-a-day newspaperman. You can have me for nothing!" Tatum pitches forward toward the camera, which is positioned on the floor, and falls into an extreme close-up, dead. "We dug a hole and put the camera there," said Wilder. "We stood in the hole with the camera" so that Douglas's face was only inches away from the lens when he collapsed. "The shot was always in my mind, but it wasn't in the script. . . . That was one of the few times I went for a bold shot like that." Wilder wanted to end on a powerful image of Tatum.[29]

"Wilder's anti-heroes are never just heels," writes Kevin Lally; "he understands their human frailty too well to deny them the potential for self-examination, no matter how repellant their behavior." Tatum somehow senses that it is only right that he should pay for his crime by succumbing to the stab wound inflicted by Lorraine. The ending, Lally states, "is certainly not a cop-out." A recurring theme in Wilder's most powerful films is that of "a wretched opportunist wistfully seeking redemption."[30]

When *Ace in the Hole* opened in July 1951, it flopped with a resounding thud. Several reviewers loathed the film, calling it an unwarranted attack on the integrity of the American press. Wilder personally was denounced as a cynic who had made a rancid movie "without a sliver of compassion for the human race," which is gleefully portrayed at its worst. Wilder had a rattlesnake's view of the world, said one critic; "this film has fangs."[31] Filmmaker Guy Maddin (*The Saddest Music in the World*) emphasizes that "most critics considered themselves newspapermen and therefore within the target range of the movie's furious contempt." So it was not surprising that several reviewers excoriated *Ace in the Hole.* "Of course the rapacious hunger of tabloid news gatherers for their scoop," he continued, "is nothing more than accurately presented in the movie."[32] Kirk Douglas noted that Wilder's treatment of the news media became more credible over time because the excesses of the tabloid press became more familiar. "Newsmen will sometimes stretch their objective reporting to make a story more sensational," he observed.[33]

Wilder stubbornly refused to acknowledge that *Ace in the Hole* was a ferocious condemnation of the human race. But he realized in retrospect that, when a director stages an incident of this kind—in which a character's life hangs in the balance—usually the audience implicitly assumes that he will show the helpless person being saved in the nick of time, thereby releasing the tension that has built up in the audience. Consequently, the audience feels cheated if the threatened peril actually overtakes the innocent party and they are denied the satisfaction of seeing the individual emerge unharmed. In depicting this gruesome calamity as he does, Wilder is rather like the director of an old silent serial, showing the heroine who is tied to the railroad tracks really being run over by the oncoming train. Wilder reflected that portraying this sympathetic man perishing in such a dreadful fashion was a cardinal sin; it elicited a severely negative audience reaction. "At the very least, I should have had Leo's demise occur off screen," he said. "But I am always rewriting my films in my head years after they are finished." In any event, he always thought of *Ace in the Hole* as "the runt of the litter."

Shortly after he read the scalding reviews of the movie, Wilder witnessed an auto accident while driving down Wilshire Boulevard. "Somebody was run over right in front of me; I wanted to help the guy who was run over." A newspaper cameraman came out of nowhere and took a picture of the injured party. Wilder called to him, "You'd better call an ambulance." The photographer replied, "I've got to get to the *Los Angeles Times;* I've got a picture here that I've got to deliver!" Wilder concluded, "You put that in a movie, and the critics think you're exaggerating."[34] Emphasizing just how callous and insensitive "the gentlemen of the press" can be, Wilder also recalled a reporter once asking him "how did I feel when I learned my mother had died at Auschwitz." He concluded, "It makes you wonder just how cynical *Ace in the Hole* really was."[35]

Panic broke out at the studio when *Ace in the Hole* failed to leave the starting gate. The American press made such an outcry against the picture that Y. Frank Freeman, who was still vice president at Paramount, dispatched relays of publicity agents to city desks around the country to explain that "the picture's depiction of trashy journalism was not directed against the

Fourth Estate as such," but only against its bad apples.[36] No dice. The mass audience still stayed away in droves.

The film was better received overseas; Europeans did not mind a Hollywood film criticizing the American press. In fact, the movie won a Golden Lion at the Venice Film Festival. Freeman decided that the favorable publicity attending the Venice award, along with a more benign title for the picture, might resuscitate the film's chances of finding an audience in the United States. He accordingly attempted to tie "a pretty bow" around the movie by retitling it *The Big Carnival* and reissuing it in the domestic market. He made this decision without Wilder's knowledge or consent; Wilder was so incensed that for the first time he began to consider leaving Paramount for good. At all events, when the picture did not go well with the substitute title, said Wilder, "they changed it back again to *Ace in the Hole;* but it was too late."[37]

Wilder had been the kingpin at Paramount; now some people around the studio shunned him. His gut reaction to his detractors at the studio was, "Fuck them all—it is the best picture I ever made!" Still, he continued, "*Ace in the Hole* cost me power at the studio."[38] The fact that it was his first picture without Brackett boded ill for Wilder's future, according to studio insiders. They were saying that *Ace in the Hole* was a flop because Wilder no longer had Brackett to guide him in writing a screenplay. Moreover, Richard Lemon notes, "He was warned that his next picture had to earn enough profit to cover both movies."[39]

In 1952 a journalist named Herbert Luft submitted a hostile essay about Wilder's films—especially *Ace in the Hole*—under the title "A Matter of Decadence," to the *Quarterly of Film, Radio, and Television.* Because it was clearly one-sided, the editors wisely invited Charles Brackett, who was now president of the Academy of Motion Picture Arts and Sciences, to supply a rebuttal. Brackett graciously agreed to do so, particularly because he wanted to demonstrate that he still had faith in his erstwhile collaborator. Brackett accordingly wrote an essay titled "A Matter of Humor." The essays were published together as "Two Views of a Director" in the Fall 1952 issue of the *Quarterly.*

Luft weighed in with the objection that Wilder, "like many Germans"— though Wilder's heritage was Austrian—"depicted only the weaknesses and shortcomings of the American people in films like *A Foreign Affair, Sunset Boulevard,* and *Ace in the Hole.*" Luft contended in his broadside against Wilder that these films denigrated America and that Wilder was himself anti-American.[40] Brackett replied emphatically that he found Wilder "sassy and brash and often unwise; but he was in love with America as I have seen few people in love with it."[41]

Luft reserved his biggest blast for *Ace in the Hole,* which in his judgment was Wilder's most corrupt film: it implies not only that newspaper reporters are prone to sensationalize the news but that Americans are insensitive sensation seekers who "take guided tours of the cave where a man is virtually buried alive."[42] Brackett maintained that, on the contrary, *Ace in the Hole* was "in the vein of American self-criticism which has been a major current in our national literature since the days of *The Octopus* and *The Jungle.*" Frank Norris's *The Octopus* (1901) and Upton Sinclair's *The Jungle* (1906) were in the muckraking tradition of American letters—social protest novels deploring the plight of the downtrodden working classes in America. In conclusion, Brackett noted Luft's contention that Wilder flayed the characters in his films and explained that Wilder rather acknowledged that "time, which flays us all mercilessly," spares no one.[43]

Wilder's brooding tale is galvanized by Kirk Douglas's astounding performance as the tormented protagonist. When Douglas won the AFI's Life Achievement Award in 1991, George Stevens Jr. paid this tribute to him: "No other leading actor was ever more ready to tap the dark, desperate side of the soul and thus to reveal the complexity of human nature. His special gift had been to show us the flaws in every hero and the virtues in every heel."[44] Douglas's Chuck Tatum certainly exemplifies Stevens's statement.

*Ace in the Hole* has been rediscovered as a picture of quality in recent years by critics and film historians. On August 16, 2002, the AFI officially proclaimed this movie as an overlooked masterpiece by presenting a special screening of the picture in Los Angeles, hosted by film director Neil LaBute (*In the Company of Men*). The rediscovery of the film was highlighted by a full week's run at New York's Film Forum in January 2007, in which a newly restored print was screened. On that occasion, Wilder was called "the most precise, indeed, relentless, chronicler of the postwar American scene, in shade as well as light, the motion pictures have ever produced." Manohla Dargis praised how nimbly *Ace in the Hole* presents Wilder's jaundiced view of American hucksterism.[45]

After Wilder's partnership with Brackett ended, he tried out a number of script collaborators, but none more than once, because, in his estimation, they did not cut the mustard. Wilder parted company with Newman and Samuels by mutual agreement after *Ace in the Hole* foundered. None of them wished to tackle another screenplay together, with that fiasco hanging over their heads. Wilder next turned to Edwin Blum, a veteran screenwriter whose credits included *The Adventures of Sherlock Holmes* (1939), Basil Rathbone's first outing as Holmes, and Jules Dassin's *The Canterville Ghost* (1944), an Oscar Wilde fantasy with Charles Laughton. Blum was under contract to Paramount, and the studio executives considered him an experienced screenwriter.

## *Stalag 17* (1953)

Wilder knew he had to be very cautious in the selection of his next project, in the wake of his recent debacle. He reasoned that a popular Broadway play would be a safe bet. "I used to go to New York every year and see the new plays," he told me, "and when I saw one I liked, I considered filming it." He eventually chose *Stalag 17,* a smash hit by Donald Bevan and Edmund Trzcinski. The production, directed by Jose Ferrer, had opened at the Forty-eighth Street Theatre on May 8, 1951. Wilder had seen it on his excursion to New York and considered it a valuable property. The play is set in a German prisoner-of-war camp during World War II—a prison camp very much like the one in which Bevan and Trzcinski had been interned.

When Wilder suggested the project to Paramount, however, he found that a reader in the story department had earlier submitted an unfavorable report on the original version of the play, which had opened in a trial run in Philadelphia on April 6, 1949, with the unwieldy title *Stalag XVII-B.* The reader's report said that the play was "monotonous and lacking in action" and recommended that the studio not acquire it for filming. But that report was filed before the revised version of the play opened on Broadway in 1951 and became a runaway success. When the play was resubmitted to Paramount, the studio brass this time around found it a very promising property. At Wilder's behest Paramount shelled out one hundred thousand dollars for the screen rights in August 1951.[46] The jungle telegraph at the studio spread the word that Wilder was once more in the studio's good graces.

Bevan and Trzcinski described the play as a comedy-melodrama about American GIs interned in a Nazi prisoner-of-war camp. It is marked by liberal doses of raucous barracks humor, but it is rooted in the despair of men confined in a squalid prison compound for the foreseeable future. Blum did not immediately understand why the play appealed to Wilder and asked him what he saw in it. Without batting an eyelash, Wilder replied, "There are guys running around in their underwear. . . . You didn't see it, so you don't appreciate it."[47] Blum was still incredulous about the merits of the play, but he had just been put on salary at one thousand dollars a week; hence he was not inclined to argue the point.

The title of the play refers to a German *Stalag,* short for *stamm lager* (prisoner-of-war camp). The real Stalag 17 was situated on the outskirts of Krems, Austria, near the Danube and less than fifty miles from Vienna.

*Stalag 17* and *The Emperor Waltz* are the only two Wilder pictures set in his native Austria. Wilder preferred to overlook that his homeland was part of the Nazi empire at the time *Stalag 17* takes place, so the setting of the film is not identified as Austria.

Wilder retained the fundamental story line of the play. The prisoners endeavor to smoke out a Nazi informer their captors have planted in their midst, disguised as an American prisoner. Their chief suspect is J. J. Sefton, a loner and a black-market profiteer whom they dislike and distrust. Hence Sefton is determined to uncover the real spy and avoid being his scapegoat.

Wilder set out to spruce up the play, first of all with some new characters. He created Sefton's minion Cookie (who would be played by Gil Stratton Jr.) to provide a voice-over narration. Stratton said, "Billy wanted the narration, so that, if something in the script needed to be explained," he could cover it with a line added to the narration. Stratton continued, "The original script opened in the Paramount barbershop, where Cookie is a barber after the war." Y. Frank Freeman, the vice president of Paramount, comes in for a haircut, and Cookie asks him, "Why haven't you made a picture about POWs, when you have made movies about flyers and infantrymen? I was a POW." With that, Cookie begins to recount his experiences in Stalag 17 to Freeman, and the events of the film are portrayed in flashback. "At the end, the picture comes back to the barbershop," Stratton explained. "Cookie tells Freeman that Sefton reenlisted when the Korean War broke out, and is now in Korea," pulling off the same kinds of scams on the other soldiers that he did in Stalag 17. Since Wilder never got along with Freeman, it is amazing that Freeman agreed to do a cameo in Wilder's movie. Be that as it may, Wilder retained the narrator but scrapped the prologue and epilogue in the barbershop. "And he was right not to use this material," concluded Stratton, since Wilder thought it was a bit arch.[48]

Another key character whom Wilder invented for the movie was Colonel von Scherbach, the commandant of the prison camp, who is referred to in the play but never appears on stage. Wilder called on his fellow Austrian émigré director Otto Preminger to play the commandant. Preminger told me, "I played only Nazis during the war, because there were no Nazis available to do it. Later on I played the Commandant for my old friend Billy Wilder in *Stalag 17*."[49] In his first scene, Preminger sets the tone for his depiction of the nasty commandant as he snarls, with maniacal glee, "Nobody has ever escaped from Stalag 17—not alive, anyway." It was ironic that Preminger played Nazis so convincingly, since he was, like Wilder, "a Jewish refugee who had to flee from Hitler."[50] Preminger's enacting the role of a

Nazi officer in the present film recalls Erich von Stroheim's playing Rommel in *Five Graves to Cairo,* although von Scherbach is certainly more stiff-necked and inflexible than Rommel in the earlier movie.

There is one strategic question that confronts any filmmaker who wants to film a stage play: To what extent should the play be opened out spatially for the screen, by including more settings than were possible in the theater, to exploit the greater flexibility of the motion picture medium? Asked this question, Wilder answered that, on the one hand, he wanted to build up the claustrophobic atmosphere of prison life in *Stalag 17* by emphasizing in his visual compositions the cramped conditions in which the prisoners live: "I wanted the audience to experience the confinement of the prisoners, and therefore I shot no scenes outside of the prison compound." Indeed, *Stalag 17* is Wilder's most enclosed film. On the other hand, Wilder said, he would not consider having the movie take place entirely on one set, barrack 4, which is crammed with bunks. He opened out the play for the screen effectively, explains Holden's biographer Bob Thomas, "by taking the action outdoors into the muddy prison yard, so he could get some of the drama out in the open."[51]

What's more, in transposing *Stalag 17* from stage to screen, Wilder decided to write into the action events that take place offstage and are merely related in dialogue passages in the play. For example, the scene in which Commandant von Scherbach interrogates Lieutenant Dunbar (played by Don Taylor in the film), a prisoner accused of sabotage, is staged in the commandant's office in the movie.

Wilder also added some incidents to the screenplay that are not in the play at all. They are built around Sefton's character as a crafty con man who learns to capitalize on the misery of his fellow inmates by pandering to the lowest tastes of his fellow prisoners of war and bartering with the prison guards for cameras, bottles of wine, and other contraband items.[52] His foot locker becomes a treasure chest of cartons of cigarettes, watches, and other amenities. Sefton obtains a makeshift telescope from one of the guards. He then charges his fellow inmates two cigarettes or a candy bar as admission for a peep show he has set up in the barracks—through the telescope, they can ogle the naked female prisoners as they parade by the dusty window of the delousing shack in the women's compound across the way. "You couldn't catch much through the steam," Cookie comments in his voice-over narration. "But believe you me, after two years in that camp, just the idea of what was behind that steam sure spurred up your voltage." Donald Bevan explained, "The Russian broads," as the GIs call them, "were not in the play, but similar incidents did happen in a POW camp."

Wilder obviously made some significant alterations in the play when he adapted it for the screen. In the process, with Blum's assistance, he rewrote most of the play's dialogue. Bevan did not mind, but his coauthor, Trzcinski, was offended by the many changes. He complained that he no longer recognized the play that he and Bevan had written. Trzcinski had a small part in the film, as a prisoner named Triz, but he stopped speaking to Wilder after shooting was finished. "If I'd been him, I would have stopped too," Wilder admitted.[53] Nevertheless, Wilder was sure that he had vastly improved the play by revising it for film as he did.

As usual, Wilder did not complete the shooting script until the last minute. The shooting script is dated January 30, 1952, four days before principal photography was scheduled to begin. Consequently, Wilder was once again tardy in making a copy of the script available to the industry censor; it was delivered to Breen's office on February 1. The rowdy barracks humor, which offers much-needed comic relief from the picture's darker moments, bothered Breen the most. He objected to the crude phrases employed by one GI to another such as, "Why don't you take this whistle and shove it?" Wilder sought to justify such rough language as typical of soldiers in wartime. One of the inmates, Stosh Krusawa, an oversexed lug, is fittingly nicknamed "Animal." He is a "brawny, unshaven retard in long johns."[54] Stosh asks a prison guard whether some of the Russian broads from the neighboring compound might visit the GIs' barracks. He urges, "Just get us a couple with big glockenspiels!"[55] Following his customary procedure in negotiating with Breen, Wilder made a token gesture of cooperation by changing a few lines, such as the one about the whistle. But he politely ignored some of Breen's other objections. Thus the double entendre about the "glockenspiels" remained in the shooting script.[56]

The Christmas party scene, which is not in the play, in particular disturbed Breen. In it Stosh gets soused on the potent schnapps Sefton brews from potato peels, which Harry, Stosh's sidekick and a real chump, says tastes like nitric acid. Strictly for laughs, Harry stuffs straw under his hat and masquerades as Betty Grable, Stosh's favorite pinup. The prisoners have voted Grable "the girl they would most like to have behind barbed wire," and Harry once promised to get Stosh a date with Grable after the war. In his woozy state, Stosh mistakes Harry for Grable. As the phonograph is playing a popular song of the time, "I Love You," Stosh timidly asks Harry for a dance. Wilder conveys Stosh's illusion by superimposing a photograph of Grable over a shot of Harry, who then turns into Grable. Stosh is in a trance until the hallucination wears off. When Stosh finally recognizes Harry as his dance partner, he bursts into tears.

"We are concerned about the scene in which Harry and Stosh dance together," Breen declared in a letter. For starters, Breen was uncomfortable with Harry's cross-dressing. "If there is any inference in the finished scene of a flavor of sex perversion, we will not be able to approve it under the Code." Breen further thought that Stosh should not be crooning some bars of "I Love You" to Harry, nor should he call Harry "darling." Breen was also unnerved by Stosh's "snuggling" with Harry as they danced because it implied a hint of sexual pleasure on Stosh's part.[57]

Wilder promised to consider Breen's suggestions carefully but not necessarily to implement them. Reportedly, Blum asked Wilder what he intended to do about the dance sequence, and Wilder replied, "Not a damned thing!" Truth to tell, the scene remained unchanged in the final shooting script, and Breen did not raise the issue again.[58] After all, innuendo is a slippery target for a censor. Furthermore, Breen, who had held his office since 1930, was soon to retire and be replaced by his chief assistant, Geoffrey Shurlock. Perhaps because his time in office was running out, Breen was not as strict about implementing the censorship code as he had been in the past.

Wilder, with Blum's aid, had turned out a fine screenplay, one that Wilder was proud of. Be that as it may, Edwin Blum, like Raymond Chandler before him, vowed never to collaborate with Wilder again. Blum regarded the writing role he had been assigned as "little more than a butler" or glorified stenographer. "My name is in the credits, but I don't think of the script as mine. Oh, I made some important contributions," especially in beefing up the characterization of Sefton. "When you work with Billy, he rules you a thousand percent. I know . . . the more he likes you, the more sarcastic he gets. But I couldn't take the insults." Blum recalled one of Wilder's insulting diatribes: "My God, I have a cretin collaborating with me! You should listen to the rotten words he uses," Wilder exclaimed to their fellow screenwriters at the writers' table in the commissary. "Eddie, when I had Charlie Brackett as my partner, he came up with exquisite words. . . . He was a literate man, not an ignoramus like you."[59]

Wilder never noticed his inconsistency in admitting that he needed a collaborator because "I speak lousy English" and criticizing Blum's vocabulary. One day, when he was really fed up, Blum retorted, "Billy, you roar like a lion; but you got no teeth. All I feel is soft, flabby gums."[60] That shut Wilder up—for the moment, at least. Asked about Blum, Wilder responded, "I worked with him on the script of a very good picture, *Stalag 17*, but I never worked with him again." In Wilder's opinion, Blum did not make a significant contribution to the script.[61] Like Chandler, Blum failed to mention when complaining about Wilder that Wilder kept him on salary throughout the production period and consulted him about script revisions along the way. This was an unusual courtesy for a screenwriter at the time.

In casting the picture, Wilder recruited some actors from the Broadway play, including Robert Strauss (Stosh) and Harvey Lembeck (Harry), who were priceless as the dimwitted prison pals. Wilder needed a major star familiar to the mass audience for Sefton; the studio at first urged Charlton Heston on Wilder. But Wilder eventually decided Sefton was too much of a conniving, hard-bitten hustler to be played by Heston, who normally played nobler types. *Stalag 17* was ahead of its time in presenting an American soldier as an antihero, before it had become fashionable in the American cinema to present such a character in unflattering light. Wilder finally picked William Holden, who had become an important star after *Sunset Boulevard*. At first Holden rejected the role; he had attended the play in New York and walked out after the first act. He found the stage play dull and thought Sefton was merely a garden-variety con man. But Holden changed his mind when he read the script, in which Wilder and Blum had cleverly built up Sefton's role and made him a heel who turns out to be a hero. With *Stalag 17* Holden became Wilder's favorite leading man. "My love will always be with Mr. Holden," he said.[62] Sig Ruman, a veteran of *Ninotchka* and *The Emperor Waltz*, played Johann Sebastian Schulz, a barracks guard who clowns around with the inmates at times (his favorite wisecrack to Harry is "Droppen sie dead!"). But Schulz is a lot slyer than he appears—he is in cahoots with the barracks informant.

Ernest Laszlo had served his apprenticeship as camera operator on *The Major and the Minor* and other films. Since then he had become a director of photography in his own right and had earned recognition for films like Rudolph Maté's film noir *D.O.A.* (1950). He did so by achieving a more realistic look for the films he photographed, instead of the usual "soft, glossy visual style" of most Paramount films.[63] As such, he was the perfect choice for *Stalag 17*. Laszlo's atmospheric cinematography captured the sordid setting of a POW camp, utilizing deep grays and blacks in keeping with the somber dramatics.

The studio allocated a budget of $1,315,000 for *Stalag 17,* somewhat less than the budget for *Ace in the Hole,* but still adequate for Wilder's needs. Wilder's fee for coauthoring the screenplay and directing and producing the picture would be $250,000. The budget was sufficient to allow the production staff to build Wilder his very own prison camp for filming exteriors at Snow Ranch in Calabasas, California, forty miles northwest of Hollywood. Production designers Franz Bachelin and Hal Pereira constructed wooden shacks and barracks for the prisoners, along with gun turrets and observation towers for the guards.

The weatherman predicted plenty of rain in Calabasas during February 1952, when Wilder would be shooting there for ten days. That guaranteed gray skies and acres of mud, which contributed to the bleak landscape of the camp. All in all, Wilder was successful in creating the degraded atmosphere of the prison compound. When the viewer sees the mud and lice that are so characteristic of a prison camp, it is difficult to believe that the film was shot almost entirely in a Hollywood studio and on a ranch in Southern California.

Principal photography began on February 2. Preminger, with his thick German accent, was central casting's concept of a Nazi. He had a reputation for berating cast and crew at the top of his voice on the set. He once endeavored to put a nervous actor at ease by glaring at him nose-to-nose and hollering, "RELAX!" On the first day of shooting *Stalag 17*, Preminger was fidgety about appearing in front of the camera for the first time in a great while. As a prank, Wilder pasted his face against Preminger's and shouted, "RELAX!" Only Wilder could have gotten away with that. One actor noted that Preminger was parodying himself in *Stalag 17*. He added that the commandant whom Preminger played was "Otto on a good day."[64]

Preminger told me, "I had trouble remembering my lines."[65] Wilder recalled that, when Preminger forgot a line, "he would get very embarrassed and say he was rusty because he hadn't acted in so many years. So he said he would send me a pound of caviar every time that he had a day when he blew his lines. Well, several pounds of caviar arrived for me in the course of shooting that film, but Preminger gave a fine performance." Wilder said elsewhere, "Directors are not difficult to direct, because they remember the problems which they have had with their actors when they are directing. As a result, they will bend over backward to be helpful."[66]

Wilder could be as stubborn as a Prussian general in dealing with the studio brass. He was summoned by the front office and advised that it was improper for Stosh and a couple of the other prisoners to be wearing filthy underwear. He was told that he must stop having the men "running around looking so dirty." Wilder responded with acrimony: "Like hell I will! I will close down the picture, and you can have somebody else do it."[67] The men wore their grungy union suits for the rest of the movie.

Holden occasionally lost his patience during shooting. The actors who had appeared in the stage play had developed a camaraderie, and they sometimes indulged in boisterous horseplay between takes. Wilder did not mind, but it irked Holden, who finally snapped one day and yelled, "Goddammit! Can't you guys shut up for a minute? Some of us are trying to get some work done!"[68] Strauss and the others who were making a commotion were startled by the scolding and complied. Holden took his role very seriously indeed. He was uneasy about the fact that Sefton was trafficking in black-market goods with the Nazi guards. Holden wanted the audience to like Sefton because he wanted them to like *him*. "Could I have a line or two that shows that I really hate the Germans?" Holden implored Wilder. But Wilder refused. Sefton was "an unsentimental opportunist," he explained to Holden. Otherwise he could not have been so successful in conning the guards and the other prisoners with his crooked deals.[69]

Some sources say that Holden did not become a problem drinker until he was making *The Bridge on the River Kwai* on location in Ceylon (now Sri Lanka) in 1956. But Gil Stratton said that he noticed Holden occasionally taking a nip from a flask when he was off the set. Holden sometimes appeared on the set with dark circles under his eyes and was a little unsteady, indicative of a night of drinking.

Because all the action of the film takes place in and around barrack 4, the central set, the scenes in the script could be shot in sequence. In this manner the actors could develop their roles as the plot evolved. As the shooting progressed, Wilder fell five days behind schedule, largely because heavy rains caused delays at Snow Ranch. In addition, Wilder and Blum had continued to revise the script scene by scene throughout the shooting period. They had on occasion gotten behind, and this held up the shooting. Don Hartman, who had followed Buddy De Sylva as head of production at Paramount, finally decreed that Wilder had one more week to finish shooting. Wilder announced that he was finished with rewrites, and he promised to shoot the remaining scenes with maximum efficiency during the last week of filming. Cast and crew agreed to make up for lost time by shooting on three nights until the wee hours of the morning. The production wrapped on March 29, 1952, almost on schedule. Wilder brought the film in for $1,661,530; the front office decided that this was close enough to the original budget, $1,315,000, and did not complain.

During the shooting period, Wilder and supervising editor Doane Harrison, along with the film's editor, George Tomasini, worked out a plan whereby, through careful editing and artful tracking shots, the tempo of the film would never drag, even though much of the action is concentrated in the narrow confines of barrack 4. Hence the final editing of the movie during postproduction went along briskly. This was the only film Tomasini edited for Wilder; he went on to edit seven pictures for Alfred Hitchcock.

Franz Waxman was on hand to compose another score for a Wilder film. Wilder's instructions to Waxman were simple: "Main title and end music;

and in certain sections a drum only." Wilder did allow for source music, as in the Christmas party scene, in which Waxman approximated a dance band playing popular songs that were ostensibly coming from the barracks phonograph. Waxman was in complete accord with Wilder in relying primarily on percussion for the background music throughout the film. Percussion instruments by themselves, Waxman noted, can sound very sinister and menacing in a melodramatic movie about prisoners of war.[70]

During the opening credits, a military band plays "When Johnny Comes Marching Home," featuring brass, snares, and a glockenspiel. The march music accompanies a tracking shot of a Nazi guard with a German shepherd patrolling along a high wire fence. As the story gets under way, it is clear that *Stalag 17* is essentially a whodunit. Sefton must finger the Nazi informer masquerading as an American prisoner if he is to quell his fellow inmates' suspicions about him—they call him a "kraut kisser."

Wilder injects some neat humor into the melodrama to keep the movie from becoming too grim. In Trzcinski's cameo as Triz, he insists on washing his socks in the same kettle in which the inmates' potato soup is boiled, despite their vigorous protests. Even Preminger does a comic turn. Commandant von Scherbach is traipsing around his office in his white silk socks while he interrogates Dunbar, who has been convicted of an act of sabotage. The commandant phones one of the high command in Berlin at one point. While waiting for the call to go through, he has his orderly help him put on his cumbersome black boots so that his superior officer can hear his heels clicking together as he stands at attention. After he hangs up, he has the orderly remove the boots. Wilder was proud of this gag.[71]

Sefton continues his efforts throughout the movie to uncover the real traitor lurking in the barracks. As luck would have it, Sefton quite by accident secretly notices Price, one of the inmates, smuggling a message to a Nazi officer. Sefton subsequently unmasks Price before his fellow inmates; they sheepishly admit that they scapegoated him. Having redeemed himself in the eyes of his fellow prisoners, Sefton then volunteers to secretly escort Dunbar out of the camp before the commandant can have him executed for sabotage. Sefton is about to follow Dunbar through the trapdoor in the barracks floor, which leads to the escape tunnel that will take them out of the compound. Before Sefton descends, Andrew Sarris writes, Sefton "bids a properly cynical adieu to his prison camp buddies": "If I ever run into any of you bums on a street corner, just let's pretend we never met before." But Wilder judged Sefton's parting words to be too spiteful, so he later added a shot of Sefton popping back up through the trapdoor "with a boyish smile and a friendly salute; he then ducks down for good."[72]

In a chilling scene, the other prisoners arrange a condign punishment for Price. They wait until dark and force him out of the front door of the barrack, right into the glare of the searchlights in the prison yard. The Nazi guards mistake him for a prisoner who is attempting to escape and immediately gun him down. Afterward the GIs lie back on their bunks. Cookie begins to whistle "When Johnny Comes Marching Home," a reprise of the march employed in the opening credits. Then, as Jay Nash and Stanley Ross write, "a full orchestra picks it up and thunders triumphantly at the finish."[73]

Audiences found Wilder's adroit mixture of raucous comedy and spine-tingling melodrama very entertaining. The movie is studded with many sharp, earthy one-liners and is also a masterful, gripping motion picture. After a successful advance screening hosted by Paramount in May 1953, the picture opened to enthusiastic notices when it was released nationwide in July. *Stalag 17* grossed $10 million in its first six months of release, making it Wilder's biggest hit for Paramount so far. The studio had warned Wilder that *Stalag 17* had to earn a profit to wipe out the deficit left over from *Ace in the Hole*. *Stalag 17* did in fact make enough money to cover both movies.

At the Academy Award ceremony on March 25, 1954, William Holden, who shrewdly underplayed the role of Sefton, won an Oscar for his assured performance. Holden's wife, Ardis, who was by all accounts a shrew, told him, "Well, you know, Bill, you really didn't get the award for *Stalag 17*," in which she felt his performance was only adequate. "They gave it to you for *Sunset Boulevard*."[74] According to Sam Staggs, "Holden's life had begun already to assume the lineaments of *The Lost Weekend*"; he drowned his resentment toward his wife in drink at an Oscar party.[75] He was still seething when they arrived home. The inebriated Holden missed the driveway and plowed into a lamppost, tearing a fender off his Cadillac. He woke the next morning, still wearing his tuxedo and sitting in an easy chair, with his golden statuette in his lap.[76]

Wilder was nominated for best director but lost to Fred Zinnemann, who won for *From Here to Eternity*. Wilder did not mind losing to his old friend. By the time of *Stalag 17*, some of the promising young filmmakers who got their start on *Menschen am Sonntag* had fallen on dark days. Robert Siodmak's Hollywood career was faltering, and he would soon reverse course by returning to Germany to make pictures. Edgar Ulmer had never risen above making low-budget program pictures for the cost-conscious independent studios collectively known as Poverty Row (where Billy's brother Willie had also wound up). Only Wilder and Zinnemann were still thriving in Hollywood.

The German censorship board banned *Stalag 17* from being exhibited in Germany in 1953. (*A Foreign Affair* had likewise been banned in Germany in 1948; it remained so until 1977.) In 1956 Wilder received a letter from George Weltner, the Paramount executive in charge of world-wide distribution, indicating that the film could be released in Germany—provided that, when the dialogue was dubbed into German, the spy hiding among the prisoners "is not a Nazi, but a Polish prisoner of war" who has sold out to the Nazis. Wilder replied to the Paramount high command, "Fuck you, gentlemen! You ask me, who lost my family in Auschwitz, to permit a change like this? Unless somebody apologizes," Wilder said, he would never make another film for Paramount. "I never heard anything from Paramount," Wilder concluded; "no apology, no nothing."[77] For the record, *Stalag 17* was not altered when it was released in Germany in 1960.[78] It was well received by the press and public there. Wilder himself was pleased with the movie. "Along with *Sunset Boulevard*, it is one of my favorites," he declared unequivocally.[79]

With *Stalag 17*, Wilder had made a successful Broadway play into an equally successful movie. By so doing, he had been reinstated as a major player at Paramount. For his next project, he chose another promising Broadway play, *Sabrina Fair*, which he would bring to the screen as *Sabrina*, a romantic comedy with Audrey Hepburn, Humphrey Bogart, and, once again, William Holden. But at this point Wilder had been associated with Paramount for sixteen years, and he was growing restless.

# 9

# Fascination

## Sabrina and The Seven Year Itch

Vexed again; perplexed again;
Thank God, I can be oversexed again.
Bewitched, bothered, and bewildered am I.
—*Lorenz Hart and Richard Rodgers,*
*"Bewitched"*

It is not uncommon for a studio to buy the screen rights to a Broadway play before it opens to get the jump on rival studios. Samuel Taylor's play *Sabrina Fair: A Woman of the World* had been submitted to Paramount in typescript months before the New York premiere in November 1953. A reader in the story department turned in an enthusiastic report on the play, and this prompted Wilder to get Paramount to purchase the film rights immediately.

Wilder's decision turned out to be a wise one; Taylor's four-act play was a hit and eventually racked up 318 performances. Sabrina is the daughter of Thomas Fairchild, the chauffeur on the estate of the wealthy Larrabee family on Long Island. Sabrina nurtures a crush on David Larrabee, an irresponsible playboy, but eventually falls for Linus, David's older, more sensible brother. Neither David nor Linus takes much notice of Sabrina, however, until she returns from a sojourn in Paris, where she has been transformed into "a woman of the world."

## *Sabrina* (1954)

Samuel Taylor was invited to Hollywood to collaborate with Wilder on the screenplay in the summer of 1953. He had absolutely no experience in writing for the screen and found Wilder an exacting taskmaster. For a start,

Wilder wanted the film to be called *Sabrina,* not *Sabrina Fair.* Taylor pointed out that he drew the play's title from John Milton's masque *Comus* (1637). Sabrina is the ancient name of the goddess of the River Severine: "Sabrina Fair . . . / Listen for dear honor's sake, / Goddess of the silver lake."[1] Wilder insisted that *Sabrina Fair* sounded like one of those dreary English rural comedies, set at a country fair, that inevitably died at the box office in America. Wilder, as usual, got his way, and the title of the film was shortened to *Sabrina.*

Obviously, Wilder did not regard Taylor's play as a sacred text, any more than he thought Bevan and Trzcinski's *Stalag 17* was scripture. Taylor was dismayed when Wilder began excising large chunks of the play's text. Wilder explained that a four-act comedy was too long for a movie under any circumstances, since most stage comedies were three acts at most. What's more, Wilder had to make cuts to make room for additional scenes in the screenplay; for example, he wished to dramatize on screen Sabrina's stint in Paris. This episode is only referred to in the play, which is set entirely in the Larrabee mansion. Wilder also aimed to make the screenplay sharper and funnier than Taylor's talky play, in which the dialogue overexplained everything. In this, Wilder succeeded.

Wilder and Taylor finished a preliminary rough draft by July 1953. By then Taylor had found working with Wilder too taxing. The frustrated playwright abruptly threw up his hands one day and announced that he was returning to New York to oversee the rehearsals of his play, scheduled to open on November 11, 1953. In the Broadway theater, Taylor reasoned, the playwright was respected and listened to, whereas in Hollywood the playwright had little control over how his work was recast for the screen. In 1974 I met Taylor in New York; by then he had received plaudits for his screenplay for Hitchcock's *Vertigo* (1958). Taylor confirmed that he had found Wilder difficult to work with. Nevertheless, he respected Wilder, like Hitchcock, "as a genuine auteur, the true author of every film he makes."

Wilder heard from William Holden about Ernest Lehman, who had just completed the screenplay for Robert Wise's *Executive Suite* (1954) at MGM. Holden was starring in the movie, which was still in production; he informed Wilder that, although *Executive Suite* was Lehman's first movie script, he clearly had an ear for good screen dialogue. In checking on Lehman with a fellow screenwriter at MGM, Wilder learned that Lehman had graduated from City College in New York and had since been freelancing as a writer. The other writer recommended Lehman to Wilder, saying that, on the grounds of Lehman's script for *Executive Suite,* it was evident that he had a gift for the tongue-in-cheek, wry repartee that had distinguished the best films of Ernst Lubitsch. That was all that Wilder had to hear to prompt him to phone Lehman and ask him to replace Taylor immediately.

Lehman told me when I met him at the Cannes Film Festival in 1976 that he inquired when Wilder wanted him to show up at Paramount, and Wilder replied, "How about this afternoon?" Wilder then explained to Lehman the sad state of affairs. Paramount had established a starting date for principal photography in the last week of September 1953, with shooting running through most of November. It was already August, and Wilder had completed only a preliminary rough draft of the script. So he had to get rolling on the final shooting script posthaste. Lehman moved over to Paramount from MGM that afternoon.

There is an old adage in Hollywood that it is suicidal to begin principal photography on a film before the final shooting script is completed. Wilder was violating that sage bromide in spades. The film was already in preproduction, and Wilder and Lehman would have to continue hammering out the final shooting script all the way through the production period. "This was a picture that was still being written and shaped as we went," Wilder moaned. "I don't write; I rewrite."[2]

Lehman was no pushover when it came to defending his point of view; in this respect Wilder had met his match. Lehman could be "as stubborn as the director; and their collaboration was stormy when it wasn't openly hostile," writes Donald Spoto.[3] Like Edwin Blum, Ernest Lehman never got used to the fact that Wilder dished out insulting wisecracks even to people he liked. Lehman told me that Wilder called him all sorts of nasty names, ranging from "a eunuch, a misogynist, and a queer" to "a middle-class Jewish prude." Lehman concluded, "Wilder never grasped how his jibes offended his friends." Not surprisingly, Lehman found collaborating with Wilder exasperating and exhausting. When Lehman tossed Wilder a line of dialogue, Wilder invariably replied, "Very good; but let's make it better."[4] What Lehman did not know was that Wilder was telling Lehman what Lubitsch had said repeatedly to him.

Despite Wilder's quarrels with Lehman, which recalled his arguments with Brackett, they turned out what Philip Kemp terms "a witty, literate, well-paced, and stylish" screenplay for *Sabrina*. Yet Richard Corliss has written off Lehman as a "mere service station attendant of other writers' vehicles." Kemp counters that Corliss's view seems "singularly inapt," in view of Lehman's shrewdly gauged collaboration with Wilder on *Sabrina*.[5]

Since preproduction was in full swing when Lehman began working on *Sabrina*, Wilder was busy with casting the picture as well as writing the final shooting script. He settled on Audrey Hepburn to play the title role; as a matter of fact, Wilder considered the movie first and foremost a vehicle for her. Hepburn's first big film was *Roman Holiday,* in which she played a runaway princess in Rome; it would not be released until September. But its director, William Wyler, assured Wilder that Hepburn had given a star-making performance. "I saw the test that Wyler made with her," Wilder remembered, "and I was absolutely crazy about her."[6] In the test she radiates poise and beauty as she recalls studying ballet when she was growing up.

When Hepburn's casting was announced, Wilder gave a press conference in which he decried "the number of drive-in waitresses" being groomed for stardom; they just "wiggle their behinds at the camera." By contrast, said Wilder, Audrey Hepburn, at age twenty-four, was known for her grace and elegance. "God kissed her on the cheek, and there she was." Hepburn had class and intelligence as well as beauty, he concluded. "She looks as if she could spell *schizophrenia.*"[7] Later on he told Hepburn that, for him, it was love at first sight when she walked onto the set. He confessed that he talked in his sleep about Audrey, but fortunately his wife's name was Audrey as well, "so I got away with it."[8] In *Sabrina* Audrey Hepburn grows up to be a fairy princess solely because of her "charm and beauty," Peter Bogdanovich writes. Wilder retained the play's Cinderella theme in his film; as he put it, there could be no more perfect Cinderella than Audrey Hepburn.[9]

Wilder had no trouble in convincing William Holden to do his third Wilder film, as David Larrabee. Casting Linus Larrabee, however, presented a knotty problem. Cary Grant had agreed to play the part of David's older brother, but he changed his mind and bowed out one week before filming was to begin. Grant had decided he did not want to play a stuffed shirt like Linus who was in love with a much younger woman. Wilder needed a star of Grant's stature, and Humphrey Bogart was available, so Wilder offered the part to Bogart. At fifty-four, Bogart was twenty-five years older than his wife, Lauren Bacall, and yet he had made four pictures with Bacall. So Bogart as Linus could be a credible love interest for Audrey Hepburn's Sabrina.

Wilder went to Bogart's home in Holmby Hills to convince him to take the part. Bogart accepted the role reluctantly; he had an inferiority complex about playing a part originally intended for Cary Grant. Still, Bogart was mollified in some degree by the substantial salary of $200,000 he would receive—considerably more than Holden ($80,000) and Hepburn ($25,000) were allotted. Bogart cited an old bromide attributed to Sam Goldwyn, "You must take the bitter with the sour."[10] Still, throughout the shoot, Bogart needled Wilder about preferring Grant to him. As a matter of fact, one of the handicaps Wilder and Lehman experienced in composing the final shooting script was that they had to tailor the role of Linus for Bogart, who, unlike Grant, had never played light romantic comedy.

This is not to say that Bogart was miscast as Linus Larrabee. Despite his tough-guy image in pictures, Bogart's background was one of "inherited wealth," as Richard Schickel is at pains to emphasize in *Bogie*. He grew up in a privileged, upper-class family in New York City. What's more, he had often played classy romantic leads on the Broadway stage in the 1920s. He was probably the first stage actor to utter to his country club companions a line that has since become a cliché: "Tennis, anyone?"[11]

Wilder managed to corral for *Sabrina* three trusted associates who had collaborated with him on previous pictures: film editor Arthur Schmidt (*Sunset Boulevard*), composer Frederick Hollander (*A Foreign Affair*), and cinematographer Charles Lang (*Ace in the Hole*). Since *Sabrina* was scheduled to go before the cameras with two weeks of location work on Long Island, Wilder, Lehman, Lang, and Doane Harrison, Wilder's longtime supervising editor, embarked for New York on September 22, 1953. The rest of the film unit would follow in a couple of days.

Wilder had no trouble securing an ideal location at Glen Cove, Long Island, to stand in for the Larrabee estate in the movie; it was the property of Barney Balaban, the president of Paramount. After shooting exteriors at Glen Cove, the cast and crew returned to Hollywood, where Wilder was scheduled to film interiors at Paramount for seven weeks. Filming resumed on October 6. The following day, Wilder submitted the shooting script to the front office. "But the shooting script was still not finished," said Wilder.[12]

By day, Wilder directed the picture while Lehman labored on the script alone. In the evenings, they worked together, with Wilder kibitzing on what Lehman had written. The writing partners continued grinding out new pages in a frenzy. But they could scarcely keep up with the shooting schedule; they wrote some scenes the night before they were to be shot. Lehman's nerves got increasingly ragged, while Wilder survived each night on black coffee and cigarettes. "It was agonizing, desperate work," Lehman remembered, "and at times our health broke down from the effort." Wilder had some sleepless nights when his back troubled him, as it always did when he was operating under a great deal of stress.

One afternoon, Wilder ambled up to Harrison, his right-hand man, and said casually, "Please get the electricians to invent some complicated lighting effects for the next scene that will take some time." Puzzled, Harrison inquired, "What for?" Without raising his voice, Wilder replied, "We haven't got the goddamed dialogue written yet!" Harrison then instructed Lang to have the crew create a varied range of gray and dark, shadowy tones for the night scene coming up, so that Wilder and Lehman could finish revising the scene. Little wonder that Lehman called *Sabrina* the scariest experience he ever had in his life.[13]

The shoot also proved to be an ordeal for most of the cast and crew, said Martha Hyer. She played David Larrabee's fiancée, whom David largely ignores once he becomes attracted to Sabrina. "There was much friction, side-taking, and intrigues during the filming," she said, especially from Bogart. Perhaps he was insecure because "he didn't feel comfortable in the part."[14] Bogart's son Stephen put it more bluntly. "Bogie seemed to bask in his role as a troublemaker," and make trouble he did on the set of *Sabrina*.[15] According to his biographer, Jeffrey Meyers, Bogart "was unstable, edgy, and somewhat paranoid" about playing high comedy. Furthermore, he was "drinking more than was good for him."[16] Bogart had always been a heavy drinker. He no longer drank his lunch, but he regularly had his secretary, Verita Petersen, bring him a glass of Scotch on the set at five o'clock, an hour before quitting time. As he sipped the whiskey between takes, Bogart became even more dyspeptic and surly.

As filming progressed, Wilder took to inviting Holden and Hepburn to his office for drinks at the end of the day. Bogart, whom Wilder did not find congenial company, was not included. When Wilder discovered that Bogart felt ostracized, however, he gave Bogart a belated invitation to join the group each afternoon. Bogart curtly turned Wilder down, since he had not been asked to join Wilder's "clique" at the outset. From then on, the battle lines were definitely drawn. Bogart resented Wilder, Holden, and Hepburn as having formed a conspiracy against him.

Wilder shrugged off Bogart's antipathy as best he could. "I get along very well with actors," he declared, "except when I have to work with sons-of-bitches like Mr. Bogart. . . . He was crazy, Bogart was; I knew I was on his list of bastards." But Wilder consoled himself that, once a picture is finished, a director's relationship with an actor is over. After all, "you're not married to them!"[17]

Bogart continued to snipe at Wilder and at his two costars. At one point Wilder handed Bogart the new script pages. After looking them over, Bogart inquired whether Wilder had any children. "Yes," Wilder responded, "a thirteen-year-old daughter." Bogart pitched the pages back at Wilder and barked, "Did she write this?"[18]

Bogart even maliciously mocked Wilder's German accent. When Wilder was under pressure, his accent became more pronounced. One day he gave a direction to Bogart, "Giff me here a little more faster." Bogart jeered at him: "Hey, Wilhelm, would you not mind translating that remark into English? I don't schpeak so good the Cherman, *jawhohl!*"[19] Bogart later explained to the press that he thought Wilder was too authoritarian. Wilder, he said, was "the kind of Prussian German with a riding crop." Bogart continued, "He's the type of director I don't like to work with. He works with the writer and excludes the actor. It irritated me, so I went to work on him. One thing led to another. This picture *Sabrina* is a crock of crap anyway."[20]

On another occasion, Bogart complained that Wilder strutted around the set like a "kraut bastard Nazi son-of-a bitch."[21] Wilder finally had had enough. After all, it was common knowledge in the film colony that Wilder's mother, stepfather, and grandmother were victims of the Holocaust. Wilder addressed Bogart in measured tones: "Mr. Bogart, some actors are talented and some actors are shits. You, Mr. Bogart, are a talented shit."[22]

Wilder told journalist Ezra Goodman a couple of years later that Bogart "surrounds himself with whipping boys, aspiring young directors like Richard Brooks," who had directed Bogart in the Korean War movie *Battle Circus* (1953). "He exposes them to ridicule; and they have to like it," because they want to direct an established star like Bogart. But experienced directors like Joseph Mankiewicz, who directed Bogart in *The Barefoot Contessa* (1954), and, of course, Billy Wilder, "don't take that from him."[23]

Bogart's paranoia particularly focused on William Holden, who was the matinee idol Bogart had once been. Bogart accused Holden of trying to steal the picture by upstaging him during their scenes together. Moreover, Bogart noticed Holden puffing on a cigarette and was certain that Holden was attempting to make him cough when saying his lines. Bogart stormed at Wilder, "That fucking Holden over there, waving cigarettes around, blowing smoke in my face, crumpling up papers. I want this sabotage ended, Mr. Wilder."[24] Wilder, who wrote "Cum Deo" on the first page of every screenplay, began to think God was deserting him. He rolled his eyes to the heavens and did not reply to Bogart. In his effort to needle Holden, Bogart called him "lover boy," ridiculing Holden's good looks. Bogart implied that "pretty boy" Holden was merely a movie star and not a serious actor.

"I hated the bastard," said Holden; "he was always stirring things up when he didn't have to."[25] Still, Holden usually lived up to Wilder's expectations as an agreeable and cooperative actor, except for those times when he was in his cups. Holden's drinking problem had become more pronounced since *Sunset Boulevard* and *Stalag 17*. Bogart too was a heavy drinker, but he was more in control of his drinking than Holden. One afternoon, after he had had a liquid lunch, Holden showed up on the set bleary-eyed, in an alcoholic stupor. He was in no condition to work, and he kept forgetting his lines. "Methinks the lad has partaken too much of the grape," Bogart sneered, adding that Holden was "a dumb prick."[26] Holden, enraged, threw a punch at his costar, and Bogart retaliated. Wilder, acting as referee, had to pull them apart; he then ordered Holden to retire to his dressing room and rest until he sobered up. Asked by a reporter for his opinion of Bogart, Holden answered with circumspection that Bogart was "an actor of consummate skill, with an ego to match." Yet the antipathy between Bogart and Holden was never visible in their performances on the screen, and as Wilder was fond of saying, "What the audience sees is all that matters."[27]

Not even the winsome Audrey Hepburn could escape Bogart's wrath, since he saw her as part of the clique with Wilder and Holden. Wilder and Lehman were still falling behind in their revisions of the shooting script, and one morning when Hepburn arrived at the studio, she was handed new pages of revised dialogue. The pages had been ripped out of Lehman's typewriter only a few hours before. When Hepburn fumbled her lines during the first take, Wilder was understanding, but Bogart, who had an uncanny facility to master his lines, smirked, "Maybe you should stay home and study your lines, instead of going out every night." Hepburn smiled graciously; she was a young, inexperienced actress and Bogart was an old pro. She was not going to bicker with a cranky star. Bogart later said to a reporter, speaking of Hepburn, "Yeah, she's great, if you can give her twenty takes."[28]

Audrey Hepburn was not going out every night, as Bogart charged, but she did spend some nights with William Holden, with whom she was having an affair. They would meet in a small apartment that Holden had rented for their secret trysts. When the picture wrapped, Holden offered to divorce Ardis and marry Audrey. "When Audrey learned that Holden was no longer able to have children, her affection cooled," writes David Hofstede. She wanted to be a mother as well as a wife; she ended the affair immediately.[29] Wilder claimed that he was not aware of their love affair while he was shooting the picture; Holden and Hepburn made every effort to conceal it from him.[30]

Bogart's "list of bastards" also included Ernest Lehman, since Bogart resented that Wilder spent more time conferring with his writing partner than with the actors. One day Lehman rushed onto the set to distribute the new script pages that he and Wilder had finished rewriting only that morning. He did not bring enough copies, however, and he ran out before he got to Bogart. "Where's mine?" Bogart demanded. "I don't have another copy," Lehman mumbled sheepishly. Bogart hollered, "Get that City College bum out of here and send him back to Monogram [a Poverty Row studio] where he belongs!"[31]

Lehman, still a young screenwriter, was devastated by Bogart's vicious outburst. Wilder called a halt to the rehearsal: "There will be no further shooting on this picture until Mr. Bogart apologizes to Mr. Lehman." Bogart walked over to Lehman and said, "Come on into my dressing room for a drink later, kid." The rehearsal resumed.[32] Like Holden, Wilder acknowledged that Bogart was "a tremendously competent actor." Nevertheless, Bogart was also a boor; "his barbs were uncouth." Wilder continued, "I learned from the master, Erich von Stroheim"; compared to him, Bogart's needling "was just child's play. You have to be much wittier than Bogart to be *that* mean."[33]

Not surprisingly, the pressure of reworking the screenplay under the gun was getting to be too much for Lehman. During one story conference, he collapsed from nervous exhaustion and began sobbing uncontrollably. Wilder put his arm around him and whispered, "Nobody's ever worked harder than you, Ernie." He told Lehman to grab a cab, go home, and rest; he then closed down production for a couple of days. Lehman's physician, Raymond Spritzler, ordered bed rest for his patient. But the irrepressible Wilder sneaked over to Lehman's house one evening to confer about the script. Soon the doctor arrived at the front door for a house call, and Wilder scrambled into the nearest closet before Spritzler entered the bedroom. After the doctor pronounced Lehman fit enough to return to work, Lehman said, "Well, Doc, I guess I can tell Mr. Wilder to come out now."[34] Wilder said casually that doctors simply did not understand the demands of the picture business.

In late November, production chief Don Hartman instructed Wilder that, since he was already over schedule, shooting must be completed by the end of the week. Wilder still had one scene that had not been revised yet. It contained a long speech, full of fatherly advice, delivered by Fairchild the chauffeur (John Williams) to his daughter Sabrina as he drives her to the pier to board the *Liberté* for her sojourn in Paris. Wilder saved the unfinished scene for the final day of filming, December 5. He and Lehman started reworking it during their lunch hour and completed it around dinnertime. Fairchild's speech was lengthy and complex, and Williams could not get it right. Legend has it that Wilder filmed seventy-two takes before Williams got his lines down; Wilder remembered only about half that many. At 9:30 P.M. Williams at last got the speech perfect, and Wilder exclaimed, "Cut! Print! That's a wrap!"[35] Wilder ended up eleven days behind schedule, with a final budget of $2,238,813, close enough to the original budget to elicit no complaints from the suits in the front office.

The picture begins with Audrey Hepburn as Sabrina introducing the film, in Wilder fashion, in a voice-over on the sound track. This prologue has the flavor of a fairy tale, prefiguring Sabrina as a Cinderella who is transformed into a graceful fairy princess by the time she returns from Paris: "Once upon a time, on the north shore of Long Island, some twenty miles from New York, there lived a small girl on a large estate. There was a chauffeur named Thomas Fairchild, who had a daughter named Sabrina. The Larrabees were giving a party . . ." The elflike Sabrina is perched in a tree, gazing dreamily at the couples waltzing on the Larrabees' terrace to the strains of "Isn't It Romantic?" Sabrina yearns to be a part of the Larrabees' high life, but she is an outsider, watching their elegant ball from afar.

Later in the picture, David Larrabee whistles "Isn't It Romantic?" as he encounters Sabrina on her return from Paris, just as Captain Pringle whistles the same tune when he is on his way to a rendezvous with Erika in *A Foreign Affair.*

A full moon shines above Sabrina as she sits on a tree branch, foreshadowing her father's repeated warning, "Don't reach for the moon, child." But Sabrina is doing just that, since she is mooning over David Larrabee, the younger of the two Larrabee sons. David, however, is little more than a feckless playboy; he is annually listed on his brother Linus's tax return as a six-hundred-dollar deduction. This is Sabrina's last night on the Larrabees' palatial estate; the following day she departs for Paris and a two-year course in a cooking school, arranged by her father.

By the time Sabrina returns from Paris, Cinderella has blossomed into a fairy princess, and David notices her; she is an intriguing mixture of sex appeal and innocence. She has eyes only for David, who is a jaunty, devil-may-care chap. By contrast, Linus appears to be a stuffy, conservative businessman. He carries an umbrella even on a sunshiny day, indicating that he is overcautious, afraid to take a chance even on the weather.

Sabrina wonders if she stands a chance in marrying David. "It's like a Viennese operetta," she reflects. "The young prince falls in love with a waitress in a cabaret, and his family tries to buy her off." As a matter of fact, Linus, ever the hardnosed businessman, endeavors to railroad David into marrying Elizabeth Tyson, heiress to a sugarcane fortune, which is overseen by her father, played by silent film star Francis X. Bushman (*Ben Hur,* 1925). This lucrative marriage would prove beneficial to a Larrabee Industries business venture. Linus pretends to court Sabrina, ostensibly to get her mind off David. But Linus's plan backfires when he begins to fall for Sabrina himself, and Sabrina eventually reciprocates his affection.

Wilder and Lehman agonized over the pivotal scene in which Sabrina

Billy Wilder on the set. (Author's collection)

Greta Garbo and Melvyn Douglas in *Ninotchka,* which Wilder cowrote. It was directed by Ernst Lubitsch, Wilder's mentor. (Jerry Ohlinger's Movie Material Store, New York)

(*Above*) Don Ameche, Claudette Colbert, and John Barrymore in *Midnight,* which Wilder cowrote. It was directed by Mitchell Leisen, with whom Wilder clashed over script changes. (Jerry Ohlinger's Movie Material Store, New York) (*Below*) Gary Cooper and Barbara Stanwyck in *Ball of Fire,* which Wilder cowrote. It was directed by Howard Hawks, a director whom Wilder admired. (Jerry Ohlinger's Movie Material Store, New York)

Ginger Rogers as Susan Applegate in *The Major and the Minor*, Wilder's first film as a Hollywood director. Rogers in the course of the story had to disguise herself as twelve-year-old Sue-Sue and later as Sue-Sue's mother. (Larry Edmunds Bookshop, Los Angeles)

Wilder, Erich von Stroheim, Anne Baxter, and Franchot Tone rehearsing *Five Graves to Cairo*. (Jerry Ohlinger's Movie Material Store, New York)

Erich von Stroheim (center) as Field Marshal Erwin Rommel, who was still leading the Nazi Afrika Korps when *Five Graves to Cairo* was made. (Jerry Ohlinger's Movie Material Store, New York)

Miles Mander (Colonel Fitzhume), Wilder, Stroheim, and Ian Keith on the set of *Five Graves to Cairo*. Cinematographer John F. Seitz is behind Stroheim. (Jerry Ohlinger's Movie Material Store, New York)

Writer Raymond Chandler and Wilder at work on *Double Indemnity*. Despite their fierce creative differences, they turned out a superior screenplay. (Department of Special Collections, Charles E. Young Research Library, University of California, Los Angeles)

*(Above)* Barbara Stanwyck and Fred MacMurray in *Double Indemnity,* a classic film noir. (Film Stills Archive, Museum of Modern Art, New York) *(Below)* Femme fatale Phyllis Dietrichson (Stanwyck) eavesdrops on Walter Neff (MacMurray) and Barton Keyes (Edward G. Robinson) in *Double Indemnity.* (Film Stills Archive, Museum of Modern Art, New York)

MacMurray and Robinson in the scene that replaced the original ending of *Double Indemnity*. (Film Stills Archive, Museum of Modern Art, New York)

Phillips Terry, Jane Wyman, and Ray Milland in *The Lost Weekend*. Milland won an Academy Award for playing an alcoholic. Wilder received Academy Awards for directing the film and coauthoring the screenplay. (Jerry Ohlinger's Movie Material Store, New York)

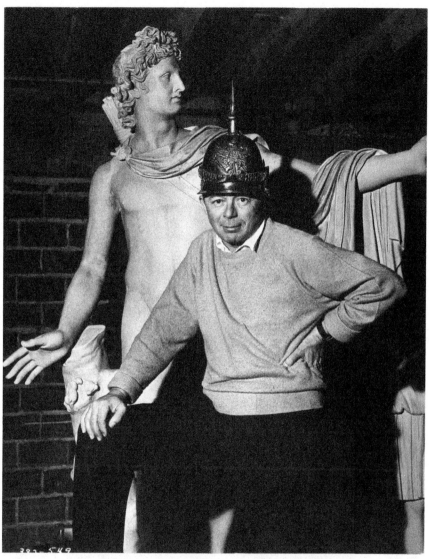

Wilder clowning on the set of his Viennese musical, *The Emperor Waltz*. As for the film, critics were not amused. (Jerry Ohlinger's Movie Material Store, New York)

Marlene Dietrich as Erika Von Schluetow, the former mistress of a Nazi officer in *A Foreign Affair*. Wilder had known Dietrich in Berlin in the 1920s. (Jerry Ohlinger's Movie Material Store, New York)

Dietrich and John Lund (Captain John Pringle) in *A Foreign Affair*. (Jerry Ohlinger's Movie Material Store, New York)

Cecil B. De Mille plays himself in *Sunset Boulevard;* Gloria Swanson as Norma
Desmond is seated behind him. (Movie Star News, New York)

Erich von Stroheim as Max von Mayerling in *Sunset Boulevard,* the role for which he is most remembered. (Film Stills Archive, Museum of Modern Art, New York)

Stroheim and Swanson in *Sunset Boulevard.* (Film Stills Archive, Museum of Modern Art, New York)

Kirk Douglas as Chuck Tatum, an opportunistic reporter, in Wilder's exposé of "cheesy tabloids," *Ace in the Hole*. (Larry Edmunds Bookshop, Los Angeles)

*(Above)* William Holden won an Academy Award for his portrayal of J. J. Sefton, an inmate in a Nazi prisoner-of-war camp in *Stalag 17.* (Jerry Ohlinger's Movie Material Store, New York) *(Below)* Preminger (Colonel von Scherbach, center) views the corpse of a prisoner who attempted to escape from the POW camp in *Stalag 17.* (Jerry Ohlinger's Movie Material Store, New York)

Wilder directs Otto Preminger, another director, as the commandant of the POW
camp in *Stalag 17*. (Jerry Ohlinger's Movie Material Store, New York)

Humphrey Bogart (Linus Larrabee) shares a toast with Audrey Hepburn (Sabrina Fairchild) in *Sabrina*. The tension between Bogart and Wilder was not evident in Bogart's performance. (Jerry Ohlinger's Movie Material Store, New York)

This legendary photo of Marilyn Monroe with her dress billowing over a subway grating in *The Seven Year Itch* has been called "the shot seen round the world." Tom Ewell looks on. (Larry Edmunds Bookshop, Los Angeles)

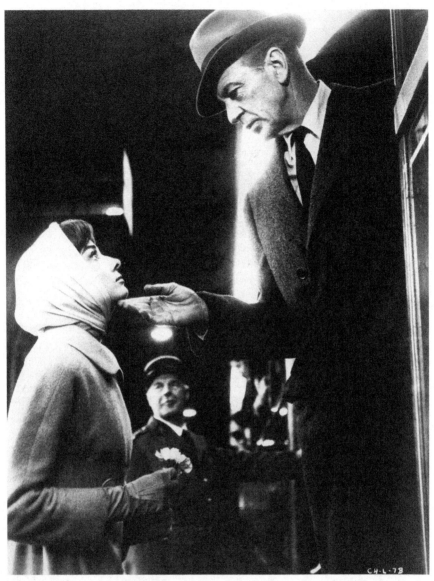

Audrey Hepburn (Ariane Chavasse) and Gary Cooper (Frank Flannagan) at the climax of *Love in the Afternoon*. (Jerry Ohlinger's Movie Material Store, New York)

Charles Laughton (Sir Wilfrid Robarts) addresses the court on behalf of his client, Tyrone Power (Leonard Vole, far right), in *Witness for the Prosecution*. (Larry Edmunds Bookshop, Los Angeles)

Marlene Dietrich as Christine Vole in *Witness for the Prosecution*, testifying in court. (Larry Edmunds Bookshop, Los Angeles)

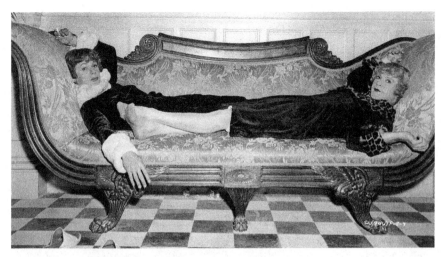

*(Above)* Tony Curtis as Joe/Josephine and Jack Lemmon as Jerry/Daphne in *Some Like It Hot*. (Cinema Book Shop, London) *(Below)* Curtis and Lemmon in disguise as Society Syncopators. Marilyn Monroe (center) crowned her career with her performance in *Some Like It Hot*. (Film Stills Archive, Museum of Modern Art, New York)

George Raft (center) as racketeer Spats Colombo is confronted by Pat O'Brien as federal agent Mulligan in *Some Like It Hot*. Raft often played gangsters and O'Brien cops in gangster films of the 1930s. (Jerry Ohlinger's Movie Material Store, New York)

Jack Lemmon and Shirley MacLaine in *The Apartment*, the peak of Wilder's career. Wilder received Academy Awards for directing the film, coauthoring the screenplay, and producing the best picture of the year. (Jerry Ohlinger's Movie Material Store, New York)

Fred MacMurray discusses his role in *The Apartment* with the author. (Long Photography, Los Angeles)

J. D. Sheldrake (MacMurray) discovers that his secretary (Edie Adams) has been gossiping about his love affairs with the office staff in *The Apartment*. (Jerry Ohlinger's Movie Material Store, New York)

James Cagney (second from left) retired from the screen after making *One, Two, Three*. He is shown here with Horst Buchholz (right). (Larry Edmunds Bookshop, Los Angeles)

Wilder reteamed Jack Lemmon and Shirley MacLaine in *Irma la Douce*, his most commercially successful movie. (Jerry Ohlinger's Movie Material Store, New York)

*(Above)* Dino (Dean Martin), Orville (Ray Walston), and Polly (Kim Novak) in *Kiss Me, Stupid* look over a ditty that Orville has composed. It was actually an unpublished song written by George and Ira Gershwin. (Jerry Ohlinger's Movie Material Store, New York) *(Below)* Walter Matthau won an Academy Award as Willie Gingrich, a crooked lawyer, in *The Fortune Cookie*. Here he badgers Ned Glass as Doc Schindler and Jack Lemmon as Harry Hinkle. (Larry Edmunds Bookshop, Los Angeles)

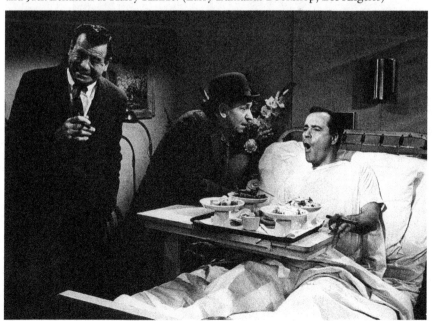

*(Above)* Sherlock Holmes (Robert Stephens) and Dr. Watson (Colin Blakely) in *The Private Life of Sherlock Holmes,* which was substantially cut before its release. This still is from one of the missing episodes. (Author's collection)  *(Below)* Holmes pretends to be homosexual to fend off the Russian ballerina's demand that he father her child. The ballet company's impresario (Clive Revill) looks on. (Jerry Ohlinger's Movie Material Store, New York)

Pat O'Brien as Hildy Johnson and Adolphe Menjou as Walter Burns (left photo) in the first film version of *The Front Page* (1930); Jack Lemmon as Hildy and Walter Matthau as Walter (right photo) in Wilder's remake (1974). (National Center for Film Study, Chicago)

Wilder, on the set of *The Front Page,* analyzes a comedic point for Matthau and Lemmon. (National Center for Film Study, Chicago)

*(Above)* Wilder gives Lemmon the proper nuance for an upcoming scene in *The Front Page*. (National Center for Film Study, Chicago) *(Below)* I. A. L. Diamond (left) on the set of *Avanti!* with Wilder. Diamond and Wilder cowrote a dozen films. (Film Stills Archive, Museum of Modern Art, New York)

Marthe Keller, in the title role of *Fedora*, confers with William Holden as Barry Detweiler, a failure in the picture business, recalling his role in *Sunset Boulevard*. (Larry Edmunds Bookshop, Los Angeles)

Walter Matthau ponders Wilder's direction on the set of *Buddy Buddy*, Wilder's last film. (Bennett's Bookstore, Hollywood, California)

Wilder received the coveted Irving G. Thalberg Memorial Award, one of the several life achievement awards bestowed on him in his later years, at the Academy Awards ceremony in 1988. (Academy of Motion Picture Arts and Sciences, Beverly Hills, California)

meets Linus in the board of directors' conference room late one night and they realize that they are genuinely falling in love. Wilder arrived on the set after lunch one Friday with only a page and a half of dialogue ready for this crucial scene. He nonchalantly sauntered over to Hepburn and asked her to stall the filming of the scene "by feigning a headache and fumbling her lines."[36] Hepburn was even willing to play the prima donna in front of the cast and crew by retreating to her dressing room for a nap. Her apparently erratic behavior enabled Wilder and Lehman to revise the scene over the weekend.

When Monday rolled around, Wilder was prepared with the script pages, and the scene came off very smoothly. Bogart played Linus as the self-sufficient, middle-aged bachelor who is forced to acknowledge his need for love, and Hepburn brought out the charm and gentleness in Sabrina that attracted Linus. The important scene was written and acted with exceptional finesse.

Linus is ashamed that he initially romanced Sabrina for an ulterior motive. Consequently, he encourages her to return to David. Sabrina, however, decides that she is fed up with both of the Larrabee brothers and opts to take the *Liberté* back to Paris. At the finale, David confronts Linus in the conference room and insists that he will not take Sabrina back because she is a gold digger who has plotted to marry into the Larrabee fortune. Outraged, Linus slugs David, who falls backward and somersaults all the way down the long conference table. "You *are* in love with her!" David proclaims; "I was just helping you to make up your mind!" Linus's kayoing David is a nod to Bogart's screen image as a tough guy. David hands Linus his hat and cane and tells him to rush down to the dock and board the *Liberté* before the ocean liner sets out for the open sea. Once on board, Linus joins Sabrina on deck and tells her the ocean voyage will be their honeymoon. As for his taking David's place in her life, he reflects, "It's all in the family."

By the time *Sabrina* premiered in September 1954, Audrey Hepburn had collected an Academy Award. Hence the cast of *Sabrina* was headlined by three Oscar winners: Holden for *Stalag 17* (1953), Hepburn for *Roman Holiday* (1953), and Bogart for *The African Queen* (1951). *Sabrina* was hailed by the critics as a charming and hugely entertaining love story; Frederick Hollander's dreamy score and Charles Lang's slick visuals were the icing on the cake. Hepburn was toasted as the alluring Sabrina that the story was waiting for.

Although Bogart still had nothing but scorn for *Sabrina*, Schickel points out that "the pictures he made thereafter are best left in something like near silence." *Sabrina* was the last blockbuster in which Bogart appeared before he retired from the screen in 1956. His final five movies lacked "the livewire energy" of Wilder's stylish high comedy.[37] Bogart succumbed to cancer on January 13, 1957. Lauren Bacall phoned Wilder shortly before the end to say that Bogie wanted to see him. Bogart wished to be reconciled with Wilder, and he apologized for his ill-tempered behavior while making *Sabrina*. Wilder replied generously, "There is nothing to apologize for; we don't have court manners around a movie set. I fight with a lot of people." Wilder always thought of Bogart afterward as a brave man because he endured his last illness "with great dignity."[38]

It goes without saying that Lehman did not wish to collaborate with Wilder again anytime soon. *Sabrina* "began in disarray and finished in sheer panic," he commented.[39] When I spoke with Lehman, he reflected, "Billy always got his own way. Somehow *Sabrina* turned out the way *he* wanted it to, and I never figured out how he did it."

*Sabrina* was the last picture in Wilder's current contract with Paramount; he decided not to renew his contract but rather to leave the studio. After eighteen years and seventeen pictures at Paramount, he believed it was time for a change. Once *Sabrina* had been launched, Wilder drove his Jaguar through the Paramount gate at 5451 Marathon Street, never to return. He was looking for fresh challenges at other studios.

Wilder was not interested in signing a long-term contract with any one studio, as he had done at Paramount. Instead, he preferred to make a deal with a major studio for one picture at a time. Each studio would arrange the financing and distribution of the film he made for it. Wilder set up shop as an independent producer-director. He would now exercise more control over the screenplay, the casting, and the direction of each film he chose to make.

While he was shopping around for his next property, Wilder was contacted by Irving "Swifty" Lazar, a Hollywood agent. Lazar had earned his nickname from the speed with which he could put together a production package for a studio. He informed Wilder that George Axelrod, the author of *The Seven Year Itch*, a smash Broadway hit, would like Wilder to consider directing the film version. The play had premiered at the Fulton Theatre in New York on November 20, 1952, and it went on to run for 1,141 performances. There was little risk in choosing to film *The Seven Year Itch*; it seemed almost guaranteed to be a blockbuster movie. The story is set in New York City during a boiling hot summer. Asked what attracted him to the play, Wilder said of the heroine, "The girl keeps her underwear in the frigidaire! Wow!!"[40]

The story centers on Richard Sherman, a middle-aged man who becomes infatuated with a woman who lives in the same apartment building while his wife and son are away for the summer. (Because *The Seven Year Itch* is a May-

December romance like *Sabrina,* Wilder had Linus Larrabee arrange to take Sabrina to see *The Seven Year Itch* on Broadway.) When a Hollywood reporter parodied the title of the play *The Seven Year Itch* as "The Lust Weekend," Wilder was convinced that the project was made to order for him. Charles Feldman, who had produced the film version of *A Streetcar Named Desire* (1951), was now producing at Twentieth Century–Fox. Feldman, who was also an agent, had arranged to buy the film rights for *The Seven Year Itch* from Axelrod for five hundred thousand dollars as a vehicle for Marilyn Monroe, one of his clients.

Wilder, along with George Cukor and Joseph Mankiewicz, was one of the few directors Monroe was willing to work with, and she very much "wanted to work with Wilder on *The Seven Year Itch,*" notes Barbara Leaming.[41] Since Monroe had an exclusive contract with Twentieth Century–Fox, Wilder would have to make the picture there. Lazar brokered a deal with the studio for Wilder to direct the movie, cowrite the screenplay with Axelrod, and coproduce the film with Feldman. Darryl Zanuck, the Twentieth Century–Fox studio chief, earmarked $250,000 for Wilder as director, cowriter, and coproducer of the picture—the same salary Wilder had gotten from Paramount for *Sabrina.*

## *The Seven Year Itch* (1955)

When Axelrod reported to Wilder's office at Twentieth Century–Fox for their first story conference in April 1954, Wilder began ribbing him from the get-go, just as he had done to the long-suffering Ernest Lehman on *Sabrina.* Axelrod had brought a copy of his play along, tucked under his arm. "I thought we might use the play as a guide," he said. Wilder took the play and dropped it on the floor, replying, "Fine; we'll use it as a door-stop."[42] Wilder's insults had offended other writers Wilder had worked with. But Axelrod merely shrugged off Wilder's barbs: "He sees the worst in everybody; but he sees it funny."[43] So the partners got along just fine.

Moreover, Axelrod did not believe he had much cause for complaint about Wilder's plans to alter his play for the screen. Wilder assured Axelrod that he would retain the fundamental narrative structure of the play and as much of Axelrod's original dialogue as the censor would allow. "For Billy I had awe," Axelrod remembered; "I didn't stand up to him" the way that Lehman had.[44]

The action of the play is limited to a single room in Richard Sherman's apartment, but Wilder decided to open out the play for the screen by having a composite set of the whole apartment constructed. In this fashion Wilder could move the action throughout the apartment. In addition, he decided to play some scenes outdoors, to avoid the charge of merely making a "photographed staged play." Wilder solved the problem of having a lengthy scene played in the same setting, such as in Richard's living room, by never allowing the pace of the action to slacken during the scene. Moreover, he gave the scene variety by covering all aspects of the action from various camera angles.

The principal problem Wilder and Axelrod encountered in adapting the play for film was coping with the industry censor. In the play, while Richard's wife Helen and his obnoxious son Ricky take a seaside vacation in Maine, Richard must stay behind in New York and endure the scorching heat. Nonetheless, he looks forward to his newfound freedom as a "summer bachelor." After seven years of marriage, Richard has developed an itch to have a fling. Specifically, Richard yens for the blonde who has sublet the apartment above his in a Manhattan triplex for the duration of the summer. He invites her to his apartment with seduction on his mind. Significantly, Richard refers to her as the Girl, implying that, to him, she is a nameless, ethereal goddess who seems just beyond his reach.

Axelrod said that he and Wilder had "a horrible problem . . . with the Breen office" in developing the play's spicy plot for the movie version.[45] In fact, Geoffrey Shurlock had replaced Joseph Breen as film censor a few months earlier, and so it was with Shurlock, not Breen, that Wilder had to negotiate. To begin with, Shurlock contended that adultery was not an appropriate topic for comedy. Adultery had reared its ominous head in *Double Indemnity* too, but that was no comedy. In the stage play, Richard does in fact have an extramarital affair with the Girl. But the industry's censorship code would not permit Richard's flirtation with the Girl to be consummated in the movie. Wilder and Axelrod were forced to substitute fantasy sequences in their screenplay in which Richard imagines that he seduces the Girl.

Wilder had hoped at least to hint that Richard did have a sexual encounter with the Girl. "I remember spending a night wondering what to do," and he finally came up with a solution to the problem. He went to Zanuck and said, "Try this: The maid of Richard's apartment is making up the bed and finds a hairpin." Wilder concluded, "And you know that they have committed the act."[46] But Zanuck refused to consider the idea, fearing that Shurlock would reject it too. Hence Wilder complained that he was straitjacketed in adapting the play for the screen: "*The Seven Year Itch* is a film about adultery, but the narrowminded morals of the 1950s made sure the climax only took place" in Richard's overheated imagination.[47]

Wilder sent the completed screenplay, dated August 10, 1954, to Geoffrey Shurlock. (He had vowed never again to go into production with a rough draft of the script, as he had done with *Sabrina*.) Shurlock objected to some naughty phrases cropping up in the script that were prohibited by the censorship code. He took exception, for example, to the Girl's line, "I feel so sorry for you with those hot pants."[48] Wilder contended that she was referring to the summer heat, not the heat of passion. Besides, Wilder maintained, some of the words and phrases that Shurlock considered improper for the film proved quite acceptable to theater audiences when they were spoken from the stage. As Axelrod put it, "We managed to bring the play in unscathed," meaning that there were no censorship problems with the dialogue in the Broadway play.[49] But Shurlock was intransigent, so phrases like "hot pants" disappeared from the movie's dialogue. Be that as it may, Wilder had a knack for saucy innuendo, which he had learned from Lubitsch, so the script as approved by the censor was "still able to offer moments of risqué dialogue."[50]

While casting the picture, Wilder was looking very hard for a suitable leading man to play Richard Sherman. He tested a young actor named Walter Matthau, who he thought was hilarious in the part. But Matthau was not as yet a star, so Zanuck insisted that they go with Tom Ewell, who had originated the role of Richard on the stage. "He knows where all the laughs are," said Zanuck.[51] Feldman, Wilder's coproducer, agreed with Zanuck, so Ewell was cast. Matthau, however, was destined to make his name as a major actor in other Wilder pictures, starting with *The Fortune Cookie*.

Wilder and Feldman were in harmony on the rest of the casting. Evelyn Keyes (*The Jolson Story*, 1946) was given the role of Richard's wife, Helen. Robert Strauss, who was selected to play Kruhulik, the superintendent of Richard's apartment building, "offers only a slightly more articulate version of his 'Animal' in *Stalag 17*."[52] The director of photography for this picture, Milton Krasner, had just filmed Jean Negulesco's *Three Coins in the Fountain* (1954) in CinemaScope and color.[53] When this wide-screen process was introduced in the early 1950s, director George Stevens quipped that "the dimensions of the widescreen were better suited to photographing a boa constrictor than a human being."[54] But Wilder was committed to wide screen as well as color for this film.

The CinemaScope process was not particularly useful in the scenes set in Richard's apartment. Wilder employed it to better advantage in the fantasy sequences, as when Richard dreams of making love to the Girl on an expansive seashore. Wilder quickly learned that the first rule of utilizing the format was that, if the action in the center of the frame was blocked out properly, the action taking place on either side would pretty much take care of itself.

Principal photography began on location in New York on September 3, 1954, and ran for two weeks. "Personally, I would prefer to shoot in the studio, because I am in control," Wilder observed years later.[55] After all, when shooting occurred in a real location, crowds of onlookers often flocked to watch the filming and got in the way. That is just what happened when Wilder was filming in the streets of Manhattan. One location scene takes place when Richard and the Girl are strolling on a sidewalk in downtown Manhattan on a hot summer night. The Girl finds the heat too much for her and decides to cool off by standing over a subway grating. As Douglas Brode describes the scene, "A train rumbles beneath, blowing the cool air upward," and sends the Girl's skirt fluttering to reveal her gorgeous legs. "Laughingly, she struggles—but not too hard—to keep it down as Richard looks on, his mouth hanging open like a hound dog's." It is in scenes like this one, Brode concludes, that Monroe proved herself to be the most authentic blonde bombshell to hit the screen since Jean Harlow.[56]

Sheer pandemonium resulted when this scene was filmed on location. Wilder had chosen to shoot it at the corner of Lexington Avenue and Fifty-second Street in the wee hours, when presumably the streets would be deserted. But Harry Brand, Twentieth Century–Fox's intrepid publicity chief, planted a notice in the newspapers of the metropolitan area that Marilyn Monroe would be filming at the site at two o'clock on Thursday morning, September 15. Consequently, nearly two thousand fans were on hand to watch the Hollywood superstar do the scene. The milling crowds were kept behind barricades, but they nevertheless were noisy and unruly.

Wilder called out, "Roll 'em!" and a train passed underneath one subway grating—actually a wind-blowing machine manned by a special effects technician. The gust of wind sent Monroe's billowy white dress flying above her shoulders, accompanied by raucous cheers from the gawking bystanders. "The scene wasn't working," Wilder remembered, so "we reshot it several times" over the next three hours.[57] Each time Marilyn's skirt blew upward, the spectators roared like the crowds at the Roman circus. Joe DiMaggio, Monroe's husband, was among the onlookers. She had been married to the legendary New York Yankees baseball hero for eight months, and their marriage was already on shaky ground. DiMaggio was outraged at what he considered his wife's indecent display. One of his friends, who was boozed up, said to DiMaggio, "Joe, what can you expect when you marry a whore?" DiMaggio yelled in response, "I've had it!"[58] After the next take, DiMaggio whispered something in Monroe's ear and marched away in a huff. Asked if her husband's angry departure had worried Monroe, Wilder replied, "No; she loved the crowds"; she was at heart an exhibitionist.[59]

Nonetheless, when Monroe returned to hotel suite 1105 at the St. Regis Hotel a couple of hours later, she had to pay the piper. She and DiMaggio had a horrendous quarrel, with DiMaggio denouncing the crass exhibition his wife had put on. Cameraman Milton Krasner, who was trying to sleep next door, "heard shouts of anger through the wall."[60] As a matter of fact, "within hours after the famous scene was shot," writes Fred Lawrence Guiles, Monroe's first biographer, "the marriage was over."[61] Two weeks later, Monroe filed for a divorce. When DiMaggio's friends told him that he had overreacted on the night when the controversial scene was filmed, he said, "I regret it, but I cannot help it." DiMaggio, who had been brought up in a morally conservative Catholic home, was convinced that the skirt-blowing scene had publicly humiliated him. "*I* would have been upset if *I* had been her husband," said Wilder in DiMaggio's defense, considering the raucous comments that were being made that night by some of the bystanders, including one of DiMaggio's friends.[62]

Tom Wood, among other Wilder biographers, believes that "Billy was perhaps indirectly responsible" for the breakup of Monroe and DiMaggio's marriage because he shot the scene in which "a blast of air sent her skirt soaring."[63] Wood seems less than fair to Wilder. The director believed that DiMaggio had for some time nursed ambivalent feelings about being married to a movie star–sex symbol. "I don't know if he was jealous of other men" giving his wife the once-over or "jealous of her getting more attention than he did. Probably both."[64]

Leaming states baldly that the sequence filmed on Lexington Avenue was nothing more than "a spectacular publicity stunt," since the footage had to be largely reshot in the studio.[65] As Wilder pointed out, however, he had every intention of using the material he filmed that night, until he discovered that much of the footage was unusable because of the chaotic conditions in which it was filmed. What's more, the censor was nervous about the sexual implications of the scene and would not approve the location footage because Monroe's skirt blew up past her waist. After all, Shurlock emphasized, the script states merely that "a subway train roars by, the breeze from it blows her skirt *a little*" (emphasis added).[66] Therefore, after the film unit returned to the Twentieth Century–Fox Studios in Hollywood on September 17, Wilder said, "We constructed a corner of the street on the back lot; and it was perfect."[67] George Axelrod added, "We used the original location shots of Marilyn," which were more revealing than what was filmed in the studio, "in the ads."[68]

Shooting would continue on the soundstages at Twentieth Century–Fox throughout the rest of September and into October. As always, Wilder worked out in advance with Doane Harrison how he would compose the shots and select the camera angles for each scene.

Monroe had an acting coach, Paula Strasberg, the wife of Lee Strasberg, the director of the Actors Studio in New York. Monroe leaned heavily on Paula Strasberg and demanded that she always be with her on the set. Hence Strasberg hovered over Monroe and was off camera giving her signals while Monroe was filming a scene. Wilder resented Strasberg's intrusive presence on the set, and he saw it as an obvious sign of Monroe's insecurity as an actress. But the front office had approved this arrangement, so Wilder had to put up with it. Still, he was frustrated by Monroe's unprofessional behavior during the shooting period. Her growing psychic instability made her increasingly difficult to deal with; it was manifested especially in her chronic habit of showing up several hours late and not knowing her lines when she finally did report for work.

Howard Hawks, who directed Monroe in *Gentlemen Prefer Blondes,* agreed with Wilder that Monroe had an inferiority complex about her acting ability. "She had to be convinced that she was good," Hawks said. He remembered not being able to find her one day when it came time to shoot a scene. After looking everywhere, it occurred to him to lift up a table in the corner of the soundstage, "and there she was, hiding like a frightened girl."[69]

It was not surprising that, by October 21, the movie was nine days behind schedule. It was largely Monroe's fault. Wilder observed that "she had trouble concentrating because there was always something bothering her." Understandably, "she was on the edge of a deep depression" because of the collapse of her marriage to DiMaggio.[70] As her tensions grew, the dosage of her sleeping pills increased, and she started mixing her medication with alcohol. Leaming writes that, as time went on, Monroe "built up a tolerance to medication, driving her to ever larger doses." Some days she showed up on the set in a groggy or dazed state. She sometimes seemed disoriented and would stumble over the simplest lines of dialogue. In short, she was a "sick, mixed-up girl."[71]

Wilder now looked back nostalgically on his quarrels with Bogart while making *Sabrina*. "At least Bogart was there on time; and he was there all day," Wilder mused. He endured such agonies while working with Monroe that Bogart seemed "amiable" by comparison.[72] Wilder was convinced, however, that "it was worth going through hell" while making fifteen to twenty takes with Monroe because, when she finally got it right, "it was the best it could be."[73] Wilder found that, once Monroe finally emerged from her dressing room, he could work with her effectively. In fact, he managed to elicit a very good performance from her in *The Seven Year Itch.*

The production at long last wrapped on November 4, 1954, thirteen working days over the original thirty-five-day schedule, and more than $1 million over budget—mostly thanks to Monroe's erratic and unpredictable behavior. So Wilder got going on the editing of the footage posthaste. Because he had planned the editing of the film with Harrison while shooting the picture, the two of them, plus editor Hugh Fowler, accomplished the final edit in record time.

Only one obstacle surfaced during postproduction: Wilder had to cope with the Legion of Decency, a Roman Catholic organization that rated the moral suitability of movies for its Catholic constituency. "Although the Legion was never officially an organ of the Catholic Church and its movie ratings were nonbinding," Bernard Dick explains, "many Catholics were still guided by the Legion's classifications."[74] In addition, in the absence of an industry rating system, which would not come to pass until 1968, the legion's ratings were followed by many non-Catholics. The studio bosses tended to do the legion's bidding to avoid receiving an objectionable rating from the legion for a movie, which would damage the film's chances at the box office. *The Seven Year Itch* was Wilder's first serious run-in with the legion. It would not be his last.

After the legion members attended a private screening of the movie, Monsignor Thomas Little, the legion's director, registered a complaint with Twentieth Century–Fox. So Zanuck arranged for Little to meet with Wilder. The offending scene was one in which the Girl, while taking a bubble bath, gets her toe stuck in the faucet. A plumber (deadpan comedian Victor Moore) accidentally drops his wrench into the suds and has to feel around in the water to find it. When he retrieves it, he takes the phallic wrench firmly in hand. The plumber's dropping the wrench in the bathtub is not in the shooting script, and therefore it must have been invented on the set. The screenplay merely says, "An elderly, shriveled plumber in overalls is trying to free her toe, working on the faucet with a monkey wrench."[75] Consequently, Wilder could not maintain that the gag the legion had found offensive was integral to the sequence. He grudgingly agreed to cut the shots of the plumber dropping the wrench in the tub and groping around in the soapy water for it. Still, *The Seven Year Itch* helped to pave the way for more artistic freedom in the making of Hollywood movies. "The picture could be done today without censorship," Wilder opined years later; "one can now tackle more daring themes."[76]

Wilder engaged Saul Bass, who was justly famous for designing the opening credits for many films, to create the title sequence for *The Seven Year Itch*. Recalling the old-fashioned French sex farces, in which a lothario is discovered hiding behind the closed door of a lady's boudoir closet, Bass designed a patchwork of multicolored doors "that one by one slide aside to reveal the film's credits lurking coyly behind them."[77]

After the credits, Wilder forged ahead with a prologue for the movie that is nowhere suggested in the play. A narrator explains that it was the custom among the Native Americans on Manhattan Island "to send their wives and children upriver for the summer. . . . The husbands would remain behind to attend to business." We see the Indian men, after they have loaded the women and children into large canoes, turn their attention to a sexy Indian maiden walking by. "Actually our story has nothing to do with Indians," the narrator explains; "it plays five hundred years later. We only wanted to show you that nothing has changed in Manhattan; husbands still send their families away for the summer." Richard Sherman puts his wife, Helen, and son, Ricky, aboard a train at Grand Central Terminal bound for Maine. He returns to his apartment to face another sweltering New York summer.

Richard soon encounters the Girl, who has sublet the apartment upstairs for the summer. In one of their chats she mentions that she is a model and also does TV commercials. The Girl later discovers a photo of herself in *U.S. Camera* and shows it to Richard. She calls it "one of those art pictures." (This seems to be a reference to the nude photograph of Monroe that appeared as the Playmate of the Month centerfold in the first issue of *Playboy* in 1950. "All I had on was the radio," Monroe recalled later.[78]) An explicit reference to the offscreen Monroe appears later in the movie when someone inquires about the identity of the vivacious blonde Richard has been hanging around with. "Wouldn't you like to know?" Richard retorts. "Maybe it's Marilyn Monroe!"

Richard is determined to remain faithful to Helen. ("I'm probably the most married man you'll ever know," he boasts.) Nevertheless, he fantasizes that he is a successful Casanova. In one of Richard's daydreams, he pictures himself making love to a beautiful young woman on a sandy beach. His playmate emotes, "Richard, your animal attraction will bother me from here to eternity." Louis Giannetti calls this fantasy a "delicious parody-homage" to Wilder's old friend Fred Zinnemann, since it is modeled on a sequence in *From Here to Eternity* in which Burt Lancaster romances Deborah Kerr on the seashore. Richard's middle-age spread, Giannetti adds, "presents an absurdly comical contrast to Burt Lancaster's manly physique."[79]

After he finally summons the courage to make his fantasies a reality, Richard invites the Girl down to his apartment for a drink. Before she arrives, he puts a recording of Rachmaninoff's Second Piano Concerto on his phonograph, muttering, "It never misses." The concerto conjures up a fantasy of Richard suavely sporting a scarlet smoking jacket and playing the concerto on the piano. The Girl, wearing an evening gown festooned with black stripes, struts around like a tigress in heat. But she is soon overcome by the strains of the lovely concerto, and she melts into Richard's arms. They kiss passionately as the daydream fades. French filmmaker François Truffaut (*The 400 Blows,* 1959), who was a cinema critic before he became a director, wrote in his critique of *The Seven Year Itch* when it was released in France that Wilder, "the libidinous old fox," parodies in this fantasy *Brief Encounter,* "the least sensual and sentimental film ever wept over." Wilder's movie, like David Lean's, is "beyond smut and licentiousness" and treats the lovers "with good humor and kindness."[80]

When the Girl really arrives, she notices Richard's wedding ring and mumbles, "A married man won't get drastic." But Richard fully intends to get drastic. He uncorks a magnum of champagne, and the foaming liquid gushes out of the bottle—another phallic symbol supplied by Wilder, "the libidinous old fox." Richard turns on his trusty Rachmaninoff recording, but the Girl shuns classical music—"No vocals," she explains. In yet another of Wilder's inexhaustible supply of baseball metaphors, Richard says, "Maybe we should send Rachmaninoff to the showers." He invites the Girl to sit next to him on the piano bench while he tickles the ivories. He makes an abortive pass at the Girl; they topple over backward onto the floor. With sublime understatement, he says apologetically, "I'm afraid this wasn't a good idea." He politely asks her to leave.

Undaunted, Richard invites the Girl to take in a movie with him. As they stroll back to their apartment building afterward, the Girl casually mentions that she has just appeared in a TV commercial for Dazzledent toothpaste. "Every time I show my teeth on TV," she says proudly, "more people see me than ever saw Sarah Bernhardt. It's something to think about!" She adds that Dazzledent leaves her breath "kissing sweet" and demonstrates by kissing Richard full on the mouth. He returns the favor.

But Richard ultimately abandons his endeavor to become a swinging summer bachelor; seized by propriety, he decides to join his family in the boondocks of Maine. When he bids farewell to the Girl, she confesses in a speech that is not in the play that she is drawn to him because he is the "shy, gentle type" that she finds "tender and kind and sweet. . . . If I were your wife," she concludes, "*I'd* be jealous of *you.*" Sarah Churchwell comments on the Girl's perceptive observations about Richard, "She is not as dumb as some writers make out. The Girl is artless and unsophisticated; but she is not stupid."[81] The Girl gives Richard an affectionate good-bye kiss, and he dashes off to catch his train.

In April 1955, two months before *The Seven Year Itch* premiered, Marilyn Monroe was interviewed by Edward R. Murrow on CBS-TV. Monroe said, "One of the best parts I've ever had is in *The Seven Year Itch*. I knew when Billy Wilder wanted me for the part that it would be very important for my career." She continued, "Billy Wilder is one of the best directors I have ever worked with. A good director contributes a lot when he is *with you* every moment on the set, helping you with your performance." She added, "I enjoy doing comedies, but I would like to do dramatic parts too."[82]

The studio brass decided to open *The Seven Year Itch* on June 1, 1955, Monroe's twenty-ninth birthday, at Loew's State Theatre on Broadway. DiMaggio accompanied Monroe to the premiere only as a publicity ploy, since they were already divorced. Twentieth Century–Fox had erected a blow-up of Monroe's skirt-blowing pose on a billboard fifty-two feet high, which towered above the theater. When she saw the poster, Monroe grumbled, "That's what they think of me." She was tired of the image of the blonde bombshell that the studio had created for her. Monroe and DiMaggio showed up half an hour late for the movie—much to Wilder's annoyance. "Marilyn made a grand entrance," he complained, "thereby taking everyone's attention away from my picture."[83] Still, there was a standing ovation at the end of the movie, which eventually grossed $5,734,471 worldwide. Zanuck had good reason to overlook the $1 million budget overrun.

*The Seven Year Itch* was enthusiastically received by reviewers as a sizzling sex farce beautifully mounted in CinemaScope. Milton Krasner's cinematography is suitably lush, with bright reds and luminescent greens, befitting Richard's garishly provocative daydreams. The Wilder-Axelrod dialogue delights in swerving off on unexpected tangents until the moment of truth is reached, while the plot is masterfully orchestrated throughout. The imaginative and inventive score was composed by Alfred Newman, head of the Twentieth Century–Fox music department. Because *The Seven Year Itch* is a romantic comedy, Newman's fulsome melodies resemble the tunes one hears in elevators. It is particularly attuned to Richard's florid fantasies.

The public adored Monroe in the picture, and she was never more radiant. Truth to tell, however, she was weary of playing sexpots that were none too bright. After Monroe completed *The Seven Year Itch*, "in a gesture of defiance against Fox, she went to New York and began attending acting classes at the Actors Studio," under the direction of the Strasbergs.[84] Twentieth Century–Fox lured her back to Hollywood in December 1955 with a lucrative contract that also gave her approval of the directors she worked with. Billy Wilder was on her short list of acceptable directors.

For his part, asked whether he would consider directing Monroe again after the anguish she had caused him while making *The Seven Year Itch,* Wilder replied that he was willing to forgive and forget. In *The Seven Year Itch* Monroe gave a fine-spun performance in one of her most appealing roles. Admittedly, "Marilyn Monroe was never on time; not once," he concluded. "Of course, I've got my Aunt Ida in Vienna, who was always on time for everything; but who would want to see her in a movie?"[85]

Wilder would indeed work with Monroe again, a few years down the road; in the meantime, he had signed with Warner Bros. to make *The Spirit of St. Louis,* a movie about Charles Lindbergh. Axelrod shuttled back to Broadway with a play titled *Will Success Spoil Rock Hunter?* (1955). And so it was that Wilder was looking for yet another collaborator on his screenplay.

# 10

# Light Up the Sky

## The Spirit of St. Louis and Love in the Afternoon

We live not as we wish, but as we can.

—*Menander, 300 B.C.*

Wilder had written a news story about Lindbergh's historic flight across the Atlantic back in 1927 for a Berlin paper, when he was a freelance reporter. He could not afford to go to France to cover Lucky Lindy's landing in Paris. Nevertheless, he never forgot this thrilling event, and his having covered it for a Berlin daily was one of the contributing factors in his directing *The Spirit of St. Louis* nearly thirty years later. "You cannot imagine now what the name of Lindbergh meant to us in Europe in 1927," he said.[1]

Ernest Lehman told me in 1976 that Wilder made the picture in part because he suspected that around Hollywood he was still thought of as a European. "Unlike many of his fellow emigrants," says Volker Schlöndorff, "Wilder never felt as if he was in exile in Hollywood. He threw himself wholeheartedly into the American popular culture, pulp, sports, and radio." *The Spirit of St. Louis* was an American subject, and "he wanted to take the most American of subjects and make it his own."[2]

Lindbergh published his autobiographical account of his celebrated flight in 1953 and won the Pulitzer Prize. Leland Hayward, a former Hollywood agent, was now a producer at Warner Bros. (*Mr. Roberts*, 1955). Hayward brought the project to Wilder, who agreed to direct the picture, coauthor the screenplay, and coproduce the film.

## *The Spirit of St. Louis* (1957)

Charles "Slim" Lindbergh was born on February 4, 1902, in Detroit, Michigan, of Swedish stock, and grew up in Little Falls, Minnesota. In 1926, while serving as an airmail pilot between St. Louis and Chicago, Lindbergh decided to compete for the $25,000 prize offered by French-born Raymond Orteig, a New York hotel proprietor, for a nonstop flight from New York to Paris in May 1927. "Think of being able to leap over the earth," Lindbergh mused.[3]

At 7:52 on the morning of May 20, 1927, Lindbergh roared aloft from Roosevelt Field, Long Island; he landed at Le Bourget Airport at 10:24 on the evening of May 21. With the completion of his thirty-three-and-a-half-hour nonstop solo flight in a tiny monoplane, Lindbergh's daring thrilled the world. President Coolidge awarded him the Distinguished Flying Cross and commissioned him as a colonel in the U.S. Army Air Corps Reserve.

In the years ahead, however, there would be some dark days. In 1932 his two-year-old son was abducted and murdered by a kidnapper. After the outbreak of the war in Europe, Lindbergh gave speeches in 1940 and 1941 endorsing America's neutrality, insisting that Britain be left to fight Nazi Germany alone. Indeed, in his public addresses he "soft-pedaled Nazi Germany's obvious menace."[4]

Wilder subscribed to a statement issued by Lindbergh's wife, Anne, who declared that, when her husband realized how wrong he had been in his judgment of the Nazis, "he completely reversed himself and entered the U.S. war effort" to make "a considerable contribution." In the wake of the Nazi V-2 rockets and the blitzkrieg of London, Lindbergh lamented, "I have seen the aircraft I loved destroying the civilization I expected them to serve."[5] He ultimately flew fifty combat missions against the Japanese in the South Pacific theater.[6] At all events, Wilder's movie would end with Lindbergh's triumphant homecoming parade in New York City in 1927 and would not touch on later events in his life.

Film historian Scott Eyman notes that the first star of talking pictures was not Al Jolson in *The Jazz Singer* (which premiered on October 6, 1927); it was Charles Lindbergh! The first sound film in wide distribution was a newsreel of Lindbergh taking off for Paris from Roosevelt Field "with a motor that sounds like a lawn mower." More impressive was the newsreel shortly thereafter that recorded Lindbergh's brief speech on the reviewing stand as part of the homecoming celebration in Manhattan. Film executive A. C. Lyles remembers, "That scene excited Hollywood tremendously. It made the possibility of sound movies so much more immediate."[7]

It was no secret that James Stewart was lobbying for the role of Lindbergh in *The Spirit of St. Louis*. Stewart had been a fan of Lindbergh's since he was in his teens. Lindbergh's flight to Paris had begun on Stewart's nineteenth birthday. At the time Stewart had hand carved a wooden model of the *Spirit* and stuck it on a map of the North Atlantic, which he proudly displayed in the window of his father's hardware store.[8] When Lindbergh subsequently landed on an airfield near Stewart's home in Indiana, Pennsylvania, as part of his personal appearance tour, Stewart attempted unsuccessfully to get his autograph. Still, he never forgot the event. Lindbergh inspired him to become a pilot himself, and during World War II Stewart flew twenty missions over Germany as a bomber pilot.[9]

Withal, Stewart was acutely aware that Jack Warner considered the forty-seven-year-old actor too old to play the twenty-five-year-old Lindbergh. "I need a star," Warner told Wilder and Hayward when they discussed the matter, "but not one that's pushing fifty."[10] After interviewing several other actors, though, Wilder and Hayward ultimately came back to Stewart. The tall, lanky actor resembled Slim Lindbergh; with a pilot's cap and goggles, Stewart might just get by as an aviator half his age. Wilder and Hayward agreed on casting Stewart, so Warner finally relented. They signed Stewart to play Lindbergh on March 22, 1955, with filming to commence in September 1955.[11]

Stewart got the opportunity to meet Lindbergh shortly after he signed for the movie. He was so awestruck at meeting his idol that "I suddenly realized I had no questions to ask him" about how to play him in the movie.[12] "I still wanted his autograph, but I was too shy to ask him for it." Finally Stewart said, "I hope I can do a good job for you." Lindbergh replied, "I hope so too."[13]

Wilder, of course, was searching for a co-screenwriter after George Axelrod's return to Broadway. His choice fell on Wendell Mayes, who had written a teleplay about a midwestern family that TV critic John Crosby had favorably reviewed in the *Los Angeles Times*. Wilder convinced Hayward that they should hire Mayes at a salary of one thousand dollars a week. As a neophyte screenwriter, the easygoing Mayes enjoyed working with Wilder. He did not take umbrage at Wilder's sassy wisecracks; he thought Wilder was very witty. The writing partners committed themselves to spending the entire summer on composing the first draft of the screenplay.

Lindbergh occasionally sat in on Wilder and Mayes's script conferences when he was in town. They met in Wilder's home because the reclusive Lindbergh would not go near the studio. Wilder found it frustrating to work with the shy, taciturn Swede; he thought Lindbergh "standoffish" and "not easy to get through to." As time went on, Wilder continued, "I found that I was beating my head against a cement wall, because I could not write into the script a single personal scene with him; only what was in the book."[14]

Lindbergh, Wilder, and Hayward went to Washington so Lucky Lindy could show them the original *Spirit of St. Louis,* which is on permanent display, suspended from the ceiling, at the Smithsonian Institution. The museum officials erected a platform alongside the plane so that Lindbergh's guests could see the interior of the aircraft at close range. It was a revelation for Wilder to see how crude the single-engine monoplane really was: a little bit of metal, canvas, and wood. The original *Spirit* cost $13,000, whereas the three replicas used in the movie cost a total of $1.3 million.

During their story conferences, Wilder and Mayes were confronted with the dilemma of how to get away from the monotony of the thirty-three and a half hours that Lindbergh spent alone in the cockpit in the course of his solo flight. They ultimately decided to fill the time between takeoff and landing with periodic flashbacks to Lindbergh's early life, accompanied by Stewart's narration in voice-over on the sound track. For example, Wilder shows Lindbergh as a barnstorming aviator performing stunts at air carnivals. Wilder also wanted to introduce a companion for Lindbergh to chat with during the flight. So he, with Lindbergh's permission, invented a fly that stows away in the monoplane, attracted to the cockpit by the sandwiches Lindbergh has brought along. Lindbergh, who sees the fly as a fellow flyer, says, "You're good luck, because nobody has ever seen a fly crash!" That line is one of the few flashes of the Wilder wit in the screenplay. Wilder joked that he had the animation department at Warner Bros. pencil the fly into the scenes it was in, because the live fly he hired refused to follow the script.

Wilder recalled the scene in *Hold Back the Dawn* in which Charles Boyer absolutely refused to address a cockroach. By contrast, James Stewart was willing to converse with an insect. "After all, they don't talk back," he explained. "Mr. Stewart did not object to talking to insects," Wilder opined, because "he had had to deal all his life with agents and producers."[15] During the shooting period, however, as time wore on, Stewart said, "I recall getting a little annoyed with the fly and asked Wilder to get rid of the bug." So Wilder had the insect fly out the window when the plane is over Newfoundland.[16] Thinking of the thousands of miles that still lie ahead for the *Spirit,* Lindbergh quips, "I don't blame you."

Wilder turned in the preliminary draft of the screenplay to Jack Warner in August 1955. Warner advised him that Stewart was committed to filming Hitchcock's *The Man Who Knew Too Much* (1956) until the end of August; shooting on the Lindbergh film was scheduled to begin in September. Stewart prepared for the role of Lindbergh by spending any spare time he had studying old newsreels of Lindbergh, the better to impersonate him in the picture. He also practiced piloting one of the three replicas of the *Spirit* built for the movie from the original plans.[17]

Meanwhile, with preproduction in full swing, Wilder and Hayward put together a crack production team, including cinematographers Peverell Marley (*The Greatest Show on Earth*, 1952) and Robert Burks, who was shooting *The Man Who Knew Too Much*. Editor Arthur Schmidt was cutting his fourth Wilder movie, and composer Franz Waxman was scoring his fourth Wilder picture.

Hayward and Wilder agreed that "it would add immeasurably to the impact and authenticity of the film to shoot as much of the flight as possible on or near the original locations," writes Arthur Rowan in the most informative article about the making of the movie. In August 1955, before principal photography was scheduled to commence, Wilder decided to get a jump on the shooting period by gathering a small production crew to film aerial footage of the first leg of Lindbergh's flight, starting at Roosevelt Field on Long Island, where the journey began.[18]

Wilder and his film unit shot footage along the route that Lindbergh had taken out of New York and went on to film above the mountains of Nova Scotia and over St. John's, Newfoundland. The crew comprised aerial cameraman Thomas Tutweiler, supervising editor and associate producer Doane Harrison, and Leland Hayward. Having completed the filming of this preliminary portion of Lindbergh's flight plan, Wilder and his team proceeded to Paris, where Wilder established a temporary production office at the Ritz Hotel.

Principal photography got under way on Friday, September 2, 1955, with the filming of Lindbergh's landing at Paris's Le Bourget Airport. Wilder shot the movie's final scene first because the weather was still mild, approximating what it was on May 21, 1927. Wilder was barred from using the real Paris airport, so he substituted Aérodrome de Guyancourt near Versailles. Wilder said, "Since it was night, who could tell?" Three thousand extras were instructed to break through the barricades near the landing strip and rush hysterically out to the plane, giving Lucky Lindy a tumultuous welcome.

Hayward reported to Jack Warner in a letter dated September 9 that he and Wilder had banked on good weather that night—until it started to drizzle. "I have to tell you, you could have bought the picture for a quarter when it started to rain, with this airport covered with these goddamed French extras. But luckily it stopped, and we got some terrific shots."[19] They finished filming at five o'clock in the morning.

Hitchcock had completed shooting *The Man Who Knew Too Much* behind schedule, with the result that Stewart could not show up in Paris for the *Spirit of St. Louis* shoot until mid-September. He had gone straight from one picture to the other, so he insisted that he be allowed to go back to Los

Angeles and rest for a week or so before beginning work in earnest on the Lindbergh picture. Weighing on Stewart's mind was the inescapable fact that Lindbergh was nearly half Stewart's age when he made his transatlantic flight. Stewart was afraid that, if he began shooting *The Spirit of St. Louis* right away, his haggard appearance would show him to be every bit of his forty-seven years.[20]

Be that as it may, Wilder had counted on Stewart's traveling with him and his camera crew so they could photograph Stewart actually flying the replica of the *Spirit* over various locations on the itinerary of Lindbergh's flight, including the Irish coast, the English Channel, and Paris itself. Wilder and Hayward took Stewart to lunch to hash out their disagreement. "Jimmy," Wilder pleaded, "for God's sake, trust me and let me get these shots of Lindbergh flying over authentic European locations!" But Stewart was implacable; he abruptly jumped up from the table, saying, "I've got to go!"[21] He went directly to his hotel, packed his bags, and caught the evening flight to Los Angeles.

After Stewart's departure, Wilder, Hayward, and the film unit continued to shoot along the flight path that Lindbergh had followed on the second leg of his journey. They filmed in the air over Ireland's Dingle Bay and the coast of Cornwall, proceeded past Land's End, crossed the Channel, and finally followed the Seine River to the outskirts of Paris. "We had unbelievable technical problems," Wilder remembered. "We had another plane in the air to film the plane we were shooting. God, it was horrendous. The weather would change from one minute to the next." If sunshine turned to clouds, the color of the sky would not match that of the earlier shots, and the camera crew would have to wrap for the rest of the day. Hayward wrote to Jack Warner on September 25, "There is no escaping the fact that this is probably the most difficult picture that anyone has tried to make—logistically, technically, and every other way it is a bitch."[22]

Wilder and the entire unit were back at Warner Bros. in Hollywood by the end of September. Wilder and his producer partner had a powwow with Warner in which they agreed that filming should not resume until the shooting script was finished. Mayes had continued working on the final draft while Wilder was supervising aerial photography in Europe, but they needed to make a joint effort to finish up. Wilder particularly favored this plan because of the dreadful experience he had had endeavoring to work on the shooting script of *Sabrina* at night while directing the picture during the day. Warner accordingly shut down production for the rest of October.

Wilder was pleased with the final draft. Although Mayes never collaborated with Wilder again, Wilder later recommended him to Otto Preminger to compose the screenplay for *Anatomy of a Murder* (1959), one of Preminger's best movies.

Filming on *The Spirit of St. Louis* resumed in November. The close shots of Lindbergh piloting his plane were filmed on a soundstage in the studio, utilizing process photography. Wilder employed the technique known as rear-screen projection, whereby an actor performs in front of a screen on which images of exterior locations (in this case panoramic shots of cloudscapes) are projected from behind. Wilder had used rear-screen projection on *Sunset Boulevard* and other films. In this instance he filmed Stewart in midflight while he was seated in a mock-up of a cockpit on a soundstage. It was a pity that Wilder did not have shots of Stewart actually flying the replica of the *Spirit* over various European locations, as he had hoped. The process shots would have to suffice for the flying sequences of Lindy at the controls of his plane.

The aerial sequences in the movie encompassed flashbacks to Lindbergh's days as an airmail pilot and as a barnstorming aviator in air carnivals. They were time-consuming and expensive to shoot. Production designer Art Loel established a large location site near Santa Maria on the California coast, complete with airfield and hangars, to film them. These sequences had to be filmed in the air from another plane. Paul Mantz, a veteran pilot of camera planes for aerial photography, piloted the plane in which Tutweiler had mounted his camera.[23]

Lindbergh came on location only once during the shooting period. Wilder was doing retakes of the *Spirit* touching down at Le Bourget on May 21, 1927. "Lindbergh turned up unannounced one day," Stewart recalled, to watch the pilot, Stan Reaver, land the plane. Just before Reaver took off, Lindbergh told him, "Don't forget to slip in for a three-point landing. Remember, I'm supposed to be flying the plane."[24]

Wilder was scheduled to finish principal photography in March 1956, but he fell behind schedule. As a result, the original 64-day shooting schedule expanded to 115 days. In the course of the grueling seven-month shoot, Wilder shot more than two hundred thousand feet of film, much of it devoted to the aerial sequences, which Schmidt, in consultation with Harrison and Wilder, had to trim to twelve thousand feet during postproduction.[25] This is the only film for which Wilder shot a huge surplus of footage. Consequently, postproduction took longer on *The Spirit of St. Louis* than on any of Wilder's previous pictures. Wilder and his editing team did not complete the edit until June 1956; it clocked in at two hours and fifteen minutes. The movie's price tag eventually climbed from $2 million to $6 million.[26]

Jack Warner decided to have the world premiere at Radio City Music

Hall in New York on February 21, 1957, hoping that the batch of early reviews would be favorable. When the film was unveiled, it began with one of Wilder's typical printed prologues: "A young man alone in a single engine airplane flew non-stop from Roosevelt Field in New York across the entire North Atlantic Ocean to Le Bourget Field in Paris, a distance of 3,610 miles. In this triumph of mind, body, and spirit, Charles A. Lindbergh influenced the lives of everyone on earth; for in the 33 hours and 30 minutes of his flight the Air Age became a reality. This is the story of that flight."

The takeoff in the rain from Roosevelt Field on Long Island is a virtuoso set piece. Wilder wanted the plane, with its heavy load of gasoline, to just barely clear the tops of the trees at the end of the runway. "I want a vivid shot of just how the treetops looked to Lindbergh as he skimmed over them on take-off," said Wilder. The sequence is superbly edited by Schmidt: "Quick cuts of the rear of the plane, then a close-up of Lindbergh, a long shot of the *Spirit,* followed by a shot of the spectators, a subjective tracking shot of the muddy runway which puts the viewer in the cockpit; and the majestic finale," as the *Spirit* clears the clump of trees.[27] As the *Spirit* lifts and soars, so do the strings of Waxman's rhapsodic background score.

One scene called for Lindbergh to perform a wing-walking stunt, with a stunt man doubling for Stewart. "Hell," Wilder bragged, "I could perform that simple feat myself." Stewart bet Wilder one hundred dollars that he would not have the nerve to do it. "Maybe he wanted a new director," Wilder mused. Wilder boarded the vintage World War I monoplane that Harlan Gurney was piloting; he was strapped in a harness "and flew, standing on the top wing with his arms outstretched," for a ten-minute ride at eight hundred feet.[28]

In still another flashback, Lindbergh recalls a priest, Father Hussman, who took flying lessons from him. Hussman gives him a St. Christopher medal, explaining, "St. Christopher helps wayfarers to cross bridgeless waters." Lucky Lindy replies that he trusts not in God but in his instrument panel and his compass. Nevertheless, a friend of his hides the medal in Lindbergh's sandwich sack just before the *Spirit* taxis down the runway for takeoff. Lindbergh discovers it in midflight, when he opens the sandwich bag, and hangs the medal on the instrument panel. Later, when he reaches Cherbourg on his way to Paris, Lindbergh realizes that he is running out of fuel. Fatigued and bewildered, Lindbergh pushes himself to the limits of endurance to reach Le Bourget. Gazing at the St. Christopher medal dangling from the control panel, he blurts out, "Oh, God help me!"

"Lindbergh finally accepts what the medal represents: a belief in a higher power whose existence he had previously doubted," Bernard Dick writes. Lindbergh then spies the brightly lit Paris, shown in breathtaking long shot; he flies over the Arc de Triomphe and the Eiffel Tower, proceeds along the Seine River, and on to Le Bourget. As the mass of well-wishers cheers him, "Wilder cuts back to the medal, enabling it to share in the applause."[29] Some reviewers were incredulous at finding an expression of faith in a Wilder film. But the director who began every script with "Cum Deo" was not averse to portraying a religious incident in a film, especially since it came from the script's source. Waxman's score throughout the sequence is marked by brass, celesta, and shimmering strings. This unearthly music spirals upward, suggesting the heights of human endeavor.

The movie concludes with the authentic newsreel footage of the frenetic ticker-tape parade filmed on the occasion of the real Lindbergh's official welcome in New York City. Some film historians call *Ace in the Hole* Wilder's "virulent hate letter to America," according to Neil Sinyard and Adrian Turner; "*The Spirit of St. Louis* is perhaps the nearest Wilder has ever come to writing a love letter to the country of his adoption."[30]

*The Spirit of St. Louis* collected a sheaf of largely positive notices when it premiered at Radio City Music Hall. "Under veteran director Billy Wilder, *Spirit* comes off as Class A picture-making," *Variety* declared. But the reviewer added a caution: "Considering that Lindbergh is today little more than Mr. Anonymous to youngsters, the spontaneous box office appeal" will perhaps not be "commensurate with the scope of the production."[31] Indeed, Warner's marketing researchers discovered that hardly anyone under forty knew who Lindbergh was.

Inevitably, more than one reviewer jeered at Stewart playing the youthful Lindbergh with a toupee, describing "a geriatric James Stewart in a henna hairpiece."[32] Other critics noted that the picture's 135-minute running time was likely to make viewers fidget at times, instead of drawing them into the story.

The movie ultimately took in only $2.6 million domestically—not even half of the production cost. It was an expensive and conspicuous flop. Jack Warner writes in his autobiography that the picture was "the most disastrous failure we ever had. Every studio has them from time to time, but this was one of the worst. I have never been able to figure out why it flopped."[33] Wilder said, "I felt sorry for Jack Warner. I thought of offering him his money back; but then I thought he might take it."[34]

Stewart attributed the movie's disappointing audience response in some degree to Lindbergh's failure to assist in promoting the picture. Lindbergh did not help matters, said Stewart, by refusing all requests for personal appearances; he would not even talk to the press. Lindbergh was not, after all, familiar to the younger generation of moviegoers, the major ticket buyers. Still, Stewart remained a champion of the Lindbergh film, calling it one of the best movies of his career. "I thought I got right into Slim's character; I guess he thought so too." In fact, Lindbergh pronounced a favorable verdict: the movie "captured the spirit of his journey."[35] Historian Joseph Roquemore declares that, except for the pesky fly in the cockpit, "Wilder's absorbing adaptation of Lindbergh's memoirs remains perfectly faithful to history . . . and beautifully staged all the way."[36]

In addition, Wilder drew skillful performances from the supporting characters who populate the flashbacks, most notably Father Hussman (Marc Connelly) and Bud Gurney (Murray Hamilton), Lindbergh's sidekick from his air circus days. Wilder tackled difficult subject matter with a sense of humanity and honesty; the result is moving and ultimately hopeful. Nonetheless, the movie's excessive length makes one wish that Wilder had made a more compressed film.

Looking back on *The Spirit of St. Louis,* Wilder confessed, "I've never done an outdoor picture before or since; I'm not an outdoors man." He explained that his idea of an outdoor scene was "a balcony of the Paris Ritz built by Alexander Trauner in the studio."[37] Actually, for Wilder's next film, a picture derived from Claude Anet's 1920 French novel *Ariane,* Trauner would create the interior of Paris's Ritz Hotel in the studio.

Since at this point Wilder was still absorbed with *The Spirit of St. Louis,* he cast about for yet another promising screenwriter who could get started on the screenplay of *Ariane.* He had recently met a young writer named I. A. L. Diamond at a Writers Guild dinner. Diamond had written a hilarious sketch for the occasion about two benighted screenwriters fresh out of ideas. Wilder met with him afterward and found him a clever, bright young writer. He had no trouble obtaining Diamond's services, since Diamond was freelancing and was interested in adapting Anet's novel for film. With a cowriter in hand, Wilder negotiated a sweetheart contract for himself with the Mirisch brothers at Allied Artists to finance and distribute the picture with a budget of $2.1 million. Wilder would receive $250,000 for directing the picture and $100,000 for coauthoring the script, plus a 10 percent share of the gross profits.[38]

Diamond was, like Wilder, Jewish and European. He was born Itek Dommnici in Ungheni, Romania, in 1920. When he was nine, he and his family relocated to Brooklyn, New York. He attended Boys High School in Brooklyn, where he was known as Isadore Diamond (which sounded more "American" to his parents) and was nicknamed "Iz." He became a mathematics wizard in high school but majored in journalism at Columbia University. In college he called himself I. A. L. Diamond; the initials stood for "Interscholastic Algebra League," of which he had been the champion in high school.

After graduating from college in 1941, Diamond went to Hollywood, aiming to be a screenwriter. He worked on pedestrian pictures like *Two Guys from Milwaukee* (1946); the only screenplay of consequence that he collaborated on during this period was Howard Hawks's *Monkey Business* (1952), which he cowrote with Ben Hecht.

Wilder had failed to find a long-term replacement for Charles Brackett—until Diamond appeared on the horizon. Personality-wise, he was a diamond in the rough: a tall, taciturn, remote individual who reminded Wilder of Slim Lindbergh. Iz Diamond's withdrawn, introverted personality "proved to be the perfect balance for Wilder's extroverted nature," writes Joanne Yeck.[39] "My husband had absolute confidence in his own ability," Barbara Diamond pointed out; consequently, he was not intimidated by Wilder's caustic manner or sarcasm.[40]

For one thing, Diamond admired Wilder because Wilder was first and foremost a screenwriter. Both of them, Diamond explained, firmly believed that "eighty per-cent of the creation of any movie lies in the writing. The other twenty per-cent is in the execution": in putting the camera in the right place and in directing the actors.[41]

## *Love in the Afternoon* (1957)

Wilder was prompted to make the present movie by his recollection of a German film version of *Ariane* (1931), which Paul Czinner directed when Wilder was a screenwriter at Ufa. The movie starred Elisabeth Bergner, whom Czinner married in 1933. The film was also released in an English version, *The Loves of Ariane*. Wilder remembered the movie as funny and touching.

Wilder updated the time frame of his remake from the 1920s to the present; Diamond came up with a new title, *Love in the Afternoon*. Wilder left Diamond to continue working on *Love in the Afternoon* while he went off to Europe to shoot *The Spirit of St. Louis*. In due course Diamond composed a detailed screen treatment for the script, which he mailed to Wilder overseas. Wilder cabled him that he heartily approved it and authorized Diamond to set to work on the first draft of the script. When Wilder returned to Hollywood to complete the Lindbergh picture, he spent as much time as he could spare collaborating with Diamond on the screenplay of *Love in the*

*Afternoon*. By the time Wilder delivered his director's cut of *The Spirit of St. Louis* to Warner Bros. in June 1956, *Love in the Afternoon* was ready to go into preproduction.

Most of Wilder's dealings with Allied Artists were with the Mirisch brothers—Walter, Harold, and Marvin—who gave him a fairly free hand in making the movie. Nevertheless, they always kept Steve Broidy, the head of the studio, posted about their projects. So they set up a meeting in Broidy's office with Wilder and Diamond.

Wilder said that Broidy began by asking him, "What are we going to do about the title? It's terrible!" Diamond had suggested the title because it implied love in the afternoon of life—that is, a mature man romancing a young girl—an implication totally lost on Broidy. Wilder responded to Broidy, "Tell me the best title you've ever heard of." Broidy hesitated, then said, "*Wichita*—because it suggests the Wild West." Allied Artists had released a Western with that title in 1955, which was well received. "Granted, *Wichita* is a good title; so is *Oklahoma!*" Wilder wisecracked. "Why not call our picture *Meanwhile, Back at the Ritz?*" Wilder added abrasively, "We have a title for this picture, and that's the way it's going to be!" Broidy said sheepishly, "Can't you take a joke?" Wilder did not answer but said to Diamond abruptly, "Let's go!"[42]

In adapting Anet's novel to the screen, Wilder retained only the kernel of its plot. Ariane, a student at a music conservatory, falls in love with a charming roué. She plays the cello; he plays the field. The lothario whom Ariane is smitten with is much more sophisticated and worldly-wise than she is. She cannot bear to admit to him that she is a virgin; instead, she boasts that she is as much a cosmopolitan lover as he is. Wilder also kept the novel's ending, in which the lovers, after multiple misunderstandings, are reunited at a train depot.

Wilder and Diamond invented the rest of the plotline. For example, they created the character of Ariane's father. In addition, they modeled Frank Flannagan, the aging playboy in their script, after Howard Hughes, the rich tycoon who was often seen in the company of Hollywood actresses during the period in which he owned RKO Studios in the 1950s.

Wilder said that he and Diamond were instantly compatible. There were never bitter quarrels between them, as there had been between Brackett and Wilder. If Wilder and Diamond did not agree on a line of dialogue, "we just went on to find something we were both nuts about."[43] Unfortunately, Diamond had already committed himself to write the script for a Danny Kaye vehicle at MGM, *Merry Andrew* (1958), before he got involved in *Love in the Afternoon*. But he promised Wilder to come back to work with him immediately afterward. When Diamond returned later on to work on *Some Like It Hot*, he became Wilder's permanent writing partner.

By the end of July 1956, Wilder decamped for Paris; he took up residence in the Hotel Raphael for the duration of the shoot. He planned to film exteriors in and around Paris and interiors at the Studios de Boulogne, just west of the heart of the city. The cameras were set to roll on September 1.

Wilder had brought together an impressive cast and production crew. To begin with, Audrey Hepburn had jumped at the chance to appear in another Wilder movie after the enormous success of *Sabrina*. She was to play Ariane, who is in her late teens in the novel; although Hepburn was twenty-seven, she could easily pass for a girl who had just turned nineteen.

Wilder had offered the role of Frank Flannagan, the graying libertine, to Cary Grant. But Grant refused the role for the same reason that he had rejected the part of Linus Larrabee in *Sabrina*. He felt uncomfortable romancing Hepburn, who was half his age and looked even younger. Wilder was keenly disappointed that Grant had turned him down yet again. To Wilder, Grant was "the best of the light comedians; . . . and I never made a picture with him—spilt milk!" What was the use of crying about it?[44]

Wilder turned to Gary Cooper, who accepted the part, although there was a disparity of more than twenty-five years between Cooper and Hepburn. Cooper's screen image in recent years had been that of a strong, silent man of integrity and honor. Nevertheless, Wilder was aware that Cooper was a lot more like Frank Flannagan in real life than he was like the upright heroes he usually played. Cooper was a confirmed womanizer; he had had affairs with several of his leading ladies, from Marlene Dietrich to Ingrid Bergman. Indeed, Cooper was "known throughout Hollywood as the actor who talked softly and carried a big prick."[45] Cooper, at this point in his career, liked to think of himself as playing "the fellow next door." Wilder laughed at that notion; "Hell, if I want to see the guy next door, I go next door."[46] Wilder well knew that during the 1930s and 1940s Cooper had become one of the great romantic leads in films like *Bluebeard's Eighth Wife* and *Ball of Fire*, both cowritten by Wilder. So Wilder was confident that Cooper could play high romantic comedy. Incidentally, the beautiful brunette who plays Flannagan's date in the Paris opera sequence is none other than Wilder's wife, Audrey.

To play Ariane's father, Claude Chavasse, a character not in the novel, Wilder chose sixty-eight-year-old Maurice Chevalier. Claude is a private detective specializing in cases of marital infidelity; he spends his time "popping flashbulbs in hotels," as the saying goes. The suave, debonair Chevalier had starred in romantic comedies in Hollywood in the early sound era, including no fewer than five pictures directed by Ernst Lubitsch, among them *The Merry Widow* (1934). Wilder was interested in making a picture at last with a star who had worked so much with Lubitsch.

Chevalier's career had been endangered during World War II by suspicions that he was collaborating with the Nazi forces when he remained to entertain in occupied France. But after some months, he went into retirement until the end of the war, and his name was eventually cleared. Nevertheless, Chevalier had not appeared in a Hollywood film since before the war. He was particularly pleased to be costarring with Audrey Hepburn in *Love in the Afternoon*. He dispatched a telegram to her, stating, "How proud I would be, and full of love I would be, if I really had a daughter like you."[47] Chevalier continued to appear in American films after *Love in the Afternoon,* including Vincente Minnelli's *Gigi* (1958).

Behind the camera, Wilder had gathered a first-rate production crew. The director of photography was William Mellor, who had earned an Academy Award for photographing George Stevens's *A Place in the Sun* (1951). Production designer Alexander Trauner was working on his first Wilder movie, but it would not be his last. Like Wilder, Trauner was a Viennese Jew, but he had worked primarily in France. During the Nazi occupation, he had gone into hiding but continued to work undercover, designing sets for such noteworthy pictures as Marcel Carné's *Les enfants du paradis* (*Children of Paradise,* 1945). As an in-joke, Wilder has Trauner appear in the opening credits, posting a photo on an outdoor display board. Finally, Franz Waxman, who had scored *Mauvaise graine,* as well as many other Wilder films, was providing the music for another Wilder picture being filmed in France.

When principal photography commenced on September 1, 1956, Wilder was concerned about Chevalier's expression of joie de vivre; he had the twinkling, roguish eyes and lubricous swagger of a romantic rascal. Jeanette MacDonald, who costarred with Chevalier in *The Merry Widow* and other films, called Chevalier "the biggest bottom pincher I have ever come across." For her part, Hepburn admired Chevalier professionally, but she did not appreciate "his brand of flirtatiousness."[48]

The cast and crew customarily gathered for drinks at the end of the shooting day, but Chevalier was never present. Hepburn assumed that Wilder had excluded him, just as he had done to Bogart during *Sabrina*. Actually, these cocktail hours were hosted by the French crew, who let it be known that they had not forgiven Chevalier's willingness to entertain during the wartime occupation. Chevalier simply ignored the snub and never mentioned it.[49]

Before filming began, Wilder was confident that, with the proper makeup and lighting, Cooper's real age could be soft-pedaled on the screen. But when he was on camera, Cooper's gaunt, lined features made him look even older than his fifty-six years. Alexander Walter assumed that Cooper's haggard face suggested that "his propensity for philandering . . . in his declining years was taking a physical toll."[50] But that was not entirely the case. What was known to only a few of Cooper's intimates was that he had been diagnosed with incurable cancer. This was certainly a contributing factor to his appearing to be a man over sixty on the screen. As a matter of fact, he had only a few years left to live.[51] In any case, Wilder instructed Mellor to photograph Cooper in close-up in soft focus and shrouded in shadows, to disguise the wrinkles on his face. Cameron Crowe defends Cooper's performance: "His is an underrated and selfless performance, always serving Audrey Hepburn, who dazzles from beginning to end."[52]

Principal photography wrapped in December 1956, and Wilder moved on to postproduction. He had two composers working on the score: Waxman was to create the incidental music, and Matty Malneck was to write the title song for the movie, "Love in the Afternoon." Wilder had met Malneck in 1926 when the latter was a member of Paul Whiteman's orchestra.[53] Malneck, who served as musical adviser on the movie, said Wilder's knowledge of hit songs of the 1920s and 1930s was encyclopedic; moreover, he knew how to integrate a song into the action, so that it heightened a moment. One such song was "Fascination," one of Wilder's favorite songs from his student days in Vienna. Walter Mirisch writes in his memoirs that one day Wilder said to him, "Come back to the office. I want you to listen to a record; it's very old and scratchy, but I think it would be wonderful" in the film. Mirisch continues, "This was the first time I heard 'Fascination.' It was incredible. The song was used in the film and is now always identified with it."[54] Wilder had Waxman work this haunting waltz into the background music for the love scenes between Ariane and Frank.

Wilder prepared the final edit of the movie with film editor Leonid Azar and supervising editor Doane Harrison. After he submitted it to the industry censor, he was notified that Geoffrey Shurlock found the film's ending unacceptable. Shurlock insisted that, instead of the lovers' merely "galloping off into the sunset," it should be made clear that they are headed for the altar.[55] The Legion of Decency, with which Wilder had had a run-in over *The Seven Year Itch*, objected to the ending on the same grounds and threatened to classify the movie in its category of condemned films. Allied Artists worried that the legion's denunciation would earn the film an unjustified reputation with the public at large as a salacious movie. The studio prevailed on Wilder to insert a brief declaration at film's end, stating firmly that Frank and Ariane were soon married. So Wilder commandeered Chevalier to record a bit of voice-over narration for the U.S. prints of the movie. Chevalier remarks that the happy couple "are now serving a life sentence in New York."

Shurlock was satisfied with this resolution of the problem, but Wilder's concession only partially mollified the Legion of Decency. The legion merely raised its rating of *Love in the Afternoon* from condemned to its still disapproving objectionable category, "films that can be a moral danger to spectators," explaining that the film "tends to ridicule the virtue of purity by reason of undue emphasis on illicit love." Wilder was livid when he got the news: "I do not have the reputation of ever having been connected with pictures of a lascivious character."[56]

Chevalier's voice-over at the end of the movie bookends his narration during the movie's prologue. Wilder later told an interviewer that the opening narration was voiced by Louis Jourdan, but Wilder's memory played him false—the voice speaking the opening and closing narration in the movie is clearly Chevalier's. As Dick points out, when the prologue ends, Chevalier's voice as the narrator "meshes with that of the character he is playing, Claude Chevasse."[57] (Jourdan, a French actor who appeared in Hollywood pictures like *Gigi* [1958], does narrate the prologue of Wilder's film *Irma la Douce* [1963].)

The prologue of *Love in the Afternoon* is a brisk tour of Paris, punctuated by Claude's rakish commentary as he presents lovers embracing passionately all over town: "In Paris," he proclaims, "people make love—well perhaps not better than anywhere else—but certainly more often." There follows a montage of kissing couples. "They do it on the Left Bank, and on the Right Bank; they do it anytime, anywhere: the butcher, the baker, and the friendly undertaker. Even poodles do it"—a shot of two dogs smooching is perhaps a reference to the amorous canines in *The Emperor Waltz*. "There is married love," Claude concludes, "and illicit love; that is where I come in." He is a private eye specializing in tracking down straying spouses.

Donald Spoto notes that "Wilder's stated intention with *Love in the Afternoon* was to honor his mentor, Ernst Lubitsch," by making a soufflé-light picture, suffused with Lubitsch's sophisticated Continental grace and wit.[58] In *Love in the Afternoon* Cooper plays a part similar to his role in Lubitsch's *Bluebeard's Eighth Wife*, that of a much-married, wealthy cad who carries on a never-ending series of love affairs with mostly married women. Frank is an executive with the Pepsi-Cola Company; a rendezvous with him is sometimes described as "the pause that refreshes" (which was actually Coca-Cola's motto).

One scene that is certainly touched by the spirit of Lubitsch occurs when Claude has Frank's hotel suite under surveillance at the behest of a woman's jealous husband. Claude observes a stream of waiters pushing carts laden with food and drink into the suite. The waiters are followed by the gypsy quartet that Frank always has on hand to establish the mood for his seductions. Impeccably clad in tuxedos, they serenade the couple with "Fascination." Soon the waiters file out of the suite, pushing the empty carts, with the gypsy musicians close behind them. The last musician shuts the door and hangs the "Do not disturb" sign on the doorknob. Wilder here employs one of Lubitsch's favorite tricks to get around the censors: he suggests that Frank and his lady of the moment are indulging beyond the closed doors in outrageous behavior, which is never shown. "If Lubitsch was an inspired 'director of doors,'" Kevin Brownlow says, "then Wilder paid him homage in this scene."[59]

While Ariane is ostensibly dusting her father's office, she surreptitiously dips into his confidential files. She comes across a file full of newspaper clippings documenting Frank's escapades. She becomes intrigued with the aging Don Juan and contrives to visit him at his hotel. When Ariane crosses the threshold into Frank's suite, the innocent ingenue is entering the adult world of an infamous philanderer, with all its secrets and lies. Ariane does not reveal her name to Frank but masquerades as a mystery woman with a notorious past. She soon falls under the lothario's spell and thus begins a series of afternoon tête-à-têtes with him. Ariane insists on seeing him in the afternoon so she can tell her father she is rehearsing with the orchestra of which she is a member.

Ariane says that Frank has an American face like a cowboy's—a reference to Cooper's sagebrush movies. Having never dated a slick American playboy before, the sheltered Ariane endeavors to fathom the personality of Frank Flannagan and his ilk. She tells a friend, "They're strange people, Americans. When they're young, they have their teeth straightened, their tonsils taken out, and gallons of vitamins pumped into them. Something happens to their insides; they become mechanized, dehumanized." She concludes, "'I'm not even sure whether he has a heart,'" since Frank maintains that all love affairs should be transitory.

Wilder himself has spoken of Americans, including himself, in an uncomplimentary fashion: "We are the most hard-boiled, undisciplined people in the world. First our heroes smack their girl's face with a grapefruit," as James Cagney does in *Public Enemy* (1931), "and then they kick mothers in wheelchairs downstairs," as Richard Widmark does in *Kiss of Death* (1947). "How much farther can we go?"[60] How far will Frank go to hold on to Ariane?

That Frank is growing jealous of Ariane's roster of former lovers is evident when he notices the ankle bracelet she is wearing. She claims that it is a gift from a former lover, when actually it is a key chain. He abruptly tears it from her ankle because he did not give it to her. Ariane's anklet recalls the provocative ankle bracelet worn by Phyllis in *Double Indemnity*.

Tormented by this nameless female's exotic tales of her former lovers, Frank goes so far as to hire Claude Chevasse to uncover her true identity. Claude soon learns that the woman he is investigating is his own daughter. To his chagrin, Claude, "the record keeper of affairs of indiscretion," realizes that his daughter has become a "candidate for one of her father's file cards."[61] Claude implores Frank to forget her. "Give her a chance," he pleads. "She's such a little fish; throw her back in the water." Frank accordingly tells Ariane that he has bought a train ticket for a holiday on the Riviera—without her. He reminds her of his cynical motto: "He who loves and runs away lives to love another day." Ariane nevertheless accompanies Frank to the depot to bid him adieu.

The following sequence begins with "a view of a smoking, chugging locomotive in a splendid vaulted railway station."[62] This is one of the very few scenes in his film that Wilder borrowed from Czinner's movie. Frank has boarded the train; it begins to move. Ariane rushes along the platform, assuring Frank through her tears that she will continue her promiscuous life after he is gone. Ariane explains the tears by saying, "It's the soot; it always happens to me at railroad stations." This is a reference to David Lean's *Brief Encounter* (1945), in which Laura, the heroine, gets a cinder in her eye while standing on the station platform, and Alec, the handsome hero, removes it for her.

Frank now realizes that his emotions have been genuinely touched by this disarming girl. At the last moment, "as the train picks up speed, Frank lifts her aboard and carries her to a seat in the back," writes Dick, who has done the best analysis of this film in English. "Be quiet, Ariane," says Frank. He calls Ariane—once his anonymous lover—by her name for the first time.[63]

Claude, who has shadowed Ariane and Frank to the train station, remains standing on the platform, along with the four gypsy musicians. They saw away with gusto at "Fascination" for the last time; since the quartet was associated with Frank's seductions, they have been left behind for good.

Wilder did not like Claude's final voice-over, assuring the audience that Frank and Ariane would soon wed. When Frank sweeps Ariane up in his arms and takes her to his compartment, "that is the real ending," said

Wilder.[64] In any case, at the fade-out, the strains of "Fascination" swell sublimely to a peak as Waxman marshals the full orchestra for the film's finale.

*Love in the Afternoon* was released in June 1957. Most critics welcomed it as "a sheer delight," "a cascade of bubbles and belly laughs," and—most significant for Wilder—"the type of sophisticated fare Lubitsch would have undertaken with delight."[65] As Brownlow notes, "If Lubitsch had lived, he'd have made just such a picture."[66] Audrey Hepburn was captivating as the wistful Ariane; her wide-eyed wonder and innocence "rang as true as a small silver bell."[67] Yet Maurice Chevalier, more than one critic noted, nearly stole the picture with his winning performance as the quirky, mischievous private eye specializing in cases of amour.

One reservation about the movie was that the aging Gary Cooper "frankly has a much longer count on the calendar" than the wispy, effervescent Audrey Hepburn. Cooper seemed to lack conviction and hence was disappointing as the protagonist. Barson quips that in *Love in the Afternoon,* "Coop sometimes looks as though he'd like to doff his tux, don his buckskin gear and ride off to hunt buffalo."[68]

Some other reviewers complained that 130 minutes was an excessive running time for a lighter-than-air love story; more decisive editing by Azar and Harrison would have provided better pacing.

François Truffaut, speaking for the young, feisty film critics at *Cahiers du cinema,* was disappointed in *Love in the Afternoon.* Truffaut griped that it was a sentimental, old-fashioned movie; he preferred the rash, somewhat cruder *Seven Year Itch.* Wilder, wrote Truffaut, had become "a lecherous old balladeer out of touch with the world."[69] But Truffaut's panning of the film did not represent the generally good notices the movie garnered throughout Europe.

Indeed, the movie made a better showing at the box office in Europe, but Allied Artists had sold the rights to the European distribution of the film to finance the making of the picture in the first place. *Love in the Afternoon* was not a moneymaker for Allied Artists. To make matters worse for the studio, William Wyler's *Friendly Persuasion* also failed to become a smash hit in America. Thus neither of Allied Artists' first two prestige pictures propelled it into the big time, as it had hoped.

When Allied Artists was forced to cut back on its ambitious plans to become a major Hollywood studio, the Mirisch brothers decided to desert it. In July 1957, only a month after the premiere of *Love in the Afternoon,* Walter, Harold, and Marvin Mirisch established the Mirisch Company, their own independent production company, with a view to releasing their pictures through United Artists (UA).

In 1919 UA had been formed by Charles Chaplin, D. W. Griffith, Mary Pickford, and Douglas Fairbanks Sr. to distribute the pictures they made. When they inaugurated UA, one Hollywood executive joked, "The lunatics have taken over the asylum."[70] But UA was still operating nearly four decades later. It did not make movies but financed and distributed films made by independent producers, who were multiplying in Hollywood as the studio system fell into decline. In the 1950s, UA, now headed by Arthur Krim, had released such successful pictures as *The African Queen* and *High Noon*. With Walter Mirisch as production chief, the Mirisch brothers arranged with Krim to base their production unit at the Samuel Goldwyn Studios in Hollywood, where UA had its headquarters. The Mirisches leased studio space on the Goldwyn lot to make their pictures.

For his part, Wilder was pleased to be working with independent production companies and no longer associated with major studios like Paramount, Twentieth Century–Fox, and Warner Bros. He put a birdcage in his office at the Goldwyn Studios, with a stuffed bird perched on top. He explained, "The bird sitting atop the cage is symbolic of my final freedom from my imprisonment by the majors: the bird has escaped the cage. I call the neighborhood where the major studios are in Hollywood the Bermuda Triangle."[71]

Edward Small, whose independent production company also released films through UA, had acquired the film rights to Agatha Christie's hit play *Witness for the Prosecution*. Small planned to produce the picture in partnership with Arthur Hornblow Jr., who had produced Wilder's first Hollywood picture, *The Major and the Minor*. They signed Wilder to cowrite the screenplay and to direct *Witness for the Prosecution*, to be made at the Goldwyn Studios for UA release. Wilder said that he was glad to be making another movie in Hollywood; filming abroad was overrated. "It's much easier technically to shoot a picture in Hollywood," because the studio facilities were second to none. "If you're going to perform a delicate operation, why not do it in the best hospital?" Moreover, France, where *Love in the Afternoon* was shot, "is a place where the money falls apart in your hand, and you can't tear the toilet paper."[72]

# 11

# Remains to Be Seen

## Witness for the Prosecution

I would win most of my cases if it weren't for my clients. They will waltz into the witness box and blurt out things that are better left unblurted.

—*Leo McKern as Horace Rumpole, barrister,*
*in the telefilm* Rumpole and the Confession of Guilt

Falling in love again, never wanted to.
What am I to do?
I can't help it.

—*Frederick Hollander, "Falling in Love Again"*
*(Marlene Dietrich's signature song)*

*Witness for the Prosecution* began its artistic life as a short story that Agatha Christie published in 1933 in Britain in a volume titled *The Hound of Death*. The story was published in the United States in 1948 in the collection *Witness for the Prosecution*. When another playwright sought permission to turn the story into a play, Christie decided to adapt it for the stage herself. The play opened at the Winter Garden Theatre in London on October 28, 1953. "When the curtain came down on my ending," Christie recalled, the play and its author were greeted with a standing ovation.[1] After a run of 468 performances in London, the production moved to Broadway on December 16, 1954. The play was a smash hit there, running for 646 performances; it won the New York Drama Critics' Circle award for best foreign play.

Independent producer Edward Small, who had produced the classic film noir *Raw Deal* (1948), purchased the screen rights to *Witness for the Prosecution* at a high price, since Agatha Christie was a popular and prolific mystery writer whose works were outsold only by Shakespeare and the Bible.[2] Small hired Billy Wilder to cowrite the screenplay and direct the picture for one hundred thousand dollars plus 5 percent of the gross profits. Small would act as executive producer; his partner, Arthur Hornblow Jr., was to produce the picture. Wilder very much wanted to work again with Hornblow, who "had given me my first chance to direct." Hence Wilder did not grumble about relinquishing the producer's chores to him. As things turned out, Wilder recalled, Hornblow "took a dark load off my shoulders."[3] It was Hornblow, not Wilder, who went to the front office to talk them out of shaving the budget.

Wilder was interested in filming a Christie mystery because he had read her work over the years. Asked about the influences on his films, he replied, "If there was any influence on me, it must come from the books and plays I read. . . . My work is not sugarcoated, I don't use the sugar tongs," he explained. "But I don't sit down and say, 'Now I'm going to make a vicious, unsentimental picture.'" The tone of the film depended on the source story.[4]

Stephen Farber points out an interesting parallel between *Witness for the Prosecution* and *Sunset Boulevard*. The relationship of Leonard Vole, the young fortune hunter, to Emily French, the wealthy widow whom he eventually murders, "is an almost identical, cut-rate version of the same parasitic relationship of Joe Gillis and Norma Desmond," once again motivated by greed and ending in violence.[5]

Small said that "Marlene Dietrich made no bones about wanting the role of the German-born Christine Vole, Leonard's wife." As she grew older, Dietrich had not been offered many worthwhile parts. She was convinced that this film would give her the opportunity to prove that she was still an accomplished actress and not merely a headliner at Las Vegas, where she periodically entertained. "Billy Wilder, her old comrade from prewar Berlin, endorsed her for the role of Christine," Small said. Both Wilder and Hornblow recommended Charles Laughton to play Sir Wilfrid Robarts, and Small approved the casting of both Dietrich and Laughton.[6]

Small himself suggested Tyrone Power for Leonard Vole. Admittedly, Power was no longer the box office knockout he had been in the 1940s, when he played the swashbuckling hero of several costume dramas. Nevertheless, Small was confident that Power's name still had marquee value. Power at first declined the role, since he suspected that he would be overshadowed by the well-known scene stealers Dietrich and Laughton. "Ty changed his mind," said Small, "when I offered him a salary of $300,000."[7] Besides, Power, like Dietrich, welcomed the chance to prove by his performance in this picture that he was a serious actor and not just a movie star. "I'm sick of all these knights in shining armor parts; I want to do something worthwhile, like plays and films that have something to say," Power said at the time. "Someday I will show the fuckers who say I was a success just because of my pretty face."[8] He also wanted to be directed by the renowned Billy Wilder. By December 1956, the leads were all cast.

With shooting only six months away, Wilder got down to writing the script in earnest. His partner this time around was Harry Kurnitz, who had twenty years of experience as a screenwriter. He had, for example, written the screenplay for Carol Reed's thriller *The Man Between* (1953). Moreover, he had authored many mystery novels under the pseudonym Mario Page. Kurnitz was not a young screenwriter who would defer to Wilder as Wendell Mayes had done. In fact, Kurnitz reminded Wilder of the intractable Raymond Chandler. Wilder thought Kurnitz was not as serious about devoting himself to the screenplay as he himself was. Kurnitz countered that he was simply not a workaholic like Wilder. He believed firmly in a nine-to-five workday and was not inclined to work overtime as Wilder pestered him to do. And, unlike Edwin Blum and other veteran screenwriters of the Wilder wars, Kurnitz was impervious to Wilder's sarcastic insults. He was a fast man with a verbal punch who bounded back with clever jokes of his own aimed at Wilder. Even Wilder had to acknowledge that Kurnitz helped him turn out a solid screenplay.

In adapting *Witness for the Prosecution* for the screen, Wilder realized that Christie concentrated primarily on the tantalizing ingenuity of the plots of her stories, while she treated characterization perfunctorily. Wilder viewed the murder mysteries she churned out as essentially exercises in puzzle solving. On the level of character delineation, Wilder observed, Christie's mysteries were like "high school plays."[9] Wilder was less interested in showing how the mystery was solved than he was in portraying the characters' encounters with the evils of a corrupt society.

Accordingly, said Wilder, "We changed a few things from the original."[10] To flesh out the barrister's character, Wilder gave the overweight Sir Wilfrid a heart condition brought on by overwork. He also gave the barrister a nurse, the peckish, fluttering, relentlessly vigilant Miss Plimsoll, who is charged with keeping Sir Wilfrid from suffering another heart attack. Wilder obtained the services of Elsa Lanchester, Laughton's wife, for the part; she was best known for playing the title role in *The Bride of Frankenstein* (1935). Sir Wilfrid views Miss Plimsoll as a meddling nuisance. In giving him "a foil in Miss Plimsoll, Wilder humanized the character by making him a flawed human being who stubbornly resents the nurse's ministrations."[11] "If you weren't a woman, Miss Plimsoll," he explodes at one point, "I would strike you!" When she confiscates his cigars and brandy—both of which are proscribed by doctor's orders—Sir Wilfrid fumes, "I'll snatch her thermometer and plunge it into her shoulder blades!" It would be "justifiable homicide." Such humorous byplay between them provides some much-needed comic relief.

Wilder and Kurnitz inserted some flashbacks into the screenplay to keep the film from bogging down into a static, talky courtroom drama. The most crucial flashback, which is based on a reference in the play's exposition, depicts how Christine came to meet Leonard, her husband-to-be, when he was a British soldier in Hamburg at the end of World War II. Wilder took the liberty of working into this flashback a cabaret scene that he had dropped from the screenplay of *A Foreign Affair*, in which a brawl breaks out when a sailor attempts to paw Erika. Steven Bach notes, "Christine is another version of Erika, singing in an off-limits dive that is nearly a replica of the earlier picture's Lorelei Club."[12] Indeed, Dietrich's performance as Christine in *Witness for the Prosecution* "stands next to her portrayal of Erika in *A Foreign Affair* in revealing her considerable but sadly underused talents."[13]

For the scene in *Witness for the Prosecution*, Dietrich needed a ribald song to sing while playing her accordion and serenading the American enlisted men in the café with her sassy charm. Frederick Hollander, who supplied the songs for Dietrich in *A Foreign Affair*, had gone back to Germany. So, with the help of Matty Malneck, who was scoring *Witness for the Prosecution*, Wilder and Dietrich dug up a German ballad about Hamburg's red-light district titled "Auf der Reeperbahn nachts um halb eins" (On the Reeperbahn at half past midnight). It was composed by Ralph Arthur Roberts, an actor-manager with whom Dietrich had worked in a cabaret in Berlin in the 1920s. Jack Brooks provided the English lyrics for the number, which became "I May Never Go Home Anymore." In the flashback, when Christine finishes the song, some sailors get rambunctious, and one of them grabs Christine. In the ensuing melee, one leg of Christine's slacks is ripped open well above the knee.

The scene required 145 extras and cost $75,000, including the construction of the nightclub set. Ean Wood opines that Wilder went to all that trouble and expense just to show off one of Dietrich's famous legs. The film, he comments, was good enough to survive "the unnecessary flashback scene."[14] On the contrary, Wilder deemed the flashback essential to the plot. The sequence establishes how Christine and Leonard fell in love on the spot. Furthermore, we see that Christine is grateful to Leonard for agreeing to marry her and bring her back to London as a war bride. The flashback shows how Christine's gratitude grows into love—much more clearly than Christie does in the play. It further helps to establish why Christine is later willing to risk prison by perjuring herself on Leonard's behalf during his murder trial. In short, the flashback sequence is Wilder's major contribution to his literary source.

After the completion of the screenplay, Kurnitz vowed never to collaborate with Wilder again, just as Lehman, Blum, and others had done. In a profile of Wilder he later published in a slick magazine, Kurnitz explained why: "Billy's associates sometimes have a hunted look, shuffle nervously, and have been known to break into tears if a door slams anywhere in the same building. . . . He has a fierce, monomaniacal devotion to whatever project is in the typewriter." Kurnitz continued, "He is a fiend for work and works nearly all the time. Let's face it, Billy Wilder at work is actually two people— Mr. Hyde and Mr. Hyde."[15] Asked to comment on Kurnitz's article, Wilder said that a journalist once quoted one of his friends as saying that "my collaborators are $50,000 secretaries." He continued, "For one thing, that individual is no friend of mine; for another, if what he said was true, I would hire my relatives and make their salaries tax-deductible!"

Principal photography began on June 10, 1957, at the Goldwyn Studios. Laughton upstaged Power in *Witness for the Prosecution,* just as Power suspected he might. Power had come to Hollywood in 1936 after some supporting roles on Broadway; he immediately established himself as a star in films like *Jesse James* (1939). After serving in the marines in World War II, he played mostly in colorful historical romances like *Captain from Castile* (1947). Like Laughton, Power returned to the stage between pictures. He was in fact directed by Laughton in a concert reading of Stephen Vincent Benet's verse drama *John Brown's Body,* with Judith Anderson and Raymond Massey. Film historian Sam Staggs mentions that Dietrich tried to vamp Power during the shooting of *Witness for the Prosecution.* This embarrassed the actor, because his orientation was apparently more homosexual than heterosexual. Wilder confirmed that Dietrich developed a crush on Power. "Everybody had a crush on Ty Power. Laughton had a crush on him; I did too. As heterosexual as you might be, it was impossible to be impervious to that kind of charm."[16]

Among Wilder's production crew on this picture, cinematographer Russell Harlan and production designer Alexander Trauner stand out. Harlan had "developed a flinty black-and-white photographic style."[17] The stark, harsh lighting style he developed for Westerns like *Red River* (1947) was carried forward intact to his hard-edged cinematography for *Witness for the Prosecution.* Trauner matched his superb work on *Love in the Afternoon* with his production design for *Witness for the Prosecution.* Particularly noteworthy was his replica of the Old Bailey, London's criminal court. He was denied permission to take photographs of the real courtroom, so he had to make detailed sketches of the architecture. Trauner built his set to scale, according to specific measurements: forty-three feet by fifty-six feet, with a twenty-seven-foot ceiling. It was constructed of sturdy Austrian oak, complete with panels in the walls, any of which could be removed to make room for the camera, if a setup called for it, "allowing filming from any angle." The price tag for the entire set was $75,000.[18]

Maria Riva's biography of her mother, Marlene Dietrich, quotes from many of Dietrich's letters to her. In a letter dated July 13, 1957, Dietrich complains that, although most observers said they could not tell the difference between the actual Old Bailey and Trauner's courtroom set, she was not one of them. "Wilder and Hornblow are proud that they have the real thing; except that it is new." She caviled that "the ceiling is painted fresh and almost white, looking like a Hollywood set. The British barrister we have on the set agreed with me that it is dirty up there from the years. The leather on the benches is brand-new too."[19]

In the same letter, Dietrich took some pot shots at Mr. and Mrs. Wilder. Dietrich frequently spent weekends with the Wilders while the film was in production, and she was not above criticizing the lifestyle of her hosts. "All they do, those two, is sit in front of the TV set! Billy even eats in front of it! They both sit there like Mister and Missus Glutz from the Bronx, eating their frozen dinners! Unbelievable! That's what happens to brilliant men when they marry low-class women. Sad!"[20] It seems that Dietrich was jealous of Wilder's wife, who was younger than she. Indeed, she sometimes ignored Audrey while she was absorbed in conversation with Billy. Wilder said that he tried to explain to his wife that Dietrich did not slight her deliberately; it was just that Audrey did not exist for her. Audrey replied that her husband's making excuses for Dietrich did not help.

If Marlene Dietrich was jealous of Audrey Wilder, Elsa Lanchester was jealous of Dietrich. Lanchester, who was one year younger than Dietrich, resented that she looked matronly while Dietrich's svelte beauty was still alluring. She gossiped to friends that Dietrich was in the makeup chair at the studio at the crack of dawn every day during filming. The makeup man, she said, would spend two hours banishing the wrinkles from her face to preserve the illusion of Dietrich's youthful glamour.[21] Noel Coward, who visited the set, noted dryly, "Marlene, with her intense preoccupation with herself, is showing signs of wear and tear. How foolish to think that one can ever slam the door in the face of age." Nevertheless, "slam it shut she did," Bach writes. "Marlene, in fact, looks uncannily young in most of *Witness*," particularly in the flashback to her warbling songs in the sleazy Hamburg nightery.[22]

Wilder was fascinated by Dietrich. "The femme fatale, with her feather boa, fake eyelashes, and long legs" was her screen personality. "At home, Dietrich scrubbed the floors on her hands and knees, fried eggs and potatoes." She doctored lovers and stagehands "with homemade remedies for hangovers and colds. . . . She was so down-to-earth."[23] As one of her multiple complaints to her daughter during filming, Dietrich felt she had reason to question Tyrone Power's personal appearance in the film. She wrote to Maria, "Ty Power sits in the prisoner's box; he wears a beautiful tweed jacket; his shirt is immaculate, cuffs freshly pressed." He was, nevertheless, playing the unemployed defendant in a murder trial. "None of the poor English appearance, the wrinkled cuffs and sleeves" of a man who is out of a job, hard up, "a man who is in prison on top of that. There he sits, a HOLLYWOOD LEADING MAN so out of character."[24] By contrast, Dietrich, who was playing the wife of an impecunious grifter, was made to wear relatively inexpensive outfits. She was miffed that Power's costumes were more elegant than hers, which did not show off her beauty. Wisely, Dietrich communicated her negative judgments to her daughter but not to Wilder.

Laughton had a reputation for being a troublesome and temperamental actor. Yet Wilder reported that Laughton's spirits were high during the shooting of *Witness for the Prosecution;* he was "full of suggestions on every aspect of filmmaking, from costumes to camera angles."[25] Wilder regularly conferred with Laughton while rehearsing a scene and considered his suggestions seriously. Dietrich resented their tête-à-têtes on the set, from which she was excluded. She wrote to Maria in her letter of July 13, "By now Laughton is co-directing me with Billy. He is a sly fox, and Billy does not notice what he is doing. There were long conferences after every one of my takes between Laughton and Billy; and I just stood there and took it. I know I have a terrible legend to overcome: that I am only interested in my looks" and did not care about acting. Dietrich could not refrain from being offended by the reluctance of her director and costar to ask for her input. After all, she had played promiscuous females all her life, "and this one they don't even think I can contribute anything to." She concluded, "I will still get Mrs. Vole on the screen" in a good performance.[26]

As a matter of fact, Wilder was more satisfied with Dietrich's performance, as filming progressed, than she realized. In retrospect, Dietrich's overriding evaluation of Wilder was likewise favorable. In her autobiography, she writes, "Billy Wilder was a master builder who knew his toolbox and used it in the best way possible to set up the framework on which he hung the garlands of his wit and wisdom."[27]

Dietrich was correct in sensing that Wilder had a very high opinion of

Laughton's acting ability. "Wilder was convinced that Laughton had the greatest range and power of any actor" he had ever directed. Nothing tests an actor's mettle like the role of a lawyer, and Laughton's larger-than-life portrayal of Sir Wilfrid is one of the craftiest and juiciest performances of his career.[28] "In our film it is Laughton who pulls the whole thing together," Wilder explained. Sir Wilfrid is a much more important character in the film than he is in the play. "Laughton is more of a three-dimensional character in the film"; he makes the barrister a knight in search of justice.[29]

In photographing the courtroom drama, Wilder often used long, uninterrupted takes to allow the camera to move about the set, so that the pace of the action never falters. In this manner he kept the movie from looking static and stagey. Moreover, an extended take, uninterrupted by cuts to other angles, enables the actor to give a sustained reading of a long speech and thus to build steadily to a dramatic climax. In one scene, for example, Sir Wilfrid has a virtuoso speech in which he exposes Christine as lying on the witness stand. Laughton's voice "rises from a whisper to a tremendous roar of fury" as he denounces her as a *liar;* the word reverberates for several seconds.[30] Laughton spoke "very low for a page-and-a-half," Wilder recalled; "and then worked up to the big line, 'Are you not a chronic and habitual LIAR?' The whole thing we did in one close-up, one take."[31] The single, unbroken take makes Laughton's delivery all the more effective.

Laughton biographer Simon Callow reports that Laughton was in such good humor during shooting "that he volunteered to read all the parts for the jury's reaction shots." The extras who played the jurors were hired for one day; passages of dialogue would be read to them off camera, and they would react. The reaction shots would later be cut in to various scenes. When Laughton asked Wilder to let him read the off camera speeches, Wilder answered, "You don't want to do this, Charles; it's donkey work. The script girl can do it." But Laughton insisted, and he presented perfect impersonations of his fellow actors. "Wilder beamed at Laughton's sheer skill," notes Callow.[32]

As the plot unfolds, a Cockney doxy phones Sir Wilfrid from Euston station, claiming to be in possession of documentation that is pertinent to the trial. Sir Wilfrid acquires the evidence from her in a hurried meeting at the depot, and it results in Leonard Vole's acquittal. The mysterious woman is subsequently revealed to be Christine Vole in disguise; she masterminded the clever ruse to save her husband from the gallows.

For this impersonation, Wilder tagged Laughton to coach Dietrich in a Cockney accent. "Marlene was forever up at our house," said Lanchester, "taking lessons in Cockney from Charles. She was obsessed with this impersonation; I never saw anyone work so hard."[33] Noel Coward was visiting Laughton and Lanchester at the time, and so he also helped Dietrich with the dialect, both at their house and on the set. "It is not easy to teach Cockney to a German glamour-puss," Coward recorded in his diary, "but she did astonishingly well."[34] Indeed, Dietrich's Cockney accent was so authentic that a rumor soon spread around the studio that her voice in the scene had been dubbed by another actress. But Jay Nash and Stanley Ross note that "production stills exist of Dietrich rehearsing the telephone scene without make-up."[35] In addition, during postproduction, Dietrich wrote in her diary, "Sept. 4th. Dubbing Cockney woman."[36]

Dietrich mastered the dialect, but there was still the question of how to disguise Christine in a way that would fool both Sir Wilfrid and the audience. The makeup artists, Gustaf Noran, Ray Sebastian, and Harry Ray, went to work on Dietrich, supplying her with a dark wig, a false nose, and a scar on her cheek. Orson Welles, for whom Dietrich had recently made a cameo appearance in *Touch of Evil* (1958), kibitzed on the fashioning of Dietrich's false nose out of putty. Wilder thought that Dietrich in full makeup looked positively grotesque. Dietrich herself suggested that the fake nose be made less prominent and that her makeup in other ways be toned down. Wilder approved the adjustments.

Wilder filmed the scene in which the Cockney trollop phones Sir Wilfrid from the train station in two ways. In one version, writes Bach, "we see it is Christine speaking with a Cockney accent. At the end of the call, she takes from her purse the wig we will later see her wear in disguise."[37] In the other version, Dietrich, already made up as the Cockney hooker, makes the call to Sir Wilfrid. Wilder was aware that there were two ways that the scene could be played: with suspense or with surprise. Viewers might be made aware in advance that the Cockney harlot was Christine's invention. That would generate suspense, because the filmgoer would be anxious to see precisely what Christine was up to. Or the viewer might be left in the dark as to the real identity of the mystery woman. That would cause surprise when Christine's masquerade was finally revealed at the film's climax. Wilder chose surprise rather than suspense, so that the audience is genuinely shocked at film's end to learn that Christine and the Cockney woman are one and the same person. Wilder wanted the audience to be caught off guard by the revelation of Christine's elaborate deception at the same time that Sir Wilfrid is.

Wilder absolutely insisted that strict secrecy be maintained about the movie's surprise ending during shooting. Throughout the production period, a placard was posted on the door of the soundstage, demanding that no one who saw the play "ever told the secret" and informing all columnists and other visitors to the set that they must sign the following pledge: "I promise not to reveal any of the secrets . . . which lead to the disclosure of the surprise ending."[38] Among the signatures on the poster was that of Noel Coward, who had helped coach Dietrich on the Cockney accent. The final ten pages of the screenplay were not distributed to cast and crew until just before it was time to film the final sequence. On the day that the finale was shot, Wilder had security guards posted at the door of the soundstage.

Principal photography wrapped on August 20, 1957. Wilder lucked out in his choice of editor for *Witness for the Prosecution*. He had not had a regular film editor for some years, although Doane Harrison continued as supervising editor, in addition to being an associate producer for Wilder. For the present film, Wilder snagged Daniel Mandell as editor; Mandell thus began an association with Wilder that would last for ten years. The veteran editor had already won two Academy Awards, for *Pride of the Yankees* (1942) and *The Best Years of Our Lives* (1946). Mandell always maintained that "the greatest accomplishment of a good editor is, ironically, that the audience is totally unaware of his work." Wilder heartily agreed. "The minute someone in the audience says, 'What a snappy piece of editing that is in that montage,' they are no longer paying attention to the story." Mandell's edit of *Witness for the Prosecution* was "an adept combination of action and intimate drama."[39]

The credits of *Witness for the Prosecution* unroll as the Old Bailey comes into session, accompanied by a solemn "Pomp and Circumstance"–type march. The film's mystery concerns a clever cad named Leonard Vole. Leonard is accused of the murder of Mrs. French, a rich widow with whom he had been friendly—so friendly, in fact, that she wrote him into her will shortly before her demise. Christie tips off the audience subtly that Leonard is not really a decent sort by giving him the last name of Vole. Yet Leonard's wife, Christine, seems devoted to him, and we learn why in the flashback to Christine's shabby basement digs in war-ravaged Hamburg: Leonard married her and brought her back to London as a war refugee. The flashback concludes just as the ceiling collapses in Christine's bombed-out flat while Leonard is with her; this disaster subtly foreshadows how the roof will cave in on both of them before the film is over.

Leonard tells his lawyer, Sir Wilfrid, that he is counting on Christine's testimony to save him from the gallows. But the barrister has a hunch that, if Leonard assumes that the unpredictable Christine is going to save him, "he is a drowning man clutching at a razor blade." Sir Wilfrid faces an open-and-shut case, but he nevertheless mounts a full-scale defense for his client, since he is convinced that Leonard is caught in a web of circumstantial evidence.

Given Christine's apparent loyalty to Leonard, Sir Wilfrid is flabbergasted when she appears in court as a witness for the prosecution. Sir Wilfrid reminds her that a wife cannot testify against her husband, but Christine counters that she and Leonard were never properly married because she was never legally divorced from her first husband, Otto Helm, who is living in East Berlin. She then proceeds to give evidence that undermines Leonard's alibi for the night of the murder. She testifies that Leonard returned home that night with blood on his sleeve after ten o'clock, allowing him ample time to have killed Emily French earlier that same evening.

After court is adjourned, Sir Wilfrid is summoned to a railway station by a phone call from a Cockney prostitute, who sells him some incriminating love letters written by Christine to Max, her lover. Christine clearly indicates in the letters that she has given false testimony against Leonard because she wanted him to be convicted so that she can go off with another man. Sir Wilfrid presents this newly acquired evidence in open court. The jury is shocked at Christine's duplicity and votes to acquit Leonard.

Once the courtroom is cleared, Christine approaches Sir Wilfrid and lapses into the Cockney accent she employed when she talked with him the night before, while she was disguised as the prostitute. Christine fabricated the documentation and then sold it to Sir Wilfrid so he could use it against her in court and win an acquittal for Leonard. Christine adds that she concocted the whole masquerade not because she thought Leonard was innocent but because she was certain of his guilt. While Sir Wilfrid is still reeling from Christine's disclosure, Leonard casually announces that he is now free to leave Christine for a younger woman. Maddened with jealousy, Christine snatches a bread knife from the evidence table and stabs him to death right in the courtroom.

Christie's original short story ends with the revelation of Christine's clever maneuvers to save Leonard from the gallows. In the play Christie engineered Christine's "private retribution" on Leonard because she was no longer satisfied to allow Leonard to go unpunished for killing the hapless Emily French. The play ends with Christine declaring, "I shall be tried for the murder of the only man I ever loved." Looking at the judge's bench, she adds, "Guilty, my lord," as the curtain descends.[40] Bach reflects, "The result is the transformation of Christine Vole from calculating bitch to desperately wronged woman."[41] The ending of the play implies that Christine herself will go to the gallows for killing Leonard.

Wilder was not completely satisfied with the play's outcome. "Wilder could no more sentence Christine to death for murdering a bounder than he could send Erika off to the labor camp without implying that she would never get there," Bernard Dick comments perceptively. So Wilder supplies an escape clause for Christine before the film's final fade-out. Sir Wilfrid agrees to defend Christine, explaining that she did not murder Leonard; "she executed him." Dick concludes, "So it was not murder, but retribution. Christine is meting out the sentence that the jury would have, if it had all the facts."[42] One knows that Sir Wilfrid will secure an acquittal for Christine. Paul Bergman and Michael Asimov write that it is "to Miss Plimsoll's despair" that "Sir Wilfrid immediately volunteers to represent Christine."[43] On the contrary, Miss Plimsoll encourages Sir Wilfrid to defend Christine. Brandishing the thermos that Sir Wilfrid pretends contains cocoa, she calls out to him, "You forgot your brandy!"

With *Witness for the Prosecution,* Wilder fashioned a film noir in the grand tradition of *Double Indemnity.* Indeed, *Witness for the Prosecution* resembles *Double Indemnity* in that it possesses the fascination of a hair-raising tale told by the tabloids; it is concerned with "the kind of people we read about so often in the less austere dailies."[44] Wilder was acclaimed for directing a film in which the courtroom is knee-deep in spirited argument, and suspense builds as witnesses reveal crucial details.

*Witness for the Prosecution* played exclusive engagements in New York and Los Angeles in December 1957 to qualify for that year's Academy Awards. When it was released in February 1958, it quickly became a box office sensation, ultimately accruing $8 million in domestic rentals alone. In the notices Laughton was singled out for praise: "Sage of the courtroom and cardiac patient, who's constantly disobeying his nurse's orders, . . . Laughton plays out the part flamboyantly and colorfully."[45]

More to the point were the critics who said that in this film Dietrich demonstrates that "she is a dramatic actress, as well as a still glamorous chanteuse."[46] This is precisely what Dietrich set out to prove when she lobbied for the role of Christine Vole. Christine sees herself as a victim when Leonard abandons her at film's end, and Dietrich expertly locates the ache at the core of Christine's character in the final scene.

Since Laughton and Dietrich had showier roles than Power, his performance as the feckless, lazy, but adorable Leonard Vole was mostly overlooked in the reviews. Yet Jeanine Basinger quite rightly states in *The Star Machine,* "Perhaps the best performance Tyrone Power ever gave was in Billy Wilder's 1957 *Witness for the Prosecution,* the one movie Power made in his postwar freelance period that really stands out today." In the film, Power does not hesitate to use his celebrated sex appeal "to play a rotting seducer well on his way to full decay as a wicked old roué."[47]

*Witness for the Prosecution* received six Academy Award nominations, including best director, actor (Charles Laughton), supporting actress (Elsa Lanchester), and editor (Daniel Mandell). Marlene Dietrich was not nominated as best actress. There are two possible explanations. The first theory is that, as Malene Sheppard Skaerved says, "Many suspected that the Cockney voice had been dubbed" by another actress. Though this was not true, the doubts kept her from being nominated.[48]

The other theory is that Wilder quietly spread the word around the studio that Dietrich should not be nominated because knowledge of her playing two roles had to be suppressed to keep from revealing the surprise ending to moviegoers who had not yet seen the film. Dietrich would not have been aware of Wilder's alleged machinations because, by the time the Oscar nominations were in the works, she had been gone from Hollywood for several months.

Maximilian Schell, director of the feature-length documentary *Marlene* (1983), favored the second theory. He told Dietrich that Wilder had discouraged her nomination and asked her whether she resented not being nominated for an Academy Award for her performance. She responded that an Oscar no longer mattered: "Rubbish! Garbo never got one either." Referring to honorary Oscars, she concluded, "They give you one on your deathbed; then you know you are dying."[49] Wilder, of course, vehemently denied sabotaging Dietrich's chances for an Oscar. He had told her after the picture wrapped that she deserved an Oscar (not that she would receive one for this movie) and he let it go at that.[50]

Irene Atkins terms *Witness for the Prosecution* "a triumph for Christie, just as the play had been."[51] Asked if he thought the film should have been deemed a triumph for himself as well, Wilder responded, "Frankly, I have never been interested in what the critics say of my films. A good review means less to me than, for instance, a comment Agatha Christie made about *Witness for the Prosecution*." Looking back, she called *Witness* the best film that had ever been derived from her mysteries.[52] "That means a great deal more to me than anything a critic has ever said of one of my films." Wilder noted.

*Witness for the Prosecution* has worn well. Released on DVD in 2001, it is a shining example of how a combination of expert remastering and intelligent packaging can invigorate a classic film. On June 17, 2008, the AFI broadcast a TV special in which the ten greatest films in ten genres were selected. *Witness for the Prosecution* was chosen as one of the top courtroom dramas of all time.

With the release of *Witness for the Prosecution*, Wilder had fulfilled his contract with Edward Small and was free to go to work for the Mirisch brothers again. He suggested to them that he make a comedy based on a 1932 German film. That in itself did not sound very promising to the Mirisches. Still, *Love in the Afternoon* had been derived from a 1931 German film, and that had turned out okay. So the Mirisches gave Wilder the go-ahead on a film that would turn out to be a milestone in his career.

# 12

# The Gang's All Here

## Some Like It Hot

Producer David Selznick told me mixing gangsters and comedy wouldn't work. In fact, it did.

—*Billy Wilder*

United Artists had an agreement with the Mirisch Company to distribute its films and serve as a financial backer. The Mirisch Company was based at the Samuel Goldwyn Studios, where UA had its offices. Walter Mirisch apprised Wilder of the company's plans to produce its own pictures and to continue its working relationship with Wilder. He agreed to make his next picture, *Some Like It Hot,* for the Mirisch Company. That began a creative association between the Mirisches and Wilder, states Walter Mirisch, "that ultimately resulted in his making his next eight films for us. I think . . . that is a record for a relationship enduring in this industry" between a director and a production company.[1]

"I. A. L. Diamond and I got the idea for *Some Like It Hot* from an earlier German film, *Fanfaren der Liebe* [*Fanfares of Love,* 1932], which was set in Bavaria," Wilder said. The original German film was cowritten by Robert Thoeren and Michael Logan, who were scriptwriters at Ufa in Berlin at the time. Thoeren was now working in Hollywood; he had repeatedly coaxed Wilder to do an American remake of the original picture. Wilder obtained a print of the German picture and screened it. (Thoeren did not live to see *Some Like It Hot;* he died in 1957.) *Fanfaren der Liebe* was about two starving musicians who don a number of disguises to get work; for example, they wear blackface to join an all-black jazz band. Only the film's final episode caught Wilder's attention. "When the two guys dressed as women and joined the girls' band called the Alpine Violets," he thought he had the makings of a farce.

Gerd Gemünden writes in his monograph on Wilder that Wilder was influenced in remaking *Fanfaren der Liebe* by the successful German remake in 1951, directed by Kurt Hoffmann. But Wilder emphasized that his movie was derived from the original film.[2] Wilder pitched the concept to Walter Mirisch, insisting that the premise of the two musicians in drag could be the basis for a classic screwball comedy. Mirisch had faith enough in Wilder to give him the go-ahead.

In its original version, Wilder said, *Fanfaren der Liebe* was a low-budget, second-class German flick "with heavy-handed, Teutonic humor." The two musicians are shown smoking cigars and shaving while in drag—rather crude jokes. Diamond pointed out that the sturdy *Charley's Aunt* was the classic example of a hero dressing as a woman in American cinema. Jack Benny starred in Archie Mayo's successful 1941 picture, playing an Oxford under-graduate in Victorian Britain impersonating an elderly dowager who chaperones young society ladies. Diamond was confident that, since *Charley's Aunt* had been a hit, the general public would accept another farce about cross-dressing.[3]

In brainstorming with Diamond about the plot, Wilder noted that *Fanfaren der Liebe* dealt with two guys who joined a girls' band simply because they needed jobs. "When we talked about it, we decided that the two guys should join the girls' band as an absolute question of life and death. Otherwise, it would seem that at any point in the picture they could simply remove their wigs and tell Sugar Kane, the band's sexy vocalist and ukulele player, that they both love her and hence are rivals for her affections—then take it from there." Wilder continued, "So we invented the fact that they had witnessed a gangland killing and had to disguise themselves to protect their lives. Then we set the story in the Roaring Twenties, in order to make this element of the plot more believable," since mob warfare was rampant in the Prohibition era. "And so we brought in an actual gangland killing, the St. Valentine's Day Massacre, as the killing which they had witnessed." Wilder concluded, "So it was not that Mr. Diamond and I just sat down and said that we were going to do a satire on the old gangster pictures. That is just how the scenario developed. As Lubitsch used to say, 'We began to have a picture.'" Like Lubitsch, Wilder loved what he lampooned. The America he depicts in the Roaring Twenties is gaudy and vulgar but also full of fun.

Wilder discarded the English title *Fanfares of Love* and replaced it with *Some Like It Hot* at Diamond's suggestion. The film is set in the Jazz Age, and the band caters to jazz lovers who "like it hot." That title, however, had been used for a low-budget Paramount picture in 1939, with Bob Hope as a sideshow owner. Walter Mirisch had to get permission to use the title from

Universal Pictures, which by that time had acquired Paramount's pre-1948 films.

Wilder initiated the casting process as soon as he and Diamond began working on the screenplay. He definitely wanted Tony Curtis to play Joe, a saxophone player. They had met while they were both working at Paramount, when Wilder was shooting *Stalag 17* and Curtis was playing the title role in *Houdini* (1953). Curtis recalled, "Harold Mirisch used to show movies in his home on Lexington Drive." One night, before a screening, Wilder took Curtis aside and offered him the part of Joe. Curtis, who very much wanted to work with Wilder, responded, "I'll do it!"[4]

UA wanted well-known actors in the leads to ensure that the film was commercially viable. Curtis was certainly a bankable star. The studio wanted Frank Sinatra to costar with Curtis as Jerry, a bass fiddle player, but Sinatra did not even respond to Wilder's offer. Accordingly, Wilder decided on Jack Lemmon, who had won a best supporting actor Academy Award for playing the rambunctious Ensign Pulver in *Mr. Roberts* (1955). Wilder offered him the role of Jerry, explaining, "You're going to be in drag for 85 percent of the picture. Do you want to do it?" Not wishing to lose out on a Wilder picture, he answered, "I'll do it!" UA hedged about Lemmon, however, because it wanted a superstar for the part.

Then, in early April 1958, Wilder unexpectedly received a letter from Marilyn Monroe, saying that she was in the market for a picture and would like to work with Wilder again. He immediately offered her the role of Sugar Kane. But Monroe's accepting the part was not a foregone conclusion. Wilder promptly dispatched to Monroe a five-page précis of the scenario, and she was enraged when she read it. Monroe was sick to death of playing dim-witted blondes in pictures. After attending acting classes at the Actors Studio in New York in the fall of 1955, she was eager to play serious roles. She had already played a seedy saloon thrush in *Bus Stop* (1956) and proved that she could act. Hence she angrily threw the synopsis of *Some Like It Hot* on the floor, declaring that "she had played dumb characters before, but never this dumb!"[5]

Monroe vehemently objected to playing a showgirl so stupid that "she can't tell that the two women she is becoming friends with are men in drag." But, as Sarah Churchwell writes, "Marilyn's character is not the only one in the film who falls for the comically bad disguise; according to the conventions of farce, all the characters are fooled by it."[6] Playwright Arthur Miller, whom Monroe had married in June 1956, encouraged her to accept the part. The scenario, he perceptively pointed out, was well structured and had the makings of a solid screenplay. Wilder was delighted. For him, Monroe was like smoking, he explained; "I knew she was bad for my health, but I couldn't give her up."[7]

Monroe finally signed for *Some Like It Hot* on April 21, 1958. She mentioned in passing that she was glad that Curtis had already signed for the picture; she had known him since 1949, when they were both new in Hollywood. Curtis remembered her as "a sweet kid" in those days, hoping for a break. They would make out in the back seat of his pale green Buick convertible. When they later met on the set of *Some Like It Hot*, Monroe inquired whether he still had the green convertible.[8]

Now that Wilder had snagged both Curtis and Monroe, UA no longer had an objection to his hiring Lemmon. "I didn't hear anything for two months" after the meeting with Wilder in the restaurant, Lemmon remembered. "I finally got a call from Billy, who said he would send me the first sixty pages of the script." They were the funniest sixty pages he ever read; "I knew God had struck!"[9]

Monroe signed for three hundred thousand dollars, plus 10 percent of the gross profit; Lemmon and Curtis would receive one hundred thousand dollars apiece, with Curtis also getting 5 percent of the gross. Wilder's salary was two hundred thousand dollars for cowriting and directing the movie, plus a hefty 18 percent of the gross. Diamond received sixty thousand dollars as coauthor of the script.

Wilder told me, "Once we set the film in 1929 for plot reasons, we decided to exploit the old gangster pictures by bringing in George Raft and Pat O'Brien," since Raft had been stereotyped as the bad guy and O'Brien as the good guy in early gangster films. "Their presence helped to give our picture more of an authentic look." Wilder had cast Gloria Swanson, Erich von Stroheim, and Cecil B. De Mille in *Sunset Boulevard* for a similar reason. Pat O'Brien said, "I always played a cop or a priest in gangster pictures like *Angels with Dirty Faces* [1938]. So in *Some Like It Hot* I was Inspector Mulligan, a sort of Eliot Ness character from *The Untouchables,* which was popular on TV at the time. Mulligan is pursuing bootlegger Spats Colombo, played by George Raft, my old friend. Raft, who was raised in New York's Hell's Kitchen, was typecast as a gangster after he played Guido Renaldo in *Scarface* [1932]. Billy also cast George E. Stone in *Some Like It Hot,*" O'Brien continued. "George Stone had played mobsters in movies like *Little Caesar* [1930], opposite Edward G. Robinson."[10]

Wilder had made jokes at Raft's expense in interviews over the years, remarking, for example, that he was glad Raft had refused the role of Walter Neff in *Double Indemnity,* because that was when he knew he was going to make a good picture. Apparently none of Wilder's jibes got back to Raft, because he was delighted to appear in *Some Like It Hot*. By his own admission, Raft was given his start in Hollywood "by friends in the underworld," and he maintained close ties with racketeers during his career.[11]

Wilder said, "I tried to get Edward G. Robinson too, but he wouldn't do it. So I got his son to play a small part." O'Brien said that Robinson refused to work with Raft, his old Warner Bros. stablemate, "after engaging in a fistfight with him on the set of *A Bullet for Joey* [1955]." Afterward Robinson vowed, "I'll never work with that guy again," O'Brien concluded, "and he never did."[12]

Raft's character in *Scarface* perpetually flips a coin in the air. In *Some Like It Hot*, Raft's Colombo notices a young hood (Edward G. Robinson Jr.) flipping a coin; he grabs the coin and snaps, "Where'd you pick up that cheap trick?" Little wonder that Wilder described *Some Like It Hot* as "*Scarface* meets *Charley's Aunt*." As Richard Armstrong notes, Raft was also obliged "to emulate his old rival James Cagney by threatening an associate with a grapefruit in the film, in a direct steal from *Public Enemy* [1931]."[13]

In still another reference to the films of the 1930s, Wilder cast comedian Joe E. Brown, whose career had peaked in the 1930s with films like *Elmer the Great* (1933), in which he played an ace baseball player. Wilder got him to play lecherous millionaire Osgood Fielding in *Some Like It Hot*. Wilder had seen some of Brown's pictures. He said to himself, "That's the guy to play Osgood!" Wilder always had a canny eye for character actors. He tagged Joan Shawlee to play Sweet Sue, the benighted leader of Sweet Sue's Society Syncopators, the all-girl band. Shawlee would reappear in later Wilder films.

"If I did not work with a writer twice," Wilder observed, he had not found the collaborator he was looking for. By contrast, Wilder had worked with I. A. L. Diamond on *Love in the Afternoon* and had already committed himself to collaborating with him on *Some Like It Hot*. That was the clue that Wilder had at last found a permanent collaborator. The souvenir program accompanying the DVD of the present film states that *Some Like It Hot* "marked Wilder's first collaboration with his new writing partner," overlooking *Love in the Afternoon*.[14]

The writing pair spent the spring of 1958 composing the first draft of the script. Wilder, who was fourteen years older than Diamond, liked working with his junior partner, whom he viewed as a younger brother. While collaborating on the screenplay, Wilder and Diamond settled into a routine which lasted for nearly a quarter of a century. They worked on the script of *Some Like It Hot* daily from nine to six. "You arrive in the morning, and you have forty-five minutes of bitching about your wife, . . . and how you saw a picture," and it was lousy. "It establishes a good atmosphere, before you get going on your own stuff." Wilder said that they worked methodically, "like two bank tellers."[15]

When they began the writing process, they would block out each scene thoroughly. Diamond would type out the draft of a scene and show it to Wilder, who would say—quoting Lubitsch—"Now we make it better."[16] Then they would revise the scene together, fine-tuning it until they were both satisfied. That is why their screenplays are models of economy.

Wilder said that his relationship with Diamond was "like a marriage; we fought all the time." But Wilder had always believed that a writing team must be able to argue about their work without destroying the relationship. Unlike Charles Brackett, Diamond was a taciturn man; he would not engage in "verbal sparring" with Wilder.[17] If Wilder occasionally threw a cantankerous temper tantrum, Diamond would simply wait it out. When it passed, they would go back to work.

The dynamic duo finished the first draft of the screenplay on May 2, 1958. They then labored on the second draft, finishing the first two-thirds of the revised script by the beginning of principal photography. They revised the last third of the screenplay during production, which is why their final shooting script is dated November 12, 1958, shortly after the conclusion of the shooting period. The last third of the script "is never finally formulated when we begin shooting," Wilder noted. The point is, "If you give the bosses the final third in advance, they can fire you at any time."[18]

Wilder was fortunate to line up some top-notch production artists. The director of photography was Charles Lang. Another Wilder alumnus, editor Arthur Schmidt, edited the present film. Orry-Kelly, who designed Monroe's strategically abbreviated, diaphanous costumes, was the only individual to win an Academy Award for *Some Like It Hot*. This is an indication that the film was not taken seriously in the film colony at the time of its release.

Doane Harrison, Wilder's perennial supervising editor, was on the set every day, standing unnoticed in the background, always making sure that Wilder had all the coverage he needed to cut a scene together. Diamond, equally unnoticed, was also on the set daily, holding on to the script as if it were the Bible, vigilantly helping Wilder protect the dialogue in the script from being altered by an actor. Wilder had arranged for Diamond to be given the status of associate producer.

Wilder had acted as his own producer on most of his films, starting with *Ace in the Hole*. One exception was his previous film, *Witness for the Prosecution*, which was produced by his old friend Arthur Hornblow. But with *Some Like It Hot*, Wilder was once more acting as both producer and director. He said he liked holding down both jobs, so he had the final say on the making of the picture, from casting to cutting.

As producer-director of *Some Like It Hot*, Wilder had to cope with Monroe's complaints during production. Monroe showed up at the studio expecting to do color tests during preproduction, only to discover that Wilder had decided that the picture would be in black and white. She promptly reminded him that her contract stipulated that all of her films were to be shot in full color, just as *The Seven Year Itch* had been. "I'm at my best in color," Monroe insisted. Wilder did not confess to Monroe that his real reason for not filming in color was simply that he hated color movies. He told her that, for one thing, he chose black and white for the movie because it was set in the era of the great gangster pictures, which were all in black and white. For another thing, the color test footage revealed a blue tint of stubble on the cheeks of her two costars. After viewing the color tests of Lemmon as Daphne and Curtis as Josephine, Monroe conceded that "the boys' make-up would appear gaudy in color." Wilder was franker; he said the color tests for Lemmon and Curtis made them look like "flaming fagots." Wilder recalled, "So Monroe said, 'Forget it!' Marilyn gave in, but not with very good grace."[19]

To help coach Lemmon and Curtis in the fine art of female imperson-ation, Wilder hired Vander Clyde, a legendary drag queen known in Europe as Barbette, whom Wilder remembered from his younger days in Berlin. Lemmon said that Clyde quit after three days. He told Wilder, "Curtis is very good; Lemmon is impossible. I'll never be able to teach him anything, and he won't do what I tell him anyway!"[20] Curtis played Josephine as a restrained, sophisticated lady, but Lemmon saw Daphne as much less lady-like. He went to Wilder and declared, "The goof I am playing wouldn't be very proficient in walking in heels. I need to be barely good enough to look like a clumsy woman."[21] Lemmon told Wilder that Clyde was too finicky, and Wilder sided with Lemmon. The two "girls," Wilder maintained, should have different personalities. "I didn't play Josephine for laughs," Curtis noted; "I tried to make her more demure, because Jack played Daphne as more gauche. I modeled Josephine after Grace Kelly. Whereas Jack loved tromping around in high heels, swinging his hips; he had a ball. He looked like a ditzy 20-cent tart."[22]

Lemmon challenged Curtis to attempt the acid test of their disguise: Lemmon, dragging a bewildered and somewhat shy Curtis behind him, went traipsing to the ladies' room in the studio lobby. They sat in front of the mirror in the lounge adjoining the women's restroom, "where they did their make-up for a good half hour. Apparently nobody batted an eye."

Then they went to Wilder's office to see if they passed his inspection. They told him of their experience in the ladies' room, and he exclaimed, "That does it—don't change a thing! This is exactly the way I want you to look!" He added humorously that Curtis resembled Joan Crawford and Lemmon resembled Mae West.[23]

By the time Wilder hired Monroe to play the female lead in *Some Like It Hot*, he discovered that her personal problems had increased and her mental health had deteriorated. Monroe was up to her old tricks, but she was more difficult to work with than ever. Because she could master only a snippet of dialogue at a time, Wilder was reduced to filming her scenes in a succession of brief shots. Curiously enough, said Wilder, when all of these bits and pieces were strung together at the editing table, a complete performance emerged.

Wilder also had to cope once again with Monroe's chronic tardiness. She set the tone of how she was going to behave during the filming of *Some Like It Hot* on the day of her makeup and wardrobe tests. She was scheduled to appear at 1:00 P.M.; she arrived at 3:30. By the time her assistants had prepared her for the camera tests, it was 6:10. Diamond recalled, "Billy had dismissed the crew at 6:00 and then departed himself—which left her ready for action—all by herself." That same night, Wilder received the first of several phone calls from Arthur Miller. Regardless of his personal feelings about his wife's behavior, Miller always defended her to Wilder. Wilder thought it demeaning for Miller to be arbitrating with him about the vagaries of Monroe's behavior. She should have had her agent, not her husband, who was a distinguished playwright, dealing with him.

Principal photography began on August 4, 1958. Monroe's erratic behavior did not improve once shooting commenced. Wilder would sometimes endeavor to make the best of a bad situation by making wry witticisms at Monroe's expense. "She has breasts of granite; she defies gravity," he fulminated one day to friends. "She has a brain like Swiss cheese—full of holes; she hasn't the vaguest conception of the time of day. She arrives late and tells you she couldn't find the studio" because she lost the address. "And she's been working there for years."[24]

Wilder said that he did not realize what a disorganized person Monroe was until one day she gave him a lift and he looked in the back of her car. "It was like she threw everything in the back helter-skelter, because there was an invasion and the enemy armies were already in Pasadena. There were blouses lying there, old traffic tickets, old plane tickets, old lovers, for all I know."[25] Elsewhere he said, "She was the most rude, mean, discourteous and completely selfish person I have ever met."[26] One day, while Wilder was waiting for her on the set with cast and crew at eleven o'clock in the morning, he dispatched the second assistant director, Sam Nelson, to her dressing room. Nelson discovered her reading Thomas Paine's *The Rights of Man*. According to Norman Mailer's book on Monroe, she looked up from her reading and barked, "Go fuck yourself!"[27] Sarah Churchwell, commenting on Monroe's profanity, writes, "Marilyn Monroe became nastier" as she became more anxious, more insecure, "and more addicted to the chemicals that were making her moods even more volatile."[28]

Wilder was appalled when he learned that Monroe had studied at the Actors Studio with Paula Strasberg after finishing *The Seven Year Itch*. "Here you have this poor girl, and all of a sudden she becomes a famous star," he said. "So now these people tell her she has to be a great actress." He was not convinced that she needed training. In fact, he was concerned that her sessions at the Actors Studio had shaken her confidence in herself. "God gave her everything she needed," Wilder continued; she is "a calendar girl with warmth and charm."[29]

One thing Monroe learned from her stint at the Actors Studio was to study her scenes to develop a concept of how she should play each one. Monroe had all the scenes in the script of *Some Like It Hot* in which she appeared bound together, and she discarded the rest. She then made marginal notes on each page of her script to help her in preparing the scene.

Paula Strasberg was omnipresent on the set, as she had been when *The Seven Year Itch* was being shot; she received fifteen hundred dollars a week for coaching Monroe. Curtis said that Wilder thought this an unnecessary expense and referred acridly to Strasberg, who inexplicably always dressed in black, as "the bat." As a result of her internship at the Actors Studio, Monroe was leaning on her acting coach even more than she had in her previous pictures. Wilder griped that Monroe worshiped the Actors Studio like a religion. Sometimes Strasberg even interfered when Wilder was conferring with Monroe on the set, to make her own suggestions. Wilder was determined to indicate to "Madame Strasberg" early on that he was running the show, said Curtis. "After each take, Marilyn wouldn't look at Billy for his reaction; she would look at Paula for her approval." One day during the first week of filming, writes Barbara Leaming, Wilder got what he needed in a single take. When he called "Cut!" Monroe glanced over at Strasberg. Wilder rose from his director's chair and shouted, "How was that for you, Paula?"[30] From then on Strasberg was relegated to the sidelines, where she could confer with Monroe in private between takes, but she was not to interfere when Wilder was directing her protégé on the set.

The production unit moved to San Diego, which was standing in for

Miami, Florida, for location shooting at the Hotel del Coronado, an ocean-front resort; it is called the Seminole-Ritz in the movie. Shooting was scheduled to start on September 8, 1958, and last for a month.

Miller did not accompany Monroe to San Diego, but, despite their constant bickering when they were together, she was desperately lonely without him. She had found the pressures of making mainstream commercial films to be more and more stressful in recent years. According to Alison Castle, the editor of the published screenplay, "her anxiety level only increased her dependency on barbiturates, which she was taking in alarming amounts." On September 11 she addressed a letter in a trembling hand to her friend the poet Norman Rosten, saying that she was aboard a ship sinking in a "rough and choppy" sea. On the hotel stationery was a sketch of the resort facing the ocean. Monroe drew a tiny stick figure drowning in the surf, shouting "Help!"[31]

The following night Monroe "swallowed an overdose of sleeping pills"; not for the first time, she attempted suicide. "Paula found her in time" and took her to the hospital.[32] Miller rushed to her bedside, and Monroe spent the weekend in the hospital. The whole affair was hushed up by the studio; the public relations department announced that Monroe was suffering from exhaustion. Later, while Miller was on hand on location, he learned that his wife was pregnant. In due course, Wilder recalled, Miller took him aside and informed him confidentially that Monroe was expecting. He accordingly requested that Wilder allow Monroe to leave at 4:30 every day, instead of the customary 6:00. Wilder was beside himself. He pointed out to Miller, "It is already 4:30, and I still don't have a take," because Monroe had not showed up until noon. He promised Miller that, "if she was on the set at 9:00 A.M., then by noon I would be finished with her," and he would let her go—not at 4:30, but at noon.[33] Whatever polite relationship had once existed between Miller and Wilder was at an end.

Wilder later confided to William Schorr, a former production assistant, that his back, which always troubled him when he was tense, was giving him severe pain, caused by his having to cope with Monroe. He added ruefully, "I don't know if I will be able to live through this."[34] At all events, location filming in San Diego finished in the first week of October 1958. The remaining month of shooting back at the Goldwyn Studios was strained. As shooting wore on, Monroe's takes were more and more "stretching into double digits," and the patience of her costars was wearing thin.[35] Wilder was bewildered by her erratic behavior. "I knew we were in midflight, and there was a nut on the plane, and they've got a bomb."[36]

Curtis remembered enduring endless takes until Monroe finally did a scene properly. "When she got it right at last, Billy would use that take," which might not be Curtis's best take, because he was tired out by then. When Curtis brought this to Wilder's attention, Wilder replied that he had to go with Monroe's best take, "because when she was on screen, the audience could not take their eyes off her." Curtis hit the ceiling when he heard this, and he became all the more disgruntled with her. He expressed his irritation with Monroe one evening while the cast and crew were viewing the rushes and she was absent. Curtis was asked what it was like to be kissed by Marilyn Monroe in a love scene. "It's like kissing Hitler," he responded curtly.[37]

Jack Lemmon claimed, "Only the cast and crew heard him say it." But his statement reached the press. Curtis denied making the remark when he was interviewed by a gossip columnist, to avoid a clash with Monroe. But, years later, Curtis admitted that he made the insulting comment. "She was very good in the movie," he said, "but she was difficult to deal with." He confessed that he was fed up with her when he made the statement. "Now she is dead, and it doesn't matter anymore."

During the final weeks of filming, the actors found it more and more frustrating to work with Monroe because "more often than not, Marilyn seemed to be tipsy," according to Diamond. "After each scene Marilyn would call out to her secretary, 'May! Coffee!' and May Reis would bring her a red thermos bottle," which contained not coffee but sweet vermouth.[38] Monroe's gynecologist warned her that her steady intake of alcohol and barbiturates "could trigger a miscarriage," writes Leaming. "Yet the red thermos remained a fixture on the set. And though Marilyn insisted that she wanted a baby more than anything, she continued to take drugs."[39]

Late in the shoot Monroe seemed to be "pilled out," as Curtis put it. "She was mixing sleeping pills and vermouth, and she had increasing difficulty in memorizing her lines."[40] Wilder recounted how Monroe blew a scene in which Sugar enters a hotel room looking for whiskey. "This is Prohibition time, and alcohol is hard to come by," Wilder explained. Sugar searches through the drawers of a bureau for the elusive bottle. It took Monroe forty-seven takes to say coherently, "Where's that bottle?" instead of "Where's the bonbon?" or "Where's the whiskey?" After the twentieth take, Wilder said to her, "Relax, Marilyn; don't worry." She asked dazedly, "Worry about what?"[41]

"Finally Wilder had the line pasted inside the dresser drawer," Roger Ebert notes. "Then she opened the wrong drawer. So he had it pasted inside every drawer."[42] Wilder, we know, would not allow any deviation from the dialogue as written in the screenplay. Churchwell declares, "His insistence on take after take until she got the line right" suggested that they were engaged in a test of wills—"indeed, a pissing contest." Someone was going to win, and it was going to be Wilder. In the last analysis, this incident indicates that "her drug use was spiraling out of control."[43] Wilder said to himself after this episode, "I'm in jail; but not for life!"[44]

When principal photography wrapped on November 7, 1958, Wilder was at last sprung from prison. Monroe returned to New York, where she and Miller had an apartment on East Fifty-seventh Street. On the night of December 16, Monroe suffered a miscarriage. In the past, when she lost a baby, she had blamed fate. This time she took the responsibility herself. She had ignored her gynecologist's warnings that her addictions to pills and liquor could harm the baby; now it was too late. Yet Miller maintained quite unfairly that his wife's miscarriage resulted from her being overworked while shooting *Some Like It Hot*. Asked by Volker Schlöndorff subsequently to comment on Wilder, Miller answered tersely, "He was a bastard."[45]

Wilder was interviewed some months later by Art Buchwald, a columnist for the European edition of the *Herald Tribune*. The irrepressible Wilder said that he had declared a truce with Monroe. When Buchwald reminded Wilder how he had earlier complained that Monroe had kept him waiting on the set for hours, Wilder retorted, "But we didn't waste those hours. We played poker; I managed to read *War and Peace* and *Les Misérables*."[46] But the capper was probably Wilder's remark in *Time* magazine around the same time. He said he was working on a script proposal about a film set in East Berlin, which was true. What was not true was that it dealt with Russian agents kidnapping an American blonde bombshell "who might be Marilyn Monroe: They take her away to brainwash her; but she beats them because she has no brain to wash."[47]

Monroe was outraged that Wilder was ridiculing her in print. But her psychiatrist, Ralph Greenson, urged her to make peace with Wilder, since she might want to make another film with him. Monroe phoned Wilder's home, but Audrey told her that Billy was not in. Monroe began in a vapid, girlish tone of voice, "I wanted to say that your husband"—then her voice took on a mean, sinister sound—"that he is the worst son-of-a-bitch who ever lived, and he can just go fuck himself!" Then she became sweet and amiable again: "But my very best to you, Audrey." Audrey Wilder said that it was almost as if some demon had possessed Monroe momentarily.[48]

Mirisch, the executive producer, declared that Monroe's coming to work late and being unprepared had cost the studio eighteen shooting days. As a result, "the film did go over budget, to the tune of $500,000." The final production cost, Mirisch reported, was $2.8 million, which at the time was a very high price tag for a comedy.

During postproduction, Arthur Schmidt was busy editing the film, with Harrison and Wilder kibitzing as usual. Wilder noticed that Curtis's voice as Josephine was a problem. "He could not maintain a high-pitched voice for Josephine during an entire take"; his voice kept slipping into a lower register. Wilder commandeered Paul Frees, an accomplished mimic, who also appeared as Mr. Provoloner, the "funeral director" of the speakeasy in the film's opening sequence, to dub the voice of Josephine on the sound track.[49]

After Schmidt had completed the preliminary edit of the movie, it was ready for scoring. The lot fell to composer Adolph Deutsch, who had won three Academy Awards, including one for *Oklahoma!* (1955). Like many great film composers, Deutsch understood that his sole function was to help the movie, not show off his handiwork. "A film musician is like a mortician," he said; "he can't bring the body back to life, but he's expected to make it look better."[50] With the assistance of music adviser Matty Malneck and Wilder, an expert on jazz, Deutsch chose songs of the period for the score, like "Running Wild" and "Stairway to the Stars," which he adroitly incorporated into his background music.

Wilder submitted the finished print of *Some Like It Hot* to Geoffrey Shurlock, the industry censor. Shurlock, with the backing of his advisory board, recognized the film as suitable for mature audiences and granted it the industry's official seal of approval. Just when Wilder thought he was home free, the Legion of Decency entered the lists by issuing a harsh statement denouncing the film: "Though *Some Like It Hot* purports to be a comedy," the treatment dwelled on gross suggestiveness that was "seriously offensive to Christian and traditional standards of morality and decency." The dialogue contained "not only double entendre, but outright smut."[51]

Monsignor Thomas Little, the legion's director, fired off an angry letter to Shurlock on March 5, 1959, accusing him of being too easy on *Some Like It Hot*. The legion contended that the picture, by openly depicting "transvestism," ran counter to the spirit of the industry's censorship code. Shurlock responded to Little on March 18, defending his decision in favor of the movie by pointing out that men masquerading as women had been a perennial source of humor throughout theater and film history. He cited the venerable *Charley's Aunt* as one of the enduring comedies in the annals of the theater. Shurlock noted that the code had been given a major overhaul in 1956, so "there are now no taboos on subject matter."[52] The legion placed *Some Like It Hot* in its morally objectionable category, where it had also relegated *Love in the Afternoon*.

Douglas Brode correctly terms *Some Like It Hot* a milestone in the trend toward "a racier style of comic picture," marked by smatterings of piquant sex.[53] Wilder concurred that it was a daring film for its time: "Two guys dressing up as dames," running around in lipstick and heels—two wolves in women's clothing. "Ten years later it could have been even bolder."

But the legion's complaints about the picture were not the end of Wilder's woes. The sneak previews were still to come. UA scheduled a sneak on a Friday night in December 1958 at the Bay Theatre in Pacific Palisades, and it was a total disaster. "Nobody laughed, except one of our friends," Wilder told me. There had been a serious picture on before the sneak: *Cat on a Hot Tin Roof,* an adaptation of a southern gothic play by Tennessee Williams. The audience did not laugh because they apparently thought *Some Like It Hot* was a serious melodrama too. Jack Lemmon remembered that people were leaving in droves, muttering, "What the hell is this?" Wilder was devastated. Joseph Mankiewicz, an old friend of Wilder's, attended the preview. He put "a consoling arm around Wilder's shoulder" and murmured, "It's alright, Billy; it happens to all of us."[54]

The Mirisch brothers huddled with Wilder in the lobby of the theater, insisting that he must cut 10 minutes from the picture; conventional wisdom dictated that 122 minutes was too long for a farce. Wilder listened politely and assured the Mirisches that he would consider ways of shortening the movie. In an editing session held at the Goldwyn Studios, Wilder removed one scene, lasting exactly 1 minute, from the picture. It was a short scene in the sleeping car on the train, while the band is on its way to Florida. "Jerry thinks he is crawling into Sugar Kane's bunk, but by mistake he gets in with me," Curtis explained. "Jerry says, 'I have a secret; I'm a man!' And I say, 'I know that!!'"[55] "Billy said the scene was expendable," Lemmon said; "it was one scene too many on the train" about the boys pretending to be girls. But, Lemmon concluded, "Billy didn't touch the rest of the film." Wilder was reluctant to cut a picture. A producer complaining about the length of a movie, he told me, "is like a motel manager demanding that his guests get out before midnight."

Wilder decided to preview the film the following Friday in Westwood, an upscale section of Los Angeles where he could expect a more sophisticated audience than had attended the first preview; he hence could hope for a more positive response to the movie. This audience laughed uproariously—not because Wilder had made one small, token cut but because the audience had been alerted that the film was a comedy.

*Some Like It Hot* had its world premiere in New York on March 29, 1959, and collected mostly great reviews. It eventually became one of the top hits of the year, turning a profit of $15 million.

Armstrong notes that "*Some Like It Hot* is essentially a spoof of the vintage Hollywood gangster pictures of the early 1930s. It is a freewheeling world of hoods in shiny Packards, bathtub gin, and jazz."[56] That Wilder is parodying the old gangster films is apparent in the opening scene. A hearse is shown speeding down the street, occupied by Colombo's thugs dressed as undertakers. Two of them are in the back of the hearse guarding the casket, which is full of bottles of illegal liquor. A squad car follows them to a speakeasy, which is decked out like a funeral parlor. Wilder gives a nod to *Sunset Boulevard* by having a look-alike for Erich von Stroheim playing the organ in the funeral parlor. As the plot unwinds, Inspector Mulligan raids the joint and arrests the racketeers for embalming their customers with cheap whiskey from the coffin. Colombo, who is modeled on Al Capone, has his mob rub out the members of the rival gang of Toothpick Charlie (George E. Stone) in a Chicago garage on St. Valentine's Day 1929. Jerry and Joe, two unemployed musicians, witness the St. Valentine's Day Massacre quite by accident; they must flee from Colombo, who wants them murdered before they can squeal on him and his gang to his nemesis, Inspector Mulligan. To save their skins, they disguise themselves as females and join an all-girl dance band that is en route to a gig in Florida.

Wilder cuts immediately from Joe and Jerry deciding to tour with Sweet Sue's orchestra to the two of them briskly walking down the train platform dressed as women. There is no montage of the guys dressing up. "We never showed where Lemmon and Curtis borrow the dresses and wigs—maybe from a girlfriend," Wilder said. He dispensed with needless exposition and simply made a sharp cut to the boys already in drag, "and the audience started screaming."[57]

Monroe then makes her first appearance in the movie, sashaying down the railway platform, carrying her ukulele case. When she saw the rushes of this scene the next day, she told Wilder that her entrance in the picture should be more memorable. Wilder assured her that he would come up with a better first look at Sugar Kane and do a retake the following day. He wanted her to know that he took her suggestions seriously. Monroe had always hoped that the time would come when a director would pay attention to her suggestions. Unfortunately, the moment may have come too late. She did not believe that Wilder planned to do a retake the next day. "I'm not going back into that fucking film until Wilder re-shoots my opening," she declared to her assistant at the end of the day. "When Marilyn Monroe comes on the screen, nobody's going to be looking at Tony Curtis playing Joan Crawford. They're going to be looking at Marilyn Monroe."[58]

True to his word, Wilder redid the shot the next morning. "Monroe walks alongside the train," said Wilder, "and I let out a blast of steam from the engine right on her fanny. It was the right lead-in for the star of the picture."[59] Walter Mirisch said, "I thought when the cloud of steam blasted at Marilyn's behind on the train platform, Billy was recalling the scene in *The Seven Year Itch* when the gust of air comes up through the subway grating and blows on her legs—Billy Wilder topping himself."

Jerry is now known as Daphne, and Joe as Josephine. Initially, both men are attracted to Sugar Kane, but they are afraid to doff their disguises to tell her who they really are, because they continue to be stalked by Colombo and his mob. While Sweet Sue's band is booked into the Seminole-Ritz Hotel in Miami, Joe continues to be much interested in Sugar, who views "Josephine" as a good friend, "a gal pal." Sugar, we learn, is a torch singer who has the right to sing the blues. She confides to Josephine that she has been exploited by a series of unscrupulous boyfriends, all of them musicians. She complains that she always gets "the fuzzy end of the lollipop," a remark whose phallic connotations are unmistakable. When a boyfriend deserts her, all he leaves behind is "a pair of old socks and a toothpaste tube all squeezed out." Sugar comes across as a girl who is savvy enough to know better but not strong enough to resist deadbeat musicians.

Meanwhile, Jerry catches the roving eye of Osgood Fielding, an elderly millionaire who, of course, believes that he is courting a young lady named Daphne. For the time being, Jerry enjoys being wined and dined by a rich tycoon. While Jerry is frolicking with Fielding, Joe decides to court Sugar in yet another disguise. He doffs his dress and wig, decks himself out in a yachtsman's outfit, and dons thick glasses. He wants to impress Sugar by posing as the heir to the Shell Oil fortune. When Wilder asked Curtis about his character masquerading as a millionaire, Curtis answered, "What would you think if I imitated Cary Grant?" Curtis had been doing impersonations of movie stars like Grant and James Cagney since he was a kid. Wilder said it would be "a wonderful plus for the picture."[60] Wilder subsequently showed the picture to Cary Grant and inquired, "How do you like that impression Tony did of you?" Grant replied, "I never talked like that!" Wilder would have liked to direct Grant in a movie, but it never happened. Hence, Curtis observes, his impersonation of Grant in *Some Like It Hot* was as close as Wilder ever got to "having Grant in a movie."[61]

Joe persuades Jerry to go nightclubbing with Osgood one night so he can romance Sugar aboard Osgood's yacht, the *Caledonia,* claiming that it is his. Monroe was aware that this love scene with Curtis was a key scene in the picture, so she made several notes in the margin of her copy of the script.

When Joe and Sugar come onboard Osgood's fabulous yacht, Sugar, who was raised on the wrong side of the tracks, is dazzled by the luxurious sitting room. Monroe wrote in the margin that Sugar feels like "Alice in Wonderland."[62]

Once Joe and Sugar are sitting cozily on a couch, Joe, in the guise of the millionaire, confesses to her that he is frigid and invites her to attempt to cure him of his affliction. Falling for his ruse, "Sugar accepts the challenge, smothering the supine Joe in loving kisses" to restore his virility.[63] Wilder points out that, if Joe were the aggressor in this scene and overpowered Sugar, it would be dirty. But if she is the aggressor and seduces him because she thinks he is impotent, it is funny. "And so *she* suggests the sex, and she fucks *him!*" Wilder explained.[64]

At first Joe tells Sugar, as he leads her on, that her kisses are "a complete washout"; they have failed to thaw the frigid tycoon. Monroe wrote in the margin next to Joe's line that Sugar takes his remark as a "personal affront." But Joe soon admits that he has been warmed by her kisses when his glasses steam up; Monroe accordingly wrote in the margin that Joe is "getting drunk on kisses."[65] Ebert notes, "When Monroe kisses Curtis while they're both horizontal on the couch, notice how his shoe rises phallically in the mid-distance. Does Wilder intend this effect? Undoubtedly."[66]

Actually, it was Curtis's idea to have "my leg go up in the air when Marilyn is kissing me." While Monroe was embracing him passionately, "she could feel that I was having an erection." She looked at him knowingly, as if to say that, ten years after they had sex in the back seat of his green convertible, she could still turn him on. So raising his leg during the scene was his "little ad-lib," a stand-in for his erection.[67] While Joe and Sugar are making love on the yacht, Osgood and Daphne are dancing a furious tango in a nearby roadhouse. Raft, who had been a dancer on the stage before becoming an actor, was willing to coach Lemmon and Brown in the tango. As Osgood and Daphne dip and twirl around the dance floor, Daphne has a rose clenched between her teeth. Wilder is here making a reference to *Charley's Aunt*, in which Jack Benny in the title role coyly has a rose in his teeth as a rich suitor proposes to him.[68] Osgood likewise proposes marriage to Daphne in the course of their night on the town, as we learn in the following scene.

When Joe returns to their hotel room, he finds Jerry doing a reprise of his tango with Osgood as he shakes a pair of maracas to a Latin beat. "When I walked on the set," Lemmon recalled, "Billy handed me a pair of maracas and said to me, 'In between every line, start dancing wildly and give a shake to the maracas.'" Lemmon said to himself, "My God, he's lost it!"[69] Actually, the maracas were a stroke of genius. Wilder explained later that he wanted a pause after each of Lemmon's punch lines because he did not want the audience's laughter to drown out the next straight line spoken by Curtis, which was setting up the next joke. Wilder therefore filled the space between each gag line with Lemmon's shaking the maracas. For example, Joe asks Jerry why he is so happy, and Jerry answers, "I'm engaged!" The gimmick with the maracas "allowed time to pass for the audience to laugh," said Lemmon, and not lose the next straight line from Joe: "Why would a guy want to marry a guy?" Jerry replies, "Security!" When Lemmon finally saw the movie with an audience, he realized that "the manner in which Wilder had paced the scene was brilliant." Wilder had "sculpted and edited" the scene to make room for laughs.[70]

For a while Jerry is mesmerized by the notion of a millionaire. He even considers contracting a marriage with Osgood—which would be unconsummated—with a view to arranging an annulment shortly thereafter and obtaining substantial alimony payments. Lemmon noted that "Jerry is from some other planet; he's crazy. That's why it is believable that the daffy Jerry would consider marrying Osgood: he's nuts!"

The climax of the film comes when Colombo and his henchmen show up at the resort hotel for a summit conference with a rival gang headed by Little Bonaparte (Nehemiah Persoff), whose character is a send-up of Edward G. Robinson's portrayal of Little Caesar. The racketeers' convention is billed as "The Friends of Italian Opera" and is highlighted by a ceremonial banquet. The crime syndicate's banquet has always been part of the iconography of the gangster picture, dating back to *Little Caesar*.

Little Bonaparte is sore at Colombo for killing Toothpick Charlie, because he and Charlie were choirboys together. Furthermore, Little Bonaparte decides to consolidate his power in the underworld by having one of his goons mow down Colombo and his mob with a machine gun at the banquet. Once Colombo and his gang are out of the way, Jerry and Joe can at last discard their disguises. Joe immediately declares his love for Sugar, but Jerry's situation is not so simple. When the persistent Osgood renews his offer of marriage to Daphne, Jerry sees that the jig is up and feels obligated to take off his wig and declare to Osgood that he cannot marry him under any circumstances. "Utterly unshakable in his love for Daphne, and trusting in his passionate instincts, Osgood overlooks all, including gender," comments Doug Tomlinson.[71] With a twinkle in his eye, the unfazed Osgood responds tranquilly to Jerry's revelation that he is a man: "Nobody's perfect."

Wilder and Diamond hit on this closing line when they were fiddling around with the final scene. Diamond had supplied the line for Osgood in the first draft of the screenplay.[72] Wilder had thought that the line was weak, though, and he was still reluctant to use it. He asked, "Do you think it's strong enough for the tag line of the picture?" Diamond answered, "I don't know." Since the final scene was to be shot the following day, Wilder decided to leave this "throwaway line" in the final scene, with the hope that overnight "we will think of something better." Diamond agreed. "It's not chiseled in marble," he commented.[73] But "Nobody's perfect" remained, and when the film was previewed for the press, the closing line brought down the house. It finally dawned on Wilder that "this was not a dummy line; it was a great line!"[74] Wilder gave Diamond full credit for thinking of it; he said he did not even supply the exclamation point. Tomlinson calls Osgood's declaration "a candidate for the funniest closing line in cinema history."[75]

Admittedly, Jerry temporarily forgets himself when he seriously considers Osgood's proposal of marriage, Wilder explained. "But even when he forgot himself," he was not consciously toying with the notion of engaging in a homosexual relationship. "It was just the idea of being engaged to a millionaire that was very appealing," because Osgood offers him "security." "But when the crunch finally comes, Jerry cannot go through with the marriage."[76] In harmony with the usual theme of Wilder's films, Jerry will do *almost* anything for money; he draws the line when it involves marrying another male.

*Some Like It Hot* was a sensation at the box office as well as a critical triumph. It remains one of the Wilder films that moviegoers recall most fondly. To Barry Norman, Monroe gave "a performance of melting charm" that, in the end, made her tiresome and troublesome behavior during production seem "worth it."[77] Wilder agreed: "Many actresses were more reliable, but no one was as convincing or had better technique."[78] In fact, Monroe won a Golden Globe award from the Foreign Press Association for *Some Like It Hot*. Monroe was generally thought to have given her two best performances in her two Wilder films, *The Seven Year Itch* and *Some Like It Hot*.

At the time of its release, the very popularity of *Some Like It Hot* was reason enough for some critics to write it off as a mere crowd pleaser. But over the years the movie has gained stature, and it is now considered one of Wilder's major achievements. The AFI presented a special on CBS-TV on June 13, 2000, honoring the top one hundred comedies of the first century of American cinema, as selected by fifteen hundred film professionals and critics. Heading the list was *Some Like It Hot*. Tomlinson said at the time that "*Some Like It Hot* combines the slapstick . . . and wit of screwball comedy, to make the funniest American film of the 1950s and one of the greatest of the genre."[79]

The recognition accorded the film has continued. In 2005 the editors of *Time* magazine selected the all-time top one hundred movies and included *Some Like It Hot* in the roster.[80] *Premiere* magazine conducted a nationwide poll in 2006 to determine the twenty-five greatest screenplays of all time; *Some Like It Hot* was highlighted on the list. Also in 2006, *Premiere*'s readership chose the fifty greatest comedies of all time. The citation for this movie read, "Billy Wilder turned the gangster film on its ear and made a timeless comic gender-bender."[81] It seems that 2006 was a banner year for this film; when *Premiere* in yet another poll selected the one hundred greatest performances of all time, Jack Lemmon was chosen for *Some Like It Hot*. Also in 2006, in a *Skye Movies* poll of the British Parliament, the 175 members voting picked *Some Like It Hot* as one of the top ten movies of all time.[82]

The film is also significant because it was the first of seven Wilder films in which Jack Lemmon starred; the Wilder-Lemmon collaboration would become one of the most enduring director-actor teams in the history of cinema. In addition, this film solidified the writing partnership of Wilder and Diamond. Their fruitful collaboration lasted for the balance of Wilder's career. What is more, they became one of Hollywood's most renowned writing teams, just as Wilder and Brackett had been.

# 13

# Love on the Dole

## *The Apartment*

Chivalry is not only dead, it is decomposed.

—*Preston Sturges*

"After I had finished *Some Like It Hot,* I wanted to make another picture with Jack Lemmon," Wilder said.[1] In considering Lemmon for his next project, Wilder began to think of him as his Everyman, says Drew Casper in the documentary *Inside "The Apartment."* In the film Lemmon would represent the Average Man, a flawed hero desperately endeavoring to get ahead.[2]

Wilder still kept a black notebook, which was locked away in a desk drawer, in which he jotted down ideas for film scenarios. He had begun this practice in earnest while he was working for Lubitsch. When he consulted the notebook this time around, he found a reference to David Lean's 1945 movie *Brief Encounter;* he remembered the picture vividly. In it Alec, a married man, is having an affair with Laura, a married woman. Alec tells Laura that he has borrowed his friend Stephen's apartment for a rendezvous, and Laura arranges to join him there. Stephen returns unexpectedly and immediately infers what is going on. He pointedly requests that Alec return his latchkey and not use it again.

What Wilder had scribbled in his trusty notebook was, "What about the friend who owned the flat" where the lovers meet?[3] Wilder saw this fellow in his proposed scenario as someone who allows other men to utilize his apartment as a place of assignation with their mistresses. As Wilder put it, "Here is a lonely bachelor who comes home to his apartment and crawls into a bed that is still warm from the lovers who had been there earlier," while he himself has no lover.[4] Wilder got together with I. A. L. Diamond to whip up a detailed proposal that he would present to the Mirisch Company and to UA. For starters, the pair decided to set the story during the Christmas holidays to provide a jarring counterpoint to the decadent atmosphere of the tale.

"We had the character and the situation," Diamond recalled, "but we didn't have a plot until we remembered a local scandal here." In 1952 an agent, Jennings Lang, was having a clandestine affair with one of his clients, actress Joan Bennett, who then was married to Walter Wanger, an independent producer. Wanger finally caught them together; in a jealous rage, he "shot Lang in the balls," though the wound was not fatal. The element of the sordid scandal that caught the writing team's attention was that Lang was using the apartment of one of his subordinates at the agency as a love nest. That, concluded Diamond, "gave us our plot."[5]

Wilder took a précis of the scenario to the studio and threw a fast pitch to Walter Mirisch and the UA front office. The proposal read in part, "This is about a young fellow who gets ahead in a big company by lending his apartment to executives for that grand old American folk ritual, the afternoon shack-up." He further described the movie as portraying "infidelity as a way of life" and "the misuse of the American Dream."[6] Mirisch agreed to serve as executive producer on the picture, and UA agreed to distribute it. The production was assigned a budget of $2,825,965. The next item on the agenda was to get Lemmon to commit to the project. After hearing Wilder's brief sketch of the plot, Lemmon enthusiastically accepted the male lead.

"When I write a screenplay, I have a particular actor in mind for the lead most of the time. Then my cowriter and I create the character with that actor in mind," Wilder said. "So when we prepared the script for *The Apartment,* we had to know that the loveable, attractive schlemiel was to be played by Jack Lemmon, who was perfect casting for the part."[7]

Wilder and Diamond began working on the screenplay, elaborating Wilder's original concept into a detailed script. It was Diamond's idea to depict the suicide attempt by the heroine, Fran Kubelik, whom the hero, Bud Baxter, is smitten with. Paul Diamond explained that another writer had told his father many years earlier about how he had broken up with his girlfriend and then come home soon after to find her lying in his bathtub, dead.[8] In the parallel scene in *The Apartment,* Bud returns to his apartment to find that Fran has attempted suicide there. The development of the scene highlights Wilder's distinctive care for narrative structure. He explained that he had to invent a physician who lives next door, Dr. Dreyfuss, who can be on hand to save Fran. "No one in the history of the movies," Neil Sinyard writes, "orchestrated the possibilities of plotting better than Wilder."[9]

Asked if it was appropriate to feature a suicide attempt in a comedy like

*The Apartment,* Wilder answered, "I don't regard *The Apartment* as a comedy. It's a slice of life that seems very naturalistic."[10] Wilder had opted to make *The Apartment* a category-breaking blend of comedy, romance, and drama. As Diamond explained, they wanted to create "a delicate balance between drama and comedy in the picture; and we were afraid if we got a laugh in the wrong place, the whole picture would go out the window."[11] Drew Casper declared that Diamond was a gentle man who brought warmth to Wilder's "cold, brittle social satire." He made Wilder "less sour."[12]

Wilder had a penchant for drawing the names of characters from real people. Fran got her surname from Rafael Kubelik, a former conductor of the Chicago Symphony Orchestra. Mr. Sheldrake, Bud's boss, is named for a professional athlete. Wilder also gave the name Sheldrake to two other characters in his films: Sheldrake is the producer who gives Joe Gillis the brush-off in *Sunset Boulevard,* and there is a Dr. Sheldrake in *Kiss Me, Stupid.*

Although Wilder was adept at writing dialogue, he also had a way of telegraphing a great deal to the audience with little or no dialogue. When Bud asks Fran how many love affairs she has had, she confesses to three but inadvertently raises four fingers. This is an adroit manner in which to suggest that Fran would like to minimize her past indiscretions but admits the truth in spite of herself. Both Bud and Fran are fundamentally decent types, writes Bernard Dick: "babes in the dirty woods of big business."[13]

Wilder and Diamond completed the first draft of the screenplay just four days before shooting began. They would continue to revise the script during filming, but these revisions amounted only to fine-tuning, since the first draft was in very good shape. Still, the writing partners did not finish revising the script until late in the shoot. Sometimes they would run into a scene where a passage of dialogue was unclear, Wilder explained, "or we needed an additional line to get someone out of the room."[14]

The casting process had continued while Wilder and Diamond labored on the first draft of the script. Wilder had his eye on Shirley MacLaine for the part of Fran and sent her part of the screenplay. MacLaine wanted to work with Wilder and accepted the role. She later said, "There were only thirty pages of script—that's all we had when we started."[15] MacLaine wrongly assumed that the thirty pages she received were all that Wilder and Diamond had written. As a matter of fact, they had finished most of the screenplay by then. Wilder sent her only the early pages of the script on principal; he did not want a fairly complete copy of the screenplay floating around the studio, particularly when it dealt with the daring subject of adultery in the workplace.

Paul Douglas (*Executive Suite*) had signed for the role of Sheldrake, but two weeks before shooting started, he succumbed to a heart attack. He was fifty-two. Wilder reasoned that, since Fred MacMurray had been so convincing as a heel in *Double Indemnity,* he would be pitch-perfect as the heel in *The Apartment.*

MacMurray's immediate response was to turn down the part. "At the time, I had a contract with Disney to make family fare like *The Shaggy Dog* [1959]. Hence, I felt that I could not jeopardize my wholesome screen image by playing a businessman who is having an extramarital affair, in a movie that takes place during the Christmas holidays no less!" But Wilder managed to coax him into taking the role. MacMurray remembered that one of his fans later expressed her dismay that he had appeared in such a "sordid" picture. "This lady accosted me on the street and underlined her anger at me by hitting me with her purse!" When he phoned Wilder about the incident, Wilder told him to console himself with the $175,000 salary he got for the movie.[16] By the way, MacMurray's two costars also received the same fee for the movie. Wilder himself was allotted $200,000 for co-writing and directing the movie, as well as 17 percent of the gross.

Wilder selected Daniel Mandell, who had edited *Witness for the Prosecution,* as the film editor on *The Apartment.* Adolph Deutsch, who composed the background music for *Some Like It Hot,* was also back again, to score *The Apartment.* Alexander Trauner, the production designer, was working on his third Wilder picture. "Whether he was exploiting the natural locations in New York City" or designing the office interiors for the insurance company in *The Apartment,* writes Andre Pozner, "Trauner excelled in creating the necessary framework for the director's narrative to unfold."[17]

In a scene near the beginning of the picture, Wilder sought to create accurately the bleak, antiseptic look of the huge office complex in which Bud labors as a member of the accounting department at Consolidated Life. The cavernous office is totally impersonal. Wilder's inspiration for the vast office set in *The Apartment* was a similar scene in King Vidor's silent film *The Crowd* (1928), about another wage slave swallowed up by a giant organization. Kevin Brownlow spoke with Vidor about Wilder's copying his scene. Vidor said he used an overhead shot to show the maze of desks and then let the camera come down and focus on "one man, one desk." Wilder has his camera facing the endless rows of desks at eye level, with Bud at his desk in the foreground. Vidor said that Wilder phoned him and inquired how many desks he had utilized in his scene.[18]

Wilder recalled, "I wanted a big room full of desks, like the set Vidor had for his picture when filming it at Metro." But that was a tall order for the Goldwyn Studios, which did not have a single soundstage the size of the one Vidor used at MGM. "So Trauner had to create the illusion of great depth by means of forced perspective."[19] According to Wilder, "We had tall extras seated behind normal desks; then shorter extras behind smaller desks; some dwarfs at miniature desks; and finally some cut-outs at toy desks."[20] Diamond testified that there were children dressed as grownups—not midgets—seated at the desks in the rear of the set.[21]

Bud spends a good deal of his time at his desk, hunched over his adding machine; as the screenplay notes, Bud's desk is just one among "several rows of steel-grey desks, steel-grey filing cabinets, and steel-grey faces under indirect lights. It is all very neat, antiseptic, impersonal."[22] Wilder lauded Trauner for his use of forced perspective, lining up the desks in parallel rows, almost to the vanishing point. "Trauner is a magician," Wilder declared; "he pulls rabbits out of hats."[23] Gerald Mast in turn praises Wilder's skilled use of the wide screen in this scene: "The geometric rows of desks, the regularity of the ceiling's fluorescent lighting, the clicking sound of business machines, the visual patterns that reduce people to mechanisms—has become a classic example of compositions for the wide screen."[24]

In *The Apartment* Wilder satirizes the regimented existence of office workers in the course of this same scene: at five o'clock sharp, three hundred clerks rise in unison from their desks and head for the nearest exit. This image is another quote from *The Crowd*.

Throughout the production period, Wilder went to great pains to give the film a realistic atmosphere. Bud lives in a walk-up apartment in a brownstone off Central Park West; his rooms look seedy and sloppy. Wilder and Trauner looked at various apartments near Central Park to get a fix on what a typical bachelor flat would look like. While dressing the apartment set, Wilder and Trauner went to resale shops in the neighborhood and selected the kinds of books and other articles that bachelors like Bud tend to collect to make their apartments—and their lives—seem less empty. And Wilder loaned the double bed from his own home to the set. It was sturdy, big bed, the kind that Wilder said he would have if he lived in a bachelor apartment. Bud's bachelor flat, like Phyllis's seedy house in *Double Indemnity,* looks lived in, not merely like a studio set that was erected immediately before the cameras turned. "We have a prefabricated loneliness in America," Wilder reflected. "With this loneliness goes the urge to better oneself and rise from the masses," which is precisely what Bud longs to do.[25]

During preproduction Wilder also conferred with the wardrobe department. He said that he did not want MacLaine outfitted in elegant costumes suitable for a movie star. Rather, she was to wear the inexpensive attire that her role as a working girl called for, just as Dietrich wore relatively simple clothes in *Witness for the Prosecution*, as befitting her character as a war refugee. "Fluffy comedies about New York working girls who earn sixty dollars a week and wear designer clothes will always be popular; but not with me," Wilder explained. "I want to go beyond the powder puff school, in favor of the starkest realism."[26] Wilder did, however, allow his wife Audrey to lend MacLaine her handsome shaggy coat, which betokened the kind of lifestyle to which Fran Kubelik aspired.

Sometimes Wilder's pursuit of realism precipitated problems with the studio's production departments. When the property department wanted to use "Lucky Chesters" or "Camel Strikes" in a scene, Wilder demanded that they supply a real pack of cigarettes, even if it meant obtaining permission from the tobacco company to use the brand in the movie.[27] Wilder also abhorred employing "stage money," instead of real legal tender, in a scene. When filming the scene in which Sheldrake offers Fran a hundred-dollar bill as a Christmas present, Wilder tossed the phony century note MacMurray was to use into the wastebasket. He then peeled an authentic bill from his own bankroll for use in the scene. Moreover, to impress on MacMurray that Sheldrake was a big wheel in the insurance company, Wilder had office stationery and memo pads with "J. D. Sheldrake" printed on them, even though no one but MacMurray would see them on Sheldrake's desk.

Similarly, in the scene in which Bud invites Fran to see a Broadway show, Wilder insisted that the title of the show be specified—even though the script merely states that Bud "is standing on the sidewalk outside the theater," waiting for Fran.[28] Wilder chose *The Music Man*, which was running on Broadway at the time, because the main character was a con man. After all, in *The Apartment*, it seems at times as if everyone is conning everybody else. Wilder accordingly shot a scene outside the Majestic Theatre, where *The Music Man* was playing, with Bud waiting in vain for Fran.

Principal photography started November 17, 1959, with location work in New York City. Wilder and Trauner picked a brownstone at 51 West Sixty-seventh Street to shoot exteriors of the apartment building where Bud lives. It is a typical neighborhood in Manhattan where the sidewalks are lined with garbage cans. Bud is reduced to sitting on a long bench in Central Park while an executive is partying with his secretary in Bud's flat. He occupies a bench in a row of benches that recede into the distance. The gloom that envelops Bud "is all the more forlorn for being stretched across the wide screen frame."[29] Moreover, throughout the film, the wide screen depicts the empty space that surrounds the characters, implying their isolation from one another. Seldom has the wide-screen format been used to better advantage than by Wilder and cinematographer Joseph LaShelle in this picture.

Since *The Apartment* takes place during the Christmas season, the bitterly cold New York weather during location shooting was appropriate for the movie, but it was tough on cast and crew. Wilder had planned to shoot several exterior shots in front of Bud's apartment building, "but it was so cold that we were always running to the nearest bar to warm ourselves" with a shot of whiskey, says Trauner in his autobiography; "we weren't making progress."[30]

"I much prefer shooting in the studio, where I am in control," Wilder declared. "I don't have to fight the weather, which is changing all the time." He would begin filming a scene on a bleak, rainy morning; "by midday the sun would come out." This made continuity difficult in the exterior scenes.[31] He finally decided to film the rest of the exteriors on a soundstage at the Goldwyn Studios, where Trauner duplicated the facades of three of the brownstones that had been used for exteriors during location shooting in New York. The film unit finished up in New York City just before Thanksgiving, and principal photography resumed at Goldwyn on November 30, 1959.

Lemmon found Wilder simpatico during the shoot at the studio, which extended into February 1960. The great thing about Wilder, he explained, was that "he doesn't impose himself on the actor before he sees what he will bring to the part." Wilder always listened to Lemmon's suggestions. Lemmon would pop into Wilder's office any time he got a brainstorm for Wilder to consider. "Don't *tell* me," Wilder would say; "*show* me."[32] Very often Wilder would accept Lemmon's suggestion. But not always.

Wilder remembered that one morning Lemmon wandered into his office just before the day's shooting was to begin. He told Wilder that he had gotten an idea the night before, when he was running his line with his wife-to-be, actress Felicia Farr, who fed him his cues. Lemmon elaborated his idea to Wilder, who shook his head no. Lemmon promptly replied that he did not like it either. In comparing notes with Wilder, Lemmon realized that his great notion was not all that great. "Jack is not an argumentative actor," Wilder told me. "We understand each other, and it is a pleasure to work with him."

Like Lemmon, MacLaine testifies that Wilder listened to her suggestions and discussed them with her until they came to some kind of agreement. Still, Lemmon recalls that she and Wilder had a serious misunderstanding on the very first day of shooting. MacLaine was not accustomed to saying her lines word for word but might nonchalantly skip a few words or alter a phrase. Other directors had not minded, but Wilder set her straight right from the get-go. "A script should be played the way it is written," he explained, "like a musical score. Every sentence has a point."[33]

Wilder decided to teach MacLaine a lesson while shooting a scene in which Fran, as an elevator operator, greets each of the executives and employees as they get on. MacLaine had two pages of dialogue, and Wilder wanted to film it in a single take. She thought she had finally nailed the scene on the fourth take. After conferring with Diamond, who, as usual, was present on the set, script in hand, Wilder informed MacLaine that she would have to do yet another take. "Those were not the exact words," he said. MacLaine had omitted a single phrase! When she did the fifth take perfectly, Wilder gave her a big kiss. He commented afterward that, once she understood that he meant business, "she got serious and worked as hard as anybody."[34]

For her part, MacLaine reflected that she came to realize that Wilder always had a complete blueprint for the movie in his mind before he started filming, "so he knows what he wants." She confessed that she never had gone to an acting school, "but I learned more from him than from anybody else in Hollywood."[35] Richard Gehman told Wilder that many stars vowed that they would "work with Billy for nothing." Always one to sidestep a patronizing compliment, Wilder retorted, "I wish they would tell that to their agents!"[36]

Wilder encountered some difficulties with LaShelle during the shoot. LaShelle recalled discussing with Wilder the scene in which Fran attempts suicide. Wilder called for an extremely low camera angle when Dr. Dreyfuss is endeavoring to revive Fran, with the camera close to the floor, shooting upward at them. LaShelle balked at this camera setup, thinking it would look pretentious. So he simply stated, "No, I don't think so." Wilder peered at him over his glasses "like an owl" and responded, "Nobody ever says 'No' to me." LaShelle stood his ground, repeating, "No!" Finally Wilder grinned and said, "Oh hell, do it the way you want."[37] LaShelle commented later that Wilder was decidedly irritated by anyone who did not follow his directions, "so you have to be damn sure you are right when you disagree with him." He called Wilder the most brilliant director he had ever known. "But," he added, "Billy is not infallible."[38] Wilder dismissed the incident by saying that LaShelle was getting grouchy because he was an elderly man. As a matter of fact, Wilder and LaShelle were both in their mid-fifties at the time. LaShelle went on to shoot three more Wilder pictures in a row, through *The Fortune Cookie*.

The shooting period wrapped on February 12, 1960, and Wilder moved on to postproduction. The film's composer, Adolph Deutsch, possessed an extensive background in classical music, which is evident in his meticulous orchestrations. Yet his score for *The Apartment* also invokes popular music, from jazz to lounge pop. His incidental music is not merely a backdrop for the action; his tunes are vividly in the foreground at times. He supplied a haunting blues number for solo saxophone that permeates the sequence in which Bud is shown in his lonely bachelor pad, cleaning up after one of his bosses' after-hours frolics and then fixing himself a frozen TV dinner.

Jack Lemmon, whose hobby was playing jazz on the piano, was impressed by Wilder's uncanny knowledge of the popular music of the past. Wilder wanted Deutsch to employ a favorite old song of his with a haunting melody as the title tune for the movie's opening credits. Wilder could hum the tune but could not remember its title. The staff of the music department at UA finally located the number: Charles Williams's "Jealous Lover." Williams was known for his miniconcerto "The Dream of Olwen," which he composed for the British film *Where I Live* (1947). He wrote "Jealous Lover" in 1949 as a pop tune. Wilder arranged to have the song retitled "Theme from *The Apartment*." It became a hit single for the duo piano team of Ferrante and Teicher. "Now it's a standard," said Lemmon.[39]

While overseeing the assembly of the footage by editor Daniel Mandell and supervising editor Doane Harrison, Wilder was observant but calm, "like the captain of a well-trained ship who no longer needs to give a lot of orders."[40] After all, both Mandell and Harrison were veterans of previous Wilder pictures. Wilder customarily allowed Mandell to do the first cut of a given scene before he looked at it, because often an editor would come up with some nifty touches on his own. Then Wilder would suggest ways to reduce any excess footage and make other adjustments. Other directors might wind up with as much as two hours of surplus footage after a picture was edited. By contrast, Wilder declared that he had "three feet of unused footage" at the end of postproduction on *The Apartment*.[41] When Wilder screened the picture for the Mirisch Company and for UA, both groups were entirely satisfied with the job he had done.

*The Apartment* concerns a loser, an accountant with a night school diploma who is always a half step behind the parade. The main plot of the picture gets under way when C. C. "Bud" Baxter decides that if his virtues as an employee of Consolidated Life are not enough to get him promoted, the vices of his philandering employers are. That is to say, Bud gains advancement in the firm by loaning his apartment to his superiors for their after-hours frolics with their secretaries.

In this, his first film after *Some Like It Hot*, Wilder manages a sly sideswipe at Marilyn Monroe by having Mr. Dobisch (Ray Walston), a middle manager at Consolidated Life, bring a Monroe look-alike (Joyce Jameson) to Bud's apartment for a tryst. Wilder asked Jameson to wear one of Monroe's gowns from *Some Like It Hot*, but the actress complained that the plunging neckline was too revealing. Wilder allowed her to wear the gown backward.

Mr. Kirkeby (David Lewis) brings Sylvia, a switchboard operator (Joan Shawlee from *Some Like It Hot*), to Bud's flat. As he and Sylvia are leaving, Kirkeby, who calls Bud "Buddy Boy," mutters to him that a promotion is in the offing for him. Bud in due course is promoted from the nineteenth-floor office pool to a wood-paneled private office on the twenty-seventh floor; he is now a junior executive. When Bud is handed his personal key to the executive washroom, Wilder implies that his rise as an organization man is a rogue's progress toward "the room at the top, the executive washroom."[42]

Bud attends the Christmas office party proudly wearing his new bowler hat, another status symbol. The screenplay describes the event as "a swinging party. Some of the employees are drinking liquor out of a paper cup" and getting smashed while singing "Jingle Bells."[43]

Earlier, Sheldrake told Bud that his current mistress had hurled her compact at him, cracking its mirror, when he broke the news to her that he had no intention of divorcing his wife to marry her. Bud, who is already picking up the "executive lingo," says to Sheldrake, "That's how it crumbles, cookie-wise." During the Christmas party Fran takes out her compact, and Bud notices the cracked mirror. "Makes me look the way I feel," she murmurs. Wilder explained, "As Bud looks into the broken makeup mirror, he knows that Fran is the girl that Sheldrake has been bringing to his apartment. We photographed the pained look of recognition on Bud's face in the cracked mirror."[44] The shattered glass symbolizes that Bud's illusions about Fran have likewise been fractured. Wilder pointed out that one shot saved ten pages of dialogue.[45]

Later in the film, Fran characterizes Sheldrake as "a taker" and herself as one "who gets took." Sheldrake says he has not bought her a Christmas present on Christmas Eve. "He then puts a hundred-dollar bill in her purse," comments Bruce Block, "just the way a John would pay off a hooker."[46] Then he picks up the gifts, all wrapped in Christmas paper, to take home to his wife and kids.

In a fit of depression, Fran stays behind in Bud's apartment after her rendezvous there with Sheldrake on Christmas Eve. Fran, who is not aware that the apartment is Bud's, then overdoses on the sleeping pills she finds in the medicine cabinet. Wilder undermines the joy of the holiday season by having Fran's suicide attempt, "provoked by both her despair and her sense of degradation, take place on Christmas Eve."[47] Bud arrives home to find Fran lying unconscious on his bed. He frantically summons Dr. Dreyfuss (Jack Kruschen) from next door to help him revive her.

Axel Madsen calls the suicide sequence "unsavory, because of the doctor's brutal treatment of the heroine after her suicide attempt."[48] Wilder personally disliked Madsen's book because Madsen suggested more than once that he was a misanthrope. "According to Madsen," Wilder stated, "the best example that I am a sadist is my having Shirley MacLaine slapped around by the doctor." Elsewhere he declared, "I had three doctors on the set whom I'd asked what you would do with a patient who had taken a dozen sleeping pills. They told me that, in order to keep her awake, to slap her, make her drink coffee, and walk without stopping." As a matter of fact, "the doctors all agreed that Jack Kruschen should have slapped her harder," but Wilder refused to reshoot the scene.[49]

At all events, Bud stays home from work to nurse Fran on the day after Christmas. When both fail to show up for work, Kirkeby smirks, "They must have had a lost weekend!" Dreyfuss wrongly assumes that Fran is Bud's girl and that her attempt at suicide was the result of a lovers' quarrel. The doctor's first inclination is to "kick Bud's keister clear around the block." He thinks better of that, however, and decides to have a fatherly chat with him. He asks Bud pointedly whether he is satisfied to remain a self-centered cad, or would he prefer to be a mensch, a decent human being. Getting back his integrity, Dreyfuss points out, will help Bud progress toward maturity. "Grow up!" he snaps at Bud.

The worm finally turns when Bud resolves not to allow Sheldrake or any other company official to use his apartment in this manner anymore. The next time Sheldrake demands the apartment key, Bud hands over to him not the key to his apartment but the key to the executive washroom. By relinquishing his status symbol, Bud shows that he is well aware that his defiance of Sheldrake will cost him his job. But Bud regains his self-esteem. He tells Sheldrake, "I've decided to become a mensch, on doctor's orders!" Sheldrake, of course, is the real villain of the piece, since he callously exploits Bud and then summarily fires him when Bud declines to be manipulated anymore.

Fran has a date with Sheldrake on New Year's Eve. He reveals that his wife has discovered his infidelities and is divorcing him. So he at long last pops the question to Fran! But Fran leaves him in the lurch when she learns from him that Bud has renounced his plushy job for her. Douglas Brode comments, "Fran gets over her feelings for her cool but contemptible boss" and falls in love instead with Bud, "a schlemiel who strains spaghetti through a tennis racket."[50] Fran ecstatically hurries down Sixty-seventh Street on her way to Bud's apartment, her hair blowing in the wind, a glowing smile on her face. Schlöndorff admires "this wonderful tracking shot of MacLaine running to rescue Lemmon from despair."[51] Wilder admitted that, because Trauner had built the facades of only three apartment buildings on the New York street set at the studio, MacLaine had to run past these same three buildings repeatedly to suggest that Fran was rushing down the entire length of the street.

Bud had earlier mentioned to Fran that he once made a bungled attempt at suicide when a love affair went sour. Hence, when Fran hears a shot ring out just as she reaches the door of Bud's bachelor flat, she fears that he has made good this suicide attempt. Fran pounds on his door, and he greets her with a foaming bottle of champagne that he has just uncorked, a present from Dr. Dreyfuss. The movie ends with Bud and Fran sitting together on the couch, contentedly playing gin rummy, as they see the new year in together. Bud rhapsodizes, "I absolutely adore you, Miss Kubelik." Fran "checks his effusiveness with mock flippancy," saying laconically, "Shut up and deal."[52] James Schamus notes that "MacLaine, cutting the cards, delivers the movie's final line in both wry acceptance of Bud's babbling protestations of love and as sage advice to the rest of us enduring the mandatory festivities of the holiday season."[53] Wilder was careful to avoid any sentimentality in the ending. "Shut up and deal" would become almost as celebrated a closing line as "Nobody's perfect!" For Bud and Fran, the game of life goes on, and they will play it together.

As mentioned before, some critics have maintained that Wilder copped out at the end of some of his films by tacking on a happy ending that was not called for. Thus some reviewers dismissed the conclusion of *The Apartment* as a conveniently romantic ending in which boy gets girl. Once again, this criticism is not valid; the ending of *The Apartment* is not as happy as it might appear to be. It is true that Bud and Fran have established a solid relationship at the fade-out, but the ending is not sentimental because of that. After all, Bud is out of work, so their future is bleak. One could say that the ending of the film is not so much happy as hopeful—there is hope that Bud and Fran can start life anew and make a go of it, as they greet the new year together. "I like to think that things will work out for them," Wilder said, "and that they will get a better apartment. But there are no guarantees; so much for the supposed happy ending of this picture." He added, "Some critics call me a cynic. I simply portray the rat race, and people who aren't rats—like Bud and Fran—who get caught up in it."

In early June 1960, I attended a sneak preview of *The Apartment* at the Albee Theatre on Fountain Square in downtown Cincinnati. UA had scheduled the sneak deep in the heart of middle America to gauge the reaction of the so-called moral majority to the movie. Some filmgoers found the mixed tone of comedy and drama bewildering, especially a suicide attempt surfacing in a comedy. Be that as it may, there were only a few walk-outs during the picture; most of the audience did not seem offended by the movie's dicey subject.

Furthermore, around this time, *The Apartment* was approved by Geoffrey Shurlock as being in harmony with the censorship code. The Legion of Decency approved the picture as suitable for mature audiences. A legion spokesman, Father Patrick Sullivan, under whose influence the legion was becoming more enlightened in its approach to serious, artistic motion pictures, made a pronouncement. He declared that, although some of the legion's consultors found the film problematic, others believed that in the movie "middle-aged lechery is shown for the pathetic and grotesque thing it is."[54] Sullivan, who was Monsignor Little's executive assistant, was impressed with the movie's theme, as expressed by Dr. Dreyfuss, when he exhorts Bud to be a mensch. It is Dr. Dreyfuss, said Sullivan, who serves as the moral compass of the picture.[55]

*The Apartment* premiered at Grauman's Chinese Theatre on June 21, 1960. The notices were decidedly mixed. On the positive side, they acknowledged that Wilder had brought a mischievous attitude to the formerly taboo subject of extramarital affairs. The movie was hailed by some as the best American comedy since Wilder's own *Some Like It Hot;* he had once again handled a potentially grim theme with wit and compassion. Like Wilder's previous film, *The Apartment* accomplished a sophisticated balancing act between cynicism and sentiment. In short, proclaimed *Variety, The Apartment* was a picture that "could only spring from a talented, imaginative" filmmaker.[56]

Nevertheless, since *The Apartment* had encountered no serious difficulties with the industry censor or with the legion, Wilder was not prepared for some of the major critics' hostile reactions to the movie. Hollis Alpert's piece in the *Saturday Review* was typical of the reviews that had nothing good to say about the picture at all. The message of this "dirty fairy tale," wrote Alpert, was that "the quickest way up the executive ladder is pimping."[57] Dwight Macdonald complained in *Esquire* about the manner in which Wilder mingled comedy and drama, "shifting gears between pathos and slapstick without any transition."[58] Damning with faint praise, Andrew Sarris felt that "only Jack Lemmon kept *The Apartment* from collapsing into the cellar of morbid psychology." Still another critic said that even Lemmon could not save the picture; his nervous, insecure rendering of Bud's character made the reviewer want to reach for a Valium.[59]

To those who charged that the movie lacked an uplifting tone, Wilder commented, "In my opinion *The Apartment* is a highly moral picture. If I wanted to show two people emancipating themselves, I had to dramatize first the mess they wanted to emancipate themselves from. . . . Every picture I make involves people making moral choices. How can I show that without showing the seamy side of the world?"[60] Bud and Fran offer the possibility of decency against which the prevailing corruption can be measured; this is the moral dimension with which Wilder imbues the tale. Still, Wilder maintained that he never intended to impart a strong moral message in his films. "Once in a while," he admitted, "maybe we smuggle in a little contraband message" for the audience to consider. "But I never ram a lecture down their throats, because they'd recoil," he explained. "I do hope they'll leave the theater a little enriched."[61]

Looking back on the movie, Wilder was particularly hurt by the epithet "dirty fairy tale" that was attached to *The Apartment*. Gehman reminded Wilder that Charles Brackett once said his work was characterized by "an exuberant vulgarity." Wilder replied, "I have been pursued for years by that nasty word *vulgarity*. The bad taste thing."[62] Moreover, Wilder was miffed that some critics would accept serious adult themes in foreign-language movies but not in American films. "If I made a picture about the sex life of fishermen in Sardinia," he groused, the critics would love it, "as long as it had a certain morbid message and was slightly out of focus." It would win a prize at some festival in Zagreb. He concluded, "What seems to make European pictures appear more adult than ours is that we don't understand the dialogue."[63]

Wilder gives *The Apartment* a wistful, melancholic quality, befitting a story that deals with an ambitious social climber. Sinyard writes of Bud, "He has a change of heart which, although belated, asserts Wilder's belief in the redemption of character."[64] The picture reflects a belief in human values, set against life in the urban jungle. Wilder saw no conflict between his cynical wit and his hope for humanity.

When Academy Awards night, April 17, 1961, rolled around, *The Apartment* boasted nine nominations and copped five awards. Alexander Trauner won for his production design and Daniel Mandell for his film editing. Wilder accepted his first Academy Award as best director since *The Lost Weekend* fifteen years before. Never known for his humility, he thanked the members of the academy "for being lovely, discerning people." When the screenplay also won an Oscar, Wilder simply said, "Thank you, I. A. L. Diamond." Diamond in turn said, "Thank you, Billy Wilder." Wilder was then awarded a third Oscar as producer of the best picture of the year; it was presented, appropriately enough, by his dear friend Audrey Hepburn. *The Apartment* is one of the very few comedies ever to win best picture.

Wilder became the second filmmaker in motion picture history to win Academy Awards for best director, best screenplay, and best picture. The triple crown had been first bestowed on Leo McCarey for *Going My Way* (1944). After presenting Wilder with the best screenplay award, playwright Moss Hart (*The Man Who Came to Dinner*) leaned over and whispered in Wilder's ear, "This is the moment to stop, Billy."[65] The remark gave Wilder pause, because he was all too aware that *The Apartment* would be difficult to top. To George Cukor, Wilder's Oscars "implicitly represented a sort of delayed recognition on the part of the film industry of Wilder's previous film, *Some Like It Hot*," which surely deserved to be crowned with an official prize from the academy.[66]

When Wilder accepted the best picture award for *The Apartment*, he noted that it really belonged to Lemmon and MacLaine, both of whom had been nominated; he termed them his "two most valuable players." Lemmon lost to Burt Lancaster, who played a Bible Belt preacher in *Elmer Gantry*; MacLaine lost to Elizabeth Taylor, who played a call girl in *Butterfield 8*.

The multiple Oscars helped *The Apartment*'s box office performance. It brought in $6.5 million in domestic rentals and an additional $2.7 million from its distribution overseas. The Mirisch Company and UA were extremely pleased with the film's performance. In addition, more than one critic felt that, in the light of *The Apartment*, Wilder had finally reached the high level of his fellow immigrant directors, including Wyler and Zinnemann.

Wilder recalled that, while he was in Berlin working on his next film, *One, Two, Three*, he was invited to a meeting of the East German Film Club, which had just run *The Apartment*. "They told me that the picture really showed the depravity of the capitalist system, how a man can further his career by filthy tricks—a typical New York story. I said this kind of thing happens in every big outfit, with the bosses having their afternoon trysts." Wilder contended that the movie was not meant to expose the crass materialism of the United States. "I said the story could happen any place, in Brussels or Bucharest." He believed the theme of the film was universal.[67]

"After one of my films went into release," Wilder told me, he often thought of things in the picture that could have been improved. "*The Apartment* is a particular favorite of mine among my own movies, because it is the one in which I made the fewest mistakes."

*The Apartment* has continued to be singled out as a masterpiece over the years. When the AFI picked the one hundred best comedies in 2000, *The Apartment* was high on the list. It was also selected in *Premiere* magazine's 2006 nationwide polls as among the greatest screenplays and the greatest comedies of all time. Finally, in 2007, the *Chicago Tribune* canvassed members of the acting community in Hollywood about their favorite films. Near the top of the list was *The Apartment.*

Wilder realized that he had reached a creative peak with *The Apartment.* But he was not prepared to accept Moss Hart's advice and quit while he was ahead. He could not promise that his next project, a comedy set in postwar Berlin, would be another top-notch picture. At the very least, "I wanted to give United Artists and the Mirisch Company a movie that was going to make some money for them."[68] He felt he owed them that.

# 14

# Love on the Run

## One, Two, Three and Irma la Douce

I've reaffirmed my lack of confidence in my fellow men.
—*Rock Hudson as Robert Talbot in the film* Come September

"Don't ask me why, but I just got the feeling I wanted to make a picture again in Germany," Wilder said; "I hadn't done one since 1948, when I did *A Foreign Affair.*"[1] He explained to a German interviewer, "Of course I was bitter after the war; but today it's a closed chapter. I have buried my anger and my hate. The wounds are healed. It is absolutely, totally forgotten. I even miss Germany again today. I'm homesick for Berlin."[2]

Wilder had a penchant for choosing story material from obscure European literary sources. These stories would be unfamiliar to American film critics, who could consequently not complain that he had not been faithful to his source story. The literary source for *Five Graves to Cairo*, for example, had been *Hotel Imperial*, a play by Lajos Biró. Wilder's next film would be derived from a play by another Hungarian playwright, Ferenc Molnar.

Wilder had seen Molnar's one-act play *Ein, zwei, drei* (One, two, three) on the stage in Berlin in 1928. Wilder remembered vividly the incredible performance on the Berlin stage of Max Pallenberg as Norrison, a high-strung Parisian banker. Pallenberg was noted for delivering his dialogue in a fast staccato, like the rapid chatter of a machine gun. The whole play takes place in Norrison's office. Lydia, the daughter of a Swedish tycoon who is one of Norrison's prize clients, is the banker's houseguest. During her stay she secretly weds Anton, a rabid Socialist taxi driver, and becomes pregnant with his child. Norrison has to hastily turn Anton into an imitation aristocrat, worthy to be the son-in-law of his wealthy client, before the industrialist meets Anton. Norrison does so with the help of an army of clothiers.

What would happen, Wilder wondered, if he set Molnar's farce in Berlin during the cold war? In Wilder's screenplay, Norrison, the banker, becomes C. R. "Mac" MacNamara, chief representative of Coca-Cola in Berlin. Scarlett Hazeltine, the scatterbrained daughter of Wendell Hazeltine, an executive at Coke's home office in Atlanta, is staying with Mac and his family in Berlin. During her sojourn she surreptitiously marries an East German Communist, Otto Piffl, and is now expecting his child, "a bouncing baby Bolshevik," according to Mac. When Wendell Hazeltine and his wife decide to come to Berlin for a visit, Mac must transform Otto, a scruffy dropout, into a capitalist and an aristocrat by means of a host of tailors and haberdashers to impress Scarlett's parents.

Although Coca-Cola plays a significant role in the script, Wilder never personally liked Coke. While a tabloid journalist in Berlin in 1929, Wilder wrote that "Coca-Cola tastes like burnt pneumatic tires."[3] He admitted privately in later years that he never had any reason to change his opinion of Coke. Wilder made Mac an executive of the Coca-Cola Company and not of a fictitious soft drink company for the same reason that Frank Flannagan, Gary Cooper's character in *Love in the Afternoon,* worked for Pepsi-Cola: Wilder abhorred the use of phony brand names in films. "When you have that," he insisted, "believability goes out the window."[4] What's more, Wilder claimed that, after the release of *Love in the Afternoon,* he had promised the Coca-Cola Company that he would one day make a film that featured a Coke executive. After all, the tie-in with Coke in a film, the bosses at Coke knew, would reap a great deal of publicity for their product.

## One, Two, Three (1961)

Wilder could think of only one actor who could deliver dialogue at the trip-hammer tempo of Max Pallenberg: James Cagney. He contacted Cagney very early in preproduction at his residence in Martha's Vineyard, to lure him to commit to the part. The sixty-one-year-old actor had been beset by some unworthy material in recent years; consequently, he was delighted to appear in a promising film like *One, Two, Three.* Wilder was glad that he got Cagney when he was still "working on eight cylinders. For me there's never been anybody better on the screen."[5] When Wilder gave Cagney the screenplay, Cagney noticed the foreword: "This piece must be played *multo furioso*—at a rapid-fire, breakneck speed: 100 miles an hour on the curves, 140 miles on the straightway."[6] "I can see why he thought of me," Cagney writes in his autobiography; "I've been a rat-a-tat talker all my life." During the shooting period, Cagney found himself spitting out his words "like bullets from a machine gun."[7]

*One, Two, Three* has some resonances of *Ninotchka*, which Wilder coscripted for Lubitsch in 1939. Otto Piffl, like Ninotchka, is saturated with Communist doctrine but eventually finds that capitalism is not so bad after all, once he experiences romance with someone from a capitalist country. *One, Two, Three* has another link to *Ninotchka:* Mac is determined to expand Coca-Cola's market into Eastern Europe at any cost. To do so, he must negotiate with (that is, bribe) three petty Russian trade commissars: Peripetchikoff (Leon Askin), Borodenko (Ralf Wolter), and Mishkin (Peter Capell). They are modeled on the three bumbling Russian envoys in *Ninotchka:* Buljanoff, Iranoff, and Kopalski. The three inept commissars in *One, Two, Three* are likewise dim bulbs. At one point, for example, the benighted Peripetchikoff declares that he and his comrades rejected a shipment of Swiss cheese because it was full of holes. Like their counterparts in *Ninotchka,* the three commissars are seduced by the decadent pleasures of the West. As Wilder opined apropos of *Ninotchka,* he thought the fact that Russian diplomats would fall prey to the onslaught of our capitalistic world was quite funny. The same holds true for the present film. In *One, Two, Three,* when someone asks Peripetchikoff, who is a devious crook at heart, "Is everybody corrupt?" he replies, "I don't know everybody!"

In adapting Molnar's play for film, Wilder and Diamond opted to retain the original title, which the German film historian Harald Keller explains this way: "One, two, three—When Mac snaps his fingers in rapid succession, his minions know to jump into position. MacNamara's impatient thwacking of 'one, two, three' stamps out the beat" of the movie.[8]

After World War II, writes Douglas Brode, "no world problem loomed more ominously than the division of Berlin into the East and West sectors," which separated capitalists from Communists.[9] In the screenplay of Wilder's movie, he and Diamond were impartial in lampooning both factions. There is, of course, the trio of Russian trade commissars. Wilder satirized the Germans on the other side of the iron curtain in the person of Schlemmer (Hanns Lothar), Mac's spit-and-polish, heel-clicking aide-de-camp. Schlemmer endeavors to hide that he served in the infamous SS corps of the Nazi army. Asked by Mac about his nation's history, Schlemmer explains that he worked in the underground—not the resistance movement but the subway system, as a motorman! He denies that he knew what the Nazis were doing aboveground. Wilder is satirizing the attitude he often encountered immediately after the war when he was attached to the OWI film unit. Many Germans maintained quite disingenuously that they were ignorant of the brutal crimes committed by the Nazis. Schlemmer inadvertently gives his Nazi past away when he recognizes a newspaper reporter "as his old SS commander."[10] He then saves face by maintaining to Mac that he did not join the SS willingly; "I was drafted!" He further explains, "I was only a pastry cook in the officers' mess."

Since Wilder and Diamond created MacNamara with Cagney in mind, it is not surprising that they quote from two of Cagney's most renowned pictures in the screenplay. When Mac gets fed up with Otto's tirades against the United States, he grabs a grapefruit from the dinner table and threatens Otto: "How would you like a little fruit for dessert?" Cagney thus recalls how he pushed a halved grapefruit in Mae Clarke's face in *The Public Enemy*. There is also a sight gag that recurs throughout *One, Two, Three*. A cuckoo clock features a flag-waving miniature figure of Uncle Sam while playing George M. Cohan's "Yankee Doodle Dandy" every hour on the hour. This is an allusion to Cagney's Oscar-winning portrayal of Cohan in the movie of the same name.

What's more, a U.S. military policeman (Red Buttons) does an imitation of Cagney's screen persona (just as another actor imitated George Raft's screen image in *Some Like It Hot*). The MP hitches up his pants with his elbows and growls, "Okay, Buster!" Cagney pretends not to notice that Buttons is parodying his mannerisms while addressing him. Cagney in turn does an impersonation of his old pal Edward G. Robinson, who also got his start in gangster pictures at Warner Bros. in the 1930s. When Mac hears that Scarlett Hazeltine's parents have learned that she is expecting a baby with her Communist husband, he mumbles, "Mother of mercy, is this the end of little Rico?" Cagney "renders that line of dialogue as an impromptu homage to Robinson," who played mobster Rico Bandello in *Little Caesar*.[11]

Kevin Lally hazards that the screenplay for *One, Two, Three* "probably contains the highest number of gags per page" of any Wilder-Diamond script.[12] The writers pitched their best jokes to Cagney's character, since Mac is obviously the center of the movie. In defending Western civilization against Otto's jibes, Mac pontificates, "Look at it this way, kid: Any world that can produce the Taj Mahal, William Shakespeare, and striped toothpaste can't be all bad." Endorsing Wilder's audacious humor, Axel Madsen writes, "Only Wilder could have planted in James Cagney's mouth," when the Communists are hijacking a shipment of Coke, this line: "And they don't even return the empties."[13]

Some early coverage in the American press about Wilder's movie criticized him for poking fun at the U.S. presence in Berlin, epitomized by MacNamara, who is a bona fide screwball. They even accused Wilder of being un-American for making this picture. "I am a very devout, naturalized

American citizen," Wilder replied; "I believe I can do more for my country with a healthy belly laugh than by waving the flag."[14]

Having spent eight months writing the script for *One, Two, Three* with Diamond, Wilder launched into preproduction. He was looking for a young German actor who could play Otto Piffl. He managed to corral Horst Buchholz, who had already gained international recognition by appearing in a Hollywood Western, *The Magnificent Seven* (1961). At a casting meeting, Wilder declared, "I'm tired of clichéd typecasting—the same people in every film." For the role of Mac's wife, Phyllis, he continued, "let's get someone whose face isn't familiar to moviegoers. Why don't we get Arlene Francis?" Francis was a television personality, known especially as a regular on the TV game show *What's My Line?* Francis played Mac's wife as "warm and sensible," two things that Mac himself decidedly was not. Since she had not appeared in a movie for more than a decade, Francis felt like a newcomer when she arrived on the set. Wilder immediately put her at ease by saying, "Now that you're here, we can start."[15]

Behind the camera, Wilder secured the services of cinematographer Daniel Fapp, who had just completed the shooting of *Let's Make Love,* a Marilyn Monroe vehicle. Because they had both done a picture with Monroe, Wilder felt that he and Fapp regarded each other with the camaraderie that characterized the survivors of the *Titanic*. Fapp was new to the Wilder camp, as was composer André Previn. Interestingly enough, Previn was himself a native of Berlin; he was born there in 1929. He studied music at the Berlin Conservatory before his family immigrated to the United States in 1939. Previn began writing film scores at MGM while still in his teens. By the time he came to write the background music for *One, Two, Three,* he had already won two Oscars: one for arranging the Lerner and Loewe score for *Gigi* (1958), and one for adapting the George and Ira Gershwin score for *Porgy and Bess* (1959).

Editor Daniel Mandell was working on his third Wilder picture, while Alexander Trauner was designing the sets for his fourth. One of Trauner's significant contributions to the film was for the sequence set in a smoky East Berlin nightclub. The nightspot brings to mind the tawdry Hamburg cabaret that Trauner designed for a flashback in *Witness for the Prosecution,* not to mention the Club Lorelei in *A Foreign Affair.* In the present movie, the nightclub scene takes place in the sleazy ballroom of the Grand Hotel Potemkin (named after Wilder's favorite silent film). In the scene as shot, there is a young man steering an older woman around the dance floor; this is an implicit reference to the Hotel Eden, where Wilder squired elderly matrons around the ballroom in 1929. Wilder also had Trauner reconstruct the arrival area of Tempelhof airport at the studio, since filming at the real airport proved impossible because of the noise of the planes passing overhead.

Principal photography was scheduled to run from June through August 1961, with exteriors filmed on location in Berlin and interiors shot in the Bavaria Film Studios in Munich. When Wilder arrived in Berlin in early June, he set up his production headquarters at the Berlin Hilton. He immediately dubbed the divided city of Berlin "Splitsville." The Berlin Wall would not be erected until mid-August, however; the Brandenburg Gate was still open to traffic between East and West Berlin. Wilder arranged with the East German authorities to do a shot of Buchholz as Otto riding a battered motorbike through the Brandenburg Gate and into East Berlin, with the camera mounted on a truck following close behind Buchholz. Unfortunately, a downpour intervened, and Wilder was unable to complete the sequence. He shut down filming for the rest of the day, with a view to returning the following morning.

By late that same afternoon, however, the East German government had gotten wind of the fact that *One, Two, Three* was a comedy and that some of the humor in the picture would be at the expense of the Communist regime. When Wilder and his crew returned the next day to complete the scene, "he found the Soviet sector out of bounds, and the Gate bustling with uniformed guards." Wilder moaned that this reversal was "Hitler's last revenge."[16] He complained that the Communists had no sense of humor. "They raised no objection until they got the idea that we were poking fun at them. But we poke fun at everybody!"[17]

Wilder was informed by the Communist authorities that he could stage the shot with Buchholz riding his motorcycle up to the gate, but Wilder and his film unit could not cross the boundary into East Berlin. Wilder made a dry run of the scene. Then he sent word to the Communist officials that their heavily armed guards were all in the shot. "While it was all right with him, he was afraid that it would give audiences the impression that East Berlin was a police state"! That message "cleared the Gate of East German policemen very fast."[18] But Wilder's troubles with the East German government were only beginning.

Much to Wilder's consternation, the Berlin Wall was erected right in the middle of shooting. In the predawn hours of August 13, 1961, East German soldiers stretched a network of barbed wire across the boundary between East and West Berlin. The wire would soon be reinforced by a fifteen-foot-high concrete wall, creating a thirty-mile-long barrier separating the Communist sector from the capitalist. In this manner the East German authorities meant "to stem the flow of refugees defecting from East Germany to the

West."[19] As Wilder put it, "They sealed off the Eastern sector and wouldn't let people come across the border. It was like making a picture in Pompeii with all the lava coming down."[20]

"Early the following morning," Diamond writes, he and Wilder "drove out to the Brandenburg Gate and found thousands of West Berliners milling silently along the border, which had been closed the night before." The reports of the Berlin crisis that reached the Los Angeles papers described the situation as a powder keg ready to explode. Accordingly, Harold Mirisch, president of the Mirisch Company, wired Wilder to bring his film unit home before there was an outbreak of violence. Wilder replied, "Don't worry." Referring to the fact that filming had been suspended, Wilder stated, "Nobody is shooting. Not even us."[21]

The upshot of the erection of the Berlin Wall was that Trauner had to construct a full-scale replica of the Brandenburg Gate on the back lot at the Bavaria Film Studios, at a cost of $150,000. Although it was constructed out of papier-mâché, Trauner's gate looked like the real thing. "When you've got the Brandenburg Gate, you don't need East Berlin," Wilder remarked. Exteriors originally scheduled to be shot in East Berlin could be filmed on the streets of West Berlin. No one would know the difference, because "East Berlin looks just like West Berlin."[22]

Wilder and Diamond had to make continuous revisions in the script to keep up with the headlines as the grim political situation continued to deteriorate. Wilder said,

> When refugees were killed trying to cross from East to West in real life, it made it harder for people to accept a comedy that took place in this setting. Filmmakers are vulnerable to this kind of risk. A situation, a political mood changes in the course of your making a film and things are not the same by the time you finish the picture as they were when you started. If you write a newspaper piece, it appears the next day. If you write a magazine article, it appears a week from Tuesday. But filmmakers who do a contemporary story have to pray that the situation that they are dealing with in the projected movie will still be valid a year in the future. Otherwise people may say that you are guilty of bad taste in treating a subject like the cold war that may have been quite different when you began.

Putting it another way, Diamond said, "A playwright can update his lines while his play is still running. But once a joke is frozen on film, you're stuck with it, come what may."[23]

Inevitably, Wilder and Diamond fell behind in revising the screenplay. One of the actors inquired flippantly, "Will we get some new pages today, or will we find them in our stockings next Christmas?"[24] Wilder and Diamond revised dialogue wherever necessary. And they even added a prologue, to be spoken by Cagney, judiciously explaining the political situation in Berlin while illustrative shots of the city appeared on the screen. The new introductory voice-over places the action of the movie between June and August 1961, the same three months when Wilder was shooting the film in Germany.

Wilder and his film unit returned to the Bavaria Film Studios, where they had filmed interiors earlier in the summer, to continue shooting throughout the balance of August and into early September. Cagney continued to rattle off pages of dialogue at ticker-tape speed. One day Wilder thought Cagney had slowed down and asked him to speak faster. "I've always been told to slow down, never to speed up," said Cagney.[25]

"Wilder asked me if I had ever played anything this fast before," Cagney writes. "I said yes, *Boy Meets Girl*," in which he costarred with Pat O'Brien. Cagney explained to Wilder that he learned on that picture "the absolute need for pacing," to prevent the dialogue from being an "unadulterated rush." He said to Wilder, "Let's take our time for one spiel," to give the audience a breather, "then pick it up and go like hell again." Wilder went along with Cagney's suggestion "to a degree," according to Cagney.[26]

Buchholz recalled coming to the studio early one morning and finding Cagney doing a soft-shoe routine in a dark corner of a soundstage. "What the hell are you doing that for?" he inquired. Cagney answered that the only way that he could get "the damned dialogue up to speed was by warming up for his scenes with a tap dance routine."[27]

Cagney reveals in his autobiography that he found Buchholz to be a headstrong young actor who attempted to upstage him. Buchholz would endeavor to maneuver Cagney around while shooting a scene with him, so that Buchholz alone would be facing the camera. Finally Wilder barked, "Stop it, Horst!" Cagney writes, "Horst Buchholz tried all kinds of scene-stealing didoes, and I had to depend on Billy Wilder to take some steps to correct this kid. If Billy hadn't, I was going to knock Buchholz on his ass, which at several points I would have been very happy to do."[28]

By contrast, Cagney was impressed by Pamela Tiffin (Scarlett), who was appearing in only her second film; she seemed to be willing to profit by Cagney's experience. He told her, for example, when she began a scene, "to plant yourself, look the other fella in the eye, tell the truth, . . . and always *mean* everything you say."[29] Cagney was gratified that she tried to do just that.

The movie's opening credits are accompanied with a zesty rendition of "The Saber Dance" by the contemporary Armenian composer Aram Khachaturian, which had gained popularity throughout America around that time. The prologue, accompanied by Cagney's voice-over, begins the movie. The narration explains that the action of the story takes place in the period leading up to the erection of the Berlin Wall. Meanwhile, the closing of the Brandenburg Gate is shown, as is a Communist youth parade with youngsters marching to "The Internationale." They are carrying balloons with the motto "Yankees Go Home."

"On Sunday, August 13, 1961, without any warning," Cagney as MacNamara intones, "the East German Communists sealed off the border between East and West Berlin. They are *real* shifty; I am stationed in Berlin, and I know. Let us go back to last June: Traffic flow is normal through the Brandenburg Gate, and one could pass from one side of the iron curtain to the other. In the Eastern sector, under Communist domination, the people still held parades. In the Western sector, the people were under Allied protection, so they had democracy." The prologue ends with a shot of a billboard displaying a pigtailed fräulein holding a bottle of Coke, with the slogan "Mach mal Pause" (The pause that refreshes). Wilder cuts to Mac walking through the huge office at the Coca-Cola headquarters in West Berlin. The clerks are working diligently at their desks, which are arranged in symmetrical rows, recalling the opening sequence in *The Apartment*.

Mac aims to expand the Coke market into Eastern Europe, which would win him the promotion to chief of European operations. "MacNamara plans to open the iron curtain just enough so he can introduce Coca-Cola to the huge untapped market in the East," Wilder explained. "Cagney was short but aggressive; as MacNamara he comes across as ambitious and ruthless. Mac would do any goddamned thing to become the number one man for Coke in Europe."[30]

Mac hopes to crack the market with the help of the three befuddled Russian trade commissars, Peripetchikoff, Borodenko, and Mishkin. He wines and dines them in the seedy ballroom of the Grand Hotel Potemkin, formerly the Grand Hotel Goering. For openers, he reminds them that their rival product, Kremlin Kola, is an abysmal failure with the Russian peasants, who use it for sheep dip.

The orchestra leader sings "Yes, We Have No Bananas" in German; a few couples dance. The band's conductor is none other than Frederick Hollander, who accompanied Marlene Dietrich on the piano as she sang his songs at the Club Lorelei in *A Foreign Affair*. Mac brings along his sexy secretary, Ingeborg (Lilo Pulver), to the festivities. She is "a bubble-headed platinum blonde, a gum-chewing, hip-swinging Marilyn Monroe clone," recalling the Monroe look-alike in *The Apartment*.[31] "I'm bilingual," Ingeborg assures MacNamara. "Don't I know it!" he retorts. Mac addresses the Russian trade delegation at one point as "my old friends, Hart, Schaffner, and Karl Marx." When Mishkin slaps Ingeborg on the behind, Mac adds, "I said *Karl* Marx, not Groucho!" Ingeborg obliges the three Russian stooges by executing a seductive dance on a tabletop, brandishing two flaming shish kebab skewers, accompanied by "The Saber Dance." There is a hint of sadomasochism in Ingeborg's dance routine as she swats the Russians with her black leather belt. The three commissars, whom Mac calls "Siberian wolves," become quite boisterous watching Ingeborg's gyrations.

Mac finds out that Scarlett Hazeltine, whom he was supposed to be chaperoning during her sojourn in Berlin, has not only secretly married Otto, a card-carrying Communist, but is expecting a blessed event. Then he learns that Scarlett's parents are coming from Atlanta for a visit. So he immediately formulates a plan to recondition Otto into a worthy son-in-law for Wendell Hazeltine (Howard St. John). Mac discovers that a German aristocrat, Count von Droste Schattenburg (Hubert von Meyerinck), is currently the men's room attendant at the Hotel Kempinski. (Sig Ruman, who appeared in *Stalag 17* and other Wilder pictures, was engaged to dub the count's lines.) The penniless count adopts Otto for four thousand marks. For an additional five marks, he throws in a sketch of his ancestral coat of arms and a photo of the ruins of the family castle. Mac summons a fleet of tailors to outfit Otto in a full wardrobe of formal attire. In this scene, Cagney had to race through two pages of dialogue while selecting various items of apparel for Buchholz's Otto. Cagney kept blowing his lines. Each time, Wilder called for another take. "Take it a little slower, Jimmy," Wilder would say; "let's go again." Finally, when Cagney had done more than forty takes, he at last got the dialogue perfect. Wilder remarked, "Send a cable to Marilyn Monroe," who had done forty-seven takes on one scene in *Some Like It Hot;* "warn her that she's got competition."[32]

This episode illustrates why Cagney stated later that he thought Wilder was "overly bossy—full of noise, a pain. Still, we did a good picture together. I didn't learn until after we were done that he didn't like me, which was fine as far as I was concerned, because I certainly didn't like him."[33] For his part, Wilder acknowledged that Cagney was a "great actor" but agreed that he and Cagney just did not get along. Wilder found Cagney "very opinionated," which was precisely what Cagney thought of Wilder. Whenever Wilder invited Cagney and his wife to a German restaurant, Cagney declined. "I did not socialize with him," said Wilder, but ultimately "we said goodbye on very good terms."[34] Cagney retired from pictures after completing *One, Two, Three*. He writes in his autobiography, "When I drove through the studio gate, and the thrill was gone, I knew it was time to quit."[35]

As the film nears its conclusion, Otto, "for love of his wife and unborn child," permits himself to be seduced by Mac into the role of a capitalist, complete with morning coat and striped trousers.[36] The movie's last scene is at the Tempelhof arrival gate, where Otto and his new wife, Scarlett, along with Mac, meet Mr. and Mrs. Hazeltine's plane. Only a couple of days before the scene was scheduled to be shot, Buchholz, while driving home from the studio, lost control of his car, spun off the road, and plowed into a clump of trees. Wilder rushed to the hospital with Buchholz's wife, the French actress Myriam Bru. The physician on duty wanted to perform an exploratory operation on her husband to ascertain whether he had sustained internal injuries. But Myriam hesitated to give her approval because she thought her husband was set against "unnecessary surgery." Wilder took her aside and said, "If there is something wrong, they will find it and fix it." He persuaded Myriam to consent to the operation. "If she had not," Buchholz maintained, "I would have died." In fact, German radio newscasters were already pronouncing him dead. "I owe my life to Billy Wilder," he concluded.[37]

Wilder's lease on the Bavaria Film Studios had expired, so he had to bring Buchholz back to Hollywood after he convalesced to shoot the closing scene at the airport. Trauner rebuilt the Tempelhof arrival gate at the Goldwyn Studios. In all, Buchholz's accident added another $250,000 to the budget.

After Wendell Hazeltine makes Otto's acquaintance at the airport, he advises Mac that he is naming his eager son-in-law, whom he sees as a promising young executive, chief of European operations for Coca-Cola. This is precisely the position that Mac has been angling for all along. Mac is being posted back to the home office in Atlanta, to the delight of his wife, Phyllis, who has a hankering to stop traipsing around Europe and return home. But Mac is deeply disappointed at losing out to the likes of Otto Piffl. Mac cheers himself up by having a Coke. He is flabbergasted to see a bottle of Pepsi-Cola coming out of the airport Coke machine. Wilder subsequently received a note from Joan Crawford, at that time a Pepsi-Cola executive, in which she chided Wilder for ending the movie with a cheap shot at Pepsi's expense. "How could you?" she asked.[38]

When *One, Two, Three* opened in December 1961, critical reaction was sharply divided. Reviewers "either loved it or hated it," said Wilder; "there was no middle ground."[39] Brendan Gill's review in the *New Yorker* was enthusiastic: "Diamond and Wilder have had the gall to manufacture a hundred outrageous wisecracks about the desperate duel Russia and the West are currently waging," he wrote. "Mr. Wilder could no doubt wring a hearty yock from the bubonic plague."[40] *Time* magazine raved that Wilder's "rapid, brutal, whambam style" had produced "an often wonderfully funny exercise in nonstop nuttiness."[41]

By contrast, Andrew Sarris noted that the unrelenting one-liners in *One, Two, Three* "were more frenzied than funny"; only "Cagney's presence" made the film worth seeing.[42] Pauline Kael went further: "*One, Two, Three* is overwrought, tasteless, and offensive—a comedy that pulls out laughs the way a catheter draws urine."[43]

"Pauline Kael and some other critics were shocked that we made fun of the cold war," Wilder said. They thought the movie exploited up-to-date issues in a crass effort to be timely. They believed it was "a great miscalculation," Wilder explains, "that we even made mention of the building of the Berlin Wall. They failed to realize that the Berlin Wall went up while we were shooting the picture." He acknowledged that "people were killed trying to escape" from the Soviet sector, "and the subject of the film no longer seemed very funny." The political climate in Berlin had conspired to make *One, Two, Three* a much darker comedy than *A Foreign Affair,* Wilder's previous Berlin film. Because *One, Two, Three* pulls no punches and lands satirical haymakers on both sides of the iron curtain, Wilder feared that "both the Communists and the capitalists would put me up against the Berlin Wall and shoot me!"[44]

Kael's acerbic review went on to assert that Wilder had been called a great director around Hollywood, when he was only a clever one. Indeed, she scolded, "His eye is on the dollar, or rather on success, on the entertainment values that bring in dollars. But he has never before . . . exhibited such brazen contempt for people," except perhaps in *Ace in the Hole.*[45] When Wilder was reminded subsequently of Kael's diatribe, he responded in kind: "I don't make pictures for the so-called intelligentsia," like Kael; "they bore the ass off me. I think they're all phonies, and it delights me to be unpopular with them. They are pretentious mezzo-brows." Kael's observation that Wilder was not a great director, just a filmmaker out to make a fast buck, particularly offended him. "I have at no time regarded myself as one of the artistic immortals. I am just making movies to entertain people, and I try to do it as honestly as I can."[46]

*One, Two, Three* cost close to $3 million. Its domestic gross was only $2 million; its foreign gross was $1.6 million. So the picture did turn a profit, though a modest one.

The 1961 Berlin International Film Festival presented a retrospective of

Wilder's films on the occasion of his return to Germany to make *One, Two, Three*. The event climaxed on the final day of the festival with Wilder's accepting an award for his achievements. He was delighted to be feted by the Germans, since his film career had begun in Berlin in the 1920s. The trophy was inscribed, "To Billy Wilder, a great artist and a great man." Wilder responded to the accolade at the reception after the ceremony with his usual bravado: "I agree."[47]

Two years after the release of *One, Two, Three*, screenwriter Abby Mann (*Judgment at Nuremberg*, 1961) took a cheap shot at the movie. Mann went to the Moscow International Film Festival in 1963 as part of the Hollywood contingent. He apologized to the Russians for movies like *One, Two, Three* and promised that "some of us will try to give you more films in the manner of *Grapes of Wrath* [1940]," a social protest movie about migrant workers in the Depression. Wilder fired off a response to the trade papers. "Who appointed Abby Mann as spokesman for the American Film World in Moscow?" Wilder inquired. "His remarks were both sophomoric and sycophantic."[48]

The fall of the Berlin Wall on November 9, 1989, occasioned fresh interest in *One, Two, Three*. After the successful revival of the film at a Paris art house in 1989, the movie was rereleased in Germany, where it became a sensation and was likewise successful on German TV. Keller hazards that moviegoers and critics alike were not prepared in 1961 for a picture that combined Marx brothers slapstick and high-class wordplay with dark drama. "The public recognition that the film deserved" came only years later, when it met with "wide acclaim from young critics and audiences that had grown in maturity."[49]

Wilder thought it was a "sporadically good picture."[50] Withal, because *One, Two, Three* was not a big moneymaker on its original release, he figured that he had to be careful in selecting his next project. He chose to make a film adaptation of *Irma la Douce* (Irma the sweet), a French musical play about a Parisian prostitute. The script for the stage play was by Alexandra Breffort, with songs by Marguerite Monnot. *Irma* premiered in Paris in 1956 and ran for five years. It was transplanted to Broadway in an English-language version in the fall of 1960 and ran for over a year.

## *Irma la Douce* (1963)

Wilder decided from the get-go that the movie version of *Irma* would not be shot in the streets of Paris, as *Love in the Afternoon* had been. In the wake of the chaotic production history of *One, Two, Three*, Wilder had again become disenchanted with making films in foreign capitals. When he wound up having to rebuild the Tempelhof airport set on a Hollywood soundstage to shoot the movie's final scenes, Wilder wondered why he had gone to the trouble and expense of filming the rest of the movie in Germany. He was convinced that *Irma* could be filmed more quickly and economically at the Goldwyn Studios in Hollywood than on location in Paris.

For *Irma* Wilder was able to reunite the two stars of *The Apartment,* Jack Lemmon and Shirley MacLaine. Since the story focuses on Irma (Shirley MacLaine), a prostitute who falls in love with Nestor (Jack Lemmon), her pimp, Louella Parsons asked Lemmon in an interview how this unsavory tale could be laundered for the movie version. "Audiences are much more mature today, and they demand maturer subject matter," Lemmon replied. "I think any subject can be handled on the screen today, provided that it's done with good taste."[51] But since Wilder had been criticized by reviewers in the past for exhibiting bad taste in his films, Parsons was not entirely reassured.

Wilder was aware that a producer who was considering a film adaptation of *Irma* back in 1959 had submitted the play script to Geoffrey Shurlock, inquiring whether the play was suitable for filming. Shurlock responded with a letter that took a decidedly dim view of *Irma*. He declared, "It's [*sic*] leading lady is a practicing prostitute who, additionally, falls in love with and lives with the leading man, bearing his child out of wedlock." He continued, "She is also carrying on a second affair with the leading man who has disguised himself as somebody else. This relationship is not treated with any semblance of the compensatory moral values or voice of morality required by the Censorship Code." In sum, "the general low and sordid tone of the story render[s] this property unacceptable" for film production.[52]

Shurlock's letter thoroughly discouraged the producer in question. Nevertheless, Wilder was optimistic about *Irma*'s potential as a viable film project. "There's no reason this film should not get" the industry's official seal of approval from Shurlock's office, Wilder asserted. "It has no orgies, no homosexuals or cannibalism."[53] Wilder was alluding to Mankiewicz's film of Tennessee Williams's *Suddenly, Last Summer,* in which a homosexual is killed and eaten by young cannibals he has previously engaged in sexual encounters. Mankiewicz's picture was in fact granted the industry's seal of approval by Shurlock.[54]

Wilder convinced Walter Mirisch that he could make *Irma* a sophisticated adult comedy. "We are doing it with taste and feeling," he assured Mirisch. "It will strike a happy medium between Tennessee Williams and Walt Disney."[55]

The Mirisch Company bought the screen rights of Breffort and Monnot's musical play for $350,000. This was a sizeable sum, but the film rights to *Witness for the Prosecution* had cost $435,000, and that investment had paid off handsomely. Wilder opted to shoot the picture in color at the behest of Walter Mirisch. *Irma* would be Wilder's first color film since *The Spirit of St. Louis*. Mirisch assigned to Wilder's color production a budget of $5 million.

Wilder had not made a musical since *The Emperor Waltz*, which was a resounding flop. He knew that musicals were not his forte, so he planned to drop some of the songs from the original score of *Irma* and concentrate on the story. As things turned out, he wound up throwing out all of the songs. "I have nothing against music," he explained, "but the more I went into that story, the better I thought it was. And for me, the numbers got in the way. So first, one of them went; then another one went. . . . More and more I could see that, if I really wanted to explore all the avenues of this story, there wasn't going to be room for *any* numbers."[56] Wilder found that the characters were two-dimensional and the story was thin, so he aimed to fill out the characterizations and fill in the story.

Diamond heartily endorsed Wilder's decision. "We saw the show in Paris" and liked the plot but not the songs, he stated. "The songs stopped the action and seemed to have nothing to do with the story."[57] Axel Madsen calls Wilder's scuttling all of the songs "a daring piece of open-heart surgery that amputated his source material of part of its identity" as a musical comedy.[58] But Wilder never regretted his decision. "I think it worked out very well," he said.[59]

Other changes developed as Wilder and Diamond worked on the screenplay. They transferred the principal setting from the bohemian Montmartre district of Paris to the neighborhood of the bustling wholesale meat market of Les Halles. Just a step away from the marketplace, in Rue Casanova, is the red-light district inhabited by the poules (harlots). "Nobody ever mentioned the symbolism of the raw meat for sale," Wilder observed.[60] Nevertheless, the implication that "the Halles 'meat market' also applies to the prostitutes on display" is hard to miss.[61]

Wilder and Diamond "hit us over the head with the old rotten jest that prostitution is . . . a way of life like any other," Pauline Kael smirked.[62] Putting it another way, Kevin Lally notes, "For its time, *Irma la Douce* is remarkably non-judgmental about the oldest profession."[63] Moustache (Lou Jacobi), the worldly proprietor of the café Chez Moustache, where the poules and their mecs (pimps) hang out, glibly pontificates at one point, "Love is illegal, but not hate—that you can do anywhere, anytime, to anybody." Moustache is the commentator on the action in the movie, as in the play. He makes constant references to his past adventures: as a soldier cashiered from the French Foreign Legion, as a croupier in a Monte Carlo casino, and so on. His hilarious recollections are always capped by the phrase, "But that's another story!"

Wilder assembled a top cast for the picture, with Lemmon and MacLaine in the leads and reliable character actors like Lou Jacobi (as Moustache) and Joan Shawlee (as a hooker named Amazon Annie) lending strong support. Furthermore, Wilder was fortunate to have several veterans of his previous films working behind the camera: cinematographer Joseph LaShelle, production designer Alexander Trauner, film editor Daniel Mandell, and composer André Previn, not to mention cowriter I. A. L. Diamond and supervising editor Doane Harrison.

Most of the movie was filmed at the Goldwyn Studios, where Trauner took up all of stage 4 with his realistic reproduction of a Paris street. The mammoth set took three months to construct and cost $350,000. This main set consisted of the facades of forty-eight buildings, including the Chez Moustache tavern and the Hotel Casanova brothel. To a visitor to the set, "it could only look false," Wilder observed, "but on the screen, believe me, everything fell into place with a stupefying authenticity."[64]

Principal photography began in August 1962, with ten days of shooting exteriors in Paris. This footage would be carefully integrated throughout the film to enliven all of the material that was filmed on the Hollywood soundstages. The location footage included several shots of the Halles marketplace, including an aerial view, and scenes along the banks of the Seine River. This river footage was filmed across from Trauner's own home on Rue des Saints-Peres.

One of the more curious plot contrivances involves a shot of Jack Lemmon in disguise emerging from the Seine. Wilder was unaware that the waters of the Seine were an unsavory mixture of mud and garbage. Lemmon contracted an intestinal virus as a result of being immersed in the river, and filming was suspended for a few days while he recovered.

Production resumed at the Goldwyn Studios on October 8 and continued until February. Wilder had to cope with the fact that, because *Irma* was set in Paris, all of the characters were French. Wilder abhorred the practice of having foreigners speak English with foreign accents. He contended that the audience would not tolerate Lemmon, MacLaine, and the other actors speaking English with a French accent for a whole movie: "It's false; it just does not work," he maintained. Wilder decided not to have the actors "simulate a French accent," since they were plainly Americans. "We had a long talk," says MacLaine, and decided that everyone in the cast should have the same American accent.[65]

Lemmon had developed a practice to soothe himself before shooting a scene. When the director was ready to shoot, Lemmon would close his eyes and say, "It's magic time." But MacLaine had no such mantra that worked for her when she was tense on the set. During the four-month shoot at the studio, Wilder followed his customary practice of endeavoring to defuse tension on the set with humor. While filming a tough scene in which Nestor and Irma discuss the possibility of her abandoning her profession, Wilder noted jokingly that Lemmon had won an Academy Award for *Mr. Roberts* and was nominated for his two previous Wilder pictures, but he "was twice screwed by very inferior talent." Three takes were spoiled when MacLaine muffed her lines. "I don't know what the fuck I'm doing!" she exclaimed. Lemmon gave her a blank stare. After several more takes, Wilder again offered a witticism to break the tension: "This is the slowest company in Hollywood." He pointed out that George Stevens had started his film of the life of Christ, *The Greatest Story Ever Told* (1965), the week before, "and Jesus is bar mitzvahed already."[66]

Principal photography wrapped in February 1963. Early in postproduction Wilder screened the rough cut of *Irma* for Previn. Wilder instructed him to "disregard all of the pratfalls" and compose a romantic score derived from the batch of songs that Marguerite Monnot had composed for the original stage production. Previn followed Wilder's directions and produced lyrical background music that accented the romance between Nestor and Irma.[67]

Wilder insouciantly stated that he fully expected *Irma* to receive the official seal of approval from the industry censor, since, he noted disingenuously, it was fundamentally a love story as "innocent as a glass of milk." In reality, Wilder had "slyly subverted the Code by making a comedy out of an otherwise taboo subject."[68] Be that as it may, Shurlock asked for only minimal cuts: the shot of MacLaine naked to the waist in the bathtub was replaced by a shot revealing only her head and shoulders, and a shot of an American GI leaving the brothel with a whore on each arm was excised.

Wilder remembered that Shurlock had demanded that Ariane and Frank marry at the end of *Love in the Afternoon* to give the movie a morally uplifting conclusion. He forestalled a similar complaint about the present film's screenplay by retaining the wedding of Irma and Nestor from the stage play. These modifications overcame Shurlock's initial objections to the scenario, as put forth in his 1959 letter. After all, Shurlock was aware of "the growing liberal climate in this country" during the "swinging Sixties," writes film historian Dawn Sova. He observed that prostitution was no longer quite as objectionable a topic for film as it once had been.[69]

The Legion of Decency knew of the cuts made in *Irma* at the behest of the industry censor but still found the movie distasteful. Monsignor Little, speaking on behalf of the legion, explained that, "in developing the story of the redemption of one prostitute, the film concentrates on details of prostitution and upon suggestiveness in costuming, dialogue, and situations." He continued, "It fails as a comedy and, as a consequence, tends to be a coarse mockery of virtue."[70] The legion therefore placed *Irma* in its morally objectionable category, where it had also relegated *Some Like It Hot.* Father Patrick Sullivan noted that the legion's consultants came down hard on *Irma* because, in retrospect, they believed their positive rating of *The Apartment* was misguided. Be that as it may, Sullivan added, the legion could have been tougher on *Irma* than it was. Eleven of its consultants voted to condemn the movie, with only eight favoring the morally objectionable category and three favoring a rating for adults. Nevertheless, the movie was not condemned.[71]

Hal Wallis, the respected producer responsible for films like *Casablanca* (1942) and *The Rose Tattoo* (1955), attended an advance screening of *Irma.* Appalled that the film had been granted a code seal, he blasted off a blistering letter to Shurlock. Wallis pronounced *Irma la Douce* "a salacious, pornographic, distasteful, obscene, offensive, degrading piece of celluloid." Audiences, he continued, could only respond to the picture in the same way that they did to stag films. "I have great admiration for Wilder's talent in some of his work," he wrote, "but this is without a doubt the filthiest thing I have ever seen on the screen." Shurlock responded to Wallis that UA had assured him that the film "would be sold strictly as an adult movie."[72] In fact, the disclaimer "This picture is for adults only" appeared in advertising layouts for the movie and in the film's trailer. Only on that condition did Shurlock, in concert with his advisory board, issue the code seal for *Irma.* UA was following the example of MGM, which received a code seal for Stanley Kubrick's controversial film *Lolita* (1962) by stating in the ads that *Lolita* was "for persons over eighteen only."[73]

Wilder was grateful to Shurlock for standing up to Wallis on his behalf; he saw signs that the guardians of film morality were becoming less strict in administering the censorship code. "We had tremendous problems in the past," he recalled. "There was a man at Paramount in charge of censorship who would constantly be snooping around the set to see whether the decolletage was too deep, whether it was permissible. It was not easy, I assure you, because they were powerful, and you had to be very smart" to get around them. Those were different days, he concluded.[74]

The credit sequence of *Irma la Douce* opens "in a mean, narrow street just off Les Halles," according to the screenplay, "and the prostitutes are out on their love patrol in full war paint." The camera moves in on Irma, "stationed beside the dimly lit entrance of a shabby hotel. . . . A customer walks over to Irma and asks her a frank question—a ten franc question. Irma nods and leads him into the hotel," the Hotel Casanova. Legend has it that Casanova slept there in 1763.[75]

There is a dissolve to a short scene that plays like a burlesque skit. Irma's customer is putting money in her purse, which lies open on the night table. "To get her Johns to dish out more dough, Irma lays it on thick and spins tales of past misfortunes," notes Heinz-Jürgen Köhler.[76] She tells this particular client that she was a concert pianist until the piano lid fell on her hand and destroyed her career. He is touched by her sob story and drops an extra bill in her purse as a tip.

Wilder follows the credit sequence with a prologue that recalls the prologue at the beginning of *Love in the Afternoon*. This time the narrator is Louis Jourdan, another French actor who appeared in Hollywood films. Jourdan's voice-over commentary accompanies a quick tour of Les Halles wholesale meat market. "This is the story of Irma la Douce," he intones, "a story of passion, bloodshed, desire, and death—everything that makes life worth living." This is one of the very few speeches in the screenplay that is taken verbatim from the stage play. The camera tracks along row after row of slabs of beef, pork, lamb, and veal. Then it moves on to a long line of harlots on the pavement. "If you are looking for some action, forget the high-rent district," the narrator goes on; "come to our neighborhood. Just step around the corner to the Rue Casanova. That is where you will find the girls, better known as poules." One of the girls, he points out, is named Lolita; she wears sunglasses with heart-shaped rims—the trademark of the title character in Kubrick's film. The girls take their coffee break in the louche Chez Moustache bistro; so do the mecs. The proprietor is known as Moustache, but "according to police records," the narrator points out, "Moustache is a Romanian thief named Constatinescu."

The narrator acknowledges that the mecs regularly pay off the local gendarmes, or flics, to cast a blind eye on the girls plying their trade on the sidewalk. "It is what the politicians call 'peaceful coexistence,' trade on the sidewalk. Then one day disaster struck: an honest cop on the beat!" With that, the narrator bows out and Nestor bows in.

Nestor Patou, a rookie policeman patrolling the Rue Casanova, is shocked to find prostitution rife on his beat. He orders a raid on the Hotel Casanova, only to learn that Chief Inspector Lefevre himself has been caught in the raid. Lefevre, Nestor's superior, personally sees to it that Nestor is kicked off the force. Nestor, out of a job, hangs around Moustache's bistro. One night Hippolyte (Bruce Yarnell), Irma's mec, roughs her up for holding back some of her earnings from him. Nestor intervenes and knocks Hippolyte's block off. He thereby inherits Irma as his poule and becomes the number one mec on the block.

Irma in due course seduces Nestor. The *Los Angeles Times* reviewer employed this scene to compare Wilder to Ernest Lubitsch. "Lubitsch, who delighted in sex farces, stopped at the bedroom door. Wilder walks right inside."[77] Indeed, the camera follows Irma and Nestor right into the bedroom; then Irma shuts the door.

Nestor, who has fallen in love with Irma, soon becomes obsessed with the notion that she is still seeing other men. Nestor concocts a scheme whereby he masquerades as a wealthy Englishman, Lord X, who will provide her with sufficient funds so that he can have her exclusive services. He disguises himself with a goatee, a set of buck teeth, and a patch over one eye. Because Nestor initially wants to sleep with Irma only as himself, Lord X tells Irma that he is impotent and seeks only her companionship. He explains that, while he was a prisoner of the Japanese, the bridge on the River Kwai fell on him when it was hit by an explosion, leaving him "half a man." Irma is incredulous: "You think you have run out of gas, but maybe you are just stalled"—a typical Wilder double entendre. In any case, to earn the francs that Lord X pays Irma for their weekly evening together playing double solitaire, Nestor must toil all night at the nearby Les Halles market. Suffice it to say that Irma eventually "cures" Lord X of his impotence.

When Nestor suspects that Irma prefers Lord X's company to his, he becomes wildly jealous and "kills off" Lord X by dumping the wardrobe he wore as Lord X in the Seine. Wilder described the film as the story of a man who becomes jealous of himself. Nestor is soon imprisoned for drowning Lord X, the imaginary British peer, in the river. While in jail, Nestor gets word that Irma is pregnant, and he escapes to be with her. Nestor disguises himself as Lord X one last time to convince the police that he did not drown Lord X. The police hear that Lord X has been inexplicably hanging around under the bridge on the Seine. Indeed, they witness Lord X emerging from the Seine, claiming to be unable to remember what happened to him.

Nestor explains to Irma hurriedly that he impersonated Lord X and that she really loved him all along. Realizing this, the visibly pregnant Irma agrees to marry Nestor. They are wed in a solemn ceremony according to the rites of the Catholic Church, which is curious, since neither Nestor nor Irma is Catholic. Irma goes into labor during the ceremony and delivers the baby in the sacristy. Chief Inspector Lefevre is on hand to inform Nestor that, since he has been cleared of the murder charge, he will be reinstated as a police officer. So Irma is no longer a poule and Nestor is no longer a mec.

Meanwhile, a lone figure steps out of a pew in the church and proceeds up the aisle toward the exit. It is none other than Lord X, complete with eye patch and goatee. This Lord X cannot be Nestor in disguise, because Nestor is busy in the sacristy with Irma and the newborn babe. Spying this impossible reappearance of Lord X, Moustache can only exclaim to the audience, "But that's another story!"

Wilder never explained the gimmicky gag with which the picture ends, but the plot has been far-fetched all along. As MacLaine puts it, the scenario does not bear close analysis, "because it was all artificial anyway."[78] Bernard Dick writes, "When a prostitute's lover masquerades as a peer, . . . without her knowing his identity," we are in the world of what the French call *boulevard comedy,* which flourished in the early twentieth century. The term refers to a small theater near a boulevard in Montmartre that specialized in "bedroom comedies" by the likes of Georges Feydeau. Dick explains, "These old-fashioned French farces subsequently influenced movie directors like Lubitsch and Wilder."[79]

Although *Irma* was big at the box office when it was released on June 5, 1963, several critics dismissed the comedy about the proverbial harlot with a heart of gold as vulgar and lacking in true comic invention. Leo Mishkin in the *New York Morning Telegraph* quite by chance echoed Wallis's angry letter to Shurlock, pronouncing *Irma* "a lewd film that belongs at a stag smoker."[80] Sam Staggs, a film historian who is usually in Wilder's corner, writes, "If high schools put on plays about French hookers, *Irma la Douce* is the kind of low farce that might have the sophomore class in stitches." He deplores "the gauche material, the facile dialogue, the in-your-face crudeness parading as wit."[81]

*Variety* did not much mind the bawdy humor but did take Wilder to task for the movie's excessive running time. The film is just under two and a half hours, "an awfully long haul for a frivolous farce. . . . A little snipping and splicing, particularly in the later stages, and the film's occasional sluggishness" could have been reduced considerably.[82] *Variety* was not alone in stating that "half-an-hour cut out would make it a better film."[83]

Withal, the movie had its fans. Bosley Crowther in the *New York Times* endorsed Wilder's "comic skill and his ability to handle raw material with deceptively silken gloves."[84] What's more, André Previn received an Academy Award for his score, which seamlessly incorporated Marguerite Monnot's original themes. That was the only Oscar accorded *Irma,* but Shirley MacLaine won a Golden Globe award for her performance.

Reflecting on *Irma la Douce,* Wilder noted, "I personally earned more out of that picture than any other picture I made," since he received a whopping 17 percent of the gross plus his usual salary. "That doesn't mean the best; it just means it made the most money."[85] The movie eventually grossed $25 million, which would be the equivalent of $80 million today. *Irma* was a huge hit, Wilder said, "but I'm not sure why." It was not a film he was particularly proud of. "It didn't come out quite the way I wanted it to. It's nothing to be ashamed of," but it was not a movie that he thought much of.[86]

"There is no guaranteeing audience reaction," Wilder said at the time of *Irma*'s release. "I've been lucky; I've taken a lot of chances in treading new ground, which could have slipped out from under me. Though I've gotten away with it about 90 percent of the time, I don't flatter myself that I can hit all the time. But I have to live in hope—or perhaps under the delusion—that if I like it, a great many other people will like it too."[87]

The 1960s, which brought an increasingly liberal climate to America (in contrast to the buttoned-down 1950s), were in full swing. *Some Like It Hot, The Apartment,* and *Irma la Douce* all dwelled on sensitive sexual issues, and all three were severely criticized by the minions of morality. Yet they were all popular with the moviegoing public. Up to this point, Wilder had successfully tested the limits of what was acceptable to the mass audience in popular entertainment. There were industry insiders, like Hal Wallis, who believed that Wilder had already pushed the envelope too far. Nonetheless, Wilder, emboldened by the extraordinary success of *Irma,* was confident that he could make another crowd-pleasing sex romp. With *Kiss Me, Stupid,* however, he would finally overplay his hand.

# 15

# Grifters

## Kiss Me, Stupid and The Fortune Cookie

Everybody lives by cheating everybody else.

—*Preston Sturges*

"The first thing you learn in Hollywood," Billy Wilder declared, was that you must not offend pressure groups. "Don't offend the Catholics, the Jews, the dentists," or any other group.[1] Wilder forgot his own advice when he made *Kiss Me, Stupid,* which offended the Catholic Legion of Decency mightily. But in 1963, Wilder was riding high. In the light of the phenomenal success of *Irma la Douce,* Harold Mirisch, the president of the Mirisch Company, issued Wilder a sweetheart contract that guaranteed him a salary of four hundred thousand dollars plus 10 percent of the gross profit for his next movie.

Wilder selected as the source of his next movie a farce by Italian playwright Anna Bonacci titled *L'ora della fantasia* (The dazzling hour). Wilder knew the play in its French translation, which had been a big hit on the Paris stage as a vehicle for Jeanne Moreau in 1953. *Irma la Douce* had also been a success in Paris. Both were naughty boulevard comedies, as Pauline Kael observes.[2] So Wilder assumed that his film version of Bonacci's farce would repeat the success of *Irma* on the screen.

The French adaptation of Bonacci's Italian play is set in Victorian England. George Sedley, a village church organist, wants to have his new oratorio performed in London. Sir Ronald, the influential sheriff of London, passes through town. George, at the suggestion of his friend Taylor, invites the sheriff to stay overnight in his home so that George can persuade him to arrange for the London premiere of his oratorio. To ingratiate himself with the sheriff, George arranges to have Geraldine, the village harlot, substitute for his wife, Mary, as Sir Ronald's companion for the night. As a result of some plot twists, Sir Ronald winds up spending the night with Mary instead of Geraldine. He agrees to sponsor the London performance of her husband's oratorio in exchange for "one dazzling hour" with Mary. George is astonished later to learn that his oratorio is to be performed in London.

## *Kiss Me, Stupid* (1964)

Although the studio had persuaded Wilder to shoot *Irma* in color, he held out for shooting the present film in black and white. Admittedly, color was in wide use for features by 1963, but Wilder continued to favor black and white. "Unlike David Lean," who needed color for his epic *Lawrence of Arabia* (1962), "my pictures are set in the bed or under the bed" and do not require color, he glibly explained.[3]

In adapting the play for the screen, Wilder changed the names of the characters and transplanted the setting from a rural village in Victorian England to a hick town in the American Southwest named Climax, Nevada. George Sedley and his sidekick Taylor are retooled into the frustrated songwriters Orville Spooner and Barney Milsap. Wilder's first Hollywood screenplay, *Music in the Air,* featured a songwriting team who served to some degree as the models for Orville and Barney.[4]

In Wilder's scenario, piano teacher Orville attempts to sell a song he and Barney wrote to Dino, a famous crooner who is stranded in Climax overnight. Following the play's plot fairly closely, the screenplay has Orville send his wife Zelda away for the night so that he can have Polly, a prostitute, pose as Zelda and spend the night with Dino. This is all part of Orville's plot to manipulate Dino into featuring the song on a TV special. But Orville's plans go awry, and the real Zelda winds up bedding down with the singer—with the understanding that Dino will introduce the song on the air. Throughout the film, Orville is jealous to the point of paranoia of any man who pays attention to his pretty young wife, a trait Wilder retained from his literary source.

I. A. L. Diamond maintained that, in fashioning the script with a spicy plot punctuated with salty double entendres, he and Wilder were aiming to create a movie like Tony Richardson's *Tom Jones* (1963). Richardson's film is a loose adaptation of the earthy Henry Fielding novel *Tom Jones* (1749), a bawdy social satire about the manners and morals of eighteenth-century England. Like the novel, the film is a very honest portrayal of the period. But "we were not interested in doing a picture about greed and sex in Victorian England," Diamond stated; "we wanted to translate it into modern times."[5]

With the script in reasonably good shape, Wilder cast the picture. He went into production with Dean Martin as the crooner Dino, Kim Novak as Polly, and Peter Sellers as Orville. Martin was the first to be cast, since Wilder needed the singer's assurance that he would not mind that the crooner in the script was modeled after his popular image. Indeed, Martin's character in the film bears his own nickname, Dino. Martin would be parodying himself in the picture, just as Otto Preminger had done in *Stalag 17*. "He's a delicious and adorable man who does what you ask him," said Wilder of Martin. "He's one of the most relaxed and talented men I know."[6]

As Polly the Pistol, the prostitute who yearns for domesticity, Novak seems to be doing a takeoff on Marilyn Monroe. "Wilder obviously had Marilyn Monroe in mind when he created the character of Polly," Bernard Dick writes. "Wilder invested Polly with the same sexy vulnerability that made Marilyn tragic and desirable."[7] Novak is quite touching as a Monroe-like wistful floozy. As it happened, Marilyn was Novak's own first name; it had been changed to Kim by the studio early on to avoid confusion with Monroe.

Wilder envisaged Peter Sellers as Orville Spooner, the jealous husband, because Sellers had the knack of making the most eccentric characters sympathetic to an audience. Felicia Farr, an accomplished actress as well as the wife of Jack Lemmon, rounded out the cast as Orville's wife Zelda.

Wilder was able to round up the same group of seasoned production artists who had collaborated with him on *Irma la Douce*. Production designer Alexander Trauner had to create Climax, Nevada, for the movie—a desolate place on the fringe of the Nevada desert, recalling the sun-baked town in *Ace in the Hole*. Wilder and Trauner scouted locations for Climax on the outskirts of Twenty-nine Palms, a small town near the California desert. They selected suitable sites for the dusty residential neighborhood where Orville lives and for the sleazy Belly Button roadhouse. The tavern is so named because the sign out front, which Trauner constructed outside a real café, features a cartoonish cocktail waitress with a fake jewel conspicuously glittering in her belly button.

Wilder needed a couple of sample songs that were supposedly composed by the team of Orville and Barney. During preproduction he had consulted an old friend, the lyricist Ira Gershwin, about the matter. Ira said that he had a trunk full of songs that he and his brother, the late George Gershwin, had never published. He volunteered to rework a couple of the numbers so that they would sound as if they were written by amateur songwriters. One was "I'm a Poached Egg," a whimsical ditty that he and George had written in the 1920s and quite rightly discarded. Ira also dusted off a love song titled

"Sophia," which had been dropped from the Fred Astaire–Ginger Rogers movie musical *Shall We Dance?* (1937).

Principal photography on *Kiss Me, Stupid* began on March 6, 1964. In addition to the location work in Twenty-nine Palms, Wilder filmed some shots of casinos on Fremont Street in Las Vegas. In addition, he shot Dino's Vegas nightclub act at the swank Moulin Rouge club on Sunset Boulevard in Hollywood. But the bulk of the picture was filmed, as usual, at the Goldwyn Studios.

Wilder, according to his custom, attempted to minimize the stress level on the set during shooting with wisecracks. In Dean Martin, Wilder met his match when it came to trading verbal punches. Martin always had a comeback for Wilder's witticisms. When Wilder issued complicated instructions to Martin on how he was to play a particular scene, Martin retorted, "Well, for Chrissakes, if you wanted an *actor,* what did you hire me for? Why didn't you go get Marlon Brando?"[8] Peter Sellers was not accustomed to incessant banter on the set. Moreover, Wilder preferred an open set and allowed his own friends, as well as guests of the cast and crew, to visit the soundstage during shooting. "The clubby atmosphere made Sellers feel like an outsider," since he was from Britain, notes Glenn Hopp.[9] To make matters worse, other directors permitted Sellers to improvise while rehearsing a scene, but Wilder did not allow any actor to do so.

Sellers kept all of his gripes against Wilder to himself. Nevertheless, the high-strung, erratic actor privately fretted about his resentment of the working conditions on a Wilder set. At night he often sought to assuage his tensions and anxieties by smoking marijuana and sniffing amyl nitrate, a habit that was pushing him toward a crisis.[10]

The crisis erupted on Sunday evening, April 5, 1964. The thirty-eight-year-old actor—after indulging in a dose of amyl nitrate—suffered a mild heart attack. He was rushed to Cedars of Lebanon Hospital. The following Tuesday, shortly after midnight, Sellers suffered a massive coronary thrombosis and was at death's door. Miraculously, he survived and was on the road to recovery very soon. The hospital's heart specialists advised Wilder that Sellers could resume work on *Kiss Me, Stupid* after six months of convalescence at home in England.[11]

Wilder sent Sellers a wire, stating, "Your heart is mended; but mine is still broken."[12] Wilder was already a month into the shooting schedule. In six months' time, the contracts of the other major players in the film would have expired, and they would move on to other projects. Wilder was saddened by the prospect of having to replace Sellers, but he had no choice.

Once he was back in London, Sellers granted Alexander Walker an interview for the *Evening Standard*, in which he declared, "I have had Hollywood, luv. At the studios they give you every creature comfort, except the satisfaction of being able to get the best work out of yourself. I used to go down to the set of *Kiss Me, Stupid* with Billy Wilder and find a bloody Cook's Tour of hangers-on and sightseers standing just off the set, right in my line of vision." These were friends of the director and the cast "who came to kibitz on Peter Sellers, actor. I should have ridden to the set on horseback and bawled out, 'Who are all these damn civilians? Get them out of the range of my cannons!'"[13]

Shortly thereafter, Sellers received a cable signed by Wilder, Martin, and Novak: "Talk about unprofessional rat finks!" "Rat fink" was Polly's description in the script of any boyfriend who had dumped her. Wilder released the telegram to the press with the comment "Heart attack? You have to have a heart before you can have a heart attack!"[14]

Sellers replied with an open letter, published in *Variety*, in which he proclaimed that he was not "an ungrateful limey," much less a "rat fink." He continued, "I went to Hollywood to work and found regrettably that the creative side of me couldn't accept the sort of conditions under which the work had to be carried out." He concluded by saying that anyone was free to say that he was the one at fault, "and no doubt will."[15]

Wilder decided against replying to Sellers's latest salvo to put a stop to the interchange. He hastily recast the part of Orville with Ray Walston, who had played one of the randy executives in *The Apartment*. Wilder began reshooting all of Sellers's scenes with Walston on April 13. A full twenty-four shooting days out of a total of eighty-five were devoted to retakes with Walston. That inevitably meant that the film would considerably exceed the film's original schedule and budget.

Wilder later observed that he admired Sellers as an actor, whatever their disagreements. He added ruefully, "We got Ray Walston, who is a fine actor, but no Peter Sellers."[16] Walston was ultimately charmless and unlikable in the role, Axel Madsen comments. Walston often assumes a grim look, "which is meant to express bewilderment, but registers as truculence."[17] One cannot help but wonder how the film would have turned out with Sellers as a more sympathetic Orville.

During postproduction Previn's background music was recorded. He adroitly integrated into his score themes from the songs that Ira Gershwin had provided. It was time then to send the picture to the industry censor.

Wilder had stopped submitting screenplays to Shurlock in the late 1950s, when Shurlock had advised him that he could not make a solid judgment about a movie on the basis of the script; he could do so only after viewing the finished film. Shurlock thus had no chance to make even a tentative judgment about *Kiss Me, Stupid* before it was screened for him and his staff. After the film unreeled, writes Jack Vizzard, Shurlock's chief assistant, Shurlock flabbergasted his advisers, who deemed the movie somewhat crude and tasteless, by announcing, "I'm going to pass it." He explained, "If this is the kind of movie they want to make; if the companies are going to put up the money for this kind of stuff and then expect me to try and stop them, they're crazy!"[18]

The provisions of the censorship code presumed that "motion pictures, unlike stage plays, appeal to mass audiences, the mature and the immature."[19] As Joseph Breen had pointed out to Wilder more than once, "Because motion pictures command a mass audience, material which may be perfectly valid for dramatization and treatment on the stage may be completely unacceptable when presented in a motion picture."[20] What the code was saying was that movies were fundamentally a family medium. *Kiss Me, Stupid* was definitely not family entertainment, nor could it be retooled into a family film. Shurlock decided to let Wilder's picture take its chances in the marketplace, and he would observe whether or not the mass audience was prepared to accept a picture with a risqué plot and ribald humor. He proposed to simply wait and see how audiences reacted to *Kiss Me, Stupid*.

The Legion of Decency took a much dimmer view of *Kiss Me, Stupid*. Monsignor Little and his staff had been concerned for some time that Hollywood's output was suffering from a creeping indecency. According to Father Patrick Sullivan, Little was exasperated by the long line of increasingly sleazy movies such as Edward Dmytryk's *The Carpetbaggers* (1964) and *Where Love Has Gone* (1964). Both movies were based on outré novels by Harold Robbins, whose books could be described as below the belt and beneath discussion. Furthermore, Little believed that in recent years Wilder films like *Irma la Douce* had been stretching the limits. With *Kiss Me, Stupid*, Little was convinced, Wilder had finally crashed and burned. In Little's view, *Kiss Me, Stupid* was about as sophisticated as a burlesque show. Little was determined to make an example of the film by taking a harsh stance toward it.[21]

Little accordingly submitted a list of offensive material to Wilder. For example, Polly's pet parrot, which is fascinated by TV Westerns, often snaps, "Bang, bang!" when Polly brings a customer into her mobile home. Moreover, when Orville shows Polly around his home, he comments, "You'll like it; it's not very big, but it's clean." Polly inquires suspiciously, "What is?" It was clear, said Little, "that Orville was not talking about his house." In addition, Dino tells Orville that he would like to go out in the garden with Zelda so "she can show me her parsley." When Wilder noted that the legion found this line suggestive, he commented with feigned innocence, "What do they want? Broccoli?"[22] Little and his staff also objected to some visual gags, such as the huge, phallic cactus plants in Orville's front yard.

Wilder took an unprecedented step for a film director by having a conference with Little. He informed Little personally that he would make some of the suggested alterations, as a gesture of his goodwill. He warned that, because the sets had already been dismantled, he could not do some of the retakes that Little had asked for. The scene in Polly's trailer, however, in which Dino has a rendezvous with Zelda, could be redone because it involved a small set, and Dean Martin and Felicia Farr were available to reshoot it.

In the trailer scene as originally filmed, Zelda goes to bed with Dino in return for his promise to plug one of her husband's songs on TV. The scene fades out with Dino and Zelda lying on the bed and kissing passionately, leaving no doubt that they will have intercourse. Wilder had quipped to one of the crew that a director was not responsible for what the characters did after the scene faded out. But Little thought otherwise.

The revamped scene concludes with Dino falling asleep on the bed while Zelda gives him a back massage. The following morning Dino creeps out of the trailer while Zelda is still asleep—after leaving five hundred dollars on the night table. Zelda's bare shoulders are visible above the bedcovers, so the money is presumably for services rendered. But the implications of the scene are left to the viewer's imagination.

Harold Mirisch recalled that Wilder tried his best to placate the legion. "We made a lot of changes, but they insisted on more of them. We couldn't do them," because Kim Novak was no longer available for retakes.[23] At the end of the day, the legion assigned *Kiss Me, Stupid* a condemned rating. This was the first condemnation of a mainstream Hollywood feature since Elia Kazan's film of Tennessee Williams's *Baby Doll* in 1956.[24] *Baby Doll* centers on the voluptuous young wife of a seedy cotton gin owner many years her senior.

The legion's official press release announcing the condemnation of *Kiss Me, Stupid* began by recalling that "Mr. Wilder's earlier film *The Apartment* was an example of effective comic satire, 'with redeeming social value'"—a term the legion had picked up from the Supreme Court's statements about controversial films. "In the case of *Kiss Me, Stupid*, however, not only has Mr. Wilder failed to create a genuine satire out of situation comedy, but he has regrettably produced a thoroughly sordid piece of realism, which is aesthetically as well as morally repulsive. Crude and suggestive dialogue, a leering treatment of marital and extra-marital sex, and a prurient preoccupation with lechery compound the film's bald condonation of immorality." The legion's broadside also pointed out that "the release of this film during the holiday season . . . is a commercial decision bereft of respect for the Judaeo-Christian sensibilities of the majority of the American people."[25] Harold Mirisch replied to Little that it was too late to postpone the movie's release on December 18, 1964.

The legion's news release wound up with one final blast, this time at Shurlock's office. It noted "with astonishment" that a film "so patently indecent and immoral" should have received the censorship code's seal of approval.[26] Shurlock responded to Little with the same reason he had given for issuing a code seal for *Irma la Douce:* he did so on condition that the movie's trailer and ad layouts would contain the warning "This picture is for adults only." The legion's public criticism of Shurlock's office made it abundantly clear that Shurlock and Little were "singing from different hymnals," notes Thomas Doherty. That the industry censor was prepared to grant a code seal to pictures like *Kiss Me, Stupid* "led to an acrimonious divorce between the two senior partners of Hollywood censorship."[27]

Once the legion had condemned *Kiss Me, Stupid,* UA, uneasy about public criticism, "turned the picture over with as little fuss as possible to its subsidiary," Lopert Pictures, for U.S. distribution.[28] Lopert specialized in foreign films released on the art house circuit. That automatically resulted in a more limited distribution for *Kiss Me, Stupid* than UA normally would have provided for a major release.

Wilder had one sneak preview for the movie in New York City and another in Los Angeles in November 1964. In both instances, several audience response cards complained about the more raucous jokes in the picture. Wilder gradually was coming to realize, however, that there was a limit to how much cosmetic surgery one could perform on a film. All he could do at this juncture was to wait and see how the reviewers reacted when the movie opened on December 18—at yuletide, no less.

The opening credits of *Kiss Me, Stupid* begin with a shot of the Vegas Strip, then move on to the marquee of the Sands Hotel, announcing Dino's appearance there. Then Wilder cuts to the Copa Room, where Dino is performing his nightclub act, surrounded by a bevy of bosomy chorus girls. The crooner points to one of the befeathered chorines and says, "Last night she was banging on my bedroom door for forty-five minutes; I wouldn't let her out!" That bit of saucy wit sets the tone of the humor in the rest of the movie.

Dino departs from Vegas the next day in his Italian sports car, headed for Los Angeles, where he is to tape a TV special. He develops car trouble on the outskirts of the desert town of Climax, Nevada. His car is hauled into town by a tow truck while he sits behind the steering wheel as if he were driving. The local gas station attendant, Barney Milsap (Cliff Osmond), recognizes Dino and immediately gets in touch with his songwriting partner, Orville Spooner, the local piano teacher. Together they concoct a conspiracy to keep Dino in town overnight so he can hear some of their songs. The duplicitous Barney informs Dino that he cannot repair his auto, a foreign make he is not familiar with, until the following day. Orville, according to plan, invites Dino to spend the night at his house, where Orville can perform some of the tunes he has composed, with Barney's lyrics.

Orville is pathologically jealous of his young wife Zelda. In fact, he goes ballistic when he suspects fourteen-year-old Johnnie Mulligan, one of his piano pupils, of having a crush on his wife. Orville suddenly turns on Johnnie and accuses him of being a "male Lolita." While they tussle, Orville tears the boy's shirt off. As he chases the bare-chested youngster around the room, the scene takes on an unwarranted hint of homoeroticism.

Barney and Orville later practice one of the songs they hope to sell Dino on. Orville accompanies Barney as he warbles "I'm a Poached Egg":

I'm a poached egg without a piece of toast;
I'm a haunted house that doesn't have a ghost;
I'm da Vinci without the Mona Lis';
I'm Vienna without the Viennese,
When I'm without you.

Ira Gershwin deliberately made the second rhyme awkward to indicate that, in the story, the lyric is by an amateur.

Orville is aware that the lecherous crooner will listen to the songs only on the condition that Orville provide him with companionship for the night. He hastily pushes a dressmaker's dummy of his wife out of sight, indicating with a single gesture that his curvaceous wife Zelda is not going to be the target of Dino's roving eye. Orville sends his wife packing before Dino arrives at the house. He then hires Polly the Pistol, a full-time cocktail waitress and part-time hooker from the Belly Button roadhouse, to pose as his wife—and serve as Dino's companion for the night.

When Orville plays "Sophia" for Dino, the singer exclaims, "I need another Italian love song like a giraffe needs strep throat!" Still, "Sophia" is a definite improvement over "I'm a Poached Egg":

Listen to me, Sophia, have you any idea
How much you mean to me-ah?
Sweet Sophia be mine,
Or from the earth I resign!

In due course Dino makes a pass at Polly, and Orville becomes jealous in spite of himself. He behaves like a protective husband, hollering, "Do you think you can buy my wife for a song?" He slugs Dino and kicks him bodily out of the house. (Hence Wilder's comment that *Kiss Me, Stupid* is a chaste film that reflects the sanctity of marriage.) Polly is deeply touched by Orville's solicitude for her.

Meanwhile, Zelda, who is not part of Orville's conspiracy to sell a song to Dino, whiles away the evening at the Belly Button tavern, getting tipsy. Big Bertha, the madam of the party girls available at the café, puts Zelda to bed in Polly's trailer, which is next door to the roadhouse. When Dino appears at the café, looking for action, the obliging bartender directs him to Polly's mobile home. Dino hopes to "shoot it out" with Polly the Pistol. Dino finds Zelda in the trailer and assumes she is Polly; Zelda does not tell him otherwise. This is a typical case of mistaken identity, so common in boulevard comedy. Polly's parrot greets Dino with a shout, "Bang! Bang!" to which Dino retorts, "No coaching from the audience!" The double entendres come thick and fast in this movie. Zelda proceeds to talk Dino into plugging "Sophia" on TV in exchange for some lovemaking. Meanwhile, back at the Spooner residence, Orville tenderly takes the real Polly, who is wistful for domesticity and enjoys pretending to be Mrs. Spooner, to bed.

One night a few weeks later, Orville and Zelda are watching a color television set in the local TV store's show window, along with other citizens who do not own a color set. Orville is dumbfounded to hear Dino launch into "Sophia" on national TV. The bewildered Orville turns to his wife and wonders out loud how this could have happened. Zelda gives him an enigmatic smile and says, "Kiss me, stupid!" Previn pours on a lushly orchestrated version of "Sophia," which carries over into the closing credits.

When the movie opened on December 18, 1964, most reviews were negative. Some critics had virtually nothing good to say about the picture. One reviewer sneered, "For Wilder, love is a four-letter word."[29] *Life* magazine had often been amiable toward Wilder's pictures in the past, but Thomas Thompson's review of *Kiss Me, Stupid* called the movie "a titanic dirty joke." He continued, "For years Billy Wilder has walked the shaky tightrope between sophistication and salaciousness; but with *Kiss Me, Stupid* he has fallen off with a resounding crash."[30] *Time* deemed the picture "one of the longest traveling salesman stories ever committed to film."[31] *Variety* noted, "Wilder, usually a director of considerable flair and inventiveness (if not always impeccable taste), has not been able this time out to rise above a basically vulgar, as well as creatively delinquent, screenplay."[32]

Billy Wilder and William Wyler had maintained a long-standing pact whereby each would accept the praise or blame for a movie the other had made, rather than endeavoring to clear up the confusion about their names. When *Kiss Me, Stupid* received a barrage of negative reviews, however, Wyler phoned Wilder and said, "All bets are off! I am not going to allow anyone to assume that I made *Kiss Me, Stupid*!" Wyler said he meant his remark as a joke, but Wilder was not amused.[33]

The single notice that gave Wilder and his picture unstinting praise came from novelist-screenwriter Joan Didion, film critic for *Vogue*. "*Kiss Me, Stupid* is suffused with the despair of an America many of us prefer not to know, . . . as witnessed by the number of people who walk out on it." There is "the desolate glare of Las Vegas; the aridity of the desert; a small town where gasoline station attendants dream of hitting the gold record, the jackpot they will never make at the slots; and cocktail waitresses who work in sleazy bars." Didion concluded, "In its feelings for such a world, for such a condition of the heart, *Kiss Me, Stupid* is quite a compelling and moving picture."[34] Didion was the wife of novelist-screenwriter John Gregory Dunne, who titled his career essay on Wilder "The Old Pornographer." The title is a reference to the note Wilder sent to Didion in appreciation of her review. "I read your piece in the beauty parlor while sitting under the hair dryer; and it sure did the old pornographer's heart good. Cheers!"[35]

The film flopped at the box office, "but its failure was ultimately due to the host of negative reviews," not the legion's condemnation, as censorship expert Frank Walsh notes.[36] "The movie was a dog," said Wilder stoically; "with Sellers it would have been 5% better."[37]

Nevertheless, Wilder's gaudy, bawdy film boasts a bravura performance by Dean Martin; he is the polished, slicked-down, self-assured embodiment of male sexuality. The movie is like a grind house picture made for the art house trade. "The pursuit of sex and money is always a major impulse in Wilder's movies, but here it becomes all-consuming," writes George Morris. "Wilder is appalled by Orville's sexual and pecuniary machinations," Morris continues, "but he can laugh at him because he understands Orville's petty dreams."[38]

Diamond contended that *Kiss Me, Stupid* was as moral as a preacher's Sunday sermon: "It is a cautionary tale—a jealous husband goes to such extremes to protect his wife's virtue that she winds up losing it." Diamond remembered that he and Wilder were consoled "by the great reviews the movie got in London and Paris." The British and French reviewers saw the picture as a stinging social satire. As the tale of a city slicker outwitted by a country bumpkin, it was *Tom Jones* in modern dress. "They understood what we were aiming at," said Diamond.[39]

Since the movie was blasted by American critics and ignored by American audiences, it was released only a short while in the United States and was seldom revived. Not surprisingly, *Kiss Me, Stupid* failed to recoup its $2 million production cost. "Okay, I made a bad picture," Wilder conceded; "but why the indignation, why the charges that I had undermined the nation's morals?" He added, "They were going to tear up my citizenship papers!"[40]

Over the years, Wilder did defend himself for making *Kiss Me, Stupid* whenever it was dismissed as a vulgar film. "This question of bad taste has followed me for years," he told me. He continued,

> When I made *Kiss Me, Stupid* the film was severely criticized. Yet I always thought that it had some tenderness in its treatment, at least in the scenes between the café girl and the husband who asks her to masquerade as his wife for an evening. This is the only taste of domesticity that she has ever experienced in her whole life and she is very touched by it. But no one seemed to see this aspect of the story.
>
> In any event the film caused a big scandal. Today *Kiss Me, Stupid* would seem like Disney fare, and I wonder what all the screaming was about.

Wilder was devastated by the hostile reception of his movie in 1964. Fair-weather friends in the film colony avoided him. "When I was lying in the gutter," he recalled bitterly, "a number of people came along and administered a kick in the groin."[41] In this period of depression and self-doubt, Wilder fled with his wife Audrey to a spa in Badgastein, Austria. This time he stayed several months, taking stock of his career; he subsequently referred to this period as his "year of hibernation." He had retired to the resort, he confessed later, to lick his wounds and to put thoughts of suicide out of his mind. "I thought of killing myself because I thought I would never make another movie."[42]

There was a beautiful waterfall at Badgastein, which prompted him to recall the Berlin apartment he had lived in when he was trying to break into the movie business in the 1920s. He could hear the water running in the leaky toilet in the restroom next to his tawdry room all night. "I'd imagine it was a beautiful waterfall, just to get my mind off the monotony of it." When he was taking the cure at Badgastein, "There I was in bed at night, listening to the waterfall; and all I could think of was that goddamned toilet! And that, like the man says, is the story of my life."[43]

At all events, Wilder's fears that he would never make another picture for the Mirisch Company or anyone else proved groundless. Five months after the disastrous opening of *Kiss Me, Stupid*, Harold Mirisch renewed Wilder's contract.

After all, *Kiss Me, Stupid* was viewed in Europe not as a prurient movie but as a film aimed at thoughtful adults. When one sees *Kiss Me, Stupid* today, now that the controversy has died down, one can see that it is a knockabout farce; that is all that it ever was. Wilder's films in the early 1960s, taken together, were landmark movies that set a trend toward more adult subject matter on the screen.

When Wilder returned from his extended stay at Badgastein, he began meeting daily with Iz Diamond in their cluttered office on the Goldwyn lot. But their discussions did not yield any viable ideas for a screenplay. Sometimes they would just sit in sullen silence for long periods of time; the phone did not even ring. But Wilder's sense of humor gradually returned. He joked that, for the first time in living memory, he received no phone calls requesting him to be a pallbearer. "In Hollywood you only want people with hit pictures to haul your coffin," he explained with mock solemnity.[44]

One afternoon Ernest Lehman, with whom Wilder had cowritten *Sabrina*, wandered into the office. He observed that Wilder was losing weight and smoking too much. He inquired how Wilder and Diamond were getting on with a new project. Wilder replied that they felt like parents who had produced a defective child. "Now we keep asking ourselves, 'Do we dare screw again?'"[45]

After three months of spinning his wheels, the ideas started flowing again. Wilder told a journalist that he realized that he had spent too much time analyzing and rethinking his failure. "All that self-torture is a waste of time; I'm already preparing another failure!"[46] He got the inspiration for a new movie while watching a football game on TV. When a husky fullback ran out of bounds with the ball, he wound up falling on a spectator on the sidelines. "That's a movie," Wilder muttered to himself, "and the guy underneath is Lemmon."[47] From this incident he and Diamond developed a scenario called *The Fortune Cookie*, about Harry Hinkle, a TV cameraman accidentally knocked cold by a football player, Luther "Boom Boom" Jackson, during a game. Harry allows his brother-in-law, "Whiplash Willie" Gingrich, a crooked lawyer, to lure him into filing a fraudulent insurance claim to acquire the fortune he needs to win back his greedy ex-wife. Walter Mirisch had faith in Wilder and green-lighted the new project with a budget of $3.7 million.

## *The Fortune Cookie* (1966)

*The Fortune Cookie* is the first of three Wilder films that are linked by an exploration of male friendship. The other two are *The Front Page* and *The Private Life of Sherlock Holmes*. In the first of the three films, Wilder applied a tongue-in-cheek approach to a subject that he had already examined with deadly seriousness in *Double Indemnity:* the gentle art of cheating an insurance company. *The Apartment* also involves an insurance company. In fact, the company that employs Bud Baxter (Jack Lemmon) in *The Apartment* is the very same insurance company that Harry Hinkle (Jack Lemmon again) hopes to swindle in *The Fortune Cookie*.

The crucial piece of casting for the present film was the role of Willie Gingrich, the shyster lawyer. Walter Matthau immediately came to Wilder's mind. While Wilder was preparing *The Fortune Cookie,* Matthau scored a major stage triumph as a sloppy, dyspeptic individual sharing a bachelor flat with another man in *The Odd Couple,* which made him a Broadway star and got him national press attention. Like James Cagney, Matthau was a product of New York's Lower East Side and could play a tough customer with a gruff voice like Willie Gingrich convincingly. Wilder saw Matthau as an up-and-comer and thought the part of Willie would jump-start his movie career. In fact, Wilder would write the part with Matthau in mind, just as he had written the role of Sir Wilfrid in *Witness for the Prosecution* specifically for Charles Laughton.

"Before we put a word on paper," Diamond remembered, "we went to New York to see Mr. Matthau."[48] After Wilder recounted the plot of *The Fortune Cookie* for Matthau, the actor said he would like to see the script. Wilder answered that there was no script as yet. Matthau, who wanted very much to work with Wilder, responded, "Okay, who needs a script? I'll do it!"[49]

Matthau was sometimes asked whether he modeled his portrayal of Willie Gingrich, a glib, cynical type, on Wilder. His reply: "I *always* play Wilder in a Wilder picture; Wilder sees me as Wilder! That is, Billy sees me as a loveable rogue, a scalawag like himself."[50] Indeed, Willie is described in the screenplay as having "a brain full of razor blades," a phrase coined by William Holden about Wilder.[51]

In *The Fortune Cookie,* Wilder paired Matthau with Lemmon for the first time. The comic duo would appear in two more Wilder pictures and in films made by other directors as well, such as the screen version of *The Odd Couple* (1968). Jack Lemmon's son Chris writes that "Pop and Walter developed an immediate friendship on *The Fortune Cookie*."[52]

After Matthau and Lemmon were cast, Wilder and Diamond set to work on the script. *The Fortune Cookie* is their most structured screenplay. It is divided into sixteen segments, each introduced on screen with a catchy title: "The Caper," "The Taste of Money," and so on. The titles are reminiscent of a TV miniseries in which the plot unfolds in individual episodes, each with a clever title.

The script's first episode is titled "The Accident." When grid star Boom Boom Jackson runs out of bounds with the football, he accidentally flattens TV cameraman Harry Hinkle, who is standing on the sidelines. Wilder, we know, was a stickler for authenticity in his films. With his customary thirst for realism, he staged the accident during a real professional football game between the Cleveland Browns, Boom Boom's team, and the Minnesota Vikings. Harry is employed by CBS-TV, and the game is played at Cleveland Municipal Stadium. No fictitious names for Wilder.

The screenplay displays flashes of the sharp wit that indicated that Wilder and Diamond were back on track. In the episode titled "The Brother-in-Law," for example, Willie shows up at St. Mark's Hospital looking very much like a shady grifter in his seedy tweed coat and battered fedora. Willie donates a dime to the collection box for unmarried mothers, a charitable cause of the nuns who operate the hospital. "Unwed mothers? I'm for that!" he says with a leer. Shortly after, Willie needs a dime to phone the *Cleveland Plain Dealer* with his hot tip that he is suing CBS-TV, the Browns, and the stadium for $1 million. An inveterate chiseler, Willie sneaks back to the collection box and retrieves the dime to make the phone call. Morris sees this irreverent gag as one example of how Wilder's wit in *The Fortune Cookie* at times seems as corrosive as that in *Ace in the Hole*. Morris writes that throughout the movie Wilder goes for the jugular as he launches "an unrelieved attack on human rapacity and corruption, as epitomized in Willie Gingrich."[53] Kevin Lally takes Willie less seriously; he sees him as "an engaging scoundrel, . . . always on the lookout for a crooked new angle."[54]

In filling out the supporting cast of the movie during preproduction, Wilder demonstrated once more his sharp eye for good character actors. He picked Ned Glass (the storekeeper in *West Side Story*) to play Doc Schindler, a veterinarian on parole for doping a racehorse. Willie instructs the doc to inject Harry with a shot of Novocain so that he will be numb when he is examined by the team of physicians representing Consolidated Life. One of the insurance company's consultants, Professor Winterhalter, is played by none other than Sig Ruman. Winterhalter from Vienna is another of Wilder's pixilated Freudian psychiatrists. He recalls that, "in the old days, when a man claimed paralysis, we threw him in the snake pit; if he climbed out, we knew he was lying." When one of the doctors asks Winterhalter for his learned opinion about Harry's claims, he replies succinctly, "Fake!" But he is outnumbered by the physicians who have been taken in by Harry's phony injuries.

A number of artists behind the camera had, like Sig Ruman, been associated with other Wilder pictures: supervising editor Doane Harrison, film editor Daniel Mandell, cinematographer Joseph LaShelle, and composer André Previn. As things turned out, all of them were collaborating with Wilder for the last time.

*The Fortune Cookie* was LaShelle's fourth film for Wilder; three of them, *The Apartment, Kiss Me, Stupid,* and the present film, were photographed in black and white. In each of these pictures, LaShelle masterfully filmed the drab living quarters of the hero in unsparing detail. Wilder admired LaShelle as an experienced cameraman, "but he was on the verge of retirement" and did in fact retire two years later.[55] By coincidence, LaShelle left Wilder's production team after shooting Wilder's last black-and-white film. In the age of color television, a feature film had to be made in color to be broadcast in prime time. So not even Wilder could hold out any longer.

Principal photography for *The Fortune Cookie* commenced on October 31, 1965, with location filming in Cleveland. For the opening sequence, shot during the Browns-Vikings game, the script called for "a gloomy, bone-chilling day."[56] The weather during the game was made to order; it was a cold, gray Sunday. Wilder had three cameras strategically stationed around the stadium to cover the action on the field. In the course of the game, a Browns halfback executed a spectacular run down the field. Wilder arranged with the Browns' owner, Art Modell, to have halfback Ernie Green repeat the run the following day so that he could film the sequence in which Boom Boom is knocked out of bounds and plows into Harry.

Accordingly, on Monday, some of the Browns—some wearing their own uniforms, others dressed as Vikings—took to the field, where Green made a mad dash with the ball. Wilder hollered "Cut!" and substituted one stunt man for Green and another for Jack Lemmon at the point where Boom Boom was to crash into Harry. Lemmon's stunt man reeled backward and landed on his back on a pile of mattresses covered with fake grass. While the scene was being filmed, Wilder stood next to the camera, puffing on a cigarette and barking commands like a top sergeant at the players and the camera crew.

Finally, on Tuesday, ten thousand extras showed up to fill the stands, lured by the raffling off of a sports car and a trip to Hollywood. Wilder needed them to stand up and cheer wildly for Boom Boom as he ran down the field. A press conference was held at which a studio press agent announced that the call for extras was the largest in Hollywood history. Wilder told the reporters present, "After my last picture I know how Modell feels" about the Browns' losing Sunday's game. "But he shouldn't worry. There'll be further disasters."[57]

After finishing location work in Cleveland, the film unit returned to Hollywood to shoot interiors at the Goldwyn Studios. Matthau developed a good working relationship with Wilder from the outset. On Matthau's first day on the set, Wilder gave Matthau, in his heavy German accent, a complicated set of directions for playing a scene. Matthau respectfully listened in silence and then inquired, "You speak kind of funny; you from out of town?" Matthau asked Lemmon, "Why are you doing this film? I have the best part." Lemmon replied, "Don't you think it's about time?"[58] Lemmon's point was that he was already a movie star by the time he made *The Fortune Cookie*, whereas Matthau was only now getting a role in pictures that would afford him his big break.

Matthau obviously had the stronger role; it was difficult for Lemmon to be funny when he spent the majority of the movie in a wheelchair. Nevertheless, Lemmon took center stage whenever the script offered him the opportunity. When Harry eagerly anticipates the return of his estranged wife, Sandi, he puts on a phonograph record of Cole Porter's "You'd Be So Nice to Come Home To" and spins around the room in a kind of wheelchair ballet. Wilder utilized the wide-screen format skillfully by holding the camera stationary and allowing Lemmon to careen around the room. Lemmon roamed from one side of the screen to the other, sometimes even disappearing momentarily from the frame. This lack of perfect pictorial composition made the scene more dynamic and spontaneous. Surprisingly, Lemmon's virtuoso ballet was accomplished in a single take.

Still, Wilder was concerned that Lemmon's performance was going to be overshadowed by Matthau's showier role. During the production period, Wilder did all he could to bolster Lemmon's part, including highlighting the wheelchair ballet. He also wrote some additional dialogue for Lemmon to give him more screen time.

Wilder's facetious prediction at the Cleveland press conference came to pass when, after nearly two months of filming on the Goldwyn lot, Walter Matthau suffered a heart attack. But there was no question of Wilder's replacing Matthau, as had happened with Peter Sellers on *Kiss Me, Stupid*.

There were only ten days left in the shooting schedule of *The Fortune Cookie,* so of course Wilder opted to wait for Matthau to recover before completing principal photography. Walter Mirisch writes that the "cast insurance policy" paid the costs of holding on to the cast members "until production could be resumed." Wilder had to shut down production for two months, so shooting did not wrap until February 1966.[59]

The last shot of Matthau that Wilder filmed before suspending production showed Willie rushing up the stairs to Harry's apartment with a settlement check from Consolidated Life. The first shot of Matthau that Wilder made when filming resumed showed Willie entering Harry's apartment with the check. But Matthau had lost weight during his convalescence. "You see me going upstairs weighing 198 pounds," he recalled. "I walk in the apartment and I'm 160 pounds." But the audience never noticed this discrepancy. "Billy told me to act heavier," Matthau explained.[60] In fact, Matthau was wearing an overcoat when he went into the apartment; the coat helped to conceal that Matthau had gotten thinner.

When Wilder screened the final cut of *The Fortune Cookie* for UA, the studio brass had one complaint: they judged the movie's title to be weak. Ever since Paramount temporarily altered the title of *Ace in the Hole* to *The Big Carnival* without Wilder's consent, however, he had it stipulated in his contract that the titles of the U.S. release prints of his movies could not be changed without his approval. UA was free, however, to retitle the picture for the British market, and it did so, calling it *Meet Whiplash Willie.*

Wilder set up a sneak preview of the movie in Westwood, his favorite neighborhood for a sneak, in June 1966. Diamond and Lemmon were on hand. Wilder told them that, before the picture started, he was going to wipe his brow "and say a few prayers." He watched the movie with the audience intermittently, when he was not pacing nervously in the theater lobby. "Do they care, the audience in there? Are they interested?"[61] Wilder said that he always asked himself those questions during previews of his pictures. He explained, "For me there are only two types of movies, interesting movies and boring movies. It's as simple as that. Does a film rivet my attention, so that I drop my box of popcorn and become part of what is happening on the screen, or doesn't it? If a film engages my interest only sporadically, the picture just hasn't got it."

After the preview of *The Fortune Cookie,* Wilder felt that the audience's reaction, as reflected in the preview cards, was fairly positive. Still, he decided to make a couple of minor adjustments: He cut three minutes of "excess baggage," that is, superfluous dialogue. He also asked Previn to replace the waltz music that accompanied Harry and Boom Boom tossing a football around the empty stadium at the fade-out with a rousing march played by a brass band. Also, because "You'd Be So Nice to Come Home To" already figured prominently in the background music, Previn employed the tune to accompany the opening credits, orchestrated with an old-fashioned big band sound.

The film's first episode, "The Accident," concludes with Harry being carted off the playing field on a stretcher. He is on his way to St. Mark's Hospital, where he will be attended by nursing sisters. Diamond quipped that, to appease the legion, instead of having hookers, as in Wilder's two previous movies, "we have nuns in this one!"[62]

"The Brother-in-Law," the next episode, begins with Whiplash Willie Gingrich, an ambulance-chasing lawyer, keeping vigil next to Harry's hospital bed. The wily, unscrupulous Willie is a grotesque figure straight out of Dickens. Matthau's performance as a hoax-peddling fraud is marked by ticks and funny vocal inflections. Willie earned his nickname because he specializes in turning whiplash cases into lucrative lawsuits. And so he badgers Harry into exaggerating his injuries to extort a hefty sum of money from the insurance company. "We're going for all the marbles, kid," Willie assures Harry with maniacal glee. Despite serious misgivings, Harry goes along with Willie's crooked scheme. Willie reassures him, "The insurance company is loaded; they will take our payoff out of petty cash!" He adds, "We're in this together—straight down the line." This is precisely what Walter says to Phyllis when they finalize their scheme to bilk the insurance company in *Double Indemnity*.

"The motives underlying this Wilderian deception are exceptionally base," Morris writes.[63] Harry agrees to the swindle only because Willie convinces him that his estranged wife, Sandy (Judi West), will be reconciled with him once he comes into a great sum of money. Harry and Sandy were married on the Fourth of July. Ironically, that was the day Harry lost his independence—he remains emotionally dependent on his erstwhile wife, though she dumped him for a failed musician.

In reality, Sandy is no prize. For one thing, she is not very bright. Sandy has read only one book—*The Carpetbaggers*. But she never got past page 19 because she found the trashy novel too sophisticated. Nevertheless, Harry wants her back. When Willie talks on the phone to Sandy in New York, Wilder adroitly uses the wide-screen format to reveal Sandy's true character. We see Sandy on the left side of the screen as she talks to Willie; she is wearing a tawdry negligee. On the right side of the screen, a naked man is asleep in a disheveled bed. As Sandy is described in the screenplay, she does not have much class, but "there is something very provocative about her."[64]

Sandy agrees to come to Cleveland, ostensibly to care for Harry, but the mercenary female actually covets her share of the insurance settlement. She has confidence in Willie as a shyster lawyer. "Willie," she later comments, "could find a loophole in the Ten Commandments."

Boom Boom (Ron Rich) is distraught when he hears that Harry is seriously injured and, for the time being, confined to a wheelchair. To make amends, he becomes Harry's caretaker once he is released from the hospital, so it is Boom Boom—not Sandy—who becomes Harry's nursemaid. The two men gradually become fast friends. Consequently, Harry develops severe scruples about inflicting a specious burden of guilt on Boom Boom.

It is significant that Wilder released *The Fortune Cookie* in 1966, when the civil rights movement was going strong, epitomized by demonstrations for racial equality led by Martin Luther King Jr. (after whom Wilder named Luther "Boom Boom" Jackson). The African American Boom Boom is one of the very few honest individuals in the picture. British critic Frieda Lockhart comments that "the Negro footballer is too good to be true."[65] Actually, it seems that Wilder conceived Boom Boom as a contrast to Willie. Indeed, Harry's conversations with Boom Boom serve to balance his encounters with Willie. As Steve Seidman puts it, Boom Boom functions as the "good conscience" figure in Harry, while Willie functions as his "bad conscience" figure. This proves to be a very effective way of dramatizing Harry's inner conflict on the screen.[66]

Meanwhile, a trio of lawyers representing Consolidated Life, known as the Legal Eagles, engage Chester Purkey (Cliff Osmond), a dogged private eye and surveillance expert, to keep tabs on Harry. "The 'respectable' insurance firm's methods, including bugging their opponent's apartment, are almost as nasty as Whiplash Willie's tactics," writes Lockhart.[67] The private detective, sneaking around in his cheap raincoat with his hidden microphones and cameras, poking clandestinely "into the most intimate activities and conversations," Stephen Farber states, "is the most repulsive character in the film."[68]

The Legal Eagles eventually decide to settle Harry's claim with a check for two hundred thousand dollars rather than face the endless courtroom battle Willie has threatened them with. But Purkey, like a crafty card sharp, has one last wild card up his sleeve. When he goes to Harry's apartment to collect his surveillance equipment, he makes calculated racial slurs about Boom Boom. He observes, "What gets me is, I'm driving an old Chevy; and I see a coon riding around in a white Cadillac." Harry, furious, finally gives the game away by rising from his wheelchair to slug Purkey. For good measure, Harry decides to sock Purkey again, so he shouts to Purkey's cameraman in the apartment across the street, "Roll 'em, Max!" This is Wilder's reference to the last sequence of *Sunset Boulevard*, in which Max is directing the newsreel cameramen who are photographing Norma. Undaunted, Willie informs Purkey that he plans to sue him for his racist remarks on behalf of the NAACP. Moreover, having realized at long last that the self-serving Sandy's concern for him was motivated solely by money, Harry kicks his ex-wife out the door.

At this point, the viewer might recall the fortune cookie that Harry opened earlier in the film. Its message quoted Abraham Lincoln's dictum, "You can fool some of the people all of the time, all of the people some of the time, but you can't fool all of the people all of the time."

Once again, Wilder was criticized for sweetening his bitter brew by providing a film with an unwarranted upbeat ending, whereby Harry experiences a sense of moral regeneration just when the insurance payoff is within his grasp. Louis Giannetti has a thought-provoking response to this objection. He reminds us that many of Wilder's films are about morally weak individuals like Harry who return to the path of virtue by film's end. "But in Wilder's world," he adds, "virtue must be its own reward." Wilder's characters might manage to save their self-respect—but that is all they salvage. "The spoils of their calculations are reluctantly sacrificed when they decide to give up their schemes," as when Harry blows the whistle on the insurance fraud. Therefore the ending of *The Fortune Cookie*, like that of *The Apartment,* is less positive than it might appear.[69]

Wilder himself responded to those critics he termed "Jack the Rippers," who claimed that the "shower bath of sentiment" at the film's end was a concession to the box office. He explained that he wanted to give the audience "a little bonus at the end," because "it would have been dismally depressing otherwise."[70]

Once Harry is able to reject his scheming brother-in-law, he reverts to his kind and honest nature.[71] In the film's epilogue, titled "The Final Score," Harry goes looking for Boom Boom to make amends for the anguish he has caused his pal. Harry locates him in the deserted football stadium. After Harry apologizes, the pair reaffirm their comradeship by contentedly tossing a football back and forth like a couple of adolescent boys. Wilder makes the same point with Harry and Boom Boom's impromptu game of touch football that he made with Bud and Fran's gin rummy game at the conclusion of *The Apartment:* it is easier to play the game of life with someone else than to have to go it alone. So the final line of *The Fortune Cookie* is Harry's shout, "Come on, play ball!" as the game of life goes on.

Dick notes that "the basic decency of Harry and Boom Boom contrasts sharply with the mendacity of Harry's ex-wife Sandy and his brother-in-law Willie." Little wonder, then, that at film's end Harry "seeks out the only person who has not sunk into the bogs of greed—Boom Boom."[72] Wilder's interest in male bonding in his movies goes back to Walter Neff and Barton Keyes in *Double Indemnity* and Sefton and Cookie in *Stalag 17*. But Farber declares that "homosexuality plays a furtive role in a number of Wilder's films," including *The Fortune Cookie*.[73] Homosexuality does surface in some of Wilder's films, but *The Fortune Cookie* is not one of them. To find homosexuality in this picture is to underestimate the value Wilder places on male friendship in his films.

*The Fortune Cookie* opened in theaters across the country on October 19, 1966, to largely favorable notices and good box office returns. Critics noted the laugh-a-minute repartee peppered with the bitter satirical asides that distinguish Wilder's work. The fundamentally positive reception of the film went a long way in aiding Wilder to put the fiasco of *Kiss Me, Stupid* behind him.

Richard Schickel found the film a wily morality tale about chicanery and deception, punctuated with Wilder's customary corrosive wit: "A jack-hammer of a film, savagely applied to those concrete areas of the human spirit where cupidity and stupidity have been so long entrenched; it is a bitterly, often excruciatingly funny movie." Wilder, he continued, "is just about the only American director of comedy who finds his material in the artful exaggeration of all-too-recognizable human and social traits. He has a cold rather than a warm comic spirit. . . . If you can stand the chill, I think you'll find plenty of truth in what he has to say." In his unqualified rave, Schickel called Matthau "the W. C. Fields of the 1960s," noting that he shared with Fields "an undeniably comic orneriness."[74] Matthau indeed steals the picture in an act of the grandest larceny, and he won an Academy Award for his role as the conniving Willie.

Wilder brought in *The Fortune Cookie* $5,000 over budget, but the Mirisch brothers did not complain. After all, the movie grossed $5 million domestically, with an additional $1.8 million coming from overseas; the film's profit was double that of its cost.

Wilder was relieved that he experienced no censorship problems with *The Fortune Cookie*. As it happened, Monsignor Little, his nemesis all the way back to *The Seven Year Itch*, retired in 1966 and was replaced by his executive assistant, Father Patrick Sullivan. Shortly after his appointment, in a press release dated December 8, 1965, Sullivan proclaimed that the Legion of Decency had changed its name to the National Catholic Office for Motion Pictures (NCOMP). The organization had dispensed with its more militant name, which seemed to connote a vigilante group, "to emphasize the more positive approach to films that the office was espousing."[75] NCOMP was more interested in endorsing good films than in spying out sensual footage in movies it disapproved of.[76]

What's more, on September 20, 1966, Geoffrey Shurlock announced that the censorship code had been revised yet again, with a view to "the expansion of the artist's freedom." This was a move that Wilder certainly welcomed, just as he had the modifications in the legion's policies. The latest revisions in the code set the stage for the unveiling on November 1, 1968, of the film industry's own rating system. The new system would evaluate movies "on a sliding scale ranging from family-friendly to adults only."[77] The film censor's office, like the legion, also acquired a new name; it became the Code and Rating Administration (CARA).

Jack Vizzard, Shurlock's chief assistant, observed that non-Catholic and Catholic moviegoers alike preferred to follow the industry's ratings rather than those of NCOMP. As a result, the studio bosses no longer allowed the Catholic organization to affect the moral content of movies.[78]

The inauguration of NCOMP and CARA made Wilder feel as if he had been let out of reform school as he began to work on his next picture, *The Private Life of Sherlock Holmes*. When it was finally released in November 1970, it would be Wilder's first feature in four years, the longest hiatus in Wilder's career. He had so many setbacks during the production of the film that it seemed that he had joined the ranks of such hard-luck filmmakers as Orson Welles.

# 16

# The Game's Afoot

## The Private Life of Sherlock Holmes

Women are not to be trusted; not the best of them—a twinkle in the eye, and the arsenic in the soup.

—*Robert Stephens as Sherlock Holmes*
*in the film* The Private Life of Sherlock Holmes

Sir Arthur Conan Doyle, like Agatha Christie, was one of the foremost writers of classic British detective stories. Conan Doyle's armchair sleuth, Sherlock Holmes, can find the solution to any mystery with his ingenious faculties of deduction. But Conan Doyle's stories are not merely exercises in puzzle solving; he portrays his hero's encounters with the evils of society in a vivid and compelling fashion.

Arthur Conan Doyle was born in Edinburgh in 1859; he was educated in a Jesuit school and at Edinburgh University, where he earned his medical degree in 1885. He decided to augment his meager income as a doctor by trying his hand at writing detective stories. The character of Sherlock Holmes was inspired by Joseph Bell, a physician who taught Conan Doyle in medical school. Bell employed his astute powers of deduction to diagnose patients' ailments and even infer details of their past lives.[1] Conan Doyle said that he created his fictional detective with similar powers of deduction, "to treat crime as Dr. Bell treated diseases." Holmes became the world's first consulting detective, a genius at unraveling the threads of a mystery.[2]

William Gillette wrote a play, *Sherlock Holmes* (1899), in which the playwright played Holmes on tour for three decades. It was Gillette who coined the celebrated phrase, "Elementary, my dear Watson." The first important Sherlock Holmes on film was John Barrymore, who starred in Albert Parker's silent film version of Gillette's play in 1922. Although some exteriors were shot in London, the film is too faithful to the Gillette original, with some scenes seeming stage bound. Still, critics thought that Barrymore had captured Holmes, as when he fixes the villain with a penetrating, hawklike stare. Gillette's play was revived on Broadway in 1974 in a production that I saw at the Broadhurst Theatre. Robert Stephens, who would play the title role in Wilder's film *The Private Life of Sherlock Holmes,* also starred in the revival in New York.[3] But the best-known interpreter of the Holmes character was Basil Rathbone, who played the detective in fourteen films between 1939 and 1946. Rathbone told me in correspondence in 1966 that the first film in which he played Holmes was also the best: *The Hound of the Baskervilles* (1939), directed by Sidney Lanfield.

At that film's end, Holmes says, "I've had a strenuous day; oh, Watson, the needle!" No screen hero had ever made such a daring and nonchalant confession to drug addiction. Not until Wilder's film thirty-one years later would Holmes indulge his drug habit on-screen. Between the release of Lanfield's film and the release of Wilder's, Geoffrey Shurlock had, on December 11, 1956, announced that, "in keeping with present-day conditions," his office was rescinding the ban on illegal drugs as a subject for films.[4] So Wilder was free to treat Holmes as an addict.

Wilder set his movie in the Victorian era, the period in which Conan Doyle wrote his stories of the great detective. In their original screenplay, Wilder and Diamond devised new adventures for Holmes, none of which were derived directly from the Conan Doyle stories. "I didn't want merely to do a remake of *The Hound of the Baskervilles,*" Wilder said. He did not incorporate any one story into his scenario; he borrowed from two stories for the cases he invented for his movie, using these two stories as points of departure.

Conan Doyle's "The Adventure of the Bruce-Partington Plans" (1905) deals with Colonel Valentine Walters's theft of the secret blueprints of a submarine from the British navy office. Walters attempts to sell the plans to a German espionage agent. This story inspired the episode in Wilder's picture that revolves around Britain's secret efforts to perfect a submarine for wartime use.[5] Queen Victoria is mentioned in the original story,[6] but she makes an actual appearance in Wilder's film. In the picture, Queen Victoria "rejects the use of a submarine as a warship" and calls a halt to the development of the submarine for wartime use. Bernard Dick comments that this is Wilder's "ironic gloss on Britain's unpreparedness for submarine warfare at the outbreak of World War I."[7]

Irene Adler is the model for Ilse von Hoffmanstahl in Wilder's movie. In "A Scandal in Bohemia," Irene is the devious female who outwits Holmes at every turn and finally manages to flee England before he can expose her for endeavoring to blackmail the king of Bohemia. Like Irene, Ilse outwits the master sleuth, "the only woman ever to do so."[8] In Conan Doyle's story, Watson says, "The best plans of Mr. Sherlock Holmes were beaten by a woman's wit. . . . When he speaks of Irene Adler, it is always under the honorable title of *the* woman."[9]

Holmes's perennial popularity helped Wilder convince Walter Mirisch, the studio chief, to approve his own Holmes movie.[10] UA, the distributor, followed suit. "The three greatest figures in fiction for the screen," Wilder said in his pitch to Mirisch, "are Robinson Crusoe, Tarzan, and Sherlock Holmes." Wilder aimed to do an in-depth study of Holmes, whom he esteemed as a most intriguing character. "I think of this picture as my valentine to Sherlock," he said.[11] Mirisch assigned the movie a $6 million budget, one of the largest of Wilder's career.[12]

"I wanted to show Holmes as vulnerable, as human," said Wilder. "In my picture he does *not* solve the mystery; no, he is deceived" by Ilse, the beautiful German spy who masquerades as Gabrielle Valladon, a Belgian damsel in distress.[13] "We treated Holmes with respect," Wilder insisted, "but not reverence."[14] The screenplay does not hesitate to examine Holmes's apparent disdain for women and his addiction to cocaine, not to mention Holmes's ambiguous relationship with Watson. "It's more *The Odd Couple* than Conan Doyle," Wilder said, "only with a Victorian backdrop—two bachelors cohabiting."[15]

Wilder conceived the film as an opulent costume drama that would run just under three hours—his longest movie. "It's not how long you make it, but how you make it long," he observed. He was confident that his Holmes movie should be a large-scale road show attraction: there would be two performances daily with a reserved seat policy "and an intermission to give your kidneys a break."[16]

Wilder aimed to settle on the actors playing Holmes and Watson early on, so that he and Diamond could write the roles with actors in mind. Wilder wanted Robert Stephens, a member of Laurence Olivier's prestigious National Theatre company in London. Wilder was mightily impressed by Stephens's performance in his latest film, *The Prime of Miss Jean Brodie* (1969), which Wilder saw at an advance screening. The role of Watson went to Colin Blakely, also associated with Olivier's company, who had appeared in the film *A Man for All Seasons* (1966). Admittedly Wilder's lead actor was not well known to American filmgoers, but Stephens looked to Wilder very much like he thought "Mr. Sherlock Holmes" should look.[17] Besides, Wilder wanted Holmes and Watson to be portrayed by actors whom viewers did not associate with other roles. Wilder cast Christopher Lee, who was likewise not familiar to American audiences, as Sherlock Holmes's older brother, Mycroft. Lee had played Sherlock Holmes in *Sherlock Holmes and the Deadly Necklace* (1962).

Wilder and Diamond perused the Holmes stories to immerse themselves in the world of Sherlock Holmes. Then they mapped out the screenplay, on which they toiled throughout 1967. "I don't think I'm being pretentious in saying that I structured my film in four parts, like a symphony," said Wilder.[18] Each of the richly detailed episodes was complete in itself. In the early winter of 1968, the writing team completed the first draft of the script—except for the ending, which they had not finalized. When Stephens said he would like to know how the story ended, Wilder replied, "So would I."[19]

One afternoon when Wilder and Diamond were chatting, Wilder exclaimed that he had a brainstorm for the episode in which the experimental submarine figures. While the sub is doing trial runs in Loch Ness in the Scottish Highlands, the Loch Ness monster materializes. Of course, it is not really the legendary sea creature but the experimental sub; the Royal Navy has camouflaged it with a gargoyle-like periscope that resembles the Loch Ness monster to scare the locals away from the area.[20] With that, Wilder and Diamond plunged into the task of finishing the shooting script.

*The Private Life of Sherlock Holmes* is the second Wilder film that foregrounds male friendship. Wilder called the movie the story of "the friendship between Holmes and Watson when they were young."[21] Their longstanding friendship is brought into relief in the episode that is labeled in the script "The Singular Affair of the Russian Ballerina."

In the screenplay, Holmes is summoned to Covent Garden, to the presence of Petrova, a neurotic Russian prima ballerina who is appearing in London, played by Tamara Toumanova (*Torn Curtain*, 1966). She wants Holmes to father her child so that their offspring will have her beauty and his brains. Holmes politely declines the invitation by owning himself a bachelor who has enjoyed several fulfilling years living with another bachelor. He hints that he is homosexually attached to Watson "through a cruel caprice of Mother Nature." Rogozhin, the ballet company's impresario (Clive Revill), tells Holmes that Petrova's first choice was Tchaikovsky, who declined because "women were not his glass of tea." Holmes responds, "Tchaikovsky was not an isolated case." Rogozhin asks, "Dr. Watson is your glass of tea?" Holmes replies, "If you want to be picturesque about it."

Chris Steinbrunner and Norman Michaels, the authors of *The Films of Sherlock Holmes,* emphasize that "Holmes is slyly utilizing this ploy to extricate himself from the situation. . . . For Holmes it is merely a way to escape the attentions of a madwoman."[22] They maintain that Holmes and Watson share nothing more or less than an easy camaraderie in the picture.

Watson is appalled when he hears of Holmes's "confession" to the ballerina; he insists that they cease to share a bachelor flat. Holmes replies, "Of course, we can continue to meet clandestinely, in the waiting rooms of suburban railway stations." This is an implicit reference to *Brief Encounter* (1945), in which the lovers meet secretly in a train depot. But Holmes in point of fact is merely suggesting a parallel between the secretive liaisons that occur between a heterosexual couple and those that occur between a homosexual couple—which some think he and Watson are. Since Watson's faith in Holmes has been shaken by this incident, he boasts that he can get several women to testify to his manhood. Then he asks Holmes pointedly, "I hope I'm not being presumptuous, but there have been women in your life?" Holmes responds icily, "The answer is yes—you are being presumptuous." And so Watson's question remains unanswered.

Other reviewers believe that Wilder meant the filmgoer to take Holmes's remarks at face value—that Holmes does seem to be homosexual in the movie. The *Variety* critic writes that Holmes "fakes a story about his being not at all masculine" to duck out of a ticklish situation. "But is he really faking?" Moreover, *Variety* notes, "Stephens plays Holmes in a rather effete fashion under Wilder's tongue-in-cheek direction."[23]

The court of last resort is, of course, Billy Wilder. He stated flatly to interviewer Doug McClelland, "I wanted to make Holmes a homosexual—that's why he is on dope. . . . But unfortunately the son of Conan Doyle," Adrian Conan Doyle, who represented his father's estate, would not allow it.[24] Wilder accordingly portrayed Holmes as homosexual very subtly. Moreover, Wilder said, he chose Stephens to play Holmes partly because he thought Stephens "looked" homosexual, even though Stephens was married and had a family. Indeed, Wilder had Stephens wear a touch of mascara in some scenes; the actor never objected.[25] Wilder told me that Adrian Conan Doyle could not pin anything down in the script to which he could take exception concerning Holmes's sexuality. The cognoscenti, concluded Wilder, perceived the implications in the ballerina sequence that Holmes was homosexual.

Film historian Richard Valley writes perceptively that "the film remains refreshingly ambivalent about Holmes's sexuality." Wilder implied that the Baker Street bachelor was homosexual, "but he never went so far as to actually say so, . . . while taking into account Holmes's fascination with Ilse, the woman in the case."[26]

The shooting script finally weighed in at 260 pages, the longest screenplay of Wilder's career. He estimated that the finished film would run ten minutes short of three hours. The film was scheduled to be shot at Pinewood Studios on the outskirts of London, where Wilder engaged British production artists like Christopher Challis and film editor Ernest Walter. Challis had photographed three movies for Michael Powell and was known for his lush color photography, particularly on *Tales of Hoffman* (1951). Walter had edited two Agatha Christie mysteries, George Pollack's *Murder, She Said* (1961) and *Murder Most Foul* (1965). In addition, Wilder enlisted composer Miklos Rozsa for the fourth time and production designer Alexander Trauner for the seventh.

Wilder asked Trauner to reconstruct Victorian London at Pinewood. Trauner built Baker Street in the 1880s on the back lot at Pinewood with staggering authenticity. The set was 150 yards long and was designed in forced perspective to create the illusion of greater length. Trauner's Baker Street set included the elaborate facades of all of the buildings facing the thoroughfare, plus a cobblestone street and period street lamps.

Holmes's bachelor flat occupied a soundstage at Pinewood. Wilder concerned himself with the set decoration of Holmes's apartment, just as he had done when dressing Baxter's Manhattan digs in *The Apartment*. Once again Wilder accompanied Trauner on a shopping tour to decorate the shelves of Holmes's Baker Street apartment. Adrian Conan Doyle, who had gotten over his disputes with Wilder about the screenplay, visited the apartment set and declared, "If Sherlock Holmes were to enter this room, he would immediately feel right at home. Everything is exactly in its place."[27]

Principal photography got under way at Pinewood in mid-February 1969. After enduring the nightmare of shooting *One, Two, Three* in Berlin, Wilder had vowed never to make another movie in Europe. But he relented when it came to *Sherlock Holmes*. "This is an English story and has to be made here," he explained. "Its cast and crew throughout the shooting will be as English as the weather."[28] Location shooting was scheduled to be done in London and in Inverness, Scotland, where Holmes goes searching after the missing husband of his Belgian client, Gabrielle Valladon (played by the French actress Genevieve Page). Scotland has seldom looked better than it does in Challis's color photography—all misty mountains and glimmering lakes.

Wilder, as usual, joked with the cast on the set. During the ballet sequence at Covent Garden, Colin Blakely was called on to execute an impromptu Russian folk dance with six women in the corps de ballet. "Colin, I want you to act like Laughton and dance like Nureyev," Wilder said. Afterward Wilder commented with mock disappointment, "Colin, why did you act like Nureyev and dance like Laughton?"[29] Ernest Walter noted, "Mr. Wilder—and he was mostly called Mr. Wilder—is a funny man; and to try to top him was not the best thing to do."[30] It would take a Walter Matthau to do that. Wilder's sense of humor did not desert him when he was shooting on location in a church cemetery near Pinewood. The gravedigger, who gives Holmes information about the occupant of a freshly dug grave, was played by Stanley Holloway, who sang "I'm Getting Married in the Morning" in *My Fair Lady* (1964). Wilder warbled "I'm getting buried in the morning" to Holloway.

For his part, Stephens found working with Wilder taxing. Wilder was determined to explore every possible way of staging the action of a scene, and he would continue rehearsing long after Stephens felt he was ready to shoot it. Stephens writes in his autobiography that he felt that he was "being put through a meat grinder every day." Wilder "would spend hours" rehearsing a scene "until the whole thing was squeezed completely dry, and you felt like running, screaming off the set, which is more or less what I did."[31]

Like Peter Sellers, who kept all of his gripes about Wilder to himself while shooting *Kiss Me, Stupid,* Stephens privately fretted about his frustrations in working with Wilder but never told him how he felt. He was not satisfied with the way he played a single scene, and he convinced himself that he was giving a second-rate performance. Halfway through the shoot, he collapsed from exhaustion and tension. Totally depressed, he swallowed a handful of sleeping pills and washed them down with scotch.

Wilder was terribly upset and confessed contritely that he had pushed Stephens too hard. Wilder promised, Stephens writes, that "we would carry on and finish the picture, and we'd go a little slower and not hurry things." But, Stephens concludes, "When I returned, it was all exactly the same."[32] As in the case of Marilyn Monroe's suicide attempt during *Some Like It Hot,* the studio hushed up Stephens's brush with suicide; the public relations department reported to the press only that Stephens was suffering from exhaustion. Stephens loyally expressed unstinting praise of Wilder to the columnists: "Fantastic! He's always good-humored and immensely knowledgeable."[33]

Wilder was just as loyal in his observations about Stephens. "He was a very fine actor, who took direction very well," said Wilder. After Stephens's try at suicide, "we had to wait until he recuperated" to finish the film.[34] As in the case of Matthau's heart attack on *The Fortune Cookie,* filming had proceeded too far to consider replacing Stephens. At any rate, principal photography wrapped on December 13, 1969. Waiting out Stephens's convalescence was one reason that the picture, scheduled for a nineteen-week shoot, lasted for twenty-nine weeks. Another was that Wilder's 260-page script took longer to shoot than either he or the studio had anticipated.

During postproduction, Ernest Walter found it easy to cut the footage together. Wilder had allowed him to spend time on the set during shooting, just as Doane Harrison had always done, and for the same reason: Wilder would plan with Walter how each scene would be edited into the completed film. "You didn't find Mr. Wilder a very easy man to get close to," Walter said, "but as long as you knew your job, there was no problem."[35]

Wilder was familiar with Miklos Rozsa's violin concerto. Rozsa writes in his autobiography that Wilder asked him to work it into his score for the present film.[36] Wilder, notes Tony Thomas, "was inspired by the fact that Holmes liked playing the fiddle."[37] Wilder wanted Rozsa's background music to reflect Holmes's sense of loss after he discovers that Gabrielle, for whom he has developed a deep regard, is a German secret agent. Rozsa accordingly employed the bittersweet romantic theme from the concerto, "but with an urgent, pulsating rhythm underneath."[38] "Rozsa's achingly lovely concerto," writes Robert Horton, "distills in the score the essence of loss" and an air of melancholy.[39] Wilder paid tribute to Rozsa by showing him conducting Tchaikovsky's *Swan Lake* in the orchestra pit at Covent Garden during the ballet sequence.

When Walter finished editing the rough cut of the film in London, it ran three hours and twenty minutes. The full-length movie is a compendium of self-contained units in which Holmes confronts a variety of cases. The first is titled "The Adventure of the Upside-Down Room." The corpse of an elderly Chinese man is found in a rented room where all of the furniture is nailed to the ceiling. On observing the bizarre crime scene and asking Watson pointed questions, Holmes astutely deduces that Watson concocted the baffling case, with a corpse borrowed from a morgue. He did so in an effort to alleviate the boredom Holmes endured between cases, which induced him to take refuge in cocaine.

The second episode is "The Dreadful Business of the Naked Honey-mooners," which takes place aboard an ocean liner in the Mediterranean. The naked bodies are found in bed in their cabin; Watson volunteers to take charge of the investigation to impress Holmes with his own powers of deduction. After disturbing the nude newlyweds, who have merely been asleep in their bed, exhausted by a night of sex, Watson discovers to his chagrin that he has led Holmes to the wrong cabin!

The third episode is "The Singular Affair of the Russian Ballerina." The fourth and longest is "The Case of the Missing Husband," discussed below. In addition, there is a flashback, titled in the screenplay, "The Adventure of the Dumbfounded Detective," which takes place at Oxford University in Holmes's student days, while he is a member of the university rowing team. His teammates hold a lottery, in which the victor is to spend the night with a prostitute. Holmes is the winner, but he is reluctant to claim his prize because he has a crush on a girl he has seen around town. He is devastated to learn that the trollop is the very girl he secretly idolizes. This flashback, of course, recalls an incident from Wilder's youth, in which the girl Wilder had been dating in Vienna turned out to be a harlot.

Wilder also prepared a prologue in the script in which a young Dr. Watson, the grandson of Holmes's confrere (also played by Colin Blakely), opens a safety deposit box at Barclays Bank and finds the manuscripts for the four adventures, which, his grandfather explains in a covering letter, were not published during his lifetime because they contained potentially scandalous material.

It seems that king-size period pictures were beginning to go out of fashion at the time, as evidenced by the box office failure of epic-scale costume dramas like *Far from the Madding Crowd* (1967). (In fact, after showing some historical epics of this sort, one small-town exhibitor is said to have written to his distributor, "Don't send me no more pictures about people who write with feathers!"[40])

UA held a disastrous preview of *Sherlock Holmes* at the Lakewood Theatre near Long Beach, after which the preview cards were "uniformly bad," Walter Mirisch writes. "We had a tremendous number of walkouts." The cards pronounced the movie too episodic. In fact, "as each of the segments ended, we lost part of our audience."[41] Mirisch and the other nervous studio officials declined to distribute the movie at its original length; they pressured Wilder into carving more than an hour out of the movie to bring it closer to average length. They also decreed that it would not be showcased as a road show presentation.

Wilder acknowledged that the rough cut was half an hour longer than he had anticipated. So he was willing to sacrifice "The Adventure of the Upside-Down Room," which ran exactly thirty minutes. But UA insisted that the film be cut to two hours or it simply would not distribute it. Wilder was already committed to go to Paris to begin work on another film, so he conferred with the Mirisches about shortening the film and then met with Ernest Walter. "I told the editor, 'Cut this, cut that,'" Wilder remembered. Then he headed for Paris.[42]

Because the film consisted of individual episodes, Wilder was able to retain intact "The Singular Affair of the Russian Ballerina" and "The Case of the Missing Husband," the two key episodes, and drop the other two. To bring the film in at two hours and five minutes, however, Walter also had to delete the Oxford flashback and the prologue. This was more than Wilder had bargained for. Still, he had no choice but to acquiesce, to honor his commitment to UA of a two-hour release print.

In all, seventy-five minutes of footage was removed from the final cut, but because of the film's structure, *The Private Life of Sherlock Holmes* in its truncated form was not marred in any essential way by UA's meddling. Still, after Wilder viewed Walter's final cut, he remarked, "I was saddened by what was left out." He added, "Perhaps enough of it remains; I hope so." But when the project that Wilder went to Paris to work on was shelved, he further regretted that he had not personally supervised Walter's final edit of *Sherlock Holmes.* "We previewed the new version in Santa Barbara," Mirisch recalls; "we had few or no walkouts." This was "somewhat of a victory for the recut version," which lost 30 percent of the original version.[43]

At least the industry censor passed the final version of the movie without any further cuts. *Sherlock Holmes* was the first Wilder film to receive a classification from the new CARA. It was classified as PG, "parental guidance suggested." That the movie flirted with the subject of homosexuality was not a problem for the present censor, Eugene Dougherty, who replaced Geoffrey Shurlock in 1968, when the new rating system began. Homosexuality was no longer a taboo subject for a Hollywood movie.

During the opening credit sequence, Dr. Watson reads a letter addressed to his heirs in voice-over on the sound track. The voice-over was incorporated into the credit sequence from the eliminated prologue. Watson explains that he intends to recount some of Holmes's cases that involve "matters of a delicate and sometimes scandalous nature." One delicate issue that is raised in the film is the question of Holmes's attitude toward the opposite sex. Holmes discusses this subject with Watson early in the movie. Essentially, Holmes explains, "I don't dislike women; I merely mistrust them" because they are unreliable. "The most affectionate female I ever knew was a murderess." She led him down the garden path "until she could steal some cyanide from my laboratory to sprinkle on her husband's steak-and-kidney pie." Holmes fears that an emotional entanglement with a female could warp his judgment and cloud his powers of deduction. Holmes's remarks about women introduce the central episode in the film, "The Case of the Missing Husband." "The time has come to reveal the most intimate aspect of Holmes's life," Watson says in his voice-over narration. "His one and only involvement with a woman."

Gabrielle Valladon comes to Holmes's Baker Street flat, seeking the private detective's assistance. She has come to London from Belgium, searching for her husband, Emile, an engineer and inventor who is missing. An item in a newspaper gives a clue to Emile's possible presence in Scotland, so Holmes, Watson, and Gabrielle take the Highland Express to Inverness. As Holmes declares, "The game's afoot!" They manage to trace Emile Valladon to a village cemetery, where his corpse has been interred. Mycroft Holmes, Sherlock's brother, who is associated with British intelligence, knows of Sherlock's presence in Scotland and invites him to a secret meeting at a Scottish castle. Mycroft informs his brother that the government has been conducting secret experiments with a type of primitive submarine. Emile Valladon was involved in the experiments and died accidentally when one of the trial runs of the submarine went awry. Mycroft then reveals that the woman his brother knows as Gabrielle Valladon is an impostor; she is actually Ilse von Hoffmanstahl, a notorious German spy. Ilse ingratiated herself with Holmes to dupe him into helping her track down Emile Valladon and uncover the secret plans for the submarine. "In helping Ilse," Mycroft concludes, "you have been in the service of the Kaiser."

It is a severe blow to Holmes's pride to acknowledge that he has allowed himself to be outwitted by the feminine wiles of a charming foreign spy. Ilse endeavors to soften the blow by saying that she volunteered for this assignment because she "couldn't resist the challenge of coming up against the best." Steinbrunner and Michaels note that, although Ilse has admitted to Holmes that she is a foreign spy, "there is an unspoken tenderness in their parting."[44] Holmes and Ilse have developed in the course of their journey together a reticent but nonetheless genuine affection for each other. Dick calls their farewell "two intelligent people saying goodbye to one another."[45]

As Ilse proceeds up the path in a carriage on her way to be exchanged by the Germans for a British prisoner, she signals to Holmes in Morse code by opening and closing her umbrella. Holmes reads her departing message: "Auf Wiedersehen" (Until we meet again). But they will not. In the movie's epilogue, Holmes learns of Ilse's execution as a foreign agent while she is on a secret mission in Japan, spying on the Yokohama Harbor naval installations. He retreats to his bedroom with the container of cocaine that is hidden in a file case to assuage his grief over the death of Ilse, with whom he shared a platonic relationship. As Holmes observes at the end of *The Sign of the Four*, "For me there still remains the cocaine bottle."[46] The scene is accompanied by Rozsa's bittersweet theme.

Jonathan Rigby writes that Holmes's emotions have been stirred by Gabrielle, a woman whose pluck and acumen he admires, so he is shattered when he learns of her execution. Stephens's "mournful Holmes is a triumph. It's by no means the standard issue Sherlock of the popular imagination, but remains much the most human and affecting interpretation on film."[47]

*The Private Life of Sherlock Holmes,* at a running time of 125 minutes, had its American premiere at Radio City Music Hall in New York City on October 19, 1970. It opened to a batch of mixed reviews. Vincent Canby in the *New York Times* found the movie amusing. Focusing on the film's treatment of the ambiguous nature of Holmes and Watson's friendship, Canby stated that the material was "rather daring" for a Sherlock Holmes picture. Nevertheless, "there is simply no reason to cavil with Billy Wilder's mostly comic, charming movie," which is fundamentally "a fond and entertaining film."[48] Pauline Kael, as usual, filed a negative report in the *New Yorker.* She thought the movie ranged from mildly diverting to downright dull: "Wilder has made a detective picture that fails to whet our curiosity," she opined. "So one must content oneself with the occasional wit," along with Trauner's magnificent Victorian production design and Challis's handsome color cinematography.[49]

The movie had been booked at the music hall in late October as its Thanksgiving attraction, but it was withdrawn before Thanksgiving in the wake of the lukewarm public reception. The film likewise proved to be a box office disappointment when it went into general release across the country. Its total domestic gross was a paltry $1.5 million.

"When the picture was released," Walter explained, "people were disappointed because they expected a thriller like *The Hound of the Baskervilles* with Basil Rathbone. But this was a more tongue-in-cheek picture, and a more personal story."[50] Moreover, writes Allen Eyles, "the downbeat epilogue was not calculated to please the masses."[51] Though the movie failed in the United States, Wilder emphasized, "in England it was popular."[52] Tom Milne's notice in the *Observer* in London was typical of the British response to the picture. Milne, who placed the movie on his "ten best list" for 1970, proclaimed that, Wilder's "acid wit" notwithstanding, the film was really "an affectionate *homage*" to Holmes.[53]

Although the film was not a notable success when it was released, it has steadily built a strong reputation among film scholars as one of the best Sherlock Holmes films. As Michael Pointer observes, it is "the only Holmes film to be made by a major director." In the course of the movie, "we are able to savor many of the delights of Wilder's unique piece, which revealed Holmes as human and fallible in a most moving way."[54]

Nowadays the film is seen as an archetype for the detective movie, with its crackling dialogue, elegant visuals, rousing score, and dark-hearted characters. It is "a masterpiece of the highest order," in George Morris's words.[55] Eyles writes in his survey of the Holmes movies, "It is the screen's most intelligent, coherent, and convincing representation of the detective and his world."[56]

When a fully restored version of *Sherlock Holmes* was scheduled for release on DVD by MGM Home Entertainment in 2003, there was renewed interest in the sequences that had been excised from the movie, for inclusion in the Special Features section of the DVD. Wilder had often said over the years, "If it takes my permission to help restore *Sherlock Holmes,* I'm delighted; if they can get ahold" of the missing material, "they can show it."[57] The restoration team found the sound track for "The Upside-Down Room" but no film footage to go with it, so they filled in the missing visuals with still photos of the episode. For "The Naked Honeymooners," the technical team uncovered all of the footage, but no sound track, so they employed subtitles for the dialogue. For both "The Adventure of the Dumbfounded Detective" and the prologue at Barclays Bank, the restoration crew utilized script excerpts, with visuals supplied by still photos. Wilder heard before his death in 2002 of the plans to recover the lost footage, but he did not live to see it in the DVD. When the DVD finally arrived in 2003, *The Private Life of Sherlock Holmes* met with fresh acclaim. It has at last come to occupy a prominent place in the canon of Wilder's work.

# 17

# The Perfect Blendship

## *The Front Page* and *Avanti!*

I was curious to see how a bunch of empty-headed nitwits would
conduct themselves.

> —*William Powell in the title role
> of the film* My Man Godfrey

Friendship, friendship!
What a perfect blendship!
When other friendships have been forgot
Ours will still be hot.

> —*Cole Porter, "Friendship"*

In 1928 Billy Wilder was a reporter on a tabloid in Berlin that specialized in crime stories and sensational feature pieces, such as his first-person account of life as a gigolo. That same year, on August 14, playwrights Ben Hecht and Charles MacArthur premiered their cynical farce about the newspaper racket, *The Front Page*, on Broadway.

The play later reminded Wilder of his years as a young reporter; he would get around to filming it some four decades later. "I loved the 1920s," he recalled. "A reporter back then was a mixture of a private eye and a dramatist. If you were any good, you could improve on the story" by adding some spicy details. "Then there was the round-the-clock dedication—no family life for the lone wolf—and the camaraderie of the newsroom."[1]

Like Wilder, Hecht always remembered fondly his years as a young reporter, in his case for the *Chicago Daily News*. He was only sixteen when he got his first job as a cub reporter, he recalled in a brief essay about *The Front Page* in his private papers. "I quit after sixteen years of chasing fires, killers, swindles, and scandals."[2] Hecht based many characters in *The Front*

*Page* on real Chicago journalists. His street-smart reporter Hildy Johnson, for example, was modeled on Hilding Johnson, a reporter for the *Chicago Herald-Examiner* who was not above picking locks and clambering through transoms in pursuit of a news story. As Sherman Duffy, one of Hecht's fellow reporters, put it, "Socially, a journalist fits somewhere between a whore and a bartender."[3] Walter Burns, the domineering managing editor in Hecht and MacArthur's play, was inspired by Walter Howey, the managing editor of the *Herald-Examiner.* Hecht described Howey this way: "He smiled like a wide-eyed sightseer from the sticks. But he could plot like Cesare Borgia and strike like Gengis Khan."[4]

Howard Hughes produced the first film version of the play in 1931. It was directed by Lewis Milestone (*All Quiet on the Western Front*). Pat O'Brien played Hildy, and Adolphe Menjou was Walter Burns. Wilder felt that Milestone's version was "handicapped by the crude conditions of making early sound pictures." In addition, it could not totally disguise its stage-bound origins.[5]

The second movie adaptation of *The Front Page* was titled *His Girl Friday* (1940). It was directed by Howard Hawks, with a screenplay by Charles Lederer, who had collaborated on the script of the 1931 movie. Hawks said that one day, after Cary Grant was set to play Walter Burns, "I had a secretary read through one of the scenes of *The Front Page* with me. I realized that Hildy Johnson's lines were better when they were read by a woman. I called Hecht and he agreed, so the part of the reporter was rewritten for Rosalind Russell."[6] Wilder, who had coscripted *Ball of Fire* for Hawks, much admired him. But he did not agree with Hawks's changing Hildy's gender. In his opinion, it placed too much emphasis on Walter's winning back his ex-wife, rather than his ace reporter. Hawks had also moved his film up to 1940. Hence his film was not *The Front Page* of Hecht and MacArthur, according to Wilder.[7]

When Jennings Lang, a vice president at Universal, by sheer coincidence inquired whether Wilder would like to direct a remake of *The Front Page*, Wilder accepted enthusiastically. (For the record, this was the same Jennings Lang whose affair with Joan Bennett some years earlier was one of the inspirations for *The Apartment*.) Wilder was drawn to the project in part because male friendship plays an important role in *The Front Page*, just as it does in *The Fortune Cookie* and *The Private Life of Sherlock Holmes*. Furthermore, Wilder's own experience as a journalist would be reflected in the movie. "I hope to show that I have a feeling for newspaper guys," he told Lang. "I understand their problems and their hang-ups."[8]

## *The Front Page* (1974)

In September 1973, Wilder and Diamond set up shop at Universal, reworking one of the classic American comedies into a screenplay. Jack Lemmon
and Walter Matthau were cast as Hildy Johnson and Walter Burns before
Wilder started on the script. Hence Wilder and his partner could write the
screenplay with these two actors in mind. Wilder pointed out that Matthau
was closer to the original conception of the gruff, surly Walter Burns in the
play than the dapper Adolphe Menjou in Milestone's version or the suave
Cary Grant in Hawks's film.

Wilder moved the setting of his film back to its original time frame.
Wilder's version of the play takes place in Chicago in 1929—in the same
town, the same year, and the same zany world as *Some Like It Hot.* As a matter of fact, there is an implicit reference to *Some Like It Hot* in *The Front
Page:* one of the reporters boasts that he scooped his fellow journalists in
covering the St. Valentine's Day Massacre. There is also an allusion to *The
Spirit of St. Louis:* Hildy recalls the hack reporters sitting around the press
room, waiting for Lindbergh to land in Paris. What's more, Wilder lifted a
line spoken by Chuck Tatum in *Ace in the Hole* for Hildy to repeat in the
present film. Tatum says that a reporter is proud of his front page story
today, and the next day somebody wraps the front page around a dead fish.
Even Ben Hecht is mentioned as having made Walter Burns furious by for-
saking the newspaper game to go to Hollywood to write scripts. Hecht had
to be smuggled out of Chicago to escape the wrath of Walter Burns. In addition, Hildy does an impersonation of James Cagney as a tough guy—which
is a bit premature, since this film is set in 1929, and Cagney went to
Hollywood in 1930.

Wilder and Diamond rewrote about 60 percent of the play's dialogue,
much to the dismay of Helen Hayes, the widow of Charles MacArthur and
one of the great actresses of the theater. Nevertheless, Wilder said that he
regarded the screenplay as a faithful opening out of the play for the screen,
and he said so to Hayes. He conceded, however, "We did much more opening out of the story than we did on *Stalag 17,* for instance. . . . Certain plays
call for being opened out more than others. Indeed, the playwright himself
might have opened up the play more had he not been straitjacketed by the
format of the stage."

Whereas the play was set entirely in the press room, "the film ranges
more naturally over Chicago," including a new scene in the Balaban and
Katz State Theatre (actually the State-Lake), where Peggy Grant, Hildy's
fiancée, plays the organ during intermission.[9] Barney Balaban, who was pres-

ident of Paramount during Wilder's tenure there, co-owned a chain of Chicago movie theaters before going to Hollywood. (The feature announced on the State's marquee is *The Phantom of the Opera,* a 1925 silent picture with Lon Chaney—a curious choice, since *The Front Page* is set well after the advent of sound pictures.)

Walter, carrying out one of his crafty ruses to sabotage the marriage of Hildy and Peggy, visits Peggy backstage and presents himself as Hildy's probation officer. He solemnly informs Peggy that Hildy is a convicted flasher. But Hildy gets wind of what Walter is up to and exposes his nefarious plot to Peggy over the phone. The description of Walter in the screenplay is one of those satirical asides that make a Wilder screenplay almost as entertaining to read as to see performed. As the scene with Peggy shows, Walter "operates in the great tradition of Machiavelli, Rasputin, and Count Dracula: No ethics, no scruples, and no private life—a fanatic, oblivious of ulcers and lack of sleep, in his constant pursuit of tomorrow's headlines."[10]

Wilder added two characters to the scenario who do not appear in the play. One of them, Dr. Eggelhofer (Martin Gabel), is a balmy Freudian psychiatrist from Vienna. Eggelhofer, who is only referred to in the play, is to provide a second opinion about the sanity of Earl Williams (Austin Pendleton), a befuddled anarchist who claims that he shot a policeman quite by accident. When Eggelhofer interprets a gun as a phallic symbol, Earl complains to the sheriff, "If he's going to talk dirty . . ." Eggelhofer asks Earl to reenact how he shot the cop, and the sheriff obligingly lends Earl his revolver for the demonstration. Earl uses the gun to escape and, in the ensuing scuffle, accidentally shoots Eggelhofer in the groin. Eggelhofer is carted off to the hospital, hollering, "Fruitcake!"—his assessment of Earl's sanity.

The other character that Wilder introduced into the picture is Rudy Keppler (Jon Korkes), a callow cub reporter who becomes the object of the affections of journalist Roy Bensinger (David Wayne). With the Bensinger character, Wilder picks up on the topic of homosexuality he had broached in *The Private Life of Sherlock Holmes.* Roy is high-strung and effeminate in the play, but Wilder presents him clearly as a mincing homosexual. Gerd Gemünden calls Bensinger "Wilder's most stereotypical portrait" of a homosexual.[11] Some of the reporters derisively term Rudy "a snot-nosed kid" because he gets so excited about Earl's escape that he wets his pants. Roy defends Rudy, insisting that the other reporters are "beastly" to him. Rudy seems to be regressing to childhood, with Roy as his father figure. Hildy warns Rudy, "Never get caught in the can with Bensinger!" Later on Roy caresses Rudy's shoulder like a lover. We subsequently see Roy and Rudy exiting the men's room together; Rudy has disregarded Hildy's advice. In fact, Wilder obviously intended the relationship of Roy and Rudy as a contrast to the male bonding of Hildy and Walter, which does not have sexual intent.

By mid-February 1974, Wilder and Diamond had completed the first draft of the script; by mid-March, the shooting script was ready. Lemmon and Matthau were appearing in their second Wilder film, eight years after he had teamed them in *The Fortune Cookie*. In rounding out the cast during preproduction, Wilder chose Carol Burnett to play Mollie Malloy, a harlot who befriends Earl. Molly is another hooker with a heart of gold, recalling Gloria from *The Lost Weekend* and, of course, Irma la Douce. Carol Burnett, like Arlene Francis, who appeared in *One, Two, Three,* was a popular television personality. So she gave the picture additional marquee value. By contrast, Wilder selected the young film actress Susan Sarandon to play Peggy. *The Front Page* was only her third picture as a supporting player.

For production designer, Wilder picked Universal's Henry Bumstead. He had won Academy Awards for *To Kill a Mockingbird* (1962) and, more recently, *The Sting* (1973), for that film's "meticulous recreation of 1920s cafés, bookie joints, and train interiors."[12] Hence Bumstead was an ideal choice for *The Front Page*. Wilder also snagged a top-notch film editor, Ralph Winters, who was likewise a two-time Oscar winner, as editor of *King Solomon's Mines* (1950) and coeditor of *Ben Hur* (1959).

Principal photography was scheduled to start on April 3, the day after the Academy Award ceremony at which Lemmon won an Oscar for *Save the Tiger* (1973), his second Academy Award. At the Oscar party afterward, Wilder said to Lemmon with tongue in cheek, "Congratulations! But don't be late for work tomorrow."[13]

Some exteriors were shot on location around Chicago, but the bulk of *The Front Page* was filmed at Universal in Hollywood. The citywide manhunt for Earl Williams was shot on Chicago streets, conjuring up the opening scene of *Some Like it Hot*.

The film's principal set is the press room of the Cook County criminal court building, where the reporters gather to wait for the latest developments in the Earl Williams case. Bumstead constructed the press room on stage 24 in all its "pristine squalor": There is a half-empty mustard jar nestled among the ragged playing cards, cigar butts, and an ancient Remington typewriter on the long center table, plus "a propeller fan revolving slowly overhead." Joseph McBride, who visited the set, describes Wilder as "a perpetual motion machine, his language as salty and sarcastic as the reporters in the story, his thick Viennese accent filtered through a mouthful of gum," now that his doctor had taken him off cigarettes.[14]

In general, the dialogue proceeds at "a rapid-fire pace," and the "machine-gun delivery of the lines" recalls the staccato pace of the dialogue in *One, Two, Three*.[15] But Wilder had learned when *One, Two, Three* was released that audiences simply could not keep up with the hectic tempo of the dialogue. He therefore decided, while making *The Front Page,* to give the audience a breather by having the dialogue of some scenes spoken at a more leisurely pace.

Matthau commented that he liked working with Wilder because "he is from the old school, where every shot is preplanned. He doesn't waste time covering a scene from multiple angles." Matthau explained, "Most directors don't know what they want, so they have a lot of takes. Wilder cuts the cloth as he sees it." Wilder concurred: "When the script is finished," he said, he knew "roughly how it will look on film." Lemmon also found Wilder pleasant to work with. "The kind of rapport that comes from making several films with a director is invaluable," he said. "It's like shorthand, he doesn't have to get more than one sentence out before I know what he has in mind."[16]

The picture wrapped in mid-June after a ten-week shoot. Since Wilder had planned with Winters how every scene would be cut, the editor did a preliminary edit of each scene right after it was filmed. As a result, Wilder and Winters put the finishing touches on the final cut less than a week after Wilder finished shooting.[17]

In 1974 Richard Heffner was appointed chief of CARA. "Wilder availed himself of the new freedom of speech" permitted by the revised code, "but just enough to stay within the boundaries of the PG rating." Hence Wilder avoided the expletive *fuck,* "which in 1974 would have meant an automatic R rating."[18] The PG rating, Heffner said, "would make the film available to a wider, younger audience than the R rating would have allowed."[19] Consequently, when Hildy announces he is leaving Chicago to take a job in Philadelphia, he exclaims, "Am I glad to get out of this friggin' town!"

The musical score for *The Front Page* was provided by Billy May, the music supervisor on the film. May stitched together melodies from popular songs of the Jazz Age, much as Matty Malneck had done for *Some Like It Hot.* He did so with the kibitzing of Wilder, the resident expert on jazz. For old times' sake, Wilder included in the movie "Button Up Your Overcoat," whose lyrics were cowritten by Buddy De Sylva, who had been a lyricist before he became production chief at Paramount during Wilder's tenure there.

A blast of ragtime music, resonant of the Roaring Twenties, introduces the movie's opening credits. The front page of the newspaper is shown being set in type: it is the morning edition of June 6, 1929. As the newspaper rolls off the presses, we see that the masthead declares, "Nothing but the Truth." Below that, the headline proclaims, "Cop Killer Sane, Must Die!"

Walter Burns, the domineering and unscrupulous editor of the *Chicago Examiner*, is bent on keeping Hildy Johnson, his star reporter, from marrying Peggy Grant because she insists that Hildy renounce the newspaper game and take a job with an advertising firm in Philadelphia. Walter craftily talks Hildy into postponing his departure from the *Examiner* so that he can cover the execution of Earl Williams, an anarchist convicted of killing a cop. Walter is confident that Hildy subconsciously wants to be rescued from a dull marriage and a boring job in advertising. Hence he is betting that, once he gets Hildy to put off leaving the *Examiner*, he can manipulate him into abandoning his plans.

Of course, Burns's subconscious motive is that he does not want to lose his best friend, any more than he wants to lose his ace reporter. Therefore *The Front Page* rightly belongs among those Wilder films that focus on a strong male relationship. George Morris comments that "the friendship between Hildy and Walter evolves obliquely" in the course of the picture. "They never express their mutual feelings in words," only in gestures.[20] For example, in the scene in which Hildy feverishly types out his article on Earl Williams, Walter intuits that Hildy wants a cigarette; he lights one and puts it in Hildy's mouth. This gesture, of course, recalls the way that Walter Neff shows his regard for Barton Keyes in *Double Indemnity* by lighting Keyes's cigar for him. It is a gesture of friendship that Keyes reciprocates at the end of that film by lighting Walter's cigarette.

In the present film, Wilder beefed up the role of Mollie Malloy from the play. Mollie takes Earl in after he has been beaten by the police for handing out leftist leaflets on a street corner. She later accuses the reporters of writing trashy copy about her relationship with Earl. She resents their saying that she was willing to marry Earl on the gallows; they respond with verbal abuse. Morris comments, "Mollie may be a whore, but her impulses are among the more decent and honest in the film."[21]

After Earl escapes because of the incompetence of Sheriff Hartman (Vincent Gardenia), the mayor (Harold Gould) organizes the manhunt for Earl. The mayor, in collusion with the sheriff, has connived all along to railroad Earl just before an election, in which the mayor and the sheriff are campaigning on a law-and-order ticket. Since the mayor wants Earl dead, he authorizes the police to shoot him on sight.

Meanwhile, Earl seeks sanctuary in the deserted press room. Hildy finds him there and conceals him in a rolltop desk. Convinced of Earl's innocence, Hildy tells Walter that he plans to publish an exposé on the mayor and sheriff's conspiracy to employ Earl as a scapegoat in their plans for reelection. But Earl is soon discovered, and Sheriff Hartman arrests Hildy and Walter for harboring a fugitive. Walter and Hildy turn the tables on the sheriff and the mayor by revealing the incriminating evidence they have about both of them. Walter announces in a solemn tone, "There is a Divine Providence that watches over the *Examiner*!"

As the picture nears its conclusion, it seems that Walter's plot to hold on to Hildy has failed. Hildy and Peggy head for the depot to board the next train for Philadelphia. But Walter, as resilient and irrepressible as ever, has not yet played his last card. He shows up at the train terminal, ostensibly to wish Hildy a fond farewell. He even bestows his own watch on Hildy as a token of his abiding esteem for his favorite reporter. But once the train has left the station, Walter shows his true colors. He sends a wire posthaste to the police in Gary, Indiana, the train's first stop. He demands that Hildy be arrested, explaining, "The son of a bitch stole my watch."

Ever since the play opened on Broadway, the final line of dialogue has ranked among the most celebrated curtain lines in theater history. It was blipped in Milestone's film and excluded from Hawks's movie because of censorship restrictions on the use of profanity. But the censorship code had been revised by the time Wilder made his movie. When a columnist asked Wilder during filming whether he planned to delete the play's closing line, he replied, "That would be like rewriting 'To be or not to be,' for God's sake. It's a classic."[22]

Wilder pointed out to me that he added "a printed epilogue that tells what happened to the characters after the end of the story. We took that idea, of course, from the epilogue of *American Graffiti* [1973]." The audience is informed that Hildy Johnson eventually became managing editor of the *Examiner*; Walter Burns, after he retired, occasionally lectured at the University of Chicago on "the ethics of journalism"; Roy Bensinger and Rudy Keppler opened an antiques shop in Cape Cod; and Dr. Eggelhofer, after Earl shot him in the balls, wrote a best-seller, *The Joys of Impotence*. Bernard Dick writes that the epilogue "is rather like an alumni newsletter, only wittier."[23]

*The Front Page* premiered on December 17, 1974, at the Century Plaza Theatre in Los Angeles. The reviews were a mixed bag. Pauline Kael delivered herself of her meanest notice of a Wilder picture since *One, Two, Three*. This time she said that Wilder had a "sharp-toothed, venomous wit. He's debauching the Hecht and MacArthur play to produce a harsh, scrambling-for-laughs gag comedy. . . . It's enjoyable on a very low level."[24] Joseph

Morgenstern in *Newsweek* opined, "Wilder is out of touch with the temper of the times."[25]

Perhaps in response to Morgenstern, Andrew Sarris noted that Wilder's brand of cynicism "seems much more contemporary than it ever did." He continued, "It is refreshing to see a director . . . who still believes in the spoken word as a vehicle of expression."[26] Sarris later wrote, "I must concede that I have greatly underrated Billy Wilder, perhaps more so than any other director. His twilight resurgence in the 1970s," with films like *The Private Life of Sherlock Holmes* and *The Front Page,* "made me rethink Wilder."[27]

Richard Armstrong states baldly that, when *The Front Page* was released, it "met neither box office success nor critical favor."[28] On the contrary, the movie had its champions from the outset, most notably Sarris. Moreover, it was a box office success, "earning $15 million against a cost of $4 million." *The Front Page* was Wilder's biggest commercial hit since *Irma la Douce.*[29]

*The Front Page* evokes the screwball comedies of the 1930s. It is laced with brittle humor and at times approximates the rough-and-tumble spirit of the golden age of screwball—as when the cop cars make a madcap dash through the streets of Chicago, dutifully following up one ridiculous false lead after another as to the whereabouts of Earl Williams.

# *Avanti!* (1972)

Wilder made another film with Jack Lemmon around this time. In endeavoring to find a viable project, he followed his old practice: when in doubt, choose a Broadway play. This time he turned to *Avanti!* by Samuel Taylor, whose hit play *Sabrina Fair* Wilder had successfully adapted for the screen in 1954 as *Sabrina. Avanti!* had not been a success on Broadway in 1968—it ran for only twenty-one performances. Nevertheless, Wilder was confident that he could improve it in adapting it for film, just as he had done with *Sabrina Fair* and other plays.

Wilder was committed to one more film for the Mirisch Company, so he pitched the project to Walter Mirisch, who acted as executive producer on Wilder's films for the Mirisch brothers. Although Wilder had made some flops in recent years, Mirisch's regard for Wilder and his talents had not diminished, so he green-lighted the project.

Taylor's play deals with the relationship between a couple who first become friends because of a common bond. Sandy, a straitlaced Baltimore industrialist, and Alison, a carefree London boutique clerk, cross paths when they come to Rome to claim the bodies of his father and her mother, who have been killed in an auto accident after a ten-year clandestine summertime romance. As the story gets going, Sandy and Alison become bosom buddies, not to say soul mates. Indeed, they are destined to become lovers and will consequently extend their parents' love affair into the next generation.

In retooling Taylor's play into a film script, Wilder decided to do a major overhaul on the source story. He even changed the names of the principals: Sandy became Wendell Armbruster Jr., and Alison became Pamela Piggott.

Wilder began work on the screenplay in the late fall of 1971. Diamond, who had scripted the movie version of *Cactus Flower* for Columbia, was called back by the studio to adapt *40 Carats*, another Broadway hit, into a movie. Consequently, Wilder teamed with screenwriter Philip Epstein (*Casablanca*) on *Avanti!* "I started out with Billy Wilder and couldn't do anything with it," Epstein remembered. "It was not a fruitful collaboration."[30] Meanwhile, Diamond was getting nowhere with *40 Carats*. So in January 1972, he returned to work with Wilder.

Taylor's single-set play takes place in a hotel room in Rome. Wilder opened it out for the screen by relocating the action at a health resort on the Italian island of Ischia. What's more, in reimagining the story for the screen, Wilder kept only Taylor's premise (the deaths of the couple's parents, which bring them to Italy) and the resolution (their adopting their parents' annual romantic ritual). "It is a bittersweet love story," said Wilder, "a little like *Brief Encounter*," which had given Wilder the basic concept for *The Apartment*.[31]

Indeed, Wendell Armbruster Jr. is the same kind of corporate executive that Linus Larrabee is in *Sabrina*. "There are lots of them in America," Wilder explained, "these young executives who drink a lot, drive Cadillacs, go to the club, play golf. They lead a luxurious life, have a telephone in the car"—one remembers Linus making phone calls in his limo. "Suddenly they discover that their existence is empty. They have no one to talk to and nothing to say on the telephone. And it wouldn't make much difference if their stock rose or fell three points. That is the reevaluation of our materialistic values that this film addresses" by examining Wendell's life.[32]

Wilder decided to drop Wendell's dour wife, Emily, from the lists. In the play, she shows up in Rome to ascertain why Wendell has not come home to stage an elaborate funeral for his father, only to find Wendell bogged down in the red tape generated by the Italian bureaucracy. The screenplay replaces her with a more comic figure, a U.S. State Department official named Joseph J. Blodgett. In the film, rather than going to Italy herself, Emily Armbruster dispatches this bumbling duffer to expedite her husband's return. Blodgett is described in the script as "a diplomat who has been working for the State

Department as a trouble shooter. He has yet to be on target."[33] Running true to form, Blodgett will not be on target in coping with Wendell, who bamboozles him. "I painted Blodgett like a humorous character," said Wilder. "Even though I exaggerated a bit, he still wasn't very far from the people I knew at the State Department."[34]

Wilder maintained a beach house near Malibu; his next-door neighbor happened to be Jack Lemmon. "I gave him, as a friend, the first half of the script to read, and he asked me for the role of Wendell Armbruster," Wilder recalled. "At first I was thinking of casting someone in his thirties. So I had to adjust the character to fit his age," which was forty-seven at the time. "Then I wrote the second half."[35]

By the spring of 1972, Wilder and Diamond had completed the screenplay. It is salted with good-natured jokes at the Italians' expense. There is, for example, the mountain of red tape that Wendell must cut through to arrange for the burial of his father's remains back in the States. "That's just the side dish," Wilder said; "the meat is the affair between the American and the English girl, who is a little too fat, but who has a nice bust. It's difficult to find a girl who is twenty pounds too heavy, who is teased for her weight, and who is nonetheless adorable, touching, and in the end erotic," Wilder continued. "We were lucky to have found Juliet Mills, a miraculous actress." Mills, the daughter of actor John Mills, had played in the Western *The Rare Breed* (1966), opposite James Stewart, and in other films. But she was chiefly known for her work on the London stage. Wilder sent her the script, and she phoned him soon after. "I want the role," she said. "I'll gain twenty pounds; give me eight weeks." Wilder recalled that she ate night and day and became very chubby "on beer, pasta, and ice cream." And she gave a superb performance as Pamela Piggott.[36]

For the role of Carlo Carlucci, the worldly and wily manager of the Grand Hotel Excelsior, Wilder considered Alberto Sordi, an Italian comic actor. He had come to prominence in Federico Fellini's early films. "But Sordi did not possess a sufficient mastery of English, and would therefore have slowed down the action," said Wilder. "He wouldn't have hit the ball back fast enough to Lemmon on the other side of the net." Wilder instead chose the British actor Clive Revill, "who could play an Italian like he played a Russian ballet master in *Sherlock Holmes*."[37] Carlucci is described in the screenplay as "a gentleman of the old school; he runs the hotel with discipline and aplomb, and with the precision of Toscanini conducting a symphony orchestra."[38] Both Revill and Edward Andrews, who played Blodgett, offer fine, broad characterizations.

Wilder had broken his resolution not to go to the expense of filming any more movies in Europe when he shot *Sherlock Holmes* in Great Britain. By the same token, he opted to make *Avanti!* entirely on location in Italy, because it was an Italian story that simply cried out to be made there. The exteriors were filmed along the Amalfi Coast and on the islands of Capri and Ischia; the interiors were shot in the Safra Palatinio Studios in Rome.

Production designer Ferdinando Scarfiotti had just come off *Death in Venice* (1971). Surveying the sets Scarfiotti had designed for *Avanti!* on the soundstages in Rome, Wilder mused, "I couldn't have shot this film anywhere but Italy. The air is Italian—even on the interior sets built in the studio. If I transported the bed, the couch, and the vase of flowers to a Hollywood studio, it wouldn't have the same look."[39]

Wilder shot the movie in the summer of 1972, with the cast and crew billeted in the Hotel Excelsior Victoria in Sorrento while on location. He selected Luigi Kuveiller as director of photography after viewing Elio Petri's *Un tranquillo posto di campagna* (*A Quiet Place in the Country*, 1968). "I loved the lucidity, the lightness, and the precision of his photography," said Wilder, and, of course, Kuveiller was an expert on local color.[40]

"Wilder was not above showing a bit of behind in the liberated 1970s," Dick observes.[41] He staged the first nude scene to be featured in a Wilder film for *Avanti!* Pamela coaxes Wendell into a rendezvous on the beach, but he is reluctant to accept her invitation to go skinny-dipping. "Where is your British reserve?" he inquires. Inevitably he gives in, and the couple swim naked in the Mediterranean Sea. When the sun comes up over Mount Vesuvius, they swim to a rock just offshore, where their parents used to sunbathe at dawn. Staggs denounces the nude swimming scene as "the least attractive scene in any movie"—from the rear, Lemmon looks like a potato. "Juliet Mills retains her dignity throughout"; Lemmon does not.[42] Conversely, Crowe judges the nudity to be "delicately layered and purposeful," since it represents the first genuine intimate moment that Wendell and Pamela share.[43]

Michel Ciment noted that Wilder had Ralph Winters come over to Italy to make the preliminary edit of each scene during shooting. As a result, Winters prepared the final cut in short order. "Although I liked it very much, at 144 minutes I thought it was far too long," writes Walter Mirisch. "It's difficult to sustain a comedy at that length. I felt it would play much better if it were shorter, but Billy disagreed."[44] Wilder pointed out that *Avanti!* had previewed better than *Sherlock Holmes* and that comments on the preview cards did not indicate conclusively that the picture warranted shortening. So Mirisch did not insist on deletions, as he had for *Sherlock Holmes*.

Wilder turned the film over to Carlo Rustichelli, who had just scored

*Alfredo, Alfredo* (1971), an Italian comedy that was a vehicle for Dustin Hoffman. Rustichelli punctuated his score with themes from Italian popular songs like "Un'ora sola ti vorrei." Since the film is set at the sunny Italian seashore, Rustichelli obliges with a lush, romantic Italian serenade, complete with mandolin, to accompany the opening credits.

Wendell Armbruster Jr. arrives at the Grand Hotel Excelsior, a health resort and spa on the island of Ischia in the Bay of Naples. He soon learns from Pamela Piggott of his father's annual rendezvous with Pamela's mother for the past decade. Shocked, Wendell blurts out, "You mean all the time we thought he was over here getting cured, he was getting laid? That dirty old man!"

"At its heart, it's a story of love between a father and a son," Wilder commented. "Wendell starts to understand a father whom he has never thought much about. He is closer to his father dead than when his father was living. That gives the story a certain bite." Wilder continued, "He discovers his father's past, and that gives the story its force. If I did not have that element in *Avanti!* I would have had the old story of the romance in Italy between Wendell and Pamela—a sort of *Debbie Reynolds Goes to Italy.*"[45]

Wendell Armbruster Sr. and Catherine Piggott, his inamorata, were killed when Wendell's father accidentally drove his car off a high cliff. In a key sequence, Wendell and Pamela must go to the municipal morgue to officially identify their parents' bodies. Scarfiotti discovered the location site for the morgue scene on the island of Ischia; it was actually a church situated high above the sea.[46] In this scene, Wilder adroitly mingles comedy and pathos. Mattarazzo, the coroner, is played by the Italian comedian Pippo Franco. For Wilder, Mattarazzo is a typical Italian bureaucrat. He goes through an elaborate ritual of whipping out rubber stamps and stamp pads from his coat pockets with maniacal precision. He then dutifully stamps both sets of legal documents in triplicate. Afterwards he slyly pinches Pamela's bottom.[47]

"Yet Wilder never trivializes the tragedy" that has brought Wendell and Pamela together, as Dick indicates. When they enter the morgue, Wilder captures the reverential hush "with a long shot that he holds until a shaft of sunlight comes through the circular window" and illuminates the mortuary.[48] Kuveiller's lighting of the morgue sequence gives it a haunting, wistful beauty. The sequence concludes with Pamela's leaving a bouquet of daffodils on each corpse. One is reminded that, after all, this film is "a narrative triggered by human mortality."[49]

Carlo Carlucci schemes to bring Wendell and Pamela together by recreating the romantic atmosphere experienced by their parents, and his plot succeeds. Wendell begins to wear his father's jacket, and Pamela dons her mother's dress. They even take to calling each other by the nicknames their parents had for each other, Willie and Kate. In short, "Wendell and Pamela are soon performing the same rituals as their parents did," including skinny-dipping in the Mediterranean at dawn.[50] Thus does Wilder depict the "growing love between Wendell and Pamela," Dick notes.[51] At one point Pamela explains to Wendell that, when the maid knocks and says, "Permisso" (Permission to enter), he should reply, "Avanti!" (Come ahead!) Accordingly, when Wendell wants to kiss Pamela, he says, "Permisso," and she responds, "Avanti!"

There is a scene in *Avanti!* that recalls the first film that Wilder cowrote for Lubitsch, *Bluebeard's Eighth Wife.* In that film, Nicole and Michael divide a pair of pajamas between them. In *Avanti!* when Wendell and Pamela are shown in bed together, he is wearing the pajama pants and she is wearing the tops. This is "an amusing Wilder touch," like a painter's signature on a canvas.[52]

Wendell eventually becomes exasperated by the mass of Italian governmental red tape he encounters while trying to arrange for his father's corpse to be exported to Baltimore for the funeral at the local Presbyterian church on the following Tuesday. Carlucci points out that that would involve preparing the body for shipment on a Sunday, and "no one works on Sunday—this is a Catholic country!" Wendell answers, "I'll get a dispensation from the pope." Carlucci replies that papal dispensations "are not granted to Presbyterians!" Finally, at the behest of Wendell's nagging wife, Emily, Joseph J. Blodgett, a pompous plutocrat representing the State Department, arrives to finalize the arrangements. Pamela intervenes and suggests to Wendell in private that they bury the deceased couple together in the local cemetery in Ischia, the island that was dear to them both.

At first, typically, Wendell rejects the notion out of hand. "Better yet, why not bury them in Venice like Romeo and Juliet?" (He means Verona.) Nevertheless, Wendell finally warms to her suggestion. He conspires with Carlucci to have an unclaimed body from the mortuary flown back to the United States as Wendell Armbruster Sr.—accompanied by Blodgett, who knows nothing of the scheme. The real Armbruster Sr. can thus be buried in Ischia with his mistress—in the Carlucci family plot, no less. Wendell and Pamela resolve to spend their annual summer holidays together in Ischia, "to continue the romantic tradition established by their parents."[53]

*Avanti!* opened on December 17, 1972, to largely negative notices. It was called, among other things, "sour chianti" from the once-rich Wilder vineyard and a movie populated with "caricatures rather than characters."[54]

Jay Cocks in *Time* wrote the picture off as a real snooze, calling it merely "passingly pleasant" and intermittently funny.[55] Wilder responded by describing *Time*'s reviews as "impish and vinegary," and Cocks in particular as seeing his films "with a jaundiced eye" and reviewing them "with karate chops."[56]

One of the very few positive reviews came from *Variety,* which termed the movie "a topnotch comedy; it is the type of divertissement all too often lacking in today's market, a whacky comedy which provides pleasurable entertainment." Yet even *Variety* complained about the movie's length.[57] Indeed, the prevailing criticism in the notices was that the film clocked in at two hours and twenty-four minutes, way too long for a romantic comedy—just as Walter Mirisch had contended. It seems that, in opening out the play for the screen, Wilder and Diamond did their job unwisely and too well, for the film is too long and heavy with plot details. *Avanti!* would have been a better movie had the ending been placed closer to the beginning.

*Avanti!* was produced at a cost of $2.7 million and grossed only a modest $4.5 million. Not surprisingly, given its Italian setting and story, *Avanti!* earned bigger box office returns in Europe than in the United States. It received no Oscar nominations. (Wilder quipped that he agreed with Bob Hope: the Oscar ceremonies should be called Passover, as far as he was concerned.) Nevertheless, the picture received six Golden Globe nominations from the Foreign Press Association, for best comedy, director, actor, actress, supporting actor (Revill), and screenplay. Lemmon alone won a Golden Globe.

The critics' gruff dismissal of *Avanti!* when it was released has softened over the years. It is now thought to be a more sophisticated and tasteful film than when it first appeared. Sarris, as mentioned, initiated the reconsideration of Wilder's 1970s films, placing *Avanti!* next to *Sherlock Holmes* as a "mellow masterpiece" of Wilder's later period.[58] Similarly, Morris writes in his revisionist essay on Wilder's later work, "In *Avanti!* Wilder accepts with equanimity the approach of age and the potential for happiness between a man and a woman. It is his most affirmative, hopeful film."[59] But at the time, Wilder was depressed by the critical and popular rejection of the movie. He later reflected that, like *Sherlock Holmes, Avanti!* was "too mild, too soft, too gentle. The picture was fifteen years too late."[60]

In making *The Front Page,* Wilder said, he had tried to be "as subtle and elegant as possible," directing it in a manner that recalled the films of his mentor, Ernst Lubitsch.[61] Wilder still looked at the motto on his office wall whenever he made a creative decision: "How would Lubitsch do it?" A journalist inquired whether it was still possible to make successful movies in the

Lubitsch style. Wilder's reply was rueful, not to say bitter: "The time of Lubitsch is past. It's just a loss of something marvelous, the loss of a style I aspired to."[62]

In 1975 he explained, "Today we are dealing with an audience that is primarily under twenty-five and devoid of any literary tradition. They prefer mindless violence to solid plotting and character development; . . . four-letter words to intelligent dialogue. Nobody *listens* anymore. They just sit there waiting to be assaulted by a series of shocks and sensations."[63] A film-maker now had to come at people with a sledgehammer, he continued. Audiences did not want to see a picture "unless Clint Eastwood has got a machine gun bigger than 140 penises," or a handgun the size of a howitzer. A movie hero has to have a dirty jockstrap and a raincoat. There is a different set of values today. Something which is warm and gentle and funny and urbane and civilized hasn't got a chance."[64]

*Avanti!* was the last movie in Wilder's contract with the Mirisch Company and its distributor, UA. Transamerica Corporation, a conglomerate that owned an insurance company and many other diverse business interests, had acquired UA in 1967. The present executives at UA, prompted by the administration of Transamerica, pressured the Mirisches not to renew the contracts of their directors.

For his part, Wilder was convinced that it was time to look for fresh challenges elsewhere. His relationship with the Mirisch Company had lasted fourteen years and yielded eight movies. He decided that freelancing was the order of the day. "Wilder was eager to move on," Walter Mirisch writes, "and so without any animus whatsoever between us," Wilder and the Mirisches went their separate ways.[65] Having made *The Front Page* for Universal, Wilder wondered whether the studio would be interested in another project he had in mind. It was a story about an aging movie queen who is no more willing to face retirement from the screen than Norma Desmond is. As a matter of fact, this movie, to be titled *Fedora,* had several echoes of Wilder's most acclaimed drama, *Sunset Boulevard.*

# 18

# Twilight Years

## *Fedora* and *Buddy Buddy*

> There's too much dirt under the carpet; it will come out sooner or later.
>
> —*Murray Hamilton as a gossip columnist in the telefilm* Death Casts a Spell

Clay Felker, the editor of *New York* magazine, phoned Wilder in the fall of 1975 to ask him to sit for a frank interview, and Wilder agreed. After *Avanti!* was lambasted by the critics and *The Front Page* received a mixed critical response, Wilder seemed to draw energy and resolve from disdain and financial adversity.

When Felker's reporter, Jon Bradshaw, showed up for the interview, he seemed pleasantly surprised that Wilder's spirit was not broken by his commercial failures. Wilder, annoyed, opened fire: "What did you expect to find when you came out here? A broken-down director? A wizened, myopic boob in his dotage? I guess you thought you'd find me playing with my old Oscars? In a wheelchair, maybe? Poor old Billy Wilder, the great director—God, you should see him now: a wreck, a ruin!" He continued, "Well, they told you wrong; I'm not just functioning in the Motion Picture Relief Home, I feel just as confident and virile as I did thirty years ago."[1] Bradshaw chose not to reply and instead wrote in his notebook that Wilder "looked younger than his sixty-nine years" and was casually dressed: slacks, a pullover, an open shirt, and loafers. He was also wearing a golf cap—when he was a journalist, reporters always wore hats indoors, and he had worn a hat in his office and on the set ever since. Wilder occupied the same office at Universal that he had when he was making *The Front Page*, and that was where he was now working on *Fedora*. His office had once been Lucille Ball's dressing room, and his next-door neighbor was Alfred Hitchcock.

"Occasionally the vineyards produce a bad vintage," said Wilder, a reference to the critic who called *Avanti!* a bottle of sour chianti. "But there will always be another harvest." Still, "I've not hit a home run in a long time; *Irma la Douce* was a home run. By contrast, *Avanti!* was a strike-out; *The Front Page* was a nice hit and drove in a run or two, that was all. It was solid; but hell, I used to hit the solid stuff over the fences." Yet he insisted that he was undismayed. "Next time up, I'm hitting for the fences."[2]

# *Fedora* (1979)

Now that Wilder was a freelancer, he considered himself a "visiting professor" at Universal. He had a contract to prepare one project for the studio. At present he and Diamond were collaborating on the screenplay for *Fedora,* the project that Wilder was hoping would put him back in the big leagues. It was derived from the first of four novellas about Hollywood in the book *Crowned Heads* by Thomas Tryon, an actor turned writer. Wilder said he and Diamond "had been kicking around a Hollywood picture, when along came the galleys of this book."[3] The story concerns a retired Hollywood actress living in Europe.

On March 16, 1976, Universal officially announced that Wilder would make *Fedora* for the studio. Wilder, sounding a bit like Norma Desmond, commented, "It's particularly thrilling to make a comeback!"[4] He submitted the first draft of the screenplay to the studio in September 1976. He vividly remembered discussing the script with a young Universal executive in the black tower, Universal's executive office building. The studio official "could barely stay awake" because the scenario was not about "car crashes and space ships."[5]

William Holden, who plays an embittered independent producer in *Fedora,* seems to be speaking for Wilder when he proclaims, "The kids with the beards" are taking over the industry. The studios were being run by young people who had no regard for anyone's record, Wilder told me. Fred Zinnemann said he remembered being asked by a young executive to name his accomplishments, and Zinnemann replied, "You first."[6] As it happened, Wilder learned later that the executives in the black tower were having second thoughts about *Fedora.* Two recent Universal films about Hollywood's golden age had flopped: *W. C. Fields and Me* (1976) and *Gable and Lombard* (1976).

On November 19, 1976, Sidney Sheinberg, the president of Universal's parent company, the Music Corporation of America, finally decided to scuttle *Fedora.* He asked Jennings Lang, who had produced *The Front Page,* to inform Wilder. Lang phoned Wilder and indicated that Sheinberg considered *Fedora* "uncommercial."[7] In the old days, Wilder reflected, "the moguls prided themselves on doing a few prestige pictures every year; if they spent $1.5 million on some deep-dish project, that was no big deal." But with the collapse of the studio system in the 1960s, "the lights went out in Hollywood," said Wilder. "The result is a terror of taking risks"; the majors became increasingly cautious about marketing a dark film to an audience glutted on placebo entertainment.[8]

Wilder walked off the Universal lot for good. While continuing to work with Diamond on the final draft of the screenplay of *Fedora,* he shopped the project around town. But he was unable to interest a major studio in it after Universal passed on it. He found himself catapulted back into the 1930s, "peddling a project nobody wanted to buy."[9]

In the screenplay, Fedora continues her glamorous Hollywood career as a youthful-looking superstar well into middle age. When she retires from the screen after her face is disfigured by plastic surgery, "she trains her daughter Antonia to assume her legend," pretending to be her. George Morris notes that "the audacity of this imposture would have made Norma Desmond green with envy."[10] Fedora herself assumes the identity of Countess Sobryanski and lives in seclusion on a remote Greek island. Fedora wanted "to go on forever," Wilder commented. "She did not want to be seen shriveled in a wheelchair, in retirement." Wilder observed that *Fedora* was something like Oscar Wilde's *The Picture of Dorian Gray,* in which Dorian sells his soul to retain his youth and beauty. Wilder mused that the film should have been called "*The Picture of Dorian Gray,* by Oscar Wilder."[11] Foster Hirsch asserts that "the real-life model for Fedora was clearly Greta Garbo," and Wilder never denied it.[12] Not only has Fedora become a recluse like Garbo in her later years, but Wilder identifies one of Fedora's greatest movies as *Anna Karenina,* in which Garbo starred in 1935.

Wilder still had a penchant for slipping wisecracks about other movies into a script. The countess recalls losing an Oscar to the actress "who played a nun with tuberculosis." Audrey Hepburn, Wilder's old friend, had played that part in *The Nun's Story* (1959), but it was for *Roman Holiday* that she won an Academy Award. And, as the *New York Times* pointed out, Wilder "shaped and toughened the story in ways that inevitably recall *Sunset Boulevard,* as does the casting of William Holden, the gigolo in *Sunset Boulevard,* as the seedy, down-on-his-luck producer Barry Detweiler, in *Fedora.*"[13]

Wilder eventually grew tired of "dragging my ass along Hollywood Boulevard" like Barry, looking in vain for a studio to fund his film.[14] In desperation he turned to his agent Paul Kohner to obtain financing for *Fedora* from a German studio, since Kohner, another refugee from Hitler's Germany, still had connections in the German film industry. Kohner put in a call to the production chief at Bavaria Film Studios in Munich, where Wilder had shot *One, Two, Three,* and inquired whether he would like Billy Wilder to make a picture there for the studio. Kohner got an affirmative response and informed Wilder that the movie would be financed through Bavaria Film Studios' subsidiary, Geria Films. The budget was fixed at $6.7 million.[15]

"I have some kind of reputation in Germany," Wilder mused; "why, I don't know, because, when I left Germany, I was just one of the writers at Ufa. Suddenly the mantle of F. W. Murnau, Fritz Lang, and Ernst Lubitsch falls on my shoulders." Geria Films held a reception for Wilder to announce the production. "My God," thought Wilder, "old Ufa is going to rise again!"[16]

Universal still held the distribution rights to *Fedora* as a result of its original investment in the project. So Wilder, nursing a grudge against the studio, bought out Universal's interest in the picture. In effect, Wilder personally reimbursed Universal for its purchase of the screen rights to the Tryon novella for him. As one Hollywood insider put it, "Sid Sheinberg not only pulled the rug out from under Billy, he tried to sell it back to him!"[17]

Wilder's original casting plan was to have the same young actress play both Fedora, now known as Countess Sobryanski, and her daughter Antonia. He would age the actress for the scenes in which she played the countess. He selected Marthe Keller after attending an advance screening of *Bobby Deerfield* (1977), in which she played opposite Al Pacino. Keller was a Swiss actress who had appeared primarily in French films. Wilder eventually decided that Keller would be satisfactory as Antonia, but he feared that she lacked the range to play the elderly countess. Moreover, he found Keller temperamental and sensed that she would be difficult enough to handle in playing the one part. So Wilder needed another actress to play Antonia's mother.

His first choice was his old confrere from his Berlin days, Marlene Dietrich, whom he had directed in two films. He quickly sent off a copy of the screenplay to the reclusive Dietrich at her Paris apartment. Wilder later remembered that she shot back the screenplay to him by return mail, "as if she couldn't get rid of it fast enough." She attached an abrupt note: "I hated the script, and I don't know why you want me to do it. How could you possibly think that?"[18] Perhaps Dietrich felt that the increasingly strained relationship of Fedora and her daughter Antonia was uncomfortably close to her problematic relationship with her own daughter, Maria Riva. Moreover, Dietrich, at her advanced age, no longer wished to be photographed.

Keller herself suggested the German actress Hildegard Knef for the part. "Twenty years Dietrich's junior, Hildegard was Marlene's protegé," writes David Riva, Dietrich's grandson; she was also one of Germany's top stars.[19] Moreover, Knef had scored a personal triumph on Broadway in 1955 in *Silk Stockings,* a Cole Porter musical derived from *Ninotchka.* She had played in some Hollywood films, but she was better known for her European pictures.

Michael York plays himself in *Fedora,* as do Arlene Francis (who was in *One, Two, Three*) and Henry Fonda, who plays the president of the motion picture academy. The presence of these individuals, Wilder pointed out, adds an authentic flavor to the film, just as the appearances by Cecil B. De Mille, Buster Keaton, and Hedda Hopper do in *Sunset Boulevard.*

Although the cinematographer Gerry Fisher (*The Go-Between,* 1971) had not worked with Wilder before, composer Miklos Rozsa and production designer Alexander Trauner were creative associates of Wilder's from way back. Rozsa was collaborating on his fifth Wilder film and Trauner on his eighth.

Principal photography began on June 1, 1977, in the Greek isles, where Fedora goes to live after her retirement from the screen. Wilder and his film unit started out on the island of Corfu, with four days of exteriors. They moved on to the island of Mandouri, where Trauner had found an isolated house that would serve as Fedora's Villa Calpyso. Wilder wanted so much to finish on time and not go over budget, to please his German investors, that he reduced the rehearsal time on each scene. Keller complained that she never felt that she had nailed her characterization of Antonia "because Billy Wilder never discussed anything. You had to do what he said; and I felt a bit like a marionette."[20]

Wilder and his production unit moved on to Bavaria Film Studios to shoot interiors. Fisher had exploited the natural locations in the Greek islands to exquisite effect. While shooting the scenes in Fedora's mansion, with its dilapidated grandeur, on the studio soundstages, Fisher gave the film a bleak look, "reflecting the wasteland of the spirit" experienced by the inhabitants. As Verina Glaessner writes, in these latter scenes Fisher helped to undercut the "inherent nostalgia" of this tale of old Hollywood.[21]

Rex McGee records that, "in late July, Wilder and Diamond viewed about an hour of the footage" already edited by Stefan Arsten, and they "decided that they needed a new editor."[22] So Wilder fired Arsten and phoned Ralph Winters, who had cut *Avanti!* and *The Front Page.* Winters was involved in another film, but he suggested Fredric Steinkamp, who had won an Academy Award for coediting *Grand Prix* (1966). Wilder was also much impressed with Steinkamp's editing of *Bobby Deerfield.*

In August Wilder and his production team moved on to Paris, to finish the shoot at the Studios de Boulogne, where he had filmed *Love in the Afternoon*. Here Wilder staged Fedora's elaborate funeral, which is held in Paris. Trauner outdid himself by constructing a huge set, complete with marble pillars, splendid candelabra, and a wrought iron gallery above the casket, where the countess and her entourage sit, presiding over the proceedings. "This is a triple-A funeral," Wilder beamed. But "behind Wilder's jauntiness on the set," journalist Mary Blume observed, "the pressure shows. He has started smoking again, trying to limit himself to a particularly nasty French cigar, of which even he can only smoke three a day." Wilder confessed that shooting indoors for long periods gave him cabin fever. "Being quarantined on a sound stage and not being able to walk down a Paris boulevard," he said, "is like being a pianist in a bordello while hearing the people screwing on every floor. It makes you crazy."[23]

Principal photography wrapped on August 31, 1977, with Wilder having gone a few thousand dollars over budget, not enough for his German investors to complain about. Within a few days, he was back in Hollywood. Wilder and Steinkamp rented an editing suite at Twentieth Century–Fox to cut the film. They finished the first cut on October 20.[24]

During postproduction, a serious problem developed for Wilder. He was convinced that Antonia and the countess should have the same voice, since the daughter was impersonating her mother throughout much of the movie. But Marthe Keller and Hildegard Knef did not sound enough alike to sustain the illusion. Wilder decided to have the same German actress, Inga Bunsch, rerecord both Keller's and Knef's dialogue. Knef resented this turn of events: "First he destroys my face," when Fedora is disfigured; "now he takes away my voice. What is left?"[25] Surprisingly, Keller accepted Wilder's decision to redub her voice, although she insisted that her own voice be employed in the final scenes of the movie, when Antonia is no longer masquerading as Fedora.

Miklos Rozsa was summoned to view the rough cut in October so he could get going on his background music. He was glad to be collaborating with Wilder again. In a 1974 interview, he said that he never forgot how Wilder went to bat for him when Louis Lipstone, head of Paramount's music department, disliked the dissonance in Rozsa's scores for Wilder's pictures. Rozsa would telephone Wilder and say, "Billy, save me from this son-of-a-bitch!" And Wilder would always oblige.[26] Rozsa recorded his score with a symphony orchestra in mid-December 1977. He matched Wilder's film about old Hollywood with a "deliberately nostalgic" accompaniment.[27]

Lorimer Productions, the American representative of Bavaria Film

Studios and Geria Films, was supposed to arrange for the distribution of the movie nationwide. On March 15, 1978, Wilder screened *Fedora* for Lorimar executives. Their verdict was that the film ran long at 128 minutes, and they declined to release the film at that length. Wilder and Steinkamp accordingly excised 15 minutes from the film.[28]

On May 12, Wilder held a preview at the State Theatre in Santa Barbara, where *Sherlock Holmes* had had a favorable sneak screening. "The first half of *Fedora* played well," McGee reports, "but midway into the film the audience began to get restless." There were a number of inexplicable laughs, known in the industry as "bad laughs."[29] David Picker, a UA executive, told me in conversation after a screening of a UA film in 1980 that he had attended the Santa Barbara preview of *Fedora*. That did not deter him from picking up the distribution rights of *Fedora* after Lorimer lost interest in the movie. He did so "for old times' sake," he explained; after all, UA had previously been Wilder's distributor for fourteen years.

*Fedora* had its official world premiere at the Cannes Film Festival on the closing night of the festival, May 30, 1978. The premiere was preceded by a retrospective of Wilder's movies. "The French are great *homage* givers," Wilder joked, with a mischievous smile; they even had one for Jerry Lewis.[30] The response to *Fedora* was sharply divided: European critics loved it. American reviewers did not cotton to it, and some sneered or laughed inappropriately. Andrew Sarris commented, "The usual collection of freeloading trend-setters were reportedly laughing at all the wrong places. There is nothing quite so hideously heartless as the idiot cackle of the in-crowd when it senses that a career may be on the skids."[31]

Still, the screening at Cannes gave the film worldwide publicity, and Wilder was keenly disappointed that UA did not release *Fedora* in the United States soon after. By then he had been involved with the picture for well over two years. "In that time I could have made three lousy pictures, instead of one," he quipped.[32] As a matter of fact, UA kept *Fedora* on the shelf until May 1979—a full year after its Cannes debut. To make matters worse, "the limited release and publicity hampered the film's chances for success," Glenn Hopp points out.[33] Wilder complained about UA's "releasing it in an insulting and perfunctory way and spending peanuts on the advertising campaign."[34]

Like *Sunset Boulevard*, *Fedora* uses a flashback format to tell its story. The present film begins with Fedora (actually Antonia) throwing herself in the path of an oncoming train, just as the tragic heroine of *Anna Karenina* does. This precredit sequence continues with Arlene Francis, playing herself, announcing Fedora's death on a TV newscast. After the opening credits, there follows Fedora's wake, held in her florid mansion in Paris. "As the crowds file past her coffin," Morris writes, "the jigsaw puzzle of Fedora's past is pieced together through the recollections of her retinue and one of the mourners, Barry Detweiler."[35] It is their reminiscences that are portrayed in flashback throughout the movie. "She was going out in style," says Barry, in voice-over on the sound track, "complete with TV cameras, like a goddamned Hollywood premiere."

The real Fedora explains to Barry in a tête-à-tête during the wake that she took the name of Countess Sobryanski after Antonia began impersonating her, since the count was Antonia's father. Nevertheless, she and the count never married; they were separated by World War II. She could not acknowledge Antonia's existence because of the morals clause in her contract with MGM. "Remember those days?" she asks Barry. "You couldn't have an illegitimate child" because that constituted "moral turpitude," which could cause an actor to be suspended indefinitely.

The countess narrates for Barry the horrific episode in which the plastic surgeon Vando's botched experiment (after two decades of success) disfigured her face. Dr. Vando (José Ferrer) explains that, after the failed treatment, "an infection set in; there were complications." He adds ominously, "You can't cheat nature without paying the price." Fedora, "wheelchairbound because of a facelift run amok," retires from the screen.[36]

Henry Fonda, playing himself, is the president of the motion picture academy. Early in the film, he makes a pilgrimage to Fedora's secluded island retreat to present her with a special Oscar for lifetime achievement. Antonia agrees to double for her mother for the occasion and succeeds in fooling Fonda. Afterward Fedora conceives the plan of continuing her career with Antonia standing in for her. For years Antonia impersonates her mother, both on- and offscreen, until Antonia becomes soured on the masquerade. Matters come to a head when she costars with Michael York, playing himself, in *The Last Waltz*, a period costume picture. Antonia is shown shooting a syrupy scene for the picture with her leading man. The opulent ballroom filled with waltzing couples recalls Wilder's own *Emperor Waltz*, indicating that Wilder was quite capable of self-parody. At heart, Antonia is still a young girl. She falls hopelessly in love with Michael, but she is prohibited by her mother from revealing her true identity to Michael in order to perpetuate the illusion of the "ageless Fedora" for her fans.

Antonia is faced with the prospect of continuing to impersonate her mother while being deprived of a life of her own. As Kevin Lally notes, Antonia's mother is able to continue her career vicariously, "by robbing her own daughter of her identity."[37] Antonia sinks into a deep depression and takes refuge in drugs, ending her film career. Barry Detweiler comes to

Europe to visit the reclusive Fedora. He hopes to coax her into making a comeback in a remake of *Anna Karenina*, called *The Snows of Yesteryear*, so that he can revive his own stalled career as a producer. Of course, it is Antonia he meets in the guise of Fedora. She declines his offer of a comeback, but they part on friendly terms. "Time catches up with us all," she says as he leaves.

Soon afterward Barry returns to Europe for Fedora's funeral; it is only then that he learns from the countess, and from others as well, the truth behind Antonia's tragic life and death. By film's end, the movie has come full circle; it concludes by returning to Fedora's wake, which is really Antonia's wake. At one point during her conference with Barry, Countess Sobryanski, the real Fedora, raises her veil to expose her withered countenance. Her action is a metaphor for the manner in which she has lifted for Barry the veil of secrecy.

Barry reflects that an actress must be sugar and spice on the surface, "but underneath, cement and steel." Antonia, unlike her mother, was not made that way. At this point, Michael York appears at the wake and approaches the coffin. He places a red rose on Antonia's chest—for him, as for the endless stream of mourners, Antonia is Fedora.

"You sure know how to throw yourself a funeral," Barry remarks to the countess. She muses that Fedora is a legend, and "a legend must not linger beyond her time. Monroe and Harlow, they were the lucky ones." Before the end credits roll, Fedora adds, "Endings are very important—the final close-up—that is what people remember; the legend must go on."

The film played first-run engagements in select cities. Richard Schickel, calling the movie "old hat" in *Time*, pronounced Wilder's "melodramatic manner of storytelling" to be old-fashioned.[38] Admittedly, Wilder responded, his care for narrative structure and character development had become unfashionable in Hollywood. "They call it old-fashioned; that's the only way I know to work." So "that's the way I'm going to do it until they take the cameras away."[39] Elsewhere he added, "They say Wilder is out of touch with the times. Frankly, I regard that as a compliment. Who the hell wants to be in touch with these times?"[40]

The negative buzz about the picture occasioned Vincent Canby's remark that "*Fedora* is such a seasoned, elegant, and funny film that it exists serenely above lobby talk." Because "Wilder's reputation is subject to more revisions than a White House press release," Canby emphasized "the necessity, finally, to recognize Billy Wilder as the major filmmaker he is." *Fedora* was the work of "a brilliant, irascible man who is nearly thirty years more experienced in the woeful ways of the world than he was when he made

*Sunset Boulevard.*"[41] The film's humor is grotesque, sometimes disturbing; the movie is a unique blend of austerity and romanticism. Moreover, Keller's performance was underrated, even by Wilder. As Antonia, she starts out fragile and then reveals strength and calculation as she attempts to evade the power of those who would control her.

*Fedora* did poorly at the box office after its initial engagements in big cities and did not reach a wide audience elsewhere. Be that as it may, the picture was well received in Europe, especially in Germany, where Knef was still a star, and in France, where Keller was popular.

Although *Fedora* received unenthusiastic notices when it appeared, like *The Private Life of Sherlock Holmes,* it has over the years earned a solid critical reputation as an elegant, entertaining film that reaches the lofty realm of tragedy. In 2002, the *Times* of London went so far as to call *Fedora* "perhaps the richest of Wilder's later films."[42] Cameron Crowe comments, "If *Fedora* missed the upper rung of Wilder's greatest work, it's only a matter of inches."[43] Morris concurs that *Fedora* "is a worthy addition to the work of one of the supreme artists of the American cinema."[44]

For William Holden, alcohol had been a problem as far back as *Sabrina*. By 1977, when he made *Fedora,* "he realized his most significant accomplishments were behind him. He grew despondent and isolated, and his drinking worsened."[45] On November 16, 1981, Holden was found dead in his apartment by the building manager. His death was caused by his tripping over a throw rug while intoxicated, "then falling into the sharp edge of a bedside table."[46] The following month, Wilder told the *New York Times,* "To be killed by a bottle of vodka and a night table—what a lousy fadeout for a great guy."[47]

Asked why he kept working if he felt out of place in the current Hollywood climate, Wilder answered, "If only to get away from the vacuum cleaner. I come to work the typewriter" in his office. In one of his more melodramatic moments, Wilder declared in a 1978 interview, "I will kill myself after this interview; I have just come to the conclusion that it's no use."[48]

Nevertheless, Wilder's thoughts inevitably turned to his next picture as he searched to find "something that is negotiable with studios." The modest ticket sales of *Fedora* had made the movie a calamity for Wilder, given his recent track record. It was tougher than ever to sell a new project to a studio. Moreover, he had to be cautious in selecting a project now that there were not many bullets left in "the elderly gun." After making *Fedora* in the Greek islands, Munich, and Paris, Wilder renewed his resolution to shoot his next movie in greater Los Angeles, since location shooting in Europe was expensive. Furthermore, "I don't have to climb any fucking mountains," he explained, and "I don't have to eat crappy food and have diarrhea." Shooting around Los Angeles, "it takes only seven minutes to get to a location."[49]

In the wake of Universal's vetoing *Fedora,* Wilder was afraid that the major studios had written him off as over the hill. He had grown tired, he said, of pitching projects to young executives who were former employees of the studio mailroom. Much to his surprise, Jay Weston, a producer at MGM, invited him to make *Buddy Buddy.* The project was offered to him, Wilder emphasized; he did not have to audition: "No screen test!" Nevertheless, it was not a project that he would have chosen; "it chose *me.*" He continued, "Maybe I was a little tired of hitting my head against the wall; maybe it was a little dented."[50] Still, one reason that Weston's offer appealed to him was that Jack Lemmon and Walter Matthau agreed to costar in the picture if Wilder directed.

## *Buddy Buddy* (1981)

The film was to be based on a French play by Francis Weber, a boulevard farce titled *L'emmerdeur.* Weber also wrote the screenplay for the 1973 French film version directed by Edouard Molinaro. The movie was also called *L'emmerdeur* but was released in the United States the following year as *A Pain in the Neck* (or *A Pain in the Ass*). Wilder's *Buddy Buddy* is a black comedy about the friendship that gradually develops between a tough Mafia hit man (Walter Matthau) and a woebegone individual (Jack Lemmon) who contemplates suicide after his wife leaves him. In the French movie version, Lino Ventura, an Italian actor, played the tough contract killer, Milan, and Jacques Brel, a popular French entertainer, played the would-be suicide, Pegnon.

One reason that Weber's play appealed to Wilder was that it carried some resonance of the first screenplay he coauthored at Ufa, *Der Mann, der seinen Mörder sucht* (The man who tried to get himself killed, 1931). In it a pathetic wretch bent on killing himself becomes involved with a thief (rather than a hit man).

On May 12, 1980, Wilder drove through the gates at MGM after an absence of four decades. The studio had changed in many ways. James Aubrey, known in the industry as "the smiling cobra," had been appointed president of MGM in 1970, with a mandate to bail the studio out of debt. Aubrey went on an economy drive while the studio was fending off its creditors. By the end of the decade, however, the studio was back on track, and

David Begelman was brought over from Columbia as production chief, with a view to stepping up production. "They want to bring back the roaring lion," said Wilder.[51] One of the first projects Begelman approved was *Buddy Buddy*.

The studio was anxious to get moving on *Buddy Buddy*, since it boasted two top stars and a major director. Wilder and Diamond were encouraged to write their screenplay with dispatch. They complied by finishing the first draft in July 1981, after only two months, a much speedier job than was customary for them. In their script Milan became Trabucco, a paid assassin who has contracted to eradicate a crucial witness in a Palm Springs land fraud scandal. Pegnon is renamed Victor Clooney, a prudish censor employed in the Office of Standards and Practices at CBS-TV. His screwball wife, Celia, is enrolled in a sex clinic called the Institute for Sexual Fulfillment, where she has fallen in love with the director, Dr. Zuckerbrot.

The screenplay bears the marks of a typical Wilder scenario. When Victor assumes, quite wrongly, that Trabucco sympathizes with him about his wife's desertion, Victor says he has always believed "in the kindness of strangers," quoting Blanche DuBois in *A Streetcar Named Desire* (1951). The stool pigeon Rudy Gambola is called "the man who knew too much," the name of a 1956 Hitchcock picture.

On the one hand, Victor's efforts to develop a friendship with Trabucco recall Wilder's trilogy about male bonding. On the other hand, there was a measure of tenderness in the friendships portrayed in *The Fortune Cookie, Sherlock Holmes,* and *The Front Page;* there is none in *Buddy Buddy*. Victor's attempts to ingratiate himself with Trabucco are ill advised, to say the least. Wilder "cast a cold eye" on the theme of male bonding in the present film. After all, notes Axel Madsen, he spent his formative years in Berlin during the Roaring Twenties, a crucible of disenchantment, a society full of decadence. He learned to reflect bitterly "upon man's essential, constitutional foolishness."[52]

In rounding out the cast of *Buddy Buddy* during preproduction, Wilder selected Paula Prentiss, a comedienne, to play Celia. Prentiss was adept at playing flighty females, as in *The World of Henry Orient* opposite Peter Sellers (1964). Wilder selected German actor Klaus Kinski to play Dr. Zuckerbrot. The brilliant but unbridled actor was best known for his German films with Werner Herzog, such as *Aguirre, der Zorn Gottes* (*Aguirre, the Wrath of God*, 1972). Joan Shawlee, whose first Wilder film was *Some Like It Hot*, was back again, this time as the receptionist at the sex clinic who cheerfully repeats to callers the institute's slogan, "Ecstasy is our business."

Wilder decided on the county courthouse in Riverside, California, about an hour's drive from Los Angeles, as an important location site for the movie. The screenplay dictated that there be a hotel across the street from the courthouse, so production designer Daniel Lomino constructed a mock-Spanish hotel facade in a parking lot facing the courthouse.

Principal photography began on February 4, 1981. Wilder filmed exteriors in and around Riverside throughout February. Cinematographer Harry Stradling Jr. (*The Way We Were*, 1973) had a reputation for being at his best while shooting outdoors with color photography. His reputation was fully justified by his camerawork around the county courthouse.

Wilder was scheduled to spend March and April shooting at MGM in Culver City. After the first two weeks of filming, he realized that he had "taken a wrong turn" in casting two comedians in the leads. "I needed someone serious as the hit man, like Clint Eastwood, instead of a comic actor like Matthau," Wilder explained. Indeed, Lino Venturo, who played the contract killer in the French film, was a serious actor who specialized in playing tough guys. Wilder complained that, if the studio had not insisted that the script be finished in a scant two months, he would have seen that he had gone wrong and taken the time to go back to the drawing board. But at this point the production was moving forward, and he had to continue. He would have liked to walk off the picture, "but if I had backed out, they would have said it was because I was too old."[53]

To make matters worse, during the eighth week of shooting, Matthau took a serious fall while rehearsing a scene in which Trabucco escapes from the police by sliding down a laundry chute in the hotel. Matthau was to land on a mattress beneath the chute, but the mattress was not placed in the proper position. So when Matthau tumbled out of the chute, he landed on his back and hit his head on the concrete floor of the soundstage. Chris Lemmon writes that his father, "beside himself with concern, thought that was the end for his good buddy. He folded up his jacket and placed it under Walter's head." Then, "with tears in his eyes, he looked down at Matthau and asked, 'Are you comfortable?'" Matthau replied, "I make a living."[54] Matthau was in the hospital for only three days, but he hobbled around on crutches and wore a neck brace for three weeks. He recalled the heart attack he suffered while filming *The Fortune Cookie*. "Every time I work with Billy Wilder," Matthau observed, "I either get a heart attack or fall down and break my back."[55]

Klaus Kinski, a great German character actor who was also a pugnacious and unruly performer, shared Dietrich's opinion of Wilder as too officious on the movie set. "No outsider can understand," he writes in his autobiography, "the blustering hysteria and the authoritarianism of shooting a picture for Billy Wilder. The so-called 'actors' are simply trained poodles, who sit up on their hind legs and jump through hoops."[56] It is somewhat surprising that middle European actors like Kinski and Dietrich did not get along with Wilder, himself a middle European, on the set.

For his part, Lemmon noticed that Wilder seemed more tense while shooting this picture than he had on any of their previous pictures together, since he wanted very much to show the studio brass that he could still make a picture on schedule and on budget. He was not as open to actors' suggestions as he had been when Lemmon worked with him before. "There was a little less freedom for the actors," and Lemmon therefore kept his suggestions to himself.[57]

Still, Wilder had not lost his sense of humor. The camera operator found "the master" intimidating; the young man would ask Wilder's "kind permission" to adjust the lens. Finally Wilder just told him what he had said to Raymond Chandler four decades earlier: "For God's sake, we don't have court manners around here." At all events, the production wrapped on April 27, 1981. After directing the last scene on the docket, Wilder turned to Diamond and said, "Nice working with you, Iz."[58]

During postproduction, *Buddy Buddy* was scored by Lalo Schifrin, who had done the music for films like *Dirty Harry* (1971). Schifrin could underscore a film in the traditional symphonic manner of composers of the Hollywood studio period like Franz Waxman and Miklos Rozsa. But his eclectic style also reflected his taste for modern music, especially jazz. By the time he wrote the music for *Buddy Buddy*, Palmer notes, Schifrin had become "the most prominent and productive member of the new generation of film composers."[59]

After Schifrin had recorded his score and Wilder had collaborated with editor Argyle Nelson on the rough cut, MGM had a test screening of the picture. The younger members of the audience found the movie dull in spots, even though the film ran only ninety-eight minutes—the shortest movie Wilder had made since *Five Graves to Cairo*. Diamond commented afterward that teenagers "watch television in fifteen-minute chunks, and they aren't interested in following a plot."[60]

*Buddy Buddy* begins with Trabucco driving down a palm-lined street in suburban California. Schifrin accompanies the scene with "The Gnomes," a bizarre theme borrowed from Modest Mussorgsky's *Pictures at an Exhibition*. Trabucco checks in at the Ramona Hotel in Riverside and sets about meticulously assembling his high-powered rifle in his hotel room. He places it on a tripod in preparation for picking off Rudy Gambola, the mobster who is to testify that afternoon in the courthouse across the street. Trabucco aims to prevent the stool pigeon from getting a chance to sing.

Meanwhile, Victor Clooney, the clumsy schnook in the room next door, plans to kill himself because his wife, Celia, has run off with Dr. Hugo Zuckerbrot, the shady director of the Institute for Sexual Fulfillment. Victor ties the rope from the window curtain around a pipe in the bathroom and stands on the toilet seat. But he is such a loser that, when he steps off the toilet seat, the pipe bursts and he is deluged with gushing water. Trabucco hears the ruckus and checks out the adjoining room. He introduces himself to Victor as an expert in "pest control." Victor tells Trabucco his sad story, and the assassin, suspecting that Victor's suicide attempts will result in the police swarming all over the hotel, cunningly offers to drive Victor to the sex clinic to see Celia.

Victor assumes that Trabucco's offer is the act of a true friend, but Trabucco tells him ruefully, "I'm nobody's friend." The naive Victor responds, "People are basically good; take you for instance." Little wonder that *Buddy Buddy* has been called Wilder's blackest comedy.

The sequence at the sex institute offered Wilder a chance to open out the play for the screen, since the play is set entirely in the hotel. Victor is shocked to learn from Celia that she has had her wedding ring melted down and that it now hangs, shaped like a gold penis, around Zuckerbrot's neck. Victor, the conservative TV censor, cannot bring himself to utter the word *penis,* so he refers to the golden keepsake with "the *p* word."

Unfortunately, Victor gets nowhere trying to win back his wife, so both he and Trabucco wind up returning to the hotel. Victor, who is determined to kill himself, tells the clerk to prepare his bill. "Are you checking out?" the clerk inquires, and Victor responds, "You might say that." Back in his hotel room, Trabucco hears what sounds like a gunshot from Victor's room, only to find that Victor has just popped the cork of a champagne bottle. He is planning to toast Celia before "checking out." This gag, of course, was lifted from the last scene of *The Apartment.* Wilder saw nothing wrong with stealing from himself.

Celia reads the suicide note that Victor left with her. Although she does not want to reconcile with him, she asks Zuckerbrot to go to the hotel and talk him out of killing himself. At the hotel Zuckerbrot runs into Trabucco and assumes that he is Victor. Zuckerbrot injects Trabucco with a sedative because Victor is "a fruitcake"—Dr. Eggelhofer's term for Earl Williams— and he thinks he is sedating Victor.

Now Trabucco, groggy from the tranquilizer, is in no condition to shoot Gambola. He convinces Victor that Gambola is a "goddamned stoolie," a sleazy Mafia hood who does not deserve to live. Wilder sees to it that the mobster is not the object of the audience's sympathy, so that they do not really care if he is assassinated. Moreover, Trabucco tells Victor, if he does not rub out Gambola, the mob will exterminate him in reprisal. Still grateful that Trabucco drove him to the sex clinic to see Celia, Victor agrees to carry out Trabucco's contract killing as a favor: "I owe you one." After assorted twists and turns in the plot, Victor succeeds in blowing Gambola away. He and Trabucco escape from the hotel by diving down a laundry chute into a laundry basket and exiting through the basement.

The cops have cordoned off the street as a crime scene. So Trabucco disguises himself as a priest, donning a Roman collar and black shirt, and places a small statue of Christ on the dashboard of his car. Trabucco talks to Captain Hubris, the officer in charge, in a phony Irish brogue. Hubris requests that he give the last rites to Gambola, an Italian Catholic. Trabucco marshals every Latin phrase he can think of and "blesses" the dying gangster: "Tempus fugit" (time flies), "e pluribus unum" (out of many, one), and "caveat emptor" (let the buyer beware). Hubris then allows Trabucco to drive through the roadblock with Victor.

In the epilogue, Trabucco has escaped to a deserted tropical island. He is in a South Sea paradise—until Victor arrives in a sailboat. Victor is likewise a fugitive, having blown up the sex clinic! Celia has deserted Zuckerbrot and taken off with the clinic's female receptionist. Victor still blindly believes that in Trabucco he has found a true friend, and the disgruntled Trabucco realizes that he is stuck with Victor indefinitely. He surreptitiously suggests to his native houseboy that the local tribe reinstate its ancient custom of making human sacrifices to the gods, with a view to offering Victor as a candidate. The movie ends with a freeze-frame of Trabucco chomping on a cigar. "It is the final black moment of Wilder's career," notes Hopp. His last film concludes with no moral awakening, no redemption for the two fugitives.[61]

The world premiere of *Buddy Buddy* took place at Avco Centre Cinemas in Westwood on Friday, December 8, 1981. The film opened on December 11 to largely disappointing reviews. On the positive side, Vincent Canby in the *New York Times* called the film "the breeziest comedy Wilder has been associated with in years."[62] On the negative side, Kevin Thomas wrote in the *Los Angeles Times* that "*Buddy Buddy* isn't all that funny." The humor on the sexual revolution of the 1970s triggered by Zuckerbrot's sex clinic was "pretty familiar by now," and the film was only "mildly amusing."[63] David Ansen weighed in with a review in *Newsweek* headed "Some Like It Not." He declared that Wilder's untypically creaky slapstick and leaden gags made him wonder when Wilder was last at the movies. Was the director who was once ahead of his time now behind the times?[64]

Dr. Jack Green, a behavioral psychologist at Rush Medical Center in Chicago, called the picture "a romp about would-be assassins, inadequate husbands, immoral therapists, and errant wives. Wilder plays out his own attitude relative to the mob, the police, and psychiatry. In other venues, Wilder has demonstrated genius. In this tribute to inadequacy, he has shown everyone in it at their worst; no one is likeable and everyone is one-dimensional. There is an aftertaste of disdain that overlays the film." A psychiatrist at the center said, "The purpose of the profit-oriented Institute of Sexual Fulfillment is total sexual freedom for all (illustrated by the nude customers and a man in a bathrobe carrying a blow-up doll), and a corrupt CEO 'Doctor' who has an affair with Victor's wife, with no regard to the consequences—Victor's suicide attempts. . . . The image of an analyst of German extraction (like Freud)" is of someone who "promotes promiscuity and sexual gratification . . . under the guise of 'research.'"[65]

The critics by and large found *Buddy Buddy* to be a rather off-center, laborious farce. The dialogue lacked sparkle, the plotting was sluggish at times, and the story never jelled. Wilder's use of verbal wit in a morally disturbing environment did not work this time around. *Buddy Buddy* emerged as a box office failure. It grossed a lackluster $6 million—it did not break even.

"*Buddy Buddy* was dead on the vine—Hollywood and Vine," Wilder confessed in retrospect; "it was a misfire."[66] Fred MacMurray said he wondered how an experienced director like Billy Wilder and the other talents involved in the movie could all go so wrong about the same picture.[67] Asked this question, Wilder replied, "Nobody in Hollywood is foolproof; nobody hits a homer every time." He continued, "When you make a particular movie, you know damned well" after two or three weeks that it is going to "fall flat like a lead pancake. You, the director, are the pilot in the cockpit; you designed the plane and you thought it was going to soar. But that goddamned plane that you've constructed is not going to fly; it is going to crash."[68]

When a Broadway play fails during the tryout on the road, it quietly closes out of town and is forgotten, Wilder said. Some of the plays of Hecht and MacArthur, for example, never made it to Broadway. "But when you make a bad picture, it pursues you the rest of your life. It comes back to haunt you." MGM sold the ancillary rights for *Buddy Buddy* to TV and home video. "It hurts to strike out on your last picture," Wilder said. If he could have chosen a movie to end his career with, it would not have been *Buddy Buddy*. "I didn't know that was going to be my swan song; if I'd known, I would have bet on a different swan."[69]

# Epilogue

## A Touch of Class

The American public was tired of the cinematic chocolate éclairs that had been stuffed down their throats. They had a great desire for knowledge of life as it is lived. I tried to give it to them in my own way.

—*Erich von Stroheim*

Hollywood is a factory town for mass production, out of which something good comes now and then.

—*Billy Wilder*

The export of European film artists to Hollywood in the 1930s, write Gerald Mast and Bruce Kawin, bled the European film industry "as steadily as a Dracula's kiss." But this exodus "would inject its powerful juices into the American film" for decades to come.[1] Billy Wilder certainly did his part to enrich American cinema. He learned during his long career in Hollywood that a director had to work hard not just to achieve artistic independence but also to keep it. Wilder went his own way in Hollywood and made films that suited his own talent, taste, and temperament. He challenged the fundamentally conformist cinema of Hollywood, bringing to his films a sophisticated middle European wit and mature view of human nature.

Still, Wilder often had difficulty in securing studio backing for a project he had developed on his own. He had to negotiate with movie executives who were wary of providing capital for a property that departed in varying degrees from the safe, commercial subject matter they tended to favor. Yet it was precisely the risky, offbeat project that often captured a large audience; movies like *The Apartment* bear out this contention. Such a film is not a gigantic spectacle concerned with sinking ocean liners or torching office towers. In the age of cookie-cutter fare at the multiplex, this type of film relies more on the director's creativity than on fancy technology.

"You have to be flexible," Wilder said. "When wide-screen came in, I considered making the love story of two dachshunds. You see, I try to make pictures that are not for cinema gourmets. I don't do cinema; I make movies—for amusement. I'm making a picture for a middle-class audience, for the people that you see on the subway; and I can only hope they'll like it."[2] It has often been said that some films age; some films date. A substantial number of the films made by Wilder belong to the first category; they demonstrate his respect for the creative freedom that he worked so hard to win.

Wilder was philosophical about the ups and downs of filmmaking. "If I were to sum up my career, I would say that I am a competent journeyman who has gotten lucky once in a while." He explained,

> Sometimes a film comes off and sometimes it doesn't and you can't always predict the outcome, which I think is clear from some of the films I've made. Don't misunderstand me. I don't say that for this failure I have this excuse and for that failure I have that excuse, but for this big hit I take all the credit! I have had good luck, too, and sometimes I have muffed it when it came my way. But look at the total canon of a supreme dramatist like George Bernard Shaw. He wrote dozens of plays of which you remember six or seven, which are still being played in the repertory. The rest are never performed.

Wilder was instrumental in bringing a mature treatment of sex to Hollywood films, particularly in his comedies. Writing of the films Wilder coauthored with I. A. L. Diamond, Joanne Yeck notes, "Witty dialogue and sophisticated situations marked their stories. They openly challenged the long-standing assumption that *all* Hollywood products should be family oriented, and provided moviegoers with tasteful, adult entertainment."[3]

Wilder was not aware that *Buddy Buddy* would be his last picture. He said at the time, "I have absolutely no intention of retiring." Using yet another baseball metaphor, he added, "This here ball game is going into extra innings."[4] But film directing had become "a young man's sport," and Wilder was a septuagenarian. Furthermore, in the wake of the debacle of *Buddy Buddy*, with the studio gossip spreading that Wilder was over the hill, no studio would grant him the right of final cut. His demand for final cut—a prerogative that he had enjoyed throughout his career—forced him into retirement.

"I was retired, and I didn't know it," he said later. Then, one day, while he and Diamond were discussing a possible feature idea, Diamond suddenly said, "I'd better tell you, I guess." He revealed that he was suffering from incurable cancer. "He only told me six weeks before he died," Wilder remembered.[5] On April 21, 1988, Iz Diamond passed away. Friends said that Wilder was "flattened" by Diamond's death. Now even Wilder acknowledged that his career was over; he had no writing partner. He missed having a collaborator who could serve as a sounding board, someone whose taste and ideas he respected. "If God would send me another Brackett or Diamond . . ." he mused; but that was not in the cards.[6]

When a film director hits seventy, he is expected to bequeath his screenplays to the Academy of Motion Picture Arts and Sciences and to appear at awards shows. Wilder kept his scripts, but he did accept awards. In addition to the many Academy Awards he received as a director, writer, and producer, he received recognition from various other quarters. "The awards keep arriving," Wilder commented. "I get offered all these prizes, . . . but no offers to make a picture."[7] His awards include a Lifetime Achievement Award from the Film Society of Lincoln Center in 1982; the prestigious Career Achievement Award presented by the Directors Guild of America in 1985; a Life Achievement Award from AFI in 1986; the coveted Irving G. Thalberg Memorial Award, which he received on April 11 at the 1988 Academy Awards ceremony in recognition for his contribution to the cinema; and an award for distinguished achievement presented to him by President George H. W. Bush at a televised gala at the Kennedy Center in 1990. In addition, Wilder received the Preston Sturges Award, presented jointly by the Writers Guild and the Directors Guild of America in 1991, and the National Medal of the Arts, presented by President Bill Clinton at the White House in 1993.

Moreover, the Library of Congress claimed the films of this native Austrian as part of the American film heritage when it bestowed a singular honor on Billy Wilder in 1995. *The Apartment, Double Indemnity, Some Like It Hot,* and *Sunset Boulevard* were selected as four of the American motion pictures to be preserved in the permanent collection of the National Film Registry of the Library of Congress as culturally, historically, and aesthetically important.

In 1997 Wilder accepted the Golden Laurel Award from the Producers Guild of America. He said at the testimonial dinner that he had run out of acceptance speeches, so he decided to tell an anecdote inspired by his having turned ninety: An elderly man went to see a doctor and complained, "I can't pee." The doctor asked him, "How old are you?" He said, "I'm ninety." The doctor's diagnosis: "You've peed enough." It was Wilder's way of acknowledging, writes Richard Corliss, "that his big carnival ride was over."[8]

Wilder received yet another singular honor when a building at Paramount Studios, where he had made several films, was dedicated to him on the studio's seventy-fifth anniversary in 1989. It stands as an enduring monument to his incalculable contribution to American cinema.

But not all such recognition has come from the United States; Wilder received laurels from other sectors of the film world. In 1995 he was given a Lifetime Fellowship by the British Academy of Film and Television Arts. During their deliberations on Wilder's candidacy, one of the members said, "I would vote for Billy Wilder, but he's dead." When the remark got back to Wilder, he replied, "Mistake! Thank God I am not dead. You see, I am the lion tamer who did not get eaten by the lions."[9]

A special Golden Bear was bestowed on Wilder at the 1993 Berlin International Film Festival. He dryly told a reporter, "I'm getting it because Lubitsch is dead." On a lighter note, he confessed that he would rather have a Volkswagen. In his acceptance speech, he quoted Norma Desmond, thanking "all those wonderful people out there in the dark." Moreover, in the spring of 1994, his native country conferred on its illustrious exile the Grand Prize of the Republic of Austria. It was presented to Wilder by the chancellor of Austria, Franz Vranitzky, on Wilder's first visit to his homeland in three decades.[10] In addition, Volker Schlöndorff, then head of production at Ufa, where Wilder began his film career as a screenwriter, arranged to have a city square near the studio on the outskirts of Berlin named Billy Wilder Plaza.

During the early months of 2002, Wilder's health began to fail significantly; he was in and out of the hospital. It became evident that this was his last illness. Billy Wilder died peacefully at eleven o'clock in the evening on Wednesday, March 27, 2002, in his apartment; his wife Audrey was by his side. Wilder had always been refreshingly unpretentious, living in a twelfth-story apartment on Wilshire Boulevard. Unlike Norma Desmond, he never felt the need to have a house with a swimming pool as a Hollywood status symbol.

In his obituary in *Time,* Richard Corliss observed how the sterner critics labeled Wilder, Hollywood's cleverest writer-director, as a cynic. "Yet, if cynic he was," he had a "shameless love for all the scoundrels who schemed to get rich, shin up the corporate ladder, and bamboozle an insurance company. . . . What knaves these mortals be!"[11] Wilder always disavowed being a cynic. He did not invent sinners, he pointed out; he just paid attention to how they operated. Diamond claimed that many of Wilder's films were decidedly not cynical; they were "whipped cream that's gotten slightly curdled." Moreover, notes Michiko Kakutani, "in some Wilder movies, the cream isn't even sour." *Sabrina* and *Love in the Afternoon,* for example, are really "fairy tales, in which a toadlike cynic is transformed by Audrey Hepburn."[12] Wilder always maintained that he was an optimist. "I carry a little hope of being immortal," he said, because his best films would endure.[13]

A scant five months after Wilder's death, in August 2002, he was chosen as one of the ten greatest film directors of all time in an international poll of 108 filmmakers and 145 film critics conducted by the British Film Institute.[14] Wilder was indeed a world-class director. But he invariably identified himself as a writer who happened to direct his own screenplays, and not as a writer-director. He admired Preston Sturges because he was the first writer to become a director; "he always had a respect for words." Asked what he would like printed on his tombstone, Wilder answered without hesitation, "Here lies a writer." He added, "It is what I am."[15]

Wilder would have been particularly pleased by a poll conducted by the Writers Guild of America in 2005, in which members chose the twenty-five best screenplays of all time. Three of them were cowritten by Wilder.[16] All three—*Sunset Boulevard, Some Like It Hot,* and *The Apartment*—were original screenplays. As Raymond Chandler once said, good original screenplays "were almost as rare in Hollywood as virgins."[17]

Perhaps one of the most touching compliments Wilder received came from British director Stephen Frears (*The Grifters*): "I identify with Billy Wilder, of course. He was a man who went to Hollywood and made a very, very elaborate range of films; yet he kept his own voice."[18] Indeed he did.

# Filmography

## *Mauvaise graine* (1933)

*Production Company:* Compagnie Nouvelle Cinématographique
*Producer:* Edouard Corniglion-Molinier
*Directors:* Alexander Esway and Billy Wilder
*Script:* Max Kolpe, H. G. Lustig, and Billy Wilder, based on an original story by Billy Wilder
*Directors of Photography:* Paul Coteret and Maurice Delattre
*Production Designer:* Robert Gys
*Music:* Walter Gray and Franz Waxman
*Cast:* Danielle Darrieux (Jeanette), Pierre Mingand (Henri Pasquier), Raymond Galle (Jean-la-Cravate), Paul Escoffier (Dr. Pasquier), Michel Duran (the boss), Jean Wall (Zebra), Marcel Maupi (man in Panama hat), Paul Velsa (man with peanuts), Georges Malkine (secretary), Georges Cahuzac (Sir), Gaby Héritier (Gaby)
*Released:* France, 1933 (premiere), 1934 (general release)
*Running Time:* 80 min.

## *The Major and the Minor* (1942)

*Production Company:* Paramount
*Producer:* Arthur Hornblow Jr.
*Director:* Billy Wilder
*Assistant Director:* C. C. Coleman Jr.
*Script:* Charles Brackett and Billy Wilder, suggested by the play *Connie Goes Home* by Edward Childs Carpenter and the story "Sunny Goes Home" by Fannie Kilbourne
*Director of Photography:* Leo Tover
*Editor:* Doane Harrison
*Production Designers:* Roland Anderson and Hans Dreier
*Music:* Robert Emmett Dolan
*Costumes:* Edith Head

*Sound:* Don Johnson and Harold Lewis

*Cast:* Ginger Rogers (Susan Applegate), Ray Milland (Major Philip Kirby), Rita Johnson (Pamela Hill), Robert Benchley (Mr. Osborne), Diana Lynn (Lucy Hill), Edward Fielding (Colonel Hill), Frankie Thomas (Cadet Osborne), Raymond Roe (Cadet Wigton), Charles Smith (Cadet Korner), Larry Nunn (Cadet Babcock), Billy Dawson (Cadet Miller), Lela E. Rogers (Mrs. Applegate), Aldrich Bowker (Reverend Doyle), Boyd Irwin (Major Griscom), Byron Shores (Captain Durand), Richard Fiske (Will Duffy), Norma Varden (Mrs. Osborne), Gretl Dupont (Miss Shackleford), Roland Kibbee (station agent), Ken Lundy (elevator boy)

*Released:* September 1942

*Running Time:* 100 min.

## *Five Graves to Cairo* (1943)

*Production Company:* Paramount

*Producer:* Charles Brackett

*Director:* Billy Wilder

*Assistant Director:* C. C. Coleman Jr.

*Script:* Charles Brackett and Billy Wilder, based on the play *Hotel Imperial* by Lajos Biró

*Director of Photography:* John F. Seitz

*Editor:* Doane Harrison

*Production Designers:* Hans Dreier and Ernst Fegte

*Set Decorator:* Bertram Granger

*Music:* Miklos Rozsa

*Costumes:* Edith Head

*Sound:* Ferol Redd and Philip Wisdom

*Cast:* Franchot Tone (Corporal John J. Bramble), Anne Baxter (Mouche), Erich von Stroheim (Field Marshal Erwin Rommel), Akim Tamiroff (Farid), Fortunio Bonanova (General Sebastiano), Peter van Eyck (Lieutenant Schwegler), Konstantin Shayne (Major von Buelow), Fred Nurney (Major Lamprecht), Miles Mander (Colonel Fitzhume), Ian Keith (Captain St. Bride)

*Released:* May 1943

*Running Time:* 96 min.

## *Double Indemnity* (1944)

*Production Company:* Paramount
*Associate Producer:* Joseph Sistrom
*Director:* Billy Wilder
*Assistant Director:* C. C. Coleman Jr.
*Script:* Raymond Chandler and Billy Wilder, based on the novella by James
    M. Cain
*Director of Photography:* John F. Seitz
*Editor:* Doane Harrison
*Production Designers:* Hans Dreier and Hal Pereira
*Set Decorator:* Bertram Granger
*Music:* Miklos Rozsa
*Sound:* Stanley Cooley
*Cast:* Fred MacMurray (Walter Neff), Barbara Stanwyck (Phyllis Dietrich-
    son), Edward G. Robinson (Barton Keyes), Porter Hall (Mr. Jackson),
    Jean Heather (Lola Dietrichson), Tom Powers (Mr. Dietrichson),
    Byron Barr (Nino Zachetti), Richard Gaines (Edward S. Norton),
    Fortunio Bonanova (Sam Garlopis), John Philliber (Joe Peters), Bess
    Flowers (Norton's secretary), Betty Farrington (Nettie, the maid),
    Sam McDaniel (Charlie)
*Released:* September 1944
*Running Time:* 107 min.

## *The Lost Weekend* (1945)

*Production Company:* Paramount
*Producer:* Charles Brackett
*Director:* Billy Wilder
*Assistant Director:* C. C. Coleman Jr.
*Script:* Charles Brackett and Billy Wilder, based on the novel by Charles R.
    Jackson
*Director of Photography:* John F. Seitz
*Process Photography:* Farciot Edouart
*Special Photographic Effects:* Gordon Jennings
*Editor:* Doane Harrison
*Production Designers:* Hans Dreier and Earl Hedrick
*Set Decorator:* Bertram Granger (supervisor on operatic sequence: Armando
    Agnini)
*Music:* Miklos Rosza; overture and opening aria of Verdi's *La traviata*

*Musical Director:* Victor Young

*Song:* "Libiamo" from *La traviata,* sung by John Garris and Thedora Lynch

*Sound:* Stanley Cooley

*Medical Adviser:* Dr. George N. Thompson

*Cast:* Ray Milland (Don Birnam), Jane Wyman (Helen St. James), Phillip Terry (Wick Birnam), Howard Da Silva (Nat, the bartender), Doris Dowling (Gloria), Frank Faylen ("Bim" Nolan, the nurse), Mary Young (Mrs. Deveridge), Anita Sharp-Bolster (Mrs. Foley, the cleaning lady), Lillian Fontaine (Mrs. St. James), Frank Orth (opera attendant), Lewis L. Russell (Mr. St. James), Clarence Muse (washroom attendant), Fred Toones (washroom attendant)

*Released:* November 1945

*Running Time:* 99 min.

## *The Emperor Waltz* (1948)

*Production Company:* Paramount

*Producer:* Charles Brackett

*Production Manager:* Hugh Brown

*Director:* Billy Wilder

*Assistant Director:* C. C. Coleman Jr.

*Script:* Charles Brackett and Billy Wilder

*Script Supervisor:* Ronald Lubin

*Director of Photography:* George Barnes

*Color Process:* Technicolor

*Process Photography:* Farciot Edouart

*Camera Operator:* Lathrop Worth

*Special Photographic Effects:* Gordon Jennings

*Editor:* Doane Harrison

*Production Designers:* Franz Bachelin and Hans Dreier

*Set Decorators:* Sam Comer and Paul Huldschinsky

*Music:* Victor Young

*Musical Associate:* Troy Sanders

*Vocal Arrangements:* Joseph J. Lilley

*Songs:* "The Emperor Waltz," melody based on music by Johann Strauss, lyrics by Johnny Burke; "Friendly Mountain," melody based on Swiss airs, lyrics by Johnny Burke; "Get Yourself a Phonograph," music by James Van Huesen, lyrics by Johnny Burke; "A Kiss in Your Eyes," music by Richard Heuberger, lyrics by Johnny Burke; "I Kiss Your Hand,

Madame" and "The Whistler and His Dog," music by Ralph Erwin and Fritz Rotter, lyrics by Arthur Pryor

*Costumes:* Edith Head and Gile Steele

*Choreography:* Billy Daniels

*Sound:* Stanley Cooley and John Cope

*Cast:* Bing Crosby (Virgil Smith), Joan Fontaine (Johanna Augusta Franziska von Stoltzenberg-Stoltzenberg), Roland Culver (Baron Holenia), Lucile Watson (Princess Bitotska), Richard Haydn (Emperor Franz Josef), Harold Vermilyea (chamberlain), Sig Ruman (Dr. Zwieback), Julia Dean (Archduchess Stephanie), Bert Prival (chauffeur), John Goldsworthy (obersthofmeister), Doris Dowling (Tyrolean girl)

*Released:* July 1948

*Running Time:* 106 min.

## *A Foreign Affair* (1948)

*Production Company:* Paramount

*Producer:* Charles Brackett

*Production Manager:* Hugh Brown

*Director:* Billy Wilder

*Assistant Director:* C. C. Coleman Jr.

*Script:* Richard Breen, Charles Brackett, and Billy Wilder, based on an original story by David Shaw

*Script Supervisor:* Harry Hogan

*Director of Photography:* Charles B. Lang Jr.

*Process Photography:* Farciot Edouart and Dewey Wrigley

*Camera Operator:* Guy Bennett

*Special Photographic Effects:* Gordon Jennings

*Editor:* Doane Harrison

*Production Designers:* Hans Dreier and Walter Tyler

*Set Decorators:* Sam Comer and Ross Dowd

*Music:* Frederick Hollander

*Musical Director:* Frederick Hollander

*Songs:* "Black Market" and "Illusions," music and lyrics by Frederick Hollander, sung by Marlene Dietrich

*Costumes:* Edith Head

*Sound:* Hugo Grenzbach and Walter Oberst

*Cast:* Jean Arthur (Phoebe Frost), Marlene Dietrich (Erika von Schluetow), John Lund (Captain John Pringle), Millard Mitchell (Colonel Rufus J. Plummer), Peter von Zerneck (Hans Otto Birgel), Stanley Prager

(Mike), William Murphy (Joe), Raymond Bond (Pennecot), Boyd Davis (Giffin), Robert Malcolm (Kramer), Charles Meredith (Yandell), Michael Raffetto (Salvatore), Damian O'Flynn (Lieutenant Hornby), Harland Tucker (General McAndrew), William Neff (Lieutenant Lee Thompson), George M. Carleton (General Finney), Gordon Jones (first MP), Freddie Steele (second MP), Bobby Watson (Hitler)

*Released:* August 1948
*Running Time:* 116 min.

## *Sunset Boulevard* (1950)

*Production Company:* Paramount
*Producer:* Charles Brackett
*Director:* Billy Wilder
*Assistant Director:* C. C. Coleman Jr.
*Script:* Charles Brackett, D. M. Marshman Jr., and Billy Wilder
*Director of Photography:* John F. Seitz
*Process Photography:* Farciot Edouart
*Special Photographic Effects:* Gordon Jennings
*Editorial Supervisor:* Doane Harrison
*Editor:* Arthur Schmidt
*Production Designers:* Hans Dreier and John Meehan
*Set Decorators:* Sam Comer and Ray Moyer
*Music:* Franz Waxman; "Salome's Dance of the Veils" by Richard Strauss
*Sound:* John Cope and Harry Lindgren
*Cast:* William Holden (Joe Gillis), Gloria Swanson (Norma Desmond), Erich von Stroheim (Max von Mayerling), Nancy Olson (Betty Schaefer), Cecil B. De Mille (himself), Fred Clark (Sheldrake), Lloyd Gough (Morino), Jack Webb (Artie Green), Franklyn Farnum (undertaker), Larry J. Blake (first finance man), Charles Dayton (second finance man), Hedda Hopper (herself), Buster Keaton (himself), Anna Q. Nilsson (herself), H. B. Warner (himself), Ray Evans (himself), Jay Livingston (himself)

*Released:* August 1950
*Running Time:* 111 min.

## *Ace in the Hole* (1951),
## originally released as *The Big Carnival*

*Production Company:* Paramount
*Producer:* Billy Wilder

*Associate Producer:* William Schorr
*Director:* Billy Wilder
*Assistant Director:* C. C. Coleman Jr.
*Script:* Walter Newman, Lesser Samuels, and Billy Wilder
*Director of Photography:* Charles B. Lang Jr.
*Editors:* Doane Harrison and Arthur Schmidt
*Production Designers:* Earl Hedrick and Hal Pereira
*Music:* Hugo Friedhofer
*Song:* "We're Coming, Leo," music by Ray Evans, lyrics by Jay Livingston
*Professional Advisers (Journalists):* Dan Burroughs, Will Harrison, Harold Hubbard, Wayne Scott, and Agnes Underwood
*Sound:* John Cope and Harold Lewis
*Cast:* Kirk Douglas (Charles Tatum), Jan Sterling (Lorraine), Robert Arthur (Herbie Cook), Porter Hall (Jacob Q. Boot), Richard Benedict (Leo Minosa), Ray Teal (sheriff), Gene Evans (deputy), Frank Cady (Mr. Federber), Frank Jaquet (Smollett), Iron Eyes Cody (copy boy)
*Released:* July 1951
*Running Time:* 111 min.

# *Stalag 17* (1953)

*Production Company:* Paramount
*Producer:* Billy Wilder
*Associate Producer:* William Schorr
*Director:* Billy Wilder
*Assistant Director:* C. C. Coleman Jr.
*Script:* Edwin Blum and Billy Wilder, based on the play by Donald Bevan and Edmund Trzcinski
*Director of Photography:* Ernest Laszlo
*Special Photographic Effects:* Gordon Jennings
*Editorial Advisor:* Doane Harrison
*Editor:* George Tomasini
*Production Designers:* Franz Bachelin and Hal Pereira
*Music:* Franz Waxman
*Sound:* Gene Garvin and Harold Lewis
*Cast:* William Holden (Sefton), Don Taylor (Lieutenant Dunbar), Otto Preminger (Colonel von Scherbach), Robert Strauss (Stosh "Animal" Krusawa), Harvey Lembeck (Harry Shapiro), Richard Erdman (Hoffy), Peter Graves (Price), Neville Brand (Duke), Sig Ruman (Schulz), Michael Moore (Manfredi), Peter Baldwin (Jonson), Robinson Stone

(Joey), Robert Shawley (Blondie), William Pierson (Marko), Gil Stratton Jr. (Cookie), Jay Lawrence (Bagradian), Erwin Kalser (Geneva man), Edmund Trzcinski (Triz), Tommy Cook (prisoner)
*Released:* July 1953
*Running Time:* 121 min.

## *Sabrina* (1954)

*Production Company:* Paramount
*Producer:* Billy Wilder
*Director:* Billy Wilder
*Assistant Director:* C. C. Coleman Jr.
*Script:* Ernest Lehman, Samuel Taylor, and Billy Wilder, based on the play *Sabrina Fair* by Samuel Taylor
*Director of Photography:* Charles B. Lang Jr.
*Editorial Adviser:* Doane Harrison
*Editor:* Arthur Schmidt
*Production Designers:* Hal Pereira and Walter Tyler
*Music:* Frederick Hollander
*Sound:* John Cope, Harold Lewis
*Cast:* Audrey Hepburn (Sabrina Fairchild), Humphrey Bogart (Linus Larrabee), William Holden (David Larrabee), Walter Hampden (Oliver Larrabee), John Williams (Thomas Fairchild), Martha Hyer (Elizabeth Tyson), Joan Vohs (Gretchen Van Horn), Marcel Dalio (Baron St. Fontanel), Marcel Hillaire (the professor), Nella Walker (Maude Larrabee), Francis X. Bushman (Tyson), Ellen Corby (Miss McCardle), Marjorie Bennett (Margaret, the cook), Emory Parnell (Charles, the butler), Nancy Kulp (Jenny, the maid), Paul Harvey (doctor)
*Released:* September 1954
*Running Time:* 114 min.

## *The Seven Year Itch* (1955)

*Production Company:* Twentieth Century–Fox; a Feldman Group Production
*Producers:* Charles K. Feldman and Billy Wilder
*Associate Producer:* Doane Harrison
*Director:* Billy Wilder
*Assistant Director:* Joseph E. Rickards
*Script:* George Axelrod and Billy Wilder, based on the play by George Axelrod

*Director of Photography:* Milton Krasner (CinemaScope)
*Color Process:* DeLuxe Color
*Color Consultant:* Leonard Doss
*Special Photographic Effects:* Ray Kellogg
*Editor:* Hugh S. Fowler
*Production Designers:* George W. Davis and Lyle Wheeler
*Set Decorators:* Stuart A. Reiss and Walter M. Scott
*Music:* Alfred Newman; Rachmaninoff's Piano Concerto no. 2
*Title Design:* Saul Bass
*Sound:* Harry M. Leonard and E. Clayton Ward
*Cast:* Marilyn Monroe (the Girl), Tom Ewell (Richard Sherman), Evelyn
    Keyes (Helen Sherman), Sonny Tufts (Tom MacKenzie), Robert Strauss
    (Kruhulik), Oskar Homolka (Dr. Brubaker), Marguerite Chapman
    (Miss Morris), Victor Moore (plumber), Roxanne (Elaine), Donald
    MacBride (Mr. Brady), Carolyn Jones (Miss Finch), Butch Bernard
    (Ricky)
*Released:* June 1955
*Running Time:* 105 min.

## *The Spirit of St. Louis* (1957)

*Production Company:* Warner Bros.
*Producers:* Leland Hayward and Billy Wilder
*Associate Producer:* Doane Harrison
*Production Consultant:* Charles Eames
*Production Manager:* Norman Cook
*Production Manager (France):* Jean-Marie Loutrel
*Director:* Billy Wilder
*Assistant Directors:* C. C. Coleman Jr. and Don Page
*Script:* Wendell Mayes and Billy Wilder, based on the book by Charles A.
    Lindbergh
*Directors of Photography:* Robert Burks and J. Peverell Marley (CinemaScope)
*Color Process:* WarnerColor
*Aerial Photographic Adviser:* Ted McCord
*Aerial Photography:* Thomas Tutwiler
*Aerial Supervisor:* Paul Mantz
*Editor:* Arthur P. Schmidt
*Production Designer:* Art Loel
*Set Decorator:* William L. Kuehl
*Special Effects:* H. F. Koenekamp and Louis Lichtenfield

*Music:* Franz Waxman
*Musical Director:* Franz Waxman
*Orchestration:* Leonid Raab
*Sound:* M. A. Merrick
*Technical Advisers:* Major-General Victor Bertrandrias (U.S. Air Force, re-
tired) and Harlan A. Gurney
*Cast:* James Stewart (Charles Augustus Lindbergh), Murray Hamilton (Bud
Gurney), Patricia Smith (mirror girl), Bartlett Robinson (B. F. Mahoney),
Marc Connelly (Father Hussman), Arthur Space (Donald Hall), Charles
Watts (O. W. Schultz), Dabbs Greer (Goldsborough), Robert Cornthwaite
(Knight), Robert Burton (Major Lambert), Richard Deacon (Levine)
*Released:* April 1957
*Running Time:* 135 min.

## *Love in the Afternoon* (1957)

*Production Company:* Allied Artists
*Producer:* Billy Wilder
*Associate Producers:* Doane Harrison and William Schorr
*Director:* Billy Wilder
*Second Unit Director:* Noel Howard
*Assistant Director:* Paul Feyder
*Script:* I. A. L. Diamond and Billy Wilder, based on the novel *Ariane* by
Claude Anet
*Director of Photography:* William Mellor
*Editor:* Leonid Azar
*Production Designer:* Alexander Trauner
*Musical Adviser:* Matty Malneck
*Musical Adaptation:* Franz Waxman, "Fascination," music by F. D. Marchetti,
lyrics by Maurice de Ferauldy
*Sound Editor:* Del Harris
*Sound:* Jo de Bretagne
*Cast:* Gary Cooper (Frank Flannagan), Audrey Hepburn (Ariane Chavasse),
Maurice Chevalier (Claude Chavasse), Van Doude (Michel), John McGiver
(Monsieur X), Lise Bourdin (Madame X), Bonifas (commissioner of po-
lice), Alexander Trauner (artist), Audrey Wilder (brunette)
*Released:* June 1957
*Running Time:* 125 min.

## *Witness for the Prosecution* (1958)

*Production Company:* Edward Small/United Artists
*Producer:* Arthur Hornblow Jr.
*Director:* Billy Wilder
*Assistant Director:* Emmett Emerson
*Script:* Harry Kurnitz and Billy Wilder, based on the play and story by Agatha Christie
*Director of Photography:* Russell Harlan
*Editor:* Daniel Mandell
*Production Designer:* Alexander Trauner
*Set Decorator:* Howard Bristol
*Music:* Matty Malneck
*Musical Director:* Ernest Gold
*Orchestration:* Leonid Raab
*Song:* "I May Never Go Home Anymore," music by Ralph Arthur Roberts, lyrics by Jack Brooks
*Sound:* Fred Lau
*Cast:* Tyrone Power (Leonard Vole), Marlene Dietrich (Christine Vole), Charles Laughton (Sir Wilfrid Robarts), Elsa Lanchester (Miss Plimsoll), John Williams (Brogan-Moore), Henry Daniell (Mayhew), Ian Wolfe (Carter), Torin Thatcher (Mr. Myers), Norma Varden (Mrs. French), Una O'Connor (Janet McKenzie), Francis Compton (judge), Philip Tonge (Inspector Hearne), Ruta Lee (Diana), Marjorie Eaton (Miss O'Brien), Ottola Nesmith (Miss Johnson), J. Pat O'Malley (shorts salesman), Molly Roden (Miss McHugh)
*Released:* February 1958
*Running Time:* 116 min.

## *Some Like It Hot* (1959)

*Production Company:* Mirisch Company/United Artists
*Producer:* Billy Wilder
*Associate Producers:* I. A. L. Diamond and Doane Harrison
*Director:* Billy Wilder
*Assistant Director:* Sam Nelson
*Script:* I. A. L. Diamond and Billy Wilder, based on the film *Fanfaren der Liebe* by Michael Logan and Robert Thoeren
*Director of Photography:* Charles B. Lang Jr.
*Editor:* Arthur Schmidt

*Production Designer:* Ted Haworth
*Set Decorator:* Edward G. Boyle
*Music:* Adolph Deutsch
*Song Supervisor:* Matty Malneck
*Songs:* "Running Wild," music by A. H. Gibbs, lyrics by Leo Wood; "I Want
    to Be Loved by You," music by Herbert Stothart, lyrics by Bert Kalmar;
    "I'm Through with Love," music by Matty Malneck, lyrics by Gus Kahn
*Sound:* Fred Lau
*Cast:* Marilyn Monroe (Sugar Kane, née Kowalczyk), Tony Curtis (Joe/
    Josephine), Jack Lemmon (Jerry/Daphne), Joe E. Brown (Osgood
    Fielding III), George Raft (Spats Colombo), Pat O'Brien (Mulligan),
    Nehemiah Persoff (Little Bonaparte), Joan Shawlee (Sweet Sue), Billy
    Gray (Sig Poliakoff), George E. Stone (Toothpick Charlie), Dave Barry
    (Beinstock), Mike Mazurki (Spats's henchman), Harry Wilson (Spats's
    henchman), Beverly Wills (Dolores), Barbara Drew (Nellie), Edward G.
    Robinson Jr. (Paradise), Marian Collier (Olga)
*Released:* March 1959
*Running Time:* 121 min.

## *The Apartment* (1960)

*Production Company:* Mirisch Company/United Artists
*Producer:* Billy Wilder
*Associate Producers:* I. A. L. Diamond and Doane Harrison
*Production Manager:* Allen K. Wood
*Director:* Billy Wilder
*Assistant Director:* Hal Polaire
*Script:* I. A. L. Diamond and Billy Wilder
*Director of Photography:* Joseph LaShelle (Panavision)
*Editor:* Daniel Mandell
*Production Designer:* Alexander Trauner
*Set Decorator:* Edward G. Boyle
*Special Effects:* Milton Rice
*Sound:* Fred Lau
*Music:* Adolph Deutsch
*Cast:* Jack Lemmon (C. C. "Bud" Baxter), Shirley MacLaine (Fran Kubelik),
    Fred MacMurray (Jeff D. Sheldrake), Ray Walston (Joe Dobisch), Jack
    Kruschen (Dr. Dreyfuss), David Lewis (Al Kirkeby), Hope Holiday
    (Margie MacDougall), Joan Shawlee (Sylvia), Naomi Stevens (Mrs.
    Mildred Dreyfuss), Johnny Seven (Karl Matuschka), Joyce Jameson

(the blonde), Willard Waterman (Mr. Vanderhof), David White (Mr. Eichelberger), Edie Adams (Miss Olsen), Benny Burt (bartender), Frances Weintraub Lax (Mrs. Lieberman), Hal Smith (Santa Claus)
*Released:* June 1960
*Running Time:* 125 min.

# One, Two, Three (1961)

*Production Company:* Mirisch Company/United Artists
*Producer:* Billy Wilder
*Associate Producers:* I. A. L. Diamond and Doane Harrison
*Production Managers:* William Calihan and Werner Fischer
*Director:* Billy Wilder
*Second Unit Director:* Andre Smagghe
*Assistant Director:* Tom Pevsner
*Script:* I. A. L. Diamond and Billy Wilder, based on the play *Ein, zwei, drei* by Ferenc Molnar
*Director of Photography:* Daniel Fapp (Panavision)
*Editor:* Daniel Mandell
*Production Designer:* Alexander Trauner
*Special Effects:* Milton Rice
*Music:* André Previn
*Sound:* Basil Fenton-Smith
*Cast:* James Cagney (C. R. MacNamara), Horst Buchholz (Otto Ludwig Piffl), Pamela Tiffin (Scarlett Hazeltine), Arlene Francis (Phyllis MacNamara), Howard St. John (Hazeltine), Hanns Lothar (Schlemmer), Leon Askin (Peripetchikoff), Ralf Wolter (Borodenko), Karl Lieffen (Fritz), Hubert von Meyerinck (Count von Droste Schattenburg), Lois Bolton (Melanie Hazeltine), Peter Capell (Mishkin), Til Kiwe (reporter), Hennig Schlüter (Doctor Bauer), Karl Ludwig Lindt (Zeidlitz), Lilo Pulver (Ingeborg), Red Buttons (MP), Christine Allen (Cindy MacNamara), John Allen (Tommy MacNamara), Frederick Hollander (orchestra leader, uncredited)
*Released:* December 1961
*Running Time:* 115 min.

# Irma la Douce (1963)

*Production Company:* Mirisch Company/United Artists
*Producer:* Billy Wilder

*Associate Producers:* I. A. L. Diamond and Doane Harrison
*Production Supervisor:* Allen K. Wood
*Director:* Billy Wilder
*Assistant Director:* Hal Polaire
*Script:* I. A. L. Diamond and Billy Wilder, based on the musical play by Alexandre Breffort and Marguerite Monnot
*Director of Photography:* Joseph LaShelle (Panavision)
*Color Process:* Technicolor
*Editor:* Daniel Mandell
*Production Designer:* Alexander Trauner
*Set Decorators:* Maurice Barnathan and Edward G. Boyle
*Music:* André Previn, adapted from the score by Marguerite Monnot
*Costumes:* Orry-Kelly
*Sound:* Robert Martin
*Cast:* Jack Lemmon (Nestor Patou), Shirley MacLaine (Irma), Lou Jacobi (Moustache), Bruce Yarnell (Hippolyte), Herschel Bernardi (Inspector Lefevre), Hope Holiday (Lolita), Joan Shawlee (Amazon Annie), Grace Lee Whitney (Kiki the Cossack), Paul Dubov (Andre), Howard McNear (concierge), Cliff Osmond (police sergeant), Diki Lerner (Jojo), Herb Jones (Casablanca Charlie), Ruth Earl and Jane Earl (Zebra Twins), Tura Satana (Suzette Wong), Lou Krugman (first customer), James Brown (customer from Texas), Bill Bixby (tattooed sailor), James Caan (soldier with radio), Louis Jourdan (narrator, uncredited)
*Released:* June 1963
*Running Time:* 147 min.

## *Kiss Me, Stupid* (1964)

*Production Company:* Mirisch Company / Lopert Films
*Producer:* Billy Wilder
*Associate Producers:* I. A. L. Diamond and Doane Harrison
*Production Manager:* Allen K. Wood
*Director:* Billy Wilder
*Assistant Director:* C. C. Coleman Jr.
*Script:* I. A. L. Diamond and Billy Wilder, suggested by the play *L'ora della fantasia* by Anna Bonacci
*Director of Photography:* Joseph LaShelle (Panavision)
*Editor:* Daniel Mandell
*Production Designer:* Alexander Trauner
*Art Director:* Robert Luthardt

*Set Director:* Edward G. Boyle

*Special Effects:* Milton Rice

*Music:* André Previn

*Songs:* "Sophia," "I'm a Poached Egg," and "All the Livelong Day," music by George Gershwin, lyrics by Ira Gershwin

*Cast:* Dean Martin (Dino), Kim Novak (Polly the Pistol), Ray Walston (Orville J. Spooner), Felicia Farr (Zelda Spooner), Cliff Osmond (Barney Milsap), Barbara Pepper (Big Bertha), James Ward (milkman), Howard McNear (Mr. Pettibone), Doro Merande (Mrs. Pettibone), Bobo Lewis (waitress), Tommy Nolan (Johnnie Mulligan), Alice Pearce (Mrs. Mulligan), John Fiedler (Reverend Carruthers), Arlen Stuart (Rosalie Schultz), Cliff Norton (Mack Gray), Mel Blanc (Dr. Sheldrake), Eileen O'Neal (showgirl), Susan Wedell (showgirl), Bernd Hoffmann (barkeeper), Henry Gibson (Smith), Alan Dexter (Wesson), Henry Beckman (truck driver)

*Released:* December 1964

*Running Time:* 122 min. (2003 restored version: 126 min.)

# *The Fortune Cookie* (1966)

*Production Company:* Mirisch Company/United Artists

*Producer:* Billy Wilder

*Associate Producers:* I. A. L. Diamond and Doane Harrison

*Production Supervisor:* Allen K. Wood

*Unit Manager:* Patrick J. Palmer

*Director:* Billy Wilder

*Assistant Director:* Jack Reddish

*Script:* I. A. L. Diamond and Billy Wilder

*Director of Photography:* Joseph LaShelle (Panavision)

*Editor:* Daniel Mandell

*Production Designer:* Robert Luthardt

*Set Decorator:* Edward G. Boyle

*Special Effects:* Sass Bedig

*Music:* André Previn

*Song:* "You'd Be So Nice to Come Home To," music and lyrics by Cole Porter

*Sound:* Robert Martin

*Cast:* Jack Lemmon (Harry Hinkle), Walter Matthau (Willie Gingrich), Ron Rich (Luther "Boom Boom" Jackson), Judi West (Sandy Hinkle), Cliff Osmond (Chester Purkey), Lurene Tuttle (Mother Hinkle), Harry

Holcombe (O'Brien), Les Tremayne (Thompson), Lauren Gilbert (Kincaid), Marge Redmond (Charlotte Gingrich), Noam Pitlik (Max), Harry Davis (Dr. Krugman), Ann Shoemaker (Sister Veronica), Maryesther Denver (nurse), Ned Glass (Doc Schindler), Sig Ruman (Professor Winterhalter), Archie Moore (Mr. Jackson), Howard McNear (Mr. Cimoli), William Christopher (intern), Dodie Heath (nun), Herbie Faye (Maury, the equipment man), Billy Beck (Maury's assistant), Judy Pace (Elvira), Helen Kleeb (receptionist), Keith Jackson (football announcer), Don Reed (newscaster), Robert DoQui (man in bar)

*Released:* October 1966

*Running Time:* 126 min.

## *The Private Life of Sherlock Holmes* (1970)

*Production Company:* Mirisch Company/United Artists

*Producer:* Billy Wilder

*Associate Producer:* I. A. L. Diamond

*Production Supervisor:* Larry De Waay

*Production Manager:* Eric Rattray

*Director:* Billy Wilder

*Assistant Director:* Tom Pevsner

*Script:* I. A. L. Diamond and Billy Wilder, based on characters created by Sir Arthur Conan Doyle

*Director of Photography:* Christopher Challis (Panavision)

*Color Process:* DeLuxe Color

*Editor:* Ernest Walter

*Production Designer:* Alexander Trauner

*Art Director:* Tony Inglis

*Set Decorator:* Harry Cordwell

*Special Effects:* Cliff Richardson and Wally Veevers

*Music:* Miklos Rozsa

*Ballet Adviser and Dance Arranger:* David Blair

*Title Design:* Maurice Binder

*Sound Editor:* Roy Baker

*Sound Recorders:* J. W. N. Daniel and Gordon K. McCallum

*Cast:* Robert Stephens (Sherlock Holmes), Colin Blakely (Dr. John Watson), Genevieve Page (Gabrielle Valladon), Christopher Lee (Mycroft Holmes), Tamara Toumanova (Petrova), Clive Revill (Rogozhin), Irene Handl (Mrs. Hudson), Mollie Maureen (Queen Victoria), Stanley Holloway (gravedigger), Catherine Lacey (old lady), Peter Madden

(Von Tirpitz), Michael Balfour (cabbie), James Copeland (guide), John Garrie (first carter), Godfrey James (second carter), Robert Cawdron (hotel manager), Alex McCrindle (baggage man), Frank Thornton (Porter), Paul Hansard (monk), Miklos Rozsa (conductor)

*Released:* November 1970

*Running Time:* 125 min. (2003 DVD version: 185 min.)

# *Avanti!* (1972)

*Production Company:* Mirisch Company/United Artists
*Producer:* Billy Wilder
*Production Manager:* Alessandro von Normann
*Director:* Billy Wilder
*Assistant Director:* Rinaldo Riccio
*Script:* I. A. L. Diamond and Billy Wilder, based on the play by Samuel Taylor
*Director of Photography:* Luigi Kuveiller (Panavision)
*Aerial Photography:* Mario Damicelli
*Color Process:* DeLuxe Color
*Editor:* Ralph E. Winters
*Production Designer:* Ferdinando Scarfiotti
*Set Decorator:* Nedo Azzini
*Musical Arrangements:* Carlo Rustichelli
*Musical Conductor:* Gianfranco Plemizio
*Sound:* Basil Fenton-Smith, William Varney, and Frank Warner
*Cast:* Jack Lemmon (Wendell Armbruster), Juliet Mills (Pamela Piggott), Clive Revill (Carlo Carlucci), Edward Andrews (Joseph J. Blodgett), Gianfranco Barra (Bruno), Francesco Angrisano (Arnoldo Trotta), Pippo Franco (Mattarazzo), Franco Acampora (Armado Trotta), Giselda Castrini (Anna), Rafaele Mottola (passport officer), Lino Coletta (Cipriani), Harry Ray (Dr. Fleischmann), Guidarino Guidi (maître d'), Giacomo Rizzo (barman), Antonino Faà di Bruno (concierge), Yanti Somer (nurse), Janet Agren (nurse), Aldo Rendine (Rossi)

*Released:* December 1972

*Running Time:* 144 min.

# *The Front Page* (1974)

*Production Company:* Universal
*Producer:* Paul Monash
*Executive Producer:* Jennings Lang

*Production Manager:* Carter De Haven Jr.

*Director:* Billy Wilder

*Second Unit Director:* Carey Lofton

*Assistant Directors:* Charles E. Dismukes, Howard G. Kazanjian, and Jack Saunders

*Script:* I. A. L. Diamond and Billy Wilder, based on the play by Ben Hecht and Charles MacArthur

*Director of Photography:* Jordan S. Cronewath (Panavision)

*Special Effects:* Nick Carey

*Color Process:* Technicolor

*Editor:* Ralph E. Winters

*Production Designers:* Henry Bumstead and Henry Larrecy

*Set Decorator:* James W. Payne

*Music Adaptation:* Billy May

*Songs:* "Button Up Your Overcoat," music by Ray Henderson, lyrics by B. G. De Sylva and Lew Brown; "Wedding Bells Are Breaking Up That Old Gang of Mine," music by Sammy Fain, lyrics by Irving Kahal and Willie Raskin; "Congratulate Me," music by Lou Handman, lyrics by Bob Rathberg

*Sound:* Martin Hoyt and Robert Martin

*Titles:* Wayne Fitzgerald

*Cast:* Jack Lemmon (Hildy Johnson), Walter Matthau (Walter Burns), Susan Sarandon (Peggy Grant), Carol Burnett (Mollie Malloy), Vincent Gardenia ("Honest Pete" Hartman), David Wayne (Roy Bensinger), Allen Garfield (Kruger), Austin Pendleton (Earl Williams), Charles Durning (Murphy), Herb Edelman (Schwartz), Martin Gabel (Dr. Max J. Eggelhofer), Harold Gould (mayor), Cliff Osmond (Officer Jacobi), Dick O'Neill (McHugh), Jon Korkes (Rudy Keppler), Lou Frizzell (Endicott), Paul Benedict (Plunkett), Doro Merande (Jennie, the janitor), Noam Pitlik (Wilson), Joshua Shelley (cab driver), Allen Jenkins (telegrapher), John Furlong (Duffy), Biff Elliot (police dispatcher), Barbara Davis (Myrtle), Leonard Bremen (Butch)

*Released:* December 1974

*Running Time:* 105 min.

# *Fedora* (1979)

*Production Company:* Geria Films/Bavaria Film Studios/United Artist

*Producers:* Helmut Jedele and Billy Wilder

*Director:* Billy Wilder

*Script:* I. A. L. Diamond and Billy Wilder, based on the novella by Thomas Tryon from his book *Crowned Heads*

*Assistant Director:* Jean-Patrick Constantini

*Director of Photography:* Gerry Fisher

*Color Process:* Technicolor

*Editors:* Stefan Arsten and Fredric Steinkamp

*Production Designer:* Alexander Trauner

*Music:* Miklos Rozsa

*Cast:* William Holden (Barry "Dutch" Detweiler), Marthe Keller (Fedora), Hildegard Knef (Countess Sobryanski), José Ferrer (Dr. Vando), Frances Sternhagen (Miss Balfour), Mario Adorf (hotel manager), Stephen Collins (Young Barry), Henry Fonda (president of the academy), Michael York (himself), Hans Jaray (Count Sobryanski), Gottfried John (Kritos), Arlene Francis (newscaster), Jacques Maury (usher), Christine Mueller (young Antonia), Rex McGee (photojournalist)

*Released:* April 1979

*Running Time:* 113 min.

# *Buddy Buddy* (1981)

*Production Company:* Metro-Goldwyn-Mayer

*Producer:* Jay Weston

*Director:* Billy Wilder

*Assistant Director:* Gary Daigler

*Script:* Billy Wilder and I. A. L. Diamond, based on the play *L'emmerdeur* by Francis Weber

*Director of Photography:* Harry Stradling Jr.

*Editor:* Argyle Nelson

*Music:* Lalo Schifrin

*Song:* "Cecilia," arranged by Peter Rugolo, sung by Michael Dees

*Cast:* Jack Lemmon (Victor Clooney), Walter Matthau (Trabucco), Paula Prentiss (Celia Clooney), Klaus Kinski (Dr. Hugo Zuckerbrot), Dana Elcar (Captain Hubris), Miles Chapin (Eddie, the bellhop), Michael Ensign (assistant manager), Joan Shawlee (receptionist), Fil Formicola (Rudy "Disco" Gambola), C. J. Hunt (Kowalski), Bette Raya (Mexican maid), Ronnie Sperling (hippie husband), Suzie Galler (pregnant wife), John Schubeck (newscaster), Ed Begley Jr. (lieutenant 1), Frank Farmer (lieutenant 2), Neile McQueen (saleswoman)

*Released:* December 1981

*Running Time:* 98 min.

# Notes

Billy Wilder granted the author an extended interview in his Hollywood office on September 30, 1975, and the present book was developed from that interview. From time to time over the years, the interview was updated by telephone. All quotations from Wilder that are not attributed to another source are from this interview.

## 1. FROM BERLIN TO HOLLYWOOD

1. Kevin Lally, *Wilder Times: The Life of Billy Wilder* (New York: Holt, 1996), 1. Wilder's first name was spelled *Billie* until he went to Hollywood, when he changed the spelling to *Billy* because *Billie* was used for females there, e.g., Billie Burke. But I use the spelling *Billy* throughout this book for the sake of consistency.

2. Hellmuth Karasek, *Billy Wilder: Eine Nahaufnahme* [Billy Wilder: A close-up] (Hamburg: Hoffman und Campe, 1992), 29–30. This book has the most complete treatment of Wilder's youth; it has not been published in an English translation. Robert Scheff translated the cited passages. Unless otherwise noted, all translations are in the Billy Wilder file, National Film Archive, British Film Institute, London.

3. Geoffrey Macnab, "Gold Leaf and Shadow-Play: Vienna in Films," *Sight and Sound,* n.s., 16, no. 9 (2006): 32.

4. Karasek, *Billy Wilder,* 34–35.

5. Maurice Zolotow, *Billy Wilder in Hollywood,* rev. ed. (New York: Limelight, 1987), 341–42; Billy Wilder, "Going for Extra Innings," interview by Joseph McBride and Todd McCarthy, *Film Comment* 13, no. 1 (1979): 42.

6. Zolotow, *Billy Wilder in Hollywood,* 26.

7. Daniel Johnson, "On the Wilder Side of Freud," *Times* (London), September 30, 1995, 2.

8. Tom Wood, *The Bright Side of Billy Wilder, Primarily* (Garden City, NY: Doubleday, 1970), 164; see also Karasek, *Billy Wilder,* 53–55.

9. Billy Wilder, interview by Richard Gehman, *Playboy,* June 1963, 58.

10. Fred Zinnemann, interview by author, London, May 15, 1994.

11. Peter Bogdanovich, *Who the Devil Made It: Conversations with Film Directors* (New York: Ballantine Books, 1998), 565.

12. Fred Zinnemann, *A Life in the Movies: An Autobiography* (New York: Scribner, 1992), 16.

13. Billy Wilder, "Wir von Filmslude" [We of the Film Studio], *Tempo*, June 23, 1929, 2. Robert Scheff translated the cited passages. Wilder and his partners called their film unit the Film Studio—an ironic title, since they were not associated with any film studio.

14. "People on Sunday," *Sight and Sound*, n.s., 15, no. 6 (2005): 86; see also Jeffrey Meyers, introduction to *The Lost Weekend: A Screenplay*, by Billy Wilder and Charles Brackett, ed. Jeffrey Meyers (Los Angeles: University of California Press, 2000), vii.

15. Zinnemann, interview.

16. Kevin Brownlow to author, July 14, 2006.

17. Wood, *Bright Side of Billy Wilder*, 174.

18. Karasek, *Billy Wilder*, 94.

19. Glenn Hopp, *Billy Wilder: The Cinema of Wit* (Los Angeles: Taschen, 2003), 10.

20. Garson Kanin, *Hollywood: Moviemakers and Moneymakers* (New York: Viking, 1974), 152.

21. Michael Blowen, "The Art of Billy Wilder," *Boston Globe*, October 22, 1989, 81.

22. Wilder, interview by Gehman, 58.

23. Gene D. Phillips, *Fiction, Film, and F. Scott Fitzgerald* (Chicago: Loyola University Press, 1986), 14.

24. Lincoln Barnett, "The Happiest Couple in Hollywood," *Life*, December 11, 1944, 104, 102.

25. John Gregory Dunne, "The Old Pornographer: Billy Wilder," *New Yorker*, November 8, 1999, 90.

26. Billy Wilder, "One Head Is Better Than Two," in *Hollywood Directors, 1941–1976*, ed. Richard Koszarski (New York: Oxford University Press, 1977), 270.

## 2. CHAMPAGNE AND TEARS

1. Ernst Lubitsch, "Film Directing," in *Hollywood Directors, 1914–1940*, ed. Richard Koszarski (New York: Oxford University Press, 1976), 273–74.

2. Scott Eyman, *Ernst Lubitsch: Laughter in Paradise* (New York: Simon and Schuster, 1993), 259.

3. Ibid., 257.

4. "Billy Wilder," in *Conversations with the Great Moviemakers of Hollywood's Golden Age at the American Film Institute*, ed. George Stevens Jr. (New York: Knopf, 2006), 302; see also Michiko Kakutani, "Ready for His Close-Up," *New York Times Magazine*, June 28, 1996, 14.

5. Jürgen Muller and Jorn Hetenbrugge, "Chaos and Illusion: Notes on the Movies of the Thirties," in *Movies of the Thirties*, ed. Jürgen Muller (Los Angeles: Taschen/BFI, 2005), 17; see also David Freeman, "*Sunset Boulevard* Revisited," *New Yorker*, June 21, 1993, 74.

6. Barry Paris, *Garbo: A Biography* (New York: Knopf, 1995), 361.

7. Ibid., 363.

8. Jay Nash and Stanley Ross, eds., *The Motion Picture Guide, 1927–1983* (Chicago: Cinebooks, 1985), 2171.

9. Wood, *Bright Side of Billy Wilder,* 39–40.

10. Zolotow, *Billy Wilder in Hollywood,* 69.

11. Louis Giannetti, *Understanding Movies,* 11th ed. (Upper Saddle River, NJ: Pearson Prentice Hall, 2008), 419.

12. David Chierichetti, *Hollywood Director: Mitchell Leisen* (Los Angeles: Photoventures Press, 1995), 123.

13. Wood, *Bright Side of Billy Wilder,* 65.

14. Manohla Dargis, "Film," *New York Times,* April 15, 2007, sec. 2, p. 4.

15. "David Kipen Picks Five Great Screenplays," *Chicago Tribune Book Review,* February 26, 2006, 8.

16. Eyman, *Ernst Lubitsch,* 257.

17. Freeman, "*Sunset Boulevard* Revisited," 74.

18. "Billy Wilder," in Stevens, *Conversations,* 305–6.

19. Billy Wilder, foreword to *Emeric Pressburger: The Life and Death of a Screenwriter,* by Kevin Macdonald (Boston: Faber and Faber, 1994), xiii.

20. Stephen Silverman, "Billy Wilder and Stanley Donen," *Films in Review* 47, nos. 3–4 (1996): 35; see also Hopp, *Billy Wilder,* 28.

21. Lally, *Wilder Times,* 103–4.

22. Howard Hawks, interview by author, Chicago, November 11, 1973.

23. Ibid.

24. Andrew Sarris, "From the Kaiser to the Oscar," *New York Times Book Review,* December 27, 1998, 5.

25. Hawks, interview.

26. Todd McCarthy, *Howard Hawks: The Grey Fox of Hollywood* (New York: Grove Press, 1997), 327.

27. "Billy Wilder," in Stevens, *Conversations,* 315–16.

28. Richard Corliss, *Talking Pictures: Screenwriters in the American Cinema* (Woodstock, NY: Overlook Press, 1988), xxi.

29. "Billy Wilder," in Stevens, *Conversations,* 317.

30. Charlotte Chandler, *Nobody's Perfect: Billy Wilder, a Personal Biography* (New York: Applause Books, 2004), 103.

31. John Russell Taylor, *Strangers in Paradise: The Hollywood Émigrés, 1933–1950* (New York: Holt, Rinehart and Winston, 1983), 205–6.

## 3. NEW DIRECTIONS

1. Zolotow, *Billy Wilder in Hollywood,* 107.

2. Billy Wilder, interview by Burt Prelutsky, in *Billy Wilder: Interviews,* ed. Robert Horton (Jackson: University Press of Mississippi, 2001), 185.

3. Leslie Halliwell, *Who's Who in the Movies,* rev. ed., ed. John Walker (New York: HarperCollins, 2005), 488.

4. Lally, *Wilder Times,* 112.

5. Dunne, "Old Pornographer," 90.

6. Zolotow, *Billy Wilder in Hollywood,* 104.

7. Chandler, *Nobody's Perfect,* 103.

8. Wood, *Bright Side of Billy Wilder,* 73–74.

9. Chandler, *Nobody's Perfect,* 107.

10. Ibid., 104.

11. Lally, *Wilder Times,* 114.

12. Richard Armstrong, *Billy Wilder: American Film Realist* (Jefferson, NC: McFarland, 2004), 20.

13. William K. Everson, *Hollywood Bedlam: Classic Screwball Comedies* (New York: Carol, 1994), 212.

14. Herbert Luft, "A Matter of Decadence," in "Two Views of a Director: Billy Wilder," *Quarterly of Film, Radio, and Television* 7, no. 1 (1952): 67.

15. Armstrong, *Billy Wilder,* 17.

16. Bernard Dick, *Billy Wilder,* rev. ed. (New York: Da Capo, 1996), 35.

17. Ibid., 34.

18. *The Graham Greene Reader: Reviews, Essays, and Interviews,* ed. David Parkinson (New York: Applause Books, 1995), 481.

19. Ed Sikov, *On Sunset Boulevard: The Life and Times of Billy Wilder* (New York: Hyperion, 1998), 189.

20. On Rommel's African campaign, see Joseph Roquemore, *History Goes to the Movies* (New York: Doubleday, 1999), 186–90.

21. Sikov, *On Sunset Boulevard,* 52.

22. Arthur Lennig, *Stroheim* (Lexington: University Press of Kentucky, 2000), 419; see also Michel Ciment, *Passport pour Hollywood* (Paris: Editions du Seuil, 1987), 71.

23. Richard Koszarski, *Von: The Life and Times of Erich von Stroheim* (New York: Limelight, 2001), 286.

24. Sikov, *On Sunset Boulevard,* 188.

25. Cameron Crowe, *Conversations with Wilder* (New York: Knopf, 2001), 268.

26. Ibid., 108.

27. James Ursini, "John F. Seitz," in *Film Noir Reader 3,* ed. Alain Silver, James Ursini, and Robert Porfirio (New York: Limelight, 2002), 101.

28. Lennig, *Stroheim,* 420.

29. Kurt Richter, interview by author, Berlin, May 20, 1977.

30. Miklos Rozsa, *Double Life* (New York: Winwood, 1989), 131.

31. Andrew Sarris, *You Ain't Heard Nothin' Yet: The American Talking Film, 1927–1949* (New York: Oxford University Press, 2000), 327.

32. Lennig, *Stroheim,* 420.

33. Lally, *Wilder Times,* 121.

## 4. THE RISE OF FILM NOIR

1. William Hare, *Early Film Noir* (Jefferson, NC: McFarland, 2003), 24.

2. John Allyn, "*Double Indemnity:* A Policy That Paid Off," *Literature/ Film Quarterly* 6, no. 2 (1978): 120.

3. Richard Schickel, *Double Indemnity* (London: British Film Institute, 1993), 31.

4. Murray Schumach, *The Face on the Cutting Room Floor* (New York: Da Capo, 1975), 64. The code was composed in 1930 but did not go into action until 1934.

5. Gaylyn Studlar, "Hard-Boiled Film Noir: *Double Indemnity,*" in *Film Analysis,* ed. Jeffrey Geiger and R. L. Rutsky (New York: Norton, 2005), 383.

6. "James M. Cain: Tough Guy," interview by Peter Brunette and Gerald Perry, in *Backstory: Interviews with Screenwriters of Hollywood's Golden Age,* ed. Pat McGilligan (Berkeley: University of California Press, 1986), 127.

7. Frank Walsh, *Sin and Censorship: The Catholic Church and the Motion Picture Industry* (New Haven, CT: Yale University Press, 1996), 187.

8. Roger Ebert, *The Great Movies* (New York: Broadway Books, 2002), 144.

9. John Irwin, *Unless the Threat of Death Is behind Them: Hard-Boiled Fiction and Film Noir* (Baltimore: Johns Hopkins University Press, 2006), 70.

10. John McCarty, *Thrillers: Classic Film Suspense* (New York: Carol, 1992), 50.

11. Jeffrey Meyers, introduction to *Double Indemnity: A Screenplay,* by Billy Wilder and Raymond Chandler, ed. Jeffrey Meyers (Los Angeles: University of California Press, 2000), x.

12. Al Clark, *Raymond Chandler in Hollywood* (Los Angeles: Silman-James, 1996), 98.

13. Frank MacShane, *The Life of Raymond Chandler* (New York: Dutton, 1976), 112; see also Woody Haut, *Heartbreak and Vine: Hardboiled Writers in Hollywood* (London: Serpent's Tail, 2002), 30.

14. Billy Wilder, "On the Fourth Floor at Paramount," interview by Ivan Moffat, in *The World of Raymond Chandler,* ed. Miriam Gross (New York: A and W, 1978), 45.

15. Schickel, *Double Indemnity,* 35.

16. Philip Kiszely, *Hollywood through Private Eyes: The Screen Adaptation of the Hard-Boiled Private Detective Novel in the Studio Era* (New York: Lang, 2006), 136.

17. "James M. Cain: Tough Guy," 125.

18. Wilder, "On the Fourth Floor at Paramount," 47.

19. Billy Wilder, interview by Robert Porfirio, in Silver, Ursini, and Porfirio, *Film Noir Reader 3,* 109.

20. Lally, *Wilder Times,* 130; see also Zolotow, *Billy Wilder in Hollywood,* 114.

21. William Nolan, "Marlowe's Mean Streets: The Cinematic World of Raymond Chandler," in *The Big Book of Noir,* ed. Ed Gorman, Lee Server, and Martin Greenberg (New York: Carroll and Graf, 1998), 30.

22. Chandler, *Nobody's Perfect,* 115.

23. MacShane, *Life of Raymond Chandler,* 107; see also "James M. Cain: Tough Guy," 127.

24. "James M. Cain: Tough Guy," 127; see also *The Raymond Chandler Papers: Selected Letters and Non-fiction,* ed. Tom Hiney and Frank MacShane (New York: Atlantic Monthly Press, 2000), 28.

25. Wilder, "On the Fourth Floor at Paramount," 48.

26. James M. Cain, *Double Indemnity* (New York: Vintage, 1992), 23–24.

27. Andrew Sarris, "Billy Wilder, Closet Romanticist," *Film Comment* 12, no. 4 (1977): 8.

28. Dunne, "Old Pornographer," 91.

29. Alan Woolfolk, "The Horizon of Disenchantment," in *The Philosophy of Film Noir,* ed. Mark Conrad (Lexington: University Press of Kentucky, 2006), 120.

30. Mark Conrad, "The Meaning and Definition of Noir," in Conrad, *Philosophy of Film Noir,* 11; see also Paul Schrader, "Notes on Film Noir," in *American Movie Critics: An Anthology from the Silents until Now,* ed. Phillip Lopate (New York: Library of America, 2008), 457.

31. Foster Hirsch, *The Dark Side of the Screen: Film Noir,* rev. ed. (New York: Da Capo, 2009), 117.

32. *Shadows of Suspense,* documentary, directed by Jonathan Gaines (New Wave Entertainment, 2006).

33. Nino Frank, "The Crime Adventure Story: A New Kind of Detective Film," trans. Barton Palmer, in *Perspectives on Film Noir,* ed. Barton Palmer (New York: Twayne, 1994), 21–22.

34. Jason Holt, "A Darker Shade," in Conrad, *Philosophy of Film Noir,* 27.

35. Alain Silver, James Ursini, and Paul Duncan, *Film Noir* (Los Angeles: Taschen, 2004), 37; see also Wilder, interview by Porfirio, 104.

36. Zolotow, *Billy Wilder in Hollywood,* 117.

37. Irwin, *Unless the Threat of Death,* 53.

38. Axel Madsen, *Billy Wilder* (London: Secker and Warburg, 1968), 91.

39. "Dialogue on Film: Billy Wilder and I. A. L. Diamond," in Horton, *Billy Wilder: Interviews,* 127. This is an edited transcript of a seminar that Wilder and Diamond gave at the American Film Institute.

40. Fred MacMurray, interview by author, Beverly Hills, CA, July 10, 1987.

41. Chandler, *Nobody's Perfect,* 118.

42. Wilder, interview by Porfirio, 116.

43. Richard Schickel, "Commentary," *Double Indemnity,* DVD, directed by Billy Wilder (Paramount Home Video, 2006).

44. Rozsa, *Double Life,* 142.

45. Robert Horton, "Music Man: Miklos Rozsa," *Film Comment* 31, no. 6 (1995): 3.

46. Schickel, *Double Indemnity,* 39.

47. Crowe, *Conversations with Wilder,* 357.

48. Peter Evans, "*Double Indemnity,*" in *The Book of Film Noir,* ed. Ian Cameron (New York: Continuum, 1992), 127.

49. Cain, *Double Indemnity,* 80.

50. Ibid., 3.

51. Evans, "*Double Indemnity,*" 169.

52. Ibid., 168; see also James A. Paris, "Murder Can Sometimes Smell like Honeysuckle: Billy Wilder's *Double Indemnity,*" in *Film Noir Reader 4: The Crucial Films and Themes,* ed. Alain Silver and James Ursini (New York: Limelight, 2004), 21.

53. Frank Krutnik, *In a Lonely Street: Film Noir, Genre, Masculinity* (New York: Routledge, 1991), 253.

54. Mark Bould, *Film Noir: From Berlin to Sin City* (Irvington, NY: Columbia University Press, 2006), 37.

55. MacMurray, interview.

56. "James M. Cain: Tough Guy," 125; see also Alain Silver and James Ursini, *The Noir Style* (Woodstock, NY: Overlook Press, 2003), 142.

57. Wilder and Chandler, *Double Indemnity: A Screenplay,* 109.

58. Dick, *Billy Wilder,* 48.

59. "James M. Cain: Tough Guy," 125.

60. Dick, *Billy Wilder,* 43.

61. Meyers, introduction to *Double Indemnity: A Screenplay,* xiii.

62. "James M. Cain: Tough Guy," 126.

63. Schickel, "Commentary."

64. Lally, *Wilder Times,* 137; Meyers, introduction to *Double Indemnity: A Screenplay,* xiv.

65. "Billy Wilder," in Stevens, *Conversations,* 331.

66. Wilder and Chandler, *Double Indemnity: A Screenplay,* 120. This is the original screenplay, which includes the execution scene, 120–23. Jeffrey Meyers claims that the execution scene is "now published for the first time" in his edition. Meyers, introduction to *Double Indemnity: A Screenplay,* xiv. As a matter of fact, the execution scene is included in the version of the script published in Sam Thomas, ed., *Best American Screenplays* (New York: Crown, 1995), 302–4.

67. James Naremore, *More Than Night: Film Noir in Its Contexts,* rev. ed. (Los Angeles: University of California Press, 2008), 91.

68. Hare, *Early Film Noir,* 45.

69. *Double Indemnity* scripts, Paramount Collection, Margaret Herrick Library, Academy of Motion Picture Arts and Sciences, Beverly Hills, CA; cf.

Billy Wilder and Raymond Chandler, *Double Indemnity: A Screenplay,* in Raymond Chandler, *Later Novels and Other Writings,* ed. Frank MacShane (New York: Library of America, 1995), 970–72. The latter is the final version of the screenplay, which has the ending as it appears in the release prints of the movie, so it does not include the execution scene.

70. Thomas Leitsch, "*Double Indemnity,*" in *Encyclopedia of Novels into Film,* ed. James Welsh and John Tibbetts (New York: Facts on File, 2005), 104.

71. Sikov, *On Sunset Boulevard,* 230; see also Schickel, *Double Indemnity,* 68.

72. Studlar, "Hard-Boiled Film Noir," 397.

73. Kanin, *Hollywood,* 152.


## 5. THROUGH A GLASS DARKLY

1. Wood, *Bright Side of Billy Wilder,* 87.

2. Lally, *Wilder Times,* 143.

3. Ibid., 143–44.

4. Zolotow, *Billy Wilder in Hollywood,* 128.

5. Wood, *Bright Side of Billy Wilder,* 88.

6. Charles Higham and Joel Greenberg, *The Celluloid Muse: Hollywood Directors Speak* (Chicago: Regnery, 1969), 249.

7. Lally, *Wilder Times,* 115.

8. Preface to *The Lost Weekend,* by Charles Jackson (New York: Time, 1963), xi.

9. Ibid., ix, xii.

10. Wilder, interview by Porfirio, 110. The staff of the Rush Medical Center in Chicago likewise assured me that Wilder's portrait of an alcoholic is an accurate one.

11. Harry Benshoff and Sean Griffin, *Queer Images: A History of Gay and Lesbian Films in America* (New York: Rowman and Littlefield, 2006), 35.

12. Jackson, *Lost Weekend,* 48–49.

13. Lally, *Wilder Times,* 145.

14. Ibid., 144.

15. Armstrong, *Billy Wilder,* 41.

16. Hirsch, *Dark Side of the Screen,* 191–92.

17. Nash and Ross, *Motion Picture Guide,* 1738.

18. Chris Columbus, "Wilder Times," *American Film,* March 1968, 27.

19. Ray Milland, *Wide-Eyed in Babylon* (New York: Morrow, 1974), 211.

20. Sarris, *You Ain't Heard Nothin' Yet,* 329.

21. Lawrence Quirk, *Jane Wyman: The Actress and the Woman* (New York: Dembner Books, 1986), 79.

22. Eileen Creelman, "Doris Dowling Discusses Her First Movie," *New York Sun,* November 24, 1945, 11.

23. Madsen, *Billy Wilder*, 26.

24. Pauline Kael, *5001 Nights at the Movies* (New York: Holt, 1991), 437.

25. John F. Seitz, interview by James Ursini, in Silver, Ursini, and Porfirio, *Film Noir Reader 3*, 207.

26. Milland, *Wide-Eyed in Babylon*, 224.

27. Nash and Ross, *Motion Picture Guide*, 1738.

28. Sikov, *On Sunset Boulevard*, 221.

29. Zolotow, *Billy Wilder in Hollywood*, 131; see also Madsen, *Billy Wilder*, 32.

30. Armstrong, *Billy Wilder*, 41.

31. Ibid., 39.

32. Judy Cornes, *Alcohol in the Movies, 1898–1962: A Critical History* (Jefferson, NC: McFarland, 2006), 125.

33. Chandler, *Nobody's Perfect*, 125.

34. Cornes, *Alcohol in the Movies*, 135.

35. Jackson, *Lost Weekend*, 277.

36. Stephen Farber, "The Films of Billy Wilder," *Film Comment* 7, no. 1 (1971–1972): 10; see also David Thomson, *The New Biographical Dictionary of Film*, rev. ed. (New York: Knopf, 2004), 962.

37. Andrew Sarris, *The American Cinema: Directors and Directions, 1929–1968*, rev. ed. (New York: Da Capo, 1996), 166.

38. Crowe, *Conversations with Wilder*, 269; see also Lally, *Wilder Times*, 150.

39. Rozsa, *Double Life*, 148.

40. Richard Ness, "Miklos Rozsa," in *International Dictionary of Films and Filmmakers*, ed. Tom Pendergast and Sara Pendergast (Detroit: St. James Press, 2000), 4:724; see also Michael Walsh, "Running Up the Score," *Time*, September 11, 1995, 78.

41. Sikov, *On Sunset Boulevard*, 253; see also Lally, *Wilder Times*, 534.

42. Lally, *Wilder Times*, 144; see also Sikov, *On Sunset Boulevard*, 222.

43. Mason Wiley and Damien Bona, *Inside Oscar: The Unofficial History of the Academy Awards* (New York: Ballantine Books, 1993), 150.

44. Lars Penning, "*The Lost Weekend*," in *Movies of the Forties*, ed. Jürgen Muller (Los Angeles: Taschen/BFI, 2005), 271–72.

45. James Agee, *Film Writing and Selected Journalism*, ed. Michael Sragow (New York: Library of America, 2005), 215; see also Clive James, "How to Write about Film," *New York Times Book Review*, June 6, 2006, 38.

46. Wiley and Bona, *Inside Oscar*, 150.

47. "*Lost Weekend*'s Author Loves the Movie," *P.M. New York*, November 25, 1945, 3.

48. Sarris, *You Ain't Heard Nothin' Yet*, 127.

49. Madsen, *Billy Wilder*, 67–68.

50. Wilder, interview by Prelutsky, 186.

51. Nash and Ross, *Motion Picture Guide,* 1738.

52. Lally, *Wilder Times,* 142; see also Crowe, *Conversations with Wilder,* 14.

53. Lally, *Wilder Times,* 156.

54. A copy of *Die Todesmühlen,* along with an English translation of the narration, is in the Records of the Office of the Chief Signal Officer, RG 111, National Archives, College Park, MD.

55. Sikov, *On Sunset Boulevard,* 249.

56. Freeman, "*Sunset Boulevard* Revisited," 75.

57. Chandler, *Nobody's Perfect,* 141.

58. Richard Lemon, "Billy Wilder's *Fortune Cookie,*" in Horton, *Billy Wilder: Interviews,* 50.

59. Sikov, *On Sunset Boulevard,* 279.

60. Lemon, "Billy Wilder's *Fortune Cookie,*" 50.

61. Crowe, *Conversations with Wilder,* 313.

62. Sikov, *On Sunset Boulevard,* 259.

## 6. WUNDERBAR

1. Sarris, "Billy Wilder, Closet Romanticist," 8.

2. Kanin, *Hollywood,* 153.

3. Crowe, *Conversations with Wilder,* 70, 256, 340.

4. Chandler, *Nobody's Perfect,* 134.

5. Sikov, *On Sunset Boulevard,* 263–64.

6. Billy Wilder and Charles Brackett, memorandum to all concerned with the production, May 31, 1946, Paramount Collection.

7. Karasek, *Billy Wilder,* 340.

8. Madsen, *Billy Wilder,* 73; see also Wood, *Bright Side of Billy Wilder,* 94.

9. Zolotow, *Billy Wilder in Hollywood,* 152.

10. Billy Wilder, notice posted on bulletin board in production office, n.d., Paramount Collection; see also Zolotow, *Billy Wilder in Hollywood,* 152.

11. Chandler, *Nobody's Perfect,* 134–35.

12. Roger Osterholm, *Bing Crosby: A Bio-bibliography* (Westport, CT: Greenwood Press, 1994), 34.

13. Chandler, *Nobody's Perfect,* 138.

14. Osterholm, *Bing Crosby,* 265.

15. Dick, *Billy Wilder,* 126.

16. Kanin, *Hollywood,* 153–54.

17. Crowe, *Conversations with Wilder,* 170; see also Chandler, *Nobody's Perfect,* 135.

18. Eyman, *Ernst Lubitsch,* 350.

19. Otto Preminger, interview by author, New York, April 22, 1979.

20. William Wyler, interview by author, Hollywood, CA, March 24, 1976.

21. Madsen, *Billy Wilder*, 74.

22. Michael Barson, *Hollywood Directors of the Sound Era* (New York: Noonday Press, 1995), 455.

23. Agee, *Film Writing and Selected Journalism*, 358.

24. Sikov, *On Sunset Boulevard*, 278.

25. Crowe, *Conversations with Wilder*, 340.

26. Steven Bach, *Marlene Dietrich: Life and Legend* (New York: Morrow, 1992), 329.

27. Zolotow, *Billy Wilder in Hollywood*, 137.

28. Sikov, *On Sunset Boulevard*, 249.

29. David Shaw, "Love in the Air," May 1947, 1, Paramount Collection.

30. Hopp, *Billy Wilder*, 62.

31. Zolotow, *Billy Wilder in Hollywood*, 155.

32. "Dialogue on Film: Billy Wilder and I. A. L. Diamond," 114.

33. Marlene Dietrich, *Marlene* (New York: Avon, 1990), 238.

34. Maria Riva, *Marlene Dietrich* (New York: Knopf, 1993), 195.

35. Ibid.

36. Ean Wood, *Dietrich: A Biography* (London: Sanctuary, 2002), 255–56; see also Bach, *Marlene Dietrich*, 332.

37. Volker Schlöndorff, interview by David Riva, in *A Woman at War: Marlene Dietrich Remembered*, ed. David Riva (Detroit: Wayne State University Press, 2006), 24. This book is a companion to David Riva's documentary about his grandmother, *Marlene Dietrich: Her Own Song* (2001).

38. Robert Dassanowsky-Harris, "Billy Wilder's Germany," pt. 1, *Films in Review* 41, no. 5 (1990): 293.

39. Oliver Kuch, "*A Foreign Affair,*" in Muller, *Movies of the Forties*, 437.

40. Crowe, *Conversations with Wilder*, 80.

41. Bach, *Marlene Dietrich*, 329.

42. Schlöndorff, interview, 24.

43. J. M. Woodstock, "The Name Dropper," *American Cinemeditor* 39, no. 4 (1990): 15.

44. "The Production Code of the Motion Picture Association of America," reprinted in Gregory D. Black, *Hollywood Censored: Morality Codes, Catholics, and the Movies* (New York: Cambridge University Press, 1994), 308.

45. See *A Foreign Affair* file, Paramount Collection.

46. *Marlene Dietrich: Her Own Song*, documentary, directed by David Riva (APG, 2001); see also Maria Riva, interview, in Riva, *Woman at War*, 133.

47. Giannetti, *Understanding Movies*, 483.

48. Wood, *Dietrich*, 258.

49. Schlöndorff, interview, 24.

50. Wood, *Dietrich*, 258; see also Crowe, *Conversations with Wilder*, 74.

51. Corliss, *Talking Pictures*, 145.

52. Sarris, *American Cinema*, 166.

53. Sarris, "Billy Wilder, Closet Romanticist," 9.

54. Dassanowsky-Harris, "Billy Wilder's Germany," pt. 1, 294.

55. Karasek, *Billy Wilder*, 394.

56. Dassanowsky-Harris, "Billy Wilder's Germany," pt. 1, 296.

57. Farber, "Films of Billy Wilder," 14; see also Robert McLaughlin and Sally Parry, *We'll Always Have the Movies: American Cinema during World War II* (Lexington: University Press of Kentucky, 2006), 296.

58. Taylor, *Strangers in Paradise*, 201.

59. Malene Sheppard Skaerved, *Dietrich* (London: Haus, 2003), 132.

60. Farber, "Films of Billy Wilder," 13.

61. Stuart Schulberg, "A Communication: A Letter about Billy Wilder," *Quarterly of Film, Radio, and Television* 7, no. 4 (1952): 434.

62. Kuch, "*Foreign Affair,*" 435.

63. Lally, *Wilder Times*, 184.

64. Kuch, "*Foreign Affair,*" 435; also see Skaerved, *Dietrich*, 132.

65. Sam Staggs, *Close-Up on Sunset Boulevard* (New York: St. Martin's Press, 2003), 20.

## 7. DARK WINDOWS

1. Billy Wilder, "Wilder Seeks Films with Bite," interview by Philip Scheuer, in Horton, *Billy Wilder: Interviews*, 127.

2. "Billy Wilder," in Stevens, *Conversations*, 306.

3. "Dialogue on Film: Billy Wilder and I. A. L. Diamond," 119.

4. Charles Brackett, "Putting the Picture on Paper" (lecture, n.d.), 1–3, Paramount Collection.

5. Ibid., 3.

6. Armand Deutsch, *Me and Bogie* (New York: Putnam, 1991), 155–56.

7. Madsen, *Billy Wilder*, 82.

8. Thomson, *New Biographical Dictionary of Film*, 656.

9. Lally, *Wilder Times*, 187.

10. Wilder, interview by Porfirio, 112; see also "Billy Wilder," in Stevens, *Conversations*, 326.

11. Billy Wilder, Charles Brackett, and D. M. Marshman Jr., "Sunset Boulevard: Draft Script," December 21, 1948, Paramount Collection.

12. Staggs, *Close-Up on Sunset Boulevard*, 61.

13. Agee, *Film Writing and Selected Journalism*, 467.

14. Joseph I. Breen to Billy Wilder, May 24, 1949, *Sunset Boulevard* file, Paramount Collection.

15. George Cukor, interview by author, Los Angeles, August 18, 1980.

16. "Billy Wilder: The Art of Screenwriting," interview by James Linville, in *The Paris Review Interviews*, ed. James Gourevitch (New York: St. Martin's Press, 2006), 1:418.

17. Chandler, *Nobody's Perfect*, 146.

18. Scott Eyman, *Mary Pickford: America's Sweetheart* (New York: Fine, 1990), 282.

19. Wilder, interview by Gehman, 65.

20. "Billy Wilder," in Stevens, *Conversations*, 303.

21. Cukor, interview.

22. Gloria Swanson, *Swanson on Swanson* (New York: Pocket Books, 1981), 494; see also Zolotow, *Billy Wilder in Hollywood*, 160.

23. Lennig, *Stroheim*, 445; see also Koszarski, *Von*, 289.

24. Lennig, *Stroheim*, 445.

25. Seitz, interview, 209.

26. Bob Thomas, *Golden Boy: The Untold Story of William Holden* (New York: St. Martin's Press, 1983), 59.

27. Milt Machler, *Libby* (New York: Tower, 1980), 12.

28. "William Holden: An Untamed Spirit," *Biography*, A&E, April 27, 1999; see also Thomas, *Golden Boy*, 61.

29. Thomas, *Golden Boy*, 228.

30. Dunne, "Old Pornographer," 91; see also Staggs, *Close-Up on Sunset Boulevard*, 72.

31. *Swanson on Swanson*, 498.

32. Staggs, *Close-Up on Sunset Boulevard*, 67.

33. Freeman, "*Sunset Boulevard* Revisited," 77.

34. Ibid.; see also Staggs, *Close-Up on Sunset Boulevard*, 67, 103.

35. Billy Wilder, Charles Brackett, and D. M. Marshman Jr., *Sunset Boulevard: A Screenplay*, ed. Jeffrey Meyers (Los Angeles: University of California Press, 1999), 43.

36. Gloria Swanson, interview, *Queen Kelly*, DVD, directed by Erich von Stroheim (Kino Video, 2003).

37. *Swanson on Swanson*, 499.

38. Seitz, interview, 208.

39. Wood, *Bright Side of Billy Wilder*, 98.

40. Katelin Trowbridge, "The War between Words and Images: *Sunset Boulevard*," *Literature/Film Quarterly* 30, no. 4 (2002): 296.

41. *Swanson on Swanson*, 499.

42. Ibid., 499–500.

43. John Meehan, "*Sunset Boulevard*," *Society of Motion Picture Art Directors Bulletin*, May–June 1951, 2.

44. Herb Lightman, "Old Master, New Tricks," *American Cinematographer* 31, no. 9 (1950): 318.

45. Sikov, *On Sunset Boulevard*, 293.

46. *Swanson on Swanson*, 220.

47. Ibid., 501.

48. Daniel Brown, "Wilde and Wilder," *PMLA* 119, no. 5 (2004): 1218.

49. Christopher Ames, *Movies about Movies: Hollywood Reflected* (Lexington: University Press of Kentucky, 1997), 200–201.

50. Wilder, Brackett, and Marshman, *Sunset Boulevard: A Screenplay*, 98.

51. Zolotow, *Billy Wilder in Hollywood*, 164.

52. Staggs, *Close-Up on Sunset Boulevard*, 147.

53. Tony Thomas, *Film Score: The View from the Podium* (London: Yoseloff, 1979), 57.

54. John Caps, "Movie Music," *Film Comment* 39, no. 6 (2003): 37.

55. Freeman, "*Sunset Boulevard* Revisited," 77.

56. Crowe, *Conversations with Wilder*, 214.

57. Karasek, *Billy Wilder*, 354; see also Chandler, *Nobody's Perfect*, 150.

58. Seitz, interview, 210; cf. Sikov, *On Sunset Boulevard*, 301.

59. Crowe, *Conversations with Wilder*, 255.

60. Avrom Fleishman, *Narrated Films: Storytelling Situations in Cinema History* (Baltimore: Johns Hopkins University Press, 1992), 96.

61. Brown, "Wilde and Wilder," 1217.

62. *Swanson on Swanson*, 500.

63. Staggs, *Close-Up on Sunset Boulevard*, 110.

64. Freeman, "*Sunset Boulevard* Revisited," 77.

65. Jeffrey Meyers, introduction to Wilder, Brackett, and Marshman, *Sunset Boulevard: A Screenplay*, xi.

66. Morris Dickstein, "*Sunset Boulevard*," in *The A List: 100 Essential Films*, ed. Jay Carr (New York: Da Capo, 2002), 282.

67. Steffen Haubner, "*Sunset Boulevard*," in Muller, *Movies of the Forties*, 543.

68. Higham and Greenberg, *Celluloid Muse*, 250.

69. Billy Wilder and Rudy Behlmer, audiotape of dialogue, November 8, 1976, Paramount Collection; see also Wood, *Bright Side of Billy Wilder*, 100.

70. Billy Wilder, interview by Richard Brown, *Reflections on the Silver Screen*, AMC, 1993.

71. *Swanson on Swanson*, 501–2.

72. Louis Giannetti and Scott Eyman, *Flashback: A Brief History of Film*, rev. ed. (Upper Saddle River, NJ: Prentice Hall, 2006), 197.

73. Staggs, *Close-Up on Sunset Boulevard*, 158.

74. Agee, *Film Writing and Selected Journalism*, 468–69.

75. Staggs, *Close-Up on Sunset Boulevard*, 185.

76. Axel Madsen, *Stanwyck* (New York: HarperCollins, 1994), 286.

77. Crowe, *Conversations with Wilder*, 35.

78. Kanin, *Hollywood*, 153.

79. Ibid.

80. Chandler, *Nobody's Perfect*, xv.

81. Wilder, interview by Prelutsky, 185.

## 8. BARBED WIRE SATIRE

1. Manny Farber, "Underground Films," in Lopate, *American Movie Critics,* 223–24.

2. Hirsch, *Dark Side of the Screen,* 83.

3. Chandler, *Nobody's Perfect,* 37.

4. Wilder, interview by Prelutsky, 184; see also Wilder, "Wilder Seeks Films with Bite," 16.

5. Robert Murray and Roger Brucker, *Trapped! The Story of Floyd Collins* (Lexington: University Press of Kentucky, 1999), 74, 170, 172.

6. Wood, *Bright Side of Billy Wilder,* 103; see also Wilder, "Wilder Seeks Films with Bite," 171.

7. Billy Wilder, Walter Newman, and Lesser Samuels, "Ace in the Hole: Draft Script," May 31, 1950, Paramount Collection.

8. J. P. Telotte, *Voices in the Dark: The Narrative Patterns of Film Noir* (Urbana: University of Illinois Press, 1989), 83.

9. Billy Wilder, Walter Newman, and Lesser Samuels, "Ace in the Hole: Unpublished Screenplay," Paramount Collection.

10. Wilder, "Wilder Seeks Films with Bite," 16; see also Armstrong, *Billy Wilder,* 56.

11. Joseph I. Breen to Billy Wilder, July 15, 1950, *Ace in the Hole* file, Paramount Collection.

12. Armstrong, *Billy Wilder,* 57.

13. Madsen, *Billy Wilder,* 93.

14. Breen to Wilder, July 15, 1950.

15. Kirk Douglas to Billy Wilder, June 19, 1950, Kirk Douglas Collection, State Historical Society of Wisconsin, Madison.

16. Chandler, *Nobody's Perfect,* 166.

17. Kirk Douglas, interview, 1984, *Ace in the Hole,* DVD, directed by Billy Wilder (Criterion, 2007).

18. Sikov, *On Sunset Boulevard,* 315.

19. *Ace in the Hole* press book, Paramount Collection.

20. Murray and Brucker, *Trapped,* 247–48.

21. Staggs, *Close-Up on Sunset Boulevard,* 251.

22. Lemon, "Billy Wilder's *Fortune Cookie,*" 54–55; see also "Billy Wilder," in Stevens, *Conversations,* 327.

23. Farber, "Underground Films," 231.

24. Tony Thomas, "Hugo Friedhofer," in Pendergast and Pendergast, *International Dictionary of Films and Filmmakers,* 4:285.

25. Thomas, *Film Score,* 213–14.

26. Madsen, *Billy Wilder,* 93; see also Chandler, *Nobody's Perfect,* 166.

27. Kirk Douglas, *The Ragman's Son: An Autobiography* (New York: Simon and Schuster, 1988), 178.

28. Dick, *Billy Wilder,* 60.

29. Crowe, *Conversations with Wilder,* 205.

30. Lally, *Wilder Times,* 212; see also Sarris, *You Ain't Heard Nothin' Yet,* 333.

31. Nash and Ross, *Motion Picture Guide,* 190.

32. Guy Maddin, "Chin Up for Mother," in *Ace in the Hole,* souvenir program (Criterion Collection, 2007), 4.

33. Douglas, interview.

34. Wilder, interview by Porfirio, 111; see also Wood, *Bright Side of Billy Wilder,* 106.

35. Chandler, *Nobody's Perfect,* 185; see also Wilder, interview by Porfirio, 111.

36. Maddin, "Chin Up for Mother," 4.

37. Chandler, *Nobody's Perfect,* 165. The film was repackaged for TV as *The Big Carnival,* but history repeated itself. When the movie was a flop on TV, the original title was once more restored for reruns. Surprisingly, a few film historians still refer to the movie as *The Big Carnival,* even though the original title was permanently reinstated.

38. Wilder, interview by Gehman, 59; see also Zolotow, *Billy Wilder in Hollywood,* 176.

39. Lemon, "Billy Wilder's *Fortune Cookie,*" 49.

40. Luft, "Matter of Decadence," 65.

41. Charles Brackett, "A Matter of Humor," in "Two Views of a Director," 66.

42. Luft, "Matter of Decadence," 65.

43. Brackett, "Matter of Humor," 69.

44. John J. O'Connor, "A Salute to Kirk Douglas for His Life," *New York Times,* May 23, 1991, C32.

45. Manohla Dargis, "The Listings," *New York Times,* January 12, 2007, B31; see also "Movies," *New Yorker,* January 15, 2007, 6.

46. Stephen Cahir, "*Stalag 17,*" in *The Encyclopedia of Stage Plays into Film,* ed. James Welsh and John Tibbets (New York: Facts on File, 2001), 279; see also "Screen Rights to *Stalag 17,*" *Variety,* August 29, 1951, 5.

47. Zolotow, *Billy Wilder in Hollywood,* 179.

48. *Stalag 17: From Reality to Screen,* documentary (Paramount Home Video, 2006). Unless specifically noted otherwise, all quotations from the cast members and Bevan in this chapter are from this source.

49. Preminger, interview.

50. Taylor, *Strangers in Paradise,* 67.

51. Thomas, *Golden Boy,* 80.

52. Madsen, *Billy Wilder,* 22.

53. Chandler, *Nobody's Perfect,* 167.

54. Armstrong, *Billy Wilder,* 65.

55. Sikov, *On Sunset Boulevard,* 338.

56. Billy Wilder and Edwin Blum, *Stalag 17: A Screenplay,* ed. Jeffrey Meyers (Los Angeles: University of California Press, 1999), 25.

57. Joseph I. Breen to Billy Wilder, February 19, 1956, *Stalag 17* file, Paramount Collection; see also Dick, *Billy Wilder,* 69.

58. Wilder and Blum, *Stalag 17: A Screenplay,* 113–14.

59. Jeffrey Meyers, introduction to Wilder and Blum, *Stalag 17: A Screenplay,* xi.

60. Zolotow, *Billy Wilder in Hollywood,* 301.

61. Crowe, *Conversations with Wilder,* 42.

62. Ibid., 305.

63. John Gallagher, "Ernest Laszlo," in Pendergast and Pendergast, *International Dictionary of Films and Filmmakers,* 6:485.

64. Foster Hirsch, *Otto Preminger* (New York: Knopf, 2007), 403.

65. Preminger, interview.

66. Bogdanovich, *Who the Devil Made It,* 606.

67. Crowe, *Conversations with Wilder,* 97.

68. Thomas, *Golden Boy,* 80.

69. Nash and Ross, *Motion Picture Guide,* 3098; see also Chandler, *Nobody's Perfect,* 168.

70. Billy Wilder to Franz Waxman, April 5, 1957, *Stalag 17* file, Paramount Collection.

71. Cahir, "*Stalag 17,*" 280.

72. Sarris, *American Cinema,* 166.

73. Nash and Ross, *Motion Picture Guide,* 3098.

74. Sikov, *On Sunset Boulevard,* 344.

75. Staggs, *Close-Up on Sunset Boulevard,* 186.

76. Thomas, *Golden Boy,* 82–83.

77. Billy Wilder, interview by Volker Schlöndorff, 1988, in *Billy Wilder Speaks,* documentary, directed by Gisela Grischow and Volker Schlöndorff (Bioskop Film, 2006). The documentary, created for German TV, aired on TCM in 2006 with English subtitles.

78. See *Stalag 17* file, Paramount Collection.

79. Alan Andres, "Anti-hero: William Holden Gambles on *Stalag 17,*" *American Movie Classics,* December 1993, 1–2.

## 9. FASCINATION

1. Dominic Head, ed., *The Cambridge Guide to Literature in English* (New York: Cambridge University Press, 2006), 231.

2. Donald Spoto, *Enchantment: The Life of Audrey Hepburn* (New York: Harmony Books, 2006), 112.

3. Ibid., 99.

4. Zolotow, *Billy Wilder in Hollywood*, 237.

5. Philip Kemp, "Ernest Lehman," in Pendergast and Pendergast, *International Dictionary of Films and Filmmakers*, 4:990.

6. Lally, *Wilder Times*, 237.

7. Ezra Goodman, *The Fifty-Year Decline and Fall of Hollywood* (New York: Simon and Schuster, 1961), 271; see also Alexander Walker, *Audrey: Her Real Story* (New York: St. Martin's Press, 1994), 86.

8. Lally, *Wilder Times*, 237.

9. Peter Bogdanovich, *Who the Hell's in It: Conversations with Hollywood's Legendary Actors* (New York: Ballantine Books, 2006), 437; see also Chandler, *Nobody's Perfect*, 174.

10. Jeffrey Meyers, *Bogart: A Life in Hollywood* (New York: Houghton Mifflin, 1997), 282.

11. Richard Schickel, "Appreciation: The Genuine Article," in *Bogie: The Life and Films of Humphrey Bogart*, by Richard Schickel and George Perry (New York: St. Martin's Press, 2006), 21.

12. Spoto, *Enchantment*, 112.

13. Richard Gehman, "Charming Billy," *Playboy*, December 1960, 90; see also Walker, *Audrey*, 97.

14. Spoto, *Enchantment*, 108.

15. Stephen Bogart, foreword to Schickel and Perry, *Bogie*, 11.

16. Meyers, *Bogart*, 282.

17. Crowe, *Conversations with Wilder*, 9, 173–74.

18. Thomas, *Golden Boy*, 85.

19. Meyers, *Bogart*, 283.

20. Goodman, *Fifty-Year Decline*, 265.

21. Stephen Bogart, *Bogart: In Search of My Father* (New York: Dutton, 1995), 179.

22. See Sikov, *On Sunset Boulevard*, 314, for a slightly different version of Wilder's insult to Bogart.

23. Goodman, *Fifty-Year Decline*, 266.

24. Thomas, *Golden Boy*, 86.

25. Meyers, *Bogart*, 284.

26. Spoto, *Enchantment*, 109; see also Ian Woodward, *Audrey Hepburn* (New York: St. Martin's Press, 1984), 117.

27. Meyers, *Bogart*, 284.

28. Crowe, *Conversations with Wilder*, 159.

29. David Hofstede, *Audrey Hepburn: A Bio-bibliography* (Westport, CT: Greenwood Press, 1994), 75; see also Spoto, *Enchantment*, 110–11.

30. Crowe, *Conversations with Wilder*, 173; see also Bogart, *In Search of My Father*, 179–81.

31. "Ernest Lehman," in Stevens, *Conversations with the Great Moviemakers*, 486.

32. Lally, *Wilder Times,* 237; see also Zolotow, *Billy Wilder in Hollywood,* 253.

33. Goodman, *Fifty-Year Decline,* 266.

34. Zolotow, *Billy Wilder in Hollywood,* 185.

35. Ibid., 156; see also Lally, *Wilder Times,* 235.

36. Hopp, *Billy Wilder,* 91.

37. Schickel, "Appreciation," 72, 76.

38. Karasek, *Billy Wilder,* 385.

39. Walker, *Audrey,* 97.

40. Lally, *Wilder Times,* 240; see also Zolotow, *Billy Wilder in Hollywood,* 140.

41. Barbara Leaming, *Marilyn Monroe* (New York: Random House, 1998), 114.

42. Madsen, *Billy Wilder,* 14.

43. Wilder, interview by Gehman, 60.

44. George Axelrod, interview by Patrick McGilligan, *Film Comment* 31, no. 6 (1995): 14.

45. Ibid., 12.

46. Wilder, interview by Brown; see also Crowe, *Conversations with Wilder,* 85.

47. Erich Stahl, "*The Seven Year Itch,*" in *Movies of the Fifties,* ed. Jürgen Muller (Los Angeles: Taschen/BFI, 2005), 225.

48. Billy Wilder and George Axelrod, *The Seven Year Itch: Unpublished Screenplay* (Los Angeles: Twentieth Century–Fox, 1954), 77.

49. Axelrod, interview, 12.

50. Rebecca Epstein, "*The Seven Year Itch,*" in Welsh and Tibbetts, *Encyclopedia of Stage Plays into Film,* 266.

51. Pat Kirkham, "Saul Bass and Billy Wilder in Conversation," *Sight and Sound,* n.s., 5, no. 6 (1995): 20.

52. Armstrong, *Billy Wilder,* 79.

53. Zolotow, *Billy Wilder in Hollywood,* 230.

54. Gene D. Phillips, *Major Film Directors of the American and British Cinema,* rev. ed. (Bethlehem, PA: Lehigh University Press, 1999), 107.

55. "Entretien avec Billy Wilder," interview by Michael Ciment, *Positif,* August 1983, 20. Bridgette Chandler translated the cited passages.

56. Douglas Brode, *The Films of the Fifties* (New York: Carol, 1993), 136.

57. "Entretien avec Billy Wilder," 1983, 21.

58. Leaming, *Marilyn Monroe,* 128.

59. Crowe, *Conversations with Wilder,* 344.

60. Anthony Summers, *Goddess: The Secret Lives of Marilyn Monroe* (New York: Macmillan, 1986), 118.

61. Fred Lawrence Guiles, *Norma Jean: The Life of Marilyn Monroe* (New York: McGraw-Hill, 1969), 157.

62. Chandler, *Nobody's Perfect,* 180.

63. Wood, *Bright Side of Billy Wilder*, 111.

64. Chandler, *Nobody's Perfect*, 180.

65. Leaming, *Marilyn Monroe*, 128; see also Sarah Churchwell, *The Many Lives of Marilyn Monroe* (New York: Holt, 2006), 47.

66. Wilder and Axelrod, *Seven Year Itch: Unpublished Screenplay*, 77.

67. Sikov, *On Sunset Boulevard*, 366.

68. "*The Seven Year Itch*," *Backstory*, AMC, August 26, 2000.

69. Hawks, interview.

70. "Billy Wilder," in Stevens, *Conversations*, 312.

71. Leaming, *Marilyn Monroe*, 33; see also Wood, *Bright Side of Billy Wilder*, 110.

72. Zolotow, *Billy Wilder in Hollywood*, 255.

73. Lally, *Wilder Times*, 243.

74. Bernard Dick, *Forever Mame: The Life of Rosalind Russell* (Jackson: University Press of Mississippi, 2006), 79.

75. Wilder and Axelrod, *Seven Year Itch: Unpublished Screenplay*, 66.

76. "Dialogue on Film: Billy Wilder and I. A. L. Diamond," 124.

77. Philip Kemp, "Saul Bass," in Pendergast and Pendergast, *International Dictionary of Films and Filmmakers*, 4:67.

78. Churchwell, *Many Lives of Marilyn Monroe*, 37; see also Chandler, *Nobody's Perfect*, 180.

79. Louis Giannetti, *Masters of the American Cinema* (Englewood Cliffs, NJ: Prentice Hall, 1981), 324.

80. François Truffaut, *The Films of My Life* (New York: Simon and Schuster, 1975), 159.

81. Churchwell, *Many Lives of Marilyn Monroe*, 59–60; see also Dick, *Billy Wilder*, 80.

82. Marilyn Monroe, interview by Edward R. Murrow, *Person to Person*, CBS-TV, April 8, 1955.

83. Sikov, *On Sunset Boulevard*, 368; see also Leaming, *Marilyn Monroe*, 137.

84. Ephraim Katz, *The Film Encyclopedia*, ed. Fred Klein and Ronald Nolen, rev. ed. (New York: HarperCollins, 2005), 989.

85. Hopp, *Billy Wilder*, 95.

## 10. LIGHT UP THE SKY

1. Chandler, *Nobody's Perfect*, 183.

2. Volker Schlöndorff, "Playing by His Rules: Billy Wilder," *Los Angeles Times Calendar*, June 18, 2006, 8; see also Armstrong, *Billy Wilder*, 80.

3. "Air Force," in *Oxford Desk Encyclopedia of World History*, ed. Edmund Wright (New York: Oxford University Press, 2006), 126; see also Lorraine Glennon, ed., *Our Times* (Atlanta: Turner, 1995), 144.

4. Roquemore, *History Goes to the Movies*, 363.

5. Kyla Dunn, "Death Defying," *New York Times Book Review*, October 7, 2007, 36; see also Chandler, *Nobody's Perfect*, 186.

6. Roquemore, *History Goes to the Movies*, 263–64.

7. *The Dawn of Sound: How Movies Learned to Talk*, documentary (Warner Bros., 2007).

8. Stark Smith, *Jimmy Stewart, Bomber Pilot* (St. Paul, MN: Zenith Press, 2005), 23.

9. Ibid.; see also Nash and Ross, *Motion Picture Guide*, 3070.

10. Roy Pickard, *Jimmy Stewart: A Life in Film* (New York: St. Martin's Press, 1992), 29–30.

11. See Steve Seidman, *The Film Career of Billy Wilder* (Pleasantville, NY: Redgrave, 1977), 89.

12. Allen Eyles, *James Stewart* (London: Allan, 1984), 131.

13. Marc Eliot, *Jimmy Stewart: A Biography* (New York: Random House, 2006), 298; see also Jhan Robbins, *Everybody's Man: A Biography of Jimmy Stewart* (New York: Putnam, 1985), 250.

14. Gary Fishgall, *Pieces of Time: The Life of James Stewart* (New York: Scribner, 1997), 258; see also Higham and Greenberg, *Celluloid Muse*, 251.

15. Sikov, *On Sunset Boulevard*, 379; see also Chandler, *Nobody's Perfect*, 185.

16. Fishgall, *Pieces of Time*, 258; see also Eliot, *Jimmy Stewart*, 299.

17. Fishgall, *Pieces of Time*, 257.

18. Arthur Rowan, "Making the Aerial Shots for *The Spirit of St. Louis*," *American Cinematographer*, June 1957, 367.

19. Leland Hayward to Jack Warner, September 9, 1955, *The Spirit of St. Louis* file, Warner Bros. Archives, Cinematic Arts Library, University of Southern California, Los Angeles.

20. Sikov, *On Sunset Boulevard*, 376–77.

21. Leland Hayward to Jack Warner, [early September 1955?], *The Spirit of St. Louis* file, Warner Bros. Archives.

22. Leland Hayward to Jack Warner, September 25, 1955, *The Spirit of St. Louis* file, Warner Bros. Archives; see also Rowan, "Making the Aerial Shots," 385.

23. Rowan, "Making the Aerial Shots," 381.

24. Leonard Mosley, *Lindbergh: A Biography* (Garden City, NY: Doubleday, 1976), 351.

25. Armstrong, *Billy Wilder*, 85.

26. Interim report, n.d., *The Spirit of St. Louis* file, Warner Bros. Archives.

27. Dick, *Billy Wilder*, 129; see also Hopp, *Billy Wilder*, 101, and Rowan, "Making the Aerial Shots," 385.

28. Sikov, *On Sunset Boulevard*, 378; see also Lally, *Wilder Times*, 253.

29. Dick, *Billy Wilder*, 129–30.

30. Neil Sinyard and Adrian Turner, *Journey down Sunset Boulevard: The Films of Billy Wilder* (Ryde, Isle of Wight: BCW, 1979), 353.

31. "*The Spirit of St. Louis,*" in *Variety Film Reviews, 1907–1996* (New Providence, NJ: Bowker, 1997), vol. 9, n.p.

32. Dunne, "Old Pornographer," 92.

33. Jack Warner, *My First Hundred Years in Hollywood* (New York: Random House, 1964), 320.

34. Pickard, *Jimmy Stewart,* 136.

35. Mosley, *Lindbergh,* 351; see also Scott Berg, *Lindbergh* (New York: Putnam, 1998), 503.

36. Roquemore, *History Goes to the Movies,* 364.

37. Chandler, *Nobody's Perfect,* 187.

38. Zolotow, *Billy Wilder in Hollywood,* 323.

39. Joanne Yeck, "I. A. L. Diamond," in Pendergast and Pendergast, *International Dictionary of Films and Filmmakers,* 4:210.

40. Murray Schumach, "Bright Diamond," *New York Times Magazine,* May 26, 1963, 80–81.

41. Wood, *Bright Side of Billy Wilder,* 117–18.

42. Wilder, interview by Schlöndorff. Sikov, *On Sunset Boulevard,* 390, erroneously states that the title that Broidy mentions is *Omaha,* which is not the name of an Allied Artists film.

43. Wilder, interview by Prelutsky, 188.

44. Lally, *Wilder Times,* 259.

45. Eliot, *Jimmy Stewart,* 341.

46. Wilder, "Going for Extra Innings," 47.

47. Walker, *Audrey,* 139–40.

48. Ibid., 142; see also Halliwell, *Who's Who in the Movies,* 95.

49. Walker, *Audrey,* 141–42; see also Lally, *Wilder Times,* 260.

50. Walker, *Audrey,* 140.

51. Katz, *Film Encyclopedia,* 299.

52. Crowe, *Conversations with Wilder,* 345.

53. Sikov, *On Sunset Boulevard,* 397.

54. Walter Mirisch, *I Thought We Were Making Movies, Not History* (Madison: University of Wisconsin Press, 2008), 81.

55. Thomas Doherty, *Hollywood's Censor: Joseph I. Breen and the Production Code Administration* (New York: Columbia University Press, 2007), 109. The book covers Shurlock's tenure as industry censor as well.

56. *Love in the Afternoon* file, Legion of Decency files, in the author's possession; Sikov, *On Sunset Boulevard,* 369.

57. Crowe, *Conversations with Wilder,* 108; Dick, *Billy Wilder,* 82.

58. Spoto, *Enchantment,* 149.

59. Brownlow to author.

60. Wilder, "Wilder Seeks Films with Bite," 15.

61. "*Love in the Afternoon,*" in *Variety Film Reviews,* vol. 9, n.p.

62. Kael, *5001 Nights at the Movies,* 438.

63. Dick, *Billy Wilder,* 85; see also Hopp, *Billy Wilder,* 110.

64. Chandler, *Nobody's Perfect,* 191.

65. Wood, *Bright Side of Billy Wilder,* 179.

66. Brownlow to author.

67. Thomson, *New Biographical Dictionary of Film,* 903.

68. Barson, *Hollywood Directors,* 457.

69. Sikov, *On Sunset Boulevard,* 396.

70. Eileen Whitaker, *Pickford: A Biography* (Lexington: University Press of Kentucky, 1997), 491.

71. *Portrait of a 60% Perfect Man: Billy Wilder,* documentary, directed by Annie Tresgol (Action Films, 1980).

72. Gehman, "Charming Billy," 61, 70.

## 11. REMAINS TO BE SEEN

1. Charles Osborne, *The Life and Crimes of Agatha Christie* (New York: HarperCollins, 1999), 268–69.

2. Edward Small, interview by author, Los Angeles, July 5, 1977.

3. Jon Tuska, *In Manors and Alleys: The American Detective Film* (New York: Greenwood Press, 1988), 320; see also Sikov, *On Sunset Boulevard,* 403.

4. Wilder, interview by Gehman, 58–59.

5. Farber, "Films of Billy Wilder," 17.

6. Small, interview.

7. Ibid.

8. Halliwell, *Who's Who in the Movies,* 382.

9. Crowe, *Conversations with Wilder,* 69.

10. Tuska, *In Manors and Alleys,* 320.

11. Dick, *Billy Wilder,* 138.

12. Bach, *Marlene Dietrich,* 384.

13. Dassanowsky-Harris, "Billy Wilder's Germany," pt. 1, 294.

14. Wood, *Dietrich,* 299; see also Wood, *Bright Side of Billy Wilder,* 185.

15. Harry Kurnitz, "Billy the Wild," *Holiday,* June 1964, 93, 95.

16. Staggs, *Close-Up on Sunset Boulevard,* 272; see also Hector Arce, *The Secret Life of Tyrone Power* (New York: Morrow, 1979), 254.

17. John Baxter, "Russell Harlan," in Pendergast and Pendergast, *International Dictionary of Films and Filmmakers,* 4:349.

18. Madsen, *Billy Wilder,* 111.

19. Riva, *Marlene Dietrich,* 681–82.

20. Ibid., 648.

21. Wood, *Dietrich,* 299.

22. Bach, *Marlene Dietrich,* 386.

23. Schlöndorff, "Playing by His Rules," 8.

24. Riva, *Marlene Dietrich*, 681.

25. Simon Callow, *Charles Laughton: A Difficult Actor* (New York: Grove Press, 1987), 242.

26. Riva, *Marlene Dietrich*, 680, 682; see also Skaerved, *Dietrich*, 142–43.

27. Dietrich, *Marlene*, 127.

28. Staggs, *Close-Up on Sunset Boulevard*, 366; see also Crowe, *Conversations with Wilder*, 346.

29. Philip Scheuer, "Outcome of Christie Play Kept Dark for Film," *Los Angeles Times*, July 14, 1957, V2.

30. Charles Higham, *Charles Laughton* (New York: Doubleday, 1976), 204.

31. Crowe, *Conversations with Wilder*, 30, 153.

32. Callow, *Charles Laughton*, 242.

33. Nash and Ross, *Motion Picture Guide*, 3889.

34. Bach, *Marlene Dietrich*, 385.

35. Nash and Ross, *Motion Picture Guide*, 3889.

36. Riva, *Marlene Dietrich*, 687.

37. Bach, *Marlene Dietrich*, 385.

38. Osborne, *Life and Crimes of Agatha Christie*, 270.

39. Patricia Hanson, "Daniel Mandell," in Pendergast and Pendergast, *International Dictionary of Films and Filmmakers*, 4:528.

40. Agatha Christie, *Witness for the Prosecution*, in *The Mousetrap and Other Plays* (New York: Dodd, Mead, 1978), 422.

41. Bach, *Marlene Dietrich*, 387.

42. Dick, *Billy Wilder*, 139.

43. Paul Bergman and Michael Asimow, *Reel Justice: The Courtroom Goes to the Movies* (Kansas City, MO: Andrew and McMeel, 1996), 185.

44. Wood, *Bright Side of Billy Wilder*, 184.

45. "*Witness for the Prosecution*," in *Variety Film Reviews*, vol. 11, n.p.; see Lally, *Wilder Times*, 274.

46. Homer Dickens, *The Complete Films of Marlene Dietrich* (New York: Citadel, 1992), 207.

47. Jeanine Basinger, *The Star Machine* (New York: Knopf, 2007), 174–75.

48. Skaerved, *Dietrich*, 143.

49. *Marlene*, documentary, directed by Maximilian Schell (Bayerischer Rundfunk, 1984). Schell was, like Dietrich, a German actor who worked in Hollywood; he won an Oscar for *Judgment at Nuremberg* (1961).

50. Donald Spoto, *Blue Angel: The Life of Marlene Dietrich* (New York: Doubleday, 1992), 264.

51. Irene Atkins, "Agatha Christie and the Detective Film," *Literature/Film Quarterly* 3, no. 3 (1973): 206.

52. G. C. Ramsey, *Agatha Christie: Mistress of Mystery* (New York: Dodd,

Mead, 1967), 220. One commentator smirked that Wilder only claimed that Christie made this statement; obviously her statement is documented.

## 12. THE GANG'S ALL HERE

1. Dan Auiler, "The Making of *Some Like It Hot:* Interviews," in Billy Wilder and I. A. L. Diamond, *Some Like It Hot: A Screenplay,* ed. Alison Castle (New York: Taschen, 2001), 236.

2. Gerd Gemünden, *A Foreign Affair: Billy Wilder's American Films* (New York: Berghahn Books, 2008), 110–11; see also Lally, *Wilder Times,* 277.

3. I. A. L. Diamond, "The Day Marilyn Monroe Needed 47 Takes to Remember to Say, 'Where's the Bourbon?'" *California,* December 1985, 132.

4. Auiler, "Making of *Some Like It Hot:* Interviews," 236.

5. Leaming, *Marilyn Monroe,* 303; see also Zolotow, *Billy Wilder in Hollywood,* 202.

6. Churchwell, *Many Lives of Marilyn Monroe,* 60.

7. Leaming, *Marilyn Monroe,* 303.

8. Auiler, "Making of *Some Like It Hot:* Interviews," 278.

9. *The Making of "Some Like It Hot,"* documentary, directed by Mike Thomas (Sony, 2006). Unless specifically noted otherwise, all quotations from the members of the cast and crew in this chapter are from this source.

10. Pat O'Brien, interview by author, Columbus, OH, June 14, 1965.

11. Jerry Vermilye, *The Films of the Thirties* (New York: Carol, 1993), 131.

12. O'Brien, interview.

13. Armstrong, *Billy Wilder,* 89.

14. *Some Like It Hot,* souvenir program (MGM Home Entertainment, 2006); see also Crowe, *Conversations with Wilder,* 38.

15. "Billy Wilder," in Stevens, *Conversations,* 305–6.

16. Auiler, "Making of *Some Like It Hot:* Interviews," 246.

17. Zolotow, *Billy Wilder in Hollywood,* 201; see also Chandler, *Nobody's Perfect,* xv.

18. Madsen, *Billy Wilder,* 43.

19. Ibid., 114; see also Gehman, "Charming Billy," 147.

20. Auiler, "Making of *Some Like It Hot:* Interviews," 160.

21. Dan Widener, *Lemmon: A Biography* (New York: Macmillan, 1975), 169.

22. Tony Curtis, interview by Leonard Maltin, *Some Like It Hot,* DVD, directed by Billy Wilder (MGM Home Entertainment, 2006).

23. Chris Lemmon, *A Twist of Lemmon: A Tribute to My Father* (New York: Algonquin Books, 2006), 43; see also Chandler, *Nobody's Perfect,* 211.

24. Madsen, *Billy Wilder,* 114.

25. James Thomas, "Wilder's Winning Ways," *Daily Express* (London), April 19, 1961, 1.

26. Blowen, "Art of Billy Wilder," 83; see also "Dialogue on Film: Billy Wilder and I. A. L. Diamond," 113.

27. Norman Mailer, *Marilyn: A Biography* (New York: Grosset and Dunlop, 1973), 17.

28. Churchwell, *Many Lives of Marilyn Monroe*, 251.

29. Leaming, *Marilyn Monroe*, 313; see also Zolotow, *Billy Wilder in Hollywood*, 257.

30. Leaming, *Marilyn Monroe*, 314.

31. Alison Castle, introduction to Wilder and Diamond, *Some Like It Hot: A Screenplay*, 18.

32. Leaming, *Marilyn Monroe*, 316; see also Castle, introduction, 18.

33. Auiler, "Making of *Some Like It Hot*: Interviews," 279.

34. Zolotow, *Billy Wilder in Hollywood*, 261.

35. Castle, introduction, 18.

36. Wood, *Bright Side of Billy Wilder*, 156.

37. Tony Curtis and Barry Paris, *Tony Curtis: The Autobiography* (New York: Morrow, 1993), 162.

38. Diamond, "Day Marilyn Monroe Needed," 135.

39. Leaming, *Marilyn Monroe*, 318.

40. Curtis, interview.

41. Wilder, interview by Schlöndorff.

42. Ebert, *Great Movies*, 426; see also Diamond, "Day Marilyn Monroe Needed," 135.

43. Churchwell, *Many Lives of Marilyn Monroe*, 251.

44. Wilder, interview by Schlöndorff.

45. Schlöndorff, "Playing by His Rules," 8.

46. Billy Wilder, interview by Art Buchwald, *Herald Tribune* (Paris), August 7, 1960, 4.

47. Billy Wilder, interview, *Time*, June 27, 1960, 75.

48. Gehman, "Charming Billy," 90; see also Wood, *Bright Side of Billy Wilder*, 162.

49. *Some Like It Hot*, souvenir program, 1.

50. Douglas Gomery, "Adolph Deutsch," in Pendergast and Pendergast, *International Dictionary of Films and Filmmakers*, 4:208.

51. Richard Barrios, *Screened Out: Playing Gay in Hollywood from Edison to Stonewall* (New York: Routledge, 2003), 268.

52. Doherty, *Hollywood's Censor*, 330.

53. Brode, *Films of the Fifties*, 283.

54. Cliff Rothman, "A 40-Year-Old Comedy That Hasn't Grown Stale," *New York Times*, August 1, 1999 (with correction appended September 5, 1999), http://www.nytimes.com/1999/08/01/movies/film-a-40-yearold-comedy-that-hasn-t-grown-stale.html; see also Zolotow, *Billy Wilder in Hollywood*, 203.

55. Cf. Wilder and Diamond, *Some Like It Hot: A Screenplay*, 71–72, for this scene, which was deleted from the release prints of the movie.

56. Armstrong, *Billy Wilder,* 88.

57. "Billy Wilder," in Stevens, *Conversations,* 320; see also Crowe, *Conversations with Wilder,* 221.

58. Richard Buskin, *Blonde Heat: The Sizzling Screen Career of Marilyn Monroe* (New York: Watson-Guptil, 2001), 218.

59. Helmut Dieter, "Marilyn Monroe: 30 Jahre nach Irem Tod" [Marilyn Monroe: 30 years after her death], *Stern,* August 6, 1992, 34. Robert Scheff translated the cited passages.

60. Curtis and Paris, *Tony Curtis,* 160.

61. Auiler, "Making of *Some Like It Hot:* Interviews," 244, 304.

62. Marilyn Monroe's copy of the screenplay, 94, private collection.

63. Armstrong, *Billy Wilder,* 93.

64. Crowe, *Conversations with Wilder,* 38.

65. Monroe's copy of the screenplay, 116, 121.

66. Ebert, *Great Movies,* 428.

67. Chandler, *Nobody's Perfect,* 208–9.

68. Bernard Dick told me in a telephone conversation in October 2008 that in *Going My Way* Risë Stevens appears in a scene from Bizet's opera *Carmen,* in which she dances with a rose in her teeth. That film was made at Paramount in 1944, when Wilder was there, so he was no doubt also reminded of Stevens's dance.

69. Auiler, "Making of *Some Like It Hot:* Interviews," 303.

70. Ibid.; see also "Billy Wilder," in Stevens, *Conversations,* 315, 348.

71. Doug Tomlinson, "*Some Like It Hot,*" in Pendergast and Pendergast, *International Dictionary of Films and Filmmakers,* 1:938.

72. Castle, introduction, 23.

73. *Some Like It Hot,* souvenir program, 3.

74. Zolotow, *Billy Wilder in Hollywood,* 204.

75. Tomlinson, "*Some Like It Hot,*" 1:938.

76. "Dialogue on Film: Billy Wilder and I. A. L. Diamond," 124.

77. Barry Norman, *The 100 Best Films of the Century* (New York: Carol, 1993), 233.

78. Schlöndorff, "Playing by His Rules," 8.

79. Tomlinson, "*Some Like It Hot,*" 1:939.

80. "*Time*'s All-Time 100 Movies," *Time,* July 20, 2005, 60.

81. "The 50 Greatest Comedies," *Premiere,* July–August 2006, 66.

82. "British Parliament Votes for Best Movies," *New York Times,* December 29, 2006, B2. *Skye Movies* is a TV show.

## 13. LOVE ON THE DOLE

1. "Billy Wilder," in Stevens, *Conversations,* 320.

2. *Inside "The Apartment,"* documentary (MGM Home Entertainment, 2008); see also Armstrong, *Billy Wilder,* 107.

3. "Billy Wilder: The Art of Screenwriting," 1:419.

4. *Portrait of a 60% Perfect Man.*

5. "Dialogue on Film: Billy Wilder and I. A. L. Diamond," 112; see also Sikov, *On Sunset Boulevard,* 431.

6. Wilder quoted in Bruce Block, "Commentary," *The Apartment,* DVD, directed by Billy Wilder (MGM Home Entertainment, 2008); see also Gehman, "Charming Billy," 69.

7. *Portrait of a 60% Perfect Man.*

8. *Inside "The Apartment."*

9. Neil Sinyard, *Directors: The All-Time Greats* (New York: Gallery Books, 1985), 94.

10. Lally, *Wilder Times,* 303.

11. "The Write Stuff: The 25 Greatest Screenplays of All Time," *Premiere,* May 2006, 85.

12. *Inside "The Apartment."*

13. Dick, *Billy Wilder,* 91.

14. Crowe, *Conversations with Wilder,* 135, 317.

15. Sikov, *On Sunset Boulevard,* 432.

16. MacMurray, interview.

17. Andre Pozner, "Alexandre Trauner," in Pendergast and Pendergast, *International Dictionary of Films and Filmmakers,* 4:831.

18. Brownlow to author.

19. Wilder, interview by Schlöndorff.

20. Billy Wilder, introduction to *Alexandre Trauner, décors de cinéma: Entretiens avec Jean-Pierre Berthomé* (Paris: Jade, Flammarion, 1988), 5.

21. Sikov, *On Sunset Boulevard,* 434; Chandler, *Nobody's Perfect,* 226.

22. Billy Wilder and I. A. L. Diamond, *The Apartment: Unpublished Screenplay* (Los Angeles: United Artists, 1959), 1.

23. *Portrait of a 60% Perfect Man.*

24. Gerald Mast, *The Comic Mind: Comedy and the Movies* (Indianapolis: Bobbs-Merrill, 1973), 275.

25. Sinyard and Turner, *Journey down Sunset Boulevard,* 161.

26. Giannetti, *Masters of the American Cinema,* 311.

27. Lemon, "Billy Wilder's *Fortune Cookie,*" 53.

28. Wilder and Diamond, *The Apartment: Unpublished Screenplay,* 50.

29. Armstrong, *Billy Wilder,* 105.

30. *Alexandre Trauner,* 152.

31. *Portrait of a 60% Perfect Man.*

32. Wood, *Bright Side of Billy Wilder,* 147; see also Lally, *Wilder Times,* 302.

33. Wood, *Bright Side of Billy Wilder,* 129.

34. Wilder, interview by Gehman, 64; see also Zolotow, *Billy Wilder in Hollywood,* 244.

35. Gehman, "Charming Billy," 90.

36. Wilder, interview by Gehman, 64.

37. Sikov, *On Sunset Boulevard*, 436.

38. Zolotow, *Billy Wilder in Hollywood*, 279.

39. "*The Apartment*," in *Variety Film Reviews*, vol. 10, n.p.; see also Zolotow, *Billy Wilder in Hollywood*, 270.

40. Lemon, "Billy Wilder's *Fortune Cookie*," 53.

41. Crowe, *Conversations with Wilder*, 58.

42. Madsen, *Billy Wilder*, 125.

43. Wilder and Diamond, *The Apartment: Unpublished Screenplay*, 56.

44. Wilder, interview by Schlöndorff.

45. Wood, *Bright Side of Billy Wilder*, 61.

46. Block, "Commentary."

47. Richard Lippe, "*The Apartment*," in Pendergast and Pendergast, *International Dictionary of Films and Filmmakers*, 1:57.

48. Madsen, *Billy Wilder*, 123.

49. "Entretien avec Billy Wilder," interview by Michel Ciment, *Positif*, October 1970, 7. The translator of the cited passages is not named.

50. Douglas Brode, *The Films of the Sixties* (New York: Carol, 1993), 32.

51. Volker Schlöndorff, "*The Apartment*," *Premiere*, April 1992, 127.

52. Dick, *Billy Wilder*, 94.

53. James Schamus, "Holiday Movies," *New York Times*, November 4, 2007, sec. 2, p. 10.

54. Patrick Sullivan, news release, June 10, 1960, *The Apartment* file, Legion of Decency files; see also Gregory D. Black, *The Catholic Crusade against the Movies, 1940–1975* (New York: Cambridge University Press, 1999), 214.

55. Patrick Sullivan, interview by author, New York, January 28, 1977.

56. "*The Apartment*," in *Variety Film Reviews*, vol. 10, n.p.

57. Hollis Alpert, "*The Apartment*," *Saturday Review*, June 11, 1960, 24.

58. Dwight Macdonald, *On Movies* (New York: Berkeley, 1971), 312.

59. Sarris, *American Cinema*, 166; see also Staggs, *Close-Up on Sunset Boulevard*, 367.

60. Gehman, "Charming Billy," 147; see also Lally, *Wilder Times*, xiii.

61. Wilder, interview by Gehman, 62.

62. Ibid.; see also Lally, *Wilder Times*, 14.

63. Gehman, "Charming Billy," 148.

64. Sinyard, *Directors*, 44.

65. Sikov, *On Sunset Boulevard*, 445.

66. Cukor, interview.

67. *Portrait of a 60% Perfect Man*.

68. Crowe, *Conversations with Wilder*, 65.

## 14. LOVE ON THE RUN

1. Kanin, *Hollywood,* 158.

2. Helmut Voss, "Billy Wilder hat Heimweh nach dem Kurfurstendamm," *Bonner Rundschau,* February 7, 1973, 1. The translator of the cited passages is not named.

3. Billy Wilder, "Hallo, Herr Menjou?" *Tempo,* August 5, 1929, 7.

4. Madsen, *Billy Wilder,* 94.

5. Kanin, *Hollywood,* 158; see also Lally, *Wilder Times,* 312.

6. Billy Wilder and I. A. L. Diamond, *One, Two, Three: Unpublished Screenplay* (Los Angeles: United Artists, 1961), 1.

7. James Cagney, *Cagney by Cagney* (Garden City, NY: Doubleday, 1976), 154; see also Hopp, *Billy Wilder,* 136.

8. Harald Keller, "*One, Two, Three,*" in *Movies of the Sixties,* ed. Jürgen Muller (Los Angeles: Taschen/BFI, 2005), 20, 22.

9. Brode, *Films of the Sixties,* 52.

10. Dassanowsky-Harris, "Billy Wilder's Germany," pt. 1, 297.

11. Sarris, *You Ain't Heard Nothin' Yet,* 72.

12. Lally, *Wilder Times,* 321.

13. Madsen, *Billy Wilder,* 147.

14. Wood, *Bright Side of Billy Wilder,* 190.

15. Arlene Francis with Florence Rome, *Arlene Francis: A Memoir* (New York: Simon and Schuster, 1978), 169.

16. Tom Wood, "In Wilder's Wilder West," *New York Times,* July 16, 1961, sec. 2, p. 1.

17. Wood, *Bright Side of Billy Wilder,* 190.

18. Wood, "In Wilder's Wild West," sec. 2, p. 1.

19. "Berlin Wall," in Wright, *Oxford Desk Encyclopedia of World History,* 69; see also Glennon, *Our Times,* 452.

20. Wilder, interview by Gehman, 62.

21. I. A. L. Diamond, "'One, Two, Three': Timetable Test," *New York Times,* December 17, 1961, sec. 2, p. 7; see also Wood, *Bright Side of Billy Wilder,* 133.

22. Wilder, interview by Schlöndorff.

23. Diamond, "'One, Two, Three': Timetable Test," sec. 2, p. 7.

24. Wood, *Bright Side of Billy Wilder,* 126.

25. Lally, *Wilder Times,* 312–13.

26. *Cagney by Cagney,* 154.

27. Keller, "*One, Two, Three,*" 22.

28. *Cagney by Cagney,* 155.

29. Ibid., 158.

30. Wilder, interview by Schlöndorff.

31. Dassanowsky-Harris, "Billy Wilder's Germany," pt. 1, 297.

32. Sikov, *On Sunset Boulevard,* 460; see also Wood, *Bright Side of Billy Wilder,* 132.

33. Douglas Warren with James Cagney, *James Cagney: The Authorized Biography* (New York: St. Martin's Press, 1983), 192–93.

34. Crowe, *Conversations with Wilder,* 16; see also Lally, *Wilder Times,* 312.

35. *Cagney by Cagney,* 156; see also Bogdanovich, *Who the Hell's in It,* 373.

36. Robert Dassanowsky-Harris, "Billy Wilder's Germany," pt. 2, *Films in Review* 41, nos. 6–7 (1990): 354.

37. Chandler, *Nobody's Perfect,* 241.

38. Wood, *Bright Side of Billy Wilder,* 194.

39. Wilder, interview by Gehman, 62.

40. Brendan Gill, "Current Cinema," *New Yorker,* January 6, 1962, 79.

41. "Bewildering Berlin," *Time,* December 8, 1961, 60.

42. Sarris, *You Ain't Heard Nothin' Yet,* 395.

43. Pauline Kael, *I Lost It at the Movies: Film Writings, 1954–1965* (New York: Boyars, 1994), 150.

44. *Portrait of a 60% Perfect Man.*

45. Kael, *I Lost It at the Movies,* 153.

46. Wilder, interview by Gehman, 63.

47. Wood, *Bright Side of Billy Wilder,* 27.

48. Dick, *Billy Wilder,* 70; see also Lemon, "Billy Wilder's *Fortune Cookie,*" 42.

49. Keller, "*One, Two, Three,*" 24.

50. Crowe, *Conversations with Wilder,* 165.

51. Louella Parsons, "Jack Lemmon, A Multi-talented Trouper," *New York Journal-American,* September 2, 1962, 3.

52. See summary in *Irma la Douce* file, Motion Picture Association of America Production Code Administration Records, Herrick Library.

53. Joe Hyams, "Poor *Irma* Left without a Song," *New York Herald Tribune,* October 21, 1967, 7.

54. Gene D. Phillips, "Blanche's Phantom Husband: Homosexuality on Stage and Screen," *Louisiana Literature* 14, no. 2 (1997): 48.

55. Sikov, *On Sunset Boulevard,* 470.

56. Kanin, *Hollywood,* 158–59.

57. Hyams, "Poor *Irma* Left," 7.

58. Madsen, *Billy Wilder,* 131.

59. Kanin, *Hollywood,* 158.

60. Chandler, *Nobody's Perfect,* 243.

61. Tony Williams, "*Irma la Douce,*" in *Video Versions: Film Adaptations of Plays,* ed. James Welsh and Thomas Erskine (Westport, CT: Greenwood Press, 2005), 169.

62. Kael, *5001 Nights at the Movies,* 370.

63. Lally, *Wilder Times,* 330.

64. Wilder, introduction, 5.

65. Lally, *Wilder Times,* 331; see also Crowe, *Conversations with Wilder,* 87.

66. Bogdanovich, *Who the Hell's in It,* 132.

67. André Previn, *No Minor Chords: My Days in Hollywood* (New York: Doubleday, 1991), 118.

68. Williams, "*Irma la Douce,*" 169; see also Wood, *Bright Side of Billy Wilder,* 198.

69. Dawn Sova, *Forbidden Films: Censorship* (New York: Facts on File, 2001), 181.

70. Thomas Little, news release, July 15, 1963, *Irma la Douce* file, Legion of Decency files.

71. Sullivan, interview.

72. Hal Wallis to Geoffrey Shurlock, July 10, 1963, and Geoffrey Shurlock to Hal Wallis, July 15, 1963, both in *Irma la Douce* file, Motion Picture Association of America Production Code Administration Records.

73. Sova, *Forbidden Films,* 181.

74. "Billy Wilder," in Stevens, *Conversations,* 128.

75. Billy Wilder and I. A. L. Diamond, *Irma la Douce: Unpublished Screenplay* (Los Angeles: United Artists, 1963), 1.

76. Heinz-Jürgen Köhler, "*Irma la Douce,*" in Muller, *Movies of the Sixties,* 161.

77. Wood, *Bright Side of Billy Wilder,* 148.

78. Lally, *Wilder Times,* 331.

79. Dick, *Billy Wilder,* 102; see also Denis Saillard, "Le Théâtre de Boulevard," *Revue d'Histoire* 93 (2007): 15–26.

80. Lally, *Wilder Times,* 332.

81. Staggs, *Close-Up on Sunset Boulevard,* 368, 370.

82. "*Irma la Douce,*" in *Variety Film Reviews,* vol. 10, n.p.

83. Nash and Ross, *Motion Picture Guide,* 77.

84. Wood, *Bright Side of Billy Wilder,* 198.

85. Kanin, *Hollywood,* 159.

86. Wilder, interview by Prelutsky, 189.

87. Wilder, interview by Gehman, 59.

## 15. GRIFTERS

1. Gehman, "Charming Billy," 69.

2. Kael, *5001 Nights at the Movies,* 399.

3. Billy Wilder, interview, *Daily Mail* (London), July 31, 1964, 3.

4. Dick, *Billy Wilder,* 109.

5. William Froug, *The Screenwriter Looks at the Screenwriter* (New York: Dell, 1972), 165; see also Chandler, *Nobody's Perfect*, 249.

6. "Entretien avec Billy Wilder," 1970, 10.

7. Dick, *Billy Wilder*, 106; see also Kael, *5001 Nights at the Movies*, 399.

8. Nick Tosches, *Dino: Living High in the Dirty Business of Dreams* (New York: Doubleday, 1992), 362.

9. Hopp, *Billy Wilder*, 149.

10. Sikov, *On Sunset Boulevard*, 42.

11. Lally, *Wilder Times*, 338.

12. Wood, *Bright Side of Billy Wilder*, 138.

13. Roger Lewis, *The Life and Death of Peter Sellers* (London: Century, 1994), 674.

14. Ibid., 673.

15. "An Open Letter from Peter Sellers," *Variety*, clipping, n.d., *Kiss Me, Stupid* file, United Artists Collection, Wisconsin Center for Film and Theater Research, Madison.

16. Wilder, interview by Prelutsky, 188.

17. Madsen, *Billy Wilder*, 139.

18. Jack Vizzard, *See No Evil: Life inside a Hollywood Censor* (New York: Simon and Schuster, 1970), 303, 305.

19. "The Production Code of the Motion Picture Association of America," reprinted in Doherty, *Hollywood's Censor*, 359. This is the code as revised in 1956.

20. Joseph I. Breen to Irene Selznick, February 1, 1949, Motion Picture Association of America Production Code Administration Records.

21. Sullivan, interview.

22. Vizzard, *See No Evil*, 302; see also Walsh, *Sin and Censorship*, 315.

23. Harold Mirisch, interoffice memorandum, November 24, 1964, *Kiss Me, Stupid* file, United Artists Collection.

24. Raymond J. Haberski Jr., *Freedom to Offend* (Lexington: University Press of Kentucky, 2007), 83–84.

25. Vizzard, *See No Evil*, 304.

26. Ibid., 305.

27. Doherty, *Hollywood's Censor*, 325–26.

28. George Morris, "The Private Films of Billy Wilder," *Film Comment* 14, no. 1 (1979): 34.

29. Madsen, *Billy Wilder*, 39.

30. Thomas Thompson, "Wilder's Dirty-Joke Film Stirs a Furor," *Life*, January 15, 1965, 55.

31. "*Kiss Me, Stupid*," *Time*, January 1, 1965, 103.

32. "*Kiss Me, Stupid*," in *Variety Film Reviews*, vol. 11, n.p.

33. Wyler, interview.

34. Joan Didion, "*Kiss Me, Stupid*: A Minority Report," *Vogue*, March 1965, 97.

35. Dunne, "Old Pornographer," 94.

36. Walsh, *Sin and Censorship,* 317.

37. Wilder, interview by Prelutsky; see also Crowe, *Conversations with Wilder,* 156.

38. Morris, "Private Films of Billy Wilder," 35.

39. Froug, *Screenwriter Looks at the Screenwriter,* 249, 165.

40. Billy Wilder, interview by Peter Bart, *New York Times,* November 7, 1965, sec. 2, p. 1.

41. Lemon, "Billy Wilder's *Fortune Cookie,*" 40.

42. Zolotow, *Billy Wilder in Hollywood,* 314.

43. Wilder, interview by Gehman, 65.

44. Wood, *Bright Side of Billy Wilder,* 215.

45. Zolotow, *Billy Wilder in Hollywood,* 322.

46. Lally, *Wilder Times,* 354.

47. Joe Baltake, *Jack Lemmon: His Films and Career* (New York: Citadel, 1986), 167.

48. I. A. L. Diamond, interview by Adrian Turner, *Films and Filming,* May 1982, 18.

49. Chandler, *Nobody's Perfect,* 251.

50. *Portrait of a 60% Perfect Man.*

51. Billy Wilder and I. A. L. Diamond, *The Fortune Cookie,* in *The Apartment and The Fortune Cookie: Two Screenplays* (London: Studio Vista, 1966), 123.

52. Lemmon, *Twist of Lemmon,* 113.

53. Morris, "Private Films of Billy Wilder," 36.

54. Lally, *Wilder Times,* 360.

55. Crowe, *Conversations with Wilder,* 62.

56. Wilder and Diamond, *Fortune Cookie,* 115.

57. Sikov, *On Sunset Boulevard,* 50; see also Lemon, "Billy Wilder's *Fortune Cookie,*" 56.

58. Todd McCarthy, "AFI Lauds Jack Lemmon," *Variety,* March 16, 1988, 6.

59. Mirisch, *I Thought We Were,* 236.

60. Lally, *Wilder Times,* 360; see also Zolotow, *Billy Wilder in Hollywood,* 243.

61. Madsen, *Billy Wilder,* 147; see also Lemon, "Billy Wilder's *Fortune Cookie,*" 59.

62. Madsen, *Billy Wilder,* 142.

63. Morris, "Private Films of Billy Wilder," 36.

64. Wilder and Diamond, *The Fortune Cookie,* 131.

65. Frieda Lockhart, "*Meet Whiplash Willie,*" *Signpost* (London), February 15, 1967, 4.

66. Seidman, *Film Career of Billy Wilder,* 72.

67. Lockhart, "*Meet Whiplash Willie,*" 4.

68. Farber, "Films of Billy Wilder," 11; see also Armstrong, *Billy Wilder,* 122.

69. Giannetti, *Masters of the American Cinema,* 322.

70. Wood, *Bright Side of Billy Wilder,* 51–52.

71. Seidman, *Film Career of Billy Wilder,* 32.

72. Dick, *Billy Wilder,* 112.

73. Farber, "Films of Billy Wilder," 16.

74. Richard Schickel, "*The Fortune Cookie,*" *Life,* November 18, 1966, 18.

75. Walsh, *Sin and Censorship,* 318.

76. Sullivan, interview.

77. Doherty, *Hollywood's Censor,* 334.

78. Jack Vizzard, interview by author, Berlin, May 19, 1977.

## 16. THE GAME'S AFOOT

1. "Sherlock Holmes Stories," in Head, *Cambridge Guide to Literature,* 1020.

2. Allen Eyles, *Sherlock Holmes: A Centenary Celebration* (New York: Harper and Row, 1986), 111.

3. Eyles, *Sherlock Holmes,* 39, 116.

4. Doherty, *Hollywood's Censor,* 324. Breen, Shurlock's predecessor, had blipped the line about the needle in the U.S. release prints of *The Hound of the Baskervilles,* but the words were restored when the movie was rereleased in the United States in 1975.

5. Charles Higham, *The Adventures of Conan Doyle: The Life of the Creator of Sherlock Holmes* (New York: Norton, 1976), 206, 267; see also Andrew Lycett, *The Man Who Created Sherlock Holmes: The Life and Times of Sir Arthur Conan Doyle* (New York: Simon and Schuster, 2008), 175.

6. Arthur Conan Doyle, "The Bruce-Partington Plans," in *The Complete Sherlock Holmes* (New York: Doubleday, 2007), 1076.

7. Dick, *Billy Wilder,* 142.

8. Ibid., 145.

9. Arthur Conan Doyle, "A Scandal in Bohemia," in *Complete Sherlock Holmes,* 194.

10. Jeremy McCarter, "Arthur Conan Doyle and Sherlock Holmes," *New York Times Book Review,* December 30, 2007, 15.

11. Mark Shivas, "Yes, We Have No Naked Girls," *New York Times,* October 12, 1967, sec. 2, p. 4. The title of the article is a joking reference to the "wild party" in *Kiss Me, Stupid.*

12. Mirisch, *I Thought We Were,* 295, 296. Some sources say the budget was $10 million, but Walter Mirisch would know the correct sum.

13. Eyles, *Sherlock Holmes,* 111.

14. Chris Steinbrunner and Norman Michaels, *The Films of Sherlock Holmes* (Secaucus, NJ: Citadel, 1978), 216.

15. Shivas, "We Have No Naked Girls," sec. 2, p. 4.

16. Wood, *Bright Side of Billy Wilder*, 232.

17. Shivas, "We Have No Naked Girls," sec. 2, p. 4.

18. Bernard Cohn, "Billy Wilder," *Positif*, October 1969, 49–50.

19. Shivas, "We Have No Naked Girls," sec. 2, p. 4; see also Wood, *Bright Side of Billy Wilder*, 150.

20. Zolotow, *Billy Wilder in Hollywood*, 325.

21. Madsen, *Billy Wilder*, 134.

22. Steinbrunner and Michaels, *Films of Sherlock Holmes*, 218.

23. "*The Private Life of Sherlock Holmes*," in *Variety Film Reviews*, vol. 12, n.p.

24. Doug McClelland, *Hollywood Talks Turkey: The Screen's Greatest Flops* (London: Faber, 1981), 279.

25. Stephen Bourne, *Brief Encounters: Homosexuality in British Cinema* (London: Cassell, 1996), 221; see also Crowe, *Conversations with Wilder*, 301, and Lally, *Wilder Times*, 372.

26. Richard Valley, *Sherlock Holmes: Classic Themes from 221B Baker Street*, CD liner notes (Studio City, CA: Varese Sarabande, 1996), 4.

27. Steinbrunner and Michaels, *Films of Sherlock Holmes*, 217.

28. Wood, *Bright Side of Billy Wilder*, 180.

29. Shivas, "We Have No Naked Girls," sec. 2, p. 4.

30. *The Making of "The Private Life of Sherlock Holmes,"* documentary (MGM Home Entertainment, 2003).

31. Robert Stephens with Michael Coveny, *Knight Errant: Memories of a Vagabond Actor* (London: Hodder and Stoughton, 1995), 96, 98.

32. Ibid., 101.

33. Shivas, "We Have No Naked Girls," sec. 2, p. 4.

34. Crowe, *Conversations with Wilder*, 301.

35. *Making of "The Private Life."*

36. Rozsa, *Double Life*, 208–9.

37. Tony Thomas, *Music for the Movies* (New York: Barnes, 1973), 96–97.

38. Rozsa, *Double Life*, 208–9.

39. Horton, "Music Man: Miklos Rozsa," 4.

40. Gene D. Phillips, *Stanley Kubrick: A Film Odyssey* (New York: Popular Library, 1975), 178.

41. Mirisch, *I Thought We Were*, 298.

42. Crowe, *Conversations with Wilder*, 350, 98.

43. Mirisch, *I Thought We Were*, 299; see also Zolotow, *Billy Wilder in Hollywood*, 328.

44. Steinbrunner and Michaels, *Films of Sherlock Holmes*, 220.

45. Dick, *Billy Wilder*, 147.

46. Arthur Conan Doyle, *The Sign of the Four*, in *Complete Sherlock Holmes*, 173.

47. Jonathan Rigby, "*The Private Life of Sherlock Holmes*," in *Sherlock Holmes on Screen: The Complete Film and TV History*, ed. Alan Barnes (London: Reynolds and Hearn, 2008), 139.

48. Vincent Canby, "'The Private Life of Sherlock Holmes,'" *New York Times*, October 30, 1970, 15.

49. Pauline Kael, *Deeper into Movies* (New York: Bantam Books, 1974), 236.

50. *Making of "The Private Life."*

51. Eyles, *Sherlock Holmes*, 112.

52. Zolotow, *Billy Wilder in Hollywood*, 328.

53. Lally, *Wilder Times*, 373.

54. Michael Pointer, "Holmes Lives!" *American Film*, November 1975, 69.

55. Morris, "Private Films of Billy Wilder," 38.

56. Eyles, *Sherlock Holmes*, 112.

57. Wilder, "Going for Extra Innings," 98.

## 17. THE PERFECT BLENDSHIP

1. Nora Sayre, "Falling Prey to Parodies of the Press," *New York Times*, January 1, 1974, 8.

2. Ben Hecht, "*The Front Page* Now and Then," November 18, 1961, Ben Hecht Papers, Newberry Library, Chicago.

3. *Ben Hecht, the Shakespeare of Hollywood*, documentary, directed by David O'Dell (Lucasfilm, 2007); see also Roquemore, *History Goes to the Movies*, 161.

4. Arthur Schlesinger Jr., "*The Front Page*," in *Past Imperfect: History According to the Movies*, ed. Mark Carnes (New York: Holt, 1995), 202.

5. Crowe, *Conversations with Wilder*, 94; see also Wilder, interview by Prelutsky, 190.

6. Hawks, interview.

7. Joseph McBride, "Shooting *The Front Page*," *Boston Real Paper*, July 31, 1974, 13.

8. Ibid., 15.

9. Joseph McBride, "In the Picture: *The Front Page*," *Sight and Sound* 43, no. 3 (1974): 212. There is considerable overlap between this article and McBride, "Shooting *The Front Page*." I quote the *Sight and Sound* version only when it contains material not included in the *Boston Real Paper* version.

10. Billy Wilder and I. A. L. Diamond, *The Front Page: Unpublished Screenplay* (Los Angeles: Universal, 1974), 9.

11. Gemünden, *Foreign Affair*, 152.

12. John Baxter, "Henry Bumstead," in Pendergast and Pendergast, *International Dictionary of Films and Filmmakers*, 4:173.

13. Deutsch, *Me and Bogie,* 161.

14. McBride, "Shooting *The Front Page,*" 132.

15. Morris, "Private Films of Billy Wilder," 38.

16. Michael Wilmington, "Saint Jack," *Film Comment* 29, no. 2 (1993): 14, 15.

17. Chandler, *Nobody's Perfect,* 283–84.

18. Dick, *Billy Wilder,* 118; see also Doherty, *Hollywood's Censor,* 334.

19. Richard Heffner, interview by author, New York, June 13, 1975.

20. Morris, "Private Films of Billy Wilder," 38.

21. Ibid.

22. McBride, "In the Picture: *The Front Page,*" 212.

23. Dick, *Billy Wilder,* 119.

24. Pauline Kael, *Reeling* (New York: Warner Books, 1977), 362.

25. Joseph Morgenstern, "*The Front Page,*" *Newsweek,* December 23, 1974, 79.

26. Andrew Sarris, "*The Front Page,*" *Village Voice,* December 25, 1974, 8.

27. Andrew Sarris, "Billy Wilder Reconsidered," in Lopate, *American Movie Critics,* 307.

28. Armstrong, *Billy Wilder,* 124.

29. Hopp, *Billy Wilder,* 169.

30. "Julius J. Epstein: A King of Comedy," interview by Pat McGilligan, in McGilligan, *Backstory,* 187.

31. Chandler, *Nobody's Perfect,* 271.

32. "Entretien avec Billy Wilder sur *Avanti!*" interview by Michel Ciment, *Positif,* January 1974, 7. Bridgett Chandler translated the cited passages.

33. Billy Wilder and I. A. L. Diamond, *Avanti! Unpublished Screenplay* (Los Angeles: United Artists, 1971), i.

34. "Entretien avec Billy Wilder sur *Avanti!*" 5.

35. Ibid., 8.

36. Ibid., 5.

37. Ibid.

38. Wilder and Diamond, *Avanti! Unpublished Screenplay,* i.

39. "Entretien avec Billy Wilder sur *Avanti,*" 6.

40. Ibid., 8.

41. Dick, *Billy Wilder,* 97.

42. Staggs, *Close-Up on Sunset Boulevard,* 369.

43. Crowe, *Conversations with Wilder,* 351.

44. Mirisch, *I Thought We Were,* 301.

45. "Entretien avec Billy Wilder sur *Avanti,*" 5, 6.

46. Ibid., 8.

47. Ibid.

48. Dick, *Billy Wilder,* 97.

49. David Sanjek, "*Avanti!*" in Welsh and Erskine, *Video Versions,* 17.

50. Seidman, *Film Career of Billy Wilder,* 110.

51. Dick, *Billy Wilder*, 98.

52. Zolotow, *Billy Wilder in Hollywood*, 332.

53. Seidman, *Film Career of Billy Wilder*, 110.

54. Geoff Brown, "A Bite as Fierce as His Bark," *Times* (London), June 18, 1996, 34.

55. Jay Cocks, "*Avanti!*" *Time*, December 25, 1972, 109.

56. Jon Bradshaw, "I Am Big. It's the Pictures That Got Small," *New York*, November 24, 1975, 40.

57. "*Avanti!*" in *Variety Film Reviews*, vol. 13, n.p.

58. Sarris, "Billy Wilder Reconsidered," 307.

59. Morris, "Private Films of Billy Wilder," 38.

60. "Dialogue on Film: Billy Wilder and I. A. L. Diamond," 125.

61. Sinyard, *Directors*, 44.

62. McBride, "Shooting *The Front Page*," 15.

63. Bradshaw, "I Am Big," 40.

64. McBride, "Shooting *The Front Page*," 15.

65. Mirisch, *I Thought We Were*, 302.

## 18. TWILIGHT YEARS

1. Bradshaw, "I Am Big," 39.

2. Ibid., 43.

3. "Dialogue on Film: Billy Wilder and I. A. L. Diamond," 130.

4. Bradshaw, "I Am Big," 43.

5. Blowen, "Art of Billy Wilder," 52.

6. Zinnemann, interview.

7. Rex McGee, "The Life and Hard Times of *Fedora*," *American Film*, February 1979, 18.

8. Stephen Farber, "A Cynic ahead of His Time," *New York Times*, December 6, 1981, C21.

9. Sikov, *On Sunset Boulevard*, 552.

10. Morris, "Private Films of Billy Wilder," 39.

11. Mary Blume, "*Fedora:* Walking on the Wilder Side," *Los Angeles Times Calendar*, October 2, 1977, 39.

12. Hirsch, *Dark Side of the Screen*, 119.

13. Vincent Canby, "Wilder's 'Fedora,'" *New York Times*, May 6, 1979, sec. 2, p. 15.

14. Wilder, "Going for Extra Innings," 44.

15. Chandler, *Nobody's Perfect*, 291.

16. Wilder, "Going for Extra Innings," 42.

17. McGee, "Life and Hard Times," 18.

18. Karasek, *Billy Wilder*, 482; see also Wilder, "Going for Extra Innings," 44.

19. Riva, *Woman at War*, 154.

20. Dan Yakir, "*Fedora:* Another 'Uneasy' Role for Marthe Keller," *New York Post,* April 13, 1979, 27.

21. Verina Glaessner, "Gerry Fisher," in Pendergast and Pendergast, *International Dictionary of Films and Filmmakers,* 4:256.

22. McGee, "Life and Hard Times," 31.

23. Blume, "Walking on the Wilder Side," 39.

24. McGee, "Life and Hard Times," 32.

25. Ibid., 31–32.

26. Miklos Rozsa, audio interview by Rudy Behlmer, 1974, *Spellbound,* DVD, directed by Alfred Hitchcock (Criterion, 2002).

27. Ness, "Miklos Rozsa," 724.

28. McGee, "Life and Hard Times," 31–32.

29. Ibid., 32.

30. Wilder, "Going for Extra Innings," 42.

31. Andrew Sarris, "*Fedora,*" *Village Voice,* April 16, 1979, 12.

32. McGee, "Life and Hard Times," 32.

33. Hopp, *Billy Wilder,* 171.

34. Aljean Harmetz, "At 73, Billy Wilder's Bark Still Has Plenty of Bite," *New York Times,* June 29, 1979, C12.

35. Morris, "Private Films of Billy Wilder," 39.

36. Staggs, *Close-Up on Sunset Boulevard,* 373.

37. Lally, *Wilder Times,* 399.

38. Richard Schickel, "Old Hat: *Fedora,*" *Time,* May 21, 1979, 86.

39. "Dialogue on Film: Billy Wilder and I. A. L. Diamond," 112.

40. McGee, "Life and Hard Times," 18.

41. Vincent Canby, "Wilder's *Fedora,*" *New York Times,* May 6, 1979, sec. 2, pp. 15, 35.

42. "Billy Wilder: Obituary," *Times* (London), March 30, 2002, 1.

43. Crowe, *Conversations with Wilder,* 352.

44. Morris, "Private Films of Billy Wilder," 39.

45. "William Holden: An Untamed Spirit."

46. "Death of William Holden," *New York Times,* November 18, 1981, 1. Martin Sopocy is at work on a book on Holden that deals in more detail with Holden's last years. It will be the first book on Holden in twenty years.

47. Farber, "Cynic ahead of His Time," C21.

48. Kenneth Geist, *Pictures Will Talk: The Life and Films of Joseph Mankiewicz* (New York: Scribner, 1978), 195.

49. Wilder, "Going for Extra Innings," 45, 41; see also Geist, *Pictures Will Talk,* 195.

50. Chandler, *Nobody's Perfect,* 299.

51. Gene D. Phillips, *Beyond the Epic: The Life and Films of David Lean* (Lexington: University Press of Kentucky, 2006), 383; see also Farber, "Cynic ahead of His Time," C21.

52. Madsen, *Billy Wilder*, 60.

53. Karasek, *Billy Wilder*, 467; see also Chandler, *Nobody's Perfect*, 300.

54. Lemmon, *Twist of Lemmon*, 117.

55. Lally, *Wilder Times*, 407.

56. Klaus Kinski, *Kinski Uncut*, trans. Joachim Neugroschel (New York: Viking, 1996), 299.

57. Lally, *Wilder Times*, 408.

58. Richard Hadley Jr., "Billy Wilder and Comedy: An Analysis of *Buddy Buddy*" (PhD diss., University of Southern California, 1989), 186.

59. Barton Palmer, "Lalo Schifrin," in Pendergast and Pendergast, *International Dictionary of Films and Filmmakers*, 4:743.

60. Diamond, interview, 21.

61. Hopp, *Billy Wilder*, 177.

62. Vincent Canby, "'Buddy Buddy,'" *New York Times*, December 11, 1981, C12.

63. Kevin Thomas, "'Buddy Buddy,'" *Los Angeles Times Calendar*, December 11, 1981, 1.

64. David Ansen, "Some Like It Not," *Newsweek*, December 14, 1981, 124.

65. I screened the film for some of the staff of Rush Medical Center, Chicago, on September 10, 2008.

66. Baltake, *Jack Lemmon*, 255; see also Chandler, *Nobody's Perfect*, 301.

67. MacMurray, interview.

68. Wilder, interview by Porfirio, 107; see also Chandler, *Nobody's Perfect*, 248.

69. Chandler, *Nobody's Perfect*, 301, 2.

## EPILOGUE

1. Gerald Mast and Bruce Kawin, *A Short History of the Movies*, rev. ed. (New York: Longman, 2008), 191.

2. *Portrait of a 60% Perfect Man.*

3. Yeck, "I. A. L. Diamond," 4:210.

4. Billy Wilder, "Movies Forever!" *New Republic*, June 9, 1982, 23. This is a transcript of Wilder's speech when he accepted the Lifetime Achievement Award from the Film Society of Lincoln Center.

5. Wilder, interview by Schlöndorff.

6. Freeman, "*Sunset Boulevard* Revisited," 79.

7. Chandler, *Nobody's Perfect*, 301, 303.

8. Richard Corliss, "The King of Comedy: Billy Wilder," *Time*, April 8, 2002, 70.

9. Kirkham, "Saul Bass and Billy Wilder," 21.

10. Sikov, *On Sunset Boulevard*, 575–78.

11. Corliss, "King of Comedy," 70.

12. Kakutani, "Ready for His Close-Up," 14.

13. Aljean Harmetz, "Billy Wilder: The Storyteller," *Modern Maturity,* February–March 1993, 31.

14. Roger Ebert, "International Poll," *Chicago Sun-Times,* August 11, 2002, A25.

15. Chandler, *Nobody's Perfect,* 324.

16. "Write Stuff," 82.

17. Gene D. Phillips, *Creatures of Darkness: Raymond Chandler, Detective Fiction, and Film Noir* (Lexington: University Press of Kentucky, 2000), 199.

18. Stephen Frears, interview by Lester Freedman and Scott Steward, in *Reviewing British Cinema,* ed. Wheeler Dixon (Albany: State University of New York Press, 1994), 237.

# Selected Bibliography

*Ace in the Hole.* Souvenir program. Criterion Collection, 2007.

Agee, James. *Film Writing and Selected Journalism.* Edited by Michael Sragow. New York: Library of America, 2005.

Allyn, John. "*Double Indemnity:* A Policy That Paid Off." *Literature/Film Quarterly* 6, no. 2 (1978): 119–22.

Arce, Hector. *The Secret Life of Tyrone Power.* New York: Morrow, 1979.

Armstrong, Richard. *Billy Wilder: American Film Realist.* Jefferson, NC: McFarland, 2004.

Axelrod, George. Interview by Patrick McGilligan. *Film Comment* 31, no. 6 (1995): 10–24.

———. *The Seven Year Itch.* New York: Dramatist Play Service, 1953.

Bach, Steven. *Marlene Dietrich: Life and Legend.* New York: Morrow, 1992.

Baltake, Joe. *Jack Lemmon: His Films and Career.* New York: Citadel, 1986.

Barnes, Alan, ed. *Sherlock Holmes on Screen: The Complete Film and TV History.* London: Reynolds and Hearn, 2008.

Barnett, Lincoln. "The Happiest Couple in Hollywood." *Life,* December 11, 1944, 100–109.

Barrios, Richard. *Screened Out: Playing Gay in Hollywood from Edison to Stonewall.* New York: Routledge, 2003.

Berg, Scott. *Lindbergh.* New York: Putnam, 1998.

Bergman, Paul, and Michael Asimow. *Reel Justice: The Courtroom Goes to the Movies.* Kansas City, MO: Andrews and McMeel, 1996.

Bevan, Donald, and Edmund Trzcinski. *Stalag 17.* New York: Dramatists Play Service, 1951.

Black, Gregory D. *The Catholic Crusade against the Movies, 1940–1975.* New York: Cambridge University Press, 1999.

Blume, Mary. "*Fedora:* Walking on the Wilder Side." *Los Angeles Times Calendar,* October 2, 1977, 39.

Bogdanovich, Peter. *Who the Devil Made It: Conversations with Film Directors.* New York: Ballantine Books, 1998.

———. *Who the Hell's in It: Conversations with Hollywood's Legendary Actors.* New York: Ballantine Books, 2006.

Bould, Mark. *Film Noir: From Berlin to Sin City.* Irvington, NY: Columbia University Press, 2006.

Bradshaw, Jon. "I Am Big. It's the Pictures That Got Small." *New York,* November 24, 1975, 39–43.

Brown, Daniel. "Wilde and Wilder." *PMLA* 119, no. 5 (2004): 1216–30.

Cagney, James. *Cagney by Cagney.* Garden City, NY: Doubleday, 1976.

Cain, James M. *Double Indemnity.* New York: Vintage, 1992.

Callow, Simon. *Charles Laughton: A Difficult Actor.* New York: Grove Press, 1987.

Cameron, Ian, ed. *The Book of Film Noir.* New York: Continuum, 1992.

Carnes, Mark, ed. *Past Imperfect: History According to the Movies.* New York: Holt, 1995.

Carr, Jay, ed. *The A List: 100 Essential Films.* New York: Da Capo, 2002.

Chandler, Charlotte. *Nobody's Perfect: Billy Wilder, a Personal Biography.* New York: Applause Books, 2004.

Chandler, Raymond. *Later Novels and Other Writings.* Edited by Frank Mac-Shane. New York: Library of America, 1995.

———. *The Raymond Chandler Papers: Selected Letters and Non-fiction, 1909–1959.* Edited by Tom Hiney and Frank MacShane. New York: Atlantic Monthly Press, 2000.

Chierichetti, David. *Hollywood Director: Mitchell Leisen.* Los Angeles: Photo-ventures Press, 1995.

Christie, Agatha. *Witness for the Prosecution.* In *The Mousetrap and Other Plays,* 337–422. New York: Dodd, Mead, 1978.

Churchwell, Sarah. *The Many Lives of Marilyn Monroe.* New York: Holt, 2006.

Conrad, Mark, ed. *The Philosophy of Film Noir.* Lexington: University Press of Kentucky, 2006.

Corliss, Richard. "The King of Comedy: Billy Wilder." *Time,* April 8, 2002, 70–71.

Cornes, Judy. *Alcohol in the Movies, 1898–1962: A Critical History.* Jefferson, NC: McFarland, 2006.

Crowe, Cameron. *Conversations with Wilder.* New York: Knopf, 2001.

Curtis, Tony, with Mark Vieria. *The Making of* Some Like It Hot. Hoboken, NJ: Wiley, 2009.

Dassanowsky-Harris, Robert. "Billy Wilder's Germany." Pts. 1 and 2. *Films in Review* 41, no. 5 (1990): 292–97; nos. 6–7 (1990): 352–55.

Diamond, I. A. L. "The Day Marilyn Monroe Needed 47 Takes to Remember to Say, 'Where's the Bourbon?'" *California,* December 1985, 132.

———. Interview by Adrian Turner. *Films and Filming,* May 1982, 16–21.

Dick, Bernard. *Billy Wilder.* Rev. ed. New York: Da Capo, 1996.

———. *Claudette Colbert: She Walked in Beauty.* Jackson: University Press of Mississippi, 2008.

Dietrich, Marlene. *Marlene.* New York: Avon, 1990.

Doherty, Thomas. *Hollywood's Censor: Joseph I. Breen and the Production Code Administration.* New York: Columbia University Press, 2007.

Doyle, Arthur Conan. *The Complete Sherlock Holmes.* New York: Doubleday, 2007.

Dunne, John Gregory. "The Old Pornographer: Billy Wilder." *New Yorker,* November 8, 1999, 88–95.

Ebert, Roger. *The Great Movies.* New York: Broadway Books, 2002.

Eliot, Marc. *Jimmy Stewart: A Biography.* New York: Random House, 2006.

Everson, William K. *Hollywood Bedlam: Classic Screwball Comedies.* New York: Carol, 1994.

Eyles, Allen. *Sherlock Holmes: A Centenary Celebration.* New York: Harper and Row, 1986.

Eyman, Scott. *Ernst Lubitsch: Laughter in Paradise.* New York: Simon and Schuster, 1993.

Farber, Stephen. "The Films of Billy Wilder." *Film Comment* 7, no. 1 (1971–1972): 8–22.

Fishgall, Gary. *Pieces of Times: The Life of James Stewart.* New York: Scribner, 1997.

Fleishman, Avrom. *Narrated Films: Storytelling Situations in Cinema History.* Baltimore: John Hopkins University Press, 1992.

Freeman, David. "*Sunset Boulevard* Revisited." *New Yorker,* June 21, 1993, 72–79.

Gehman, Richard. "Charming Billy." *Playboy,* December 1960, 69–70, 90, 145–48.

Geiger, Jeffrey, and R. L. Rutsky, eds. *Film Analysis.* New York: Norton, 2005.

Gemünden, Gerd. *A Foreign Affair: Billy Wilder's American Films.* New York: Berghahn Books, 2008.

Giannetti, Louis. *Understanding Movies.* 11th ed. Upper Saddle River, NJ: Pearson Prentice Hall, 2008.

Goodman, Ezra. *The Fifty-Year Decline and Fall of Hollywood.* New York: Simon and Schuster, 1961.

Gorman, Ed, Lee Server, and Martin Greenberg, eds. *The Big Book of Noir.* New York: Carroll and Graf, 1998.

Greene, Graham. *The Graham Greene Reader: Reviews, Essays, and Interviews.* Edited by David Parkinson. New York: Applause Books, 1995.

Gross, Miriam, ed. *The World of Raymond Chandler.* New York: A and W, 1978.

Haberski, Raymond J., Jr. *Freedom to Offend.* Lexington: University Press of Kentucky, 2007.

Halliwell, Leslie. *Film Guide.* Rev. ed. Edited by David Gritten. New York: HarperCollins, 2008.

———. *Who's Who in the Movies.* Rev. ed. Edited by John Walker. New York: HarperCollins, 2005.

Hare, William. *Early Film Noir.* Jefferson, NC: McFarland, 2003.

Harmetz, Aljean. "Billy Wilder: The Storyteller." *Modern Maturity,* February–March 1993, 31.

Haut, Woody. *Heartbreak and Vine: Hardboiled Writers in Hollywood*. London: Serpent's Tail, 2002.

Hecht, Ben, and Charles MacArthur. *The Front Page*. In *Sixteen Famous American Plays,* edited by Bennett Cerf and Van Cartmell, 71–140. New York: Modern Library, 1941.

Higham, Charles. *Charles Laughton*. New York: Doubleday, 1976.

Higham, Charles, and Joel Greenberg. *The Celluloid Muse: Hollywood Directors Speak*. Chicago: Regnery, 1969.

Hirsch, Foster. *The Dark Side of the Screen: Film Noir*. Rev. ed. New York: Da Capo, 2009.

———. *Otto Preminger*. New York: Knopf, 2007.

Hopp, Glenn. *Billy Wilder: The Cinema of Wit*. Los Angeles: Taschen, 2003.

Horton, Robert, ed. *Billy Wilder: Interviews*. Jackson: University Press of Mississippi, 2001.

———. "Music Man: Miklos Rozsa." *Film Comment* 31, no. 6 (1995): 2–4.

Irwin, John. *Unless the Threat of Death Is behind Them: Hard-Boiled Fiction and Film Noir*. Baltimore: Johns Hopkins University Press, 2006.

Jackson, Charles. *The Lost Weekend*. New York: Time, 1963.

Kael, Pauline. *5001 Nights at the Movies*. New York: Holt, 1991.

———. *I Lost It at the Movies: Film Writings, 1954–1965*. New York: Boyars, 1994.

———. *Reeling*. New York: Warner Books, 1977.

Kakutani, Michiko. "Ready for His Close-Up." *New York Times Magazine,* July 28, 1996, 14.

Kanin, Garson. *Hollywood: Moviemakers and Moneymakers*. New York: Viking, 1974.

Karasek, Hellmuth. *Billy Wilder: Eine Nahaufnahme* [Billy Wilder: A close-up]. Hamburg: Hoffman und Campe, 1992.

Katz, Ephraim. *The Film Encyclopedia*. Rev. ed. Edited by Fred Klein and Ronald Nolen. New York: HarperCollins, 2005.

Kirkham, Pat. "Saul Bass and Billy Wilder in Conversation." *Sight and Sound,* n.s., 5, no. 6 (1995): 18–21.

Kiszely, Philip. *Hollywood through Private Eyes: The Screen Adaptation of the Hard-Boiled Private Detective Novel in the Studio Era*. New York: Lang, 2006.

Koszarski, Richard, ed. *Hollywood Directors, 1914–1940*. New York: Oxford University Press, 1976.

———, ed. *Hollywood Directors, 1941–1976*. New York: Oxford University Press, 1977.

———. *Von: The Life and Times of Erich von Stroheim*. New York: Limelight, 2001.

Kurnitz, Harry. "Billy the Wild." *Holiday,* June 1964, 93–95.

Lally, Kevin. *Wilder Times: The Life of Billy Wilder*. New York: Holt, 1996.

Leaming, Barbara. *Marilyn Monroe*. New York: Random House, 1998.

Lemmon, Chris. *A Twist of Lemmon: A Tribute to My Father.* New York: Algonquin Books, 2006.

Lennig, Arthur. *Stroheim.* Lexington: University Press of Kentucky, 2000.

Lindbergh, Charles. *The Spirit of St. Louis.* New York: Scribner, 1953.

Lopate, Phillip, ed. *American Movie Critics: An Anthology from the Silents until Now.* New York: Library of America, 2008.

Madsen, Axel. *Billy Wilder.* London: Secker and Warburg, 1968.

Maltin, Leonard, ed. *Movie Guide.* Rev. ed. New York: New American Library, 2009.

Mast, Gerald, and Bruce Kawin. *A Short History of the Movies.* Rev. ed. New York: Longman, 2008.

McBride, Joseph. "In the Picture: *The Front Page.*" *Sight and Sound* 43, no. 3 (1974): 212.

McCarter, Jeremy. "Arthur Conan Doyle and Sherlock Holmes." *New York Times Book Review,* December 30, 2007, 15.

McGee, Rex. "The Life and Hard Times of *Fedora.*" *American Film,* February 1979, 17–22, 31–32.

McGilligan, Pat, ed. *Backstory: Interviews with Screenwriters of Hollywood's Golden Age.* Berkeley: University of California Press, 1986.

Meyers, Jeffrey. *Bogart: A Life in Hollywood.* New York: Houghton Mifflin, 1997.

Milland, Ray. *Wide-Eyed in Babylon.* New York: Morrow, 1974.

Mirisch, Walter. *I Thought We Were Making Movies, Not History.* Madison: University of Wisconsin Press, 2008.

Morris, George. "The Private Films of Billy Wilder." *Film Comment* 14, no. 1 (1979): 34–39.

Muller, Jürgen, ed. *Movies of the Thirties.* Los Angeles: Taschen/BFI, 2005.

———, ed. *Movies of the Forties.* Los Angeles: Taschen/BFI, 2005.

———, ed. *Movies of the Fifties.* Los Angeles: Taschen/BFI, 2005.

———, ed. *Movies of the Sixties.* Los Angeles: Taschen/BFI, 2005.

Murray, Robert, and Roger Brucker. *Trapped! The Story of Floyd Collins.* Lexington: University Press of Kentucky, 1999.

Naremore, James. *More Than Night: Film Noir in Its Contexts.* Rev. ed. Los Angeles: University of California Press, 2008.

Nash, Jay, and Stanley Ross, eds. *The Motion Picture Guide, 1927–1983.* Chicago: Cinebooks, 1985.

Osborne, Charles. *The Life and Crimes of Agatha Christie.* New York: HarperCollins, 1999.

Palmer, Barton, ed. *Perspectives on Film Noir.* New York: Twayne, 1994.

Paris, Barry. *Garbo: A Biography.* New York: Knopf, 1995.

Pendergast, Tom, and Sara Pendergast, eds. *International Dictionary of Films and Filmmakers.* Rev. ed. 4 vols. Detroit: St. James Press, 2000.

Pointer, Michael. "Holmes Lives!" *American Film,* November 1975, 68–70.

Riva, David, ed. *A Woman at War: Marlene Dietrich Remembered*. Detroit: Wayne State University Press, 2006.

Riva, Maria. *Marlene Dietrich*. New York: Knopf, 1993.

Roquemore, Joseph. *History Goes to the Movies*. New York: Doubleday, 1999.

Rowan, Arthur. "Making the Aerial Shots for *The Spirit of St. Louis*." *American Cinematographer*, June 1957, 366–87.

Sarris, Andrew. *The American Cinema: Directors and Directions, 1929–1968*. Rev. ed. New York: Da Capo, 1996.

———. "Billy Wilder, Closet Romanticist." *Film Comment* 12, no. 4 (1977): 7–9.

———. "From the Kaiser to the Oscar." *New York Times Book Review*, December 27, 1998, 5.

———. *You Ain't Heard Nothin' Yet: The American Talking Film, 1927–1949*. New York: Oxford University Press, 2000.

Schickel, Richard. *Double Indemnity*. London: British Film Institute, 1993.

Schickel, Richard, and George Perry. *Bogie: The Life and Films of Humphrey Bogart*. New York: St. Martin's Press, 2006.

Seidman, Steve. *The Film Career of Billy Wilder*. Pleasantville, NY: Redgrave, 1977.

Sikov, Ed. *On Sunset Boulevard: The Life and Times of Billy Wilder*. New York: Hyperion, 1998.

Silver, Alain, and James Ursini, eds. *Film Noir Reader 4: The Crucial Films and Themes*. New York: Limelight, 2004.

Silver, Alain, James Ursini, and Paul Duncan. *Film Noir*. Los Angeles: Taschen, 2004.

Silver, Alain, James Ursini, and Robert Porfirio, eds. *Film Noir Reader 3*. New York: Limelight, 2002.

Silverman, Stephen. "Billy Wilder and Stanley Donen." *Films in Review* 47, nos. 3–4 (1996): 34–36.

Sinyard, Neil, and Adrian Turner. *Journey down Sunset Boulevard: The Films of Billy Wilder*. Ryde, Isle of Wight: BCW, 1979.

*Some Like It Hot*. Souvenir program. MGM Home Entertainment, 2006.

Sova, Dawn. *Forbidden Films: Censorship*. New York: Facts on File, 2001.

Staggs, Sam. *Close-Up on Sunset Boulevard*. New York: St. Martin's Press, 2003.

Stevens, George, Jr., ed. *Conversations with the Great Moviemakers of Hollywood's Golden Age at the American Film Institute*. New York: Knopf, 2006.

Swanson, Gloria. *Swanson on Swanson*. New York: Pocket Books, 1981.

Taylor, Samuel. *Sabrina Fair, or A Woman of the World*. New York: Random House, 1954.

Telotte, J. P. *Voices in the Dark: The Narrative Patterns of Film Noir*. Urbana: University of Illinois Press, 1989.

Thomas, Bob. *Golden Boy: The Untold Story of William Holden*. New York: St. Martin's Press, 1983.

Thomson, David. *The New Biographical Dictionary of Film*. Rev. ed. New York: Knopf, 2004.

Trauner, Alexandre. *Alexandre Trauner, décors de cinéma: Entretiens avec Jean-Pierre Berthomé*. Paris: Jade, Flammarion, 1988.

Trowbridge, Katelin. "The War between Words and Images: *Sunset Boulevard*." *Literature/Film Quarterly* 30, no. 4 (2002): 294–303.

"Two Views of a Director: Billy Wilder." *Quarterly of Film, Radio, and Television* 7, no. 1 (1952): 58–69.

*Variety Film Reviews, 1907–1966*. 24 vols. New Providence, NJ: Bowker, 1997.

Vizzard, Jack. *See No Evil: Life inside a Hollywood Censor*. New York: Simon and Schuster, 1970.

Walker, Alexander. *Audrey: Her Real Story*. New York: St. Martin's Press, 1994.

Walsh, Frank. *Sin and Censorship: The Catholic Church and the Motion Picture Industry*. New Haven, CT: Yale University Press, 1996.

Welsh, James, and Thomas Erskine, eds. *Video Versions: Film Adaptations of Plays*. Westport, CT: Greenwood Press, 2005.

Welsh, James, and John Tibbetts, eds. *Encyclopedia of Novels into Film*. Rev. ed. New York: Facts on File, 2005.

———. *Encyclopedia of Stage Plays into Film*. New York: Facts on File, 2001.

Widener, Don. *Lemmon: A Biography*. New York: Macmillan, 1975.

Wilder, Billy. "Entretien avec Billy Wilder." Interview by Michel Ciment. *Positif,* October 1970, 4–17.

———. "Entretien avec Billy Wilder." Interview by Michel Ciment. *Positif,* August 1983, 15–28.

———. "Entretien avec Billy Wilder sur *Avanti!*" Interview by Michel Ciment. *Positif,* January 1974, 3–9.

———. "Going for Extra Innings." Interview by Joseph McBride and Todd McCarthy. *Film Comment* 13, no. 1 (1979): 40–48.

———. Interview by Richard Gehman. *Playboy,* June 1963, 57–66.

———. "Movies Forever!" *New Republic,* June 9, 1982.

Wilder, Billy, and George Axelrod. *The Seven Year Itch: Unpublished Screenplay*. Los Angeles: Twentieth Century–Fox, 1954.

Wilder, Billy, and Edwin Blum. *Stalag 17: A Screenplay*. Edited by Jeffrey Meyers. Los Angeles: University of California Press, 1999.

Wilder, Billy, and Charles Brackett. *The Lost Weekend: A Screenplay*. Edited by Jeffrey Meyers. Los Angeles: University of California Press, 2000.

Wilder, Billy, Charles Brackett, and D. M. Marshman Jr. *Sunset Boulevard: A Screenplay*. Edited by Jeffrey Meyers. Los Angeles: University of California Press, 1999.

Wilder, Billy, Charles Brackett, and Walter Reisch. *Ninotchka: A Screenplay*. In *The Best Pictures, 1939–40*, edited by Jerry Wald and Richard Macaulay, 79–128. New York: Dodd, Mead, 1940.

Wilder, Billy, and Raymond Chandler. *Double Indemnity: A Screenplay.* Edited by Jeffrey Meyers. Los Angeles: University of California Press, 2000.

Wilder, Billy, and I. A. L. Diamond. *The Apartment: Unpublished Screenplay.* Los Angeles: United Artists, 1959.

———. *Avanti! Unpublished Screenplay.* Los Angeles: United Artists, 1971.

———. *The Fortune Cookie.* In *The Apartment and The Fortune Cookie: Two Screenplays.* London: Studio Vista, 1966.

———. *The Front Page: Unpublished Screenplay.* Los Angeles: Universal, 1974.

———. *Irma la Douce: Unpublished Screenplay.* Los Angeles: United Artists, 1963.

———. *One, Two, Three: Unpublished Screenplay.* Los Angeles: United Artists, 1961.

———. *The Private Life of Sherlock Holmes: Unpublished Screenplay.* Los Angeles: United Artists, 1970.

———. *Some Like It Hot: A Screenplay.* Edited by Alison Castle. New York: Taschen, 2001.

Wood, Ean. *Dietrich: A Biography.* London: Sanctuary, 2002.

Wood, Tom. *The Bright Side of Billy Wilder, Primarily.* Garden City, NY: Doubleday, 1970.

Wright, Edmund, ed. *Oxford Desk Encyclopedia of World History.* New York: Oxford University Press, 2006.

"The Write Stuff: The 25 Best Screenplays of All Time." *Premiere,* May 2006, 82–87.

Young, Desmond. *Rommel, the Desert Fox.* New York: Harper, 1950.

Zolotow, Maurice. *Billy Wilder in Hollywood.* Rev. ed. New York: Limelight, 1987.

# Index